DICTIONARY OF
BRITISH PORTRAITURE

Volume 3

Dictionary of
British Portraiture

IN FOUR VOLUMES

EDITED BY RICHARD ORMOND AND MALCOLM ROGERS

WITH A FOREWORD BY JOHN HAYES
DIRECTOR OF THE NATIONAL PORTRAIT GALLERY

VOLUME

3

The Victorians · Historical figures born between 1800 and 1860

COMPILED BY ELAINE KILMURRAY

B.T.BATSFORD LIMITED · *LONDON*
IN ASSOCIATION WITH
THE NATIONAL PORTRAIT GALLERY · *LONDON*

ISBN 0 7134 1472 3

Filmset in 'Monophoto' Bembo by
Servis Filmsetting Ltd, Manchester
and printed in Great Britain by
Robert Maclehose Ltd
Glasgow
for the publishers
B.T.Batsford Ltd
4 Fitzhardinge Street
London W1H 0AH

Foreword

This four-volume *Dictionary of British Portraiture* was the idea of Sam Carr, Director of Batsford. He was correct in his view that there exists no comprehensive handbook to the portraits of famous British men and women. Specialized surveys and studies there are, but no compact work to which the researcher or layman can turn easily for information about the likeness of this or that individual. The present dictionary cannot claim to be a complete or exhaustive study; inevitably there has to be a degree of selection in the people represented, and the portraits that have been listed. This is explained in the introduction. But within these limitations it does offer a reliable guide to the portraiture of a wide range of eminent British men and women from the Medieval period to the present day.

The dictionary relates directly to the purposes for which the National Portrait Gallery was founded in 1856: the collection, preservation and study of historical portraits. It has been compiled mainly from the Gallery's own immense archive, and I am delighted that its resources should be made available in this way. The information in the archive has been gathered slowly over the course of the last century or so by many devoted scholars and members of staff, and I think it is only right that I should first record our debt to them. Without their labours such a dictionary could never have been compiled. I would also like to pay a special tribute to the staff of the Guthrie Room, who maintain the archive, add to its holdings, and answer so many questions so patiently and efficiently. The work of editorial supervision has been handled most competently by my colleagues, Richard Ormond and Malcolm Rogers, who originally discussed the project with Sam Carr, and have guided all four volumes through the press. To Sam Carr himself we are grateful for his continuing enthusiasm and support, without which the project would never have materialised. Mrs Underwood and Vanessa Fergusson undertook the task of typing the entries with unusual thoroughness and accuracy. Finally, I must thank our two hard-working and dedicated compilers, who took on the daunting job of recording and researching the thousands of portraits listed here. It is a tribute both to their enthusiasm and to their composure in the face of sometimes inadequate, sometimes confusing records, that the work has been completed so expeditiously. We are deeply grateful to them for the skill and accuracy with which they have carried out their task.

JOHN HAYES

Introduction

The aim of the present dictionary is to provide a listing of the portraits of famous figures in British history that are either in galleries, institutions and public companies, or in collections accessible to the public. It is intended for the general researcher and student who needs a reliable guide to portraits on public view of which illustrations can be obtained relatively easily. It is not concerned with the intricacies of iconography, though decisions have had to be taken about the likely authenticity of particular images, nor is it comprehensive. The decision to exclude portraits in private collections was dictated by the need to limit the scope of the work, by the difficulty of obtaining permission from owners to use their names, and by the impossibility of directing readers to the specific location of privately-owned works. In a few entries it has been indicated that a privately-owned portrait is the only known likeness, or the most significant likeness, of a particular person.

Each volume of this dictionary covers a different historical period. Though there were arguments in favour of dividing the dictionary alphabetically, it was decided on balance that it would be more useful to make each volume self-contained. The chronological dividing-lines are inevitably arbitrary, and will mean that certain figures, whose contemporaries appear in one volume, are by accident of birth in another. But provided that the reader knows the birth date of his or her chosen subject, there should be no problem in turning to the correct volume.

The question of selection was a thorny one. We have relied heavily, though not exclusively, on the *Dictionary of National Biography*, and, for those sitters who died after 1960, on *Times Obituaries*, 3 vols (1951–75). Readers will no doubt be disappointed by some omissions, but it is important to remember that the non-appearance of a particular figure may simply reflect the fact that no authentic portrait of him or her is known.

The Gallery's archive is, in general, weak in the field of twentieth-century portraiture, and there are no catalogues for a number of important collections. It proved impossible to follow up the large photographic libraries, both public and commercial, and reliance has been placed on the Gallery's own holdings. The National Photographic Record was established by the National Portrait Gallery in 1917, to document well-known contemporary figures, and its work continued until 1970.

The entries themselves are cast in a condensed form, but we hope they will be comprehensible once the format has been mastered.

The arrangement of the entries is as follows:

Surname of the sitter, with Christian names (peers are listed under their titles)
Birth and death dates, where known
Profession or occupation
Known portraits, recorded under:

P	Paintings	SC	Sculpture
D	Drawings	T	Tapestry
M	Miniatures	W	Stained-glass windows
MS	Manuscripts	PR	Prints
SL	Silhouettes	C	Caricatures
G	Groups	PH	Photographs

Within each category portraits are listed chronologically, and then alphabetically by name of artist where known.

Information on individual portraits is arranged as follows:

name of artist
date of portrait where known
size (ie half length, whole length, etc)
other distinguishing features (with Garter, in a landscape, etc)
medium, in the case of drawings, groups, prints and caricatures
location, with accession number in the case of national galleries and museums

For further details see abbreviations opposite.

The absence of illustrations will be a cause of complaint. But the only possible solution would have been to illustrate everything (a selection would have satisfied few), and that would have made the series prohibitively large and expensive. In any case the dictionary has been conceived as a reference work and not a picture book, and it is as such that it must stand or fall.

RICHARD ORMOND

MALCOLM ROGERS

Abbreviations

A

ABBEY, Edwin Austin (1852-1911) artist.
sc Sir Thomas Brock, bust, The British School at Rome.
c Sir Leslie Ward ('Spy'), wl with palette, chromo-lith, for *Vanity Fair*, 29 Dec 1898, NPG.
ph Window and Grove, tql, cabinet, NPG x1.

ABBOTT, Charles Stuart Aubrey, see 3rd Baron Tenterden.

ABBOTT, Edwin Abbott (1838-1926) teacher and scholar.
p Sir Hubert von Herkomer, City of London School.
ph W. & D.Downey, hs, woodburytype, for Cassell's *Cabinet Portrait Gallery*, vol II, 1891, NPG. John Russell & Sons, hs, print, for *National Photographic Record*, vol I, NPG.

ABBOTT, Evelyn (1843-1901) classical scholar.
d Unknown, hs, semi-profile, pencil, Balliol College, Oxford.

ABBOTT, Sir James (1807-1896) general.
d B.Baldwin, 1841, hl, w/c, NPG 4532.

À BECKETT, Arthur William (1844-1909) humorist.
c Harry Furniss, pen and ink sketch, NPG 3619.

À BECKETT. Gilbert Abbott (1811-1856) comic author.
m Attrib Charles Couzens, 1855, hl, w/c, over a photograph, NPG 1362.

À BECKETT, Gilbert Arthur (1837-1891) comic author.
pr 'R.T.', after a photograph by A.Bassano, hs, wood engr, for *Illust London News*, 24 Oct 1891, NPG.

ABEL, Sir Frederick Augustus, Bart (1827-1902) chemist.
p Margaret Thomas, 1877, Institution of Electrical Engineers, London. Frank Bramley, 1900, tql seated, NPG 4926.
ph W. & D.Downey, hs, woodburytype, for Cassell's *Cabinet Portrait Gallery*, vol I, 1890, NPG x260. H.J.Whitlock, hl as a young man, carte, NPG (Album 40). Unknown, two prints, Chemical Society, London.

ABERCONWAY, Charles Benjamin Bright McLaren, 1st Baron (1850-1934) barrister and business man.
ph Sir Benjamin Stone, 1906, two prints, both wl, NPG. Walter Stoneman, 1924, hs, NPG (NPR).

ABERCORN, James Hamilton, 1st Duke of (1811-1885) lord lieutenant of Ireland.
p Stephen Catterson Smith (finished by his son), exhib 1877, Dublin Castle.
d Frederick Sargent, c1870–80, hl, profile, pencil, NPG 1834a.
pr G.Cook, after a photograph by A.Bassano, hl, profile, stipple and line, NPG. Maclure & Macdonald, hs, coloured lith, for Cassell's *Modern Portrait Gallery*, vol III, 1877, NPG.
c Carlo Pellegrini ('Ape'), wl, profile, chromo-lith, for *Vanity Fair*, 25 Sept 1869, NPG.
ph Camille Silvy, 1861, wl, carte, NPG AX7424. Lock & Whitfield, hs, oval, for *Men of Mark*, vol I, 1876, NPG.

ABERCORN, James Hamilton, 2nd Duke of (1838-1913) conservative politician.
p W.F.Osborne, Masonic Hall, Dublin.
d Sir Edwin Landseer, 1843, with his sister, Lady Harriet, and a fortune teller, pencil, Shugborough (NT), Staffs. Jules Massé, pastel, oval, Shugborough.
pr C.Laurie, hs with masonic chain of office, line, NPG.

ABERCROMBY, Robert William Duff, see Duff.

ABERDARE, Henry Austin Bruce, 1st Baron (1815-1895) statesman.
p Unknown, c1850, tql seated, DoE (Southbridge).
sc J.Milo Griffith, RA 1889, marble bust, University College, Cardiff. Herbert Hampton, statue, Cardiff. Herbert Hampton, plaster bust, National Museum of Wales 1226, Cardiff. Unknown, plaster bust, Royal Geographical Society, London.
pr C.Holl, after H.T.Wells, hs, stipple, one of 'Grillion's Club' series, BM, NPG.
c Carlo Pellegrini ('Ape'), wl, chromo-lith, for *Vanity Fair*, 21 Aug 1869, NPG.
ph John Watkins, c1860s, hs, carte, NPG (Album 136).

ABERDEEN and TEMAIR, Ishbel Maria Gordon, née Marjoribanks, 1st Marchioness of (1857-1939) promoter and patron of social service enterprises.
g A.E.Emslie, 'Dinner at Haddo House, 1884', oil, NPG 3845.
ph Barraud, tql, print, for *Men and Women of the Day*, vol IV, 1891, NPG AX5534. Dudley Glanfield, wl seated with her husband, print, NPG (*Daily Herald*).

ABERDEEN and TEMAIR, John Campbell Gordon, 7th Earl and 1st Marquess of (1847-1934) statesman.
p James Sant, RA 1882?, Haddo House, Grampian region, Scotland. Charles Furse, RA 1890?, Dublin Castle. Baron Barnekow, Town and County Hall, Aberdeen.
g A.E.Emslie, 'Dinner at Haddo House, 1884', oil, NPG 3845.
sc Robert Tait Mackenzie, 1921, bronze relief plaque, SNPG 1349.
c Sir Leslie Ward ('Spy'), wl, chromo-lith, for *Vanity Fair*, 6 Feb 1902, NPG.
ph Walter Stoneman, 1921, hs, NPG (NPR). Dudley Glanfield, wl with his wife, print, NPG (*Daily Herald*). John Russell & Sons, hl, print, for *National Photographic Record*, vol I, NPG. Hay Wrightson, hs, print, NPG (*Daily Herald*).

ABNEY, Sir William de Wiveleslie (1843-1920) photographic chemist and education official.
sc Edouard Lanteri, c1903?, bronze bust, Royal Society, London.
ph John Russell & Sons, hs, print, for *National Photographic Record*, vol II, NPG. Unknown, Royal Society.

ABRAHAM, Charles John (1814-1903) first bishop of Wellington, New Zealand.
pr F.Holl, after G.Richmond of 1849 or 1853, hs, stipple, NPG. Unknown, hs, woodcut, for *Illust London News*, 1859, NPG.

ABRAHAM, William (1842-1922) labour politician and trade-union leader.
pr Unknown, hs, woodcut, NPG.
ph Sir Benjamin Stone, 1901, two wl prints, NPG.

ACLAND, Sir Arthur Herbert Dyke, 13th Bart, of Columb John, Devon (1847-1926) politician and educational reformer.
ph W. & D.Downey, tql, woodburytype, for Cassell's *Cabinet Portrait Gallery*, vol V, 1894, NPG.

ACLAND, Sir Henry Wentworth (1815-1900) physician.
p Sir Hubert von Herkomer, 1888, tql seated, Ashmolean Museum, Oxford.

D SIR JOHN EVERETT MILLAIS, 1853, pencil and w/c, Education Trust Ltd, Ruskin Galleries, Bembridge School.
SC ALEXANDER MUNRO, c1857, plaster bust, Bodleian Library, Oxford. SIR J.E.BOEHM, 1887, bronze bust, University Museum, Oxford.
PR C.HOLL, after G.Richmond, hs, stipple, one of 'Grillion's Club' series, BM, NPG. D.J.POUND, after a photograph by Maull and Polyblank, tql seated, stipple and line, NPG.
PH TAUNT & CO, c1890?, wl with Dr Benjamin Jowett, cabinet, NPG x5146. UNKNOWN, hs, profile, print, NPG x5586.

ACTON, Charles Januarius Edward (1803-1847) cardinal.
P UNKNOWN, hs, as a boy, Coughton Court (NT), Warwicks. VINCENZO MORANI, 1844, hl seated with book and crucifix, Coughton Court.
PR G.A.PERIAM, after T.Uwins, hl seated, aged 27, line, BM. UNKNOWN, hs, line, oval, NPG.

ACTON, Sir John Emerich Edward Dalberg Acton, 8th Bart and 1st Baron (1834-1902) historian and moralist.
P F.S.VON LENBACH, c1879, hl, NPG 4083; copy by COUNTESS LEOPOLDINE ARCO-VALLERY, hs, Trinity College, Cambridge.

ACWORTH, Sir William Mitchell (1850-1925) expert on railway economics.
PH WALTER STONEMAN, 1925, hs, NPG (NPR).

ADAM, Patrick William (1854-1929) artist.
SC CHARLES MATTHEW, 1889, bronzed medallion, SNPG 1587.

ADAM, William Patrick (1823-1881) Liberal Whip.
PH BARRAUD, hs, profile, cabinet, NPG x266. MOFFAT, hs, print, NPG x5147.

ADAM SMITH, Sir George, see Smith.

ADAMS, James Williams (1839-1903) army chaplain in India.
PH ELLIOTT & FRY, c1890, hs, print, National Army Museum, London.

ADAMS, John Couch (1819-1892) astronomer and mathematician.
P THOMAS MOGFORD, 1851, hl seated, St John's College, Cambridge. SIR HUBERT VON HERKOMER, 1888, tql seated, Pembroke College, Cambridge; hs replica, NPG 1842.
D LUCETTE E.BARKER, 1869, St John's College. FAWKS, St John's College. UNKNOWN, hs, St John's College.
SC N.N.BURNARD, RA 1849, marble bust, Royal Astronomical Society, London. ALBERT BRUCE JOY, RA 1873?, marble bust, St John's College. H.C.FEHR, 1903, marble bust, Launceston Library, Cornwall. UNKNOWN, plaster bust, St John's College. A.BRUCE JOY, portrait medallion, Westminster Abbey, London.
W UNKNOWN, St John's College Chapel, Cambridge.
C UNKNOWN, 1872, pen, St John's College.
PH A.G.DEW SMITH, as an old man, St John's College.

ADAMS, Sarah Flower (1805-1848) poet.
PH UNKNOWN, after a drg by Margaret Gillies, hs, touched with chalk, NPG 1514.

ADAMS, William (1814-1848) author of *Sacred Allegories.*
PR W.H.MOTE, after G.Richmond, hl seated, stipple, for *Bonchurch,* by J.W., 1849, BM, NPG. J.H.LYNCH, tql seated, lith, V & A.

ADAMS, William Davenport (1851-1904) journalist and compiler.
PH ALFRED ELLIS, c1894, hs, woodburytype, NPG x7405.

ADAMSON, Robert (1821-1848) pioneer photographer.
PH D.O.HILL and ROBERT ADAMSON, two prints: tql seated, NPG p6(181), and 'The Adamson Family', 1844-5, NPG p6(153).

ADDERLEY, Charles Bowyer, see 1st Baron Norton.

ADDINGTON, John Gellibrand Hubbard, 1st Baron (1805-1889) director of the Bank of England.
PR J.R.JACKSON, after G.Richmond, tql, aged 65, stipple and line, Bank of England.

ADDISON, Laura (1827-1852) actress.
PR G.HOLLIS, after a daguerreotype by Mayall, wl as Queen Mary in Schiller's *Mary Stuart,* stipple and line, for Tallis's *Drawing Room Table Book,* 1851, BM. G.HOLLIS, after a daguerreotype by Paine, wl as Imogen in *Cymbeline,* stipple and line, pl to same work, BM.

ADLER, Hermann (1839-1911) British chief rabbi.
C SIR LESLIE WARD ('Spy'), wl, chromo-lith, for *Vanity Fair,* 31 March 1904, NPG.
PH H.S.MENDELSSOHN, 1890, hs, profile, cabinet, NPG x15. W. & D.DOWNEY, tql seated in robes, woodburytype, for Cassell's *Cabinet Portrait Gallery,* vol III, 1892, NPG.

ADLER, Nathan Marcus (1803-1890) chief rabbi.
P UNKNOWN, tql, Adler House, London.
PH BARRAUD, hs, print, for *Men and Women of the Day,* vol II, 1889, NPG AX5465.

ADYE, Sir John Miller (1819-1900) general.
PR MACLURE and MACDONALD, after a photograph by Fradelle, hs with orders, chromo-lith, NPG.
PH UNKNOWN, c1880s, with a painting of The Rock of Gibraltar, The Convent, Gibraltar.

AGNEW, Sir William, 1st Bart (1825-1910) fine art dealer.
P UNKNOWN, Manchester Reform Club.
G HENRY JAMYN BROOKS, 'Private View of the Old Masters Exhibition, 1888', oil, NPG 1833.
C HARRY FURNISS, c1880-1910, hl, pen and ink, for *Punch,* NPG 3413.

AGUILAR, Grace (1816-1847) novelist.
PR J.COCHRAN, hl, stipple and line, NPG.

AINGER, Alfred (1837-1904) writer, humorist and divine.
P H.G.RIVIERE, 1904, posthumous, Trinity Hall, Cambridge.
D GEORGE DU MAURIER, c1881, tql seated, w/c, NPG 2660.
SC MRS S.G.BAINSMITH, bust, Bristol Cathedral.
C SIR LESLIE WARD ('Spy'), hl in pulpit, chromo-lith, for *Vanity Fair,* 13 Feb 1892, NPG.

AINSWORTH, William Harrison (1805-1882) novelist.
P DANIEL MACLISE, c1834, hl, NPG 3655. D.MACLISE, c1834, hl, unfinished, Walker Art Gallery, Liverpool. H.W.PICKERSGILL, RA 1841, hs, Chetham's Hospital and Library, Manchester.
D D.MACLISE, 1827, wl seated, V & A. GEORGE CRUIKSHANK, hs, pencil, BM.
G D.MACLISE, 'The Fraserians,' drg, 1835, V & A. G.CRUIKSHANK, 'Sir Lionel Flamstead and his Friends', etch, V & A.
PR R.J.LANE, after W.Greatbach, hl, profile, lith, pub 1839, BM. R.J.LANE, after A.D'Orsay, hl, profile, lith, 1844, NPG.
PH LOCK & WHITFIELD, hs, semi-profile, woodburytype, for *Men of Mark,* 1881, NPG. HENNAH & KENT, tql, carte, NPG x5151. LONDON STEREOSCOPIC COMPANY, hs, semi-profile, carte, NPG x20. SOUTHWELL BROS, tql, carte, NPG AX7510.

AIRD, Sir John, 1st Bart (1833-1911) contractor.
C SIR LESLIE WARD ('Spy'), wl, profile, w/c study, for *Vanity Fair,* 20 June 1891, NPG 5014.
PH SIR BENJAMIN STONE, 1897, wl, print, NPG.

AIREDALE, James Kitson, 1st Baron (1835-1911) iron and steel manufacturer.
SC SPRUCE, bust, Leeds Town Hall.
PH SIR BENJAMIN STONE, wl, print, NPG.

AIREY, Sir James Talbot (1812-1898) general.
PR UNKNOWN, wl, 'Presentation of Native Indian Officers to the Duke of Cambridge in the Governor's Palace, Malta', woodcut, for *Illust London News*, 13 July 1878, NPG.

AIREY, Richard Airey, Lord (1803-1881) general.
P UNKNOWN, c1870, wl seated, in uniform, The Convent, Gibraltar.
PH LOCK & WHITFIELD, hs, profile, woodburytype, for *Men of Mark*, 1878, NPG.

AIRY, Sir George Biddell (1801-1892) Astronomer Royal.
P JAMES PARDON, 1833-4, tql, Observatories Syndicate, Cambridge.
D MISS ANNOT AIRY (his daughter), after John Collier of 1884, tql seated, w/c, Royal Astronomical Society.
G Two photographs by W.T.MORGAN & CO, 1891, with his family, NPG X1222 and X1223. MORGAN & KIDD, c1891-2, with his family, photograph, NPG X1224.
SC J.DEVILLE, 1823, plaster bust, Observatories Syndicate.
PR I.W.SLATER, after T.C.WAGEMAN, tql seated, lith, BM.
PH Various photographs, NPG: ERNEST EDWARDS, 1860's, both tql seated, NPG X1213 and X1214; LOCK & WHITFIELD, c1877, hs, woodburytype, NPG X24; MAULL & POLYBLANK, wl, carte, NPG X22; MAULL & POLYBLANK, tql seated, print, NPG X1215; JOHN WATKINS, hs, carte, NPG X23.

AITCHISON, George (1825-1910) architect.
P SIR LAWRENCE ALMA TADEMA, RA 1901?, tql seated, RIBA, London.
PH RALPH W.ROBINSON, tql, print, for *Members and Associates of the Royal Academy of Arts, 1891*, NPG X7347.

AITKEN, Sir William (1825-1892) pathologist.
P W.R.SYMONDS, RA 1888, tql, Royal Victoria Hospital, Netley, Hants; replica, RAMC, London.

AKERMAN, John Yonge (1806-1873) numismatist; secretary of the Society of Antiquaries.
PR H.A.OGG, hl, profile, etch, BM, NPG.

AKERS-DOUGLAS, Aretas, see 1st Viscount Chilston.

ALBANI, Dame Marie Louise Cécilie Emma, née Lajeunesse (1852-1930) singer.
PH P.PINSONNEAULT, c1897, hs, profile, cabinet, NPG X5152. LAFAYETTE, 1905, hs, postcard, NPG X30. JOHN RUSSELL & SONS, hs, print, for *National Photographic Record*, vol I, NPG. UNKNOWN, hl, woodburytype, carte, NPG AX7735.

ALBANY, Prince Leopold, 1st Duke of (1853-1884) son of Queen Victoria.
P F.X.WINTERHALTER, 1859, hs, Royal Coll.
D GEORGE DAWE, hl with Princess Charlotte, Royal Coll.
M WILLIAM WATSON, c1854, hs, oval, Royal Coll.
G F.X.WINTERHALTER, 1856, with Prince Arthur and Princess Louise, Royal Coll. JOHN PHILLIP, 'The Marriage of the Princess Royal', oil, 1858, Royal Coll. G.H.THOMAS, 'The Marriage of Princess Alice to Prince Louis of Hesse', oil, 1862, Royal Coll. SIR J.D.LINTON, 'The Marriage of the Duke of Albany', oil, 1882, Royal Coll.
SC F.J.WILLIAMSON, 1883, marble bust, Royal Coll.
C SIR LESLIE WARD ('Spy'), wl, w/c study, for *Vanity Fair*, 21 April 1877, NPG 4711. FAUSTIN, wl, lith, NPG.
PH L.CALDESI, 1857, with members of the Royal Family, print, NPG P26. MAYALL, 1861, wl, carte, NPG. MAYALL, 1863, wl with Prince Arthur, Royal Coll. W. & D.DOWNEY, 1868, with members of the Royal Family at Balmoral, carte, NPG X3610. HILLS & SAUNDERS, 1883-4, hl seated with his daughter Alice, cabinet, NPG AX5552.

ALBERMARLE, William Coutts Keppel, 7th Earl of (1832-1894) politician.
PR D.J.POUND, after a photograph by Mayall, tql seated, stipple and line, NPG.
PH JOHN EDWARDS, 1882?, with 6th and 8th (and possibly 9th) Earls, cabinet, NPG X6072.

ALBERT Francis Charles Augustus Emmanuel, Prince Consort of England (1819-1861) Prince Consort of Queen Victoria.
P G.E.VAN EBART, c1824, with his mother and brother, Royal Coll. JOHN PARTRIDGE, 1840, tql in uniform, Royal Coll. JOHN PARTRIDGE, 1841, hl, Royal Coll. F.X.WINTERHALTER, 1842, tql, Royal Coll. SIR EDWIN LANDSEER, 1842, Albert and Queen Victoria as Edward III and Queen Philippa for a bal costumé, Royal Coll. JOHN LUCAS, 1842, wl, Musée de Versailles et des Trianons; version, formerly United Service Club, London (c/o the Crown Commissioners). F.X.WINTERHALTER, 1845, wl in military uniform, Royal Coll. F.X.WINTERHALTER, 1846, wl in court dress, Lady Lever Art Gallery, Port Sunlight. SIR FRANCIS GRANT, RA 1846, wl in uniform, beside a horse, Christ's Hospital, Horsham. F.R.SAY, RA 1849, in court dress, Examination Schools, Cambridge. E.BOUTIBONNE and J.F.HERRING, 1856, on horseback, Royal Coll. JOHN PHILLIP, RA 1858, in highland dress, Aberdeen Corporation. F.X.WINTERHALTER, 1859, wl, Royal Coll; version, NPG 237. SIR WILLIAM BOXALL, RA 1859, wl as Master of Trinity House, Trinity House, London. J.G.MIDDLETON, RA 1862, as colonel of the Hon Artillery Company, Hon Artillery Company. J.C.HORSLEY, c1862, Royal Society of Arts, London.
D L.VON MEYERN HOHENBERG, 1839, hl, Royal Society of Arts. Various w/cs by C.HAAG, Royal Coll. F.X.WINTERHALTER, Albert and Queen Victoria dressed as Charles II and Catherine of Braganza, for a bal costumé, Royal Coll.
M SIR W.C.ROSS, 1839, hs, Royal Coll. SIR W.C.ROSS, 1840, hl, profile, Royal Coll. JOHN HASLEM, c1840, Derby Art Gallery. SIR W.C.ROSS, 1841, tql in evening dress, with orders, Royal Coll. ROBERT THORBURN, 1843, tql in armour, Royal Coll.
G SIR GEORGE HAYTER, 'The Marriage of Queen Victoria and Prince Albert', oil, 1840, Royal Coll. SIR EDWIN LANDSEER, 'Windsor Castle in Modern Times', oil, 1840-5, Royal Coll. C.R.LESLIE, 'The Christening of the Princess Royal at Buckingham Palace', oil, 1841, Royal Coll. SIR G.HAYTER, 'The Christening of the Prince of Wales', oil, 1842, Royal Coll. EUGÈNE LAMI, 'Reception of Queen Victoria at the Château d'Eu', oil, 1843, Musée de Versailles. F.X.WINTERHALTER, with the Queen and his children, oil, 1846, Royal Coll. SIR EDWIN LANDSEER, 'Royal Sports on Hill and Loch, 1850', oil, Royal Coll. F.X.WINTERHALTER, 'The First of May, 1851', oil, Royal Coll. H.W.PHILLIPS, 'The Royal Commissioners for the Great Exhibition, 1851', oil, V & A. H.C.SELOUS, 'Royal Opening of the Great Exhibition', oil, 1851, Royal Coll. E.M.WARD, 'The Queen Investing Napoleon III with the order of the Garter', oil, 1855, Royal Coll. E.M.WARD, 'The Queen visiting the Tomb of Napoleon I', oil, 1855, Royal Coll. ALEXANDER BLAIKLEY, 'Faraday Lecturing at the Royal Institution', lith coloured in oils, 1855, Hunterian Museum, University of Glasgow. JOHN PHILLIP, 'The Marriage of the Princess Royal', oil, 1858, Royal Coll. G.H.THOMAS, 'Queen Victoria at a Military Review in Aldershot', oil, 1859, Royal Coll. THOMAS JONES BARKER, 'Queen Victoria Presenting a Bible in the Audience Chamber at Windsor', oil, c1861, NPG 4969. UNKNOWN, 'The Last Minutes of the Prince Consort', oil, 1861, Wellcome Institute, London.
SC EMIL WOLFF, 1839, marble bust, Royal Coll. E.H.BAILY, 1841, marble bust, V & A. R.W.SIEVIER, RA 1842, bust, Royal Coll. JOHN

FRANCIS, RA 1844, marble bust, Guildhall Museum, London; related plaster bust, NPG 1736. J.G.LOUGH, 1846, statue, Royal Exchange, London. E.WOLFE, 1846, marble statue, Osborne House, Isle of Wight. BARON CARLO MAROCHETTI, 1849, marble bust, Royal Coll. J.FRANCIS, 1850, marble bust, with Queen Victoria, Geological Museum, London. MATTHEW NOBLE, 1859, marble bust, City Hall, Manchester. WILLIAM THEED, 1860, bust, Grocers' Company, London. JOHN THOMAS, 1860, marble bust, Midland Institute, Birmingham. SUSAN DURANT, 1860, medallion, Royal Coll. WILLIAM THEED, 1862, marble statue, Osborne House, Isle of Wight. MATTHEW NOBLE, 1865, statues: Peel Park, Salford; Manchester; Leeds. THOMAS THORNYCROFT, 1866, bronze statue on horseback, Liverpool. WILLIAM THEED, 1868, marble statue with Queen Victoria, as ancient Saxons, Royal Coll. CHARLES BACON, 1874, statue, on horseback, Holborn Circus, London. UNKNOWN, memorial, St George's Chapel, Windsor.

PR Self-portrait, 1840, etch, Royal Coll. Various popular prints, BM, NPG.

C Several, BM, NPG.

PH ROGER FENTON, 1854, wl seated with Queen Victoria, V & A. L.CALDESI, 1857, with the Royal Family, print, NPG P26. MAYALL, 1861, tql seated, NPG X7263. Various prints, NPG, Royal Coll.

ALBERTAZZI, Emma, née Howson (1813-1847) singer.

PR F.CORBAUX, wl as Zerlina in *Don Giovanni*, lith, pub 1837, BM. E.FECHNER, tql as Rosina in *Barbier de Seville*, lith, BM. WELD TAYLOR, after F.Salabert, tql seated in private dress, lith, BM. Several theatrical prints, NPG.

ALBERY, James (1838-1889) dramatist.

PH UNKNOWN, hs, woodburytype, NPG X276.

ALCESTER, Frederick Beauchamp Paget Seymour, Baron (1821-1895) admiral.

PR UNKNOWN, after a photograph by Mr J.Maclardy, hl, line, oval, NPG.

PH BARRAUD, tql, print, for *Men and Women of the Day*, vol IV, 1891, NPG AX5530.

ALCOCK, Sir Rutherford (1809-1897) diplomat.

P After A.J.FOSTER, 1887, Westminster Hospital, London.

PH LOCK & WHITFIELD, hs, woodburytype, for *Men of Mark*, 1877, NPG.

ALDENHAM, Henry Hucks Gibbs, 1st Baron (1819-1907) merchant and scholar.

PR JAMES FAED, after G.F.Watts, hs, mezz, NPG.

C 'PET', wl, chromo-lith, NPG.

PH VALENTINE BLANCHARD, hs, profile, carte, NPG X4946. MAULL & Co, hs, profile, cabinet, NPG X4947.

ALDERSON, Sir Edwin Alfred Hervey (1859-1927) lieutenant-general.

PH WALTER STONEMAN, 1917, hs in uniform, NPG (NPR).

ALEXANDER, Mrs, see Annie French HECTOR.

ALEXANDER, Mrs Cecil Frances (1818-1895) hymn-writer.

P C.N.KENNEDY, 1894, wl seated, The Bishop and the Dean of Derry, N Ireland.

ALEXANDER, Sir George (1858-1918) actor-manager.

C HARRY FURNISS, 1905, pen and ink, for *The Garrick Club*, NPG 4095(1). SIR BERNARD PARTRIDGE, 1909, wl, w/c, NPG 3663. SIR MAX BEERBOHM, wl, V & A. SIR MAX BEERBOHM ('Max'), wl, Hentschel-colourtype, for *Vanity Fair*, 20 Jan 1909, NPG.

PH FALK, c1885, tql in costume, print, NPG X5153. ELLIS & WALERY,

1900, wl in *Rupert of Hentzau*, print, NPG AX5475. DOVER STREET STUDIOS, hs, postcard, NPG X32. UNKNOWN, hs, print, NPG X3770. Various photographs, various sizes, NPG X280-304.

ALEXANDER, Sir James Edward (1803-1885) general.

PR R.J.LANE, 1827, hs, lith, NPG.

ALEXANDER, Robert (1840-1923) artist.

P J.R.ABERCROMBY, hs, SNPG 1191.

PH OLIVE EDIS, 1904, hs, print, NPG X35. OLIVE EDIS, 1904, wl seated with dog, print, NPG X36.

ALEXANDER, Samuel (1859-1938) philosopher.

D FRANCIS DODD, 1932, head, chalk, NPG 4422.

SC JACOB EPSTEIN, 1925, bust, Manchester University.

PH WALTER STONEMAN, 1917 and 1931, hs and hl, NPG (NPR).

ALEXANDER, William (1824-1911) archbishop of Armagh.

P C.N.KENNEDY, 1894, wl seated, The Bishop & The Dean of Derry. H.HARRIS BROWNE, hs, NGI 622.

C SIR LESLIE WARD ('Spy'), w/c study, for *Vanity Fair*, 21 Nov 1895, NGI 2701.

PH ELLIOTT & FRY, hs, NPG (Anglican Bishops).

ALEXANDER, William Lindsay (1808-1884) congregational divine.

P NORMAN MACBETH, RA 1874?, tql seated, SNPG 93.

SC HUTCHINSON, marble bust, Augustine Church, Edinburgh.

PH JOHN MOFFAT, tql seated, carte, NPG (Album 102).

ALEXANDRA Caroline Mary Charlotte Louise Julia (1844-1925) of Denmark, queen-consort of King Edward VII.

P RICHARD LAUCHERT, 1863, tql, Royal Coll. ALBERT GRAEFLE, 1864, hl, profile, Royal Coll. F.X.WINTERHALTER, 1864, tql with fan, Royal Coll. SIR W.B.RICHMOND, 1892?, hl, Royal Coll. SIR LUKE FILDES, 1894, tql seated with dog, Royal Coll; replica, NPG 1889. SIR LUKE FILDES, 1905, wl in coronation robes, Royal Coll. EDWARD HUGHES, wl in coronation robes, Royal Coll. EDWARD HUGHES, wl in ordinary dress, Royal Coll. EDWARD HUGHES, wl in mourning, Royal Coll. LAURITS TUXEN, 1902, sketch for the coronation of Queen Alexandra, Det Nationalhistoriske Museum paa Frederiksborg, Denmark. SIR JOHN GILBERT, c1902, wl with Edward VII, Royal Coll. FRANÇOIS FLAMENG, 1908, wl seated, Royal Coll.

M WILLIAM POWELL FRITH, 1867, hl in bridal dress, oil, oval, Royal Coll. C.J.TURRELL, RA 1884, hs, Royal Coll.

G W.P.FRITH, 'The Marriage of the Prince of Wales', oil, 1863, Royal Coll. G.H.THOMAS, 'The Marriage of the Prince of Wales', oil, 1863, Royal Coll. HEINRICH VON ANGELI, 1876, tql seated with the Prince of Wales and their children, Royal Coll. LAURITS TUXEN, wl with King Edward and the Duke of Clarence, oil, 1884, Det Nationalhistoriske Museum paa Frederiksborg. LAURITS TUXEN, 'The Royal Family at the time of the Jubilee', oil, 1887, Royal Coll.

SC JOHN GIBSON, 1863, marble bust, Royal Coll. MARY THORNYCROFT, 1863, marble bust, Royal Coll. MATTHEW NOBLE, 1866, marble bust, Gawsworth Hall, Cheshire. PROSPER D'EPINAY, 1868, marble bust, DoE (British Embassy, Paris). COUNT VON GLEICHEN, 1875, marble bust, Royal Coll. COUNT VON GLEICHEN, 1879, marble bust, Walker Art Gallery, Liverpool. HENRY GARLAND, 1883, marble bust, NPG 3059. COUNT VON GLEICHEN, 1891, marble statue, Royal College of Music, London. COUNTESS FEODORA VON GLEICHEN, RA 1895, marble bust, Constitutional Club, London. G.E.WADE, 1908, bronze bust, Whitechapel High Street, London.

PR Various prints and popular prints, BM, NPG.

PH Two photographs, with her family and with the Prince of Wales and her family, Royal Library, Copenhagen. Various photographs, singly, with Edward VII, and in groups, Royal Coll and NPG.

ALFORD, Henry (1810-1871) dean of Canterbury.
P LOWES DICKINSON, 1857, tql, The Deanery, Canterbury.
PR J.H.BAKER, hl, line, BM.
PH LONDON STEREOSCOPIC CO, wl, carte, NPG (Album 40). MAULL & POLYBLANK, tql seated, carte, NPG AX7484. UNKNOWN, tql, print, NPG AX7320.

ALFORD, Marianne Margaret Alford, Viscountess (1817-1888) artist.
PR G.ZOBEL, after J.R.Swinton, wl in evening dress, mezz, pub 1863, BM, NPG.

ALFRED Ernest Albert, Duke of Edinburgh and Duke of Saxe-Coburg and Gotha (1844-1900) second son of Queen Victoria and Prince Albert.
P F.X.WINTERHALTER, 1852, hs, Royal Coll. F.R.SAY, 1861, wl, South African Library, Montagu, Cape Province, South Africa. GEORG KOBERWEIN, RA 1876, wl, Trinity House, London. BARON HEINRICH VON ANGELI, c1892, tql, Royal Coll. A.L.BAMBRIDGE, c1893?, tql, The Admiralty, Devonport.
D F.X.WINTERHALTER, wl with Princess Alice, w/c, Royal Coll.
M SIR W.C.ROSS, 1845, Royal Coll.
G F.X.WINTERHALTER, 'The Royal Family, 1846', oil, Royal Coll. F.X.WINTERHALTER, wl seated with Princess Alice and Princess Helena, w/c, 1847, Royal Coll. JOHN PHILLIP, 'The Marriage of the Princess Royal', oil, 1858, Royal Coll. G.H.THOMAS, 'The Marriage of Princess Alice to Prince Louis of Hesse', oil, 1862, Royal Coll. NICHOLAS CHEVALIER, 'The Marriage of the Duke of Edinburgh', oil, 1874, Royal Coll. NICHOLAS CHEVALIER, three hunting portraits, one shooting the big elephant, two tiger shooting in India, Royal Coll.
SC MARY THORNYCROFT, marble bust, as a child, Royal Coll. MARY THORNYCROFT, 1848, statuette, as Autumn, Royal Coll. CHARLES SUMMERS, RA 1873, marble bust, Melbourne Art Gallery, Australia. SIR J.E.BOEHM, 1879, marble bust, Royal Coll. SIR JOHN STEELL, plaster bust, SNPG 170.
PR Various prints and popular prints, BM, NPG.
C CARLO PELLEGRINI ('Ape'), 1873, wl, profile, chromo-lith, NPG. C.PELLEGRINI, tql, profile, with violin, chromo-lith, for Vanity Fair, 10 Jan 1874, NPG; study, Carrington Album, Royal Coll.
PH L.CALDESI, 1857, with Queen Victoria and other members of the Royal Family, print, NPG P26. W.BAMBRIDGE, 1862, with Queen Victoria, Princess Royal and Princess Alice, print, NPG P27. W. & D.DOWNEY, 1860s, with Edward VII, carte, NPG X3606. ABEL LEWIS, c1875-80, tql in naval uniform, cabinet, NPG X6859. RUSSELL & SONS, hl, cabinet, NPG AX5555. Various other prints, singly and in groups, NPG, Royal Coll.

ALICE Maud Mary, Princess of Great Britain and Ireland, Duchess of Saxony, Grand Duchess of Hesse-Darmstadt (1843-1878) third child of Queen Victoria and Prince Albert.
P SIR EDWIN LANDSEER, 1843, when nine days old, in cradle, with the dog, Dandie Dinmont, Royal Coll. SIR EDWIN LANDSEER, wl as a child, with 'Eos', Royal Coll. F.X.WINTERHALTER, 1859, tql, oval, Royal Coll.
D QUEEN VICTORIA, several drgs, some with her brothers and sisters, Royal Coll. F.X.WINTERHALTER, 1850, with Princess Royal in eighteenth century costumes, w/c, Royal Coll.
M EDWARD MOIRA, RA 1860?, Royal Coll.
G F.X.WINTERHALTER, 'The Royal Family, 1846', oil, Royal Coll. F.X.WINTERHALTER, with Prince Alfred and Princess Helena of Schleswig Holstein, w/c, 1847, Royal Coll. F.X.WINTERHALTER,

'The Four Daughters of Queen Victoria', oil, 1849, Royal Coll. JOHN PHILLIP, 'The Marriage of the Princess Royal', oil, 1858, Royal Coll. G.H.THOMAS, 'The Marriage of Princess Alice to Prince Louis of Hesse', oil, 1862, Royal Coll.
SC MRS MARY THORNYCROFT, statuette, as Spring, as a child, Royal Coll. MRS THORNYCROFT, 1861, marble bust, Royal Coll. JOSEPH KOPF, 1874, marble bust, Royal Coll. SIR J.E.BOEHM, 1879, marble bust, Royal Coll. MISS SUSAN D.DURANT, medallion, NPG 2023a.
PR Various prints and popular prints, BM, NPG.
PH L.CALDESI, 1857, wl with Queen Victoria and other members of the Royal Family, print, NPG P26. W.BAMBRIDGE, 1862, wl with Queen Victoria, Princess Royal and Prince Alfred, print, NPG P27. W. & D.DOWNEY, 1860s, wl with the Duke of Hesse, NPG X3603. MAYALL & CO, 1861, wl, profile, print, NPG X4190. W. & D.DOWNEY, 1862?, tql with the Duke of Hesse and Edward VII, carte, NPG X3609. Various photographs, singly and in groups, NPG and Royal Coll.

ALINGTON, Henry Gerard Sturt, 1st Baron (1825-1904) sportsman.
PR J.BROWN, hs, stipple, for Baily's Mag, 1869, BM.
C SIR LESLIE WARD ('Spy'), wl, profile, chromo-lith, for Vanity Fair, 8 July 1876, NPG.

ALISON, Sir Archibald, 2nd Bart (1826-1907) soldier.
SC K.A.FRASER TYTLER, 1883, plaster bust, SNPG 944.
PR MACLURE & MACDONALD, hs, chromo-lith, supplement to The Pictorial World, 28 Oct 1882, NPG.

ALLAN, Sir Henry Marshman Havelock, see HAVELOCK-Allan.

ALLAN, Sir William (1837-1903) engineer and politician.
P TREVOR HADDON, probably RA 1899, National Liberal Club, London.
PH SIR BENJAMIN STONE, 1897, wl, print, NPG.

ALLBUTT, Sir Thomas Clifford (1836-1925) physician.
P SIR WILLIAM ORPEN, c1920, tql seated, Fitzwilliam Museum, Cambridge.
SC MARY G.GILLICK, 1928, bronze relief plaque, hl, profile, Department of Medicine, Cambridge.
PH JOHN RUSSELL & SONS, hs, print, for National Photographic Record, vol II, NPG.

ALLEN, Charles Grant Blairfindie (1848-1899) author.
PR SIR WILLIAM ROTHENSTEIN, 1897, hl seated, lith, NPG 3998.
PH BARRAUD, tql, print, for Men and Women of the Day, vol IV, 1891, NPG AX5539.

ALLEN, George (1832-1907) engraver and publisher.
P FRED YATES, 1890, tql seated, George Allen & Unwin Ltd, London.

ALLEN, Sir James (1855-1942) New Zealand statesman.
PH WALTER STONEMAN, 1921 and 1926, both hs, NPG (NPR).

ALLERTON, William Lawies Jackson, 1st Baron (1840-1917) politician.
P H.A.OLIVIER, tql seated, Museum of British Transport, York.
PR H.ADLARD, hs, stipple, BM.
C SIR LESLIE WARD ('Spy'), wl, profile, chromo-lith, for Vanity Fair, 31 Aug 1899, NPG.
PH LONDON STEREOSCOPIC CO, hs, print, for Our Conservative Statesmen, vol I, NPG (Album 16).

ALLINGHAM, William (1824-1889) poet.
D HELEN ALLINGHAM (his wife), 1876, tql seated, profile, w/c, NPG 1647. H.ALLINGHAM, c1884, hl, profile, w/c, NGI 2641. ARTHUR HUGHES, hs, pen, ink and pencil, oval, Whitworth Art Gallery,

Manchester. CHARLES FAIRFAX MURRAY, hs, Fitzwilliam Museum, Cambridge.

SC ALEXANDER MUNRO, probably related to RA 1855, plaster bust, NGI 8116. VINCENT BREEN, 20th century, bust, outside Allied Irish Bank, Ballyshannon, Co Donegal, N Ireland.

PH UNKNOWN, c1857, two copy negs by Emery Walker, hs and wl seated, NPG X307 and X308. UNKNOWN, copy neg by Emery Walker, hl seated, profile, NPG (Emery Walker Box 872).

ALLMAN, George James (1812-1898) botanist and zoologist.

P E.M.BUSK, 1897, Linnean Society, London.

D SIR F.W.BURTON, chalk, NGI 2351.

PR T.H.MAGUIRE, tql seated, lith, one of set of *Ipswich Museum Portraits*, 1851, BM, NPG.

ALLOM, Thomas (1804-1872) architect.

PR UNKNOWN, hs, woodcut, BM.

ALLON, Henry (1818-1892) congregational minister.

PR J.COCHRAN, after W.Gush, tql seated, stipple and line, NPG. J.COCHRAN, after a photograph, hs, profile, stipple, NPG. UNKNOWN, hs, profile, lith, NPG.

PH LOCK & WHITFIELD, hs, wooodburytype, for *The Congregationalist*, 1879, NPG X45. W. & D.DOWNEY, c1890, hs, woodburytype, for Cassell's *Cabinet Portrait Gallery*, vol I, 1890, NPG X44.

ALLPORT, Sir James Joseph (1811-1892) general manager of the Midland Railway.

PR G.W.EMERY, after J.E.Williams, tql seated, mezz, BM.

ALMA-TADEMA, Laura, Lady, née Epps (d1909) artist and second wife of Sir Lawrence Alma-Tadema.

P SIR LAWRENCE ALMA-TADEMA, 1876, hs, Williamson Art Gallery, Birkenhead.

G UNKNOWN, 1871, hs, with a companion portrait of her husband, Fries Museum, Leeuwarden, The Netherlands. H.J.BROOKS, 'Private View of the Old Masters' Exhibition, Royal Academy, 1888', oil, NPG 1833. SIR LAWRENCE ALMA-TADEMA, 'A Family Group', oil, 1896, Royal Academy, London.

ALMA-TADEMA, Sir Lawrence (1836-1912) painter.

P Self-portrait, 1852, hl, profile, at easel, Fries Museum, Leeuwarden, The Netherlands. Self-portrait, 1883, hs, Aberdeen Art Gallery. Self-portrait, 1896, hs at easel, Uffizi Gallery, Florence. Self-portrait, 1912, hs at easel, a portrait of his mother in the background, R Academia Romana di San Luca.

D S.P.HALL, 1895, hs, profile, pencil, NPG 4388. WILLIAM STRANG, 1908, hs, chalk, Royal Coll. FLORA LION, 1912, head, pencil, NPG 3946.

G Self-portrait, hs with his half brother Jelte Zacharius, his mother and his sister Atje, 1859, Fries Museum, Leeuwarden. UNKNOWN, 1871, hs, with a companion portrait of his wife, (a double portrait), Fries Museum, Leeuwarden. H.J.BROOKS, 'Private View of the Old Masters Exhibition, Royal Academy, 1888', oil, NPG 1833. G.GRENVILLE MANTON, 'Conversazione at the Royal Academy, 1891', w/c, NPG 2820. REGINALD CLEAVER, 'Hanging Committee, Royal Academy, 1892', pen and ink, NPG 4245. S.P.HALL, 'St John's Wood Art Club', chalk and wash, 1895, NPG 4404.

SC EDWARD ONSLOW FORD, RA 1896, bronze bust, Royal Academy, London.

C HARRY FURNISS, c1900, with Sir Henry Irving, pen and ink, Museum of London. CARLO PELLEGRINI ('Ape'), drg for *Vanity Fair*, BM.

PH UNKNOWN, 1863, wl kneeling, measuring ruins and examining marble at Pompeii, Birmingham University Library. LENA CONNELL, tql with his wife Laura, print, NPG X47. LOCK & WHITFIELD, hs, profile, oval, woodburytype, NPG X311. LONDON

STEREOSCOPIC CO, tql seated, cabinet, NPG X5155. WALERY, tql, print, NPG X6020.

ALVERSTONE, Richard Everard Webster, Viscount (1842-1915) lord chief justice.

P SIR A.S.COPE, 1903, Lincoln's Inn, London. JOHN COLLIER, 1911, tql seated in robes, Royal Institution of Chartered Surveyors, London. UNKNOWN, Harvard Law Library, Cambridge, USA.

D S.P.HALL, 1888-9, hl, pencil, one of sketches of people attending the Parnell Commission, NPG 2233. S.P.HALL, 1889, related to the Parnell Commission illustrations, pencil, NPG 2300. FREDERICK PEGRAM, 1889, several drgs, as illustrations of the Parnell Commission, for the *Pictorial World*, V & A. SEYMOUR LUCAS, 1902, hl seated, chalk, NPG 4337.

G SYDNEY PRIOR HALL, with several other figures, for the Parnell Commission, drg, 1889, NPG 2250.

PR F.DODD, hl in robes, etch, BM. G.J.STODART, after H.T.Wells, hs, stipple, one of, 'Grillion's Club', series, BM, NPG.

C FRANCOIS VERHEYDEN, 1883, hl, profile, w/c, drawn for *Vanity Fair*, 26 May 1883, NPG 2698. SIR LESLIE WARD ('Spy'), hl seated at bench, chromo-lith, for *Vanity Fair*, 1 Nov 1900, NPG. 'W.H.', hl seated at bench, chromo-lith, for *Vanity Fair*, 15 Jan 1913, NPG.

PH RUSSELL & SONS, c1895, hs, print, NPG X50. LONDON STEREOSCOPIC CO, hl in robes, cabinet, NPG X5156.

AMHERST of Hackney, William Amhurst Tyssen-Amherst, 1st Baron (1835-1909) bibliophile and Norfolk landowner.

C SIR LESLIE WARD ('Spy'), wl, chromo-lith, for *Vanity Fair*, 10 March 1904, NPG.

AMPHLETT, Sir Richard Paul (1809-1883) judge.

PR UNKNOWN, hs, woodcut, for *Illust London News*, 7 Feb 1874, NPG.

PH T.R.WILLIAMS, hs, carte, NPG (Album 120).

AMPTHILL, Odo William Leopold Russell, 1st Baron (1829-1884) diplomat.

SC UNKNOWN, relief marble tablet, Russell Chapel, St Michael's Church, Chenies, Bucks.

PR R.C.CLOUSTON, after C.Holroyd, hl seated, mezz, BM.

ANCASTER, Gilbert Henry Heathcote-Drummond-Willoughby, 1st Earl of (1830-1910) politician.

PR J.BROWN, hs, stipple, for *Baily's Mag*, 1875, BM.

C SIR LESLIE WARD ('Spy'), wl, profile, w/c study, for *Vanity Fair*, 30 July 1881, NPG 4712.

ANDERSON, Alexander (1845-1909) poet.

P CHARLES MARTIN HARDIE, 1883, hl, SNPG 697.

D J.D.GILRUTH, pencil, SNPG 1720.

ANDERSON, Elizabeth Garrett (1836-1917) physician and pioneer of the professional education of women.

P J.S.SARGENT, tql seated, Johns Hopkins University, Baltimore, Maryland, USA; copies, Elizabeth Garrett Anderson Hospital, London, and Royal Free Hospital School of Medicine, London. UNKNOWN, hl, Wellcome Institute, London. UNKNOWN, British Medical Association, London.

PH ELLIOTT & FRY, c1870, hs, profile, carte, NPG X65. FREDERICK HOLLYER, hl, profile, seated, V & A (Hollyer Albums). OLIVE EDIS, c1910, tql seated, print, NPG X66. OLIVE EDIS, tql, print, NPG X317. WALERY, tql, print, NPG.

ANDERSON, James Robertson (1811-1895) actor.

P UNKNOWN, wl as Ion, Garrick Club, London.

D DANIEL MACLISE, tql, w/c, SNPG 648.

G HENRY NELSON O'NEIL, 'The Billiard Room of the Garrick Club', oil, 1869, Garrick Club.

PR Two theatrical prints, NPG.

ANDERSON, John (1805-1855) missionary.
PR E.BURTON, after J.W.GORDON, tql seated, mezz, pub 1851, BM.

ANDERSON, John Henry (1815-1874) conjurer and actor.
PR UNKNOWN, wl, woodcut, NPG.

ANDERSON, Mary (Madame de Navarro) (1859-1940) actress.
G G.GRENVILLE MANTON, 'Conversazione at the Royal Academy, 1891', w/c, NPG 2820.
PR F.S.HADEN, hs, profile, etch, BM. Various popular prints, NPG.
PH Various photographs, some in character, various sizes, by BARRAUD, BASSANO, DOWNEY, ELLIOTT & FRY and VAN DER WEYDE, NPG X67-X83. BARRAUD, c1888, tql, print, for *Men and Women of the Day*, vol I, 1888, NPG AX5405. W. & D.DOWNEY, hs, profile, cabinet, NPG X318. VAN DER WEYDE, hs, as Juliet, cabinet, NPG X4184.

ANDERSON, Thomas (1832-1870) botanist.
P J.D.HOOKER, tql, Royal Botanic Gardens, Edinburgh.
PH FELICE BEATO, 1857-8, wl in a group of the Sikh Horse, National Army Museum, London.

ANDERSON, William (1805-1866) miscellaneous writer.
PR A.D'ORSAY, 1846, hl, profile, lith, BM, NPG.

ANDREWES, Sir Frederick William (1859-1932) pathologist and bacteriologist.
PH WALTER STONEMAN, 1923, hs, NPG (NPR).

ANDREWS, Thomas (1813-1885) surgeon and chemist.
P UNKNOWN, hs, oval, Royal Belfast Academical Institution.

ANNANDALE, Thomas (1838-1907) professor of clinical surgery.
PR WILLIAM HOLE, wl, etch, for *Quasi Cursores*, 1884, NPG.

ANSDELL, Richard (1815-1885) painter.
P SIR A.S.COPE, 1883, hs, oval, MacDonald Collection, Aberdeen Art Gallery.
G W.MURDEN, 'Associates of the Royal Academy in 1861', woodcut, for *Illust London News*, 25 July 1863, BM.
SC HENRY WEEKES, RA 1873?, marble bust, Walker Art Gallery, Liverpool.
PR H.SCHEU, after J.E.Hodgson, seated by river, with Frederick Walker who is fishing, woodcut, BM.
C UNKNOWN, wl, woodcut, for *The Hornet*, 22 Nov 1876, NPG.
PH DAVID WILKIE WYNFIELD, c1862-4, hs, NPG P70 and P89. C.A.DUVAL & Co, wl, carte, NPG (Album 104). ELLIOTT & FRY, hs, carte, NPG (Album 104). LOCK & WHITFIELD, hs, woodbury-type, for *Men of Mark*, 1883, NPG. JOHN & CHARLES WATKINS, tql seated, carte, NPG AX7554. J. & C.WATKINS, hs, carte, NPG (Album 106).

ANSON, Sir William Reynell, 3rd Bart (1843-1914) warden of All Souls College, Oxford.
P SIR HUBERT VON HERKOMER, 1895?, tql seated, All Souls College, Oxford.
SC JOHN TWEED, recumbent figure on marble monument, All Souls College Chapel.
C SIR LESLIE WARD ('Spy'), wl, profile, chromo-lith, for *Vanity Fair*, 13 June 1901, NPG.
PH SIR BENJAMIN STONE, 1901, two wl prints, NPG.

ANSTED, David Thomas (1814-1880) geologist.
PR T.H.MAGUIRE, tql seated, lith, one of set of *Ipswich Museum Portraits*, 1851, BM, NPG.
PH ERNEST EDWARDS, wl seated, for *Men of Eminence*, ed L.Reeve, vol III, 1864, NPG. MAULL & POLYBLANK, (probably rightly called), wl, carte, NPG X90.

ANSTEY, F., see Thomas Anstey GUTHRIE.

ANSTIE, Francis Edmund (1833-1874) physician.
PR C.H.JEENS, head, line, for *The Practitioner*, vol XVI, BM. UNKNOWN, after a photograph by Barraud & Jerrard, hs, woodcut, for *Illust London News*, 26 Sept 1874, NPG.

'APE', see Carlo PELLEGRINI.

ARCH, Joseph (1826-1919) politician, improved conditions of agricultural workers.
PR UNKNOWN, hs, woodcut, for *Illust London News*, 20 April 1872, NPG. UNKNOWN, two woodcuts, hl and tql profile, NPG.
C SIR LESLIE WARD ('Spy'), wl, chromo-lith, for *Vanity Fair*, 26 June 1886, NPG.
PH SIR BENJAMIN STONE, 1897, wl, print, NPG.

ARCHER, Frederick (1857-1886) jockey.
P EMIL ADAM, 1887, wl equestrian, with John Porter, his trainer, The Jockey Club, London. ROSA CORDER, hl, J.A.Allen & Co Ltd, London.
D 'C.W.S.', 1888, hs, chalk, NPG 3961.
G L.PROSPERI ('Lib'), a group at Newmarket, chromo-lith, for *Vanity Fair*, 30 Nov 1885, NPG.
PR R.JOSEY, after Rosa Corder, hl in racing dress, mezz, pub 1884, BM, NPG.
C OTTO BROWER, 1878, two w/cs, wl on horseback, NPG 2648 and 2649. SIR LESLIE WARD ('Spy'), wl, chromo-lith, for *Vanity Fair*, 28 May 1881, NPG. ALFRED ROGERS, wl as bird in a cage, for Supplement to *Society*, 26 May 1883, NPG.

ARCHER, Frederick Scott (1813-1857) inventor of collodion process.
PH R.CADE, 1855, tql seated, Science Museum, London.

ARCHER, James (1823-1904) painter.
P Self-portrait, RA 1899?, hs, SNPG 725.
PH UNKNOWN, hs, carte, NPG (Album 104).

ARCHER, William (1856-1924) dramatic critic and journalist.
PR W.ROTHENSTEIN, hl, lith, 1897, BM, NPG.
C Several cartoon drgs by SIR MAX BEERBOHM: one 1904 and one undated, University of Texas, USA; 1904, Municipal Gallery of Modern Art, Dublin; 1908, Ashmolean Museum, Oxford; 1911, Lilly Library, Indiana University, Bloomington, Indiana, USA.
PH UNKNOWN, hs, for *The Theatre*, 1886, BM (Engr Ports Coll).

ARCHIBALD, Sir Thomas Dickson (1817-1876) judge.
PR UNKNOWN, after a photograph by John Watkins, hs, woodcut, for *Illust London News*, 4 Jan 1873, NPG.

ARDAGH, Sir John Charles (1840-1907) major-general of the Royal Engineers.
P EMILY M.MERRICK, RA 1899?, tql, Royal Engineers HQ Mess, Chatham, Kent.
PR G.B.BLACK, 1880, hs in uniform, lith, NPG.
PH EMERY WALKER, after J.Russell & Sons, hs, profile, in uniform, photogravure, NPG X325.

ARDILAUN, Sir Arthur Edward Guinness, 1st Baron (1840-1915) philanthropist.
SC SIR THOMAS FARRELL, 1891, bronze statue, St Stephen's Green, Dublin.
PR UNKNOWN, hl seated, lith, NPG.

ARDMILLAN, James Craufurd, Lord (1805-1876) judge.
PR UNKNOWN, after a photograph by J.Horsburgh, hs, woodcut, for *Illust London News*, 23 Sept 1876, NPG.

ARGYLL, George Douglas Campbell, 8th Duke of (1823-1900) statesman.
P G.F.WATTS, c1860, hs, semi-profile, NPG 1263. Several portraits at Inveraray Castle, Strathclyde region, Scotland: SIR JOHN

WATSON-GORDON, RA 1851, hl, oval; HEINRICH VON ANGELI, exhib 1878, tql in highland dress (copy, H.KOBERWEIN-TERRELL, 1892, Royal Coll); G.P.JACOMB HOOD, 1890, hl; S.P.HALL; PRINCESS LOUISE (his daughter-in-law). JOHN PETTIE, hs, SNPG 857. UNKNOWN, University of St Andrews.

D J.R.SWINTON, 1852, hs, Inveraray Castle. GEORGE RICHMOND, probably 1861, hs, Inveraray Castle, engr W.Holl, stipple, one of 'Grillion's Club', series, BM, NPG. S.P.HALL, 1893, pencil, NPG 2338.

SL F.S.BADEN POWELL, 1895, head, NPG.

G SIR JOHN GILBERT, 'The Coalition Ministry, 1854', pencil and wash, NPG 1125.

SC LAWRENCE MACDONALD, 1844, marble bust, Inveraray Castle. WILLIAM BRODIE, 1855, bust, Dunrobin Castle, Highland region, Scotland. GEORGE FRAMPTON, 1905, marble bust, Palace of Westminster, London. G.FRAMPTON, RA 1908, recumbent effigy, Iona Cathedral.

C CARLO PELLEGRINI ('Ape'), wl, profile, chromo-lith, for *Vanity Fair*, 17 April 1869, NPG.

PH CALDESI, BLANFORD & Co, wl, carte, NPG AX5054. ELLIOTT & FRY, tql seated, cabinet, NPG (Album 47). MAYALL, hs, carte, NPG (Album 136). W.WALKER & SONS, tql seated, carte, NPG X93. JOHN & CHARLES WATKINS, hs, carte, NPG X92. UNKNOWN, hs, woodburytype, carte, NPG X91.

ARGYLL, John Douglas Sutherland Campbell, 9th Duke of (1845-1914) governor-general of Canada.

P J.M.BARCLAY, c1872, wl in Highland dress with dog and gun, Inveraray Castle, Strathclyde region, Scotland. HEINRICH VON ANGELI, 1875, hs with orders, Royal Coll. SIR J.E.MILLAIS, c1884, tql, profile, The National Gallery of Canada, Ottawa. S.P.HALL, 1910, tql seated in library, Inveraray Castle.

G S.P.HALL, 'Marriage of Princess Louise and the Marquess of Lorne, 1871', oil, Royal Coll.

SC COUNT GLEICHEN, RA 1871, marble bust, Inveraray Castle.

PR W.H.MOTE, after W.S.Herrick, tql with his mother, stipple and line, pub 1855, NPG.

C CARLO PELLEGRINI ('Ape'), 1870, wl, profile, w/c, for *Vanity Fair*, 19 Nov 1870, NPG 4629; pencil study, Royal Coll.

PH STUART of Glasgow, wl as a young man in Highland costume, carte, NPG X96. BENJAMIN STONE, 1898, wl, outside the Houses of Parliament, print, NPG. W. & D.DOWNEY, hs, oval, carte, with companion oval of Princess Louise, NPG. ELLIOTT & FRY, hs, profile, carte, NPG X97 and X1508; related photograph by ELLIOTT & FRY, carte, NPG X98. LONDON STEREOSCOPIC Co, hs, profile, cabinet, NPG X99. LONDON STEREOSCOPIC Co, hs, carte, NPG X95. T.RODGER, tql, carte, NPG AX7427. G.W.WILSON of Aberdeen, tql seated, carte, NPG X94.

ARGYLL, Princess Louise Caroline Alberta, Duchess of, see Princess LOUISE.

ARMES, Philip (1836-1908) professor of music at Durham.

PR UNKNOWN, tql seated, process block, for *Musical Times*, 1900, BM.

ARMITAGE, Edward (1817-1896) painter.

P Self-portrait, 1882, hs, oval, MacDonald Collection, Aberdeen Art Gallery.

SC SIR J.E.BOEHM, c1877, terracotta bust, Royal Academy, London.

PR Four woodcuts after photographs, in the NPG: hs, for *Illust London News*, 1867; hs, for *Magazine of Art*, 1894, vol 17; hs, for *Magazine of Art*, 1896, vol 19; for *Illust London News*, 1896.

ARMSTEAD, Henry Hugh (1828-1905) sculptor.

P J.E.HODGSON, 1884, hs, oval, MacDonald Collection, Aberdeen Art Gallery.

PR Two woodcuts after photographs, in NPG; hs, for *Illust London News*, 1875; hs, for *Magazine of Art*, 1880.

PH LOCK & WHITFIELD, hs, oval, woodburytype, for *Men of Mark*, 1883, NPG. UNKNOWN, hs, woodburytype, NPG X100.

ARMSTRONG, Sir Alexander (1818-1899) naval medical officer.

P UNKNOWN, hs, Hasler Hospital, Gosport.

ARMSTRONG, Sir George Carlyon Hughes, 1st Bart (1836-1907) newspaper proprietor.

PR UNKNOWN, hs, woodcut, for *Illust London News*, 27 Aug 1892, NPG.

C SIR LESLIE WARD ('Spy'), nearly wl, chromo-lith, for *Vanity Fair*, 8 Nov 1894, NPG.

ARMSTRONG, Henry Edward (1848-1937) chemist and educationist.

P T.C.DUGDALE, 1927, tql, Royal Institution, London.

SC After CLACK, bronze bust, Imperial College, London.

ARMSTRONG, Thomas (1832-1911) artist.

SC UNKNOWN, metal plaque, profile, St Lawrence the Martyr Church, Abbots Langley, Herts.

PR UNKNOWN, hl, for *Art Journal*, 1891, NPG.

ARMSTRONG, Walter (1850-1918) director of the National Gallery, Dublin.

P WALTER OSBORNE, RA 1896, NGI 1389.

SC EDWARD ONSLOW FORD, RA 1894, bronze bust, NGI 8143.

ARMSTRONG, Sir William George Armstrong, Baron of Cragside (1810-1900) inventor.

P MARY L.WALLER, 1882, hs, NPG L161.

SC ALEXANDER MUNRO, 1861, marble bust, Literary and Philosophical Society, Newcastle-upon-Tyne. SIR WILLIAM HAMO THORNYCROFT, statue, Barras Bridge, Newcastle-upon-Tyne.

PH LOCK & WHITFIELD, hs, oval, woodburytype, for *Men of Mark*, 1882, NPG, similar print, NPG X102. W. & D.DOWNEY, tql seated, woodburytype, for Cassell's *Cabinet Portrait Gallery*, vol I, 1890, NPG X101.

ARNOLD, Sir Edwin (1832-1904) poet and journalist.

D A.P.COLE, 1903, hs, pencil, NPG 2455.

SL S.BADEN-POWELL, hs, NPG.

PR BEN DAMMAN, after a photograph, hs, etch, NPG; woodcut, after same photograph, for *Illust London News*, 1892, NPG.

PH W. & D.DOWNEY, hs, woodburytype, for Cassell's *Cabinet Portrait Gallery*, vol IV, 1893, NPG.

ARNOLD, Matthew (1822-1888) poet and critic.

P G.F.WATTS, 1880, hs, profile, NPG 1000. L.C.DICKINSON, 1896, hs, Oriel College, Oxford. HENRY WEIGALL, The Athenaeum, London.

D T.B.WIRGMAN, 1882, pencil, Art Institute of Chicago, USA.

SC WILLIAM TYLER, probably RA 1889, marble bust, Balliol College, Oxford. ALBERT BRUCE JOY, marble bust, Westminster Abbey, London.

PR J.J.CADE, hs, stipple and line, for *The Eclectic*, NPG. F.HOLLYER, after a photograph by Elliott & Fry, hs, etch, NPG. UNKNOWN, after a photograph by Sarony, hs, woodcut and engraving, NPG. R.TAYLOR, after a photograph by Elliott & Fry, hs, semi-profile, woodcut, for *Illustrated Review*, vol III, 1872, NPG.

C J.J.TISSOT, nearly wl, chromo-lith, for *Vanity Fair*, 11 Nov 1871, NPG.

PH ELLIOTT & FRY, three hs cartes, NPG X109, X110 and X329. CAMILLE SILVY, 1861, wl, carte, NPG (Album 5).

ARNOLD, Thomas (1823-1900) professor of English Literature.

SC UNKNOWN, tablet, Catholic University Church, Dublin.

ARNOLD-FORSTER, Hugh Oakeley (1855-1909) politician.
P R.P.HARRIS BROWN, c1900, tql seated, The Athenaeum, London.
D S.P.HALL, pencil sketch, NPG 2328.
C SIR LESLIE WARD ('Spy'), wl, chromo-lith, for *Vanity Fair*, 24 Aug 1905, NPG.
PH ELLIOTT & FRY, hs, print, for *Our Conservative and Unionist Statesmen*, vol II, (Album 25), NPG. SIR BENJAMIN STONE, 1899, two prints, both wl, NPG.

ARNOT, William (1808-1875) Scottish minister.
PH JOHN GIBSON of Belfast, wl seated, carte, NPG X108.

ARROL, Sir William (1839-1913) engineer.
SC D.W.STEVENSON, plaster bust, SNPG 613.
PH SIR BENJAMIN STONE, 1897, two wl prints, NPG.

ARTHUR, Duke of Connaught and Strathearn, see Connaught.

ARTHUR, William (1819-1901) Wesleyan divine.
PR J.COCHRAN, after W.Gush, hl, stipple, NPG. UNKNOWN, hs, lith, NPG. UNKNOWN, hs, stipple, NPG.

ASHBOURNE, Edward Gibson, 1st Baron (1837-1913) lord chancellor of Ireland.
PR J.BROWN, after H.T.Wells, hs, stipple, one of 'Grillion's Club' series, BM, NPG.
C SIR LESLIE WARD ('Spy'), wl, w/c study for *Vanity Fair*, 4 July 1885, NPG 3932.
PH J.RUSSELL & SONS, c1892, hs, print, for *Our Conservative Statesmen*, vol I, NPG X113.

ASHER, Alexander (1835-1905) solicitor-general for Scotland.
P SIR W.Q.ORCHARDSON, RA 1902, tql, Faculty of Advocates, Parliament Hall, Edinburgh.

ASHMEAD BARTLETT, Sir Ellis (1849-1902) politician.
PR UNKNOWN, hs, lith, NPG.
C SIR LESLIE WARD ('Spy'), wl, profile, chromo-lith, for *Vanity Fair*, 21 Oct 1882, NPG.
PH RUSSELL & SONS, c1892, hs, print, for *Our Conservative Statesmen*, vol II, NPG X116. SIR BENJAMIN STONE, 1897, two wl prints, NPG. G.C.BERESFORD, two negs, 1905, and 1909, both hs, the second in uniform, NPG X6433 and X6434.

ASHTON of Hyde, Thomas Gair Ashton, 1st Baron (1855-1933) industrialist, philanthropist and politician.
PH WALTER STONEMAN, 1917, hs, NPG (NPR).

ASPULL, George (1813-1832) pianist.
PR UNKNOWN, hs, profile, aged 16, lith, for his *Posthumous Works*, 1837, BM.

ASQUITH, Herbert Henry, 1st Earl of Oxford and Asquith, see OXFORD and Asquith.

ASTLEY, Sir John Dugdale, 3rd Bart (1828-1894) sportsman.
D JOHN FLATMAN, wl on horseback, w/c, NPG 2775.
SL PHIL MAY, 1889, wl, NPG 3173.
PR J.BROWN, from a photograph, hs, stipple, for *Baily's Mag*, 1872, BM. W.J.ALLINGHAM, after a photograph by Bassano, tql, stipple and line, pub 1894, NPG. V.BROOKS, tql, lith, NPG.
C SIR LESLIE WARD ('Spy'), two chromo-liths, both wl, for *Vanity Fair*, 17 Nov 1877, and 26 July 1894, NPG.

ASTON, William George (1841-1911) Japanese scholar.
D MINNIE COHEN, 1911, hl seated, pencil, NPG 1775.

ATKINSON, John Atkinson, Baron (1844-1932) judge.
P JOHN ST HELIER LANDER, King's Inns, Dublin.

ATKINSON, Thomas (1801?-1833) poet and bookseller.
P UNKNOWN, Royal Technical College, Glasgow.
SL AUGUSTIN EDOUART, SNPG 785.

ATLAY, James (1817-1894) bishop of Hereford.
P After JOHN COLLIER of c1893, Bishop's Palace, Hereford.
SC FORSYTH, marble recumbent effigy, Hereford Cathedral.
PH LOCK & WHITFIELD, hs, oval, woodburytype, for *Men of Mark*, 1878, NPG X131.

AUSTEN, Sir William Chandler Roberts, see ROBERTS – Austen.

AUSTEN LEIGH, Augustus (1840-1905), see Leigh.

AUSTIN, Alfred (1835-1913) poet laureate.
G R.TAYLOR & Co. 'Modern Poets', woodcut, for *Illust London News*, 15 Oct 1892. BM, NPG.
C SIR LESLIE WARD ('Spy'), wl, profile, w/c study, for *Vanity Fair*, 20 Feb 1896, NPG 1768; variant, NPG 4845. SIR MAX BEERBOHM, 1900, holding a drum and two drumsticks, Kipling beside him, with lyre, The William Andrews Clark Memorial Library, University of California at Los Angeles, USA.
PH BARRAUD, hs, cabinet, NPG X135.

AUSTIN, Sir Horatio Thomas (1801-1865) admiral.
P STEPHEN PEARCE, 1860, hl with orders, NPG 1218.

AVEBURY, Sir John Lubbock, 1st Baron (1834-1913) banker, scientist and writer.
D GEORGE RICHMOND, 1869, hs, chalk, NPG 4869.
PR G.B.BLACK, 1871, hl, lith, NPG. M.KLINKICHT, after a photograph, hs, woodcut, supplement to *Illust London News*, 1890, BM. MACLURE & MACDONALD, hs, lith, NPG. UNKNOWN, after a photograph by London Stereoscopic Co, hl, lith, NPG.
C 'PET', wl, chromo-lith, supplement to *The Monetary Gazette*, 10 Jan 1877, NPG. SIR LESLIE WARD ('Spy'), nearly wl seated, chromo-lith, for *Vanity Fair*, 23 Feb 1878, NPG.
PH BARRAUD, tql seated, print, for *Men and Women of the Day*, vol II, 1889, NPG X137.

AVERY, John (1807-1855) surgeon.
M Attrib HENRY COLLEN, c1840–50, hl, NPG 1893.

AVORY, Sir Horace Edmund (1851-1935) judge.
P BEATRICE BRIGHT, RA 1919, tql seated in robes, Inner Temple, London. CHARLES WINZER, hl in robes, Corpus Christi College, Cambridge.
C SIR LESLIE WARD ('Spy'), tql, profile, chromo-lith, for *Vanity Fair*, 2 June 1904, NPG. E.X.KAPP, 1924, coloured lith, for pl 6 of *Law Journal*, 4 April 1925, V & A. E.X.KAPP, 1931, Barber Institute of Fine Arts, Birmingham. E.X.KAPP, lith, V & A. HARRY FURNISS, pen and ink, NPG 3415.
PH WALTER STONEMAN, two, both hs, one in robes dated 1930, NPG (NPR).

AYRTON, Acton Smee (1816-1886) politician.
SC G.A.W.WILKIE, 1877, marble bust, DoE (Law Courts).
PR UNKNOWN, after a photograph by Mayall, hl, woodcut, for *Illust London News*, 16 May 1857, NPG.
C CARLO PELLEGRINI ('Ape'), wl, w/c, for *Vanity Fair*, 23 Oct 1869, NPG 4713. FAUSTIN, head, body in shape of a beast, chromo-lith, NPG.

AYRTON, William Edward (1847-1908) electrical engineer and inventor.
PH W. & D.DOWNEY, tql, woodburytype, for Cassell's *Cabinet Portrait Gallery*, vol IV, 1893, NPG.

AYTOUN, William Edmondstoune (1813-1865) poet.
D JAMES ARCHER, 1855, hs, pencil and w/c, SNPG 125.
SC PATRIC PARK, c1851, plaster bust, NPG 1544.
PR UNKNOWN, hs, woodcut, for *Illust London News*, 19 Aug 1865, NPG.

C B.CROMBIE, 1848, wl, coloured etch, reprinted in *Modern Athenians*, 1882, NPG.
PH T.RODGER of St Andrews, hs, carte, NPG X355. T.RODGER, wl, carte, NPG AX7542.

B

BABINGTON, Charles Cardale (1808-1895) botanist and archaeologist.
P W.VIZARD, 1888, hl, Department of Botany, Cambridge. W.VIZARD, 1896, probably after a photograph, hl, St John's College, Cambridge.
PH ERNEST EDWARDS, wl seated, for *Men of Eminence*, ed L.Reeve, vol III, 1865, NPG.

BADEN-POWELL, Robert Stephenson Smyth Baden-Powell, 1st Baron (1857-1941) founder of the Boy Scouts and Girl Guides.
P G.F.WATTS, RA 1902, hs in South African Constabulary uniform, Charterhouse School, London. SIR HUBERT VON HERKOMER, RA 1903, tql in South African Constabulary uniform, Cavalry and Guards Club, London. DAVID JAGGER, 1929, hl, Baden Powell House, London. DAVID JAGGER, 1930, hl, Mercers' Company, London. SIMON ELWES, 1931, in scout uniform, seated at desk, Girl Guides Association headquarters, London.
D SHIRLEY SLOCOMBE, 1916, hs, chalk, NPG 4100. AUGUSTUS JOHN, 1936, hs, Collection of the 13th/18th Royal Hussars.
SC ALFRED DRURY, 1918?, bronze bust, Baden Powell House. A.G.ATKINSON, c1931, relief bronze, hs, Mercers' Company. UNKNOWN, c1931, bronze bust, Girl Guides Association headquarters. DON POTTER, 1961, statue, Baden Powell House.
W UNKNOWN, posthumous, wl talking to some Scouts, St James-the-Less, Sussex Gardens, London.
C 'DRAWL', wl, profile, chromo-lith, for *Vanity Fair*, 5 July 1900, NPG. 'APE junior', wl, profile, Hentschel-Colourtype, for *Vanity Fair*, 19 April 1911, NPG.
PH WALTER STONEMAN, 1927, hs, NPG (NPR). WALTER STONEMAN, three negs (for NPR, x535 a, b and c), two tql, one wl, NPG x357-9. UNKNOWN, wl in group at Farnham, print, NPG.

BAGEHOT, Walter (1826-1877) economist and journalist.
PR NORMAN HIRST, hs, profile, mezz, NPG.

BAGGALLAY, Sir Richard (1816-1888) judge and politician.
P JAMES SANT, RA 1877, wl in robes of lord justice, Merchant Taylors' Company, London.
C CARLO PELLEGRINI ('Ape'), wl, profile, chromo-lith, for *Vanity Fair*, 11 Dec 1875, NPG. FAUSTIN, wl, chromo-lith, NPG.
PH LOCK & WHITFIELD, hs, woodburytype, for *Men of Mark*, 1876, NPG; similar print, NPG x146. LOCK & WHITFIELD, wl, carte, NPG (Album 120).

BAGGS, Charles Michael (1806-1845) catholic bishop and antiquary.
PR UNKNOWN, hl seated, stipple, BM.

BAIKIE, William Balfour (1825-1864) naturalist and philologist.
PR UNKNOWN, hl seated, woodcut, for *Illust London News*, 28 Jan 1865, NPG.

BAILEY, Philip James (1816-1902) author of *Festus*.
P J.E.WILLIAMS, Castle Art Gallery, Nottingham.
SC JOHN ALEXANDER MACBRIDE, marble bust, SNPG 242.
PR G.B.BLACK, after I.D.Broadhead, hs, lith, NPG.
PH H.J.WHITLOCK, tql seated, carte, NPG x148.

BAILLIE, Alexander Cochrane-, see 1st Baron Lamington.

BAINES, Sir Edward (1800-1890) journalist.
P RICHARD WALLER, 1874, Corporation of Leeds. WALTER WILLIAM OULESS, 1885, Leeds City Art Galleries.
G B.R.HAYDON, 'The Anti-Slavery Society Convention, 1840', oil, NPG 599.
PR W.HOLL, after a photograph, tql seated, stipple and line, NPG. D.J.POUND, after a photograph by Mayall, tql, stipple and line, presented with *Illust News of the World*, BM, NPG.

BAINES, Thomas (1806-1881) journalist.
PH WINDOW & GROVE, hs, carte, NPG x4949.

BAINES, Thomas (1822-1875) artist and explorer.
PR UNKNOWN, tql seated with sketch pad, woodcut, for *Illust News of the World*, 27 Feb 1858, NPG.

BAKER, Sir Benjamin (1840-1907) civil engineer.
P J.C.MICHIE, hs, Imperial College, London.
D UNKNOWN, hs in uniform, pastel, Museum of London Transport.

BAKER, Sir Samuel White (1821-1893) traveller and explorer.
PR C.H.JEENS, hs, oval, with another of Lady Baker, line, for his *Albert Nyanza*, 1866, BM, NPG. C.H.JEENS, tql in dress of Turkish pasha, line, for his *Ismailia*, 1874, BM, NPG.
PH LOCK & WHITFIELD, hs, woodburytype, for *Men of Mark*, 1880, NPG; similar print, NPG x159. MAULL & CO, two cartes, tql, and wl seated, NPG x157 and x369. H.J.WHITLOCK, tql seated, carte, NPG (Album 40). UNITED ASSOCIATION OF PHOTOGRAPHERS LTD, hs, carte, NPG x160.

BAKER, Valentine (1827-1887) cavalry officer, 'Baker Pacha'.
C CARLO PELLEGRINI ('Ape'), wl, profile, chromo-lith, for *Vanity Fair*, 9 March 1878, NPG.

BAKER, William (1841-1905) Headmaster of Merchant Taylors' School.
C 'WAG', 1901, wl, profile, w/c study, for *Vanity Fair*, 21 March 1901, NPG 3300.

BALDWIN, Robert (1804-1858) Canadian statesman.
P THOMAS WATERMAN WOOD, 1855, hs seated, oil on paper, NPG 1721.
SC UNKNOWN, marble bust, Assembly Chamber, Ottawa, Canada.

BALDWIN BROWN, Gerard, see Brown.

BALFE, Michael William (1808-1870) composer.
P Attrib RICHARD ROTHWELL, (identity doubtful), c1840, tql seated, NPG 1450. UNKNOWN, Irish Academy of Music, Dublin.
D DANIEL MACLISE, c1844, hl seated, profile, NGI 2685. JOHN WOOD, hl in costume, chalk, NGI 2327.
SC L.A.MALEMPRÉ, RA 1874, marble statue, Drury Lane Theatre, London. L.A.MALEMPRÉ, marble medallion, Irish Academy of Music. SIR THOMAS FARRELL, 1878, marble bust, NGI 8044. BALLANTINE, memorial window, St Patrick's Cathedral, Dublin. UNKNOWN, medallion, Westminster Abbey, London.
PR Several liths and woodcuts, some after photographs, BM, NPG,

Harvard Theatre Collection.
PH RUSSELL & SONS, c1882, a copy after an original of 1840s, hs, cabinet, NPG X176. HERBERT WATKINS, 1860s, wl, carte, NPG X5158. MAYER, 1861, wl, carte, NPG (Album 38).

BALFE, Victoire, later Lady Crampton (1837-1871) soprano singer.
PR D.J.POUND, after a photograph by Mayall, tql, stipple and line, NPG.

BALFOUR, Arthur James Balfour, 1st Earl of (1848-1930) statesman and philosopher.
P SIR LAWRENCE ALMA-TADEMA, RA 1891, tql seated, NPG 2949. SYDNEY HODGES, c1894, tql seated, Constitutional Club, London. SIR GEORGE REID, c1900, tql, Edinburgh University. S.P.HALL, c1902-3, hl with Joseph Chamberlain, NPG 5114. JOHN SINGER SARGENT, 1908, wl, Carlton Club, London. PHILIP DE LÁSZLÓ, hl, NPG 2497. PHILIP DE LÁSZLÓ, nearly wl in DCL robes, Trinity College, Cambridge. CHARLES SIMS, wl, SNPG 1098. GEORGE FIDDES WATT, Eton College, Berks.
D GEORGE RICHMOND, 1877, hs, chalk, NPG 4987. S.P.HALL, hl, profile, pencil, NPG 2331.
G SIR JAMES GUTHRIE, 'Statesmen of World War I, 1914–18', oil, 1921–30, NPG 2463; sketch for this group, SNPG 1466 and tql study of Balfour, SNPG 1132. SIR WILLIAM ORPEN, 'A Peace Conference at the Quai D'Orsay', oil IWM London. SIR WILLIAM ORPEN, 'The Signing of Peace in the Hall of Mirrors, Versailles, 28th June, 1919', oil IWM. CHARLES SIMS, 'The Introduction of Lady Astor to the House of Commons, 1st December 1919', oil, 1923, Palace of Westminster, London.
SC EDWARD ONSLOW FORD, c1892, plaster bust, SNPG 691. UNKNOWN, 1916, bronze medal, SNPG 924.
PR VIOLET, DUCHESS OF RUTLAND, 1888, hs, lith, NPG.
C SIR JOHN TENNIEL, 'April Showers, or a Spoilt Easter Holiday', pencil, for *Punch*, 23 April 1892, Fitzwilliam Museum, Cambridge. Several drgs by SIR MAX BEERBOHM: 1900, The William Andrews Clark Memorial Library, University of California at Los Angeles, USA; 1909, Ashmolean Museum, Oxford, and Lilly Library, Indiana University, USA; 1912, Merton College, Oxford; 1920, 'Enfin Seuls', National Gallery of Victoria, Melbourne, Australia. SIR BERNARD PARTRIDGE, two drgs for *Punch*, 6 May 1903 and 16 Sept 1903, NPG. 'XIT', wl, profile, Hentschel-Colourtype, for *Vanity Fair*, 27 Jan 1910, NPG. Several ink drgs by SIR FRANCIS CARRUTHERS GOULD: hl with Joseph Chamberlain and another, NPG 2864; wl seated, NPG 2864a; tql with Campbell-Bannerman, NPG 2866. HARRY FURNISS, two ink drgs, hs and wl seated, NPG 3337 and 3338.
PH RUSSELL & SONS, 1887, hs, print, for *Our Conservative and Unionist Statesmen*, vol III, NPG; similar print, NPG X5159. G.C.BERESFORD, 1902, hs, neg, NPG X6430. LONDON STEREOSCOPIC Co. 1902, tql, cabinet, NPG X177. OLIVE EDIS, 1914, autochrome, NPG X7175. WALTER STONEMAN, 1921, hl, neg, for NPR, NPG X376. LONDON STEREOSCOPIC Co, hs, print, for *Our Conservative and Unionist Statesmen*, vol III, NPG; similar print, NPG X374. SIR BENJAMIN STONE, 1899, wl, print, and one undated print, NPG. Several photographs by W. & D.DOWNEY, OLIVE EDIS and LONDON STEREOSCOPIC Co, various dates, various sizes, NPG X179-187, JOHN RUSSELL & SONS, hs, print, for *National Photographic Record*, vol I, NPG.

BALFOUR, Clara Lucas, née Liddell (1808-1878) lecturer and authoress.
PR UNKNOWN, hs, woodcut, NPG.

BALFOUR, Edward Green (1813-1889) surgeon-general and writer on India.
P? UNKNOWN, Government Museum, Madras, India.

BALFOUR, Francis Maitland (1851-1882) naturalist.
SC ADOLF VON HILDEBRANDT, 1883?, after J.Collier, bronze bust, Department of Zoology, Cambridge; version, Trinity College, Cambridge.
PR UNKNOWN, hs, woodcut, for *Illust London News*, 19 Aug 1882, NPG.

BALFOUR, Gerald William Balfour, 2nd Earl of (1853-1945) politician and psychical researcher.
P G.F.WATTS, 1899, hl, profile, Watts Gallery, Compton, Surrey.
C SIR LESLIE WARD ('Spy'), wl, profile, chromo-lith, for *Vanity Fair*, 10 Dec 1896, NPG.
PH SIR BENJAMIN STONE, 1897, wl, print, NPG. WALTER STONEMAN, 1921, hs, NPG (NPR). A.C.HOSKINS, hs, print, for *Our Conservative and Unionist Statesmen*, vol III, NPG (Album 20).

BALFOUR, Jabez Spencer (1843-1916) radical politician.
C SIR LESLIE WARD ('Spy'), wl, w/c study, for *Vanity Fair*, 19 March 1892, NPG 4606.

BALFOUR, John Blair, see 1st Baron Kinross.

BALFOUR, John Hutton (1808-1884) botanist.
P JOHN HORSBURGH, 1878, hl seated, SNPG 1442. SIR DANIEL MACNEE, RA 1878, wl, Edinburgh University.
PR L.GHÉMAR, tql seated, with botanical specimens, lith, NPG. WILLIAM HOLE, hs, etch, for *Quasi Cursores*, 1884, NPG.

BALFOUR, Thomas Graham (1813-1891) physician.
PR WILLIAM STRANG, hs, etch, NPG.

BALFOUR of Burleigh, Alexander Hugh Bruce, 6th Baron (1849-1921) statesman.
P CHARLES MARTIN HARDIE, 1899, hs, profile, SNPG 872. UNKNOWN, University of St Andrews, Scotland.
D SIR GEORGE REID, head, pencil, Oriel College, Oxford.
C SIR LESLIE WARD ('Spy'), nearly wl, chromo-lith, for *Vanity Fair*, 14 Aug 1902, NPG.
PH RUSSELL & SONS, c1891, hs, profile, woodburytype, NPG X189. WALTER STONEMAN, 1917, hs, NPG (NPR). MELHUISH & GALE, hs, print, for *Our Conservative and Unionist Statesmen*, vol II, NPG.

BALL, John (1818-1889) man of science and politician.
PH UNKNOWN, hs, Royal Botanic Gardens, Kew.

BALL, John Thomas (1815-1898) lord chancellor of Ireland.
P WALTER OSBORNE, King's Inns, Dublin.
PR UNKNOWN, after a photograph by John Watkins, hs, woodcut, for *Illust London News*, 23 Jan 1875, NPG.

BALL, Robert (1802-1857) naturalist.
SL AUGUSTIN EDOUART, wl, NGI 2689.
PR T.H.MAGUIRE, tql seated, lith, for *Ipswich Museum Portraits*, 1851, BM, NPG.

BALL, Sir Robert Stawell (1840-1913) astronomer and mathematician.
P SARAH PURSER, c1892, hl, Trinity College, Dublin.
D RUDOLPH LEHMANN, 1894, hs, chalk, BM.
C SIR LESLIE WARD, wl, w/c study for *Vanity Fair*, 13 April 1905, NPG 4544. HARRY FURNISS, tql, pen and ink, NPG 3417.
PH W. & D.DOWNEY, hs, print, for *Cassell's Cabinet Portrait Gallery*, vol II, 1891, NPG; similar print, NPG X193.

BALLANCE, John (1839-1893) prime-minister of New Zealand.
PH UNKNOWN, Alexander Turnbull Library, Wellington, New Zealand.

BALLANTINE, James (1808-1877), see Ballantyne.

BALLANTINE, William (1812-1887) serjeant-at-law.
C UNKNOWN, wl, chromo-lith, for *Vanity Fair*, 5 March 1870, NPG.

FAUSTIN, wl, chromo-lith, NPG.
PH UNKNOWN, three woodburytypes, two hs, one hl seated, NPG X197-9.

BALLANTYNE, James (1808-1877) author, stained glass artist.
P UNKNOWN, hl, SNPG 1370.
D JOHN FRED, hl with Sir William Fettes Douglas and Thomas Faed, wash, SNPG 1589.
G D.O.HILL and ROBERT ADAMSON, two prints, hl with D.O.Hill and Dr George Bell, NPG P6(141) and P6(143).
PH D.O.HILL and ROBERT ADAMSON, two prints, both hl, profile, NPG P6(82) and P6(95).

BALLANTYNE, Robert Michael (1825-1894) author of stories for boys.
P JOHN BALLANTYNE (his brother), wl seated, NPG 4128.
PR UNKNOWN, after a photograph by Fradelle & Young, hl seated, process engr, for *Illust London News*, 17 Feb 1894, NPG.

BALY, William (1814-1861) physician.
P JOHN PRESCOTT KNIGHT, RA 1863, tql, St Bartholomew's Hospital, London.
PR UNKNOWN, after a photograph by Maull and Polyblank, hl, woodcut, for *Illust London News*, 9 Feb 1861, NPG.

BANBURY of Southam, Sir Frederick George Banbury, 1st Baron (1850-1936) politician.
P JOHN COLLIER, 1923, wl, National Railway Museum, York.
C UNKNOWN, wl, profile, mechanical repro, for *Vanity Fair*, 16 April 1913, NPG.
PH SIR BENJAMIN STONE, 1899, wl, print, NPG.

BANCROFT, Marie Effie Bancroft, Lady, née Pleydell Witton (1839-1921) actress.
P T.J.BARKER, hl, NPG 2122.
SC COUNT GLEICHEN, RA 1880?, bust, Garrick Club, London.
PR Several prints and popular prints, NPG.
PH Several photographs by LOCK & WHITFIELD, ELLIOTT & FRY, HEATH & BEAU, WINDOW & GROVE and others, NPG X207-13. BARRAUD, 1885, tql with her husband, panel, NPG X1525. WALERY, tql, print, NPG X5160.

BANCROFT, Sir Squire Bancroft (1841-1926) actor-manager.
P W.W.OULESS, RA 1884, The Athenaeum, London. HUGH GOLDWIN RIVIERE, 1900, tql, NPG 2121; replica, Garrick Club, London.
D DAVID N.INGLES, hs, charcoal, Garrick Club.
SC COUNT GLEICHEN, RA 1881?, bust, Garrick Club.
PR Several prints and popular prints, NPG, Harvard Theatre Collection, Cambridge, Mass, USA.
C SIR LESLIE WARD ('Spy'), wl, w/c study, for *Vanity Fair*, 13 June 1891, Garrick Club. SIR MAX BEERBOHM, several drgs, for example: 1903, University of Texas, USA; V & A. HARRY FURNISS, 1905, wl seated, pen and ink, for *The Garrick Gallery*, NPG 4095(2). CARLO PELLEGRINI ('Ape'), wl, profile, w/c study, for *Vanity Fair*, NPG 5072.
PH Several photographs by W. & D.DOWNEY, BARRAUD, LONDON STEREOSCOPIC CO, WALERY and others, various dates and sizes, NPG X202-6 and X550-2. BARRAUD, 1885, tql with his wife, panel, NPG X1525. CLAUDE HARRIS, c1917, hs, print, NPG X5597.

BANKES, Sir John Eldon (1854-1946) judge.
C SIR LESLIE WARD ('Spy'), wl, profile, mechanical repro, for *Vanity Fair*, 29 March 1906, NPG.
PH WALTER STONEMAN, 1917 and 1936, hs, and hl, profile, NPG (NPR).

BANKS, George Linnaeus (1821-1881) writer

PR R. & E.TAYLOR, hs, profile, woodcut, for *The Illustrated Review*, 25 Sept 1873, NPG.

BANKS, Sir John Thomas (1815?-1908) physician.
SC OLIVER SHEPPARD, bronze medallion, NGI 8159.

BANNERMAN, Sir Henry Campbell, see CAMPBELL-Bannerman.

BARBOUR, Sir David Miller (1841-1928) Indian civil servant and economist.
PH WALTER STONEMAN, 1917, hs, NPG (NPR).

BARCAPLE, Edward Francis Maitland, Lord (1803?-1870) Scottish judge.
SC WILLIAM BRODIE, marble bust, Faculty of Advocates, Parliament Hall, Edinburgh.

BARDSLEY, Sir James Lomax (1801-1876) physician.
PR UNKNOWN, after a daguerreotype by D.Fabronius, hs, lith, NPG.

BARDSLEY, John Wareing (1835-1904) bishop of Carlisle.
PH BASSANO, 1897, four negs, NPG X618-621. UNKNOWN, hs, profile, print, NPG (Anglican Bishops).

BARING, Evelyn, see 1st Earl of Cromer.

BARING, Thomas George, see 1st Earl of Northbrook.

BARING-GOULD, Sabine (1834-1924) divine and author.
P SYDNEY CARTER, 1922, tql, Devon Record Office, Exeter.
D CONSTANCE MORTIMORE, 1896, hs, profile, pencil, NPG 4353.
PH W. & D.DOWNEY, hs, woodburytype, for Cassell's *Cabinet Portrait Gallery*, vol IV, 1893, NPG.

BARKER, Frederick (1808-1882) bishop of Sydney.
PR UNKNOWN, hs, woodcut, for *Illust London News*, 13 May 1882, NPG.

BARKLY, Arthur Cecil Stuart (1843-1890) colonial governor.
PR UNKNOWN, after a photograph by G. Friederichs, hs, profile, woodcut, for *Illust London News*, 11 Oct 1890, NPG.

BARKLY, Sir Henry (1815-1898) colonial governor.
SC CHARLES SUMMERS, marble bust, State Library of Victoria, Australia.
C SIR LESLIE WARD ('Spy'), wl, chromo-lith, for *Vanity Fair*, 9 July 1887, NPG.
PH UNKNOWN, tql seated, print, NPG (Album 38).

BARLING, Sir (Harry) Gilbert, Bart (1855-1940) surgeon.
P EDWARD F.HARPER, 1915, Birmingham General Hospital. G.FIDDES WATT, 1924, Birmingham University.
PH WALTER STONEMAN, 1931, hs, NPG (NPR).

BARLOW, Henry Clark (1806-1876) writer on Dante.
D CARL CHRISTIAN VOGEL, hl, Staatliche Kunstsammlungen, Dresden.

BARLOW, Sir Thomas, 1st Bart (1845-1945) physician.
P SIR OSWALD BIRLEY, c1935, hl, University College Medical School, London. HERMAN SALOMON, 1960, tql, Wellcome Institute, London.
D CATHERINE DODGSON, 1935, hs, chalk, The Athenaeum, London.
C SIR LESLIE WARD ('Spy'), wl, mechanical repro, for *Vanity Fair*, 12 April 1906, NPG.
PH WALTER STONEMAN, 1923, hs, profile, NPG (NPR).

BARLOW, Thomas Oldham (1824-1889) mezzotint engraver.
P W.W.OULESS, 1882, hs, oval, MacDonald Collection, Aberdeen Art Gallery. SIR J.E.MILLAIS, RA 1886, tql, Corporation of Oldham.
PR UNKNOWN, tql seated, working on a plate, woodcut, BM.

PH DAVID WILKIE WYNFIELD, c1862–4, hs, print, NPG P71. RALPH W.ROBINSON, c1891, wl seated, for *Members and Associates of the Royal Academy of Arts 1891*, NPG X7349.

BARLOW, William Henry (1812-1902) civil engineer.
P JOHN COLLIER, 1880, tql seated, Institution of Civil Engineers, London.

BARNARD, Frederick (1846-1896) humorous artist.
G UNKNOWN, 'Our Artists – Past and Present', woodcut, for *Illust London News*, 14 May 1892, BM, NPG.
C HARRY FURNISS, wl seated, pen and ink, NPG 3419.

BARNARDO, Thomas John (1845-1905) philanthropist.
SC SIR GEORGE FRAMPTON, 1908, bronze relief medallion on monument, The Village, Barkingside, Ilford, Essex.
PH Various, Dr Barnardo's, Head Office, London.

BARNATO, Barnett Isaacs (1852-1897) financier.
C HARRY FURNISS, hl, pen and ink, NPG 3431.

BARNBY, Sir Joseph (1838-1896) musician.
P SIGISMUND GOETZE, 1894, tql, Corporation of London. Attrib J.W.KNOWLES, City of York Art Gallery.
SC HERBERT HAMPTON, bronze bust, Royal Albert Hall, London.
C SIR LESLIE WARD ('Spy'), wl, profile, chromo-lith, for *Vanity Fair*, 1 Nov 1894, NPG.
PH W. & D.DOWNEY, hs, woodburytype, for Cassell's *Cabinet Portrait Gallery*, vol IV, 1893, NPG.

BARNES, George Nicoll (1859-1940) statesman.
P SIR WILLIAM ORPEN, 1919, hs, Bradford City Art Gallery. MURRAY URQUHART, c1934, tql, seated, International Labour Office, Geneva.
G SIR JAMES GUTHRIE, 'Statesmen of World War I, 1914–18', oil, NPG 2463; sketch for group, SNPG 1466, and tql study of Barnes, SNPG 1134.
PH BENJAMIN STONE, 1907, wl, print, NPG, Birmingham Reference Library. WALTER STONEMAN, before 1917, hl, NPG (NPR). JOHN RUSSELL & SONS, hs, print, for *National Photographic Record*, vol I, NPG.

BARNES, John Gorell, see 1st Baron GORELL of Brampton.

BARNES, Robert (1817-1907) physician.
P HORSBURGH, tql, Wellcome Institute, London.

BARNES, William (1801-1886) poet.
P JOHN THORNE, c1845, tql seated, Dorset County Museum, Dorchester. GEORGE STUCKEY, c1870, hl, profile, NPG 3332. UNKNOWN, hl in clerical costume, Dorset County Museum. CONSTANCE EMILY BARNES, hs, as an old man, Dorset County Museum. Self-portrait, Dorset County Museum.
D Attrib BARNES, c1815, w/c, Dorset County Museum. JOHN LESLIE, two w/cs, hl, and wl profile, Dorset County Museum. UNKNOWN, as a young man, w/c, Dorset County Museum.
SC E.R.MULLINS, statue, St Peter's Church, Dorchester; model, Dorset County Museum.
PH UNKNOWN, tql seated, as an old man, Dorset County Museum.

BARNES, William Emery (1859-1939) divine.
D SIR WILLIAM ROTHENSTEIN, 1933, Peterhouse, Cambridge.
SC F.ALLIOTT, 1911, portrait on relief clay medallion, Divinity School, Cambridge.

BARNETT, Dame Henrietta Octavia Weston, née Rowland (1851-1936) social reformer.
PH ELLIOTT & FRY, c1905, tql seated with her husband, print, NPG X696. LAFAYETTE, 1932, tql, print, NPG X224. Attrib OLIVE EDIS, c1932, tql, print, NPG X534.

BARNETT, John (1802-1890) composer.

P CHARLES BAUGNIET, c1839, hl seated, NPG 1587.
PR C.BAUGNIET, hl, lith, 1845, BM, NPG.

BARNETT, Morris (1800-1856) actor.
PR J.BRANDARD, wl as Monsieur Jacques, lith, BM, NPG.

BARNETT, Samuel Augustus (1844-1913) canon of Westminster and social reformer.
P G.F.WATTS, 1887, hs, NPG 2893.
D FRANCIS DODD, c1906–13, hl seated, chalk, NPG 4419.
SC SIR GEORGE FRAMPTON, wl as a sower, on relief memorial tablet, Westminster Abbey, London.
PR F.DODD, hs, etch, BM.
PH ELLIOTT & FRY, c1905, tql with his wife, NPG X696.

BARON, Bernhard (1850-1929) tobacco manufacturer and philanthropist.
P SIR WILLIAM ORPEN, 1927, Carreras Rothmans Ltd, Basildon, Essex.

BARR, Archibald (1855-1931) inventor of range-finders.
P G.FIDDES WATT, c1913, University of Glasgow.

BARRETT, Lucas (1837-1862) geologist and naturalist.
PR UNKNOWN, hs, woodcut, for *Illust London News*, 14 Feb 1863, NPG.

BARRETT, Wilson (1846-1904) actor.
PR S.HALL, wl as Wilfred Denver in *The Silver King*, chromo-lith, NPG.
C SIR MAX BEERBOHM, 1896, as Marcus Superbus in 'The Sign of the Cross', drg, Lilly Library, Indiana University, USA.
PH W. & D.DOWNEY, c1891, tql in character, print, for Cassell's *Cabinet Portrait Gallery*, vol II, 1891, NPG; similar print, NPG X227. BARRAUD, tql seated, as Othello, photogravure, NPG X6407.

BARRETT BROWNING, Elizabeth, see Browning.

BARRINGTON, Rutland (1853-1922) actor and singer.
PH ELLIOTT & FRY, 1881, wl seated in character, for *Patience*, by Gilbert and Sullivan, print, NPG X634. UNKNOWN, hl, postcard, NPG X4941.

BARROW, John (1808-1898) archivist to the admiralty.
P STEPHEN PEARCE, c1850, hl, NPG 905.
G S.PEARCE, 'The Arctic Council, 1851', oil, NPG 1208.

BARRY, Alfred (1826-1910) primate of Australia and canon of Windsor.
D T.C.WAGEMAN, 1849, w/c, Trinity College, Cambridge.
PH LOCK & WHITFIELD, hs, woodburytype, for *Men of Mark*, 1883, NPG.

BARRY, Edward Middleton (1830-1880) architect.
G W.MURDEN, 'Associates of the Royal Academy in 1861', woodcut, for *Illust London News*, 23 Feb 1861, BM, NPG.
SC THOMAS WOOLNER, RA 1882, marble bust, Royal Academy, London.

BARRY, Sir John Wolfe Wolfe, see WOLFE-Barry.

BARRY, Martin (1802-1855) physician.
D CARL CHRISTIAN VOGEL, hs, profile, Staatliche Kunstsammlungen, Dresden.

BARRY, Sir Redmond (1813-1880) lawyer.
SC THOMAS WOOLNER, c1879, bust, Melbourne Public Library, Australia. CHARLES SUMMERS, marble bust, State Library of Victoria, Melbourne.

BARTLETT, Sir Ellis Ashmead, see Ashmead.

BARTLETT, William Henry (1809-1854) artist and writer.
PR B.HOLL, after H.Room, hl seated, stipple, pub 1839, BM, NPG.

BARTLEY, Sir George Christopher Trout (1842-1910)

founder of the National Penny Bank.

PH SIR BENJAMIN STONE, 1897 and 1898, two wl prints, NPG.

BARTON, Sir Dunbar Plunkett, 1st Bart (1853-1937) lawyer.

P ERNEST MOORE, exhib 1937, tql seated in robes, Gray's Inn, London.

C HARRY FURNISS, wl seated, pen and ink, NPG 3421.

PH WALTER STONEMAN, hs, NPG (NPR).

BARTON, Sir Edmund (1849-1920) Australian statesman.

C SIR LESLIE WARD ('Spy'), wl, profile, chromo-lith, for *Vanity Fair*, 16 Oct 1902, NPG.

BASHAM, William Richard (1804-1877) physician.

P SIR GEORGE HAYTER, 1858, (probably rightly named), Westminster Hospital, London.

BASING, George Sclater-Booth, 1st Baron (1826-1894) lawyer and politician.

C FAUSTIN, wl, profile, a 'Figaro cartoon', process block, BM.

PH UNKNOWN, hs, profile, woodburytype, NPG x252.

BASS, Michael Arthur, see 1st Baron Burton.

BATEMAN, John Frederic La Trobe (1810-1889) civil engineer.

P CLEGG WILKINSON, after a photograph, Institution of Civil Engineers, London.

BATEMAN, Kate, see Crowe.

BATEMAN, Thomas (1821-1861) archaeologist.

PR H.ADLARD, after P.W.Justyne, tql seated, stipple, BM, NPG.

BATES, Henry Walter (1825-1892) naturalist.

PH JOHN THOMSON, hs, photogravure, NPG x6409.

BATTENBERG, Henry Maurice, Prince of (1858-1896) third son of Prince Alexander of Hesse.

G R.C.WOODVILLE, 'The Marriage of Prince Henry to HRH Princess Beatrice, at Whippingham, Isle of Wight, 1885', oil, Royal Coll.

SC COUNT VON GLEICHEN, 1897, marble bust, Royal Coll.

PH BARRAUD, c1891, hs, print, for *Men and Women of the Day*, vol IV, 1891, NPG AX5545. W. & D.DOWNEY, tql in highland dress, woodburytype, for Cassell's *Cabinet Portrait Gallery*, vol v, 1894, NPG.

BATTENBERG, Prince Louis Alexander of, see 1st Marquess of Milford Haven.

BAXTER, Charles (1809-1879) painter.

PH UNKNOWN, tql seated, BM (Engr Ports Coll). JOHN & CHARLES WATKINS, hs, carte, NPG (Album 104).

BAYLEE, Joseph (1808-1883) theological writer.

PR R.J.LANE, after L.T.?, tql seated, lith, NPG.

BAYLEY, F.W.N. (1808-1853) journalist and miscellaneous writer.

PR R.J.HAMMERTON, hl, lith, NPG.

BAYLEY, Sir Steuart Colvin (1836-1925) administrator in India.

SC HAMO THORNYCROFT, c1896, statue, Calcutta.

PH WALTER STONEMAN, 1917, hs, NPG (NPR).

BAYLY, Ada Ellen ('Edna Lyall') (1857-1903) writer.

PR E.WHYMPER, hs, woodcut, BM.

BAYNES, Thomas Spencer (1823-1887) philosopher.

P UNKNOWN, University of St Andrews, Scotland.

BAZALGETTE, Sir Joseph William (1819-1891) civil engineer.

B

P ALESSANDRO OSSANI, 1878, hl seated with plans, Institution of Civil Engineers, London.

SC GEORGE SIMONDS, 1889, bronze bust on mural monument, Victoria Embankment, London.

PH UNKNOWN, hs, woodburytype, NPG x646.

BEACH, Sir Michael Edward Hicks, see 1st Earl St Aldwyn.

BEACH, Thomas Miller (1841-1894) secret service agent, known as 'Major Le Caron'.

D Several pencil sketches by S.P.HALL for *The Graphic*, 1889: three hl, NPG 2236-8; hl in court, with Sir Henry James, Patrick John Murphy and Sir Charles Russell, NPG 2239; wl with Parnell and Sir George Henry Lewis, NPG 2244.

BEACONSFIELD, Benjamin Disraeli, 1st Earl of (1804-1881) statesman and novelist.

P SIR FRANCIS GRANT, 1851, hl, Hughenden (NT), Bucks. T.J.BARKER, 1862, hs, oval, Hughenden. CHARLES LUCY, c1869, hl, V & A. HEINRICH VON ANGELI, 1877, hl, Royal Coll. T.BLAKE WIRGMAN, 1877, hl, Weston Park, Salop. HENRY WEIGALL, 1880, in court dress, Burghley House, Northants. HENRY WEIGALL, Royal Commonwealth Society, London. SIR J.E.MILLAIS, 1881, tql, NPG 3241.

D DANIEL MACLISE, 1828, tql seated, pencil, Hughenden. A.E.CHALON, 1840, hl, w/c, Hughenden. MRS J.BLACKBURN, 1873, two drgs, 'Disraeli Attending Chapel at Glasgow University', and 'Being Sworn in as Rector', Hughenden.

M Attrib RICHARD COSWAY, hs, as a child, oval, Hughenden.

SL UNKNOWN, 1812, hs, profile, Hughenden.

G JOHN PHILLIP, 'The House of Commons in 1860', Palace of Westminster, London. W.P.FRITH, 'The Marriage of the Prince of Wales', oil, 1863, Royal Coll. HENRY GALES, 'The Derby Cabinet, 1867', w/c, NPG 4893. HENRY BARRAUD, 'The Lobby of the House of Commons, 1872-3', oil, Palace of Westminster. CHARLES MERCIER, 'The Disraeli Cabinet, 1874', Junior Carlton Club, London. FREDERICK SARGENT, 'Disraeli Addressing the House of Lords', wash drg, c1880, Palace of Westminster.

SC S.FRUGONI, 1827, marble bust, Hughenden. WILLIAM BEHNES, 1847, marble bust, Hughenden. LORD RONALD SUTHERLAND GOWER, 1878-9, plaster bust, NPG 652. COUNT GLEICHEN, 1880, marble bust, Royal Coll. R.C.BELT, 1881, bronze bust, Wallace Collection, London, and c1881, medallion on memorial, Hughenden Church. R.GLASSBY, 1881, wax death mask, NPG 2655. SIR WILLIAM HAMO THORNYCROFT, 1881, plaster statuette, NPG 4671. SIR J.E.BOEHM, 1883, marble statue, Westminster Abbey, London; related bust model and statuette, 1881, NPG 860 and 1760. C.B.BIRCH, 1883, bronze statue, St George's Hall, Liverpool. COUNT GLEICHEN, 1883, marble statue, Palace of Westminster. MARIO RAGGI, 1883, bronze statue, Parliament Square, London. H.T.MARGETSON, 1884, statue, Moorgate, Ormskirk. T.RAWCLIFFE, 1887, statue, Queen's Park, Bolton. JOHN ADAMS ACTON, bust, DoE (10 Downing St).

C By or after DANIEL MACLISE, c1833, wl, pen and ink, for *Fraser's Mag*, VII, 1833, NPG 3093. CARLO PELLEGRINI, two chromo-liths, for *Vanity Fair*, 30 Jan 1869 and 2 July 1878, NPG, and SIR LESLIE WARD ('Spy'), chromo-lith, for *Vanity Fair*, 16 Dec 1879, NPG. RANDOLPH CALDECOTT, hs, chalk, NPG 3031. JOHN DOYLE, several cartoons, NPG, and related drgs, BM. RICHARD DOYLE, two pen and ink drgs: 'Lord Derby conferring the DCL on Disraeli', and hs with Lord John Russell, BM. HARRY FURNISS, several pen and ink sketches, NPG 3339-42. Various miscellaneous caricatures, BM, NPG.

PH MAYALL, 1860's, two cartes, NPG AX5060 and 5061. Various photographs by W. & D.DOWNEY, JABEZ HUGHES, LOCK & WHITFIELD, LONDON STEREOSCOPIC CO, MAYALL, HENRY TAUNT

& Co, and others, various dates and sizes, NPG x648–657, x659 and x660, and x662–9. Several cartes, one as a young man, Hughenden.

BEALE, Dorothea (1831-1906) principal of Cheltenham Ladies' College.
P B.R.NORTON, 1874, wl seated, Cheltenham Ladies' College. J.J.SHANNON, hs, in later life, Cheltenham Ladies' College.
G UNKNOWN, with her staff at Cheltenham Ladies' College, photograph, NPG x1679.
PH G.H.MARTYN & SONS, hs, photogravure, NPG x671.

BEALE, Lionel Smith (1828-1906) physician and microscopist.
P HENRY TANWORTH WELLS, 1876, hl seated, Royal College of Physicians, London.

BEARD, Charles (1827-1888) unitarian divine.
SC SIR J.E.BOEHM, marble relief bust, Unitarian Church, Ullet Road, Liverpool.

BEARSTED, Marcus Samuel, 1st Viscount (1853-1927) joint founder of the Shell Transport and Trading Company.
P SIR WILLIAM ORPEN, hl, Guildhall Art Gallery, London.
PH LONDON STEREOSCOPIC CO, c1902, hs, print, NPG x673. WALTER STONEMAN, 1921, hs, print, NPG (NPR).

BEATRICE Mary Victoria Feodore, Princess (1857-1944) fifth daughter of Queen Victoria.
P G.O.REID, 1891, hs, profile, Royal Scottish Academy, Edinburgh, JOAQUIN SOROLLA Y BASTIDA, c1908, tql seated, profile, NPG 5166. SIR W.LLEWELLYN, c1909 Burghley House, Northants.
D NOEL PATON, 1863, hl, profile, Royal Coll.
M EDWARD TAYLER, 1864, hs, oval, Royal Coll. EDUARDO DE MOIRA, RA 1883, Royal Coll.
G R.C.WOODVILLE, 'The Marriage of Prince Henry of Battenberg to HRH Princess Beatrice, at Whippingham, Isle of Wight, 1885', oil, Royal Coll.
SC PRINCESS LOUISE, 1864, marble bust, Royal Coll.
PR Various prints and popular prints, BM, NPG.
PH L.CALDESI, 1857, with members of the Royal Family at Osborne House, print, NPG P26. W. & D.DOWNEY, 1860s, wl, carte, NPG x3605. W.BAMBRIDGE, 'Royal mourning group, 1862', print, NPG P27. WILSON, WHITLOCK & DOWNEY, 1868, wl, NPG P22(8). W. & D.DOWNEY, 1868, with Queen Victoria, the Prince of Wales, Princes Arthur and Leopold, Princess Louise and the Duchess of Athol, at Balmoral, carte, NPG x3610. W. & D.DOWNEY, c1890, hl with her son, the Marquess of Carisbrooke, cabinet, NPG AX5554. W. & D.DOWNEY, 1907, a Royal Family group at Windsor, NPG x1585. Various prints, as a child, with her husband, singly and in groups, by BASSANO, W. & D.DOWNEY, OLIVE EDIS, HILLS & SAUNDERS, JABEZ HUGHES, LAFAYETTE, MAYALL, RUSSELL & SONS and others, various dates and sizes, NPG.

BEAUCHAMP, Frederick Lygon, 6th Earl of (1830-1891) privy councillor.
P RUDOLPH LEHMANN, 1878, hl, Keble College, Oxford.
PR T.H.MAGUIRE, after G.Richmond, hs, lith, NPG.
PH JOHN WATKINS, c1866-8, hs, carte, NPG AX5062.

BECKER, Lydia Ernestine (1827-1890) advocate of women's suffrage.
P SUSAN ISABEL DACRE, hs, Manchester City Art Gallery.

BECKETT, Sir Edmund, 5th Bart, see 1st Baron Grimthorpe.

BEDFORD, Francis Charles Hastings Russell, 9th Duke of
(1819-1891) politician.
P GEORGE RICHMOND, 1869, hl, Woburn Abbey, Beds. H.T.WELLS, 1874, tql, Woburn Abbey.
PR W.HOLL, after G.Richmond, hs, profile, stipple, one of 'Grillion's Club' series, BM, NPG.

BEDFORD, Herbrand Arthur Russell, 11th Duke of (1858-1940) president of the Zoological Society, created Whipsnade Zoo.
P JOHN COLLIER, 1913, wl seated, Middlesex Guildhall, London. SIR GEORGE REID, wl, Woburn Abbey, Beds. JOHN HANSON WALKER, hl in scarlet uniform, Woburn.
D S.P.HALL, hl, profile, pencil, NPG 2337.
C SIR FRANCIS CARRUTHERS GOULD, hl seated with Paul Kruger, 'Birds of a Feather', pen and ink, Woburn.
PH WALTER STONEMAN, 1921, hs, NPG (NPR).

BEDFORD, John (1810-1879) Wesleyan.
PR J.H.BAKER, after G.P.Green, hs, stipple, NPG. T.W.HUNT, after an unknown artist, hl seated, stipple, NPG.

BEDFORD, William Kirkpatrick Riland (1826-1905) antiquary and genealogist.
PH CAMILLE SILVY, 1861, wl, carte, NPG (Album 2).

BEETON, Isabella Mary, née Mayson (1836-1865) author of *Household Management* and journalist.
PH MAULL & CO, tql seated, print, NPG P3.

BEGBIE, James Warburton (1826-1876) physician.
SC SIR JOHN STEELL, 1879, bust, Royal College of Physicians, Edinburgh.

BEGG, James (1808-1883) free church minister.
P SIR DANIEL MACNEE, 1869, tql seated, SNPG 437.

BEILBY, Sir George Thomas (1850-1924) industrial chemist.
PH WALTER STONEMAN, 1918, hs, NPG (NPR).

BEIT, Alfred (1853-1906) financier and benefactor.
SC PAUL MONTFORD, relief bust, with Sir Charles Werner, Imperial College, London.

BELCHER, John (1841-1913) architect.
P SIR FRANK DICKSEE, RA 1908, tql, semi-profile, with plans, RIBA, London.
SC HAMO THORNYCROFT, c1882, bronze bust, Royal Academy, London.

BELFAST, Frederick Richard Chichester, Earl of (1827-1853) author.
SC PATRICK MACDOWELL, 1855, statue, Free Library, Belfast.

BELL, Alexander Graham (1847-1922) scientist, inventor of the telephone.
P W.W.RUSSELL, 1930, Institution of Electrical Engineers, London.
SC MOSES WAINER DYKAAR, 1922, marble bust, National Portrait Gallery, Smithsonian Institute, Washington DC, USA.
PR UNKNOWN, after a photograph, hl, process block, for *Das neunzehnte Jahrhundert in Bildnissen*, BM.

BELL, Charles Frederick Moberley (1847-1911) managing director of *The Times*.
P EMIL FUCHS, hl, The Times Newspapers Ltd, London.
PH G.C.BERESFORD, c1900s, hs, print, NPG x694. G.C.BERESFORD, 1909, hs, neg, NPG x6437.

BELL, Sir Francis Henry Dillon (1851-1936) New Zealand lawyer and statesman.
P A.F.NICOLL, three portraits: National Gallery, Wellington, New Zealand; Parliament House, Wellington; Wellington Club,

Wellington.
PH WALTER STONEMAN, hs, NPG (NPR).

BELL, Henry Glassford (1803-1874) sheriff and man of letters.
SC JOHN MOSSMAN, 1874, marble bust, SNPG 843.

BELL, Jacob (1810-1859) founder of the Pharmaceutical Society and patron of art.
PR R.J.LANE, after Miss Jessica Landseer, 1858, hs, profile, lith, pub 1860, NPG. T.LANDSEER, after E.Landseer, hl, line, pub 1869, BM, NPG.

BELL, John (1811-1895) sculptor.
PR UNKNOWN, after a photograph by Chapman and Son, hs, profile, woodcut, for *Illust London News*, 6 April 1895, NPG.

BELL, Robert (c1800-1867) author.
PH CLARKINGTON, c1860, wl seated, carte, NPG X699. J. & C.WATKINS, c1860, nearly wl seated, carte, NPG X700.

BELLAMY, James (1819-1909) president of St John's College, Oxford.
P FRANK HOLL, RA 1886, tql seated, St John's College, Oxford.
D WILLIAM STRANG, 1906, hs, chalk, St John's College.

BELLEW, John Chippindall Montesquieu (1823-1874) author and preacher.
PR D.J.POUND, after a photograph, tql, line, for *The Drawing Room Portrait Gallery of Eminent Persons*, BM.
C F. W., wl, mechanical repro, NPG.
PH MAYALL, c1860, hs, carte, NPG X705. R.W.THRUPP, c1860, hl, carte, NPG X704. SOUTHWELL BROS, wl, carte, NPG AX7488.

BELLOT, Joseph René (1826-1852) arctic explorer.
P STEPHEN PEARCE, 1851, hs, NPG 1227.
SC PHILIP HARDWICK, 1855, statue, Greenwich Hospital.
PR UNKNOWN, after a photograph by Claudet, hs, woodcut, for *Illust London News*, 15 Oct 1853, NPG.

BELLWOOD, Bessie (d1896) music-hall comedienne.
D UNKNOWN, wl on stage, ink, NPG 3968.

BENDALL, Cecil (1856-1906) professor of Sanskrit at Cambridge.
D UNKNOWN, hs, sepia, Institute of Oriental Studies, Cambridge.

BENDIGO, see William Thompson.

BENEDICT, Sir Julius (1804-1885) musician.
D CHARLES BAUGNIET, hl, w/c, BM, engr C.Baugniet, lith, pub 1844, BM. THEODORE BLAKE WIRGMAN, tql, pencil, Royal College of Music, London.
C SIR LESLIE WARD ('Spy'), wl, chromo-lith, for *Vanity Fair*, 27 Sept 1873, NPG. F. G., hl, playing piano, process block, BM. UNKNOWN, wl, 'Fashionable Music', lith, BM.
PH ERNEST EDWARDS, c1864, wl seated, print, for *Men of Eminence*, ed L.Reeve, vol II, 1864, NPG; similar print, NPG X722. FRADELLE & MARSHALL, c1876, hs, woodburytype, carte, NPG X718. LOCK & WHITFIELD, hs, semi-profile, woodburytype, for *Men of Mark*, 1881, NPG; similar print, NPG X721.

BENJAMIN, Judah Philip (1811-1884) lawyer.
PR UNKNOWN, hs, woodcut, for *Illust London News*, 17 May 1884, NPG.

BENNET, Charles Augustus, see 6th Earl of Tankerville.

BENNETT, Charles Henry (1829-1867) draughtsman on wood.
PH UNKNOWN, hs, profile, carte, NPG (Album 103).

BENNETT, Edward Hallaran (1837-1907) surgeon.
SC OLIVER SHEPPARD, relief bust on bronze panel, Trinity College, Dublin.

BENNETT, George John (1800-1879) actor.
PR Several theatrical prints, BM, NPG.

BENNETT, James Gordon (1800-1872) journalist, founder of *The New York Herald*.
PR UNKNOWN, hs, profile, woodcut, for *Illust London News*, 10 Aug 1872, NPG.

BENNETT, Sir James Risdon (1809-1891) physician.
D FREDERICK PIERCY, 1899, hs, chalk, Royal College of Physicians, London; related pastel drg by L.S.BRESLAU, 1908, hs, Royal College of Physicians.

BENNETT, Sir John (1814-1897) sheriff of London and Middlesex.
C UNKNOWN, wl on horseback, for *The Hornet*, 3 April 1872, NPG. 'PET', two wl chromoliths, both in supplements to *The Monetary Gazette*, 13 Dec 1876 and 21 July 1877, NPG.

BENNETT, John Hughes (1812-1875) physician and physiologist.
PR WILLIAM HOLE, hs, etch, for *Quasi Cursores*, 1884, NPG.

BENNETT, John Joseph (1801-1876) keeper of botanical department, British Museum.
P E.U.EDDIS, Linnean Society, London.
SC HENRY WEEKES, busts, BM, and Linnean Society.
PR UNKNOWN, hs, lith, BM.

BENNETT, Sir William Sterndale (1816-1875) musical composer.
P UNKNOWN, hl, oval, King's College, Cambridge.
PR C.BAUGNIET, hl, lith, 1844, BM, NPG. T.O.BARLOW, after J.E.Millais of c1873, tql seated, mezz, BM, NPG. D.J.POUND, after a photograph by Mayall, tql, stipple and line, for *The Drawing Room Portrait Gallery of Eminent Personages*, NPG. WEGER, after a photograph, hs, stipple and line, BM.
PH ERNEST EDWARDS, wl, print, for *Men of Eminence*, ed L.Reeve, vol I, 1863, NPG. LONDON STEREOSCOPIC CO, hl seated, carte, NPG (Album 99).

BENSON, Edward White (1829-1896) archbishop of Canterbury.
P SIR HUBERT VON HERKOMER, 1890, tql seated, Lambeth Palace, London. W.E.MILLER, 1900, hs, Trinity College, Cambridge.
SC ALBERT BRUCE JOY, RA 1885, marble bust, Lambeth Palace; related plaster and bronze busts, NPG 2058 and 2058a. THOMAS BROCK, RA 1899, marble effigy on monument, Canterbury Cathedral. A.BRUCE JOY, c1899, medallion on memorial, Rugby School Chapel, Warwicks. UNKNOWN, plaster death mask, NPG 2353.
PR C.W.SHERBORN, after H.T.Wells, hs, etch, one of 'Grillion's Club' series, BM.
C SIR LESLIE WARD ('Spy'), wl, profile, chromo-lith, for *Vanity Fair*, 30 July 1887, NPG. SIR FRANCIS CARRUTHERS GOULD, tql seated with Frederick Temple, pen and pencil, NPG 2870-1.
PH BARRAUD, hs, semi-profile, for *Men and Women of the Day*, vol II, 1889, NPG AX5472. Several prints by FREDERICK ARGALL, FRADELLE, LONDON STEREOSCOPIC CO, RUSSELL & SONS, ELLIOTT & FRY, W. & D.DOWNEY and LOCK & WHITFIELD, various dates and sizes, NPG X741-8. EMERY WALKER, after Mayall, tql seated, copy neg, NPG.

BENSON, Sir Frank Robert (1858-1939) actor-manager.
P HUGH RIVIÈRE, 1910, tql seated, Shakespeare Memorial Picture Gallery, Stratford-upon-Avon. R.G.EVES, 1924, hl seated, NPG 3777.
PH J.CASWALL SMITH, c1906, hs, semi-profile, as Richard II, postcard, NPG X749. WALTER STONEMAN, 1924 and 1934, both hs, NPG

(NPR). MRS A.BROOM, tql, profile, print, NPG x750 (neg x927). CHANCELLOR & SON, two photogravures, as Theseus in *A Midsummer Night's Dream*, and as Timon of Athens, NPG x6410 and x6411.

BENSON, Richard Meux (1824-1915) divine and founder of a religious order.
PH C.L.DODGSON, hl seated, print, NPG P7(13).

BENTHAM, George (1800-1884) botanist.
P LOWES DICKINSON, RA 1871, Linnean Society, London.
D UNKNOWN, hl, aged 10, w/c, Linnean Society. CHARLES LEBLANC, wl, aged 34, w/c, Linnean Society.

BENTINCK, Lord George Cavendish (1802-1848) statesman and sportsman.
P SAMUEL LANE, c1836, tql, NPG 1515. UNKNOWN, Hughenden (NT), Bucks.
D JOHN DOYLE, two drgs, Hughenden.
SC SIR RICHARD WESTMACOTT, 1835, statue, Calcutta. E.H.BAILY, 1842, marble bust, Russell-Cotes Museum, Bournemouth. THOMAS CAMPBELL, 1848, marble bust, NPG 134. T.CAMPBELL, 1851, bronze statue, Cavendish Square, London.
PR Attrib R.J.LANE, after A.D'ORSAY of 1840, hs, profile, lith, BM. R.J.LANE, after A.D'ORSAY of 1848, hl, profile, lith, BM, NPG. C.B., after a daguerreotype, hs, lith, pub 1848, BM, NPG. J.B.HUNT, after a photograph by Claudet, hl seated, stipple and line, pub 1848, NPG. UNKNOWN, after A.D'ORSAY, wl, profile, on racecourse, line, pub 1849, BM. T.C.W., wl, lith, BM, NPG.
C Several cartoons, drgs, BM.

BENTLEY, George (1828-1895) publisher and author.
PR UNKNOWN, after F.M.Sutcliffe, hs, profile, woodcut, for *Illust London News*, 8 June 1895, NPG.

BENTLEY, John Francis (1839-1902) architect.
P RENÉ LE BRUN, c1899, tql, Westminster Cathedral, London. W.C.SYMONS, 1902, tql seated, NPG 4479.
SC HENRY MCCARTHY, medallion on memorial, Church of the Holy Rood, Watford.
PH OSMOND BENTLEY (his son), 1896, hs, semi-profile, copy print, NPG.

BENTLEY, Robert (1821-1893) botanist.
PR UNKNOWN, after a photograph by Martin & Sallnow, hs, woodcut, for *Illust London News*, 6 Jan 1894, NPG.
PH H.J.WHITLOCK, hs, carte, NPG (Album 40).

BERESFORD, Lord Charles William de la Poer Beresford, Baron (1846-1919) admiral.
P C.W.FURSE, 1903, tql, NPG 1935.
SC EDOUARD LANTERI, 1910, bronze bust, formerly United Service Club, London (c/o The Crown Commissioners).
PR MACLURE & MACDONALD, after a photograph by London Stereoscopic Co, hs, chromo-lith, supplement to *The Pictorial World*, 1882, NPG. VIOLET, DUCHESS OF RUTLAND, hs, lith, 1890, NPG.
C SIR LESLIE WARD ('Spy'), two wl chromo-liths, for *Vanity Fair*, 12 Aug 1876, and 3 Jan 1895, NPG. 'CLOISTER', wl, chromo-lith, for *Vanity Fair*, 6 July 1899, NPG. SIR MAX BEERBOHM, 1913, 'Beresford balancing personal grievances with national despairs, and so remaining breezy', pencil and wash, Ashmolean Museum, Oxford.
PH Several prints by RUSSELL & SONS, W. & D.DOWNEY, LOCK & WHITFIELD and an unknown photographer, various dates and sizes, NPG x752–5. BARRAUD, tql, print, for *Men and Women of the Day*, vol II, 1889, NPG AX5460. SIR BENJAMIN STONE, 1899, two wl prints, NPG. WALTER STONEMAN, 1918, hl, NPG (NPR).

BERESFORD, Marcus Gervais (1801-1885) archbishop of Armagh.
PR J.R.JACKSON, after S.Catterson Smith, wl, mezz, NPG.

BERKELEY, George Charles Grantley Fitzhardinge (1800-1881) writer and sportsman.
P SIR GEORGE HAYTER, c1833, hl, study for NPG 54, Berkeley Castle, Gloucs.
G SIR GEORGE HAYTER, 'The House of Commons, 1833', oil, NPG 54.
PR J.BROWN, after a photograph, hs, stipple, pub 1865, NPG.

BERKELEY, Miles Joseph (1803-1889) botanist.
P JAMES PEEL, 1878, Linnean Society, London.
PH ERNEST EDWARDS, wl seated, print, for *Men of Eminence*, ed L.Reeve, vol II, 1864, NPG. UNKNOWN, Christ's College, Cambridge.

BERLIOZ, Harriet Constance, see Smithson.

BERNAL OSBORNE, Ralph, see Osborne.

BERNARD, Mountague (1820-1882) international lawyer.
SC E.E.GEOFLOWSKI, 1873?, plaster bust, Bodleian Library, Oxford.

BERNAYS, Albert James (1823-1892) chemist.
D WILLIAM BROCKEDON, hs, pencil and chalk, NPG 2515(102).

BERRY, Sir Graham (1822-1904) prime minister of Victoria.
PH BARRAUD, tql, print, for *Men and Women of the Day*, vol IV, 1891, NPG AX5535.

BERTIE of Thame, Francis Leveson Bertie, 1st Viscount (1844-1919) diplomat.
D LUCIE LAMBERT, 1911, wl in Bath robes, pastel, DoE (British Embassy, Paris).

BESANT, Annie, née Wood (1847-1933) theosophist, educationalist and Indian politician.
PH BARRAUD, tql, print, for *Men and Women of the Day*, vol IV, 1891, NPG AX5543. UNKNOWN, c1926, hl, print, NPG (*Daily Herald*). UNKNOWN, c1927, hl, print, NPG (*Daily Herald*). KLEIN & PEYERL, 1933, her funeral at Madras, NPG (*Daily Herald*).

BESANT, Sir Walter (1836-1901) novelist.
P A.J.STUART WORTLEY, 1882, hl with James Rice, NPG 2280. DANIEL A. WEHRSCHMIDT, 1887, Christ's College, Cambridge.
SC GEORGE FRAMPTON, 1904, relief bust on memorial, Victoria Embankment, London.
PH BARRAUD, hs, semi-profile, print, for *Men and Women of the Day*, vol I, 1888, NPG AX5417.

BESSBOROUGH, Frederick George Brabazon Ponsonby, 6th Earl of (1815-1895) barrister and cricketer.
C SIR LESLIE WARD ('Spy'), wl, profile, chromo-lith, for *Vanity Fair*, 20 Oct 1888, NPG.

BESSBOROUGH, John George Brabazon Ponsonby, 5th Earl of (1809-1880) man of affairs.
D COUNT ALFRED D'ORSAY, 1834, hl, profile, pencil and chalk, NPG 4026(6).
PR JOSEPH BROWN, after a photograph by J.E.Mayall, hs, profile, stipple, for *Baily's Mag*, 1863, NPG. MORRIS & CO, hs, lith, NPG.

BESSEMER, Sir Henry (1813-1898) engineer and inventor.
P RUDOLPH LEHMANN, RA 1870, tql seated, Metals Society, London.
SC E.W.WYON, 1867, bust, Institution of Civil Engineers, London.
C SIR LESLIE WARD ('Spy'), wl, profile, chromo-lith, for *Vanity Fair*, 6 Nov 1880, NPG.
PH LOCK & WHITFIELD, hs, woodburytype, for *Men of Mark*, 1881, NPG. LONDON STEREOSCOPIC CO, tql seated, carte, NPG (Album 40).

BEST, William Thomas (1826-1897) organist.

SC CHARLES J.PRAETORIUS, bronze relief, hs, profile, NPG 1455.

PR UNKNOWN, after a photograph by Freeman, hs, profile, woodcut, for *Illust London News*, 22 May 1897, NPG. UNKNOWN, tql seated, oval, process block, BM.

BETHELL, Richard, see 1st Baron Westbury.

BEVAN, Anthony Ashley (1859-1933) orientalist and biblical scholar.

D LEON UNDERWOOD, 1929, pencil, Trinity College, Cambridge.

PH WALTER STONEMAN, 1920, hs, NPG (NPR).

BEVERLEY, William Roxby (1814?-1889) scene-painter.

PR UNKNOWN, after a photograph by Elliott & Fry, hs, woodcut, for *Illust London News*, 1 June 1889, NPG.

BHOWNAGGREE, Sir Mancherjee Merwanjee (1851-1933) lawyer and politician.

C SIR LESLIE WARD ('Spy'), wl, semi-profile, w/c study, for *Vanity Fair*, 18 Nov 1897, NPG 4241.

PH SIR BENJAMIN STONE, 1897, wl, print, NPG, Birmingham Reference Library. SIR BENJAMIN STONE, 1902, wl, print, Birmingham Reference Library. WALTER STONEMAN, 1931, hs, NPG (NPR).

BICKERSTETH, Edward (1850-1897) bishop of South Tokyo, Japan.

PH UNKNOWN, hs, print, NPG (Anglican Bishops).

BICKERSTETH, Edward Henry (1825-1906) bishop of Exeter.

P SIR A.S.COPE, RA 1899, tql, Bishop's Palace, Exeter.

PH ELLIOTT & FRY, hs, cabinet, NPG x6864. UNKNOWN, hs, print, NPG (Anglican Bishops).

BICKERSTETH, Robert (1816-1884) bishop of Ripon.

P G.F.WATTS, c1878, hl seated, Bishop Mount, Ripon.

PR SKELTON, hs, lith, pub 1852, NPG. D.J.POUND, after a photograph by Mayall, tql seated, stipple and line, for *Drawing Room Portrait Gallery*, 1859, BM, NPG. W.A.WRAGG, tql seated, lith, BM.

PH MAULL & POLYBLANK, two cartes, wl seated and wl, NPG x948 and x7808. W.WALKER & SONS, wl seated, carte, NPG AX7469.

BIDDER, George Parker (1806-1878) the 'calculating boy'; civil engineer.

P Two portraits by unknown artists, one as a child, the other c1870, Institution of Civil Engineers, London.

D J.S.COTMAN, 1819, head, profile, pencil, V & A, etch Mrs D.Turner, BM, NPG. WILLIAM BROCKEDON, c1825, hs, chalk, NPG 2515(15).

G JOHN LUCAS, 'Conference of Engineers at Britannia Bridge', oil, 1851, Institution of Civil Engineers.

SC H.C.FEHR, 1899, marble bust, Institution of Civil Engineers. UNKNOWN, marble bust, NPG 5163.

PR S.FREEMAN, after J.King, tql, aged 9, stipple, BM, NPG. H.MEYER, after W.Waite, wl, aged 11, stipple and aquatint, pub 1817, BM, NPG. J.H.ROBINSON, after Miss Hayter, tql, aged 13, line, pub 1819, BM, NPG. R.COOPER, after W.S.Lethbridge, hl, aged 13, stipple, pub 1819, BM. J.LUCAS, tql, mezz, pub 1848, BM.

BIDDULPH, Sir Michael Anthony Shrapnel (1823-1904) general.

PR UNKNOWN, after a photograph by Maull & Fox, hs, woodcut, for *Illust London News*, 21 Dec 1895, NPG.

C SIR LESLIE WARD ('Spy'), wl, w/c study, for *Vanity Fair*, 21 Nov 1891, NPG 3931.

BIDDULPH, Sir Robert (1835-1918) general.

PH UNKNOWN, The Convent, Gibraltar.

BIDDULPH, Sir Thomas Myddleton (1809-1878) general.

P HEINRICH VON ANGELI, hs with Bath star, Royal Coll; version,

Chirk Castle, Clwyd, North Wales.

BIGG, Charles (1840-1908) classical scholar and theologian.

PH UNKNOWN, hs, print, NPG (The Club Portraits: Portfolio 4).

BIGGAR, Joseph Gillis (1828-1890) Irish politician.

D S.P.HALL, 1889, hl seated in court, pencil, for *The Graphic*, NPG 2282.

C SIR LESLIE WARD ('Spy'), wl, chromo-lith, for *Vanity Fair*, 21 July 1877, NPG. FREDERICK PEGRAM, two pencil sketches made during the sessions of the Parnell Special Commission, for *The Pictorial World*, 1888, V & A.

BIGGE, Arthur John, see Baron Stamfordham.

BIGHAM, John Charles, see 1st Viscount Mersey.

BINGHAM, George Charles, see 3rd Earl of Lucan.

BIRCH, Charles Bell (1832-1893) sculptor.

PH RALPH W.ROBINSON, wl seated, print, for *Members and Associates of the Royal Academy of Arts, 1891*, NPG x7350.

BIRCH, Samuel (1813-1885) egyptologist.

PR UNKNOWN, hs, woodcut, for *Illust London News*, 16 Jan 1886, NPG.

BIRD, Henry Edward (1830-1908) chess player.

G A.ROSENBAUM, 'Chess Players', oil, 1880, NPG 3060.

BIRD, Isabella Lucy, see Bishop.

BIRDWOOD, Sir George Christopher Molesworth (1832-1917) Anglo-Indian official and author.

SC ALFRED GILBERT, RA 1892, bronze bust, Royal Society of Arts, London.

BIRKS, Thomas Rawson (1810-1883) divine and philosopher.

D T.C.WAGEMAN, w/c, Trinity College, Cambridge.

BIRRELL, Augustine (1850-1933) man of letters and politician.

P SIR WILLIAM ORPEN, 1909, hl, Municipal Gallery of Modern Art, Dublin. AMBROSE MCEVOY, 1918, hs, National Gallery of Canada, Ottawa. ROGER FRY, 1928, hl seated, Trinity Hall, Cambridge.

D SIR WILLIAM ORPEN, 1909, hl, chalk, NPG 2791. EDMOND KAPP, 1913, Barber Institute of Fine Arts, Birmingham. RANDOLPH SCHWABE, 1927, hs, chalk, NPG 4431.

C SIR LESLIE WARD ('Spy'), wl, profile, w/c study, for *Vanity Fair*, 18 Jan 1906, NPG 3126. HARRY FURNISS, two ink drgs, tql and hl seated, NPG 3343 and 3344. SIR DAVID LOW, head, pencil, NPG 4529(32).

PH ELLIOTT & FRY, c1880s, hs, carte, NPG x970. SIR BENJAMIN STONE, 1899, three wl prints, NPG. OLIVE EDIS, c1925, hs, autochrome, NPG x7176. O.EDIS, hl, profile, print, NPG x5212 and several prints, hs and hs profile, NPG x971-7. HOWARD COSTER, hs, print, NPG x1741 and several negs, c1930, hs, NPG x2980-5. H.J.WHITLOCK & SONS, hl seated, print, NPG x978.

BISHOP, Ann, née Rivière (1814-1884) soprano.

PR D.J.POUND, after a photograph by Mayall, tql, stipple and line, for *Illust News of the World*, 1859, NPG.

BISHOP, Isabella Lucy, née Bird (1831-1904) traveller and writer.

PR UNKNOWN, hs, woodcut, for *Illust London News*, 27 June 1891, NPG.

BLACHFORD, Frederic Rogers, Baron (1811-1889) a founder of the *Guardian* newspaper.

M FREDERICK SARGENT, hs, profile, pencil, NPG 3810.

BLACK, William (1841-1898) novelist.

P JOHN PETTIE, hs, SNPG 932.
G P.NAUMANN & R.TAYLOR & CO, 'Our Literary Contributors – Past and Present', woodcut, for *Illust London News*, 1892, BM.
PR J.J.CADE, hs, stipple, for *The Eclectic Mag*, NPG. MACLURE & MACDONALD, hs, oval, chromo-lith, NPG.
C SIR LESLIE WARD ('Spy'), wl, chromo-lith, for *Vanity Fair*, 21 Feb 1891, NPG.
PH LOCK & WHITFIELD, hs, profile, print, for *Men of Mark*, 1877, NPG. BARRAUD, hs, print, for *Men and Women of the Day*, vol III, 1890, NPG AX5502. ELLIOTT & FRY, hs, photogravure, NPG X984.

BLACKBURN, Colin Blackburn, Baron (1813-1896) judge.
PH LONDON STEREOSCOPIC CO, hs, carte, NPG (Album 40).

BLACKBURNE, Joseph Henry (1841-1924) chess player.
G A.ROSENBAUM, 'Chess Players', oil, 1880, NPG 3060.
C CARLO PELLEGRINI ('Ape'), wl, profile, chromo-lith, for *Vanity Fair*, 2 June 1888, NPG.

BLACKIE, John Stuart (1809-1895) classical scholar and teacher.
P JAMES ARCHER, 1874, tql, Royal Scottish Academy, Edinburgh. J.H.LORIMER, RA 1881, tql, Edinburgh University. SIR GEORGE REID, RA 1894, tql, SNPG 676. SOMERLED MACDONALD, hs, NPG 2670.
SC WILLIAM BRODIE, plaster bust, SNPG 742.
PR WILLIAM HOLE, wl with S.H.Butcher, etch, for *Quasi Cursores*, 1884, NPG. HAHNISCH, hs, lith, BM. CASSELL, PETTER & GALPIN, hs, semi-profile, lith, NPG.
PH BARRAUD, tql, print, for *Men and Women of the Day*, vol III, 1890, NPG AX5481. W. & D.DOWNEY, tql, print, NPG X991. ELLIOTT & FRY, hs, profile, carte, NPG X990. J.MOFFAT, wl, carte, NPG X989.

BLACKLOCK, William James (c1815-1858) landscape painter.
M THOMAS HEATHFIELD, hs, w/c on marble, Carlisle City Art Gallery.

BLACKMORE, Richard Doddridge (1825-1900) novelist and barrister.
SC UNKNOWN, relief medallion on memorial tablet, Exeter Cathedral.
PH FREDERICK JENKINS, hs, oval, photogravure, NPG X7343.

BLACKWELL, Elizabeth (1821-1910) the first woman doctor of medicine.
D UNKNOWN, after a pencil sketch, Royal Free Hospital School of Medicine, London.

BLACKWOOD, Frederick Temple Hamilton-Temple, see 1st Marquess of DUFFERIN and Ava.

BLACKWOOD, Helen Selina, see Countess of DUFFERIN and Claneboye.

BLACKWOOD, John (1818-1879) third editor of *Blackwood's Magazine*.
P SIR JOHN WATSON GORDON, RA 1857, tql seated, Messrs Blackwood & Sons Ltd, Edinburgh.
PR UNKNOWN hl, etch, sepia, NPG. UNKNOWN, after a photograph by L. Suscipi, hs, woodcut, for *Illust London News*, 15 Nov 1879, NPG.

BLADES, William (1824-1890) printer and bibliographer.
PR UNKNOWN, after a photograph by Done & Ball, hs, woodcut, for *Illust London News*, 10 May 1890, NPG.

BLAGROVE, Henry Gamble (1811-1872) musician.
PR UNKNOWN, after a photograph by C.V.Bark, hs, oval, woodcut, for *Illust London News*, 28 Dec 1872, NPG.

BLAIKIE, William Garden (1820-1899) professor of theology.
P PERCIVAL NOVICE, 1853, SNPG 2025.
PH J.MOFFAT, hl, carte, NPG (Album 101).

BLAKESLEY, Joseph Williams (1808-1885) dean of Lincoln.
SC DOMINIK BIEMANN, c1841-5, hs, profile, glass plaque, V & A.

BLANCHARD, Edward Litt Laman (1820-1889) miscellaneous writer.
PR UNKNOWN, after a photograph by Herbert Watkins, hs, woodcut, for *The Illust Review*, 13 Feb 1873, NPG. UNKNOWN, hs, woodcut, for *Illust London News*, 14 Sept 1889, NPG.
PH BARRAUD, hs, semi-profile, woodburytype, for *The Theatre*, 1st Oct 1885, NPG X998.

BLANCHARD, Samuel Laman (1804-1845) author.
D DANIEL MACLISE, pencil, V & A.
G DANIEL MACLISE, 'Charles Dickens reading *The Chimes* to his friends in John Forster's chambers, 58 Lincoln's Inn Fields, 2 Dec 1844', pencil, V & A.
PR S.FREEMAN, after D.Maclise, tql seated, stipple, for his *Sketches of Life*, 1846, BM, NPG.

BLAND-SUTTON, Sir John, Bart (1855-1936) surgeon.
P JOHN COLLIER, Royal Society of Medicine, London. JOHN COLLIER, 1925, tql seated, Royal College of Surgeons, London.
D GEORGE BELCHER, 1925, Middlesex Hospital, London.
SC SIR GEORGE FRAMPTON, c1922, marble bust, Institute of Pathology, Middlesex Hospital.
C 'ELF', wl, Hentschel-Colourtype, for *Vanity Fair*, 3 Feb 1910, NPG.
PH ELLIOTT & FRY, c1913, hs, for *The Reign of George V*, vol II, NPG X1003. WALTER STONEMAN, 1924, hs, NPG (NPR).

BLATCHFORD, Robert Peel Glanville (1851-1943) journalist.
PR JOSEPH SIMPSON, hs, chromo-lith, NPG.
PH UNKNOWN, tql seated, sepia photogravure, NPG X1004.

BLOCHMANN, Henry Ferdinand (1838-1878) orientalist.
SC UNKNOWN, marble bust, Asiatic Society, Bengal, India.

BLOMFIELD, Sir Arthur William (1829-1899) architect.
PH RALPH ROBINSON, hl seated, print, for *Members and Associates of the Royal Academy of Arts, 1891*, NPG X7351.

BLOMFIELD, Sir Reginald Theodore (1856-1942) architect.
P SIR J.J.SHANNON, RA 1915, tql seated, RIBA, London.
D SIR WILLIAM ROTHENSTEIN, head, chalk, NPG 4764.
SC SIR WILLIAM REID DICK, 1927, bronze bust, NPG 3929.
PR W.STRANG, hl, etch, BM.
PH JOHN RUSSELL & SONS, hl, print, for *National Photographic Record*, vol I, NPG. UNKNOWN, hs, print, NPG X1085.

BLOOD, Sir Bindon (1842-1940) general.
P E.HALL NEALE, 1910 and 1932, both tql, the former in uniform, the latter in robes and with insignia, Royal Engineers, Chatham, Kent.
PH WALTER STONEMAN, 1917 and 1932, both hs, the latter in uniform, NPG (NPR).

BLOOMFIELD, John Arthur Douglas Bloomfield, 2nd Baron (1802-1879) diplomat.
P SIR THOMAS LAWRENCE, 1819, hs, semi-profile, NPG 1408.
PR G.COOK, hl seated, stipple, NPG.

BLOUET, Léon Paul, 'Max O'Rell' (1848-1903) humorous writer.

PH BARRAUD, hs, print, for *Men and Women of the Day*, vol II, 1889, NPG AX5462.

BLOXAM, Andrew (1801-1878) naturalist.
G J.M.W.TURNER, 'The funeral of Sir Thomas Lawrence, January 1830', w/c, BM.

BLOXAM, John Rouse (1807-1891) historian of Magdalen College, Oxford.
G J.M.W.TURNER, 'The funeral of Sir Thomas Lawrence, January 1830', w/c, BM. WILLIAM HOLMAN HUNT, 'May Morning on Magdalen Tower', oil, 1890, Lady Lever Art Gallery, Port Sunlight.
PH UNKNOWN, c1850, tql seated in robes, Magdalen College, Oxford.

BLOXAM, Matthew Holbeche (1805-1888) antiquary.
G J.M.W.TURNER, 'The funeral of Sir Thomas Lawrence, January 1830', w/c, BM.

BLUMENTHAL, Jacques (1829-1908) composer of songs.
P G.F.WATTS, c1878, hl, Royal College of Music, London.
PH JULIA MARGARET CAMERON, c1867, Gernsheim Collection, University of Texas, USA.

BLUNT, Arthur Cecil, see Cecil.

BLUNT, Wilfred Scawen (1840-1922) traveller, politician and poet.
D HENRY HOLIDAY, pencil sketch, NGI.
PR TRISTRAM ELLIS, 1883, tql in Arab dress, with horse, etch, NPG.
C CARLO PELLEGRINI ('Ape'), wl, profile, chromo-lith, for *Vanity Fair*, 31 Jan 1885, NPG.
PH Two cartes by BASSANO and MAULL & FOX, both c1870, tql and hl seated, profile, NPG X1113 and X1114 UNKNOWN, wl on horseback, sepia snapshot, NPG X1115. ELLIOTT & FRY, after 1910, two prints, hl seated, profile, and hl seated, NPG X1116 and X1185. UNKNOWN, copy by Emery Walker of a carte, wl seated, NPG.

BODICHON, Barbara Leigh Smith (1827-1891) benefactress of Girton College.
P Miss E.M.OXBORNE, 1884, Girton College, Cambridge.
PR UNKNOWN, after S.Laurence, 1861, hs, profile, lith, NPG.
PH UNKNOWN, hs, profile, oval, print, NPG P137.

BODINGTON, Sir Nathan (1848-1911) vice-chancellor of Leeds University.
P ARTHUR HACKER, University of Leeds.

BODLEY, George Frederick (1827-1907) architect.
SC THOMAS MURPHY, 1911, plaster bust, Bodleian Library, Oxford.
PR UNKNOWN, hs, profile, woodcut, for *Illust London News*, 29 April 1882, NPG.

BODLEY, John Edward Courtney (1853-1925) historian and writer.
D R.KASTOR, 1903, hs, profile, pen and ink, NPG 2278.

BODY, George (1840-1911) canon of Durham.
PH SAMUEL A.WALKER, c1889, tql, print, NPG.

BOEHM, Sir Joseph Edgar, 1st Bart (1834-1890) sculptor.
P JOHN PETTIE, 1883, hs, MacDonald Collection, Aberdeen Art Gallery.
SC ROBERT GLASSBY, marble bust, Royal Coll.
G H.J.BROOKS, 'Private view of the Old Masters Exhibition, Royal Academy, 1888', oil, NPG 1833.
PR J.M.JOHNSTONE, after a photograph, hl, woodcut, for *Magazine of Art*, BM, NPG. UNKNOWN, hs, woodcut, BM.
C SIR LESLIE WARD ('Spy'), wl, profile, chromo-lith, for *Vanity Fair*, 22 Jan 1881, NPG.
PH UNKNOWN, c1880, hs, cabinet, NPG X1131. LOCK & WHITFIELD,

hs, woodburytype, for *Men of Mark*, 1883, NPG. RALPH W.ROBINSON, wl seated, print, for *Members and Associates of the Royal Academy of Arts*, 1891, NPG X7352. J.P.MAYALL, wl seated in his studio, photogravure, NPG. WALERY, tql seated, print, NPG.

BOLTON, Sir Francis John (1831-1887) soldier and electrician.
PR UNKNOWN, after a photograph by W. & D.Downey, hs, woodcut, for *Illust London News*, 19 Jan 1884, NPG.

BOLTON, William Henry Orde-Powlett, 3rd Baron (1818-1895) conservative politician.
D FREDERICK SARGENT, c1870-80, hl, pencil, NPG 1834b.

BOMPAS, William Carpenter (1834-1906) bishop of Selkirk.
PH UNKNOWN, tql seated, print, NPG (Anglican Bishops).

BONAR, James (1852-1941) political economist.
PH WALTER STONEMAN, c1932, hs, neg, for NPR, NPG X383.

BONAR LAW, Andrew, see Law.

BOND, Sir Edward Augustus (1815-1898) principal librarian of British Museum.
PR UNKNOWN, hs, woodcut, for *Illust London News*, 8 Feb 1879, NPG.

BOND, William Bennett (1815-1906) primate of all Canada from 1904.
PH UNKNOWN, hl, profile, print, NPG (Anglican Bishops).

BONINGTON, Richard Parkes (1802-1828) painter.
P Self-portrait? (or by his father?), c1814-15, hs, oval, Castle Museum, Nottingham. MARGARET CARPENTER, c1827, hs, NPG 444; related chalk drg, NPG 492, and w/c copy, 1834, Castle Museum, Nottingham.
D Self-portrait, c1820-25, identity uncertain, wl, his back to spectator, w/c, NPG 1729. ALEXANDRE COLIN, 1829, hs, pencil, Ashmolean Museum, Oxford; related lith, BM, NPG.
SC F.W.POMEROY, RA 1910, marble statue, Nottingham School of Art.
PR DAMOUR, after R.P.Bonington, c1820, hs, aquatint, BM, NPG. E.SCRIVEN, after A.Shaw, hs, stipple, for *Library of the Fine Arts*, 1832, BM, NPG.

BONNAR, William (1800-1853) painter.
P Self-portrait, exhib 1853, NGS 642.

BOOLE, George (1815-1864) mathematician.
D UNKNOWN, 1847, hs, profile, pencil, NPG 4411.
W UNKNOWN, wl seated, memorial, University College, Cork.
PR UNKNOWN, after a photograph, hs, woodcut, for *Illust London News*, 21 Jan 1865, NPG.

BOOT, Jesse, see 1st Baron Trent.

BOOTH, Catherine, née Mumford (1829-1890) 'mother of the Salvation Army'.
P J.EARLE-MORRELL, 1886, Salvation Army International Headquarters, London.
SC GEORGE WADE, 1929, statue, William Booth Memorial Training College.
PR UNKNOWN, after a daguerreotype, tql seated, mixed engr, NPG.
PH Several, Salvation Army International Headquarters.

BOOTH, Charles (1840-1916) shipowner and sociologist.
P SIR WILLIAM ROTHENSTEIN, 1908, tql seated, University of Liverpool. G.F.WATTS, hl, NPG 4131.
D SIR WILLIAM ROTHENSTEIN, 1910, head, semi-profile, pencil, NPG 4765.

BOOTH, William (1829-1912) 'General Booth', founder of the Salvation Army.
P J.EARLE-MORRELL, 1887, tql, William Booth Memorial Training

College, Denmark Hill, London. SIR HUBERT VON HERKOMER, 1897, tql seated, William Booth Memorial Training College. N.D.DAVIS, Castle Art Gallery, Nottingham. D.N.INGLES, hl seated, NPG 2042.

D S.P.HALL, hl, profile, pencil, NPG 2383. OTTO SCHOLDERER, pastel, Castle Art Gallery, Nottingham.

SC HERBERT HAMPTON, bust, Salvation Army International Headquarters, London. H.HAMPTON, group bronze panel, Victoria Memorial, Lancaster. GEORGE WADE, 1929, statue, William Booth Memorial Training College.

PR UNKNOWN, hs, lith, NPG.

C STEPHEN REID, 1906, hl, profile, pen and ink, NPG 2275. COLIN CAMPBELL, hl, pen and ink, NPG 2932. FRANCIS DODD, tql, profile, pen and ink, BM, etch in reverse, NPG 1783a.

PH O. & K.EDIS, 1902, hs, semi-profile, print, NPG X1166. HERBERT F.JOYCE, 1906, wl, print, NPG X1538. ERNEST H.MILLS, hs, photogravure, supplement to *Illust London News*, NPG. Several, Salvation Army International Headquarters.

BOOTH, William Bramwell (1856-1929) Salvation Army leader.

P JOHN COLLIER, 1924, Salvation Army International Headquarters, London. UNKNOWN, Salvation Army International Headquarters.

PR UNKNOWN, hs, mixed, NPG.

PH ERNEST H.MILLS, wl with his wife, photogravure, supplement to *Illust London News*, NPG. Several, Salvation Army International Headquarters.

BOOTHBY, Louisa Cranstoun, Lady, see Nisbett.

BORDEN, Sir Robert Laird (1854-1937) prime-minister of Canada.

P SIR WILLIAM ORPEN, c1917-19, hs, Public Archives of Canada, Ottawa, Canada. DOROTHY VICAGI, 1925, Law Courts, Halifax, Nova Scotia, Canada. JOHN MACGILLIVRAY, Acadia University, Wolfville, Nova Scotia.

G SIR JAMES GUTHRIE, 'Statesmen of World War I, 1914–18', oil, NPG 2463; oil sketch, SNPG 1466, and tql study, SNPG 1140.

PH WALTER STONEMAN, 1917 and 1936, hs and hl, NPG (NPR).

BORROW, George (1803-1881) philologist and writer.

P JOHN BORROW (his brother), c1821 or c1824, hl, NPG 1651. H.W.PHILLIPS, after his portrait of 1843, hl, NPG 1841.

SC UNKNOWN, c1824, plaster mask, Castle Museum, Norwich.

BORTHWICK, Algernon, see Baron Glenesk.

BORTHWICK, Peter (1804-1852) editor of the *Morning Post* and politician.

PR UNKNOWN, tql, woodcut, for *Illust London News*, 7 Jan 1843, NPG.

BORTON, Sir Arthur (1814-1893) general and governor of Malta.

G UNKNOWN, after a sketch by Lieutenant Allan Gilmore, 'Presentation of Native Indian Officers to the Duke of Cambridge in the Governor's Palace, Malta', woodcut, for *Illust London News*, 13 July 1878, NPG.

BOSANQUET, Bernard (1848-1923) philosopher.

PH WALTER STONEMAN, 1917, hs, NPG (NPR).

BOSANQUET, Sir Frederick Albert (1837-1923) common serjeant.

C SIR LESLIE WARD ('Spy'), tql in court, chromo-lith, for *Vanity Fair*, 21 Nov 1901, NPG.

BOTFIELD, Beriah (1807-1863) bibliographer.

P THOMAS PHILLIPS, c1828-30, wl, Longleat, Wilts.

SC LAWRENCE MACDONALD, 1846, marble bust, Harrow School, Middx. WILLIAM BEHNES, bust, Longleat. WILLIAM BEHNES,

relief figure on marble monument to his mother, All Saints' Church, Norton, Northants.

PH CAMILLE SILVY, c1861, wl, carte, NPG (Album 2).

BOUCH, Sir Thomas (1822-1880) civil engineer.

PR UNKNOWN, after a photograph by J.Moffat, hs, woodcut, for *Illust London News*, 13 Nov 1880, NPG.

BOUCICAULT, Dion (1820?-1890) actor and dramatist.

SC JOHN ROGERS, c1875, bronze statues, in the role of *The Shaughran* with Tatters, NGI 8013, and The New York Historical Society, USA.

C HARRY FURNISS, wl, pen and ink, NPG 3554. MACLURE & MACDONALD, wl in *The Shaughran*, chromo-lith, NPG.

PH LONDON STEREOSCOPIC CO, c1865-70, hs, profile, carte, NPG X1176.

BOUCICAULT, Dion (1859-1929) actor-manager.

PR CHARLES BUCHEL, hs, lith, and HASSALL, wl as the Chancellor in *Trelawny of the Wells*, lith, NPG.

C 'SEM', two wl w/cs, NPG.

BOUGH, Samuel (1822-1878) landscape painter.

P JOHN PHILLIP, 1856, tql seated with palette, SNPG 693. ROBERT ANDERSON, tql, SNPG 2053.

D WILLIAM PERCY, 1846, hs, w/c, Carlisle City Art Gallery. THOMAS FAIRBAIRN, 1854, pencil and chalk, SNPG 1080. MARY SLEE, after William Percy, hs, w/c, SNPG 2030.

SC JOHN MOSSMAN, 1850, cameo, SNPG 673. W.G.STEVENSON, bronze statuette, SNPG 1809.

PH NESBITT & LOTHIAN, hs, carte, NPG (Album 106).

BOUGHTON, George Henry (1833-1905) painter and illustrator.

P Self-portrait, 1884, hs, MacDonald Collection, Aberdeen Art Gallery.

D A.L.BALDRY, two heads, profile, pencil, NPG 2612.

PH RALPH W.ROBINSON, wl seated with palette, at easel, print, for *Members and Associates of the Royal Academy of Arts, 1891*, NPG X7353.

BOURCHIER, James David (1850-1920) *The Times* correspondent in Balkan peninsula.

P N.MICHAILOWZ, 1908, at Sofia, in national costume, The Times Newspapers Ltd, London.

BOURKE, Richard Southwell, see 6th Earl of Mayo.

BOURKE, Robert, see 1st Baron Connemara.

BOUVERIE, Edward Pleydell (1818-1889) politician.

PR UNKNOWN, after a photograph by Beard, hs, woodcut, for *Illust London News*, 20 July 1850, NPG.

BOVILL, Sir William (1814-1873) judge.

PR UNKNOWN, hs, woodcut, for *Illust London News*, 15 Dec 1866, NPG.

C CARLO PELLEGRINI ('Ape'), wl, chromo-lith, for *Vanity Fair*, 8 Jan 1870, NPG.

PH CAMILLE SILVY, c1861, wl, carte, NPG (Album 2). LONDON STEREOSCOPIC CO, tql seated, carte, NPG X1193.

BOWEN, Charles Synge Christopher Bowen, Baron (1835-1894) judge.

SC SIR THOMAS BROCK, RA 1895, marble bust, Balliol College, Oxford.

C SIR LESLIE WARD ('Spy'), hs at bench, chromo-lith, for *Vanity Fair*, 12 March 1892, NPG.

BOWER, Frederick Orpen (1855-1948) botanist.

P SIR WILLIAM ORPEN, University of Glasgow.

PH UNKNOWN, 1889, hl seated, photogravure, NPG. WALTER

STONEMAN, 1937, hs, NPG (NPR).

BOWES-LYON, Claude George, see 14th and 1st Earl of STRATHMORE and Kinghorne.

BOWLBY, Sir Anthony Alfred, 1st Bart (1855-1929) surgeon.
P SIR WILLIAM LLEWELLYN, 1921, tql in uniform, St Bartholomew's Hospital, London.
G FRANK O.SALISBURY, King George V and Queen Mary visiting the battle areas of France in 1917, oil, Royal Exchange, London. MOUSSA AYOUB, 'The Council of the Royal College of Surgeons of England, 1926–7', oil, Royal College of Surgeons, London.
PH WALTER STONEMAN, 1919, hs, NPG (NPR).

BOWLES, Thomas Gibson (1842-1922) politician and editor of *Vanity Fair.*
C SIR LESLIE WARD ('Spy'), wl, chromo-lith, for *Vanity Fair,* 13 July 1889, and wl, profile, chromo-lith, for *Vanity Fair,* 19 Oct 1905, NPG.
PH SIR BENJAMIN STONE, 1897, wl, print, NPG.

BOWLY, Samuel (1802-1884) Quaker and anti-slavery agitator.
G B.R.HAYDON, 'The Anti-Slavery Society Convention, 1840', oil, NPG 599.

BOWMAN, Sir William (1816-1892) ophthalmic surgeon.
PR J.C.WEBB, after W.W.Ouless, tql seated, mezz, BM.
PH LOCK & WHITFIELD, hs, oval, woodburytype, for *Men of Mark,* 1880, NPG X1202.

BOWYER, Sir George, 7th Bart (1811-1883) lawyer and politician.
C SIR LESLIE WARD ('Spy'), tql, profile, chromo-lith, for *Vanity Fair,* 18 Jan 1879, NPG.

BOXALL, Sir William (1800-1879) painter, director of the National Gallery.
P MICHEL ANGELO PITTATORE, 1870, hl, NPG 937. ANNA LEA MERRITT, tql seated, as an old man, with his dog Garibaldi, Royal Academy, London.
PH ELLIOTT & FRY, hs, profile, carte, NPG (Album 103). F.JOUBERT, wl seated, carte, NPG (Album 104). JOHN & CHARLES WATKINS, tql seated, carte, NPG (Album 105).

BOYCE, George Price (1826-1897) artist.
D DANTE GABRIEL ROSSETTI, 1858, hl at easel with Fanny Cornforth, pen and ink, Carlisle Museum and Art Gallery.

BOYCOTT, Charles Cunningham (1832-1897) captain and land agent.
C SIR LESLIE WARD ('Spy'), wl, profile, chromo-lith, for *Vanity Fair,* 29 Jan 1881, NPG.

BOYD, Andrew Kennedy Hutchinson (1825-1899) minister of Church of Scotland.
PH UNKNOWN, wl seated, carte, NPG X1382.

BOYD, Archibald (1803-1883) dean of Exeter.
PR S.COUSINS (?), after H.W.Phillips, tql, mezz, BM.

BOYD, Henry (1831-1922) principal of Hertford College, Oxford.
P SIR HUBERT VON HERKOMER, 1901, tql seated, Hertford College, Oxford.
PH SOLVEIG LUND, wl seated, cabinet, NPG X1380.

BOYD, Sir Thomas Jamieson (1818-1902) lord provost of Edinburgh.
P OTTO T.LEYDE, The Merchant Company of Edinburgh.
PR UNKNOWN, after a bust by William Brodie, woodcut, for *Illust London News,* 27 July 1872, NPG.

BOYD-CARPENTER, William (1841-1918) bishop of Ripon.
P H.G.RIVIERE, RA 1916, Ripon Hall, Oxford.
C SIR LESLIE WARD ('Spy'), wl, chromo-lith, supplement to *Vanity Fair,* 8 March 1906, NPG.
PH BARRAUD, tql seated, print, for *Men and Women of the Day,* vol II, 1889, NPG AX5453. W. & D.DOWNEY, hs, woodburytype, for Cassell's *Cabinet Portrait Gallery,* vol II, 1891, NPG X5703. ELLIOTT & FRY, hs, cabinet, NPG X5701. ELLIOTT & FRY, tql seated, cabinet, NPG X5702. LAFAYETTE, hs, postcard, NPG X5704.

BOYS, Sir Charles Vernon (1855-1944) physicist.
D SIR RICHARD PAGET, 1929, tql seated, pen sketch, The Athenaeum, London.

BOYS, Thomas Shotter (1803-1874) water-colour painter and lithographer.
SC EMILE AUBERT LESSORE, 1856, hs, ceramic plaque, NPG 4820.

BRABAZON, Hercules Brabazon (1821-1906) painter.
P JOHN SINGER SARGENT, 1900, National Museum of Wales 1012, Cardiff.
D SIR WILLIAM ROTHENSTEIN: 1894, hs, profile, chalk, BM; hs, chalk, NPG L168(1).

BRABAZON, Reginald, see 12th Earl of Meath.

BRABOURNE, Edward Hugessen Knatchbull – Hugessen, 1st Baron (1829-1893) politician.
P SIR HUBERT VON HERKOMER, 1883, tql seated, County Hall, Maidstone.
C CARLO PELLEGRINI ('Ape'), wl, chromo-lith, for *Vanity Fair,* 11 June 1870, NPG.

BRACKENBURY, Charles Booth (1831-1890) major-general.
PR UNKNOWN, hs, woodcut, for *Illust London News,* 28 June 1890, NPG.

BRACKENBURY, Sir Henry (1837-1914) general.
PR UNKNOWN, after a photograph by Denque & Co, hs, profile, woodcut, for *Illust London News,* 17 June 1882, NPG.

BRADDON, Mary Elizabeth, see Maxwell.

BRADFORD, Sir Edward Ridley Colborne, 1st Bart (1836-1911) Anglo-Indian administrator and commissioner of the Metropolitan Police, London.
PR UNKNOWN, hs, woodcut, for *Illust London News,* 28 June 1890, NPG.
C SIR LESLIE WARD ('Spy'), wl, chromo-lith, for *Vanity Fair,* 15 Nov 1890, NPG.

BRADLAUGH, Charles (1833-1891) radical politician.
P W.R.SICKERT, *c*1891, hs, National Liberal Club, London. W.R.SICKERT, *c*1892–3, wl at the bar of the House of Commons, Manchester City Art Gallery.
D S.P.HALL, several pencil drgs, NPG 2313–4, 2316 and 2332. W.R.SICKERT, hs, profile, pencil, NPG 2206.
SC GEORGE TINWORTH, terracotta statue, Abington Square, Northampton.
PR W.STRANG, hs, etch, BM, NPG.
C SIR LESLIE WARD ('Spy'), tql, profile, chromo-lith, for *Vanity Fair,* 12 June 1880, NPG. SIR FRANCIS CARRUTHERS GOULD, tql with F.O'Driscoll, chalk, NPG 2868. HARRY FURNISS, wl, pen and ink, NPG 3555.
PH UNKNOWN, hs, carte, NPG X1212. UNKNOWN, hs, carte, NPG (Album 40).

BRADLEY, Andrew Cecil (1851-1935) literary critic.
P GEORGE HENRY, tql seated, University of Glasgow.
PH WALTER STONEMAN, 1917, hs, NPG (NPR).

BRADLEY, George Granville (1821-1903) dean of Westminster and schoolmaster.
P UNKNOWN, Westminster Deanery, London.
C SIR LESLIE WARD ('Spy'), wl, profile, chromo-lith, for *Vanity Fair*, 29 Sept 1888, NPG.
PH J.E.MAYALL, hs, oval, woodburytype, for *Men of Mark*, 1883, NPG. SIR BENJAMIN STONE, 1902, wl, print, Birmingham Reference Library. UNKNOWN, hl seated, cabinet, NPG X4951. UNKNOWN, Westminster Deanery.

BRADLEY, Henry (1845-1923) philologist and lexicographer.
PH HILLS & SAUNDERS, c1913, hs, print, NPG X1351. WALTER STONEMAN, 1917, hs, NPG (NPR). ERNEST HALL, 1922, tql seated, print, NPG X1350. ELLIOTT & FRY, hs, cabinet, NPG X1349. UNKNOWN, hl seated at desk, print, NPG X1352.

BRADSHAW, Ann Maria, née Tree (1801-1862) actress and singer.
D SAMUEL DE WILDE, wl as Susanna in *The Marriage of Figaro*, w/c, and ALEXANDER POPE, hs, pastel, both Garrick Club, London.
M LOUISA SHARPE, RA 1821, tql as Viola in *Twelfth Night*, Garrick Club.
PR G.H.PHILLIPS, after R.Westall, tql, mezz, pub 1828, NPG.

BRADSHAW, George (1801-1853) originator of railway guides.
P RICHARD EVANS, 1841, hl seated, NPG 2201.
PR UNKNOWN, hs, stipple, pub 1853, NPG.

BRADSHAW, Henry (1831-1886) librarian of Cambridge University.
P SIR HUBERT VON HERKOMER, 1881, King's College, Cambridge.
SC UNKNOWN, 1886, plaster bust, Old Schools, Cambridge. SIR WILLIAM HAMO THORNYCROFT, RA 1888, marble bust, University Library, Cambridge.
PH UNKNOWN, 1886, hs, print, NPG X5173.

BRADY, Henry Bowman (1835-1891) naturalist and pharmacist.
PH DEW SMITH, 1886, two prints, hs, profile, NPG X1101 and X1102.

BRAGGE, William (1823-1884) engineer and antiquary.
SC E.W.WYON, c1866, marble medallion, Mappin Art Gallery, Sheffield.

BRAHAM, Frances Elizabeth Anne, see Countess Waldegrave.

BRAMLEY-MOORE, John (1800-1886) chairman of the Liverpool docks.
P EDWARD BENSON, 1845, nearly wl seated, Walker Art Gallery, Liverpool.

BRAMPTON, Henry Hawkins, 1st Baron (1817-1907) judge.
SC J.W.SWYNNERTON, marble bust, Guildhall Art Gallery, London.
C SIR LESLIE WARD ('Spy'), wl, profile, chromo-lith, for *Vanity Fair*, 21 June 1873, NPG. HARRY FURNISS, head, pen and ink, NPG 3466.
PH LOCK & WHITFIELD, hs, woodburytype, for *Men of Mark*, 1877, NPG. BARRAUD, tql, print, for *Men and Women of the Day*, vol II, 1889, NPG AX5457. W. & D.DOWNEY, tql seated, woodburytype, for Cassell's *Cabinet Portrait Gallery*, vol II, 1891, NPG. LONDON STEREOSCOPIC CO, two prints, both hs, NPG X4267 and X4268. MAULL & CO, hl seated, carte, NPG AX5069.

BRAMWELL, Sir Byrom (1847-1931) physician.
P DAVID ALISON, c1923, Royal College of Physicians, Edinburgh.

BRAMWELL, Sir Frederick Joseph, Bart (1818-1903) engineer.

P FRANK HOLL, tql, Institution of Civil Engineers, London. SEYMOUR LUCAS, hs, Royal Society of Arts, London.
SC EDWARD ONSLOW FORD, bust, Royal Institution, London.
C SIR LESLIE WARD ('Spy'), wl, profile, chromo-lith, for *Vanity Fair*, 27 Aug 1892, NPG.

BRAMWELL, George William Wilshere Bramwell Baron (1808-1892) judge.
C SIR LESLIE WARD ('Spy'), tql seated, in court, chromo-lith, for *Vanity Fair*, 29 Jan 1876, NPG.
PH LONDON STEREOSCOPIC CO, after 1862, hs, carte, NPG X4269.

BRAND, Sir Henry Bouverie William, see 1st Viscount Hampden.

BRAND, Henry Robert, see 2nd Viscount Hampden.

BRAND, Sir Johannes Henricus (Jan Hendrik) (1823-1888) president of The Orange Free State.
PR UNKNOWN, hs, woodcut, for *Illust London News*, 2 April 1881, NPG.

BRANDRAM, Samuel (1824-1892) reciter.
PH J.E.MAYALL, hs, cabinet, NPG X4270.

BRANWHITE, Charles (1817-1880) landscape painter.
D G.W.BRAIKENRIDGE, c1835, w/c, City Art Gallery, Bristol.
PR UNKNOWN, after a photograph by J.H.Morgan, hs, profile, woodcut, for *Illust London News*, 20 March 1880, NPG.

BRASSEY, Anna or Annie Brassey, Baroness, née Allnutt (1839-1887) traveller and writer.
PR UNKNOWN, hs, lith, BM. UNKNOWN, tql, profile, with umbrella, lith, NPG.

BRASSEY, Thomas (1805-1870) railway contractor.
SC M.WAGMÜLLER, 1871, marble bust, Institution of Civil Engineers, London.
PR G.B.BLACK, tql seated with compasses, oval, lith, BM.

BRASSEY, Thomas Brassey, 1st Earl (1836-1918) politician.
P After FRANK HOLL, tql with telescope, Indian Institute, Oxford.
C CARLO PELLEGRINI ('Ape'), tql, profile, chromo-lith, for *Vanity Fair*, 6 Oct 1877, NPG.
PH LONDON STEREOSCOPIC CO, two prints, both hs, NPG X4276 and X4277.

BRAY, Charles (1811-1884) educationist.
PR H.ADLARD, after a photograph, hs, aged 72, line, BM, NPG.

BRAY, Sir Reginald More (1842-1923) judge.
C SIR LESLIE WARD ('Spy'), hl at bench, mechanical reproduction, for *Vanity Fair*, 17 Oct 1906, NPG.

BRAYBROOKE, Richard Cornwallis Neville, 4th Baron (1820-1861) archaeologist.
PH MAYER BROS, tql seated, carte, NPG X4280.

BREEKS, James Wilkinson (1830-1872) Indian civil servant.
PH CAMILLE SILVY, 1860, wl, carte, NPG (Album 2).

BRENCHLEY, Julius Lucius (1816-1873) traveller and writer.
P W.C.DOBSON, hs, Maidstone Museum and Art Gallery, Kent.
SC JOSEPH DURHAM, 1873, marble bust, Maidstone Museum and Art Gallery.

BRETT, John (1831-1902) landscape painter.
P Self-portrait, 1883, hs, MacDonald Collection, Aberdeen Art Gallery.
SC THOMAS STIRLING LEE, 1890, bust, The Art Workers' Guild, London.
PH UNKNOWN, hl seated, print, NPG X5175.

BRETT, Reginald Baliol, see 2nd Viscount Esher.

BRETT, Sir William Baliol, see 1st Viscount Esher.

BRIDGE, Sir John (1824-1900) police magistrate.
c SIR LESLIE WARD ('Spy'), hl at bench, chromo-lith, for *Vanity Fair*, 25 April 1891, NPG.

BRIDGE, Sir John Frederick (1844-1924) organist, composer and musical antiquary.
PR UNKNOWN, seated, playing the organ, process block, for *Musical Times*, 1907, BM.
c SIR LESLIE WARD ('Spy'), wl, profile, chromo-lith, for *Vanity Fair*, 14 April 1904, NPG.

BRIDGES, John Henry (1832-1906) positivist philosopher.
P FREDERICK YATES, 1904, hl seated, Royal College of Physicians, London.

BRIDGES, Robert Seymour (1844-1930) poet laureate.
P C.W.FURSE, 1893, tql seated, Eton College, Berks.
D WILLIAM ROTHENSTEIN, 1916, head, profile, pencil, Eton College. WILLIAM STRANG, head, gold-point, NPG 2773.
SC THEODORE SPICER-SIMSON, c1922, plasticine medallion, hs, profile, NPG 2044.
PR WILLIAM ROTHENSTEIN, 1897, hl, lith, BM, NPG. WILLIAM STRANG, 1898, hs, profile, etch, BM, NPG.
c SIR MAX BEERBOHM, 'The Old and Young Self', 1924, Ashmolean Museum, Oxford.
PH FREDERICK HOLLYER, 1888, hs, profile, sepia photogravure, NPG X4297. ALVIN LANGDON COBURN, hs, profile, photogravure, for *Men of Mark*, 1913, NPG AX7799. MRS M.G.PERKINS, 1913, wl seated, photogravure, for *Testament of Beauty*, 1929, NPG. WILL STROUD, 1923, two hs prints, NPG X4298 and X4299. LADY OTTOLINE MORRELL, 1924, wl seated at clavichord, neg, NPG X4300.

BRIERLEY, Benjamin (1825-1896) Lancashire dialect writer.
P GEORGE PERKINS, Failsworth Liberal Club, Lancashire.
SC JOHN CASSIDY, c1898, statue, Queen's Park, Manchester.

BRIERLY, Sir Oswald Walters (1817-1895) marine painter.
PR UNKNOWN, hs, woodcut, for *Illust London News*, 2 Jan 1886, NPG.

BRIGHT, Sir Charles Tilston (1832-1888) chief engineer of the Atlantic Telegraph Company.
SC COUNT GLEICHEN, plaster bust, Institution of Electrical Engineers, London.
PR UNKNOWN, hl seated, woodcut, for *Illust London News*, 4 Sept 1858, NPG.

BRIGHT, Henry (1814-1873) artist.
PR UNKNOWN, after a photograph by Elliott & Fry, hs, woodcut, for *Illust London News*, 25 Oct 1873, NPG.

BRIGHT, Jacob (1821-1899) radical politician.
c SIR LESLIE WARD ('Spy'), wl, chromo-lith, for *Vanity Fair*, 5 May 1877, NPG.

BRIGHT, James Franck (1832-1920) master of University College, Oxford.
P SIR GEORGE REID, tql, University College, Oxford.

BRIGHT, John (1811-1889) statesman and orator.
P GIUSEPPE FAGNANI, 1865, two portraits, New York Chamber of Commerce, and Union League Club, New York. CHARLES LUCY, 1869, V & A. LOWES DICKINSON, 1874, Reform Club, London. W.W.OULESS, 1879, tql seated, NPG 817. W.T.RODEN, 1879, City Museum and Art Gallery, Birmingham. ROBERT FOWLER, after Sir J.E.Millais of 1880, tql, Palace of Westminster, London. FRANK HOLL, 1882, tql seated, City Museum and Art Gallery, Birmingham. EYRE CROWE, 1883, wl seated, Reform Club. FRANK HOLL, 1887, Reform Club.
D FREDERICK SARGENT, hs, profile, pencil, NPG 3808. S.P.HALL, 1887, hs, sketch, pencil, NPG 2322.
G S.BELLIN, after J.R.Herbert of 1847, 'The Anti-Corn Law League', mixed, pub 1850, BM, NPG. JOHN PHILLIP, 'The House of Commons, 1860', oil, Palace of Westminster. GEORGE CRUIKSHANK, 'Bright Reform Bomb', oil, 1860, Palace of Westminster.
SC JOHN ADAMS-ACTON, c1870, marble bust, National Liberal Club, London. WILLIAM THEED, c1877, marble statue (?), Manchester City Hall. SIR J.E.BOEHM, 1881, plaster bust, NPG 868. SIR W.H.THORNYCROFT, 1891, bronze statue, Rochdale. ALBERT BRUCE JOY, 1891, marble statue on monument, Albert Square, Manchester, and c1892, marble statue, City Museum and Art Gallery, Birmingham. SIR ALFRED GILBERT, 1896, statue, National Liberal Club. UNKNOWN, marble bust, Lady Lever Art Gallery, Port Sunlight.
PR S.W.REYNOLDS jun, after C.A.Du Val, tql, mixed, pub 1843, BM, NPG. T.O.BARLOW, after J.E.Millais, tql, mezz, pub 1882, BM, NPG.
c HONORE DAUMIER, c1856, several liths, for *Le Charivari*, NPG. JOHN DOYLE, several political drgs, BM. HARRY FURNISS, tql seated, pen and ink, NPG 3345. Several prints by CARLO PELLEGRINI ('Ape'), and others, BM, NPG.
PH Various cartes by W. & D.DOWNEY, ELLIOTT & FRY, MAUJEAN, MAYALL, RUPERT POTTER, RUSSELL & SONS, ABRAHAM THOMAS and H.J.WHITLOCK, various dates and sizes, NPG. Several prints by BARRAUD, MAYALL and RUPERT POTTER, and a cabinet by BASSANO, various dates and sizes, NPG.

BRIGHT, Mynors (1818-1883) decipherer of Pepys.
P LOWES DICKINSON, Magdalene College, Cambridge.

BRIGHTMAN, Frank Edward (1856-1923) liturgiologist.
PH WALTER STONEMAN, 1930, hs, NPG (NPR).

BRINTON, William (1823-1867) physician.
P EDWARD ARMSTRONG, c1864, hs, semi-profile, Royal College of Physicians, London.

BRISE, Sir Evelyn John Ruggles-, see RUGGLES-Brise.

BRISTOWE, John Syer (1827-1895) physician.
P BEATRICE M.BRISTOWE (his daughter), tql, St Thomas's Hospital, London.
PR UNKNOWN, after a photograph by Jerrard, hs, woodcut, for *Illust London News*, 31 Aug 1895, NPG.

BROADBENT, Sir William Henry, 1st Bart (1835-1907) physician.
c SIR LESLIE WARD ('Spy'), tql seated, profile, chromo-lith, for *Vanity Fair*, 30 Oct 1902, NPG.
PH BASSANO, 1898, four negs, various sizes, NPG X4262-5.

BROADHURST, Henry (1840-1911) stonemason and politician.
c SIR LESLIE WARD ('Spy'), wl, chromo-lith, for *Vanity Fair*, 9 Aug 1884, NPG.
PH BENJAMIN STONE, 1897, wl, print, NPG, Birmingham Reference Library. OLIVE EDIS, tql, print, NPG X1343.

BROCK, Sir Thomas (1847-1922) sculptor.
P THEODORE BLAKE WIRGMAN, 1888, hl, MacDonald Collection, Aberdeen Art Gallery.
G REGINALD CLEAVER, 'Hanging Committee, Royal Academy, 1892', pen and ink, NPG 4245. SIR HUBERT VON HERKOMER, 'The Council of the Royal Academy', oil, 1908, TATE 2481.
c SIR LESLIE WARD ('Spy'), wl, chromo-lith, for *Vanity Fair*, 21 Sept 1905, NPG.

PH RALPH W.ROBINSON, wl in studio, print, for *Members and Associates of the Royal Academy of Arts, 1891*, NPG X7354. RUSSELL & SONS, after 1901, hs, cabinet, NPG X4675. MAULL & FOX, hs, cabinet, NPG X4676.

BROCK, William (1807-1875) dissenting divine.
G B.R.HAYDON, 'The Anti-Slavery Society Convention, 1840', oil, NPG 599.
PR UNKNOWN, after a photograph by London Stereoscopic Co, hs, woodcut, for *Illust London News*, 27 Nov 1875, NPG. J.R.DICKSEE, tql seated, lith, BM. J.R.DICKSEE, tql, stipple, NPG. UNKNOWN, tql, stipple, NPG.

BRODIE, William (1815-1881) sculptor.
P JOHN PHILLIP, 1859, hs, oval, Royal Scottish Academy, Edinburgh.
PH NESBITT & LOTHIAN, hs, carte, NPG (Album 106).

BRODRICK, George Charles (1831-1903) political writer.
P ROBERT MACBETH, 1898–9, tql, Merton College, Oxford. WILLIAM CARTER, 1899, tql seated, Merton College.
D S.P.HALL, 1888–9, hs, pencil sketch, NPG 2271.
C SIR LESLIE WARD ('Spy'), wl, profile, chromo-lith, for *Vanity Fair*, 30 Aug 1884, NPG. SIR MAX BEERBOHM, two drgs: 1890, wl; 1891?, study for a statue, Merton College.

BRODRICK (William) St John (Fremantle), see 9th Viscount and 1st Earl of Midleton.

BRODSKY, Adolf (1851-1929) violinist and teacher of music.
P WILLIAM CARTLEDGE, 1924, Royal Northern College of Music, Manchester.
D SIR WILLIAM ROTHENSTEIN, 1899, hl seated, pencil, NPG 4766. WILLIAM WEATHERBY, 1926, hs, profile, w/c and gouache, Manchester City Art Gallery.
PR SIR W.ROTHENSTEIN, 1899, tql seated, lith, NPG.
PH Various prints, Royal Northern College of Music. UNKNOWN, in a group with Hallé and Richter, Hallé Library, Manchester.

BROMBY, Charles Henry (1814-1907) second bishop of Tasmania.
PR UNKNOWN, tql, woodcut, for *Illust London News*, 8 Oct 1864, NPG.
PH W.WALKER & SONS, tql, carte, NPG AX7464. UNKNOWN, hl, print, NPG (Anglican Bishops).

BROMFIELD, William Arnold (1801-1851) botanist.
PR R.J.LANE, after Miss Knowles, hs, lith, NPG.

BROMLEY, Valentine Walter (1848-1877) artist.
PR UNKNOWN, hs, woodcut, for *Illust London News*, 19 May 1877, NPG.

BRONTË, Anne (1820-1849) novelist.
D CHARLOTTE BRONTË, w/c, Brontë Parsonage Museum, Haworth.
G BRANWELL BRONTË, 'The Brontë Sisters', oil, c1834, NPG 1725.

BRONTË, Charlotte (Mrs A.B.Nicholls) (1816-1855) novelist.
D GEORGE RICHMOND, 1850, hs, chalk, NPG 1452.
G BRANWELL BRONTË, 'The Brontë Sisters', oil, c1834, NPG 1725.

BRONTË, Emily Jane (1818-1848) novelist.
P BRANWELL BRONTË, c1833, hl, profile, NPG 1724.
G BRANWELL BRONTË, 'The Brontë Sisters', oil, c1834, NPG 1725.

BROOKE, Sir Charles Anthony Johnson (1829-1917) second raja of Sarawak.
C SIR LESLIE WARD ('Spy'), wl, chromo-lith, for *Vanity Fair*, 19 Jan 1899, NPG.

BROOKE, Gustavus Vaughan (1818-1866) actor.
P UNKNOWN, hl as Shylock, Garrick Club, London.

SC CHARLES SUMMERS, 1869, marble bust, State Library of Victoria, Australia.
PR D.J.POUND, after a daguerreotype, tql seated, oval, stipple and line, NPG. Several theatrical prints, NPG.

BROOKE, Sir James (1803-1868) Rajah of Sarawak.
P SIR FRANCIS GRANT, 1847, tql, NPG 1559.
SC THOMAS WOOLNER, 1858, marble bust, NPG 1426. GEORGE GAMMON ADAMS, 1868, plaster bust, NPG 1200.
PR W.J.EDWARDS, after a photograph by H.Watkins, hl seated, stipple, NPG.
PH MAULL & POLYBLANK, wl, carte, NPG X4690. Attrib MAULL & POLYBLANK, tql seated, print, NPG AX7309.

BROOKE, Stopford Augustus (1832-1916) writer and divine.
P G.F.WATTS, c1868, hs, NPG 3077.
D SIR WILLIAM ROTHENSTEIN, 1917–18, hs, pencil, NPG 4767. SIR WILLIAM ROTHENSTEIN, hs, pencil, NPG 4774.
PR G.PILOTELL, head, dry point, BM. UNKNOWN, tql seated, process block, BM.
PH BARRAUD, tql seated, print, for *Men and Women of the Day*, vol II, 1889, NPG AX5468. BERESFORD, 1903 and 1905, two hs negs, NPG X6447 and X6446. ELLIOTT & FRY, hs, carte, NPG X4689. N.S.KAY, hl, profile, print, NPG X1452.

BROOKFIELD, William Henry (1809-1874) divine.
PH JULIA MARGARET CAMERON, 1864, hs, print, NPG P18(17).

BROOKS, Charles William Shirley (1816-1874) editor of *Punch*.
G HENRY NELSON O'NEIL, 'Forty Three Members in the Billiard Room of the Garrick Club', oil, Garrick Club, London.
PR Several woodcuts, after photographs by ELLIOTT & FRY, MAYALL and others, hs, hs profile, and hl, NPG, and a group 'Editors of Punch', woodcuts and reproductions, for *Illust London News*, 18 July 1891, BM, NPG.
PH ELLIOTT & FRY, hs, profile, carte, NPG X4693. ELLIOTT & FRY, tql, carte, NPG AX7511. H.N.KING of Bath, wl seated, carte, NPG X4692.

BROOME, Sir Frederick Napier (1842-1896) colonial governor.
PR UNKNOWN, after a photograph by Gale, hs, woodcut, for *Illust London News*, 12 Dec 1896, NPG.

BROUGH, Lionel (1836-1909) actor.
P CHARLES BUCHEL, c1905, tql as Verges in *Much Ado About Nothing*, Museum of London.
D LUCIEN BESCHE, wl in character, w/c, NPG.
PR UNKNOWN, hs, lith, NPG.
C HARRY FURNISS, tql, profile, pen and ink, NPG 3556. SIR LESLIE WARD ('Spy'), wl, chromo-lith, for *Vanity Fair*, 30 March 1905, NPG.
PH LOCK & WHITFIELD, c1876, hs, carte, NPG X4704. ST JAMES'S PHOTOGRAPHIC CO, hs, print, for *The Theatre*, 1884, NPG X4705. HAINES, hs, postcard, NPG X4706. T.C.TURNER, tql, photo-gravure, NPG X6420.

BROUGHAM, John (1814-1880) actor and dramatist.
PH Four cartes, by SOUTHWELL BROS, ERNEST EDWARDS, LONDON STEREOSCOPIC CO and ADOLPHE BEAU, various sizes and dates, NPG X4708–11. ERNEST EDWARDS and HEATH & BEAU, two cartes, both wl, NPG (Album 108).

BROUGHTON, Rhoda (1840-1920) novelist.
PH BARRAUD, tql, print, for *Men and Women of the Day*, vol II, 1889, NPG AX5443.

BROWN, Ford Madox (1821-1893) painter.

P Self-portrait, 1855, tql seated with his wife, Emma Hill, 'The Last of England', Birmingham City Art Gallery; reduced version, 1860, Fitzwilliam Museum, Cambridge.

D D.G.ROSSETTI, 1852, hl, pencil, NPG 1021. WALKER HODGSON, 1892, tql, and a hs profile sketch, pencil and w/c, NPG 4041(4). FREDERIC J.SHIELDS, after a death mask, chalk, Manchester City Art Gallery.

SC CONRAD DRESSLER, plaster bust, Manchester City Art Gallery.

PR J.M.JOHNSTONE, after F.M.Brown, hl with palette, aged 55, woodcut, BM.

PH W. & D.DOWNEY, tql, carte, NPG AX7568. ELLIOTT & FRY, hs, profile, carte, NPG (Album 104).

BROWN, Frederick (1851-1941) professor of fine art.

P Several self-portraits: 1911, University College, London; 1926, hl, Ferens Art Gallery, Kingston-upon-Hull; 1932, tql, TATE 4702. DAME ETHEL WALKER, Bradford City Art Gallery.

D AUBREY BEARDSLEY, c1892, wl, pencil, pen and ink, TATE 4235. PHILIP WILSON STEER, head, profile, chalk, NPG 2816.

G SIR WILLIAM ORPEN, 'The Selecting Jury of the New English Art Club, 1909', oil, NPG 2556. D.G.MACLAREN, 'Some Members of the New English Art Club', w/c, NPG 2663.

PH G.C.BERESFORD, 1904, hs, profile, neg, NPG X6448. G.C.BERESFORD, hs, sepia print, NPG X4728.

BROWN, George (1818-1880) Canadian politician.

SC WILLIAM BRODIE, 1880, statue, Toronto, Canada.

PR UNKNOWN, after a photograph by Ellisson and Co, of Quebec, hl, woodcut, for *Illust London News*, 12 Nov 1864, NPG.

BROWN, Gerard Baldwin (1849-1932) art historian.

SC C.D'O.PILKINGTON JACKSON, c1930, bronze bust, Edinburgh University.

PR WILLIAM HOLE, wl, etch, for *Quasi Cursores*, 1884, NPG.

BROWN, Hugh Stowell (1823-1886) dissenting minister at Liverpool.

PR D.J.POUND, after a photograph, tql, supplement to *Illust News of the World*, BM.

BROWN, John (1810-1882) physician and author of *Rob and his Friends*.

P SIR GEORGE REID, 1881, hs, SNPG 290. SIR WILLIAM FETTES DOUGLAS, SNPG 852.

D JAMES RANNIE SWINTON, 1874, hs, chalk, SNPG 275. SIR JOHN WATSON GORDON, tql seated, pencil, SNPG 1813.

SC ROBERT CAUER, 1862, marble bust, SNPG 986.

PH J.MOFFAT, hs, carte, NPG X4730. T.RODGER, hs, carte, NPG X4731. UNKNOWN, wl seated with dog, carte, NPG X1374.

BROWN, Sir John (1816-1896) industrialist.

SC E.W.WYON, c1866, marble bust, Graves Art Gallery, Sheffield.

PR UNKNOWN, hs, woodcut, for *Illust London News*, 5 Oct 1867, NPG. UNKNOWN, after a photograph by Yates of Sheffield, hs, woodcut, for *Illust London News*, 9 Jan 1897, NPG.

BROWN, John (1826-1883) personal servant to Queen Victoria.

P CARL SOHN, 1883, wl in Highland dress, Scottish Tartans Society, Comrie, Ayrshire.

G SIR EDWIN LANDSEER, with Queen Victoria and two of her daughters, oil, 1866, Royal Coll.

PR W.H.EMMETT, wl, profile, with four dogs, Queen Victoria is writing at a table under trees, lith, BM. UNKNOWN, after a photograph, wl on Scottish moor, chromo-lith, BM. UNKNOWN, after a photograph by W. & D.Downey, hs, woodcut, for *Illust London News*, 7 April 1883, NPG.

PH W. & D.DOWNEY, 1860s, wl with Queen Victoria and Louise, Duchess of Argyll, carte, NPG X3608. W. & D.DOWNEY, 1868,

two prints, wl with Queen Victoria on horseback, and wl, NPG P22(4, 9). HILLS & SAUNDERS, wl, profile, with dogs, cabinet, NPG X4732. Various prints, Royal Coll.

BROWN, Oliver Madox (1855-1874) novelist and painter in water-colour.

P FORD MADOX BROWN (his father), 1860, hs, 'The English Boy', Manchester City Art Gallery.

D FORD MADOX BROWN, hs, chalk, Ashmolean Museum, Oxford.

BROWN, Robert (1842-1895) geographical compiler.

PR UNKNOWN, after a photograph by S.E.Pollard and Co, hs, woodcut, for *Illust London News*, 2 Nov 1895, NPG.

BROWN, Samuel (1817-1856) chemist and poet.

P DAVID SCOTT, hl, NGS 1877.

PH D.O.HILL & R.ADAMSON, 1844 with Rev George Gilfillan, Gernsheim Collection, University of Texas, USA.

BROWN, Thomas Edward (1830-1897) the Manx poet.

P SIR WILLIAM RICHMOND, Clifton College, Bristol.

BROWN, William Haig (1823-1907) master of Charterhouse.

P FRANK HOLL, RA 1884, tql seated, Charterhouse School, Surrey.

SC HARRY BATES, c1899, bronze seated statue, Charterhouse School.

C SIR MAX BEERBOHM, 'Some Masters of Forty Years Ago', Charterhouse School. SIR MAX BEERBOHM, 'Vague random memories of some of them', The William Andrews Clark Memorial Library, University of California at Los Angeles, USA.

BROWNE, Edward Harold (1811-1891) bishop of Winchester.

P G.F.WATTS, RA 1876, hl, Emmanuel College, Cambridge. UNKNOWN, St David's University College, Lampeter.

PR UNKNOWN, after a photograph by J. & C. Watkins, hl, woodcut, for *Illust London News*, 14 May 1864, NPG.

PH LOCK & WHITFIELD, hs, oval, woodburytype, for *Men of Mark*, 1876, NPG. ELLIOTT & FRY, 1890, tql seated in his study at Farnham Castle, sepia photogravure, NPG X4735. W. & D.DOWNEY, hs, carte, NPG X4734. SAMUEL A.WALKER, hs, carte, NPG X4742. W.WALKER & SONS, tql seated, carte, NPG AX7462.

BROWNE, George Forrest (1833-1930) minister and academic.

PH UNKNOWN, c1907, hs, postcard, NPG X4738. RUSSELL & SONS, hs, cabinet, NPG X4743. UNKNOWN, hs, print, NPG (Anglican Bishops).

BROWNE, Hablot Knight (1815-1882) water-colour painter and book-illustrator, known as 'Phiz'.

G UNKNOWN, 'Our Artists – Past and Present', woodcuts, for *Illust London News*, 14 May 1892, BM, NPG.

PR F.W.PAILTHORPE, hs, profile, etch, NPG. UNKNOWN, hs, woodcut, for *Illust London News*, 29 July 1882, NPG.

BROWNE, Sir James Crichton (1840-1938) physician and psychologist.

PR UNKNOWN, hs, woodcut, for *Illust London News*, 30 Jan 1886, NPG.

PH WALTER STONEMAN, 1917, hs, NPG (NPR).

BROWNE, Sir James Frankfort Manners (1823-1911) soldier.

PH BASSANO, 1898, four negs, various sizes, NPG X4223–6.

BROWNE, Sir Samuel James (1824-1901) general.

PR Various woodcuts for *Illust London News* illustrating events in the Afghan war, eg: at the Chapter of the Star of India at Allahabad (8 April 1876); tql in uniform (14 Dec 1878); entering Fort Ali

Musjid (4 Jan 1879); a Durbar at Jellalabad (15 Feb 1879); wl equestrian, his arrival into Jellalabad (15 Feb 1879); Reception of Sirdar Wali Mohammed at Jellalabad (24 May 1879); Conclusion of the Afghan War – Arrival of the Ameer Mahomed Yakoob Khan at Gundamuk (14 June 1879).
PH JABEZ HUGHES, print, National Army Museum, London.

BROWNE, Valentine Augustus, see 4th Earl of Kenmare.

BROWNHILL, Thomas Robson (1822?-1864), see Robson.

BROWNING, Elizabeth Barrett (1806-1861) poet.
P T.B.READ, 1853, Pennsylvania Historical Society, USA. MICHELE GORDIGIANI, 1858, hl seated, NPG 1899.
D UNKNOWN, c1820, crayon, Wellesley College Library, Mass, USA. W.M.THACKERAY, 1845, with the artist and Mrs Brookfield, Huntington Library and Art Gallery, San Marino, USA. RUDOLPH LEHMANN, 1859, hs, pencil, BM. FIELD TALFOURD, 1859, hl, chalk, NPG 322.
SC W.W.STORY, 1861, posthumous bust, Keats and Shelley Memorial Museum, Rome.
PR G.COOK, after C.Hayter, wl, aged 9, line and stipple, for vol I of her *Poetical Works*, 1889–90, BM. J.BROWN, after Mayou, as a child, stipple, for vol II of her *Poetical Works*, 1889–90, BM. T.O.BARLOW, after a photograph by Macaire of Le Havre (1858), tql, line and stipple, for vol III of her *Poetical Works*, 1889–90, BM.
PH UNKNOWN, Gernsheim Collection, University of Texas, USA.

BROWNING, Oscar (1837-1923) schoolmaster, Cambridge don and historian.
P IGNACIO ZULOAGA, 1900, King's College, Cambridge COLIN GRILL, 1914, King's College. TEAGUE, Eton College, Berks.
C 'HAY', wl, chromo-lith, for *Vanity Fair*, 24 Nov 1888, NPG. SIR MAX BEERBOHM, 'Mid-Term Tea at Mr Oscar Browning's', chalk and w/c, 1908, King's College.

BROWNING, Robert (1812-1889) poet.
P WILLIAM FISHER, 1854, Wellesley College, Mass, USA. WILLIAM PAGE, 1854, Baylor University, Texas, USA. MICHELE GORDIGIANI, 1858, hl seated, NPG 1898. SAMUEL LAURENCE, 1866, Baylor University. G.F.WATTS, 1866, hs, profile, NPG 1001. Several portraits by R.B.BROWNING (his son): 1874, St Andrews School, Tennessee; 1882, Balliol College, Oxford; 1889, Baylor University. RUDOLPH LEHMANN, 1875, tql, Baylor University; version, 1884, NPG 839. W.FISHER, 1877, Baylor University. ALPHONSE LEGROS, 1879, V & A. FELIX MOSCHELES, 1884, Wesleyan University, Ohio, USA.
D D.G.ROSSETTI, 1855, hs, w/c, Fitzwilliam Museum, Cambridge. RUDOLPH LEHMANN, 1859, hs, crayon, BM. FIELD TALFOURD, 1859, hs, chalk, NPG 1269. G.D.GILES, 1889, Baylor University.
SC HARRIET HOSMER, 1853, bronze cast of Browning's right hand clasping that of his wife, NPG 3165. THOMAS WOOLNER, 1856, bronze medallion, City Museum and Art Gallery, Birmingham. W.W.STORY, 1861, bust, Keats and Shelley Memorial Museum, Rome. R.B.BROWNING, 1886, bust, Browning Hall, Walworth, Conn, USA. H.S.MONTALBA, 1889, bust, Oxford University (?).
PR ROBERT BRYDEN, 1898, V & A.
C CARLO PELLEGRINI ('Ape'), wl, chromo-lith, for *Vanity Fair*, 20 Nov 1875, NPG.
PH LONDON STEREOSCOPIC CO, 1860s, tql seated, carte, NPG AX5076. ERNEST EDWARDS, hs, carte, NPG AX7521. EVELEEN MYERS, hs, print, NPG X1501. Several prints by BARRAUD, ELLIOTT & FRY, W.H.GROVE, W.JEFFREY, LOCK & WHITFIELD, LONDON STEREOSCOPIC CO, and E.MYERS, various dates and sizes, cartes, cabinets etc, NPG X4818–28. JULIA MARGARET CAMERON, hs, carte, NPG. UNKNOWN, a death bed portrait, print, Poetry Society, London, and Baylor University.

BRUCE, Alexander Hugh, see 6th Baron BALFOUR of Burleigh.

BRUCE, Sir David (1855-1931) surgeon-general; discoverer of the causes of Malta fever and sleeping sickness.
PH WALTER STONEMAN, 1918, hs, NPG (NPR).

BRUCE, Sir George Barclay (1821-1908) civil engineer.
P WILLIAM MAINWARING PALIN, 1888, tql seated, Institution of Civil Engineers, London.
PH OLIVE EDIS, c1902, tql seated, print, NPG X4830.

BRUCE, George Wyndham Hamilton Knight-, see KNIGHT-Bruce.

BRUCE, Henry Austin, see 1st Baron Aberdare.

BRUCE, James (1811-1863), see 8th Earl of Elgin.

BRUCE, John Collingwood (1805-1892) antiquary.
P UNKNOWN, hl, mezz, BM.

BRUCE, Victor Alexander, see 9th Earl of Elgin.

BRUNEL, Isambard Kingdom (1806-1859) civil engineer.
P JOHN CALLCOTT HORSLEY, 1848, wl, Museum of British Transport, York. J.C.HORSLEY, 1857, tql seated, NPG 979.
D CARL VOGEL, Küpferstichkabinett, Staatliche Kunstsammlungen, Dresden.
G JOHN LUCAS, 'Conference of Engineers at Britannia Bridge, Clifton', oil, c1853, Institution of Civil Engineers, London.
SC E.W.WYON, c1862, marble bust, Great Western Railway Museum, Swindon, Wilts. BARON CARLO MAROCHETTI, 1877, bronze statue on monument, Victoria Embankment, London.
PR D.J.POUND, after a photograph by Mayall, c1858, tql, line, pub with *Illust News of the World*, NPG.
PH ROBERT HOWLETT, 1857, wl standing before the chains of the 'Great Eastern', print, NPG P112; related carte, by Howlett, NPG X4836. UNKNOWN, 1859, wl, print, Brunel University. UNKNOWN, with 7th Earl Carlisle, Lord Alfred Paget, Mr Yates and the harbour master, print, NPG X4994. UNKNOWN, two groups relating to the launching of the Great Eastern Steamship, prints, 1857 and 1858, Brunel University.

BRUNTON, Sir Thomas Lauder, 1st Bart (1844-1916) physician.
P SIR HUBERT VON HERKOMER, 1913, tql seated, St Bartholomew's Hospital, London. HERMAN SALOMON, 1925, tql seated, Wellcome Institute, London.

BRYCE, David (1803-1876) architect.
D UNKNOWN, chalk, SNPG 1432.
SC GEORGE MACCALLUM, 1868, marble bust, SNPG 1090.

BRYCE, James Bryce, 1st Viscount (1838-1922) jurist, historian and statesman.
P JOSEPH WILSON FORSTER, 1899, hl seated, Trinity College, Oxford. SIR GEORGE REID, c1905, hs, Oriel College, Oxford. ERNEST MOORE, 1907, hl seated, profile, NPG 1970. SYDNEY SEYMOUR THOMAS, 1912, National Liberal Club, London. SIR WILLIAM ORPEN, RA 1917, hs, Aberdeen Art Gallery.
D S.P.HALL, wl seated with Sir John Day, pencil, NPG 2249. SIR WILLIAM ROTHENSTEIN, hs, chalk, SNPG 878.
C WRIGHT ('Stuff'), wl, chromo-lith, for *Vanity Fair*, 25 Feb 1893, NPG. Several drgs in the NPG: two pen and ink sketches by HARRY FURNISS, NPG 3425 and 3557; BOARDMAN ROBINSON, 1913, hl with Uncle Sam, pen and ink, NPG 4551.
PH W. & D.DOWNEY, hl seated, woodburytype, for Cassell's *Cabinet Portrait Gallery*, vol IV, 1893, NPG. SIR BENJAMIN STONE, 1898, wl, print, NPG. G.C.BERESFORD, 1902, hs, print, NPG X4839. G.C.BERESFORD, 1902, hs, neg, NPG X6451. JOHN RUSSELL &

SONS, hs, print, for *National Photographic Record*, vol II, NPG. WALTER STONEMAN, before 1917, hs, NPG (NPR).

BRYDON, William (1811-1873) army surgeon.
PR R. & E.TAYLOR, after a photograph by J.Stuart of Cromarty, hs, woodcut, for *Illust London News*, 19 April 1873, NPG.

BUCCLEUCH, Walter Francis Scott, 5th Duke of, and 7th Duke of Queensberry (1806-1884) Lord Privy Seal.
P Attrib JOHN JACKSON, hl, a leaving portrait, Eton College, Berks. Several portraits, Buccleuch Estates, Selkirk, Scotland: WILLIAM INGALTON, 1822, wl with Lord Scott at Eton; SIR JOHN WATSON GORDON, 1842, wl on horseback, and a hl study; SIR DANIEL MACNEE, 1877, tql in uniform; KNIGHTON WARREN, 1884, wl seated at desk. Several portraits at Beaulieu, Hants: UNKNOWN, tql; KNIGHTON WARREN, 1884, hs, profile. SIR FRANCIS GRANT, c1861, wl, Archer's Hall, Edinburgh. F.R.SAY, tql, SNPG 906.
D GEORGE RICHMOND, 1864, hs, Beaulieu, Hants. GEORGE RICHMOND, hs, chalk, Buccleuch Estates.
G SIR FRANCIS GRANT, 'A Hill Run with the Duke of Buccleuch's Hounds', oil, c1841, Buccleuch Estates. SIR GEORGE HAYTER, 'The Christening of the Prince of Wales', oil, 1842, Royal Coll.
SC THOMAS CAMPBELL, 1835, bust, Boughton House, Northants (Buccleuch Estates). HENRY WEEKES, 1861, bust, Boughton.
PH WINDOW & BRIDGE, two cartes: tql seated, profile, NPG X4851; wl seated, NPG AX7409.

BUCHANAN, Sir George (1831-1895) physician.
PR UNKNOWN, after a photograph by Fradelle and Young, hs, profile, wood engr, for *Illust London News*, 18 May 1895, NPG.

BUCHANAN, Sir George William (1854-1924) diplomat.
SC KATHLEEN SCOTT (Lady Kennet), bronze bust, DoE (British Embassy, Rome).
PH ADÈLE, wl, as a young man, cabinet, NPG X4855. WALTER STONEMAN, 1919, hs, NPG (NPR).

BUCHANAN, James (1804-1870) minister of North Leith.
PR W.WALKER, after S.Mackenzie, hs, stipple, pub 1838, BM, NPG.

BUCHANAN, James (1849-1935), see 1st Baron Woolavington.

BUCHANAN, Robert (1802-1875) Free Church leader.
D UNKNOWN, hs, chalk, SNPG 1861.

BUCHANAN, Robert Williams (1841-1901) author.
G R.TAYLOR & Co, 'Modern Poets', woodcuts, for *Illust London News*, 15 Oct 1892, BM, NPG. P.NAUMANN & R.TAYLOR & Co, 'Our Literary Contributors – Past and Present', woodcuts, for *Illust London News*, 14 May 1892, BM, NPG.
SC UNKNOWN, bust on monument, St John The Baptist Churchyard, Southend-on-Sea, Essex.
PR W.ROFFE, after a photograph by Elliott & Fry, hs, stipple and line, NPG.
PH UNKNOWN, hs, print, NPG X11853.

BUCKINGHAM and CHANDOS, Richard Plantagenet Campbell Temple Nugent Brydges Chandos Grenville, 3rd Duke of (1823-1889) statesman.
G HENRY GALES, 'The Derby Cabinet of 1867', w/c, NPG 4893.
PR C.A.TOMKINS, after A.Buckingham and Chandos (his second wife), tql, aged 65, with mantle and collar of the order of the star of India, mezz, BM. C.W.WALTON, hs, lith, NPG.
C CARLO PELLEGRINI ('Ape'), wl, profile, chromo-lith, for *Vanity Fair*, 29 May 1875, NPG.

BUCKLAND, Francis Trevelyan (1826-1880) naturalist.
PR UNKNOWN, hs, woodcut, for *Illust London News*, 1 Jan 1881, NPG.

BUCKLAND, William Warwick (1859-1946) lawyer.
P SIR JAMES GUNN, Gonville and Caius College, Cambridge.

PH UNKNOWN, 1932, hs, print, NPG X4857.

BUCKLE, George Earle (1854-1935) editor of *The Times*.
P UNKNOWN, c1878, The Times Newspapers Ltd, London.
D FREDERICK PEGRAM, c1888-9, pencil sketch, made during the sessions of the Parnell Special Commission, V & A.

BUCKLEY, Henry Burton, see 1st Baron Wrenbury.

BUCKNILL, Sir John Charles (1817-1897) physician.
PR Two wood engrs by unknown artists, the first after a photograph by Debenham & Gould, the second after a photograph by Elliott and Fry, both hs, for *Illust London News*, 2 June 1894, and 31 July 1897, NPG.

BUCKSTONE, John Baldwin (1802-1879) comedian and dramatist.
P DANIEL MACLISE, c1836, tql seated, NPG 2087. J.P.KNIGHT, hl seated, Garrick Club, London.
PR D.J.POUND, after a photograph by Mayall, tql, stipple and line, pub 1860, NPG. D.MACLISE, wl seated, lith, no 78 of his 'Portrait Gallery of Illustrious Literary Characters', for *Fraser's Mag*, 1836, NPG. Various theatrical and popular prints, BM, NPG, Harvard Theatre Collection, Cambridge, Mass, USA.
C ALFRED BRYAN, wl, w/c, NPG 3071.
PH Several cartes by ELLIOTT & FRY, FRADELLE & LEACH, and W.WALKER & SONS, various dates and sizes, NPG X4861-7. UNKNOWN, tql, print, NPG X6421.

BUDGE, Sir (Ernest Alfred Thompson) Wallis (1857-1934) Egyptian scholar.
PH SIR BENJAMIN STONE, 1906, wl, print, Birmingham Reference Library.

BUFTON, Eleanor (afterwards Mrs Arthur Swanborough) (1840?-1893) actress.
PH Four cartes, three hs, one wl, NPG X4869-72.

BUIST, George (1805-1860) Anglo-Indian journalist, editor of the *Bombay Times*.
PH D.O.HILL & ROBERT ADAMSON, 1845, hl seated, print, NPG P6(41).

BULLEN, George (1816-1894) Keeper of printed books at the British Museum.
PR UNKNOWN, after a photograph by Barraud, hs, profile, wood engr, for *Illust London News*, 20 Oct 1894, NPG.

BULLER, Charles (1806-1848) liberal politician.
SC HENRY WEEKES, 1848, marble bust on monument, Westminster Abbey, London.
PR E.SCRIVEN, after B.E.Duppa, hl, stipple, for J.Saunders's *Political Reformers*, 1840, BM, NPG.

BULLER, Sir Redvers Henry (1839-1908) general.
SC BERTRAM MACKENNAL, c1911, bronze recumbent effigy, Winchester Cathedral.
PR G.J.STODART, after H.T.Wells, hs, stipple, one of 'Grillion's Club' series, BM, ZAPP & BENNETT, hs, lith, NPG.
C SIR LESLIE WARD ('Spy'), wl, profile, chromo-lith, for *Vanity Fair*, 18 Jan 1900, NPG.
PH ELLIOTT & FRY, hs in uniform, photogravure, NPG X4878. UNKNOWN, tql in uniform, postcard, NPG X4877.

BULWER, William Henry Lytton Earle, see Baron DALLING and Bulwer.

BULWER-LYTTON, Edward George Earle Lytton (1803-1873), see 1st Baron Lytton.

BULWER-LYTTON, Edward Robert (1831-1891), see 1st Earl of Lytton.

BULWER-LYTTON, Rosina, see Lady Lytton.

BUNSEN, Sir Maurice William Ernest De, see DE Bunsen.

BURCHETT, Richard (1815-1875) artist.
PR UNKNOWN, hs, woodcut, 1875, NPG.

BURDETT-COUTTS, Angela Georgina Burdett-Coutts, Baroness (1814-1906) philanthropist.
P After S.J.STUMP of 1828, head, Coutts & Co, London. J.R.SWINTON, RA 1865, wl, Royal Marsden Hospital, London, engr G.Zobel, mezz, BM, NPG. Attrib JULIUS JACOB, tql seated, City of Edinburgh Museums and Art Galleries.
M SIR WILLIAM CHARLES ROSS, c1847, wl, NPG 2057.
G A.P.TILT, 'A Garden Party Given by Baroness Burdett Coutts for the International Medical Congress, London, 1881', oil, Wellcome Institute, London.
PR UNKNOWN, hs, lith, NPG.
C THÉOBALD CHARTRAN, wl, w/c, Coutts & Co, lith for *Vanity Fair*, 3 Nov 1883, NPG.
PH SKEOLAN, 1860s, hl seated, carte, NPG X4892. LONDON STEREOSCOPIC CO, before 1877, tql, semi-profile, carte, NPG X4890, and LONDON STEREOSCOPIC CO, before 1877, similar pose, print, NPG X4891.

BURDON, John Shaw (1826-1907) missionary bishop of Victoria, Hong Kong.
PH UNKNOWN, hs, profile, print, NPG (Anglican Bishops).

BURDON-SANDERSON, Sir John Scott, Bart (1828-1905) physiologist and pathologist.
P W.W.OULESS, 1886, hl, NPG 4297. JOHN COLLIER, RA 1894, wl seated, University Museum, Oxford. C.W.FURSE, 1900, hl seated, University Museum.
D RUDOLPH LEHMANN, 1893, hs, BM.
SC H.R.HOPE PINKER, 1907, marble bust, University Museum, Oxford.
C SIR LESLIE WARD ('Spy'), wl, chromo-lith, for *Vanity Fair*, 17 May 1894, NPG.

BURGES, William (1827-1881) architect.
PR UNKNOWN, after a photograph by Van der Weyde, hs, woodcut, for *Illust London News*, 30 April 1881, NPG.

BURGESS, John Bagnold (1830-1897) artist.
P Self-portrait, 1884, Aberdeen Art Gallery.
G S.P.HALL, 'The St John's Wood Arts Club, 1895', Burgess is probably rightly identified in the group, chalk and wash, NPG 4404.
PH RALPH W.ROBINSON, wl seated at easel, print, for *Members and Associates of the Royal Academy of Arts, 1891*, NPG X7355.

BURGH CANNING, Hubert George de, see 15th Earl and 2nd Marquess of Clanricarde.

BURGON, John William (1813-1888) dean of Chichester.
D W.E.MILLER, 1882, hs, crayon, Oriel College, Oxford.

BURKE, Sir John Bernard (1814-1892) Ulster King of Arms.
PR UNKNOWN, after a painting, wl in heralds' dress, process block, BM. UNKNOWN, tql seated, line, NPG.

BURKE, Robert O'Hara (1820-1861) Australian explorer.
SC CHARLES SUMMERS, statue on monument, with statue of W.J.Wills, Collins Street, Melbourne, Australia.
PR E.GILKS, hs, lith, NPG.

BURKE, Thomas Henry (1829-1882) Under Secretary for Ireland.
P AUGUSTUS BURKE, NGI.
D WALTER OSBORNE, after Augustus Burke, photographs and memory, pencil, NGI 2350.

BURKE, Thomas Nicholas (1830-1883) Dominican preacher

and lecturer.
P G.F.MULVANY, NGI 928.

BURN, Robert (1829-1904) classical scholar.
P ALPHONSE LEGROS, 1880, hs, profile, Fitzwilliam Museum, Cambridge.

BURNABY, Frederick Gustavus (1842-1885) soldier, traveller and balloonist.
P J.J.TISSOT, 1870, wl seated, NPG 2642.
SC UNKNOWN, medallion portrait on obelisk, St Philip's Churchyard, Birmingham.
PR E.A.ARMSTRONG, after M.Reed, hs, etch, BM.
C SIR LESLIE WARD ('Spy'), wl, chromo-lith, for *Vanity Fair*, 2 Dec 1876, NPG. HARRY FURNISS, c1880-c1910, wl, pen and ink, NPG 3428.
PH LOCK & WHITFIELD, hs, woodburytype, for *Men of Mark*, 1877, NPG. DONOVAN, hs, profile, carte, NPG X4900.

BURNAND, Sir Francis Cowley (1836-1917) editor of *Punch*.
G UNKNOWN, 'Editors of *Punch*', woodcuts and reproductions, for *Illust London News*, 18 July 1891, BM, NPG.
C CARLO PELLEGRINI ('Ape'), wl, profile, chromo-lith, for *Vanity Fair*, 8 Jan 1881, NPG. HARRY FURNISS, two pen and ink drgs, wl and hl seated, NPG 3429-30.
PH UNKNOWN, c1899, wl and wl seated (double portrait of the sitter), cabinet, NPG X4904. WALTER H.BARRETT, 1902, tql, carte, NPG X4903. JOHN RUSSELL & SONS, hs, print, for *National Photographic Record*, vol II, NPG. WALERY, tql, print, NPG. UNKNOWN, hs, woodburytype, for *The Theatre*, NPG X4915.

BURNE-JONES, Sir Edward Coley, 1st Bart (1833-1898) painter and designer.
P ALPHONSE LEGROS, 1868, hs, sketch, V & A. G.F.WATTS, 1870, hs, City Museum and Art Gallery, Birmingham. SIR PHILIP BURNE-JONES (his son), 1898, almost wl, profile, with palette, at easel, NPG 1864. ALPHONSE LEGROS, hs, Aberdeen Art Gallery.
D SIMEON SOLOMON, 1859, head, pencil, Ashmolean Museum, Oxford. GEORGE HOWARD, later Earl of Carlisle, 1875, three sketches, wl seated, hl profile, and hs profile, pencil, Carlisle Museum and Art Gallery. S.P.HALL, c1886-1903, pencil sketch, NPG 2287. ALPHONSE LEGROS, hs, w/c, V & A.
G SIR EDWARD BURNE-JONES, 'The Annunciation and the Adoration of the Magi', (Burne-Jones as a shepherd), oil, 1861, TATE 4143. G.GRENVILLE MANTON, 'Conversazione at the Royal Academy, 1891', w/c, NPG 2820.
C HARRY FURNISS, c1880-1910, pen and ink sketch, NPG 3432. Self-portrait, two sketches of himself climbing through a canvas, BM.
PH UNKNOWN, tql seated, profile, as a young man, carte, NPG (Album 104). UNKNOWN, c1874, wl seated with William Morris, print, NPG X3763. H.R.STILES, 1895, two prints, both tql seated, the first with two grandchildren, the second with one grandchild, NPG X3690 and X3691. ELLIOTT & FRY, hs, profile, cabinet, NPG X6422. FREDERICK HOLLYER, hs, profile, cabinet, NPG X4905. F.HOLLYER, wl seated, V & A (Hollyer Albums). UNKNOWN, wl seated, sepia print, NPG X3688. Several prints, Hammersmith Public Libraries.

BURNES, Sir Alexander (1805-1841) Indian political officer.
D WILLIAM BROCKEDON, 1834, hs, chalk, NPG 2515(20).
PR E.FINDEN, after D.Maclise, hs in Bokhara costume, stipple, pub 1835, NPG.

BURNETT, Frances Eliza Hodgson (1849-1924) novelist.
PH BARRAUD, wl, print, for *Men and Women of the Day*, vol I, 1888, NPG AX5434.

BURNEY, Sir Cecil, 1st Bart (1858-1929) admiral.

P SIR JOHN LAVERY, IWM.
D FRANCIS DODD, 1917, charcoal and w/c, IWM.
G A.S.COPE, 'Naval Officers of World War 1, 1914–18', oil, 1921, NPG 1913.
PH WALTER STONEMAN, 1917, hs, NPG (NPR).

BURNHAM, Edward Levy-Lawson, 1st Baron (1833-1916) Newspaper proprietor.
C SIR MAX BEERBOHM, several drgs, eg: 1903, hl seated, ink, w/c and crayon, NPG 5343; 'Mr Max Beerbohm receives an influential, though biassed, deputation, urging him, in the cause of our common humanity, and of good taste, to give over', 1908, Art Institute of Chicago; a fresco containing heads of King Edward and others, 1922, University of Texas, USA; 'The Baptism of Sir Edward Lawson', and a wl, profile sketch, Merton College, Oxford. HARRY FURNISS, tql seated, pen and ink, NPG 3433.
PH ELLIOTT & FRY, tql, sepia print, NPG X4914.

BURNS, Jabez (1805-1876) nonconformist divine.
PR D.J.POUND, after a photograph by Mayall, tql, line, for *Drawing Room Portrait Gallery*, 1861, NPG. RANDALL DALE, after Robert James, tql, semi-profile, mezz, NPG.

BURNS, John Elliott (1858-1943) labour leader and politician.
P JOHN COLLIER, 1889, tql, NPG 3170. A.J.FINBERG, 1897, speaking in a park, Battersea Library, London. G.F.WATTS, 1897, hs, semi-profile, Watts Gallery, Compton, Surrey. HAROLD SPEED, 1909, National Liberal Club, London. G.W.LEECH, posthumous, Battersea Town Hall, London.
D HAROLD SPEED, 1907, hs, pastel, NPG 5124. S.P.HALL, hs, profile, pencil, NPG 2290.
C SIR LESLIE WARD ('Spy'), wl, chromo-lith, for *Vanity Fair*, 15 Oct 1892, NPG. HARRY FURNISS, c1880–c1910, tql, pen and ink, NPG 3346. SIR FRANCIS CARRUTHERS GOULD, 1908, wl, profile, ink, for *Pall Mall Gazette*, NPG 2826. SIR MAX BEERBOHM, wl, 'You've jolly well *got* to be free!', w/c, NPG 3851.
PH W. & D.DOWNEY, tql, woodburytype, for Cassell's *Cabinet Portrait Gallery*, vol IV, 1893, NPG. BENJAMIN STONE, several prints: 1897, wl; 1901, two, both wl; 1902, wl with Lloyd George; 1905, wl, NPG. G.C.BERESFORD, 1902, hs, neg, NPG X6453. Several prints by G.C.BERESFORD, W. & D.DOWNEY, DUSA, REGINALD HAINES and LONDON STEREOSCOPIC CO, various dates and sizes, NPG X4920–27.

BURNS, William Chalmers (1815-1868) missionary in China.
PR DALZIEL, wl in Chinese dress, woodcut, BM.

BURNSIDE, William (1852-1927) mathematician.
PH WALTER STONEMAN, 1917, hs, NPG (NPR).

BURROWS, Sir George, 1st Bart (1801-1887) physician.
P J.P.KNIGHT, RA 1865, tql, St Bartholomew's Hospital, London. GEORGE RICHMOND, 1871, hl seated in President's gown, Royal College of Physicians, London.
SC MICHAEL WAGMÜLLER, 1873, marble bust, Royal College of Physicians.

BURROWS, Sir John Cordy (1813-1876) surgeon.
SC E.B.STEPHENS, 1878, marble statue, Pavilion Grounds, Brighton.

BURT, Thomas (1837-1922) trade-unionist and liberal politician.
PR UNKNOWN, after a photograph by W. & D.Downey, hs, woodcut, for *Illust London News*, 7 March 1874, NPG.
PH SIR BENJAMIN STONE, 1901, wl, print, NPG.

BURTON, Decimus (1800-1881) architect.
PR M.GAUCI, after E.U.Eddis, hl, lith, BM, NPG.

BURTON, Sir Frederic William (1816-1900) painter and director of the National Gallery.
P H.T.WELLS, 1863, hl seated, profile, NPG 1701. Attrib G.F.MULVANY, hl seated, NGI 538.
D Self-portrait, head, pencil, NGI 2400.
G H.J.BROOKS, 'Private View of the Old Masters Exhibition, Royal Academy, 1888', oil, NPG 1833.
SC JOHN HUGHES, marble life mask, NGI 8134.
PH CUNDALL, DOWNES & CO, 1860s, tql seated, carte, NPG AX5077.

BURTON, Isabel, Lady (1831-1896) wife of Sir Richard Francis Burton, traveller and writer.
D LOUIS DESANGES, 1861, hs, w/c, oval, with a companion portrait of her husband, Orleans House Gallery, Twickenham.

BURTON, John Hill (1809-1881) historian.
P W.B.HOLE, 1882, wl, Messrs Blackwood & Sons Ltd, Edinburgh.
SC ALEXANDER RHIND, after William Brodie of 1859, marble bust, SNPG 148.

BURTON, Michael Arthur Bass, 1st Baron (1837-1909) brewer.
G H.J.BROOKS, 'Private view of the Old Masters Exhibition, Royal Academy, 1888', oil, NPG 1833.
C SIR LESLIE WARD ('Spy'), wl, semi-profile, Hentschel-Colourtype, for *Vanity Fair*, 25 Nov 1908, NPG.

BURTON, Sir Richard Francis (1821-1890) explorer and writer.
P FREDERIC, LORD LEIGHTON, 1876, hl, NPG 1070. MARIE DE GUTMANSTHAL, 1879, hs, School of Oriental and African Studies, London University. Several portraits by ALFRED LETCHFORD: 1889 (made to look as in c1861), wl in fencing dress; wl in Arab dress; seated at his desk in his study, all at Orleans House Gallery, Twickenham.
D LOUIS DESANGES, 1861, hs, w/c, oval, with a companion portrait of his wife, Orleans House Gallery. MARIAN COLLIER, 1878, head, pencil, NPG 3148. ALFRED LETCHFORD, on his death bed, ink, Orleans House Gallery.
C CARLO PELLEGRINI ('Ape'), wl, profile, chromo-lith, for *Vanity Fair*, 24 Oct 1885, NPG.
PH ERNEST EDWARDS, wl seated in oriental fashion, for *Men of Eminence*, ed. L.Reeve, vol III, 1865, NPG. LOCK & WHITFIELD, hs, woodburytype, for *Men of Mark*, 1876, NPG.

BURTON, William Evans (1804-1860) actor, manager and playwright.
PR Various theatrical prints, Harvard Theatre Collection, Cambridge, Mass, USA.

BURTON, William Shakespeare (1825-1916) painter.
D Self-portrait, hs, chalk, NPG 3042.

BURY, William Coutts Keppel, Viscount, see 7th Earl of Albermarle.

BUSHNELL, Catherine (1825-1861), see Hayes.

BUSK, George (1807-1886) scientist.
P E.M.BUSK, hl, Linnean Society, London; replica, Royal College of Surgeons, London.

BUSK, Hans (1815-1882) a pioneer of the volunteer movement.
PR UNKNOWN, hs, woodcut, for *Illust London News*, 25 March 1882, NPG.

BUTCHER, Samuel Henry (1850-1910) professor of Greek at Edinburgh University.
PR WILLIAM HOLE, wl with J.S.Blackie, etch, for *Quasi Cursores*, 1884, NPG.

BUTE, John Patrick Crichton Stuart, 3rd Marquess of (1847-1900) scholar and benefactor.

P SIR HUBERT VON HERKOMER, 1892, wl, Cardiff Town Council. Two portraits by E.T.HAYNES: 1895?, hs in lord rector's robes, University of St Andrews, and 1898, hs in provost's robes, Rothesay Town Council.

PR Two woodcuts by unknown artists, for *Illust London News*, 27 April 1872, NPG: his marriage to the Hon Gwendaline Howard, at the Oratory, Brompton, and hs, oval, after a photograph by Russell and Sons, with a companion oval of his wife.

BUTLER, Arthur Gray (1831-1909) headmaster of Haileybury.

P GEORGE RICHMOND, 1867, hl, Haileybury College, Herts.

BUTLER, Edward Joseph Aloysius (Dom Cuthbert) (1858-1934) Benedictine abbot and scholar.

P W.C.SYMONS, Downside, Somerset.

BUTLER, Elizabeth Southerden, Lady, née Thompson (1846-1933) artist.

P Self-portrait, 1869, hs, oval, on card, NPG 5314.

PR UNKNOWN, hl, lith, NPG.

PH FRADELLE & MARSHALL, hs, carte, NPG (Album 104).

BUTLER, Frank Hedges (1855-1928) balloonist and pioneer of flying.

C SIR LESLIE WARD ('Spy'), hl, in balloon, Hentschel-Colourtype, for *Vanity Fair*, 11 Dec 1907, NPG.

PH UNKNOWN, Hedges & Butler Ltd, London.

BUTLER, Henry Montagu (1833-1918) master of Trinity College, Cambridge.

P SIR HUBERT VON HERKOMER, 1883, tql seated, Harrow School, Middx. Three portraits by SIR WILLIAM ORPEN, all tql seated in robes: 1911, Trinity College, Cambridge; 1911, on loan to Fitzwilliam Museum, Cambridge; study, Royal Academy, London.

D SIR WILLIAM ROTHENSTEIN, 1916, hs in academic robes, chalk, Trinity College; version, NPG 4768.

PR F.STERNBERG, after Sir H.von Herkomer of 1887, tql seated, mezz, BM, NPG.

C 'HAY', wl, w/c study, for *Vanity Fair*, 18 May 1889, NPG 3277.

PH Various prints, Trinity College: 1855, tql seated; as a young man, tql seated, reading; ELLIOTT & FRY, hs, profile; HILLS & SAUNDERS, tql, carte; ETHEL GLAZEBROOK, 1911, four prints, all tql seated; 1912, two group prints with George V and others.

BUTLER, Josephine Elizabeth, née Grey (1828-1906) social reformer.

P G.F.WATTS, hl seated, NPG 2194.

D GEORGE RICHMOND, 1851, hs, semi-profile, pastel, NPG L172.

SC ALEXANDER MUNRO, two marble busts, Walker Art Gallery, Liverpool, and Girton College, Cambridge.

PH ELLIOTT & FRY, hs, profile, print, Liverpool University.

BUTLER, Samuel (1835-1902) author of *Erewhon* and *The Way of All Flesh*.

P CHARLES GOGIN, 1896, hs, NPG 1599.

PH UNKNOWN, hl seated, aged 54, photogravure, BM (Engr Ports Coll). UNKNOWN, wl, print, Alexander Turnbull Library, Wellington, New Zealand.

BUTLER, William Archer (1814?-1848) professor of moral philosophy at Dublin.

PR C.GREY, tql seated, lith, NPG.

BUTLER, Sir William Francis (1838-1910) lieutenant-general and author.

C SIR LESLIE WARD ('Spy'), wl, mechanical reproduction, for *Vanity Fair*, 9 Jan 1907, NPG.

BUTLER, William John (1818-1894) dean of Lincoln.

SC CHAVALLIAUD, 1896, alabaster recumbent effigy, Lincoln Cathedral.

BUTLIN, Sir Henry Trentham, 1st Bart (1845-1912) surgeon.

P JOHN COLLIER, 1903, tql, St Bartholomew's Hospital, London.

BUTT, Sir Charles Parker (1830-1892) judge.

C CARLO PELLEGRINI ('Ape'), hs at bench, chromo-lith, for *Vanity Fair*, 12 Feb 1887, NPG.

BUTT, Isaac (1813-1879) founder of the Irish Home Rule Party.

D JOHN BUTLER YEATS, hs, chalk, NPG 3831 and NGI.

PR J.KIRKWOOD, wl at lectern, lith, NPG.

C 'FAUSTIN', wl, a *Figaro* cartoon, chromo-lith, NPG. LESLIE WARD 1879, hs, profile, pencil and w/c, NPG.

BUTTERFIELD, William (1814-1900) architect.

D JANE FORTESCUE COLERIDGE, 1874, hs, profile, charcoal, Keble College, Oxford.

BUXTON, Sydney Charles Buxton, Earl (1853-1934) statesman.

P EDWARD ROWORTH, House of Assembly, Cape Town, South Africa.

PR W.STRANG, hs, semi-profile, etch, NPG.

C SIR LESLIE WARD ('Spy'), wl, profile, mechanical reproduction, for *Vanity Fair*, 2 Jan 1907, NPG.

BYNG, George Henry Charles, see 3rd Earl of Strafford.

BYNG, George Stevens, see 2nd Earl of Strafford.

BYRNE, Sir Edmund Widdrington (1844-1904) judge.

C SIR LESLIE WARD ('Spy'), tql, profile, in court, chromo-lith, for *Vanity Fair*, 30 Jan 1896, NPG.

BYRON, Henry James (1834-1884) dramatist and actor.

PR H.C.MAGUIRE, wl as Sir Simon Simple, chromo-lith, NPG. E.MATTHEWS & SONS, hs, semi-profile, lith, NPG. UNKNOWN, hs, woodcut, for *The Illust Review*, 6 Dec 1873, NPG. Several prints, Harvard Theatre Collection, Cambridge, Mass, USA.

C Several woodcuts and liths, Harvard Theatre Collection.

PH Two woodburytypes by unknown photographers, both hs, the second for *The Theatre*, NPG x4939-40.

BYWATER, Ingram (1840-1914) professor of Greek at Oxford.

P JOHN SINGER SARGENT, 1901, TATE 3012.

PR W.ROTHENSTEIN, tql seated, lith, BM.

C SIR MAX BEERBOHM, c1892, two drgs, Ashmolean Museum, Oxford, and Merton College, Oxford.

C

CADBURY, George (1839-1922) cocoa and chocolate manufacturer and social reformer.

P FRANCIS DODD, c1920–22, tql seated, Cadbury Schweppes Ltd, Birmingham.

PH UNKNOWN, hs, as an old man, print, Cadbury Schweppes Ltd.

CADOGAN, George Henry Cadogan, 5th Earl (1840-1915) conservative statesman.

PR J.BROWN, after a photograph, hs, stipple, for *Baily's Mag*, 1881, BM. C.W.WALTON, after a photograph by Bassano, hs, lith, NPG.

C SIR LESLIE WARD ('Spy'), wl, profile, chromo-lith, for *Vanity Fair*, 4 June 1881, NPG.

PH BARRAUD, hs, print, for *Our Conservative and Unionist Statesmen*, vol I, NPG (Album 16).

CAILLARD, Sir Vincent Henry Penalver (1856-1930) administrator.

C SIR LESLIE WARD ('Spy'), wl, profile, chromo-lith, for *Vanity Fair*, 11 Feb 1897, NPG.

CAINE, Sir (Thomas Henry) Hall (1853-1931) novelist.

PR WALTER TITTLE, 1922, hs, lith, NPG.

C SIR BERNARD PARTRIDGE, wl, w/c study, for *Vanity Fair*, 2 July 1896, NPG 3667. HARRY FURNISS, three pen and ink sketches, all wl, NPG 3434–6.

H W. & D.DOWNEY, hs, woodburytype, for Cassell's *Cabinet Portrait Gallery*, vol III, 1892, NPG. G.C.BERESFORD, 1904, two negs, both hs, NPG x6455–6. LONDON STEREOSCOPIC CO, before 1915, hs, cabinet, NPG x5001. GEORGE B.COWEN, with his family and others in a carriage, print, NPG x5002. WALERY, tql seated, print, NPG x5000.

CAINE, William Sproston (1842-1903) politician and temperance advocate.

H SIR BENJAMIN STONE, 1901, two wl prints, NPG.

CAIRD, Edward (1835-1908) master of Balliol College, Oxford.

P SIR GEORGE REID, 1886, tql, University of Glasgow. JOHN COLLIER, 1904, tql seated, Balliol College, Oxford.

C SIR LESLIE WARD ('Spy'), hl seated at desk, chromo-lith, for *Vanity Fair*, 4 April 1895, NPG.

H THOMAS ANNAN, hl seated, carte, NPG x5006. MACNAB, wl, semi-profile, as a young man, carte, NPG (Album 102).

CAIRD, Sir James (1816-1892) agriculturist and author.

R UNKNOWN, tql, lith, for *The County Gentleman*, 13 Aug 1881, NPG.

CAIRD, John (1820-1898) principal of Glasgow University.

P SIR J.E.MILLAIS, RA 1881, University of Glasgow.

CAIRNS, Hugh McCalmont Cairns, 1st Earl (1819-1885) lord chancellor.

P LOWES DICKINSON, 1876, wl in lord chancellor's robes, Hughenden (NT), Bucks.

G JOHN PHILLIP, 'House of Commons, 1860', oil, Palace of Westminster, London.

C ALBERT BRUCE JOY, 1888, marble bust, DoE (Law Courts, London). ALBERT BRUCE JOY, 1894, marble bust, Lincoln's Inn, London.

R W.HOLL, after G.Richmond, hs, stipple, one of 'Grillion's Club'

series, BM. D.J.POUND, after a photograph by Mayall, tql, line, presented with *Illust News of the World*, BM, NPG. F.SARGENT, hs, etch, NPG. G.J.STODART, after a photograph by E.Debenham, hl seated, stipple and line, NPG. UNKNOWN, hl, lith, for *Civil Service Review*, 1877, BM. Several popular prints, NPG.

C CARLO PELLEGRINI ('Ape'), wl, profile, chromo-lith, for *Vanity Fair*, 31 July 1869, NPG.

PH Two cartes by MAYALL: 1860s, tql seated, profile, NPG x1697, and 1861, wl, NPG AX5080. LOCK & WHITFIELD, hs, oval, woodburytype, for *Men of Mark*, 1881, NPG. BINGHAM, tql, carte, NPG x5007. JOHN WATKINS, hs, carte, NPG (Album 99). UNKNOWN, hs, carte, NPG x5008.

CAIRNS, John (1818-1892) United Presbyterian divine.

P JOHN EDGAR, 1862, hl, SNPG 1389. UNKNOWN, SNPG 1417.

CAITHNESS, James Sinclair, 14th Earl of (1821-1881) scientist.

D FREDERICK SARGENT, hl, pencil, NPG 1834c.

PH VERNON HEATH, hs, carte, NPG AX7452.

CALDECOTT, Randolph (1846-1886) artist.

P Self-portrait, 1884, hs, oval, MacDonald Collection, Aberdeen Art Gallery.

CALDERON, Philip Hermogenes (1833-1898) painter.

P G.F.WATTS, 1871, hl, Watts Gallery, Compton, Surrey. SIR GEORGE REID, 1881, hs, oval, MacDonald Collection, Aberdeen Art Gallery.

G H.J.BROOKS, 'Private view of the Old Masters Exhibition, Royal Academy, 1888', oil, NPG 1833. G.GRENVILLE MANTON, 'Conversazione at the Royal Academy, 1891', w/c, NPG 2820. H.T.WELLS, 'Friends at Yewden', oil, Hamburger Kunsthalle, Hamburg.

PH DAVID WILKIE WYNFIELD, c1862–4, hs, print, NPG P72. LOCK & WHITFIELD, hs, semi-profile, woodburytype, for *Men of Mark*, 1882, NPG. RALPH W.ROBINSON, wl seated with palette, at easel, print, for *Members and Associates of the Royal Academy of Arts, 1891*, NPG x7356. JOHN & CHARLES WATKINS, two cartes, both tql seated, NPG AX7560 and NPG (Album 104).

CALDERWOOD, Henry (1830-1897) philosopher.

PR W.HOLE, tql, etch, for *Quasi Cursores*, 1884, NPG.

CALLAGHAN, Sir George Astley (1852-1920) admiral.

PH WALTER STONEMAN, 1918, hs in uniform, NPG (NPR).

CALLOW, John (1822-1878) painter.

PH Possibly F.F.COTTON, 1860, tql seated with Aaron Penley, sepia print, NPG x5013. ELLIOTT & FRY, hs, profile, carte, NPG (Album 104).

CALLOW, William (1812-1908) water-colour painter.

D E.R.HUGHES, hs, profile, pastel, NPG 2937. UNKNOWN, hs, w/c, NPG 2356.

PH ELLIOTT & FRY, hs, profile, carte, NPG (Album 104).

CALVERLEY, Charles Stuart (1831-1884) poet and parodist.

PR G.J.STODART, hs, stipple, NPG. UNKNOWN, mezz, Christ's College, Cambridge.

CAMBRIDGE, George William Frederick Charles, 2nd

Duke of (1819-1904) commander-in-chief of the army.
p John Lucas, RA 1838, tql, Royal Coll. J.P.Knight, RA 1866, wl, Christ's Hospital, Horsham, Sussex. Herman G.Herkomer, 1893, wl in uniform, Royal Engineers HQ Mess, Chatham, Kent. Sir A.S.Cope, 1897, wl in uniform, formerly United Service Club, London (c/o The Crown Commissioners). F.X.Winterhalter, Royal Coll. Unknown, wl in uniform, National Army Museum, London. Unknown, tql in uniform, Kneller Hall, Twickenham. Unknown, DoE (Ministry of Defence).
d S.F.Diez, 1841, tql, pencil and wash, Staatliche Museen zu Berlin. Frederick Sargent, 1870–80, hl, pencil, NPG 1834d. Rudolph Lehmann, 1893, BM.
g A.J.Dubois Drahonet, 1832,· wl with Queen Victoria and Prince George of Cumberland, Royal Coll. Several groups depicting royal occasions, Royal Coll.
sc William Behnes, 1831, marble bust, Royal Coll. Count Gleichen, RA 1883, marble bust, Army and Navy Club, London. G.G.Adams, 1888, marble bust, Royal Coll. F.J.Williamson, RA 1897, marble bust, Corporation of London. Adrian Jones, bronze equestrian statue, Whitehall, London.
pr Various prints and popular prints, BM, NPG.
c Alfred Thompson (Atń), hl seated, chromo-lith, for *Vanity Fair*, 23 April 1870, NPG.
ph Several prints by John Clarck, Maull & Polyblank and others, various dates and sizes, NPG 5023–7. W. & D.Downey, c1876, tql in uniform, photogravure, NPG x5184. W. & D.Downey, hs in uniform, woodburytype, for Cassell's *Cabinet Portrait Gallery*, vol III, 1892, NPG. W. & D.Downey, hl in uniform, cabinet, NPG x6857. Fenton, tql seated, print, NPG x6843. Walery, tql, print, NPG. Two cartes by unknown photographers, tql seated and wl, NPG (Album 123). Unknown, in a large group, sepia print, NPG x5028.

CAMERON, Julia Margaret (1815-1879) pioneer photographer.
p G.F.Watts, 1850–2, hs, NPG 5046.
ph H.Cameron, hl, print, V & A. Unknown, wl seated with her niece, Julia Stephen, sepia print, NPG x1587. Lord Somers, c1860, tql, print, NPG.

CAMERON, Verney Lovett (1844-1894) African explorer.
pr Several woodcuts, for *Illust London News*, NPG.
c Sir Leslie Ward ('Spy'), wl, semi-profile, chromo-lith, for *Vanity Fair*, 15 July 1876, NPG.
ph Lock & Whitfield, hs, oval, woodburytype, for *Men of Mark*, 1878, NPG. Maull & Co, hl, carte, NPG x5018.

CAMPBELL, Frederick Archibald Vaughan, see 3rd Earl Cawdor.

CAMPBELL, Sir George (1824-1892) Indian administrator and author.
c Sir Leslie Ward ('Spy'), tql, profile, chromo-lith, for *Vanity Fair*, 21 Sept 1878, NPG.

CAMPBELL, George Douglas, see 8th Duke of Argyll.

CAMPBELL, Gertrude Elizabeth, Lady, née Blood (1858-1911) writer and journalist.
p Giovanni Boldini, c1897, wl seated, NPG 1630.
ph W. & D.Downey, tql, woodburytype, for Cassell's *Cabinet Portrait Gallery*, vol IV, 1893, NPG.

CAMPBELL, James Henry Mussen, see 1st Baron Glenavy.

CAMPBELL, John (1817-1904) army surgeon.
p J.R.Reid, 1893, hs, NPG 2523.

CAMPBELL, John Douglas Sutherland, see 9th Duke of Argyll.

CAMPBELL, Lewis (1830-1908) classical scholar.
p Unknown, University of St Andrews.
ph G.C.Beresford, 1904, tql seated, neg, NPG x6458.

CAMPBELL-BANNERMAN, Sir Henry (1836-1908 prime-minister.
p Sir James Guthrie, SNPG 775. Miss Brenda Morgan, afte J.Colin Forbes, National Liberal Club, London.
d Harold Speed, 1907, hs, chalk, NPG 5120. Sir Francis Car ruthers Gould, hl, w/c, NPG 3537.
pr The Autotype Company, after J.H.F.Bacon, tql, NPG.
c Sir Leslie Ward ('Spy'), wl seated, profile, chromo-lith, fo *Vanity Fair*, 10 Aug 1899, NPG. Sir Francis Carruthers Gould several ink drgs, NPG 2826 and 2830–2, and with 1st Earl Balfou NPG 2866.
ph Sir Benjamin Stone, 1897 and 1898, two prints, both wl, NPG G.C.Beresford, 1902, hs, neg, NPG x6457. G.C.Beresford, h profile, photogravure, NPG x5186. London Stereoscopic C hs, print, NPG x5044.

CANDLISH, Robert Smith (1806-1873) Free Church leade
c B.W.Crombie, 1839, wl, coloured etch, for *Modern Athenian* 1882, NPG.
ph Elliott & Fry, two cartes, both hs, NPG x5614 and x561 Moffat, hs, carte, NPG (Album 102).

CANNAN, Charles (1858-1919) scholar and universi publisher.
ph Emery Walker, c1918, hl, profile, photogravure, NPG x5616.

CANNING, Charles John Canning, Earl (1812-1862 governor-general of India.
p C.A.Mornewick, Government House, Calcutta. Sir Georg Hayter, exhib 1868, hl, Harewood House, W Yorks.
d George Richmond, 1851, head, chalk, NPG 1057.
m William Barclay, RA 1836, Harewood House.
g John Partridge, 'The Fine Arts Commissioners, 1846', NP 342,3. William Simpson, 'Canning's Return Visit to th Maharajah of Kashmir, 1860', w/c, India Office Library an Records, London.
sc J.H.Foley, two statues, 1862, Westminster Abbey, London, an 1874, equestrian, Calcutta.
pr W.Roffe, after a photograph by Mayall, tql seated, profil stipple, BM, NPG.
ph Studio of Richard Beard, hs, daguerreotype, NPG p11 Mayall, c1860, two cartes, both tql seated, NPG x5617 an x5619.

CANNING, Hubert George de Burgh, see 2nd Marquess Clanricarde.

CANNING, Sir Samuel (1823-1908) civil engineer an pioneer of submarine telegraphy.
p Beatrice Bright, 1897, tql seated, NPG 4925.
sc Unknown, bust, Institution of Civil Engineers, London.

CANTELUPE, Sir Charles Richard Sackville-West, 6t Viscount, see 6th Earl and 12th Baron DE La Warr.

CANTERBURY, John Henry Thomas Manners-Sutto 3rd Viscount (1814-1877) governor of Trinidad.
pr Unknown, hs, semi-profile, woodcut, for *Illust London News*, July 1877, NPG.

CANTON, William (1845-1926) poet and journalist.
ph John Russell & Sons, hs, print, for *National Photographic Recor* vol I, NPG.

CAPEL, Thomas John (1836-1911) Roman Catholic prelat

Argyll.

ᴾʀ UNKNOWN, tql, lith, for *The Whitehall Review*, 24 August 1878, NPG.

ᴄ C.A.LOYE ('MD'), wl, w/c study, for *Vanity Fair*, 7 Sept 1872, NPG 2567.

ᴾʜ LOCK & WHITFIELD, hs, woodburytype, for *Men of Mark*, 1876, NPG. LONDON STEREOSCOPIC CO, two cartes, tql, NPG x5622, and hl, NPG (Album 99).

CARADORI-ALLAN, Maria Caterina Rosalbina (1800-1865) singer.

ᴾʀ Various theatrical prints, BM, NPG, Harvard Theatre Collection, Cambridge, Mass, USA.

CARDEN, Sir Robert Walter, Bart (1801-1888) lord mayor of London.

ᴾʀ D.J.POUND, after a photograph by Mayall, tql seated in robes, stipple and line, NPG.

ᴄ SIR LESLIE WARD ('Spy'), hl, w/c study for *Vanity Fair*, 11 Dec 1880, NPG 2568. Two popular prints, lith, NPG.

CARDWELL, Edward Cardwell, Viscount (1813-1886) statesman.

ᴾ GEORGE RICHMOND, tql, NPG 767.

ᴅ FREDERICK SARGENT, hl, profile, pencil, NPG 1834e.

ɢ JOHN PHILLIP, 'House of Commons, 1860', oil, Palace of Westminster, London. L.C.DICKINSON, 'Gladstone's Cabinet of 1868', oil, NPG 5116.

ᴾʀ W.HOLL, after G.Richmond, hs, stipple, one of 'Grillion's Club' series, BM, NPG.

ᴄ CARLO PELLEGRINI ('Ape'), wl, w/c study for *Vanity Fair*, 3 April 1869, NPG 2569.

ᴾʜ LOCK & WHITFIELD, hs, woodburytype, for *Men of Mark*, 1878, NPG. Three cartes: L.CALDESI & CO, wl, NPG (Album 136); W.WALKER & SONS, tql seated, NPG x5628; JOHN WATKINS, hs, NPG (Album 99).

CARLILE, Wilson (1847-1942) founder of the Church Army.

ᴾ L.R.GALESTA, Church Army headquarters, London.

ᴾʜ JOHN RUSSELL & SONS, hs, print, for *National Photographic Record*, vol I, NPG.

CARLINGFORD, Chichester Samuel Parkinson Fortescue, Baron (1823-1898) statesman.

ᴾ JAMES TISSOT, 1871, wl, Examination Schools, Oxford.

ɢ UNKNOWN, 'The Cabinet Council, 1883', lith, for *Vanity Fair*, NPG.

ᴄ F.M.TAUBMANN, monument, Waldegrave Chapel, Chewton Mendip, Somerset.

ʀ UNKNOWN, two engrs, both hs, stipple, NPG.

ᴄ CARLO PELLEGRINI ('Ape'), wl, profile, chromo-lith, for *Vanity Fair*, 14 Aug 1869, NPG.

ᴾʜ W. & D.DOWNEY, tql seated, carte, NPG (Album 136). LOCK & WHITFIELD, hs, woodburytype, for *Men of Mark*, 1883, NPG. UNKNOWN, hs, carte, NPG (Album 38). UNKNOWN, hs, profile, sepia print, NPG x4109.

CARLISLE, George James Howard, 9th Earl of (1843-1911) politician and artist.

ᴾ SIR W.B.RICHMOND, Castle Howard, N Yorks. G.F.WATTS, Castle Howard.

ᴅ H.T.WELLS, 1893, crayon, Castle Howard.

ᴴ G.C.BERESFORD, 1903, two negs, hs and tql, NPG x6463 and x6464.

CARLISLE, George William Frederick Howard, 7th Earl of (1802-1864) Viceroy of Ireland.

ᴾ UNKNOWN, hl, a leaving portrait, Eton College, Berks. STEPHEN CATTERSON SMITH, Dublin Castle. JOHN PARTRIDGE, Castle Howard, N Yorks. C.SCOTT, after a photograph, Castle Howard.

ᴅ Several drgs, Castle Howard, N Yorks: WILLIAM ROSS, 1818, head, pencil; UNKNOWN, 1823, pencil; HENRY SMITH, 1838, crayon; GEORGE RICHMOND, 1850, hs, crayon; E.REITSCHEL, c1853, wl, w/c.

ᴍ T.H.CARRICK, probably RA 1843, on marble, Castle Howard.

ɢ SIR GEORGE HAYTER, 'The House of Commons, 1833', oil, NPG 54. SIR DAVID WILKIE, 'The Queen Presiding Over her First Council', oil, 1837, Royal Coll. C.R.LESLIE, 'Queen Victoria Receiving the Sacrament at her Coronation', oil, 1838, Royal Coll. JOHN PARTRIDGE, 'The Fine Arts Commissioners, 1846', oil, NPG 342,3.

ꜱᴄ CHRISTOPHER MOORE, 1839, marble bust, NGI 8088. J.H.FOLEY, 1870, statue, Carlisle. J.H.FOLEY, two busts, Castle Howard.

ᴾʀ F.C.LEWIS, after J.Slater, hs, stipple, one of 'Grillion's Club' series, BM, NPG. D.J.POUND, after a photograph by Mayall, tql seated, stipple and line, NPG.

ᴄ Various political satires by JOHN DOYLE, drgs, BM.

ᴾʜ T.CRANFIELD, wl seated, carte, NPG x5634. UNKNOWN, hs, carte, NPG AX5084. UNKNOWN, with Lord Alfred Paget, I.K.Brunel, Mr Yates and the harbour master, sepia print, NPG x4994. UNKNOWN, with members of a Cricket Club, carte, NPG AX5085.

CARLISLE, Rosalind Frances Howard, Countess of (1845-1921) promoter of women's political rights and of temperance reform.

ᴾ SIR W.B.RICHMOND, 1880, Castle Howard, N Yorks.

ᴅ D.G.ROSSETTI, 1870, hs, chalk, Ashmolean Museum, Oxford.

CARLYLE, Jane Baillie, née Welsh (1801-1866) letter writer, wife of Thomas Carlyle.

ᴾ SAMUEL LAURENCE, c1852, hl, profile, NPG 1175.

ᴍ KENNETH MACLEAY, SNPG 1123.

ᴾʜ W.JEFFREY, two cartes, wl and wl seated, NPG x5663-4. UNKNOWN, tql seated, sepia print, NPG x5665.

CARLYLE, John Aitken (1801-1879) physician.

ᴾʀ UNKNOWN, hs, semi-profile, woodcut, NPG.

CARLYLE, Sir Robert Warrand (1859-1934) Indian civil servant and scholar.

ᴾʜ WALTER STONEMAN, 1918, hs, NPG (NPR).

CARMICHAEL, Sir Thomas David Gibson-Carmichael, 11th Bart, Baron (1859-1926) overseas administrator and art connoisseur.

ᴾʜ SIR BENJAMIN STONE, 1897, wl, print, NPG.

CARNARVON, Henry Howard Molyneux Herbert, 4th Earl of (1831-1890) statesman.

ᴾ PHILIP MORRIS, tql in masonic dress, with star and collar of St Patrick, United Grand Lodge of England, London.

ᴾʀ JUDD & CO, tql, lith, for *The Whitehall Review*, 16 Feb 1878, NPG. W.HOLL, after G.Richmond, hs, stipple, one of 'Grillion's Club' series, BM. E.STODART, after a photograph by London Stereoscopic Co, hl seated, stipple and line, NPG. Several popular prints, NPG.

ᴄ CARLO PELLEGRINI ('Ape'), wl, semi-profile, chromo-lith, for *Vanity Fair*, 11 Sept 1869, NPG.

ᴾʜ LOCK & WHITFIELD, hs, profile, woodburytype, for *Men of Mark*, 1880, NPG.

CARNARVON, Henry John George Herbert, 3rd Earl of (1800-1849) politician.

ᴾ THOMAS KIRKBY, hs, a leaving portrait, Eton College, Berks.

ᴾʀ H.ROBINSON, after W.Walker, hl in uniform, octagon, stipple and line, for *Eminent Conservative Statesmen*, BM, NPG.

CARNEGIE, Andrew (1835-1919) manufacturer and philanthropist.

P B.J.BLOMMERS, *c*1912, Palace of Peace, The Hague; study, Dundee City Art Gallery. E.A.WALTON, 1913, University of St Andrews. CATHERINE OULESS, after W.W.Ouless, hl, SNPG 1003.

SC SIR WILLIAM GOSCOMBE JOHN, 1914, marble bust, Palace of Peace, The Hague.

C SIR LESLIE WARD ('Spy'), wl, chromo-lith, for *Vanity Fair*, 29 Oct 1903, NPG.

CARNEGIE, James, see 9th Earl of Southesk.

CARNOCK, Sir Arthur Nicolson, 1st Baron (1849-1928) diplomat.

PH UNKNOWN, *c*1888, hs, sepia cabinet, NPG X5671.

CARPENTER, Edward (1844-1929) sociologist.

P HENRY BISHOP, 1907, hs, NPG 3832. ROGER FRY, wl, NPG 2447.

PH ALVIN LANGDON COBURN, 1905, hs, print, NPG P48. ELLIOTT & FRY, hs, profile, photogravure, NPG X12530. FREDERICK HOLLYER, hl, print, V & A. (Hollyer Albums).

CARPENTER, Joseph Estlin (1844-1927) Unitarian divine.

P HOWARD SOMERVILLE, two portraits, Manchester College, Oxford. MINNA TAYLER, Essex Hall, London.

CARPENTER, Mary (1807-1877) philanthropist.

PR UNKNOWN, after a photograph by Cyrus Voss Bark of Clifton, hs, woodcut, for *Illust London News*, 7 July 1877, NPG.

CARPENTER, William Benjamin (1813-1885) naturalist.

P JOHN COLLIER, RA 1880, tql, University of London.

PR T.H.MAGUIRE, tql seated, lith, for *Ipswich Museum Portraits*, 1851, BM, NPG.

PH ERNEST EDWARDS, wl seated, print, for *Men of Eminence*, vol III, ed L.Reeve, 1864, NPG. LOCK & WHITFIELD, hs, woodburytype, for *Men of Mark*, 1883, NPG. MAULL & CO, tql, carte, NPG X5698.

CARPENTER, William Boyd-, see BOYD-Carpenter.

CARRICK, Thomas Heathfield (1802-1875) miniature painter.

M Self-portrait, hl, on marble, Tullie House Museum, Carlisle.

CARRINGTON, Charles Robert Wynn-Carrington, 1st Earl (1843-1928) politician.

D HAROLD SPEED, 1910, hs, chalk, NPG 5121.

PR UNKNOWN, after D.A.Wehrschmidt of 1901, wl as Lord Great Chamberlain, mezz, NPG.

C CARLO PELLEGRINI ('Ape'), wl, profile, driving a carriage, chromo-lith, for *Vanity Fair*, 7 Feb 1874, NPG. SIR LESLIE WARD ('Spy'), wl, profile, mechanical repro, for *Vanity Fair*, 11 Sept 1907, NPG.

CARRINGTON, Sir Frederick (1844-1913) general.

D PHIL MAY, 1897, with Cecil Rhodes, pen and ink sketch, Africana Museum, Johannesburg.

CARRODUS, John Tiplady (1836-1895) violinist.

PR UNKNOWN, after a photograph by Russell & Sons, hs, wood engr, for *Illust London News*, 20 July 1895, NPG.

CARROLL, Lewis, see Charles Lutwidge DODGSON.

CARSON, Edward Henry Carson, Baron (1854-1935) Ulster leader and advocate.

P SIR JOHN LAVERY, 1922, tql seated, Ulster Museum, Belfast. P.A.DE LÁSZLÓ, tql seated, Middle Temple, London.

SC L.S.MERRIFIELD, *c*1933, statue, Parliament Buildings, Stormont, Belfast. L.S.MERRIFIELD, marble bust, Belfast Corporation.

PR J.G.DAY, 1913, hs, profile, etch, NPG 2916.

C LIBERIO PROSPERI ('Lib'), wl, profile, chromo-lith, for *Vanity Fair*, 9 Nov 1893, NPG. WALLACE HESTER, wl, Hentschel-Colourtype, for *Vanity Fair*, 8 Feb 1911, NPG. 'W.H.', wl, profile, chromo-lith for *Vanity Fair*, 17 Jan 1912, NPG. SIR MAX

BEERBOHM, 1913, wl, w/c, NPG 3852. SIR BERNARD PARTRIDGE pen and ink sketch, for *Punch*, 26 Nov 1913, NPG. HARRY FURNISS pen and ink sketch, NPG 3347.

PH SIR BENJAMIN STONE, 1898, wl, print, NPG. G.C.BERESFORD 1903, two negs, hs, and hs profile, NPG X6466–7. G.C.BERESFORD 1923, hs, neg, NPG X6465. G.C.BERESFORD, 1923?, hs, profile print, NPG X5684.

CARTE, Richard D'Oyly (1844-1901) promoter of English Opera.

C SIR LESLIE WARD ('Spy'), wl, chromo-lith, for *Vanity Fair*, 14 Feb 1891, NPG.

PH ALFRED ELLIS & WALERY, hs, print, Theatre Museum, V & A.

CARTER, Robert Brudenell (1828-1918) ophthalmic surgeon.

C (Possibly H.C.SEPPING) WRIGHT ('Stuff'), wl, profile, w/c study for *Vanity Fair*, 9 April 1892, NPG 3298.

CARTER, Thomas Thellusson (1808-1901) tractarian divine.

P MARGARET CARPENTER, hs, a leaving portrait, Eton College Berks.

CARTON, Richard Claude (1856-1928) playwright.

PH ALFRED ELLIS, hl, sepia print, for *The Theatre*, Jan 1893, NPG X5693.

CARVER, Alfred James (1826-1909) master of Dulwich College.

P S.MELTON FISHER, RA 1882, tql, Dulwich College Picture Gallery, London. E.HASTAIN, hl seated, Dulwich College Picture Gallery.

CARY, Francis Stephen (1808-1880) painter and teacher of art.

D JAMES HAYLLAR, 1851, head, pencil and chalk, NPG 3896.

CASSEL, Sir Ernest Joseph (1852-1921) financier and philanthropist.

PR A.L.ZORN, 1909, hl, etch, NPG 3995.

C SIR LESLIE WARD ('Spy'), wl, chromo-lith, for *Vanity Fair*, 7 Dec 1899, NPG.

PH WALTER STONEMAN, 1917, hl, NPG (NPR).

CASSELL, John (1817-1865) publisher.

P UNKNOWN, tql, Cassell and Collier Macmillan Publishers London.

CASWALL, Edward (1814-1878) hymn writer.

PH R.W.THRUPP, hl, carte, NPG X5711.

CATES, William Leist Readwin (1821-1895) chronologist

D CHARLOTTE PEARSON, head, profile, pencil, NPG 3078.

CATTERMOLE, George (1800-1868) painter.

D Self-portrait, *c*1820, hs, chalk, BM. Self-portrait, pencil, V & A UNKNOWN, wl seated at easel, profile, crayon, NPG 4579.

CAVAGNARI, Sir Pierre Louis Napoleon (1841-1879 diplomat.

PR Several woodcuts, *c*1879, for *Illust London News*, NPG.

PH J.BURKE, wl with Amir Yakub Khan, General Daob Shah Habeebula Moustafi and Mr Jenkyns, print, National Army Museum, London.

CAVE, George Cave, Viscount (1856-1928) statesman.

P R.G.EVES, 1925, tql seated in wig and robes, Inner Temple London. FRANCIS DODD, tql in robes, St John's College, Oxford G.F.KELLY, Merchant Taylors' School, Northwood, London W.R.SYMONDS, 1911, tql, County Hall, Kingston-upon Thames, Surrey.

D FRANCIS DODD, 1925, hs, chalk, NPG 4421.

CAVE, Sir Lewis William (1832-1897) judge.

c SIR LESLIE WARD ('Spy'), tql in court, chromo-lith, for *Vanity Fair*, 7 Dec 1893, NPG.

H LOCK & WHITFIELD, hs, oval, woodburytype, for *Men of Mark*, 1883, NPG.

CAVE, Sir Stephen (1820-1880) politician.

PR UNKNOWN, hs, woodcut, for *Illust London News*, 11 Dec 1875, NPG.

c CARLO PELLEGRINI ('Ape'), wl, chromo-lith, for *Vanity Fair*, 3 Oct 1874, NPG.

H LOCK & WHITFIELD, hs, oval, woodburytype, for *Men of Mark*, 1878, NPG.

CAVENDISH, Ada (1839-1895) actress.

R Various theatrical prints, Harvard Theatre Collection, Cambridge, Mass, USA. Two prints, NPG.

H Several prints by BARRAUD, ELLIOTT & FRY, SOUTHWELL BROS and unknown photographers, various dates and sizes, NPG X5719-23 and AX7720.

CAVENDISH, Lord Frederick Charles (1836-1882) statesman.

c ALBERT BRUCE JOY, c1884, bronze statue, Cavendish Square, Barrow-in-Furness. THOMAS WOOLNER, 1885, marble recumbent effigy on monument, Cartmel Priory, Lancs.

PR J.D.MILLER, after W.B.Richmond of c1874, hl seated, mezz, NPG.

H B.W.BENTLEY, wl, cabinet, NPG X5718. LONDON STEREOSCOPIC CO, hs, carte, NPG X5717. JOHN & CHARLES WATKINS, hs, carte, NPG (Album 136).

CAVENDISH, Spencer Compton, see 8th Duke of Devonshire.

CAVENDISH, Sir William, see 7th Duke of Devonshire.

CAWDOR, Frederick Archibald Vaughan Campbell, 3rd Earl (1847-1911) politician.

H ELLIOTT & FRY, hs, print, NPG X5724.

CAYLEY, Arthur (1821-1895) scholar.

P LOWES DICKINSON, 1874, tql seated, Trinity College, Cambridge, W.H.LONGMAID, 1884, hl seated, Trinity College.

c HENRY WILES, marble bust, Trinity College; plaster model, Philosophical Library, Cambridge.

CECIL, Arthur (1843-1896) actor.

D WALFORD GRAHAM ROBERTSON, two w/cs, tql as the Hon Vere Queckett in *The School Mistress*, and wl seated, profile, as Mr Poskett in *The Magistrate*, Garrick Club, London.

c SIR LESLIE WARD ('Spy'), wl, profile, chromo-lith, for *Vanity Fair*, 28 Dec 1889, NPG; w/c study, Garrick Club. AUBREY BEARDSLEY, in character in *Diplomacy*, pen and ink, for *The Pall Mall Budget*, 23 Feb 1893, V & A.

H UNKNOWN, c1878, hs, print, NPG X1118. ALFRED ELLIS, c1895, hs, profile, print, for *The Theatre*, July 1895, NPG X5735. Four similar cartes by FRADELLE & MARSHALL, hs, NPG X5732-4 and AX7702.

CECIL, Robert Arthur Talbot Gascoyne-, see 3rd Marquess of Salisbury.

CÉLESTE-ELLIOTT, Celine (1814?-1882) actress and dancer.

R Various theatrical prints, BM, NPG, Harvard Theatre Collection, Cambridge, Mass, USA.

H MAYALL, wl, carte, NPG X5729.

CELLIER, Alfred (1844-1891) composer and orchestral director.

R UNKNOWN, hs, woodcut, Harvard Theatre Collection, Cambridge, Mass, USA.

CHADWICK, Sir Edwin (1801-1890) reformer.

SC ADAM SALOMON, c1863, marble bust, NPG 849.

PR UNKNOWN, tql seated, woodcut, for *Illust London News*, 22 Jan 1848, NPG. UNKNOWN, after a photograph by Mayall & Co, hs, woodcut, for *Illust London News*, 23 March 1889, NPG.

CHAFFERS, William (1811-1892) standard authority on hallmarks and potters' marks.

PR UNKNOWN, hs, woodcut, for *Illust London News*, 30 April 1892, NPG.

CHALMERS, George Paul (1826-1878) painter.

P JOHN PETTIE, 1862, hs, SNPG 856. SIR GEORGE REID, 1878, hs, MacDonald Collection, Aberdeen Art Gallery. Two self portraits, hl, and hs, profile, SNPG 1245 and Royal Scottish Academy. JOSEPH FARQUHARSON, hl, SNPG 881.

CHALMERS, Sir Mackenzie Dalzell (1847-1927) judge, parliamentary draftsman and civil servant.

P T.M.RONALDSON, posthumous, Trinity College, Oxford.

CHALMERS of Northiam, Robert Chalmers, Baron (1858-1938) civil servant and master of Peterhouse, Cambridge.

P ANDRÉ CLUYSENAAR, c1920, DoE (Treasury). UNKNOWN, Peterhouse, Cambridge.

PH OLIVE EDIS, c1926, hs, profile, print, NPG X5208.

CHAMBERLAIN, Joseph (1836-1914) statesman.

P FRANK HOLL, 1886, tql, NPG 1604. J.S.SARGENT, 1896, tql, NPG 4030. S.P.HALL, c1902-3, hl seated with 1st Earl of Balfour, NPG 5114. C.W.FURSE, 1904, unfinished, Cordwainers' Hall, London; copy by SIR OSWALD BIRLEY, City Art Gallery, Birmingham. EDWIN WARD, tql seated, Reform Club, London.

D GEORGE R.HALKETT, 1893, tql, wash, Palace of Westminster, London. S.P.HALL, pencil sketch, NPG 2330. SIR HUBERT VON HERKOMER, 1903, tql seated, chalk, NPG 2779. WILLIAM STRANG, 1903, hs, chalk, Chequers, Bucks.

SC JOHN TWEED, 1916, marble bust, Westminster Abbey, London. JOHN TWEED, 1927, marble statue, Palace of Westminster, London. COURTENAY POLLOCK, plaster bust, NPG 3096.

PR W.STRANG, 1903, hs, drypoint, NPG.

c SIR MAX BEERBOHM, several cartoons, various dates, V & A, Merton College, Oxford, Birmingham University Library, Ashmolean Museum, Oxford, and Gallery of Fine Arts, Columbus, Ohio, USA. Several drgs by SIR FRANCIS CARRUTHERS GOULD and HARRY FURNISS, various dates and sizes, NPG 2829, 2864, 3348-50. PHIL MAY, wl seated, pen and ink, NPG 3020. SIR LESLIE WARD ('Spy'), wl, profile, chromo-lith, for *Vanity Fair*, 7 March 1901, NPG. 'WHO', wl, Hentschel-Colourtype, for *Vanity Fair*, 29 Jan 1908, NPG.

PH LOCK & WHITFIELD, hs, oval, woodburytype, for *Men of Mark*, 1881, NPG. BARRAUD, tql seated, print, for *Men and Women of the Day*, vol I, 1888, NPG AX5410. SIR BENJAMIN STONE, 1902, four prints, NPG. JOHN RUSSELL & SONS, hs, print, for *Our Conservative and Unionist Statesmen*, vol VI, NPG (Album 23). H.J.WHITLOCK, hs, carte, NPG (Album 136). Several prints by BARRAUD, HISTED, LONDON STEREOSCOPIC CO, RUSSELL & SONS, H.J.WHITLOCK and others, various dates and sizes, NPG X5745-54.

CHAMBERLAIN, Thomas (1810-1892) member of the Tracterian movement.

PH C.L.DODGSON ('Lewis Carroll'), tql seated, print, NPG P7(3).

CHAMBERS, George (1803-1840) marine painter.

PR AUGUSTUS BUTLER, hs, lith, for his *Life and Career*, by John Watkins, 1841, NPG.

CHAMBERS, Robert (1802-1871) publisher and author.

P CHARLES LEES, Royal and Ancient Golf Club, St Andrews, Scotland.

D RUDOLPH LEHMANN, 1851, hs, crayon, BM.
PR R.C.BELL, after J.R.Fairman, hs with his brother William, line, for W.Chambers' *Memoirs of Robert Chambers*, 1872, BM.

CHAMBERS, Sir Thomas (1814–1891) recorder of London.
C SIR LESLIE WARD ('Spy'), wl, profile, chromo-lith, for *Vanity Fair*, 22 Nov 1884, NPG.
PH JOHN & CHARLES WATKINS, hs, carte, NPG (Album 136).

CHAMBERS, William (1800–1883) publisher.
PR R.C.BELL, after J.R.Fairman, hs with his brother Robert, line, for his *Memoir of Robert Chambers*, 1872, BM. D.J.POUND, after a photograph by Mayall, tql seated, line, for *The Drawing Room Portrait Gallery of Eminent Personages*, BM. UNKNOWN, hs, chromo-lith, NPG.

CHAMPNEYS, Basil (1842–1935) architect.
PH FARREN, tql seated, carte, NPG x5742.

CHAMPNEYS, Sir Francis Henry, 1st Bart (1848–1930) obstetrician.
P J.P.BEADLE, hl, Royal Society of Medicine, London.

CHAMPNEYS, William Weldon (1807–1875) dean of Lichfield.
PR D.J.POUND, after a photograph by Mayall, tql seated, line, for *The Drawing Room Portrait Gallery of Eminent Personages*, BM, NPG.

CHANCE, Sir James Timmins, 1st Bart (1814–1902) manufacturer and lighthouse engineer.
P JOSEPH GIBBS, 1902, posthumous, Smethwick Town Hall, W Midlands.
SC After SIR WILLIAM HAMO THORNYCROFT of c1894, bronze bust, West Smethwick Park.

CHANDLER, Henry William (1828–1889?) scholar.
P S.P.HALL, hl, Pembroke College, Oxford.
D S.P.HALL, wl equestrian, pencil, Pembroke College.
PH Two prints, one as a boy, Pembroke College.

CHANNELL, Sir Arthur Moseley (1838–1928) judge.
C SIR LESLIE WARD ('Spy'), hl at bench, chromo-lith, for *Vanity Fair*, 17 Feb 1898, NPG.
PH JOHN RUSSELL & SONS, hl seated, print, for *National Photographic Record*, vol I, NPG.

CHAPLIN, Henry Chaplin, 1st Viscount (1840–1923) politician and sportsman.
P SIR A.S.COPE, 1908, tql seated, NPG 4865.
G LIBERIO PROSPERI ('Lib'), 'The Lobby of the House of Commons, 1886', oil, NPG 5256.
PR JOSEPH BROWN, after a photograph by J.E.Mayall, hs, stipple, for *Baily's Mag*, 1865, NPG. Two popular prints, NPG.
C CARLO PELLEGRINI ('Ape'), 1872, wl, profile, lith, NPG. C.PELLEGRINI, wl, profile, w/c study, for *Vanity Fair*, 5 Dec 1874, NPG 3189. C.PELLEGRINI, wl, sketch, Royal Coll. 'BEDE', 'A Fox Hunting Constellation', mechanical repro, for *Vanity Fair*, 7 Dec 1905, NPG. SIR MAX BEERBOHM, several drgs, eg wl, w/c, NPG 3853, and a w/c cartoon, University of Texas, USA. Two pen and ink sketches by HARRY FURNISS, NPG 3439–40, and a sketch by SIR FRANCIS CARRUTHERS GOULD, NPG 2828. E.T.REED, 'Now *do* I look like a Parson!?', ink, V & A.
PH BASSANO, hs, semi-profile, print, for *Our Conservative and Unionist Statesmen*, vol V, NPG (Album 22). W. & D.DOWNEY, tql, print, for Cassell's *Cabinet Portrait Gallery*, vol V, 1894, NPG. SIR BENJAMIN STONE, 1897, wl, print, NPG.

CHAPMAN, Sir Frederick Edward (1815–1893) general.
P UNKNOWN, hl in uniform, Royal Engineers HQ Mess, Chatham, Kent.

CHAPMAN, John (1822–1894) physician, author and publisher.
P BENJAMIN CONSTANT, Castle Museum and Art Gallery, Nottingham.

CHARD, John Rouse Merriott (1847–1897) colonel, Royal Engineers and hero of Rorke's Drift.
SC After E.G.PAPWORTH, c1898, bronze bust, Shire Hall, Taunton.
PR UNKNOWN, hs, semi-profile, woodcut, for *Illust London News*, March 1879, NPG. UNKNOWN, after a sketch by Lieutenant N.Newnham Davis, 'Investiture of Major Chard with the Victoria Cross', woodcut, for *Illust London News*, 6 Sept 1879, NPG.
PH LOCK & WHITFIELD, hs, profile, oval, woodburytype, for *Men of Mark*, 1881, NPG.

CHARLES, Elizabeth, née Rundle (1828–1896) author.
PR UNKNOWN, hs, profile, wood engr, for *Illust London News*, April 1896, NPG.

CHARLEY, Sir William Thomas (1833–1904) lawyer.
PR UNKNOWN, after a photograph by London Stereoscopic Co, hs, woodcut, for *Illust London News*, 27 April 1878, NPG.

CHARRINGTON, Frederick Nicholas (1850–1936) philanthropist and temperance reformer.
P UNKNOWN, c1930, hs, Tower Hamlets Mission, London.

CHARTERIS, Archibald Hamilton (1835–1908) biblical critic.
P J.H.LORIMER, Church of Scotland, Edinburgh.
PR WILLIAM HOLE, hl seated at desk, etch, for *Quasi Cursores*, 1884, NPG.

CHASE, Drummond Percy (1820–1902) last principal of St Mary Hall, Oxford.
P CHARLES NAPIER KENNEDY, 1878, tql seated, Oriel College, Oxford. W.R.SYMONDS, 1883, tql seated, Oriel College.

CHASE, Frederic Henry (1853–1925) bishop of Ely.
P H.G.RIVIERE, 1921, Queens' College, Cambridge. GEORGE HENRY, The Palace, Ely.
PH UNKNOWN, hl seated, postcard, NPG x6001.

CHATTERTON, John Balsir (1802?–1871) harpist.
PR C.BAUGNIET, tql seated playing the harp, oval, lith, BM.

CHAVASSE, Francis James (1846–1928) bishop of Liverpool.
PH JOHN RUSSELL & SONS, 1924, tql seated, print, NPG (Anglican Bishops). BROWN, BARNES & BELL, tql seated, postcard, NPG x6007.

CHELMSFORD, Frederic Augustus Thesiger, 2nd Baron (1827–1905) general.
PR JUDD & CO, hs, lith, for *The Whitehall Review*, 8 March 1879, NPG. Several woodcuts in various numbers of *Illust London News*, 1879, NPG.
C SIR LESLIE WARD ('Spy'), wl seated, profile, chromo-lith, for *Vanity Fair*, 3 Sept 1881, NPG.
PH ELLIOTT & FRY, 1882, tql, cabinet, NPG x6012. LOCK & WHITFIELD, hs in uniform, oval, woodburytype, for *Men of Mark*, 1882, NPG.

CHENERY, Thomas (1826–1884) editor of *The Times*.
PR UNKNOWN, hs, woodcut, for *Illust London News*, 23 Feb 1884, NPG.
C SIR LESLIE WARD ('Spy'), wl, profile, chromo-lith, for *Vanity Fair*, 4 Oct 1879, NPG.

CHESNEY, Charles Cornwallis (1826–1876) military critic.
P UNKNOWN, hl in uniform, Royal Engineers HQ Mess, Chatham, Kent.

PR UNKNOWN, hs, woodcut, for *Illust London News*, 1 April 1876, NPG.

CHESNEY, Sir George Tomkyns (1830-1895) general.
PR UNKNOWN, after a photograph by Maull & Fox, hs, wood engr, for *Illust London News*, 6 April 1895, NPG.

CHEYLESMORE, Herbert Francis Eaton, 3rd Baron (1848-1925) major-general.
SC VICTOR ROUSSEAU, statue, Westminster Embankment, London.
C SIR LESLIE WARD ('Spy'), wl, profile, in uniform, chromo-lith, for *Vanity Fair*, 3 Oct 1891, NPG. 'WH', wl, profile, chromo-lith, for *Vanity Fair*, 17 July 1912, NPG.

CHEYNE, Thomas Kelly (1841-1915) Old Testament scholar.
D MRS G.A.COOKE, 1910, wl seated, w/c, Oriel College, Oxford.

CHEYNE, Sir (William) Watson, 1st Bart (1852-1932) surgeon.
P W.C.PENN, 1906, tql, Royal College of Surgeons, Edinburgh. HERMAN SALOMON, tql seated, Wellcome Institute, London.

CHICHESTER, Frederick Richard, see Earl of Belfast.

CHICHESTER, Henry Thomas Pelham, 3rd Earl of (1804-1886) reformer of the management and distribution of church revenues.
P FRANK HOLL, RA 1886, tql seated, County Hall, Lewes, engr J.Scott, mezz, BM.
PR UNKNOWN, hs, woodcut, NPG.

CHILDERS, Hugh Culling Eardley (1827-1896) statesman.
P EMILY M.E.CHILDERS (his daughter), 1891, wl seated, NPG 1631.
G L.C.DICKINSON, 'Gladstone's Cabinet of 1868', oil, NPG 5116.
PR Several popular prints, NPG.
C CARLO PELLEGRINI ('Ape'), wl, chromo-lith, for *Vanity Fair*, 19 June 1869, NPG.
PH LOCK & WHITFIELD, hs, profile, oval, woodburytype, for *Men of Mark*, 1878, NPG. JOHN WATKINS, two cartes, both hs, NPG (Album 99 and Album 102). UNKNOWN, wl seated, carte, NPG X5991.

CHILD-VILLIERS, Margaret Elizabeth, see Countess of Jersey.

CHILD-VILLIERS, Victor Albert George, see 7th Earl of Jersey.

CHILSTON, Aretas Akers-Douglas, 1st Viscount (1851-1926) statesman.
C PHIL MAY, wl, w/c, NPG 4991.
PH RUSSELL & SONS, c1894, hs, print, for *Our Conservative and Unionist Statesmen*, NPG (Album 16). MAYALL & CO, hs, print, for *Our Conservative and Unionist Statesmen*, NPG (Album 19). SIR BENJAMIN STONE, wl, print, NPG.

CHIPPENDALE, Mary Jane (d1888) actress.
PR 'H.W.', hs in character, woodcut, Harvard Theatre Collection, Cambridge, Mass, USA.
PH UNKNOWN, two cartes, both hs, NPG X5998 and AX7709.

CHIPPENDALE, William Henry (1801-1888) actor.
PR Several popular prints and one caricature, Harvard Theatre Collection, Cambridge, Mass, USA.
PH ELLIOTT & FRY, hs, print, NPG X5995. W.WALKER & SONS, tql seated, profile, carte, NPG X5994.

CHIROL, Sir Ignatius Valentine (1852-1929) traveller, journalist and author.
P JOHN COLLIER, 1909, hl, NPG 4271. J.COLLIER, Lady Margaret School, Parsons Green, London.

C

CHISHOLM, Caroline, née Jones (1808-1877) philanthropist, founder of the 'Family Colonisation Loan Society'.
PR UNKNOWN, after Angelo Hayter of 1850, hs, woodcut, for *Illust London News*, 14 April 1877, NPG. J.B.HUNT, after Claudet, tql seated, stipple and line, pub 1853, NPG. UNKNOWN, hl seated at desk, engr, Mitchell Library, Sydney, Australia.

CHITTY, Sir Joseph William (1828-1899) judge.
PR C.W.SHERBORN, after H.T.Wells, hs, etch, one of 'Grillion's Club' series, BM.
C SIR LESLIE WARD ('Spy'), hs at bench, chromo-lith, for *Vanity Fair*, 28 March 1885, NPG.
PH LOCK & WHITFIELD, hs, oval, woodburytype, for *Men of Mark*, 1883, NPG. LONDON STEREOSCOPIC CO, hl seated in robes, cabinet, NPG X6000. UNKNOWN, c1900, tql seated in robes, photogravure, NPG.

CHORLEY, Henry Fothergill (1808-1872) music critic.
D COUNT ALFRED D'ORSAY, 1841, hl seated, profile, pencil and chalk, NPG 4026 (13).

CHRISTIE, Sir William Henry Mahoney (1845-1922) astronomer.
PH UNKNOWN, hs, print, NPG (Album 38). WALTER STONEMAN, 1920, hs, NPG (NPR).

CHRISTY, Henry (1810-1865) ethnologist.
SC THOMAS WOOLNER, 1867, bust, BM.

CHRYSTAL, George (1851-1911) mathematician.
PR W.HOLE, tql, etch, for *Quasi Cursores*, 1884, NPG.

CHURCH, Richard William (1815-1890) dean of St Paul's.
D W.E.MILLER, 1882, head, crayon, Oriel College, Oxford.
PR UNKNOWN, after a photograph by Elliott & Fry, hs, woodcut, for *Illust London News*, 13 Dec 1890, NPG.
C LIBERIO PROSPERI ('Lib'), tql, profile, in pulpit, chromo-lith, for *Vanity Fair*, 30 Jan 1886, NPG.
PH ELLIOTT & FRY, hs, profile, photogravure, NPG X6053. LOCK & WHITFIELD, hs, oval, woodburytype, for *Men of Mark*, 1882, NPG.

CHURCH, Sir William Selby, 1st Bart (1837-1928) physician.
P Style of P.A.DE LÁSZLÓ, tql, Royal Society of Medicine, London.
PH JOHN RUSSELL & SONS, hs, print, for *National Photographic Record*, vol I, NPG.

CHURCHILL, Jennie, née Jerome, Lady (1854-1921) society beauty and public servant.
D JOHN SINGER SARGENT, hs, charcoal, Chartwell (NT), Kent.
SC UNKNOWN, marble bust, Chartwell.
PR VIOLET, DUCHESS OF RUTLAND, hs, lith, NPG. Several popular prints, NPG.
C 'K', wl seated, chromo-lith, for *Vanity Fair*, 20 Nov 1912, NPG.
PH BARRAUD, tql, print, for *Men and Women of the Day*, vol I, 1888, NPG. BASSANO & VANDYK, hl, neg, NPG. W. & D.DOWNEY, hl, cabinet, NPG X3815.

CHURCHILL, John Winston Spencer, see 7th Duke of Marlborough.

CHURCHILL, Lord Randolph Henry Spencer (1849-1895) statesman.
P EDWIN LONG, exhib 1888, tql seated, NPG 5113. EDWIN WARD, hl, semi-profile, seated at desk, Reform Club, London.
G LIBERIO PROSPERI ('Lib'), 'The Lobby of the House of Commons, 1886', oil, NPG 5256.
SC WALDO STORY, statue, in Chancellor's robes, Chapel, Blenheim Palace, Oxon, and posthumous marble bust in Chancellor's robes, Palace of Westminster, London.

PR C.LAURIE, hs, etch, BM. LEOPOLD LOWENSTAM, after a photograph by Bassano, etch, Palace of Westminster. UNKNOWN, hs, etch, BM. UNKNOWN, hs, lith, BM. Several popular prints, NPG.

C Three pen and ink sketches by HARRY FURNISS, NPG 3351, 3352 and 3559. PHIL MAY, head, profile, pen and ink, NPG 3032. SIR JOHN TENNIEL, pencil drg, for *Punch*, 28 Nov 1885, V & A. SIR LESLIE WARD ('Spy'), wl with Gorst, Balfour and Wolff, chromo-lith, for *Vanity Fair*, 1 Dec 1880, NPG. 'LIB', wl, profile, chromo-lith, for *Vanity Fair*, 5 Jan 1889, NPG.

PH A.KEN, *c*1862, wl as a boy, carte, NPG AX5098. BASSANO, *c*1886, hs, cabinet, NPG X6115. BASSANO, hs, print, for *Our Conservative Statesmen*, NPG X6118. NADAR, hs, print, for *Our Conservative and Unionist Statesmen*, 1889, NPG X6117. UNKNOWN, hs, oval, woodburytype, NPG X6116.

CLANRICARDE, Hubert George de Burgh Canning, 15th Earl and 2nd Marquess of (1832-1916) Irish landed proprietor.

P SIR LESLIE WARD, 1919, wl seated, Harewood House, W Yorks.

D HENRY TONKS, posthumous, wl, Harewood House.

C SIR LESLIE WARD ('Spy'), wl, profile, chromo-lith, for *Vanity Fair*, 24 May 1900, NPG.

CLANWILLIAM, Richard James Meade, 4th Earl of (1832-1907) admiral of the fleet.

P After RUDOLPH LEHMANN, *c*1899, tql in uniform, HMS Mercury. VAL PRINSEP, hs, in uniform, Uppark (NT), W Sussex.

C SIR LESLIE WARD ('Spy'), wl in uniform, chromo-lith, for *Vanity Fair*, 22 Jan 1903, NPG.

CLARENDON, George William Frederick Villiers, 4th Earl of (1800-1870) foreign secretary.

P A.E.DYER, after Stephen Catterson Smith of 1861, Shire Hall, Hertford. JAMES SANT, hs, semi-profile, DoE (British Embassy, Madrid).

G SIR JOHN GILBERT, 'The Coalition Ministry, 1854', pencil and wash, NPG 1125.

SC JOHN BELL, 1874, marble statue, DoE (Foreign Office, London).

PR E.DESMAISONS, tql seated, lith, BM. W.HOLL, after G.Richmond, hs, stipple, one of 'Grillion's Club' series, BM. C.HUTCHINS, after E.Hayes, hl, lith, BM. G.SANDERS, after C.Smith, tql in court dress, mezz, BM. G.SANDERS, after C.Smith, tql seated with insignia of order of St Patrick, mezz, BM. W.WALKER, after F.Grant, hl with ribbon and star, mezz, pub 1847, BM, NPG.

PH CAMILLE SILVY, wl seated, carte, NPG (Album 38). W.WALKER & SONS, tql seated, carte, NPG X6078. JOHN WATKINS, hs, profile, carte, NPG X6077.

CLARK, Albert Curtis (1859-1937) classical scholar.

C Two caricatures, one by A.W.LLOYD, 1902, and one monogrammed, Queen's College, Oxford.

PH WALTER STONEMAN, 1917, hs, NPG (NPR).

CLARK, Sir Andrew, Bart (1826-1893) physician.

P FRANK HOLL, 1888, tql seated, Royal College of Physicians, London. G.F.WATTS, 1893, hs, profile, NPG 1003. RUDOLPH LEHMANN, 1894, tql seated, in robes, Royal College of Physicians.

M UNKNOWN, 1893, hs, semi-profile, oval, Royal College of Physicians.

SC HENRY BAIN-SMITH, 1888, marble(?) bust, Royal College of Physicians.

PH LOCK & WHITFIELD, hs, woodburytype, oval, for *Men of Mark*, 1878, NPG.

CLARK, Edwin (1814-1894) engineer.

P UNKNOWN, Institution of Civil Engineers, London.

G JOHN LUCAS, 'Conference of Engineers at Britannia Bridge', oi Institution of Civil Engineers.

CLARK, John Willis (1833-1910) man of science an[d] archaeologist.

D A.GOFFANTI, 1912, hs, chalk, Department of Zoology, Cam bridge University.

C SIR LESLIE WARD ('Spy'), wl, profile, chromo-lith, for *Vanit[y] Fair*, 10 May 1894, NPG.

CLARK, Josiah Latimer (1822-1898) engineer.

G JOHN LUCAS, 'Conference of Engineers at Britannia Bridge', oi[l] Institution of Civil Engineers, London.

CLARK, William George (1821-1878) Shakespearia[n] scholar.

P Probably F.TUTTLE, tql, Trinity College, Cambridge.

CLARKE, Sir Andrew (1824-1902) lieutenant-general an[d] colonial official.

SC Probably by EDWARD ONSLOW FORD, *c*1890, bronze bus[t] Victoria Memorial Hall, Singapore.

CLARKE, Sir Casper Purdon (1846-1911) director of th[e] Metropolitan Museum, New York.

C HARRY FURNISS, tql, pen and ink, NPG 3441.

CLARKE, Sir Edward George (1841-1931) lawyer an[d] politician.

P E.A.PRYNNE, 1887, tql, Lincoln's Inn, London. SOLOMON J.SOLOMON, probably RA 1916, tql, DoE (Law Courts, London)[.]

PR MALCOLM OSBORNE, etch, Russell-Cotes Art Gallery Bournemouth.

C HARRY FURNISS, wl, pen and ink sketch, NPG 3442. SIR LESLIE WARD ('Spy'), wl, chromo-lith, for *Vanity Fair*, 13 March 1880[,] NPG. SIR LESLIE WARD, hl, at bench, w/c study, for *Vanity Fair*, 11 June 1903, NPG 2700.

PH BASSANO, hs, profile, print, for *Our Conservative and Unionist Statesmen*, vol V, NPG (Album 22). SIR BENJAMIN STONE, 1898, two wl prints, NPG. WALTER STONEMAN, 1917, hs, NPG (NPR).

CLARKE, George Sydenham, see Baron SYDENHAM of Combe.

CLARKE, Mary Victoria Cowden-, née Novello (1809-1898) author.

PH G.B.SCIUTTO & Co, hs, oval, carte, NPG X1472. 'A.J.L.', hs, cabinet, NPG X6157.

CLAUGHTON, Piers Calverley (1814-1884) bishop of Colombo.

SC UNKNOWN, medallion portrait on memorial tablet, St Paul'[s] Cathedral, London.

CLAUGHTON, Thomas Legh (1808-1892) bishop of St Albans.

P G.P.JACOMB-HOOD, RA 1890, hl seated, Trinity College, Oxford.

PR UNKNOWN, hs, stipple.

PH UNKNOWN, tql seated in robes, carte, NPG (Album 38).

CLAUSEN, Sir George (1852-1944) painter.

P Self-portrait, 1918, hs, Fitzwilliam Museum, Cambridge. Self-portrait, hs, The Art Workers' Guild, London.

D Self-portrait, 1895, hs, pen and ink, NPG 3041. Self-portrait, 1908[,] hs, charcoal, BM.

PR Self-portrait, hs, etch, BM.

PH UNKNOWN, *c*1915, hs, print, NPG X6086. WALTER STONEMAN[,] 1930, hs, NPG (NPR).

CLAY, Frederick (1839-1889) musician.

G HENRY NELSON O'NEIL, 'The Billiard Room of the Garrick Club', oil, 1869, Garrick Club, London.

PH UNKNOWN, hs, profile, woodburytype, NPG x6087.

CLAYDEN, Peter William (1827-1902) journalist and author.
P SAVAGE COOPER, National Liberal Club, London.

CLAYTON, John (1843-1888) actor.
D HENRY WOODS, hl as Hugh Trevor in *All For Her*, grisaille sketch, Garrick Club, London.
PR Several woodcuts and a lithograph, Harvard Theatre Collection, Cambridge, Mass, USA. E.MATTHEWS & SONS, hs, semi-profile, lith, NPG.
PH Two cartes by ELLIOTT & FRY, *c*1872, both with Amy Fawsitt and William Farren in *School for Scandal*, NPG x4334 and x4335. Several prints by LONDON STEREOSCOPIC CO, WINDOW & GROVE and unknown photographers, various sizes, one in character, NPG x6090-3.

CLEASBY, Sir Anthony (1804-1879) judge.
D UNKNOWN, chalk, Trinity College, Cambridge.
PR UNKNOWN, after a photograph by J.Watkins, hl seated in robes, woodcut, for *Illust London News*, 23 Jan 1869, NPG.
C SIR LESLIE WARD ('Spy'), hs, profile, at bench, w/c study, for *Vanity Fair*, 5 Feb 1876, NPG 2701; related sketch, NPG 2897.
PH LOCK & WHITFIELD, hs, woodburytype, for *Men of Mark*, 1880, NPG.

CLERK, Sir Dugald (1854-1932) mechanical engineer.
P HAROLD SPEED, 1910, Institution of Civil Engineers, London.
D A.S.HARTRICK, 1906, hl, pencil, crayon and w/c, SNPG 1224.
PH WALTER STONEMAN, three prints, one 1917 and two 1927, NPG (NPR).

CLERK-MAXWELL, James (1831-1879) physicist.
P WILLIAM DYCE, 1835, hl with his mother, Birmingham City Art Gallery. LOWES DICKINSON, hl seated, Trinity College, Cambridge. JEMIMA BLACKBURN, hs, Department of Physics, Cavendish Laboratory, Cambridge. UNKNOWN, tql with his wife, in landscape, Cavendish Laboratory, Cambridge.
M UNKNOWN, after a photograph, hl, w/c on china, NPG 1189.
SC SIR J.E.BOEHM, 1879, after an engr by G.J.Stodart, bust, Cavendish Laboratory, Cambridge.

CLIFFORD, Sir Henry Hugh (1826-1883) major-general.
P J.RAMSAY, wl seated as a boy, in landscape with dog, Ugbrooke Park, Devon. FRANCESCO PODESTI, tql in uniform, Ugbrooke.

CLIFFORD, John (1836-1923) Baptist leader.
P JOHN COLLIER, 1906, tql, The Baptist Union, London. JOHN COLLIER, 1924, replica of portrait of 1906, hs, NPG 2037.
D EDMOND KAPP, 1913, Barber Institute of Fine Arts, Birmingham.
PH G.C.BERESFORD, two prints, both hs, NPG x6171-2. R.HAINES, hs, postcard, NPG x6170.

CLIFFORD, William Kingdon (1845-1879) mathematician and philosopher.
P JOHN COLLIER, 1878, hl, Royal Society, London. JOHN COLLIER, 1899, replica, NPG 1231.
PR C.H.JEENS, after a photograph, hs, line, for his *Lectures and Essays*, 1879, BM.

CLINT, Alfred (1807-1883) etcher and marine painter.
M Attrib to himself, hl, NPG 4616.

CLINTON, Henry Pelham Fiennes Pelham, see 5th Duke of Newcastle.

CLODD, Edward (1840-1930) banker and writer.
P JOHN COLLIER, 1914, Rationalist Press Association Ltd, London.
D HELEN BEDFORD, 1928, hs, chalk, NPG 2749.
PH E.O.HOPPÉ, *c*1909, hl seated, print, NPG P103.

CLOUGH, Anne Jemima (1820-1892) first principal of Newnham College, Cambridge.
P SIR W.B.RICHMOND, 1882, Newnham College, Cambridge. J.J.SHANNON, 1890, Newnham College. SIR WILLIAM NICHOLSON, 1924, posthumous, hl seated, Newnham College.
PH UNKNOWN, hs, cabinet, NPG x6175.

CLOUGH, Arthur Hugh (1819-1861) poet.
D SAMUEL WORCESTER ROWSE, *c*1860, hs, chalk, NPG 3314; copy by Samuel Lawrence, Oriel College, Oxford. UNKNOWN, (called Clough), hs, National Museum of Wales, Cardiff.
SC THOMAS WOOLNER, 1863, marble bust, Rugby School, Warwicks; related plaster bust, NPG 1694. UNKNOWN, death mask and cast of his hand, Balliol College, Oxford. F.W.DE WELDON, modern bust, said to be based on an early etch, City Hall, Charleston, USA.

COBDEN, Richard (1804-1865) statesman.
P GIUSEPPE FAGNANI, 1860-1, hl seated, New York Chamber of Commerce, New York; replica, 1865, NPG 201. CHARLES LUCY, 1868, V & A. LOWES DICKINSON 1870, wl seated, NPG 316; version, Reform Club, London.
D L.SAULINI, 1827?, hs, profile, chalk, Küpferstichkabinett, Staatliche Kunstsammlungen, Dresden.
G S.BELLIN, after J.R.Herbert of 1847, 'The Anti-Corn Law League', mixed engr, pub 1850, NPG. JOHN PHILLIP, 'The House of Commons, 1860', oil, Palace of Westminster, London. C.G.LEWIS, after T.J.Barker, 'Intellect and Valour of Great Britain', mixed engr, pub 1865, NPG.
SC SAMUEL NIXON, 1846, bronze statuette, Marshall Library of Economics, Cambridge. G.G.ADAMS, 1862, bronze statue, St Peter's Square, Stockport. MATTHEW NOBLE, two marble busts, 1865 and 1866, Dunford Museum, Midhurst, W Sussex, and Reform Club, London. THOMAS WOOLNER, 1866, marble bust, Brighton Art Gallery; replica, NPG 219. M.NOBLE, 1867, statue, Peel Park, Salford. MARSHALL WOOD, *c*1867, bronze statue, St Anne's Square, Manchester. W. & T.WILLS, 1868, marble statue, Hampstead Road, Camden Town, London.
PR F.C.LEWIS, after C.A.Duval, hl seated, stipple, pub 1843, NPG. Various prints and popular prints, some after photographs, BM, NPG.
C HONORE DAUMIER, 1856, several cartoons, liths, for *Le Charivari*, NPG.
PH Several cartes by W. & D.DOWNEY, C.A.DUVAL, MAUJEAN and unknown photographers, various dates and sizes, NPG x6187-93. MAUJEAN, two cartes, with John Bright and Michel Chevalier, NPG x4325-6. W. & D.DOWNEY, tql seated, print, NPG AX7342. UNKNOWN, tql, print, NPG x8010.

COBDEN-SANDERSON, Thomas James (1840-1922) bookbinder and printer.
PH PAOLO LOMBARDI, 1881, two prints, one wl, and one wl reclining, in both he is with his wife, Jane Morris and Mrs Flower, NPG x6953 and x6955.

COBURG, Alfred Ernest Albert, Duke of, see Alfred.

COCHRANE, Douglas Mackinon Baillie Hamilton, see 12th Earl of Dundonald.

COCHRANE-BAILLIE, Alexander, see 1st Baron Lamington.

COCKBURN, Sir Alexander James Edmund (1802-1880) lord chief-justice of England.
P A.D.COOPER, hs, NPG 933. G.F.WATTS, hl seated in robes, Trinity Hall, Cambridge; copy, 1895, Middle Temple, London.
D DANIEL MACLISE, V & A.
PR T.L.ATKINSON, tql seated in robes, mezz, pub 1871, NPG. Several

woodcuts and popular prints, NPG.

C CARLO PELLEGRINI ('Ape'), hl seated at bench, chromo-lith, for *Vanity Fair*, 11 Dec 1869, NPG. FAUSTIN, *c*1874, lith, V & A.

PH HENNAH & KENT, hs, carte, NPG X6288. LONDON STEREOSCOPIC Co, hs in robes, carte, NPG X6287.

CODRINGTON, Sir Henry John (1808-1877) admiral of the fleet.

P LOWES DICKINSON, 1857-63, tql seated with orders, NMM, Greenwich.

CODRINGTON, Sir William John (1804-1884) general.

P SIR WILLIAM BOXALL, hl in uniform, The Convent, Gibraltar. UNKNOWN, over a photograph?, tql in uniform, Harrow School, Middx.

D SIR GEORGE HAYTER, *c*1812, tql seated, with his brother Edward, study for a miniature, pencil, pen, ink and wash, NPG 883(8).

PR UNKNOWN, hl in uniform, coloured lith, pub 1856, NPG. UNKNOWN, wl with horse, woodcut, for *Illust Times*, 9 Aug 1856, NPG. UNKNOWN, after a photograph by Mayall, hs, for *Illust London News*, 16 May 1857, NPG. L.DICKINSON, after F.Cruikshank, hl in uniform, lith, NPG.

COKE, Thomas William, see 2nd Earl of Leicester.

COLE, George (1810-1883) painter.

PR UNKNOWN, hs, woodcut, for *Illust London News*, 29 Sept 1883, NPG.

COLE, George Vicat (1833-1893) landscape painter.

P SIR A.S.COPE, 1886, hs, MacDonald Collection, Aberdeen Art Gallery.

PR Several woodcuts after photographs, NPG.

PH UNKNOWN, hs, woodburytype, NPG X6306.

COLE, Sir Henry (1808-1882) secretary of the Department of Science and Art.

D SAMUEL LAURENCE, 1865, hs, chalk, NPG 1698. RICHARD DOYLE, hs, pen and ink, BM.

G H.W.PHILLIPS, 'The Royal Commissioners for the Exhibition of 1851', oil, V & A.

SC SIR J.E.BOEHM, 1875, plaster bust, NPG 865.

PR Two woodcuts, for *Illust London News*, 1851 and 1873, NPG.

C Attrib J.J.TISSOT, wl with dog, chromo-lith, for *Vanity Fair*, 19 Aug 1871, NPG.

PH LOCK & WHITFIELD, hs, semi-profile, woodburytype, oval, for *Men of Mark*, 1877, NPG.

COLENSO, John William (1814-1883) bishop of Natal.

P SAMUEL SIDLEY, 1866, tql seated, NPG 1080.

D T.C.WAGEMAN, w/c, Trinity College, Cambridge.

C CARLO PELLEGRINI ('Ape'), wl, profile, chromo-lith, for *Vanity Fair*, 28 Nov 1874, NPG.

PH ERNEST EDWARDS, wl seated, print, NPG X6310. LONDON STEREO-SCOPIC Co, tql, carte, NPG X6307. MAULL & Co, hs, carte, NPG (Album 40). UNKNOWN, hs, profile, carte, NPG X6308. H.N.KING, nearly wl seated, carte, NPG AX7460.

COLERIDGE, Bernard John Seymour Coleridge, 2nd Baron (1851-1927) judge.

P DAMPIER MAY, 1914, hl seated, Trinity College, Oxford.

C SIR LESLIE WARD ('Spy'), tql seated, w/c study, for *Vanity Fair*, 13 Jan 1909, NPG 3281.

PH WALTER STONEMAN, 1922, hs, NPG (NPR).

COLERIDGE, Derwent (1800-1883) author.

P UNKNOWN, hl seated, College of St Mark and St John, Chelsea.

COLERIDGE, Sir John Duke Coleridge, 1st Baron (1820-1894) judge.

P MARGARET CARPENTER, hs, a leaving portrait, Eton College,

Berks. MRS SHEE, after E.U.Eddis of 1878, tql seated in robes, Middle Temple, London.

D UNKNOWN, hs, profile, pencil, Balliol College, Oxford.

SC F.J.WILLIAMSON, 1892, marble bust, DoE (Law Courts).

PR C.HOLL, after J.T.Coleridge, hs, stipple, one of 'Grillion's Club' series, BM.

C ALFRED THOMPSON ('Atñ'), wl, profile, chromo-lith, for *Vanity Fair*, 30 April 1870, NPG. CARLO PELLEGRINI ('Ape'), hl, w/c study, for *Vanity Fair*, 5 March 1887, NPG 2702.

PH UNKNOWN, hl seated in robes, carte, NPG (Album 38).

COLERIDGE, Sara (1802-1852) writer; daughter of Samuel Taylor Coleridge.

D MARGARET CARPENTER, hs, charcoal and chalk, BM.

M EDWARD NASH, 1820, hl seated with her cousin Edith Southey (later Mrs J.W.Warter), NPG 4029.

PR R.J.LANE, after S.Laurence of 1848, hs, lith, NPG.

COLERIDGE, Stephen William Buchanan (1854-1936) author and anti-vivisectionist.

C 'ELF', wl seated with dog, Hentschel-Colourtype, for *Vanity Fair*, 27 July 1910, NPG.

COLES, Cowper Phipps (1819-1870) captain in the navy.

PR UNKNOWN, hs, woodcut, for *Illust London News*, 19 April 1862, NPG. UNKNOWN, after a photograph by J.Forris, hs, woodcut, fo *Illust London News*, 24 Sept 1870, NPG.

PH J.HARRIS, tql seated in uniform, carte, NPG (Album 102).

COLLEY, Sir George Pomeroy (1835-1881) major-general.

PR UNKNOWN, after a photograph by Maull & Co, hs, woodcut, fo *Illust London News*, 21 June 1879, NPG. 'W.G.S.', wl, 'How Colley Died!', lith, for *The Whitehall Review*, 10 March 1881 NPG.

PH UNKNOWN, tql, woodburytype, NPG X6312.

COLLIER, John (1850-1934) painter and writer on art.

P Self-portrait, 1907, hs, Uffizi Gallery, Florence.

D S.P.HALL, *c*1895, hl seated, possibly a study for NPG4404, pencil NPG 4390. E.X.KAPP, 1930 and 1931, two sketches, hs and wl Barber Institute of Fine Arts, Birmingham.

G S.P.HALL, 'The St John's Wood Arts Club, 1895', chalk and wash, NPG 4404.

PH JOHN RUSSELL & SONS, hs, print, for *National Photographic Record* vol I, NPG.

COLLIER, Robert Porrett, see 1st Baron Monkswell.

COLLINGS, Jesse (1831-1920) politician.

P PRATT JONATHAN, City Art Gallery, Birmingham.

C SIR FRANCIS CARRUTHERS GOULD, with Joseph Chamberlain, ink and w/c, V & A. SIR LESLIE WARD ('Spy'), wl, profile, chromo-lith, for *Vanity Fair*, 1 Dec 1888, NPG.

PH SIR BENJAMIN STONE, 1897, two wl prints, NPG.

COLLINS, Charles Allston (1828-1873) artist.

PR UNKNOWN, after a photograph by John Watkins, hs, woodcut for *The Illust Review*, 24 April 1873, NPG.

COLLINS, John Churton (1848-1908) author and professo of English Literature.

P T.W.HOLGATE, Bodleian Library, Oxford.

D GEORGE PHOENIX, head, w/c, Balliol College, Oxford.

COLLINS, Sir Richard Henn Collins, Baron (1842-1911) judge.

C 'QUIZ', tql, profile, at bench, chromo-lith, for *Vanity Fair*, 14 Ja 1893, NPG.

COLLINS, William Wilkie (1824-1889) novelist.

P SIR J.E.MILLAIS, 1850, tql seated, NPG 967. CHARLES ALLSTON

COLLINS, 1853, hl seated at desk, Fitzwilliam Museum, Cambridge. RUDOLPH LEHMANN, 1880, hs, NPG 3333.

D E.M.WARD, sketch for portrait (RA 1846), hs, Dickens House, London. RUDOLPH LEHMANN, 1862, hs, BM.

PR UNKNOWN, after a photograph by Herbert Watkins of 1858, hl, profile, seated, woodcut, NPG. R. & E.TAYLOR, hs, semi-profile, woodcut, for *The Illust Review*, 10 July 1873, NPG. UNKNOWN, hs, chromo-lith, BM.

C ADRIANO CECIONI, wl, w/c study, for *Vanity Fair*, 3 Feb 1872, NPG 2703.

PH CUNDALL, DOWNES & CO, hl, semi-profile, oval, print, NPG X6322. CUNDALL, DOWNES & CO, tql seated, carte, NPG X6323. LOCK & WHITFIELD, hs, woodburytype, oval, for *Men of Mark*, 1881, NPG. HERBERT WATKINS, two cartes, wl, profile, and wl, NPG X6324-5. UNKNOWN, hs, woodburytype, NPG X6326.

COLLINSON, Sir Richard (1811-1883) admiral.

P STEPHEN PEARCE, 1855, hl in uniform, NPG 1221; replica, NPG 914.

PR UNKNOWN, hs, woodcut, for *Illust London News*, 29 Sept 1883, NPG.

PH LOCK & WHITFIELD, hs, woodburytype, oval, for *Men of Mark*, 1877, NPG. UNKNOWN, Royal Geographical Society, London.

COLNAGHI, Martin Henry (1821-1908) picture dealer and collector.

P J.C.HORSLEY, 1889, TATE 2286.

COLOMB, Sir John Charles Ready (1838-1909) writer on imperial defence.

C CARLO PELLEGRINI ('Ape'), wl, profile, chromo-lith, for *Vanity Fair*, 26 March 1887, NPG.

PH SIR BENJAMIN STONE, 1898, wl, print, NPG.

COLVIN, Sir Sidney (1845-1927) literary critic and art historian.

P SIR EDWARD POYNTER, 1896, tql seated, Society of Dilettanti, Brooks's Club, London.

D ALPHONSE LEGROS, 1893, hs, pencil, BM.

PR SIR WILLIAM ROTHENSTEIN, 1897, hl seated, lith, NPG 3999.

PH JOHN RUSSELL & SONS, hl seated, print, for *National Photographic Record*, vol II, NPG. WALTER STONEMAN, 1924, hs, NPG (NPR). UNKNOWN, hs, photogravure, NPG X6333. UNKNOWN, tql seated, print, BM (Engr Ports Coll).

COMMERELL, Sir John Edmund (1829-1901) admiral.

P M.MURRAY COOKESLEY, The Admiralty, Portsmouth.

C THÉOBALD CHARTRAN ('T'), wl, semi-profile, w/c study, for *Vanity Fair*, 24 Dec 1881, NPG 4060. SIR LESLIE WARD ('Spy'), wl, profile, in uniform, chromo-lith, for *Vanity Fair*, 3 Aug 1889, NPG.

PH LOCK & WHITFIELD, hs, semi-profile, woodburytype, oval, for *Men of Mark*, 1883, NPG.

COMMON, Andrew Ainslie (1841-1903) astronomer.

PR WILLIAM NICHOLSON, lith, Royal Astronomical Society, London.

COMPTON, Lord Alwyne Frederick (1825-1906) bishop of Ely.

G S.P.HALL, 'The Bench of Bishops, 1902', w/c, NPG 2369.

PH UNKNOWN, tql seated, print, NPG (Anglican Bishops).

COMPTON, Henry (Charles Mackenzie) (1805-1877) actor.

PR Several popular and theatrical prints, BM, NPG. Various prints and caricatures, Harvard Theatre Collection, Cambridge, Mass, USA.

PH Four cartes and one woodburytype print, by LONDON STEREOSCOPIC CO, W.WALKER & SONS and unknown photographers,

NPG X6338-42.

CONINGTON, John (1825-1869) classical scholar.

D ALEXANDER MACDONALD, 1918, hl seated, profile, Corpus Christi College, Oxford.

CONNAUGHT and STRATHEARN, Arthur William Patrick Albert, 1st Duke of (1850-1942) field-marshal, son of Queen Victoria.

F.X.WINTERHALTER, tql, as a child, with doll, Royal Coll; copy, Wellington Museum, Apsley House, London. F.X.WINTERHALTER, 1859, hs, circle, Royal Coll. SIR HUBERT VON HERKOMER, c1900, in general's uniform, Royal Coll. J.S.SARGENT, c1908, tql, in uniform of the Grenadier guards, Royal Coll. SIR A.S.COPE, 1913, wl in uniform, Trinity House, London. SIR A.S.COPE, c1922, wl in Garter robes, United Grand Lodge of England. E.C.DINGLI, c1927, wl in Garter robes, Army and Navy Club, London. P.A.DE LÁSZLÓ, 1937, hl, profile, in Garter robes, Royal Society of Arts, London. GERTRUDE DES CLAYES, hl in uniform, Montreal Museum of Fine Arts, Canada.

D F.X.WINTERHALTER, wl, aged 5, in uniform of Scots' guard, Royal Coll.

G F.X.WINTERHALTER, 'The First of May, 1851', oil, Royal Coll. F.X.WINTERHALTER, 1856, with Prince Leopold and Princess Louise, Royal Coll. F.X.WINTERHALTER, 'The Opening of the Royal Albert Infirmary, 1865', oil, NPG 3083. S.P.HALL, his marriage to Princess Louise Margaret of Prussia, in St George's Chapel, Windsor, March 1879, oil, Royal Coll. J.B.E.DETAILLE, wl equestrian with Edward VII (when Prince of Wales), reviewing troops at Aldershot, oil, c1898, Royal Coll.

SC F.J.WILLIAMSON, 1885, marble bust, Royal Coll. GEORGE WADE, bronze statue, Hong Kong.

PR Various prints and popular prints, BM, NPG.

C SIR LESLIE WARD ('Spy'), wl, profile, chromo-lith, for *Vanity Fair*, 17 June 1876, NPG. SIR LESLIE WARD ('Spy'), wl, profile, in uniform, chromo-lith, for *Vanity Fair*, 2 Aug 1890, NPG.

PH L.CALDESI, 1857, with members of the Royal Family, NPG P26. W. & D.DOWNEY, 1860s, with Princess Louise, Duchess of Argyll, NPG X3604. WALERY, hs in uniform, cabinet, NPG AX5558. Several Royal Family groups, NPG. Various photographs, singly and in groups, Royal Coll.

CONNEMARA, Robert Bourke, 1st Baron (1827-1902) governor of Madras.

P UNKNOWN, Government House, Madras.

C SIR LESLIE WARD ('Spy'), wl, profile, chromo-lith, for *Vanity Fair*, 28 April 1877, NPG.

CONOLLY, Arthur (1807-1842) Asiatic traveller.

D JAMES ATKINSON, c1840, hs, profile, w/c, NPG 825.

M ROBERT THORBURN, hs, SNPG 1298.

CONQUEST, George Augustus (1837-1901) actor, dramatic author and manager.

C Several woodcuts, various dates and sizes, for *Entr'acte*, Harvard Theatre Collection, Cambridge, Mass, USA.

PH ALFRED ELLIS, c1895, hs, woodburytype, NPG X6359. UNKNOWN, hs, profile, carte, NPG X6358.

CONRAD, Joseph (1857-1924) novelist.

P ELLEN HEATH, 1898, hs, semi-profile, Leeds City Art Gallery. WALTER TITTLE, 1924, two portraits, tql seated, profile, and tql seated, NPG 2220, and University of Texas, Austin, USA.

D SIR WILLIAM ROTHENSTEIN, two drgs: 1903, hs, pastel, NPG 2097, and 1916, hs, pencil, NPG 2207. PERCY ANDERSON, 1918, hs, chalk and wash, NPG 1985.

SC JACOB EPSTEIN, 1924, bronze bust, NPG 4159.

PR CARTON MOORE-PARK, 1922, hl seated, lith, V & A. SIR MUIRHEAD

BONE, 1923–5, tql seated, listening to music, etch, NPG, Fitzwilliam Museum, Cambridge. WALTER TITTLE, 1924, hs, etch, NPG 2482.

c SIR DAVID LOW, two pencil studies, NPG 4529 (93, 94).

PH G.C.BERESFORD, 1904, one print, and one neg, both hs, NPG x6360 and x6475. WILL CADBY, 1914, hs, neg, NPG x4340. ALVIN LANGDON COBURN, 1916, hl, photogravure, for *More Men of Mark*, 1922, NPG AX7832. J.CRAIG ANNAN, 1923, Gernsheim Collection, University of Texas, USA. UNKNOWN, head, with his son, postcard, NPG x3714.

CONSTABLE, Thomas (1812-1881) printer and publisher.
SC WILLIAM BRODIE, 1870, marble bust, SNPG 1612.

CONWAY of Allington, William Martin Conway, Baron (1856-1937) art critic and collector and mountaineer.
SC E.O.FORD, 1893, medallion, NPG 4019. AVRAM MELNIKOFF, bronze head, IWM.
PH W. & D.DOWNEY, tql, woodburytype, for Cassell's *Cabinet Portrait Gallery*, vol IV, 1893, NPG. BASSANO, 1895, six negs, various sizes, NPG x1052–7. OLIVE EDIS, hs, print, NPG x6363.

COODE, Sir John (1816-1892) civil engineer.
P CLEGG WILKINSON, tql, Institution of Civil Engineers, London.
PR UNKNOWN, after a photograph, hs, woodcut, for *Illust London News*, 27 April 1872, NPG.

COOK, Sir Edward Tyas (1857-1919) journalist.
c SIR LESLIE WARD ('Spy'), wl, chromo-lith, for *Vanity Fair*, 24 Aug 1899, NPG.
PH JOHN RUSSELL & SONS, hl, print, for *National Photographic Record*, vol I, NPG.

COOK, Eliza (1818-1889) poet.
PR H.ADLARD, after T.Smart, hl, stipple, NPG. H.ADLARD, after W.Trautschold, hl, stipple, BM, NPG. D.J.POUND, after a photograph by John Watkins, tql seated, stipple and line, for *The Drawing Room Portrait Gallery of Eminent Personages*, NPG. H.B.WILLIS, after J.Watkins, wl seated, lith, BM, NPG. UNKNOWN, tql seated, line, BM.
PH F.W.EVANS, wl seated, carte, NPG x6367.

COOK, Sir Francis, 1st Bart (1817-1901) merchant and art collector.
SC UNKNOWN, bust, Queen Alexandra's House, South Kensington, London.
PR UNKNOWN, hs, woodcut, for *Illust London News*, 19 March 1887, NPG.

COOK, John Mason (1834-1899) tourist agent.
PR R. T., hs, wood engr, for *Illust London News*, 25 July 1891, NPG.

COOK, Samuel (1806-1859) water-colour painter.
D FIELD TALFOURD, hs, chalk, BM.

COOK, Thomas (1808-1892) tourist agent.
PR Two woodcuts, both hs, for *Illust London News*, 25 July 1891 and 30 July 1892, NPG.

COOKE, Edward William (1811-1880) marine painter.
PR UNKNOWN, hs, woodcut, for *Illust London News*, 13 Aug 1864, NPG.
PH JOHN & CHARLES WATKINS, tql seated, carte, NPG (Album 104).

COOKE, George Wingrove (1814-1865) man of letters.
PR UNKNOWN, after a photograph by Maull and Polyblank, hl, woodcut, for *Illust London News*, 15 July 1865, NPG.

COOKE, Sir William Fothergill (1806-1879) electrician.
P M.THOMAS, 1876, Institution of Electrical Engineers, London.

COOPER, Sir Alfred (1838-1908) surgeon.
c SIR LESLIE WARD ('Spy'), wl, w/c study, for *Vanity Fair*, 30 Dec 1897, NPG.

COOPER, Antony Ashley, see 7th Earl of Shaftesbury.

COOPER, Charles Henry (1808-1866) Cambridge antiquary.
SC TIMOTHY BUTLER, 1868, bust, Cambridge Town Hall.

COOPER, Sir Daniel, 1st Bart (1821-1902) Australian merchant.
PR UNKNOWN, after a photograph by T.Fall, hs, semi-profile, woodcut, for *Illust London News*, 20 Dec 1879, NPG.
c SIR LESLIE WARD ('Spy'), wl, profile, chromo-lith, for *Vanity Fair*, 21 Jan 1882, NPG.

COOPER, Thomas (1805-1892) chartist.
PR H.LINTON, after H.Anelay, hl seated, woodcut, NPG.
PH FRED BRYANT, hs, cabinet, NPG x6371.

COOPER, Thomas Sidney (1803-1902) painter.
P Self-portrait, 1835, Royal Museum, Canterbury. WALTER SCOTT, c1841, hs, NPG 3236. JOHN PRESCOTT KNIGHT, 1843, Royal Museum. W.W.OULESS, 1889, tql seated with palette, Royal Museum; related portrait by Ouless, 1891, hs, oval, MacDonald Collection, Aberdeen Art Gallery.
PR G.J.STODART, after J.Scott, hs, aged 38, oval, stipple, pub 1890, BM, NPG. UNKNOWN, hs, woodcut, for *Illust London News*, 6 July 1867, NPG.
c GEORGE GOURSAT ('Sem'), wl, w/c, Ashmolean Museum, Oxford.
PH ELLIOTT & FRY, hs, semi-profile, carte, NPG (Album 106). H.S.MENDELSSOHN, hs, profile, boudoir, NPG x6372. RALPH W.ROBINSON, tql seated at easel, print, for *Members and Associates of the Royal Academy of Arts, 1891*, NPG x7357. JOHN & CHARLES WATKINS, tql seated, carte, NPG (Album 104).

COPE, Sir Arthur Stockdale (1857-1940) painter.
PH H.WALTER BARNETT, tql seated, print, NPG x6870. WALTER STONEMAN, 1930, hs, NPG (NPR). UNKNOWN, hs, print, NPG x6869.

COPE, Charles West (1811-1890) historical painter.
P Self-portrait, 1879, hs, NPG 5321. SIR A.S.COPE, 1884, hs, semi-profile, MacDonald Collection, Aberdeen Art Gallery.
D RICHARD REDGRAVE, seated, sketching, in a cottage, with others, w/c, V & A.
c GEORGE GOURSAT ('Sem'), wl, w/c, Ashmolean Museum, Oxford.
PH JOHN & CHARLES WATKINS, tql seated, carte, NPG AX7575. UNKNOWN, hs, carte, NPG (Album 103). UNKNOWN, wl seated, carte, NPG (Album 104).

COPELAND, Ralph (1837-1905) astronomer.
PR UNKNOWN, after a photograph by J.E.Munro, hs, woodcut, for *Illust London News*, 16 Feb 1889, NPG.

CORBET, Mathew Ridley (1850-1902) painter.
P JOHN McLURE HAMILTON, 1893, hl seated, NPG 1867.

CORDER, William (1804-1828) murderer.
PR Several popular prints, BM.

CORELLI, Marie, see Mary Mackay.

CORNISH, Francis Warre Warre-, see WARRE-Cornish.

CORNWALLIS-WEST, Mrs George, see Lady Jennie Churchill.

CORRIGAN, Sir Dominic John (1802-1880) physician.
P STEPHEN CATTERSON SMITH sen, 1863, wl seated, Royal College of Physicians of Ireland, Dublin.
SC J.H.FOLEY, 1863, plaster statuette, NGI 8191. J.H.FOLEY, 1869, marble statue, Royal College of Physicians of Ireland.

PR UNKNOWN, after a photograph by T.Cranfield, hs, woodcut, for *Illust London News*, 17 March 1866, NPG.

CORRY, Henry Thomas Lowry (1803-1873) politician.
G SIR GEORGE HAYTER, 'The House of Commons, 1833', oil, NPG 54. HENRY GALES, 'The Derby Cabinet of 1867', w/c, NPG 4893.
PR R. & E.TAYLOR, after a photograph by John Watkins, hs, woodcut, for *Illust London News*, 22 March 1873, NPG.

CORRY, Montagu William Lowry, see Baron Rowton.

CORY, John (1828-1910) philanthropist, coal-owner and ship-owner.
SC SIR WILLIAM GOSCOMBE JOHN, 1906, bronze statue, Cathays Park, Cardiff.

COSTA, Sir Michael Andrew Angus (1810-1884) composer and conductor.
SC J.P.DANTAN, 1834, bust, Musée Carnavalet, Paris.
PR UNKNOWN, after a drawing, tql seated, lith, pub 1835, BM, NPG. C.A.TOMKINS, after C.Perugini, hs, mezz, oval, BM, pub 1862, NPG. D.J.POUND, after a photograph by Mayall, tql, stipple and line, for *Illust News of the World*, BM. O.TASSAERT, after a drawing by F.Bouchot, hl, lith, BM. G.ZOBEL, after a photograph, hl, oval, mezz, BM. Several popular prints, NPG.
C UNKNOWN, tql seated, profile, chromo-lith, for *Vanity Fair*, 6 July 1872, NPG.
PH BASSANO, hs, profile, print, NPG (Album 38). J.E.MAYALL, hs, woodburytype, oval, for *Men of Mark*, 1883, NPG. UNKNOWN, wl, carte, NPG (Album 108). UNKNOWN, hs, carte, NPG AX7695.

COTTON, George Edward Lynch (1813-1866) bishop of Calcutta.
PR UNKNOWN, hs, woodcut, for *Illust London News*, 10 Nov 1866, NPG. UNKNOWN, tql, stipple, NPG.

COTTON, Sir Henry (1821-1892) judge.
D GEORGE RICHMOND, 1875, head, chalk, NPG 4240.
C SIR LESLIE WARD ('Spy'), hs at bench, w/c study, for *Vanity Fair*, 19 May 1888, NPG 2704.
PH LOCK & WHITFIELD, hs, woodburytype, oval, for *Men of Mark*, 1881, NPG. BARRAUD, tql, print, for *Men and Women of the Day*, vol I, 1888, NPG AX5426. UNKNOWN, hs, woodburytype, oval, NPG X6899.

COTTON, Sir St Vincent, Bart (1801-1863) gambler and driver of the Brighton coach.
PR 'T.C.W.', wl, profile, seated on box, driving, lith, BM.

COTTON, Sir William James Richmond (1822-1902) lord mayor of London.
PR UNKNOWN, after a photograph by Maull & Co, hs in mayor's robes, woodcut, for *Illust London News*, 6 Nov 1875, NPG.
C SIR LESLIE WARD ('Spy'), wl, profile, w/c study, for *Vanity Fair*, 5 Sept 1885, NPG 3282.

COUCH, Sir Richard (1817-1905) judge.
PR UNKNOWN, 'Trial of the Guicowar', woodcut, for *Illust London News*, 3 April 1875, NPG.

COULTON, George Gordon (1858-1947) historian and controversialist.
PH WALTER STONEMAN, 1930, hs, NPG (NPR).

COURTENAY, William Reginald, see 11th Earl of Devon.

COURTNEY, William Leonard (1850-1928) philosopher and journalist.
P SIR HUBERT VON HERKOMER, New College, Oxford.
PR UNKNOWN, hs, wood engr, for *Illust London News*, 13 Oct 1894, NPG.
C HARRY FURNISS, pen and ink sketch, NPG 3443.

PH JOHN RUSSELL & SONS, tql seated, print, for *National Photographic Record*, vol I, NPG.

COURTNEY of Penwith, Leonard Henry Courtney, 1st Baron (1832-1918) statesman and journalist.
D ALPHONSE LEGROS, 1883, hs, pencil, Fitzwilliam Museum, Cambridge. S.P.HALL, pencil sketch, NPG 2321.
PR R.JOSEY, after W.Carter, hs, mezz, BM, NPG.
C THÉOBALD CHARTRAN ('T'), wl, profile, w/c study, for *Vanity Fair*, 25 Sept 1880, NPG 4633.
PH W. & D.DOWNEY, hs, woodburytype, for Cassell's *Cabinet Portrait Gallery*, vol III, 1892, NPG. ELLIOTT & FRY, hs, print, NPG X6904. LONDON STEREOSCOPIC CO, hs, print, NPG X6903. SIR BENJAMIN STONE, 1898-9, wl, print, NPG.

COUSINS, Samuel (1801-1887) engraver.
P JAMES LEAKEY, 1843, hl seated, NPG 1447. FRANK HOLL, 1879, tql seated, TATE 4065; pen, wash and body colour study, NPG 1751. SIR A.S.COPE, 1883, hs, MacDonald Collection, Aberdeen Art Gallery. EDWIN LONG, RA 1883, tql seated, Royal Albert Memorial Museum, Exeter.
D C.W.COPE, c1862, hs, sketch, with sketches of S.A.Hart and others, pencil, NPG 3182(3).
PH F.JOUBERT, hs, carte, NPG AX7564. UNKNOWN, wl, carte, NPG (Album 105).

COWAN, Henry Vivian (1854-1918) soldier.
D I.SHELDON-WILLIAMS, 1900, tql seated, pencil and w/c sketch, NPG 4039(1).

COWDRAY, Weetman Dickinson Pearson, 1st Viscount (1856-1927) contractor and benefactor.
P After JOHN SINGER SARGENT, tql, DoE (Mexico City).
SC HERBERT C.GRIMWOOD, bronze bust, Borough of Colchester.
PH VANDYK, hs, profile, print, NPG X11620.

COWELL, Edward Byles (1826-1903) scholar and man of letters.
P C.E.BROCK, c1896, Corpus Christi College, Cambridge. UNKNOWN, after a photograph, Sanskrit College, Calcutta.

COWELL, Samuel Houghton (1820-1864) actor and singer.
PR Various theatrical prints, Harvard Theatre Collection, Cambridge, Mass, USA.

COWEN, Sir Joseph (1800-1873) radical politician.
P EMILE A.VENTURI, 1858, University of Newcastle. EMMERSON, 1864, University of Newcastle.
PR UNKNOWN, tql seated, stipple and line, NPG. UNKNOWN, after a photograph by W. & D.Downey, hs, woodcut, for *Illust London News*, 10 Jan 1874, NPG.
C UNKNOWN, wl, chromo-lith, for *Vanity Fair*, 26 Oct 1872, NPG.

COWEN, Joseph (1831-1900) politician and journalist.
P Several portraits at University of Newcastle: E.A.VENTURI, 1857; S. or E.SAWYER, 1864; IRVING, c1880; JOHN DICKENSON, 1883; WILLIAM IRVING, 1891.
PR UNKNOWN, after a photograph by W. & D.Downey, hs, woodcut, for *Illust London News*, 2 May 1874, NPG.
C UNKNOWN, wl, chromo-lith, supplement to *The Monetary Gazette*, 1 Sept 1877, NPG. SIR LESLIE WARD ('Spy'), wl, profile, chromo-lith, for *Vanity Fair*, 27 April 1878, NPG.
PH LOCK & WHITFIELD, hs, woodburytype, oval, for *Men of Mark*, 1881, NPG.

COWIE, Benjamin Morgan (1816-1900) dean of Exeter.
D T.C.WAGEMAN, w/c, Trinity College, Cambridge.

COWIE, William Garden (1831-1902) bishop of Auckland.
PH UNKNOWN, hs, semi-profile, print, NPG (Anglican Bishops).

COWLEY, Henry Richard Charles Wellesley, 1st Earl (1804-1884) diplomat.
PR A.LEMOINE, tql seated, lith, BM, NPG.

COWPER, Charles Spencer (1816-1879) son of 5th Earl Cowper.
D COUNT ALFRED D'ORSAY, 1845, hl, profile, pencil and chalk, NPG 4026(16).

COWPER, Francis Thomas de Grey Cowper, 7th Earl (1834-1905) lord lieutenant of Ireland.
PR H.COOK, after W.C.Ross, hl as a boy, stipple, BM, NPG. VIOLET, DUCHESS OF RUTLAND, 1894, hs, profile, lith, NPG. C.W.WALTON, hs, lith, NPG.

COWPER, William Francis, see Baron Mount-Temple.

COX, Edward William (1809-1879) serjeant-at-law.
PR UNKNOWN, after a photograph by London Stereoscopic Co, hs, woodcut, for *Illust London News*, 6 Dec 1879, NPG.

COX, Harold (1859-1936) economist and journalist.
C HARRY FURNISS, pen and ink sketch, NPG 3560.
PH H.J.WHITLOCK & SONS, hs, print, NPG x6914.

COXE, Henry Octavius (1811-1881) palaeographer.
P G.F.WATTS, 1876, hl seated, Bodleian Library, Oxford.
D FREDERICK TATHAM, 1833, hl seated, w/c, Bodleian Library. R.A.J.TYRWHITT, c1853, two pencil drgs, both hs, Worcester College, Oxford. R.ST JOHN TYRWHITT, head, profile, sepia, Corpus Christi College, Oxford. SMITH, based on a photograph, 1870, hs seated, w/c, Bodleian Library.

COXWELL, Henry (Tracey) (1819-1900) aeronaut.
PR UNKNOWN, hs, profile, woodcut, for *Illust London News*, 20 Jan 1884, NPG.
PH UNKNOWN, hl with James Glaisher in a balloon, carte, NPG (Album 38).

COZENS-HARDY, Herbert Hardy Cozens-Hardy, 1st Baron (1838-1920) judge.
P R.G.EVES, 1910?, wl seated in robes, Lincoln's Inn, London; related hs sketch, DoE (Public Record Office, London).
C SIR LESLIE WARD ('Spy'), two chromo-liths: wl, profile, for *Vanity Fair*, 13 April 1893, and hs at bench, for *Vanity Fair*, 24 Jan 1901, NPG.

CRAIGMYLE, Thomas Shaw, 1st Baron (1850-1937) lawyer and politician.
P GEORGE FIDDES WATT, hl, SNPG 2130.
PH SIR BENJAMIN STONE, 1897–1908, five prints, all wl, NPG.

CRAIK, Dinah Maria, née Mulock (1826-1887) novelist.
P SIR HUBERT VON HERKOMER, 1887, tql seated, NPG 3304.
D AMELIA ROBERTSON HILL, 1845, hl seated, and hs sketch on reverse, NPG 2544.
SC H.H.ARMSTEAD, 1890, medallion on monument, Tewkesbury Abbey.
PH B.WOLLASTON, hs, photogravure, NPG x6999.

CRAIK, Sir Henry, 1st Bart (1846-1927) politician, civil servant and man of letters.
PH SIR BENJAMIN STONE, 1909, wl, print, NPG.

CRAMPTON, Victoire, Lady, see Balfe.

CRANBROOK, Gathorne Gathorne-Hardy, 1st Earl of (1814-1906) statesman.
P After FRANK HOLL, c1882–4, Carlton Club, London.
D GEORGE RICHMOND, 1857, hs, pencil, NPG 1449. W.E.MILLER, 1877, hs, chalk, Hughenden (NT), Bucks. SEBASTIAN EVANS, 1883, hs, profile, pencil, NPG 2173(46).
G HENRY GALES, 'The Derby Cabinet of 1867', w/c, NPG 4893.

PR T.G.APPLETON, after F.Holt, tql seated, mezz, BM. E.STODART, after a photograph by W. & D.Downey, hl seated, stipple and line, NPG. UNKNOWN, hl, semi-profile, lith, for *Civil Service Review*, 1877, BM. Several popular prints, NPG.
C HARRY FURNISS, pen and ink sketch, NPG 3353.
PH LOCK & WHITFIELD, hs, profile, woodburytype, oval, for *Men of Mark*, 1881, NPG. W. & D.DOWNEY, tql seated, woodburytype, for Cassell's *Cabinet Portrait Gallery*, vol II, 1891, NPG.

CRANE, Walter (1845-1915) artist.
P G.F.WATTS, 1891, hs, profile, NPG 1750. Self-portrait, 1912, hl with palette, Uffizi Gallery, Florence.
SC GEORGE SIMONDS, RA 1889, bust, Art Workers' Guild, London.
PR W.ROTHENSTEIN, three studies, in different attitudes, lith, BM, NPG. Self-portrait, hs, aged 60, BM.
PH ELLIOTT & FRY, c1875?, tql seated, cabinet, NPG x7002. BARRAUD, tql seated, print, for *Men and Women of the Day*, vol IV, 1891, NPG AX5523. T.A.GOTCH, 1906, wl with Sir Reginald Blomfield at Clare, Suffolk, print, RIBA, London. UNKNOWN, c1910?, hs, profile, print, NPG x7003.

CRAUFURD, James, see Lord Ardmillan.

CRAVEN, Henry Thornton (1818-1905) actor and dramatist.
PR PACKER & GRIFFIN, after a photograph, wl in character, lith, Harvard Theatre Collection, Cambridge, Mass, USA.
C UNKNOWN, wl, woodcut, for *Entr'acte*, 7 July 1877, Harvard Theatre Collection.

CRAWFORD, Alexander William Crawford Lindsay, 25th Earl of (1812-1880) writer and book-collector.
PH THOMAS RODGER, tql with his wife, who is seated, print, NPG x5712.

CRAWFORD, James Ludovic Lindsay, 26th Earl of (1847-1913) astronomer, collector and bibliophile.
SC Attrib GEORGE FOUCHARD, head in cannel coal, Wigan Public Libraries.
C SIR LESLIE WARD ('Spy'), tql, w/c study, for *Vanity Fair*, 11 May 1878, NPG 2705. SIR LESLIE WARD ('Spy'), wl, Hentschel-Colourtype, for *Vanity Fair*, 12 Aug 1908, NPG.

CREALOCK, Henry Hope (1831-1891) soldier, artist and author.
P ROBERT RUSS, 1869, hs, oval, NPG 2191.
D Self-portrait, with others at the charge of the 3rd Dragoon Guards in the action of Dhoodea Khera, India, 24 Nov 1858, pen and ink, National Army Museum, London.
C SIR LESLIE WARD ('Spy'), wl, w/c study, for *Vanity Fair*, 15 March 1879, NPG 2898.

CREASY, Sir Edward Shepherd (1812-1878) historian.
PH LOCK & WHITFIELD, hs, woodburytype, oval, for *Men of Mark*, 1878, NPG.

CREIGHTON, Mandell (1843-1901) bishop of London.
P HENRY HARRIS BROWN, RA 1896, Emmanuel College, Cambridge. SIR HUBERT VON HERKOMER, 1899, tql, enamel on metal, Merton College, Oxford. SIR HUBERT VON HERKOMER, 1902, tql seated, Fulham Palace, London; version, NPG 1335.
SC SIR WILLIAM HAMO THORNYCROFT, RA 1906, bronze statue on monument, St Paul's Cathedral, London. SIR W.HAMO THORNYCROFT, bronze bust, Lambeth Palace, London.
C DALTON ('F.T.D.'), wl, w/c study, for *Vanity Fair*, 22 April 1897, NPG 2706.
PH W. & D.DOWNEY, hs, woodburytype, for Cassell's *Cabinet Portrait Gallery*, vol IV, 1893, NPG. UNKNOWN, hs, print, NPG (Anglican Bishops).

CREMER, Sir William Randal (1838-1908) peace advocate.
SC P.R.MONTFORD, RA 1911, bronze bust, Palace of Westminster, London.
PH SIR BENJAMIN STONE, 1904, wl, print, NPG.

CRESWICK, Thomas (1811-1869) landscape painter.
G HENRY NELSON O'NEIL, 'The Billiard Room of the Garrick Club', oil, 1869, Garrick Club, London.
PR M.JACKSON, after T.Scott, hl, woodcut, BM. UNKNOWN, after a photograph by John Watkins, hs, woodcut, for *Illust London News*, 8 Jan 1870, NPG. UNKNOWN, after a photograph by John Watkins, tql seated at easel, woodcut, for *The Graphic*, 8 Jan 1870, NPG.
PH JOHN & CHARLES WATKINS, hs, carte, NPG (Album 104).

CRESWICK, William (1813-1888) actor.
D ALFRED BRYAN, tql, w/c, NPG 2450.
PR Several theatrical prints, BM, NPG. Various theatrical prints and caricatures, Harvard Theatre Collection, Cambridge, Mass, USA.
PH UNKNOWN, hs, woodburytype, carte, NPG X7022.

CREWE, Robert Offley Ashburton Crewe-Milnes, 2nd Baron Houghton and 1st Marquess of (1858-1945) statesman.
P WILLIAM CARTER, RA 1893, University of Sheffield. W.F.OSBORNE, before 1903, tql, NPG 3849. AMBROSE MCEVOY, 1918, Greater London Council.
D SIR WILLIAM ROTHENSTEIN, 1918, head, semi-profile, pencil, NPG 4772. SIR W.ROTHENSTEIN, 1918, hl in vice-chancellor's robes, pastel, University of Sheffield.
C SIR LESLIE WARD ('Spy'), wl, chromo-lith, for *Vanity Fair*, 10 Dec 1892, NPG. SIR MAX BEERBOHM, two cartoons: 1919, 'The Birthday Surprise', Savile Club, London, and 1924, 'The Old and the Young Self', Ashmolean Museum, Oxford. HARRY FURNISS, pen and ink sketch, NPG 3354.
PH BASSANO, 1895, five negs, various sizes, NPG X404–8. JOHN RUSSELL & SONS, hl seated, print for *National Photographic Record*, vol I, NPG. WALTER STONEMAN, 1925 and 1938, hs, and hs profile, NPG (NPR).

CRICHTON-BROWNE, Sir James, see Browne.

CRIPPS, Charles Alfred, see 1st Baron Parmoor.

CROFT, John (1833-1905) surgeon.
G HENRY JAMYN BROOKS, 'The Council of the Royal College of Surgeons of England of 1884–5', oil, Royal College of Surgeons, London.

CROFTS, Ernest (1847-1911) painter; Keeper of the Royal Academy.
G SIR HUBERT VON HERKOMER, 'The Council of the Royal Academy', oil, 1908, TATE 2481.
SC A.G.WYON, memorial plaque, Holy Trinity Church, Blythburgh, Suffolk.
PR Two woodcuts, both hs, one for *Illust London News*, 20 July 1878, NPG. UNKNOWN, hs, woodcut, BM.
PH RALPH W.ROBINSON, wl at easel, print, for *Members and Associates of the Royal Academy of Arts, 1891*, NPG X7358.

CROMER, Evelyn Baring, 1st Earl of (1841-1917) statesman, diplomat and administrator.
P JOHN SINGER SARGENT, 1902, tql seated, NPG2901.
D WILLIAM STRANG, 1908, hs, chalk, Royal Coll.
SC SIR WILLIAM GOSCOMBE JOHN, portrait medallion on memorial tablet, Westminster Abbey, London.
PR VIOLET, DUCHESS OF RUTLAND, 1898, hs, lith, NPG.
C SIR LESLIE WARD ('Spy'), wl, profile, chromo-lith, for *Vanity Fair*, 2 Jan 1902, NPG.
PH G.C.BERESFORD, 1903, hs, neg, NPG X6479. Several photographs, by LONDON STEREOSCOPIC CO, BASSANO and G.C.BERESFORD, various dates and sizes, NPG X7032–7037. JOHN RUSSELL & SONS, hl seated, print, for *National Photographic Record*, vol I, NPG.

CROMPTON, Rookes Evelyn Bell (1845-1940) engineer.
P Two portraits, one by GEORGE HARCOURT, c1935, and another by an unknown artist, Institution of Electrical Engineers, London.
D GERTRUDE HALL (his daughter), Institution of Mechanical Engineers, London.
C 'WHO', wl, Hentschel-Colourtype, for *Vanity Fair*, 30 Aug 1911, NPG.
PH WALTER STONEMAN, 1933, hl, NPG (NPR).

CROOKES, Sir William (1832-1919) chemist.
P ALBERT LUDOVICI, 1884, hl, NPG 1846. E.A.WALTON, exhib 1910, hl seated, semi-profile, Royal Society, London.
D WILLIAM STRANG, 1910, hs, chalk, Royal Coll.
C SIR LESLIE WARD ('Spy'), wl, chromo-lith, for *Vanity Fair*, 21 May 1903, NPG.
PH G.C.BERESFORD, 1906, hs, neg, NPG X6480. ELLIOTT & FRY, hs, photogravure, NPG X7044. WALTER STONEMAN, hs, NPG (NPR).

CROOKS, William (1852-1921) Socialist politician.
C HARRY FURNISS, pen and ink sketch, NPG 3561. SIR LESLIE WARD ('Spy'), wl, chromo-lith, for *Vanity Fair*, 6 April 1905, NPG.
PH SIR BENJAMIN STONE, 1905, wl, print, NPG. WALTER STONEMAN, 1918, hl, NPG (NPR).

CROSS, Mary Ann or Marian, née Evans (1819-1880) 'George Eliot'; novelist.
P FRANCOIS D'ALBERT DURADE, replica (1849), hl seated, NPG 1405.
D CAROLINE BRAY, 1842, hl seated, w/c, NPG 1232. SAMUEL LAURENCE, 1860, hs, chalk, BM. SAMUEL LAURENCE, 1860, hs, crayon, Girton College, Cambridge. SIR F.W.BURTON, 1865, hs, chalk, NPG 669. SIR F.W.BURTON, drg, Birmingham City Art Gallery. LOWES CATO DICKINSON, 1872, head, profile, ink, NPG 4961. LADY LAURA THERESA ALMA-TADEMA, two pencil sketches, both head, profile, the first dated 1877, NPG 1758 and NPG 2211.
SL UNKNOWN, hs, profile, NPG 2645.

CROSS, Richard Assheton Cross, 1st Viscount (1823-1914) secretary of state.
P SIR HUBERT VON HERKOMER, 1882, tql, NPG 2946. SYDNEY HODGES, RA 1891, Lancaster Castle.
PR UNKNOWN, hl, lith, for *Civil Service Review*, 1877, BM. G.COOK, after a photograph by London Stereoscopic Co, tql seated, stipple and line, NPG. Several popular prints, NPG.
C CARLO PELLEGRINI ('Ape'), wl, chromo-lith, for *Vanity Fair*, 16 May 1874, NPG.
PH FRADELLE & YOUNG, hs, print, for *Our Conservative Statesmen*, vol II, NPG (Album 17). LOCK & WHITFIELD, hs, woodburytype, oval, for *Men of Mark*, 1880, NPG. RUSSELL & SONS, hs, semi-profile, woodburytype, NPG X7049. UNKNOWN, hs, woodburytype, oval, NPG X7065.

CROSSLEY, Sir Francis (1817-1872) carpet manufacturer and philanthropist.
SC JOSEPH DURHAM, RA 1861, statue, People's Park, Halifax.
PR C.BAUGNIET, 1856, tql, lith, NPG. D.J.POUND, after a photograph by Mayall, tql seated, stipple and line, for *Drawing Room Portrait Gallery*, 1859, NPG. Two woodcuts, one for *Illust London News*, 20 Jan 1872, NPG. UNKNOWN, tql, stipple and line, NPG.
PH MOIRA & HAIGH, tql, carte, NPG (Album 136).

CROSSLEY, James (1800-1883) author.
P JOHN HANSON WALKER, 1875, tql, Chetham's Library, Manchester.

CROWE, Eyre (1824-1910) artist.
PR UNKNOWN, after a photograph by George Crowe, hs, woodcut, for *Illust London News*, 6 May 1876, NPG.
PH RALPH W.ROBINSON, wl seated at easel, print, for *Members and Associates of the Royal Academy of Arts, 1891*, NPG X7359.

CROWE, Sir Joseph Archer (1825-1896) journalist and art critic.
P LOUIS KOLITZ, 1877, hl, NPG 4329.

CROWE, Kate Josephine, née Bateman (1842-1917) actress.
D UNKNOWN, 1904, head, pencil, NPG 2620.
PR UNKNOWN, hs, lith, NPG. Several theatrical prints, BM, NPG.
PH Four cartes, by an unknown photographer, W. & D.Downey and SARONY & Co, various dates and sizes, NPG X240-43.

CROWQUILL, Alfred, see Alfred Henry Forrester.

CROWTHER, Samuel Adjai (1809?-1892) bishop of the Niger territory.
PH ERNEST EDWARDS, wl, carte, NPG AX7481.

CUBITT, Joseph (1811-1872) civil engineer.
PR UNKNOWN, hs, woodcut, for *The Builder*, 22 Jan 1870, NPG.

CUBITT, William George (1835-1903) colonel Indian staff corps.
G CHEVALIER DESANGES, wl equestrian at the retreat from Chinhut, 1857, where he saved the lives of three men of the 32nd regiment, oil, National Army Museum (on display at the Royal Military Academy, Sandhurst).

CULLEN, Paul (1803-1878) cardinal.
PR UNKNOWN, after a photograph by London Stereoscopic Co, hs, woodcut, for *Illust London News*, 2 Nov 1878, NPG.

CULLINGWORTH, Charles James (1841-1908) gynaecologist and obstetrician.
PH UNKNOWN, St Thomas's Hospital, London.

CUMMING, John (1807-1881) minister of the Scottish church, Covent Garden.
PR D.J.POUND, after a photograph by J.Eastham, tql, stipple and line, NPG. J.THOMSON, after W.Booth, tql, stipple, BM. Several popular prints, NPG.
C UNKNOWN, hl in pulpit, chromo-lith, for *Vanity Fair*, 13 April 1872, NPG.
PH W. & D.DOWNEY, hs, profile, carte, NPG (Album 102). W. & D.DOWNEY, wl seated, carte, NPG AX7493. ELLIOTT & FRY, hs, carte, NPG (Album 40). MASON & Co, c1860, wl, carte, NPG X7068. J. & C.WATKINS, c1860, hs, profile, carte, NPG X7070.

CUMMING, Sir William Gordon-, 4th Bart, see GORDON-Cumming.

CUNLIFFE-OWEN, Sir Francis Philip (1828-1894) director of the South Kensington Museum.
PR UNKNOWN, after a photograph by Fritz Luckhardt, hs, woodcut, for *Illust London News*, 8 Nov 1873, NPG. SMEETON & TILLY, hl, woodcut, oval, for *L'Art*, 1878, BM. UNKNOWN, hs, lith, for *The Whitehall Review*, 12 Oct 1878, NPG. UNKNOWN, hs, woodcut, for *Illust London News*, 31 July 1886, NPG.
C SIR LESLIE WARD ('Spy'), tql, chromo-lith, for *Vanity Fair*, 23 Nov 1878, NPG.
PH W. & D.DOWNEY, hs, cabinet, NPG X7075. LOCK & WHITFIELD, hs, woodburytype, oval, for *Men of Mark*, 1880, NPG. WALERY, tql, print, NPG X12629.

CUNNINGHAM, Daniel John (1850-1909) professor of anatomy at Dublin and Edinburgh.
SC OLIVER SHEPPARD, bronze panel, Trinity College, Dublin; replica, Edinburgh University.

CUNNINGHAM, Francis (1820-1875) author and critic.
SC SIR FRANCIS CHANTREY, marble bust, SNPG 1495.

CUNNINGHAM, John (1819-1893) historian.
P UNKNOWN, St Mary's College, University of St Andrews, Scotland.

CUNNINGHAM, Peter (1816-1869) antiquary.
D CHARLES MARTIN, c1859, hs, chalk, NPG 1645.
PR UNKNOWN, after a photograph by Cundall, tql seated, woodcut, for *Illust London News*, 23 Feb 1856, NPG.

CUNNINGHAM, William (1805-1861) principal of the Free Church College, Edinburgh.
P WILLIAM BONNAR, tql seated, SNPG 688. SIR JOHN WATSON GORDON, hl, SNPG 617.
PR L.GHÉMAR, hl seated, lith, BM.

CUNNINGHAM, William (1849-1919) historian of economics.
P ERIC HENRI KENNINGTON, 1908, tql seated, NPG 4021; related portrait, Trinity College, Cambridge.
D WILLIAM STRANG, 1908, hs, profile, chalk and w/c, SNPG 1839.

CUNNINGHAME GRAHAM, Robert Bontine, see Graham.

CUNYNGHAME, Sir Arthur Augustus Thurlow (1812-1884) general.
PR UNKNOWN, after a photograph by W.Hermann of Cape Town, hs, woodcut, for *Illust London News*, 23 March 1878, NPG.

CURETON, Sir Charles (1826-1891) general.
PR UNKNOWN, hs in uniform, wood engr, for *Illust London News*, 18 July 1891, NPG.

CURETON, William (1808-1864) Syriac scholar.
D GEORGE RICHMOND, 1861, hs, semi-profile, chalk, NPG 3164.
PR UNKNOWN, after a daguerreotype by Beard, hl in pulpit, woodcut, for *Illust London News*, 29 April 1854, NPG.

CURRIE, Sir Donald (1825-1909) ship-owner, benefactor and art collector.
P W.W.OULESS, 1908, tql seated in doctoral robes and insignia of his order, SNPG 2064; version, Edinburgh University. W.W.OULESS, University College (Medical School), London.
C CARLO PELLEGRINI ('Ape'), wl, profile, w/c study, for *Vanity Fair*, 21 June 1884, NPG 2707.

CURWEN, John (1816-1880) writer on music.
P WILLIAM GUSH, hl, NPG 1066. G.H.SWINSTEAD, hl, National Museum of Wales 149, Cardiff.

CURZON, Robert, see 14th Baron Zouche.

CURZON of Kedleston, George Nathaniel Curzon, Marquess (1859-1925) statesman.
P P.A.DE LÁSZLÓ, 1913, hl seated in robes, All Souls College, Oxford. SIR GEORGE REID, 1913, tql seated in robes, Government House, Calcutta. SIR HUBERT VON HERKOMER, 1914, nearly wl seated in robes, Examination Schools, Oxford. J.S.SARGENT, 1914, hl, Royal Geographical Society, London; copy by JOHN COOKE, NPG 2534.
D MELTON PRIOR, c1903, two pencil drgs: Lord Curzon investing the Maharaja of Cochin with the Order of the Star of India at the Coronation Durbar, Delhi; the Departure of the Viceroy and the Duke of Connaught from Delhi at the end of the Durbar, India Office Library and Records, London.
SC F.W.POMEROY, c1912, statue, Calcutta. SIR WILLIAM HAMO THORNYCROFT, 1918, bronze statue, Victoria Memorial Hall, Calcutta. SIR BERTRAM MACKENNAL, bronze statue, Carlton House Terrace, London.

c Sir Max Beerbohm, several political cartoons, drgs, eg 1908, Ashmolean Museum, Oxford, and 1909. All Souls College, Oxford. Harry Furniss, pen and ink sketch, NPG 3355. Sir Francis Carruthers Gould, ink and w/c sketch, V & A. Sir Bernard Partridge, two cartoons, for *Punch*, 8 Feb 1922 and 16 May 1923, NPG. Sir Leslie Ward ('Spy'), wl, profile, chromolith, for *Vanity Fair*, 18 June 1892, NPG.

PH London Stereoscopic Co, hs, print, NPG X7089. Russell & Sons, hs, semi-profile, print, for *Our Conservative and Unionist Statesmen*, vol IV, NPG (Album 21). Sir Benjamin Stone, 1898, wl, print, NPG.

CUST, Sir Lionel Henry (1859–1929) art historian.
PH Unknown, 1905, tql, print, NPG X7093.

CUST, Robert Needham (1821–1909) orientalist.
P Margaret Carpenter, hl, profile, Eton College, Berks.

D

D'ABERNON, Sir Edgar Vincent, Viscount (1857-1941) financier and diplomat.
P AUGUSTUS JOHN, 1927–31, wl in robes of the order of the Bath, TATE 5936.
D FRANCIS DODD, 1931, hs, pencil, NPG 3862.
SC ANDREW O'CONNOR, 1934, bronze bust, TATE 4853.
C SIR LESLIE WARD ('Spy'), wl, profile, chromo-lith, for *Vanity Fair*, 20 April 1899, NPG. SIR MAX BEERBOHM, 1931, cartoon, Lilly Library, Indiana University, Bloomington, Indiana, USA.
PH BASSANO, 1895, five negs, various sizes, NPG X418–22. SIR BENJAMIN STONE, 1901, two prints, both wl, NPG. G.C.BERESFORD, 1903 and 1915, two negs, hs and hs profile, NPG x6608 and x6482. WALTER STONEMAN, 1917, hs, NPG (NPR).

DACRE, Sir Henry Bouverie William Brand, 23rd Baron, see 1st Viscount Hampden.

DACRES, Sir Sidney Colpoys (1805-1884) admiral.
PR UNKNOWN, after a photograph by John Watkins, hs in uniform, woodcut, oval, for *Illust London News*, 5 April 1873, NPG.
PH LOCK & WHITFIELD, hs in uniform, woodburytype, oval, for *Men of Mark*, 1883, NPG.

DADD, Richard (1817-1886) painter.
PH UNKNOWN, c1856, tql seated at easel, in Bethlem Hospital, print, The Bethlem Royal Hospital, Beckenham, Kent.

DALE, Robert William (1829-1895) congregational minister.
SC EDWARD ONSLOW FORD, statue, Birmingham City Art Gallery.
PH H.J.WHITLOCK, hs, carte, NPG (Album 40).

DALE, Thomas Pelham (1821-1892) ritualistic divine.
PR UNKNOWN, two sketches, hs, profile, after a photograph by Fradelle, and wl in prison, woodcuts, for *Illust London News*, 20 Nov 1880, NPG.

DALHOUSIE, Fox Maule Ramsay, 11th Earl of (1801-1874) statesman.
P COLVIN SMITH, 1861, wl, Church of Scotland Assembly Hall, Edinburgh. SIR JOHN WATSON GORDON, SNPG 2139.
D THOMAS DUNCAN, c1838, hl, wash, NPG 2537.
PR J.PORTER, after T.Duncan, tql with bust of C.J.Fox, mezz, pub 1838, BM, NPG. F.SCHENCK, after a drg by W.Crawford of 1845, hs, lith, BM, NPG. D.J.POUND, after a photograph by Mayall, tql seated, stipple and line, for *Drawing Room Portrait Gallery*, 1859, BM, NPG. POSSELWHITE, after same photograph, tql (sitter in masonic dress), stipple, oval, BM, NPG.
PH MAULL & POLYBLANK, tql seated, print, NPG X7967. SOUTHWELL BROS, wl, carte, NPG AX7433.

DALHOUSIE, Sir James Andrew Broun Ramsay, 10th Earl and 1st Marquess of (1812-1860) governor-general of India.
P Several portraits by SIR JOHN WATSON GORDON: c1835, wl in uniform of Royal Company of Archers, Archers' Hall, Edinburgh; 1847, wl in robes of the lord clerk register of Scotland, NPG 188; c1858, wl seated on throne, Legislative Council Chamber, Calcutta, study for this portrait, SNPG 1119.
G SIR GEORGE HARVEY, with the Marquess of Breadalbane and Lords Cockburn and Rutherfurd, oil, SNPG 1497.

SC SIR JOHN STEELL, 1864, marble statue, Victoria Memorial Hall, Calcutta; plaster cast, SNPG 177.
PR H.ROBINSON, after G.Richmond, hs, stipple, pub 1845, BM, NPG.

DALHOUSIE, John William Ramsay, 13th Earl of (1847-1887) politician.
P JAMES ARCHER, 1889, probably after a photograph, tql, semi-profile, Dundee City Art Gallery.
C SIR LESLIE WARD ('Spy'), wl, profile, chromo-lith, for *Vanity Fair*, 28 Feb 1880, NPG.

DALLEY, William Bede (1831-1888) Australian politician.
SC SIR J.E.BOEHM, medallion portrait, St Paul's Cathedral, London. CAVALIERI ATTILIO SIMONETTI, marble bust, Legislative Council Chamber of New South Wales, Sydney, Australia.
PR UNKNOWN, hs, woodcut, for *Illust London News*, 23 Oct 1886, NPG.

DALLING and BULWER, William Henry Lytton Earle Bulwer, Baron (1801-1872) diplomat.
P GIUSEPPE FAGNANI, 1865, hs, NPG 852.
PR W.SHARP, after Kreiger, hs, lith, NPG. UNKNOWN, after a photograph by O.Schoefft, hs, profile, woodcut, for *The Illustrated Review*, 15 Aug 1872, NPG.
C JOHN DOYLE, c1847, 'The Mask of Comus, as now being Performed at the Theatre Royal, Madrid', pen and pencil, BM. CARLO PELLEGRINI ('Ape'), wl, profile, pencil study, for *Vanity Fair*, 27 Aug 1870, NPG 3969.

DALLINGER, William Henry (1842-1909) Wesleyan minister and biologist.
P Attrib E.THOMAS, tql seated with microscope, Wellcome Institute, London.
PR H.C.BALDING, after a photograph by J.Hawke, hl seated, profile, stipple, NPG.

DALY, Sir Henry Dermot (1821-1895) general.
PR JOSEPH BROWN, after a photograph by Debenham, hs, stipple, for *Baily's Mag*, 1887, NPG.

DALZIEL, Edward (1817-1905) draughtsman and woodengraver.
PH UNKNOWN, hs, profile, carte, NPG (Album 103). UNKNOWN, 1897, hl, semi-profile, print, NPG x6429. UNKNOWN, hl, print, BM (Engr Ports Coll).

DALZIEL, George (1815-1902) draughtsman and woodengraver.
PH ELLIOTT & FRY, hs, profile, carte, NPG (Album 105). UNKNOWN, hs, carte, NPG (Album 103). UNKNOWN, hl, print, BM (Engr Ports Coll).

DANBY, James Francis (1816-1875) painter.
PR UNKNOWN, hs, woodcut, 1875, NPG.
PH JOHN WATKINS, hs, carte, NPG (Album 106).

DANE, Sir Louis William (1856-1946) Indian civil servant.
P JOHN ST HELIER LANDER, 1914, Lawrence Hall, Lahore, Pakistan.

DANIEL, Charles Henry Olive (1836-1919) scholar and printer.
P C.W.FURSE, 1905, tql in robes, (unfinished), Worcester College, Oxford.

D SIR WILLIAM ROTHENSTEIN, 1896, hl, semi-profile, pencil, Worcester College.

DANIELL, Edward Thomas (1804-1843) archaeologist.
P JOHN LINNELL, tql seated, Castle Museum, Norwich.

DARBY, John Nelson (1800-1882) Plymouth brother and founder of the Darbyites.
D EDWARD PENSTONE, hs, w/c, NPG 4870.

D'ARCY, Charles Frederick (1859-1938) archbishop of Armagh and primate of all Ireland.
P SIR JOHN LAVERY, 1928, Belfast Museum and Art Gallery. FREDERIC WHITING, Bishop's Palace, Armagh, N Ireland.
PH UNKNOWN, hl, print, NPG (Anglican Bishops).

DARLING, Charles John Darling, 1st Baron (1849-1936) judge.
P C.W.FURSE, 1890, tql, NPG 3546. E.I.HALLIDAY, 1928, hl, Inner Temple, London. R.G.EVES, The Arts Club, London.
D G.C.JENNIS, sketch, V & A.
C SIR LESLIE WARD ('Spy'), wl, chromo-lith, for *Vanity Fair*, 15 July 1897, NPG. SIR LESLIE WARD ('Spy'), wl, mechanical repro, for *Vanity Fair*, 8 May 1907, NPG; related hs, w/c study, NPG 2708. SIR BERNARD PARTRIDGE, cartoon, for *Punch's Almanack*, 1922, V & A.

DARLING, Grace Horsley (1815-1842) heroine of a sea rescue.
P Probably by HORATIO McCULLOCH, 1838, hs, profile, Grace Darling Museum, Bamburgh, Northumberland. T.M.JOY, 1839, hs, Dundee City Art Gallery. H.P.PARKER & J.W.CARMICHAEL, rescuing passengers from SS *Forfarshire*, Grace Darling Museum; mezz, D.Lucas, Grace Darling Museum, and Marine Society, London.
D H.P.PARKER, 1838, two pencil and w/c drgs, hl seated and head, NPG 1662-3 and two related oil sketches by H.P.PARKER, Grace Darling Museum. ROBERT WATSON, 1838, w/c sketch, Grace Darling Museum. J.W.CARMICHAEL, two imaginary w/cs of the rescue, Grace Darling Museum.
SC DAVID DUNBAR, 1838, marble bust, NPG 998. RAYMOND SMITH, 1846, recumbent effigy, Bamburgh Cemetery.
PR L.CORBAUX, after a drg by E.Hastings, hl, lith, 1838, NPG. W.TAYLOR, after J.Reay, hl, lith, Grace Darling Museum. M.GAUCI, after G.Harrison, hl, lith, pub 1838, BM. C.COOK, after G.Cook, tql in cloak, octagon, stipple, for *New Monthly Belle Assemblée*, 1843, BM, NPG.

DARWIN, Charles Robert (1809-1882) naturalist; author of *Origin of Species*.
P W.W.OULESS, 1883, replica of his portrait of 1875, hs, Christ's College, Cambridge. SIR W.B.RICHMOND, c1879-80, tql seated in gown, Department of Zoology, University of Cambridge. ALBERT GOODWIN, 1880, with his wife, seated outside Down House, Down House, Kent. JOHN COLLIER, 1881, tql, Linnean Society, London; replicas, 1883, NPG 1024, 1924, The Athenaeum, London and 1928, Royal College of Surgeons, Down House, Kent.
D GEORGE RICHMOND, 1840, tql seated, Down House. SAMUEL LAURENCE, 1853, hs, semi-profile, chalk, Down House, Kent; related drg, c1853, hs, Sedgwick Museum of Geology, Cambridge. MARIAN COLLIER, c1878, tql seated, pencil, NPG 3144.
SC THOMAS WOOLNER, 1869, marble bust, Department of Botany, University of Cambridge. ALPHONSE LEGROS, 1881, bronze portrait medallion, Manchester City Art Gallery, SIR J.E.BOEHM, 1883, marble statue, seated, BM (Natural History); related terracotta bust, NPG 761. ALLAN WYON, RA 1891, medal, Royal Society, London. H.R.HOPE PINKER, c1896, stone statue,

University Museum, Oxford. HORACE MONTFORD, RA 1898, bronze statue, Public Library, Castlegate, Shrewsbury. H.MONTFORD, posthumous terracotta bust, NPG 1395.
PR C.H.JEENS, after a photograph, hs, profile, stipple, for *Nature*, 1874, BM. M.KLINKICHT, hl, woodcut, BM. T.H.MAGUIRE, tql seated, lith, for *Ipswich Museum Portraits*, 1851, BM. G.PILOTELL, hs, dry-point, BM. Various popular prints, NPG.
C J.J.TISSOT, wl seated, chromo-lith, for *Vanity Fair*, 30 Sept 1871, NPG.
PH Various prints by BARRAUD, ELLIOTT & FRY, LOCK & WHITFIELD, LONDON STEREOSCOPIC CO, MAULL & FOX etc, cartes, cabinets and photogravures, various dates and sizes, NPG X5930-40. MAULL & POLYBLANK, c1855, tql seated, print, NPG P106(7). JULIA MARGARET CAMERON, 1868, hs, profile, print, NPG P8. ERNEST EDWARDS, late 1860s, hl, profile, print, NPG X1500.

DARWIN, Sir Francis (1848-1925) botanist.
P SIR WILLIAM ROTHENSTEIN, 1905, tql seated, Department of Botany, University of Cambridge.
PH J.PALMER CLARKE, c1907, hs, oval, print, NPG X4613. WALTER STONEMAN, 1918, hs, NPG (NPR).

DARWIN, Sir George Howard (1845-1912) mathematician and astronomer.
P MARK GERTLER, 1912, hl, NPG 1999.
D GWENDOLEN RAVERAT (his daughter), wl seated, profile, drg on canvas, NPG 2101; copy by MISS D.PERTZ, w/c, Trinity College, Cambridge.
PH ELLIOTT & FRY, tql seated, semi-profile, cabinet, NPG X5943.

DAVEY, Horace Davey, Baron (1833-1907) judge.
P SOLOMON J.SOLOMON, RA 1906, tql seated in peer's robes. University College, Oxford.

DAVID, Sir (Tannatt William) Edgeworth (1858-1934) geologist.
P NORMAN CARTER, hl, National Museum of Wales 490, Cardiff.
PH WALTER STONEMAN, 1927, hs, NPG (NPR).

DAVIDS, Thomas William Rhys (1843-1922) oriental scholar.
PH WALTER STONEMAN, 1917, hs, NPG (NPR).

DAVIDSON, Alexander Dyce (1807-1872) divine.
P SIR JOHN WATSON GORDON, Aberdeen Art Gallery.
PR E.BURTON, after J.W.Gordon, hl seated, mezz, BM.

DAVIDSON, Andrew Bruce (1831-1902) Hebraist and theologian.
P SIR GEORGE REID, New College, Edinburgh.

DAVIDSON, Charles (1824-1902) water-colour painter.
PH JOHN WATKINS, tql seated, carte, NPG (Album 104).

DAVIDSON, John (1857-1909) poet.
D SIR WILLIAM ROTHENSTEIN, 1894, hl seated, pastel, BM.
C SIR MAX BEERBOHM, several cartoons, eg one c1922 and one undated, University of Texas, USA, and 1925, Ashmolean Museum, Oxford.
PH ELLIOTT & FRY, called Davidson, hs, cabinet, NPG X11604.

DAVIDSON, Samuel (1806-1898) theologian.
D MATILDA SHARPE, hs, chalk, NPG 1539.
PH CRELLIN, tql seated, carte, NPG X11605.

DAVIDSON of Lambeth, Randall Thomas Davidson, Baron (1848-1930) Archbishop of Canterbury.
P H.G.RIVIERE, 1905, tql seated, Trinity College, Oxford. J.S.SARGENT, 1910, tql seated in robes, Lambeth Palace, London. P.A.de LÁSZLÓ, 1926, wl seated, Church House, Westminster.
D LUCY GRAHAM SMITH, 1893, hs, w/c, SNPG 2059.

G S.P.HALL, 'The Bench of Bishops, 1902', w/c, NPG 2369.

SC NEWBERRY TRENT, 1927, bronze bust, Harrow School, Middx. CECIL THOMAS, 1934, recumbent effigy, Canterbury Cathedral. LE MARCO, bronze bust, Lambeth Palace, London.

PR N.P.ZAROKILLI, hl seated, etch, BM. UNKNOWN, hs, etch, BM.

C SIR FRANCIS CARRUTHERS GOULD, sketch, NPG 2863. SIR LESLIE WARD ('Spy'), wl, profile, chromo-lith, for *Vanity Fair*, 19 Dec 1901, NPG. SIR LESLIE WARD ('Spy'), 1910, wl, w/c study, for *Vanity Fair*, NPG 2956.

PH OLIVE EDIS, two prints, hs and tql seated, NPG X5201 and X5203. JOHN RUSSELL & SONS, hl, print, for *National Photographic Record*, vol I, NPG. WALTER STONEMAN, before 1917, hs, NPG (NPR). UNKNOWN, two prints, both hs, NPG (Anglican Bishops).

DAVIES, John Llewelyn (1826-1916) theologian.

PR UNKNOWN, hs, wood engr, for *Illust London News*, 8 Oct 1892, NPG.

DAVIES, (Sarah) Emily (1830-1921) promoter of women's education.

P RUDOLPH LEHMANN, exhib 1880, tql seated, Girton College, Cambridge.

DAVIES, Thomas (1837-1891) mineralogist.

PR UNKNOWN, after a photograph by J.Perryman, hs, wood engr, for *Illust London News*, 14 Jan 1893, NPG.

DAVIS, Charles Edward (1827-1902) architect and antiquary.

P LEONARD SKEATES, Grand Pump Room, Bath.

DAVIS, Henry William Banks (1833-1914) artist.

P Self-portrait, 1883, hs, profile, MacDonald Collection, Aberdeen Art Gallery.

PR UNKNOWN, hs, woodcut, NPG.

PH RALPH W.ROBINSON, wl carrying a canvas, print, for *Members and Associates of the Royal Academy of Arts, 1891*, NPG X7360.

DAVIS, Joseph Barnard (1801-1881) craniologist.

P J.BARNARD DAVIS (his son), Royal College of Surgeons, London.

SC UNKNOWN, plaster bust, Royal College of Surgeons.

DAVIS, Thomas Osborne (1814-1845) poet and politician.

P HENRY MACMANUS, Aras an Uachtarain (President's Residence), Dublin, Eire.

D SIR F.W.BURTON, two pencil drgs, NGI 2032.

DAVITT, Michael (1846-1906) Irish revolutionary and labour agitator.

P SIR WILLIAM ORPEN, hl seated, Municipal Gallery of Modern Art, Dublin.

D SIR WILLIAM ORPEN, Municipal Gallery of Modern Art, Dublin. FREDERICK PEGRAM, pencil sketch, V & A.

PH W. & D.DOWNEY, hs, profile, print, for Cassell's *Cabinet Portrait Gallery*, vol II, 1891, NPG. SIR BENJAMIN STONE, 1897, wl, print, NPG.

DAWKINS, Sir William Boyd (1837-1929) geologist, palaeontologist and antiquary.

PH WALTER STONEMAN, 1920, hs, NPG (NPR).

DAWSON, George (1821-1876) preacher.

PR D.J.POUND, after a photograph by H.N.King, tql, stipple and line, NPG.

DAWSON, Henry (1811-1878) painter.

P SYLVANUS REDGATE, Castle Art Gallery, Nottingham. Self-portrait, Castle Art Gallery, Nottingham.

DAWSON, John (1827-1903) trainer of race horses.

C SIR LESLIE WARD ('Spy'), 'On the Heath', wl in a group, chromo-lith, for *Vanity Fair*, 26 Nov 1896, NPG.

DAWSON, Sir John William (1820-1899) geologist.

P UNKNOWN, wl, Redpath Museum, McGill University, Quebec, Canada.

PR UNKNOWN, after a photograph by Notman and Sandham of Montreal, hs, woodcut, for *Illust London News*, 4 Sept 1886, NPG.

DAWSON, Matthew (1820-1898) trainer of race horses.

C LIBERIO PROSPERI ('Lib'), wl, profile, chromo-lith, for *Vanity Fair*, 4 Dec 1886, NPG. SIR LESLIE WARD ('Spy'), 'On the Heath', wl in a group, chromo-lith, for *Vanity Fair*, 26 Nov 1896, NPG.

DAY, Sir John Charles Frederic Sigismund (1826-1908) judge.

P UNKNOWN, Harvard Law Library, Cambridge, Mass, USA.

D S.P.HALL, three pencil drgs, the second with Viscount Bryce, and the third with Lord Hannen, NPG 2285, 2249 and 2296. FREDERICK PEGRAM, pencil sketch, V & A.

C SIR LESLIE WARD ('Spy'), hs at bench, chromo-lith, for *Vanity Fair*, 27 Oct 1888, NPG.

DAY, Lewis Foreman (1845-1910) decorative artist.

D E.R.HUGHES, 1897, hs, The Art Workers' Guild, London.

DAY, William Henry (1823-1908) trainer and breeder of race-horses.

PR G.R.BLACK, after a photograph by Elliott & Fry, 1875, hs, semi-profile, lith, NPG.

PH BARRAUD, tql, print, for *Men and Women of the Day*, vol IV, 1891, NPG AX5526.

DEAKIN, Alfred (1856-1919) Australian politician.

C SIR LESLIE WARD ('Spy'), tql, profile, mechanical repro, for *Vanity Fair*, 2 Sept 1908, NPG.

DEANE, Sir Henry Bargrave (1846-1919) judge.

C SIR LESLIE WARD ('Spy'), wl, w/c study, for *Vanity Fair*, 4 Aug 1898, NPG 3284.

DEANE, Sir Thomas Newenham (1828-1899) architect.

SC JOHN HUGHES, posthumous bronze bust, NGI 8097.

DEANE, William Wood (1825-1873) architect and painter.

PR UNKNOWN, hs, woodcut, BM.

DEAS, Sir George Deas, Lord (1804-1887) Scottish judge.

P JOHN GRAHAM GILBERT, 1864, tql seated in robes, Faculty of Advocates, Parliament Hall, Edinburgh.

DE BEGNIS, Claudine, née Ronzi (1800-1853) actress.

D A.E.CHALON, c1823, wl as Fatima in *Pietro L'Eremita*, w/c, NPG 1328.

PR NUMA BLANC, tql seated with roll of music, lith, BM. P.LEGRAND, after Colin, hl, stipple, Harvard Theatre Collection, Cambridge, Mass, USA. UNKNOWN, hl, lith, pub 1828, Harvard Theatre Collection.

DE BUNSEN, Sir Maurice William Ernest, Bart (1852-1932) diplomat.

PH WALTER STONEMAN, 1918, hs, NPG (NPR).

DE BURGH CANNING, Hubert George, see 15th Earl and 2nd Marquess of Clanricarde.

DE GEX, Sir John Peter (1809-1887) law reporter.

SC FRANK THEED, 1887, marble bust, Lincoln's Inn, London.

DE GREY, Thomas, see 6th Baron Walsingham.

DE KEYSER, Sir Polydore (1832-1897) lord mayor of London.

P JOHN CALLER, wl with lord mayor's chain and sceptre, Dendermonde, Belgium.

SC UNKNOWN, marble bust, Dendermonde Town Hall.

C SIR LESLIE WARD ('Spy'), wl, profile, w/c study, for *Vanity Fair*, 26 Nov 1887, NPG 2570.

DELANE, John Thadeus (1817-1879) editor of *The Times*.
P H.A.G.SCHIOTT, 1862, hs, NPG 1593.
PH ERNEST EDWARDS, wl, carte, NPG AX7538.

DE LA RAMÉE, Marie Louise (1839-1908) 'Ouida', novelist.
D VISCONDE GIORGIO DE MORAES SARMENTO, 1904, two chalk drgs: hl, NPG 1508 and Moyse's Hall Museum, Bury St Edmunds, Suffolk.
SC E.G.GILLICK, 1909, medallion monument on memorial drinking fountain, Bury St Edmunds.
PR UNKNOWN, after a crayon drg by Alice Danyell, 1878, hl seated with dogs, lith, NPG. A.WEGER sen, probably after the photograph by A.Beau, hs, profile, oval, stipple, NPG.
PH ADOLPHE BEAU, hs, profile, oval, cabinet, NPG.

DE LA RUE, Warren (1815-1889) inventor.
C SIR LESLIE WARD ('Spy'), wl, semi-profile, chromo-lith, for *Vanity Fair*, 2 Aug 1894, NPG.
PH MAULL & POLYBLANK, 1855, tql, print, NPG P120(38). ERNEST EDWARDS, wl seated, print, for *Men of Eminence*, ed L.Reeve, vol III, 1865, NPG. LOCK & WHITFIELD, hs, oval, woodburytype, for *Men of Mark*, 1882, NPG.

DE LA WARR, Sir Charles Richard Sackville-West, 6th Earl and 12th Baron (1815-1873) major-general.
PR R. & E.TAYLOR, after a photograph by John Watkins, hs, woodcut, for *Illust London News*, 17 Feb 1872, NPG.

DE MORGAN, Augustus (1806-1871) mathematician.
D Self-portrait, pen and ink, Royal Astronomical Society, London.
SC THOMAS WOOLNER, posthumous marble bust, University of London.
PR UNKNOWN, hl seated, woodcut, for *Illust London News*, 22 April 1854, NPG.
PH MAULL & POLYBLANK, wl, carte, NPG. UNKNOWN, hl, carte, NPG (Album 40).

DE MORGAN, Campbell Greig (1811-1876) surgeon.
SC J.G.LOUGH, c1875, marble bust, Middlesex Hospital, London.

DE MORGAN, William Frend (1839-1917) artist, potter and novelist.
P EVELYN DE MORGAN (his wife), 1909, after a photograph, wl with pot, William De Morgan Foundation, London.
D J.K.LAWSON, 1908, head, profile, pencil, NPG 2116.
PH MONTABONE, c1898, hs, cabinet, NPG X1348. ALVIN LANGDON COBURN, 1908, hs, photogravure, NPG AX7788. JOHN RUSSELL & SONS, hs, print, for *National Photographic Record*, vol I, NPG.

DE NAVARRO, Madame, see Mary Anderson.

DENISON, Albert, see 1st Baron Londesborough.

DENISON, Edward (1801-1854) bishop of Salisbury.
P H.W.PICKERSGILL, RA 1838, tql, Merton College, Oxford.
PR J.H.LYNCH, after F.Sandys, head, lith, BM.

DENISON, Edward (1840-1870) philanthropist.
D JOHN HAYTER, 1845, hl, with his sister Louisa, chalk, NPG 4480.

DENISON, George Anthony (1806-1896) archdeacon of Taunton.
PR D.J.POUND, after a photograph by Mayall, tql seated, stipple and line, for *The Drawing Room Portrait Gallery of Eminent Personages*, BM, NPG.
PH BASSANO, hs, carte, NPG (Album 38). H.HERING, wl, carte, NPG. HILLS & SAUNDERS, 1878, hl seated, cabinet, NPG (Somerset Worthies). LOCK & WHITFIELD, hs, oval, woodburytype, for *Men of Mark*, 1876, NPG. SAMUEL A.WALKER, hs, carte, NPG (Album 40). Two prints by unknown photographers, hl seated,

oval, and tql seated, NPG (Somerset Worthies).

DENISON, John Evelyn, see 1st Viscount Ossington.

DENMAN, George (1819-1896) judge.
P SAMUEL CARTER, Repton School, Derbys. H.T.WELLS, RA 1893, tql seated in robes, East Sussex County Council; version, Trinity College, Cambridge.
PR UNKNOWN, after a photograph by John Watkins, hs, oval, woodcut, for *Illust London News*, 16 Nov 1872, NPG.
C (Possibly H.C.SEPPING) WRIGHT ('Stuff'), hs, w/c study, for *Vanity Fair*, 19 Nov 1892, NPG 3299.
PH W.WALKER & SONS, c1860s, tql seated, carte, NPG (Album 136). LOCK & WHITFIELD, hs, woodburytype, oval, for *Men of Mark*, 1882, NPG.

DENMAN, Thomas Denman, 2nd Baron (1805-1894) lawyer.
PR UNKNOWN, after a photograph by J.Horsburgh, hs, wood engr, for *Illust London News*, 18 Aug 1894, NPG.

DENNISTOUN, James (1803-1855) Scottish antiquary.
SL AUGUSTIN EDOUART, SNPG 795.

DERBY, Edward Henry Stanley, 15th Earl of (1826-1893) statesman.
P W.E.MILLER, after George Richmond of 1864, hs, Trinity College, Cambridge. JAMES HAWKINS, after Sir Francis Grant of 1866, wl, Hughenden (NT), Bucks.
D SAMUEL LAURENCE, hs, chalk, NPG 948.
G HENRY GALES, 'The Derby Cabinet of 1867', w/c, NPG 4893.
SC SIR THOMAS BROCK, RA 1896, marble bust, Palace of Westminster, London.
PR J.BROWN, after a photograph, hs, stipple, BM, NPG. J.COCHRAN, after F.G.Hurlstone, with his mother, stipple, for *English Annual*, 1837, BM. W.HOLL, after G.Richmond, hs, stipple, one of 'Grillion's Club' series, BM. HOLL, after a photograph by Mayall, hl, stipple and line, NPG. L.LOWENSTAM, hl, etch, BM. D.J.POUND, after a photograph by Mayall, tql seated, stipple and line, presented with *Illust News of the World*, BM. G.J.STODART, after a photograph by Elliott & Fry, hl seated, profile, stipple and line, NPG. Several popular prints, NPG.
C SIR MAX BEERBOHM, c1900, cartoon, Merton College, Oxford. HARRY FURNISS, pen and ink sketch, NPG 3356. CARLO PELLEGRINI ('Ape'), wl, profile, chromo-lith, for *Vanity Fair*, 26 June 1869, NPG. 'PET', wl, chromo-lith, for *The Monetary Gazette*, 2 May 1877, NPG.
PH W. & D.DOWNEY, hs, woodburytype, for Cassell's *Cabinet Portrait Gallery*, vol II, 1891, NPG. LOCK & WHITFIELD, hs, oval, woodburytype, for *Men of Mark*, 1881, NPG. MAULL & POLYBLANK, tql seated, print, NPG AX7308. HERBERT WATKINS, hs, print, NPG AX7913. Several cartes by CALDESI, BLANFORD & CO, MAYALL, S.A.WALKER & CO, various sizes, NPG (Album 113). Several cartes, NPG.

DERBY, Frederick Arthur Stanley, 16th Earl of (1841-1908) governor-general of Canada.
SC F.W.POMEROY, 1911, marble statue, St George's Hall, Liverpool. SIR WILLIAM GOSCOMBE JOHN, bust, Preston Town Hall.
PR UNKNOWN, hs, lith, NPG.
C CARLO PELLEGRINI ('Ape'), wl, chromo-lith, for *Vanity Fair*, 24 May 1879, NPG.
PH JOHN RUSSELL & SONS, hl, print, for *National Photographic Record*, vol I, NPG. JOHN RUSSELL & SONS, hs, print, for *Our Conservative Statesmen*, vol II, NPG (Album 17).

DESBOROUGH, William Henry Grenfell, 1st Baron (1855-1945) athlete, sportsman and public servant.
P SIR A.S.COPE, 1918, hl, profile, Firle Place, E Sussex.

PR UNKNOWN, hs, oval, woodcut, in series depicting the Oxford Crew for the University Boat Race, 1877, for *Illust London News*, 24 March 1877, NPG.

C SIR LESLIE WARD ('Spy'), wl in riding dress, chromo-lith, for *Vanity Fair*, 20 Dec 1890, NPG.

PH OLIVE EDIS, tql seated, print, NPG X5213. WALTER STONEMAN, 1933, hs, NPG (NPR).

DESPARD, Charlotte, née French (1844-1939) suffragette and social worker.

P MARY EDIS, exhib 1916, hl, NPG 5007. Attrib C.M.HORSFALL, hs, NPG 4345.

PH MRS ALBERT BROOM, hl, print, NPG. JAMES JARCHE, wl speaking in Trafalgar Square, June 1933, neg, NPG (*Daily Herald*).

DEUTSCH, Emanuel Oscar Menahem (1829-1873) Semitic scholar.

D RUDOLPH LEHMANN, 1868, hs, pencil, BM.

DE VERE, Aubrey Thomas (1814-1902) poet and author.

PH JULIA MARGARET CAMERON, 1864, hs, print, NPG P18(15).

DE VILLIERS, John Henry de Villiers, 1st Baron (1842-1914) South African judge.

PR UNKNOWN, after a photograph by Gribble, hs, wood engr, NPG.

DEVON, William Reginald Courtenay, 11th Earl of (1807-1888) politician and philanthropist.

P GEORGE RICHMOND, 1874, tql, Powderham Castle, Exeter. ARCHIBALD STUART WORTLEY, RA 1889, Scottish Amicable Life Assurance Society.

SC E.B.STEPHENS, *c*1880, statue, Bedford Circus, Exeter.

PR W.HOLL, after G.Richmond, hs, stipple, one of 'Grillion's Club' series, BM.

PH UNKNOWN, (probably rightly called), wl seated, carte, NPG X8025.

DEVONPORT, Hudson Ewbanke Kearley, 1st Viscount (1856-1934) business man.

P P.A.DE LÁSZLÓ, Port of London Authority.

D FREDERICK SARGENT, 1893, wl seated, pencil, NPG 4483.

PH G.C.BERESFORD, 1903, two negs, hs and hs profile, NPG X6485-6. JOHN RUSSELL & SONS, hs, print, for *National Photographic Record*, vol II, NPG. SIR BENJAMIN STONE, two prints, both wl, NPG.

DEVONSHIRE, Spencer Compton Cavendish, 8th Duke of (1833-1908) liberal statesman.

P SIR J.E.MILLAIS, 1886, tql, Chatsworth, Derbys. SIR HUBERT VON HERKOMER, 1897, tql seated, NPG 1545.

D LADY ABERCROMBY, 1888, hs, profile, w/c, NPG 1598. S.P.HALL, pencil sketch, NPG 2335.

G L.C.DICKINSON, 'Gladstone's Cabinet of 1868', oil, NPG 5116.

SC ALFRED DRURY, statue, Western Lawns, Eastbourne. HERBERT HAMPTON, bronze statue, in peers robes, Horse Guards Avenue, Whitehall.

PR E.SCRIVEN, after J.Lucas, as a child, seated in landscape, stipple, for Miss Fairlie's *Children of the Nobility*, BM, NPG. C.A.TOMKINS, after H.T.Munns, tql, mezz, pub 1883, BM. VIOLET, DUCHESS OF RUTLAND, 1888, hs, lith, NPG. Several popular prints, NPG.

C CARLO PELLEGRINI ('Ape'), wl, profile, w/c study for *Vanity Fair*, 27 March 1869, NPG 4715. SIR LESLIE WARD ('Spy'), wl, w/c study, for *Vanity Fair*, 21 July 1888, NPG 3191. SIR LESLIE WARD ('Spy'), wl seated, chromo-lith, for *Vanity Fair*, 15 May 1902, NPG. SIR MAX BEERBOHM, drg, Lilly Library, Indiana University, Bloomington, Indiana, USA. SIR FRANCIS CARRUTHERS GOULD, two sketches, NPG 2833-4.

PH BARRAUD, tql seated, semi-profile, print, for *Men and Women of the Day*, 1888, NPG AX5404. BARRAUD, hs, profile, cabinet, NPG. BASSANO, hs, profile, print, for *Our Conservative and Unionist*

Statesmen, vol I, NPG (Album 24). LONDON STEREOSCOPIC CO, hs, profile, carte, NPG. JOHN & CHARLES WATKINS, wl, carte, NPG.

DEVONSHIRE, Sir William Cavendish, 7th Duke of (1808-1891) politician and promoter of science and industry.

P G.F.WATTS, 1883, tql seated in robes, Fitzwilliam Museum, Cambridge.

G SIR GEORGE HAYTER, 'The House of Commons, 1833', oil, NPG 54.

SC SIR WILLIAM GOSCOMBE JOHN, *c*1901, bronze seated statue, Devonshire Place, Eastbourne; related bronze, Fitzwilliam Museum.

PR W.ROFFE, after a photograph, hl seated, stipple, BM.

PH BARRAUD, hs, print, for *Men and Women of the Day*, vol II, 1889, NPG AX5445. MAULL & POLYBLANK, wl seated, carte, NPG. W.WALKER & SONS, wl, carte, NPG AX7406.

DEWAR, Sir James (1842-1923) chemist.

P SIR W.Q.ORCHARDSON, RA 1894, hl seated with chemical apparatus, Peterhouse, Cambridge; copy by EDMUND DYER, SNPG 1089. T.W.DEWAR (his nephew), 1900, hs, profile, SNPG 603. RENÉ DE L'HÔPITAL, Chemical Society, London.

G HENRY JAMYN BROOKS, 'Sir James Dewar lecturing on liquid hydrogen at the Royal Institution, 1904', oil, Royal Institution, London.

SC CERNIGLIARI MELILLI, 1906, bronze statuette, NPG 2118. G.D.MACDOUGALD, 1910, bronze bust, NPG 2119. SIR BERTRAM MACKENNAL, bronze portrait panel, Royal Institution.

PH Attrib ETHEL GLAZEBROOK, *c*1902, wl in the laboratory of the Royal Institution, print, NPG X5197. OLIVE EDIS, *c*1920?, tql seated, in the laboratory of the Royal Institution, print, NPG X5198.

DE WET, Christiaan Rudolph (1854-1922) Boer general and politician.

C 'EBN', wl, chromo-lith, for *Vanity Fair*, 31 July 1902, NPG.

DE WINTON, Sir Francis Walter (1835-1901) major-general and South African administrator.

PR UNKNOWN, after a photograph by J.Thomson, hs, wood engr, for *Illust London News*, 10 May 1890, NPG.

DE WORMS, Henry, see 1st Baron Pirbright.

DEWRANCE, Sir John (1858-1937) mechanical engineer.

PH WALTER STONEMAN, 1930, hs, NPG (NPR).

DIAMOND, Hugh Welch (1809-1886) photographer.

PR UNKNOWN, hs, woodcut, for *Richmond and Twickenham Times*, June 1886, NPG.

DIBBS, Sir George Richard (1834-1904) premier of New South Wales.

PR UNKNOWN, hs, wood engr, for *Illust London News*, 16 July 1892, NPG.

DICEY, Albert Venn (1835-1922) jurist.

P DESIRÉE LAUGÉE, RA 1873, hl seated, Trinity College, Oxford.

DICKENS, Charles John Huffam (1812-1870) novelist.

P DANIEL MACLISE, 1839, wl seated, NPG 1172. FRANCIS ALEXANDER, 1842, hl seated at desk, Boston Museum of Fine Arts, USA. AUGUSTUS EGG, 1850, hs as Sir Charles Coldstream in *Used Up*, Dickens House, London. ARY SCHEFFER, 1855-6, hl, NPG 315. W.P.FRITH, 1859, tql seated in his study, V & A; related oil sketch, The Free Library of Philadelphia, USA.

D GEORGE CRUIKSHANK, 1836-7, wl seated, pencil, V & A. SAMUEL LAURENCE, 1838, hs, chalk, NPG 5207. R.J.LANE, *c*1840, hs, profile, pencil, Royal Coll. COUNT ALFRED D'ORSAY, 1841 and 1842, two drgs, both hs, profile, chalk, Dickens House. DANIEL MACLISE, 1843, hs, profile, with hs profiles of his sister-in-law

and his wife, V & A. RUDOLPH LEHMANN, 1861, hs, pencil, BM.
M JANET BARROW, 1830, hs, Dickens House, London.
G CLARKSON STANFIELD, 1842, with Maclise, Forster and the artist in Cornwall, V & A. DANIEL MACLISE, 1844, Dickens reading *The Chimes* to his friends, pencil, V & A.
SC ANGUS FLETCHER, 1839, marble bust, Dickens House. HENRY DEXTER, 1842, bust, Dickens House. W.W.GALLIMORE, 1870, Parian ware bust, Lady Lever Art Gallery, Port Sunlight. G.G.FONTANA, 1872, marble bust, Walker Art Gallery, Liverpool.
PR H.K.BROWNE ('Phiz'), wl seated, etch, for *Court Mag.*, 1837, BM. J.C.ARMYTAGE, after M.Gillies of c1843, hs, stipple, pub 1844, NPG. T.H.MAGUIRE, after C.R.Leslie of c1846, wl seated as Captain Bobadil in Jonson's *Every Man in his Humour*, lith, BM. C.BAUGNIET, hl, lith, pub 1858, BM. Various other prints, some after photographs, BM, NPG.
C RICHARD DOYLE, two pen sketches, one with John Forster, and one with Forster and Douglas Jerrold, BM, HARRY FURNISS, several pen and ink sketches, posthumous, various sizes, NPG 3445-6, 3563-6.
PH Various prints by BEN GURNEY, MAYALL, MASON & CO, HERBERT WATKINS, JOHN & CHARLES WATKINS and others, various dates and sizes, NPG, Dickens House.

DICKENS, Sir Henry Fielding (1849-1933) lawyer; son of Charles Dickens.
C SIR LESLIE WARD ('Spy'), wl, profile, w/c study, for *Vanity Fair*, 13 May 1897, NPG 3285.
PH UNKNOWN, Dickens House, London.

DICKSEE, Sir Francis Bernard (1853-1928) painter.
P Self-portrait, 1883, hs, oval, MacDonald Collection, Aberdeen Art Gallery.
PH LOCK & WHITFIELD, hs, profile, oval, woodburytype, for *Men of Mark*, 1883, NPG. RALPH W.ROBINSON, wl seated, print, for *Members and Associates of the Royal Academy of Arts, 1891*, NPG x7361. W. & D.DOWNEY, tql, woodburytype, for Cassell's *Cabinet Portrait Gallery*, vol IV, 1893, NPG. WALTER STONEMAN, 1917, hs, NPG (NPR). UNKNOWN, hs, print, NPG.

DICKSON, Alexander (1836-1887) botanist.
PR WILLIAM HOLE, wl, etch, for *Quasi Cursores*, 1884, NPG.

DICKSON, Sir Collingwood (1817-1904) general.
P UNKNOWN, Royal Regiment of Artillery, Woolwich.

DIGBY, William (1849-1904) Anglo-Indian publicist and secretary of the National Liberal Club.
P JOHN COLIN FORBES, National Liberal Club, London.

DILKE, Sir Charles Wentworth, 1st Bart (1810-1869) commissioner for the exhibitions of 1851 and 1862.
G H.W.PHILLIPS, 'The Royal Commissioners for the Great Exhibition 1851', oil, V & A.
PR DALZIEL, after J.Scott, hs, circle, woodcut, BM.

DILKE, Sir Charles Wentworth, 2nd Bart (1843-1911) politician and author.
P H.LENTHALL, National Liberal Club, London. G.F.WATTS, 1873, hs, NPG 1827.
D E.T.REED, c1902, wl, pencil, NPG 5154. HAROLD SPEED, 1907, chalk, National Liberal Club. HAROLD SPEED, 1908, hs, chalk, NPG 5122. WILLIAM STRANG, 1908, hs, profile, pencil, NPG 3819.
SC OSCAR ROTY, 1900, bronze plaque, NPG 1883.
PR DALZIEL, hs, circle, woodcut, BM. Several popular prints, NPG.
C HARRY FURNISS, pen and ink sketch, NPG 3357. UNKNOWN, wl, semi-profile, chromo-lith, for *Vanity Fair*, 25 Nov 1871, NPG.
PH LOCK & WHITFIELD, hs, profile, oval, woodburytype, for *Men of Mark*, 1881, NPG. W. & D.DOWNEY, tql seated with his wife,

woodburytype, for Cassell's *Cabinet Portrait Gallery*, vol V, 1894, NPG. SIR BENJAMIN STONE, 1897, wl, print, NPG. LONDON STEREOSCOPIC CO, two prints, hs, cabinet, and hs, profile, carte, NPG.

DILKE, Emilia Frances Dilke, Lady, née Strong (1840-1904) philanthropist and art historian.
P PAULINE, LADY TREVELYAN and LAURA CAPEL LOFFT (afterwards Lady Trevelyan), c1864, wl seated, painting, NPG 1828a. SIR HUBERT VON HERKOMER, 1887, tql, NPG L131.
M CHARLES CAMINO, 1882, hl seated, NPG 1828.
PH W. & D.DOWNEY, tql with her husband, woodburytype, for Cassell's *Cabinet Portrait Gallery*, vol V, 1894, NPG.

DILLON, Emile Joseph (1854-1933) philologist, author and journalist.
P SIR WILLIAM ORPEN, probably RA 1916, NGI 976.
SC FLORENCIO CUAIRAN, marble bust, Municipal Gallery of Modern Art, Dublin.
C 'OWL', wl, profile, mechanical repro, for *Vanity Fair*, 5 Nov 1913, NPG.
PH JOHN RUSSELL & SONS, hs, print, for *National Photographic Record*, vol II, NPG.

DILLON, Harold Arthur Lee-Dillon, 17th Viscount (1844-1932) antiquary.
P GEORGINA BRACKENBURY, 1894, hs, NPG 2623.
D MAURICE CODNER, Society of Antiquaries, London. SIR GEORGE SCHARF, head, w/c, NPG 4834.
SC S.W.CARLINE, 1913, lead medallion, NPG 3259. UNKNOWN, head, Tower of London.
W UNKNOWN, kneeling figure, St Kenelm Church, Enstone, Oxon.
PH JOHN RUSSELL & SONS, hs, profile, print, for *National Photographic Record*, vol I, NPG. WALTER STONEMAN, hs, NPG (NPR).

DILLON, John (1851-1927) Irish politician.
D HENRY HOLIDAY, pencil sketch, NGI.
C HARRY FURNISS, 'Force No Remedy', with Parnell, chromo-lith, for *Vanity Fair*, 7 Dec 1881, NPG. CARLO PELLEGRINI ('Ape'), wl, profile, chromo-lith, for *Vanity Fair*, 7 May 1887, NPG. SIR FRANCIS CARRUTHERS GOULD, two sketches, NPG 2835 and 2872.
PH SIR BENJAMIN STONE, 1898, four wl prints, NPG.

DILLON, John Blake (1816-1866) Irish politician.
P HENRY MACMANUS, hs, NGI 547.

DIRCKS, Henry (1806-1873) civil engineer and author.
PR J.COCHRAN, after a photograph by Negretti & Zambra, hl seated, stipple, NPG.

DISRAELI, Benjamin, see 1st Earl of Beaconsfield.

DIXIE, Lady Florence Caroline, née Douglas (1857-1905) traveller.
PR A.MACLURE, tql on horseback, lith, for *Whitehall Review*, 1877, BM, NPG.
C THÉOBALD CHARTRAN ('T'), wl seated, chromo-lith, for *Vanity Fair*, 24 March 1883, NPG.

DIXON, Richard Watson (1833-1900) historian, poet and divine.
D SIR WILLIAM ROTHENSTEIN, 1897, tql seated, profile, lithographic chalk, NPG 3171.

DIXON, William Hepworth (1821-1879) historian and traveller.
PR MACLURE & MACDONALD, hs, lith, NPG. UNKNOWN, hs, semi-profile, circle, woodcut, for *The Illust Review*, 11 Sept 1873, NPG. UNKNOWN, hs, oval, stipple, NPG.
C UNKNOWN, wl, chromo-lith, for *Vanity Fair*, 27 April 1872, NPG.
PH A.CLAUDET, wl with a child, carte, NPG (Album 113). ELLIOTT &

FRY, two cartes, both hs, one in Album 40, NPG. F.JOUBERT, wl, carte, NPG (Album 113). LOCK & WHITFIELD, hs, oval, woodburytype, for *Men of Mark*, 1881, NPG.

DOBELL, Bertram (1842-1914) bookseller and man of letters.
PR UNKNOWN, after a pen drg, hl seated, process block, NPG.
PH UNKNOWN, hs, profile, photogravure, BM, NPG.

DOBELL, Sidney Thompson (1824-1874) poet and critic.
D BRITON RIVIERE, hs, pencil, NPG 2060.
PR UNKNOWN, after a photograph by C.R.Pottinger of Cheltenham, hs, woodcut, for *Illust London News*, 3 Oct 1874, NPG.

DOBSON, Henry Austin (1840-1921) poet and man of letters.
P SYLVIA GOSSE, 1908, hs, NPG 1964. FRANK BROOKS, 1911, hs, NPG 2176.
PR WILLIAM STRANG, three etchings: hl, profile; hs, profile; hl seated, profile, BM.
C A.N.FAIRFIELD, 1874, wl, profile, chalk, NPG 2208.
PH BARRAUD, hs, print, for *Men and Women of the Day*, vol IV, 1891, NPG AX5544. JOHN RUSSELL & SONS, c1897, hs, photogravure, NPG X4614. JOHN RUSSELL & SONS, hl seated, print, for *National Photographic Record*, vol I, NPG. Three snapshots by unknown photographers, one hs, two wl, NPG.

DOBSON, William Charles Thomas (1817-1898).
P Self-portrait, 1884, hs, oval, MacDonald Collection, Aberdeen Art Gallery.
PR Several woodcuts, hs, NPG.
PH LOCK & WHITFIELD, hs, oval, woodburytype, for *Men of Mark*, 1881, NPG. MAULL & POLYBLANK, wl, carte, NPG (Album 104).

DODGSON, Charles Lutwidge (1832-1898) 'Lewis Carroll', mathematician, writer and photographer.
P SIR HUBERT VON HERKOMER, posthumous, based on photographs, hs, semi-profile, Christ Church, Oxford.
C HARRY FURNISS, three pen and ink sketches: hs, profile, head, profile, and wl with Harry Furniss, NPG 2609, 3629 and 3567.
PH Possibly by REGINALD SOUTHEY, c1856, tql seated, print, NPG P7 (26). O.G.REJLANDER, 1863, tql seated, holding a photographic lens, print, Gernsheim Collection, University of Texas, USA. HILLS & SAUNDERS, hl seated, profile, print, NPG X5181. Two prints by unknown photographers, wl, and tql seated, profile, NPG P38 and P39. UNKNOWN, hl seated, in middle age, print, Dodgson family collection, Muniment Room, Guildford. SKEFFINGTON LUTWIDGE, the Dodgson family at Croft Rectory, print, NPG P32.

DODGSON, George Haydock (1811-1880) water-colour painter.
PR UNKNOWN, after a photograph by J.Waller of Whitby, hs, woodcut, for *Illust London News*, 26 June 1880, NPG.

DODS, Marcus (1834-1909) Presbyterian minister and biblical scholar.
P SIR JAMES GUTHRIE, New College, Edinburgh.
C JOHN STEVENSON RHIND, bronze medallion, SNPG 1207.
PH MACLURE & MACDONALD, tql seated, photogravure, NPG.

DODSON, John George, see 1st Baron MONK-Bretton.

DOLBY, Charlotte Helen Sainton-, see SAINTON-Dolby.

DOLLING, Robert William Radclyffe (1851-1902) divine and social reformer.
PH Two cabinets: one by W.V.AMEY, hs, and one by an unknown photographer, tql seated, NPG.

DOLMETSCH, (Eugene) Arnold (1858-1940) musician and historian of music.

D SIR WILLIAM ROTHENSTEIN, three chalk drgs, all heads, NPG 4641-2. EDMOND KAPP, 1921, hs, Barber Institute of Fine Arts, Birmingham. EDMUND KAPP, Bedales School, Hants.
PH HERBERT LAMBERT, tql seated with lute, print, NPG P108.

DON, Sir William Henry (1825-1862) actor.
PR UNKNOWN, tql seated, lith, and similar hl, woodcut, Harvard Theatre Collection, Cambridge, Mass, USA.

DONALDSON, Sir James (1831-1915) educationist, classical and patristic scholar.
P SIR GEORGE REID, University of St Andrews.

DONALDSON, Sir Stuart Alexander (1812-1867) Australian statesman.
PH CAMILLE SILVY, 1860, wl, carte, NPG (Album 2).

DORAN, John (1807-1878) writer.
PR J.A.VINTER, after a photograph by Dr Diamond, tql seated, lith, BM. J.BROWN, after a photograph by Herbert Watkins, hl seated, stipple, NPG.
C SIR LESLIE WARD ('Spy'), wl, w/c study, for *Vanity Fair*, 6 Dec 1873, NPG 1648.
PH ELLIOTT & FRY, hs, profile, carte, NPG.

DORRIEN, Sir Horace Lockwood Smith-, see SMITH-Dorrien.

D'ORSAY, Alfred Guillaume Gabriel, Count (1801-1852) artist and man of fashion.
P SIR GEORGE HAYTER, 1839, tql, NPG 5061. JOHN WOOD, 1841, hl, profile, Hughenden (NT), Bucks.
D SIR FRANCIS GRANT, 1836, pencil study for equestrian portrait, BM. R.J.LANE, 1841, hs, profile, chalk, NPG 4540. SIR EDWIN LANDSEER, boxing with the artist, chalk, BM. SIR EDWIN LANDSEER, two pen and ink drgs, hs, profile, and on horseback, NGS.
G DANIEL MACLISE, 'The Fraserians', lith, for *Fraser's Mag*, 1835, BM.
SC WILLIAM BEHNES, RA 1843 or RA 1847, bust, Royal Coll. Self portrait, marble bust, on loan to NPG (3548).
PR SIR EDWIN LANDSEER, 1840, with Bulwer-Lytton and Lady Blessington, lith, Royal Coll. R.J.LANE, hl, profile, lith, pub 1833, NPG. F.C.LEWIS, after F.Grant, wl on horseback, mezz, BM. D.MACLISE, wl, lith, for Maginn's *Gallery of Illustrious Literary Characters*, 1873, BM, NPG. UNKNOWN, hl, lith, BM. Two liths by unknown artists, one on horseback, the other standing by a horse, NPG.
C JOHN DOYLE, three drgs, on horseback, two chalk, one pencil, BM. SIR EDWIN LANDSEER, c1832-5, wl, profile, pen and wash, NPG 4922.

DOUBLEDAY, Edward (1811-1849) entomologist, assistant in the British Museum.
PR G.H.FORD, after a medallion by Bernard Smith, 1844, hs, profile, lith, NPG. T.H.MAGUIRE, hl, lith, one of set of *Ipswich Museum Portraits*, 1851, BM, NPG.

DOUGHTY, Charles Montagu (1843-1926) poet and traveller.
P By his daughter, Downing College, Cambridge.
D ERIC HENRI KENNINGTON, 1921, head, pastel, NPG 2113.
SC THEODORE SPICER-SIMSON, bronze medallion, Golders Green Crematorium, London.
PR FRANCIS DODD, hs, drypoint, NPG.
PH Three prints, various dates, Downing College.

DOUGLAS, Sir John Sholto, see 8th Marquess of Queensbury.

DOUGLAS, William Alexander Anthony Archibald, see 11th Duke of Hamilton.

DOUGLAS, Sir William Fettes (1822–1891) artist.
P SIR GEORGE REID, 1883, hs, oval, MacDonald Collection, Aberdeen Art Gallery.
D JOHN FAED, hl with James Ballantyne and Thomas Faed, wash, SNPG 1589. W.GRAHAM BOSS, pencil, SNPG 1700.

DOUGLAS-PENNANT, Edward, see 1st Baron Penrhyn.

DOUGLAS-PENNANT, George Sholto, see 2nd Baron Penrhyn.

DOULTON, Sir Henry (1820–1897) potter.
P ELLIS ROBERTS, tql seated, Doulton & Co Ltd, London. UNKNOWN, Doulton & Co Ltd.
D FREDERICK SANDYS, 1861, hs, semi-profile, Doulton & Co Ltd.
SC GEORGE TINWORTH, terracotta bust, Doulton & Co Ltd.
PH W. & D.DOWNEY, c1890, hs, cabinet, NPG.

DOVE, Dame (Jane) Frances (1847–1942) founder of Wycombe Abbey School.
P SIR WILLIAM RICHMOND, Wycombe Abbey School, Bucks.
PH WALTER STONEMAN, 1930, hs, NPG (NPR).

DOWDEN, Edward (1843–1913) scholar and critic.
P WALTER OSBORNE, 1891, NGI 774. JOHN BUTLER YEATS, Municipal Gallery of Modern Art, Dublin.

DOWDEN, John (1840–1910) bishop of Edinburgh.
SC SIR ROBERT LORIMER, 1911, bronze memorial tablet, wl in episcopal robes, Edinburgh Cathedral.
PH UNKNOWN, tql, print, NPG (Anglican Bishops).

DOWSE, Richard (1824–1890) Irish judge.
PR UNKNOWN, after a photograph by Chancellor & Son of Dublin, hs, woodcut, for *Illust London News*, 22 March 1890, NPG.
C CARLO PELLEGRINI ('Ape'), wl, profile, chromo-lith, for *Vanity Fair*, 25 March 1871, NPG.

DOYLE, Sir Arthur Conan (1859–1930) novelist.
P H.L.GATES, 1927, hl, NPG 4115.
C SIR BERNARD PARTRIDGE, wl seated, chained to figure of Sherlock Holmes, pencil, ink and wash, for *Punch*, 12 May 1926, NPG 3668.
PH STUDIO CIGARINI, hs, print, NPG X8038. LONDON STEREOSCOPIC Co, 1900, print, Gernsheim Collection, University of Texas, Austin, USA. JOHN RUSSELL & SONS, hs, print, for *National Photographic Record*, vol I, NPG.

DOYLE, Sir Charles Hastings (1805–1883) general.
C SIR LESLIE WARD ('Spy'), wl, profile, w/c study, for *Vanity Fair*, 23 March 1878, NPG 2709.

DOYLE, Sir Francis Hastings Charles, 2nd Bart (1810–1888) poet and civil servant.
PR UNKNOWN, hs, woodcut, for *Illust London News*, 23 June 1888, NPG.
C SIR LESLIE WARD ('Spy'), wl, profile, w/c study, for *Vanity Fair*, 24 Nov 1877, NPG 2710.

DOYLE, Henry Edward (1827–1892) director of the National Gallery of Ireland.
G HENRY JAMYN BROOKS, 'Private View of the Old Masters Exhibition, Royal Academy, 1888', oil, NPG 1833.

DOYLE, Richard (1824–1883) artist.
P H.E.DOYLE (his brother), NGI 423.
PR UNKNOWN, head, woodcut, BM.
PH JOHN & CHARLES WATKINS, tql seated, carte, NPG AX7559. UNKNOWN, hs, profile, carte, NPG (Album 104).

D'OYLY CARTE, Richard, see Carte.

DRAPER, John William (1811–1882) scientist.
PH Two prints, one by NAPOLEON SARONY, 1878, the other by an unknown photographer, c1880, both hs, National Portrait Gallery, Smithsonian Institution, Washington DC, USA.

DRESCHFELD, Julius (1846–1907) physician and pathologist.
P GEORGE HARCOURT, posthumous, University of Manchester Medical School.

DREW, Sir Thomas (1838–1910) architect.
P WALTER OSBORNE, 1891, NGI 931.

DRIVER, Samuel Rolles (1846–1914) regius professor of Hebrew and canon of Christ Church, Oxford.
P BRITON RIVIÈRE, RA 1910, tql seated, Christ Church, Oxford.

DRUCE, George Claridge (1850–1932) botanist.
P P.A.DE LÁSZLÓ, Radcliffe Science Library, Oxford; copy, City Hall, Oxford.
SC FRANK LASCELLES, bronze bust, Department of Botany, Oxford University.
PH WALTER STONEMAN, 1931, hs, NPG (NPR).

DRUITT, Robert (1814–1883) medical writer.
PR R.B.PARKES, hl, mezz, BM.

DRUMMOND, Sir George Alexander (1829–1910) senator in the parliament of Canada.
P JOLIFFE WALKER, Mount Royal Club, Montreal, Canada. PIERRE TROUBETSKOY, National Gallery of Canada, Ottawa.

DRUMMOND, Henry (1851–1897) theological writer.
PR UNKNOWN, after a photograph by Lafayette, hs, woodcut, for *Illust London News*, 20 March 1897, NPG.

DRUMMOND, James (1816–1877) painter.
PH D.O.HILL & ROBERT ADAMSON, tql, print, NPG P6 (34).

DRUMMOND-HAY, Sir John Hay (1816–1893) diplomat.
PH BARRAUD, hs, photogravure, NPG.

DRURY, (Edward) Alfred (Briscoe) (1856–1944) sculptor.
D PAUL DRURY (his son), 1937, hs, profile, crayon, BM.
PH UNKNOWN, hs, print, NPG.

DRURY-LOWE, Sir Drury Curzon (1830–1908) lieutenant-general.
PH BASSANO, 1898, five negs, in uniform, various sizes, NPG X4208–12.

DUCIE, Henry George Francis Reynolds-Moreton, 2nd Earl of (1802–1853) agriculturist.
G S.BELLIN, after J.R.Herbert, 'Meeting of the Council of the Anti Corn Law League', mixed engr, pub 1850, BM, NPG.

DUCKWORTH, Sir Dyce, 1st Bart (1840–1928) physician.
PR UNKNOWN, after a photograph by Barraud, hs, woodcut, for *Illust London News*, 3 April 1886, NPG.

DUFF, Alexander (1806–1878) missionary in India.
SC JOHN HUTCHISON, plaster bust, SNPG 640.
PR JAMES FAED, after John Faed, tql seated, mezz, pub 1851, BM, NPG. UNKNOWN, wl, mezz, BM. C.H.JEENS, hs, as an old man, stipple, NPG.

DUFF, Andrew Halliday, see HALLIDAY.

DUFF, Sir Mountstuart Elphinstone Grant-, see GRANT Duff.

DUFF, Sir Robert William (1835–1895) governor of New South Wales.
PR UNKNOWN, cutting from *Illust London News*, 1893, BM.
C UNKNOWN, wl, profile, chromo-lith, for *Vanity Fair*, 16 June 1883, NPG.

DUFF-GORDON, Lady Lucy, née Austin (1821-1869) writer.

PR C.H.JEENS, hs, profile, stipple, for her *Last Letters from Egypt*, 1875, BM, NPG.

DUFFERIN and AVA, Frederick Temple Hamilton-Temple Blackwood, 1st Marquess of (1826-1902) diplomat and administrator.

P G.F.WATTS, 1881, hs, NPG 1315. BENJAMIN CONSTANT, *c*1893, hl, Edinburgh University. HENRIETTA RAE, RA 1901, tql seated, Royal Ulster Yacht Club, Belfast. ERNEST NORMAN, hs, profile, DoE (British Embassy, Paris).

SL UNKNOWN, NPG.

PR D.WEHRSCHMIDT, after F.Holl of *c*1885, tql, mezz, BM. KLINKICHT, after a photograph, hs, woodcut, supplement to *Illust London News*, 14 Nov 1891, BM. C.HOLL, after H.T.Wells, hs, profile, stipple, one of 'Grillion's Club' series, BM, NPG. MACLURE & MACDONALD, hs, lith, NPG. C.W.WALTON, hs, lith, BM.

C ALFRED THOMPSON ('At*η*'), wl, chromo-lith, for *Vanity Fair*, 9 April 1870, NPG.

PH LOCK & WHITFIELD, hs, profile, woodburytype, for *Men of Mark*, 1876, NPG. CAMILLE SILVY, carte, V & A. JOHN WATKINS, hs, carte, NPG (Album 99). UNKNOWN, hs, semi-profile, photogravure, NPG X7763. UNKNOWN, hl, carte, NPG (Album 38).

DUFFERIN and CLANEBOYE, Helen Selina Sheridan, Countess of (1807-1867) song-writer.

PR H.ROBINSON, after F.Stone, tql, octagon, stipple, for Finden's *Female Aristocracy of the Court of Queen Victoria*, 1849, BM, NPG. T.HODGETTS, after R.Rothwell, tql, mezz, BM. W.H.MOTE, after Miss La Monte, hl, oval, stipple, BM, NPG. UNKNOWN, hs, lith, NPG.

PH CAMILLE SILVY, *c*1860, wl, carte, NPG (Album 2).

DUFFY, Sir Charles Gavan (1816-1903) Irish and colonial politician.

P UNKNOWN, after a daguerreotype, NGI 546.

SC M.DE CARNAWSKY, 1891, terracotta plaque, NGI.

PR H.O'NEILL, after a daguerreotype, hl, oval, lith, BM. J.C.MCRAE, hs, oval, stipple, NPG.

DUFFY, Sir Frank Gavan (1852-1936) Australian judge.

P W.B.MCINNES, High Court Buildings, Melbourne, Australia.

PH LAFAYETTE, hl seated, print, NPG.

DUKE, Henry Edward, see 1st Baron Merrivale.

DU MAURIER, George Louis Palmella Busson (1834-1896) novelist and illustrator.

P Self-portrait, *c*1879-80, hs, NPG 3656. SIR JOHN EVERETT MILLAIS, 1882, hs, oval, MacDonald Collection, Aberdeen Art Gallery.

D E.J.SULLIVAN, 1891, hs, pen and ink, NPG 2899.

PR UNKNOWN, woodcut, BM.

C SIR LESLIE WARD ('Spy'), wl seated, w/c study, for *Vanity Fair*, 23 Jan 1896, NPG 2711. HARRY FURNISS, *c*1880-1910, two pen and ink sketches, NPG 3568-9.

PH W. & D.DOWNEY, hs, woodburytype, for Cassell's *Cabinet Portrait Gallery*, vol II, 1891, NPG. ELLIOTT & FRY, tql seated, cabinet, NPG.

DUNCAN, Edward (1804-1882) landscape painter.

P GEORGE LANCE, Royal Institution of South Wales Museum, Swansea.

G UNKNOWN, 'Our Artists – Past and Present', hs, one of a series of woodcuts, for *Illust London News*, 14 May 1892, NPG.

PH JOHN & CHARLES WATKINS, wl seated, carte, NPG (Album 104). UNKNOWN, hs, carte, NPG (Album 103).

DUNCAN, Francis (1836-1888) colonel.

C CARLO PELLEGRINI ('Ape'), wl, chromo-lith, for *Vanity Fair*, 19

March 1887, NPG.

DUNCAN, James Matthews (1826-1890) physician.

PR UNKNOWN, after a photograph by Bassano, hs, semi-profile, woodcut, for *Illust London News*, 13 Sept 1890, NPG.

DUNCAN, John (1805-1849) African explorer.

PR G.COOK, after C.Durham, hs in uniform, line, for *Bentley's Miscellany*, 1847, BM.

DUNCAN, Thomas (1807-1845) painter.

P Self-portrait, 1844, hl, NGS 182. ROBERT SCOTT LAUDER, SNPG 292. SIR DANIEL MACNEE, SNPG 1289.

SC PATRIC PARK, bust, Royal Scottish Academy.

PR J.SMYTH, after T.Duncan, tql seated, line, for *Art Union*, 1847, BM.

DUNCANNON, Frederick George Brabazon Ponsonby, 3rd Baron, see 6th Earl of Bessborough.

DUNDAS, Sir Richard Saunders (1802-1861) vice-admiral.

G M.ALOPHE, 'Les Défenseurs du Droit et de la Liberté de l'Europe', lith, pub 1854, BM.

DUNDONALD, Douglas Mackinnon Baillie Hamilton, 12th Earl of (1852-1935) lieutenant-general.

C SIR LESLIE WARD ('Spy'), two chromo-liths, 'A General Group', for *Vanity Fair*, 29 Nov 1900, and wl in uniform, for *Vanity Fair*, 8 May 1902, NPG.

PH UNKNOWN, wl in uniform, print, NPG.

DUNEDIN, Andrew Graham Murray, 1st Viscount (1849-1942) lord of appeal.

P SIR JAMES GUTHRIE, 1910, wl in privy counsellor's uniform, Faculty of Advocates, Parliament Hall, Edinburgh.

D ROBIN GUTHRIE, 1937, head, pen and ink, NPG 3935.

C SIR LESLIE WARD ('Spy'), wl, chromo-lith, for *Vanity Fair*, 22 Oct 1896, NPG.

PH WALTER STONEMAN, 1926 and 1936, both hs, the second in uniform, NPG (NPR).

DUNKIN, Alfred John (1812-1879) antiquary and historian.

PR PENSTONE, after a photograph by Bright, hs, mixed engr, NPG.

DUNLOP, John Boyd (1840-1921) inventor and pioneer of the pneumatic rubber tyre.

P UNKNOWN, after a photograph by Lafayette, *c*1904, hl, Dunlop Ltd, London.

PH Several prints, some with his family, Dunlop Ltd.

DUNMORE, Charles Adolphus Murray, 7th Earl of (1841-1907) explorer.

C SIR LESLIE WARD ('Spy'), wl, chromo-lith, for *Vanity Fair*, 14 Dec 1878, NPG.

DUNRAVEN and MOUNT-EARL, Windham Thomas Wyndham-Quin, 4th Earl of (1841-1926) Irish politician.

P SIR A.S.COPE, RA 1921, wl seated with ribbon of order of St Patrick, Adare Manor, Co Limerick, Eire. SIR JOHN LAVERY, exhib 1923, Municipal Gallery of Modern Art, Dublin.

PR W.ROFFE, after a photograph by Debenham, tql seated, stipple and line, pub 1893, NPG.

C CARLO PELLEGRINI ('Ape'), wl, chromo-lith, for *Vanity Fair*, 4 May 1878, NPG. SIR LESLIE WARD ('Spy'), in a group 'At Cowes', chromo-lith, for *Vanity Fair*, 6 Dec 1894, NPG.

PH SWAINE, tql, print, NPG. SWAINE, hl seated, photogravure, NPG.

DUPRÉ, August (1835-1907) chemist.

PH MAYALL & Co, hs, photogravure, Chemical Society, London.

DURAND, Sir Henry Marion (1812-1871) major-general Royal Engineers.

P UNKNOWN, tql, Royal Engineers, Gordon Barracks, Chatham, Kent.

DURAND, Sir Henry Mortimer (1850-1924) Indian civil servant and diplomat.

P DOROTHY DEANE, hl seated, DoE (British Embassy, Teheran). W.T.SMITH, 1904, hs, NPG 2128.

C SIR LESLIE WARD ('Spy'), wl, profile, chromo-lith, for *Vanity Fair*, 12 May 1904, NPG.

PH G.C.BERESFORD, 1902, hs, semi-profile, neg, NPG X6491. G.C.BERESFORD, hs, profile, print, NPG.

DURHAM, Joseph (1814-1877) sculptor.

PR UNKNOWN, hs, woodcut, for *Illust London News*, 9 June 1866, NPG.

PH LOCK & WHITFIELD, hs, profile, oval, woodburytype, for *Men of Mark*, 1878, NPG. Two cartes, both by unknown photographers, both hs, NPG (Album 103 and Album 104).

DURNFORD, Richard (1802-1895) bishop of Chichester.

SC BODLEY & GARNER, 1898, recumbent effigy, Chichester Cathedral.

PR C.A.TOMKINS, after W.W.Ouless (RA 1890), tql seated, mezz, (print exhib RA 1892), mezz, NPG.

PH LOCK & WHITFIELD, hs, oval, woodburytype, for *Men of Mark*, 1877, NPG. UNKNOWN, hl, semi-profile, cabinet, NPG X4959.

DURNFORD, Sir Walter (1847-1926) provost of King's College, Cambridge.

P SIR A.S.COPE, 1914, tql seated, Eton College, Berks. SIR WILLIAM ORPEN, 1924, King's College, Cambridge.

C SIR LESLIE WARD ('Spy'), wl, profile, chromo-lith, for *Vanity Fair*, 4 Dec 1902, NPG.

DUVEEN, Sir Joseph Joel (1843-1908) art dealer and benefactor.

P EMIL FUCHS, 1903, TATE 5999.

DYCE, William (1806-1864) painter.

D JOHN PARTRIDGE, 1825, hs, pencil, NPG 3944 (30). DAVID SCOTT, 1832, wl seated in gondola, sketching, w/c, SNPG 208. CARL CHRISTIAN VOGEL, 1837, hs, profile, Staatliche Kunstsammlungen, Dresden.

SL AUGUSTIN EDOUART, SNPG 797.

SC E.G.PAPWORTH, RA 1865, marble bust, Aberdeen Art Gallery. G.G.ADAMS, c1866, medallion, for the Art Union (1875), NPG. UNKNOWN, memorial brass portrait, wl seated, St Leonard's Church, Streatham, London.

PH JOHN & CHARLES WATKINS, wl, carte, NPG X7570.

DYCE-SOMBRE, David Ochterlony (1808-1851) eccentric.

P UNKNOWN, Government House, Allahabad, Uttar Prad, India.

DYER, Sir William Turner Thiselton, see THISELTON-Dyer.

DYKE, Sir William Hart, 7th Bart (1837-1931) politician.

P G.W.BALDREY, hl, Hughenden (NT), Bucks.

PR UNKNOWN, hs in uniform, woodcut, for *Illust London News*, 7 Dec 1867, NPG.

C CARLO PELLEGRINI ('Ape'), wl, profile, chromo-lith, for *Vanity Fair*, 4 Sept 1875, NPG.

PH MAULL & FOX, hs, print, for *Our Conservative and Unionist Statesmen*, vol II, NPG (Album 17).

DYKES, John Bacchus (1823-1876) musician and theologian.

PR UNKNOWN, hs, process block, BM.

E

EADY, Charles Swinfen, see 1st Baron Swinfen.

EARDLEY, Sir Culling Eardley, 3rd Bart (1805-1863) religious philanthropist.

PR G.SANDERS, after W.Roeting, tql, mezz, pub 1865, BM.

EARDLEY-WILMOT, Sir Sainthill, see Wilmot.

EARLE, William (1833-1885) major-general.

SC C.B.BIRCH, c1886, bronze statue, St George's Hall, Liverpool.
PR UNKNOWN, after a photograph by Mayall, hs, woodcut, for *Illust London News*, 12 Aug 1882, NPG.
PH UNKNOWN, tql seated in uniform, cabinet, NPG x6866.

EAST, Sir Alfred (1849-1913) painter and etcher.

P SIR FRANK BRANGWYN, tql seated, profile, NPG 4826. Self-portrait, 1912, tql with palette, Uffizi Gallery, Florence.
PH G.C.BERESFORD, two prints, both hs, NPG. ELLIOTT & FRY, tql seated, cabinet, NPG. SIR BENJAMIN STONE, 1899, wl, print, Birmingham Reference Library.

EASTLAKE, Elizabeth, Lady, née Rigby (1809-1893) writer.

M COKE SMYTH, hs, w/c, NPG 2533.
PR FERRIER, after a photograph by John & Charles Watkins, hs, oval, woodcut, for *The Lady's Own Paper*, 9 March 1867, NPG. UNKNOWN, hs, lith, NPG.
PH D.O.HILL & ROBERT ADAMSON, several prints, various sizes, one with Anne Rigby, NPG P6 (124, 125, 130, 134, 136 and 163).

EATON, Sir Frederick (1838-1913) secretary of the Royal Academy.

G HENRY JAMYN BROOKS, 'Private View of the Old Masters Exhibition, Royal Academy, 1888', oil, NPG 1833. REGINALD CLEAVER, 'Hanging Committee, Royal Academy, 1892', pen and ink, NPG 4245.
PH UNKNOWN, wl, carte, NPG x4960. UNKNOWN, hs, cabinet, NPG.

EATON, Herbert Francis, see 3rd Baron Cheylesmore.

EBRINGTON, Hugh Fortescue, Viscount, see 4th Earl Fortescue.

EBURY, Lord Robert Grosvenor, 1st Baron (1801-1893) politician and writer.

G SIR GEORGE HAYTER, 'The House of Commons, 1833', oil, NPG 54.
PR F.C.LEWIS, after J.Slater, hs, stipple, one of 'Grillion's Club' series, BM, NPG. D.J.POUND, after a photograph by Mayall, tql seated, line, BM, NPG.
C CARLO PELLEGRINI ('Ape'), wl, chromo-lith, for *Vanity Fair*, 15 April 1871, NPG.
PH JOHN & CHARLES WATKINS, tql seated, carte, NPG AX7428.

EDEN, Sir Ashley (1831-1887) Indian official.

P JOHN HANSON WALKER, RA 1883, The Chamber of Commerce, Calcutta.

EDEN, Robert (1804-1886) bishop of Moray, Ross and Caithness.

PR S.COUSINS, after G.Richmond, tql, mezz, BM, NPG.

EDGE, Sir John (1841-1926) Indian judge.

PH WALTER STONEMAN, 1924, hs, NPG (NPR).

EDGEWORTH, Francis Ysidro (1845-1926) economist and statistician.

PH WALTER STONEMAN, 1917, hs, NPG (NPR).

EDINBURGH, Alfred Ernest Albert, Duke of, see Alfred.

EDOUIN, Willie (1846-1908) comedian.

D UNKNOWN, wl, w/c sketch, NPG.
PR Two liths by unknown artists, both hs, Harvard Theatre Collection, Cambridge, Mass, USA.

EDWARD VII (1841-1910) Reigned 1901–1910.

P Several portraits by F.X.WINTERHALTER in the Royal Coll: 1846, wl in dress of a British sailor; 1846, with Queen Victoria; 1849, wl in Highland dress, with Prince Alfred; 1852, hs; 1859, hl in uniform as colonel in the Guards; 1864, tql in Hussar's uniform. SIR JOHN WATSON GORDON, RA 1862, wl, Examination Schools, Oxford. LOUIS DESANGES, 1877, wl in masonic regalia, United Grand Lodge of England. FRANK HOLL, 1884, wl, Middle Temple, London. FRANK HOLL, 1887, wl in uniform, Trinity House, London. ARCHIBALD STUART-WORTLEY, c1893, hl in evening dress with insignia of Garter and Bath, (cut down from a wl portrait), Carlton Club, London. LUKE FILDES, RA 1902, wl in coronation robes, Royal Coll; replica, NPG 1691. SIR JOHN GILBERT, c1902, wl with Queen Alexandra, Royal Coll. LUKE FILDES, 1905, hs with Garter ribbon and star, Royal College of Physicians, London. HAROLD SPEED, c1905, wl in Garter robes, Belfast Corporation. COLIN FORBES, c1906, wl, Canadian Houses of Parliament, Ottawa, Canada. SIR A.S.COPE, 1907, hl, semi-profile, in Garter robes, Broadlands, Hants. PHILIP TENNYSON COLE, RA 1908, wl, Russell-Cotes Art Gallery and Museum, Bournemouth. SIR E.J.POYNTER, 1909, wl seated in robes, Royal Academy, London. LAURITS TUXEN, 1909, wl in uniform, on board ship, Det National historiske Museum Paa Frederiksborg, Hillerod, Denmark. HENRY WEIGALL, Wellington College, Berks.
D WILHELM HENSEL, wl seated as a baby, Hensel Albums, National Gallery, Berlin. E.M.WARD, 1857, hs, profile, pencil, Royal Coll. GEORGE RICHMOND, 1858, hs, pastel, NPG 5217. G.F.WATTS, c1874, head, chalk, NPG 3983. FRED ROE, 1905–6, head, pencil, NPG 4367. MRS M.A.BARNETT, 1908, hs, w/c, NPG 3967. JOHN SINGER SARGENT, 1910, hs, profile, on his deathbed, charcoal, Royal Coll.
M SIR W.C.ROSS, 1846, hs, oval, Royal Coll.
G There are various groups depicting royal occasions in the Royal Coll. SIR GEORGE HAYTER, 'The Christening of the Prince of Wales in St George's Chapel, 1842', oil, Royal Coll. SIR FRANCIS GRANT, with Queen Victoria and the Princess Royal, oil, 1842, Royal Coll. SIR EDWIN LANDSEER, with Queen Victoria and the Princess Royal, oil, 1842, Royal Coll. F.X.WINTERHALTER, with the Royal Family, oil, 1846, Royal Coll. SIR EDWIN LANDSEER, 'The Queen Sketching at Loch Laggan with the Prince of Wales and the Princess Royal', oil, 1847, Royal Coll. W.P.FRITH, 'The Marriage of the Prince of Wales, 1863', oil, Royal Coll. J.C.HORSLEY, 'Queen Victoria and her children', oil, 1865, (but made to look as in c1850), Royal Society of Arts, London. Several groups depicting incidents in the Indian tour of 1875, Royal Coll. HEINRICH VON ANGELI, 1876, tql with his wife and

children, Royal Coll. LAURITS TUXEN, wl seated with Queen Alexandra and Prince Albert Victor, oil, 1884, Det National historiske Museum Paa Frederiksborg. LAURITS TUXEN, 'The Royal Family at the Time of the Jubilee', oil, 1887, Royal Coll. EDOUARD DETAILLE, with the Duke of Connaught at Aldershot, oil, 1895, Royal Coll. SIR W.Q.ORCHARDSON, 'The Four Generations', oil, 1897, Royal Agricultural Society, London; oil study, NPG 4536. EDWIN AUSTIN ABBEY, 'The Coronation of King Edward VII, 1902', oil, 1904, Royal Coll.

sc MARY THORNYCROFT, 1846, marble bust, Royal Coll. M.THORNYCROFT, 1847, statuette, as Winter, Royal Coll. N.N.BURNARD, 1847, marble bust, Royal Polytechnic Society, Falmouth, Cornwall. MATTHEW NOBLE, 1868, marble bust, Gawsworth Hall, Cheshire. SIR J.E.BOEHM, c1872, bronze equestrian statuette, Royal Coll. SIR J.E.BOEHM, 1875, marble bust, Royal Coll. COUNT GLEICHEN, 1875, marble bust, Royal Coll. SIR J.E.BOEHM, c1878, equestrian statue, as colonel of the 10th Hussars, Bombay. COUNT GLEICHEN, c1885, marble bust, Walker Art Gallery, Liverpool. COUNT GLEICHEN, 1891, statue in uniform, Royal College of Music, London. SYDNEY MARCH, 1901, bronze bust, NPG 2019. SYDNEY MARCH, 1902, bust, in robes, Royal Coll. THOMAS BROCK, 1911, marble bust, Royal Coll. ALFRED DRURY, RA 1912, marble statue, University of Birmingham. PERCY BRYANT BAKER, c1913, statue, Huddersfield. SIR GEORGE FRAMPTON, c1913, marble memorial, Bolton Town Hall. SIR BERTRAM MACKENNAL, c1912–14, bronze equestrian statue, Waterloo Place, London. SIR WILLIAM GOSCOMBE JOHN, 1916, equestrian statue, Liverpool. SIR J.E.BOEHM, marble statue, at the junction of Fleet St and the Strand, London. JOHN CASSIDY, bronze bust, in uniform, Royal Coll. JOHN CASSIDY, statue on monument, in Garter robes, Whitworth Park, Manchester.

PR Numerous prints and popular prints, BM, NPG, Royal Coll.

c There are various prints and drgs. SIR MAX BEERBOHM, drgs: 1900, Princeton University Library, USA; 1906, Harvard College Library, Cambridge, Mass, USA; 1909, Fitzwilliam Museum, Cambridge; 1912, Gallery of Fine Arts, Columbus, Ohio, USA; 1921, Ashmolean Museum, Oxford. Various prints by CARLO PELLEGRINI ('Ape'), SIR LESLIE WARD ('Spy'), and others, NPG.

PH Numerous prints and negs, singly, with Queen Alexandra, and in family, royal and other groups by MRS A.BROOM, BYRNE & CO, L.CALDESI, BARON DE MEYER, E.DESMAISONS, W. & D.DOWNEY, GHÉMAR FRÈRES, GUNN & STUART, HILLS & SAUNDERS, F.JOUBERT, LAFAYETTE, MASON & CO, MAYALL, A.J.MELHUISH, RUSSELL & SONS, CAMILLE SILVY, SOUTHWELL BROS, JOHN WATKINS, G.W.WEBSTER and others, NPG, Royal Coll and Gernsheim Collection, University of Texas, Austin, USA.

EDWARD of Saxe-Weimar, Prince (1823-1902) field-marshal.

P FLORENCE MARKS, Goòdwood, W Sussex.

D JOSIAH SLATER, 1832, hl, pencil and wash, Royal Coll.

G SIR GEORGE HAYTER, 'The Christening of HRH Edward, Prince of Wales, 1842', oil, Royal Coll.

PR CARLO PELLEGRINI ('Ape'), 1872, tql, lith, NPG.

EDWARD, Thomas (1814-1886) naturalist.

D SIR GEORGE REID, hs, ink, SNPG 163; related etch by P.RAJON, 1876, BM, NPG.

EDWARDES, Sir Herbert Benjamin (1819-1868) major-general.

P HENRY MOSELEY, c1850, wl in oriental dress, NPG 1391. UNKNOWN Territorial Association Centre, Shrewsbury.

sc WILLIAM THEED, 1868, marble monument, Westminster Abbey London. J.H.FOLEY, 1870, marble bust, India Office Library and Records, London.

PR E.MORTON, after a miniature by a native artist of 1848, hs, lith India Office Library and Records. S.FREEMAN, after Morrison hs, stipple, pub 1850, NPG. C.BAUGNIET, hs in uniform, oval, lith pub 1858, NPG. C.BAUGNIET, tql in oriental dress, oval, lith, BM

PH ROSS & THOMSON of Edinburgh, c1860, two prints, tql with h wife, NPG X1370–71. H.LENTHALL, hs, carte, NPG X1369.

EDWARDS, Alfred George (1848-1937) successively bisho of St Asaph and first archbishop of Wales.

P JOHN ST HELIER LANDER, c1922, tql seated, Howell's Schoo Denbigh, Clwyd. SOLOMON J.SOLOMON, c1924, hl seated, Jesu College, Oxford. SOLOMON J.SOLOMON, National Museum Wales 549, Cardiff. SIR W.Q.ORCHARDSON, replica, Bishop Palace, St Asaph, Clwyd.

PH ROTARY PHOTO, hl, semi-profile, postcard, NPG. WALTE STONEMAN, 1925, hs, profile, NPG (NPR). UNKNOWN, hs, prin NPG (Anglican Bishops).

EDWARDS, Amelia Ann Blanford (1831-1892) noveli and egyptologist.

D UNKNOWN, hs, pastel, Somerville College, Oxford.

sc PERCIVAL BALL, 1873, marble bust, NPG 929.

PR A.WEGER, after a photograph, tql, stipple, NPG.

PH F.R.WINDOW, tql, carte, NPG.

EDWARDS, Edwin (1823-1879) painter and etcher.

P HENRI FANTIN-LATOUR, 1875, tql seated with his wife, TATE 195

D C.S.KEENE, four sketches, TATE 4372.

PR C.S.KEENE, two etchings, wl seated in garden, reading, and w seated at an easel, painting, BM.

EDWARDS, John Passmore (1823-1911) newspaper edito and philanthropist.

P G.F.WATTS, 1894, hs, NPG 3958.

sc SIR GEORGE FRAMPTON, c1898, bronze bust, South London A Gallery.

c CARLO PELLEGRINI ('Ape'), wl, chromo-lith, for *Vanity Fair*, Oct 1885, NPG.

EDWARDS, Thomas Charles (1837-1900) divine.

P SIR HUBERT VON HERKOMER, 1897, University College of Wal Aberystwyth.

EGERTON, Francis, see 1st Earl of Ellesmere.

EGERTON, Sir Philip de Malpas Grey-, see GREY Egerton.

EGG, Augustus Leopold (1816-1863) subject painter.

P Self-portrait, 1858, Hospitalfield Trust, Arbroath, Scotlan JOHN PHILLIP, RA 1859, tql seated, Royal Academy, London.

D C.H.LEAR, 1845, head, profile, chalk, NPG 1456(5).

PR J.SMYTH, after W.P.Frith, hl, line, for *Art Union*, 1847, BM, NP

PH UNKNOWN, tql at easel, print, NPG X5180.

EGLINTON, Archibald William Montgomerie, 13th Ea of, and 1st Earl of Winton (1812-1861) lord lieutenant Ireland.

P SIR HENRY RAEBURN, wl as a boy, at his mother's knee, Upt House (NT), Warwicks. STEPHEN CATTERSON SMITH, Dub Castle. LAPORTE, Upton House.

sc MATTHEW NOBLE, 1865, statue, Ayr, Scotland. PATRICK Ma DOWELL, 1866, statue, St Stephen's Green, Dublin.

PR E.BURTON, after J.G.Gilbert, wl in uniform, mezz, pub 1850, B

PH CAMILLE SILVY, 1861, wl, carte, NPG AX7444.

ELGAR, Sir Edward William, Bart (1857-1934) compos

P SIR PHILIP BURNE-JONES, c1913, tql, profile, Guildh

Worcester.

D WILLIAM STRANG, 1911, hs, profile, chalk, Royal Coll. EDMOND KAPP, 1913 and 1914, two studies, conducting, Barber Institute of Fine Arts, Birmingham. SIR WILLIAM ROTHENSTEIN, 1917, head, chalk, NPG 3868. SIR W.ROTHENSTEIN, 1919, hs, chalk, City Museum and Art Gallery, Birmingham.

SC PERCIVAL HEDLEY, 1927, bronze bust, NPG 2219.

PH E.T.HOLDING, c1905, two photogravures, hs, and hs, profile, NPG. HERBERT LAMBERT, hs, semi-profile, photogravure, for *Modern British Composers*, 1923, NPG AX7741. HERBERT LAMBERT, 1933, hl, profile, seated at desk, print, NPG P107. DR GRINDROD, hs, print, NPG. ROTARY CO, tql seated, postcard, NPG. UNKNOWN, hs, semi-profile, postcard, NPG.

ELGIN, James Bruce, 8th Earl of (1811-1863) governor general of India.

P SIR FRANCIS GRANT, RA 1862, wl, Dunfermline Town Hall.

SC WILLIAM BEHNES, 1861, marble bust, Federal Government of Canada, on loan to Lord Elgin Hotel, Ottawa, Ontario, Canada. J.B.PHILIP, 1868, medallion on monument, with four bas-reliefs, Calcutta Cathedral, engr as a woodcut for *Illust London News*, 4 Dec 1869, NPG.

PR C.MAYER, hl, line, for *Almanach de Gotha*, 1861, BM. T.FAIRLAND, after J.R.Swinton, hs, tinted lith, BM. W.HOLL, after G.Richmond, hs, stipple, one of 'Grillion's Club' series, BM, NPG. D.J.POUND, after a photograph by John Watkins, tql seated, stipple and line, presented with *Illust News of the World*, NPG. JOHN SARTAIN, after a photograph by Faris, hs, process engr, NPG.

PH Three cartes by Disderi: wl, NPG (Album 102); wl with his son, NPG (Album 113); wl seated, NPG.

ELGIN, Victor Alexander Bruce, 9th Earl of (1849-1917) statesman and Viceroy of India.

P CHARLES MARTIN HARDIE, 1899, hs, SNPG 871.

PR F.SARGENT, hs, etch, NPG.

C SIR LESLIE WARD ('Spy'), wl, chromo-lith, for *Vanity Fair*, 27 April 1905, NPG.

ELIAS, Ney (1844-1897) explorer and diplomat.

PR UNKNOWN, after a photograph by Maull & Fox, hs, wood engr, for *Illust London News*, 12 June 1897, NPG.

PH CAMILLE SILVY, 1860, wl, print, NPG (Album 2).

ELIOT, George, see Mary Ann Cross.

ELLENBOROUGH, Charles Edmund Law, 3rd Baron (1820-1890) soldier.

C SIR LESLIE WARD ('Spy'), wl, profile, w/c study, for *Vanity Fair*, 16 Sept 1886, NPG 3286.

ELLENBOROUGH, Jane Elizabeth, née Digby, Countess of (1807-1881) famous beauty.

P JOSEPH STIELER, 1831, hs, semi-profile, Schloss Nymphenburg, Munich.

D SIR GEORGE HAYTER, c1825, hl, pencil and w/c, study for a miniature, NPG 883(10).

PR I.W.SLATER, after J.Slater, head, lith, BM. UNKNOWN, tql seated, stipple, BM. T.WRIGHT, after a miniature by H.Collen (RA 1829), hs, oval, stipple, NPG. Various prints, BM, NPG.

ELLESMERE, Francis Egerton, 1st Earl of (1800-1857) statesman.

M ROBERT THORBURN, SNPG 1299.

G THOMAS PHILLIPS, with his two sisters, Lady Charlotte and Lady Elizabeth, oil, 1806, Dunrobin Castle, Highland region, Scotland. S.COUSINS, after E.Landseer, 'Earl of Ellesmere and Family', mezz, pub 1840, BM. E.M.WARD, 'The Queen Investing Napoleon III with the Order of the Garter', oil, 1855, Royal Coll.

D

SC MATTHEW NOBLE, 1858, marble bust, NPG 2203. MATTHEW NOBLE, 1860, marble recumbent effigy, St Mark's Church, Worsley, Greater Manchester.

PR D.MACLISE, wl seated, lith, for *Fraser's Mag*, 1835, NPG; related drg, V & A. H.COUSINS, after J.Bostock, tql, mezz, pub 1837, BM. F.HOLL, after G.Richmond of 1852, hs, lith, NPG. F.C.LEWIS, after J.Slater, hs, stipple, one of 'Grillion's Club' series, BM, NPG. J.STEPHENSON, after O.de Manara, hs, line, NPG. F.W.WILKIN, hs, lith, BM.

ELLICOTT, Charles John (1819-1905) bishop of Gloucester.

PR CASSELL, PETTER & GALPIN, after a photograph by London Stereoscopic Co, hs, lith, NPG. UNKNOWN, tql seated, stipple and line, NPG.

C SIR LESLIE WARD ('Spy'), wl, profile, chromo-lith, for *Vanity Fair*, 18 July 1885, NPG.

PH BARRAUD, tql seated, print, for *Men and Women of the Day*, vol IV, 1891, NPG AX5512. BASSANO, c1898, two negs, NPG X4816-17. JOHN BEATTIE, hl seated, carte, NPG AX7461. LONDON STEREOSCOPIC CO, two hl prints, NPG. Attrib MAULL & POLYBLANK, tql seated, print, NPG AX7317.

ELLIOT, Gilbert John Murray Kynynmond, see 4th Earl of Minto.

ELLIOT, Sir Henry George (1817-1907) diplomat.

PR UNKNOWN, 'The Eastern Question: The Conference at the Admiralty, Constantinople', woodcut, for *Illust London News*, 6 Jan 1877, NPG.

C SIR LESLIE WARD ('Spy'), wl, profile, chromo-lith, for *Vanity Fair*, 17 March 1877, NPG.

ELLIS, Alexander John (1814-1890) philologist and mathematician.

PH NAUDIN & CO, tql seated, carte, NPG.

ELLIS, Frederick Startridge (1830-1901) bookseller and author.

PH WINDOW & GROVE, 1895-96, hs, carte, NPG X3679.

ELLIS, Henry Havelock (1859-1939) pioneer in the scientific study of sex; writer and critic.

P HENRY BISHOP, 1924-25, hs, semi-profile, Royal College of Physicians, London. EDMOND KAPP, 1937, hs, sketch, NPG 5242. H.CHANNING STEPHENS, hs, Royal College of Physicians.

D BERNARD SLEIGH, 1931, hs, City Museum and Art Gallery, Birmingham. SIR WILLIAM ROTHENSTEIN, 1931, hs, profile, chalk, NPG 3177.

SC A.G.WALKER, RA 1912, bronze bust, Ipswich Museum. UNKNOWN, bust, National Book League, London.

PH HOWARD COSTER, 1934, seven negs, hs, hl, and hs, profile, NPG X11563-69. HOWARD COSTER, 1934, hs, print, NPG AX3488.

ELLIS, Robert Leslie (1817-1859) scientist.

D T.C.WAGEMAN, 1844, w/c, Trinity College, Cambridge. SAMUEL LAURENCE, 1849, hs, crayon, Trinity College.

SC THOMAS WOOLNER, 1867, marble bust, Trinity College.

ELLIS, Robinson (1834-1913) classical scholar.

P G.P.JACOMB-HOOD, 1889, tql seated, Trinity College, Oxford.

SC A.BROADBENT, RA 1918, bronze bust, Bodleian Library, Oxford.

C SIR MAX BEERBOHM, c1893, Merton College, Oxford. SIR LESLIE WARD ('Spy'), wl, profile, chromo-lith, for *Vanity Fair*, 24 May 1894, NPG.

ELMORE, Alfred (1815-1881) painter.

G HENRY NELSON O'NEIL, 'The Billiard Room of the Garrick Club', oil, 1869, Garrick Club, London.

PR C.BAUGNIET, hs, lith, pub 1857, BM.

PH CALDESI, BLANFORD & CO, wl at easel, carte, NPG (Album 104).

LOCK & WHITFIELD, hs, oval, woodburytype, for *Men of Mark*, 1881, NPG. MAULL & POLYBLANK, wl, carte, NPG AX7573.

ELPHINSTONE, Sir Howard Crawfurd (1829-1890) major-general.

P HERMANN SCHMEICHEN, Royal Engineers Headquarters, Aldershot, Hants.

PR UNKNOWN, after a photograph by Reichard and Lindner of Berlin, hs in uniform, wood engr, for *Illust London News*, 22 March 1890, NPG.

ELPHINSTONE, John Elphinstone, 13th Baron (1807-1860) governor of Bombay.

D UNKNOWN, tql, w/c, SNPG 1974.

SC J.H.FOLEY, 1864, statue, Bombay. MATTHEW NOBLE, recumbent figure in Bath robes, on monument, St Peter's Church, Limpsfield, Surrey.

PR A.D'ORSAY, hl, profile, lith, BM, NPG.

ELTON, Charles Isaac (1839-1900) lawyer and antiquary.

C SIR LESLIE WARD ('Spy'), wl, profile, chromo-lith, for *Vanity Fair*, 6 Aug 1887, NPG.

ELVEY, Sir George Job (1816-1893) organist and composer.

PH LOCK & WHITFIELD, hs, oval, woodburytype, for *Men of Mark*, 1882, NPG.

ELWES, Henry John (1846-1922) traveller, botanist and entomologist.

PH MAULL & FOX, hs, carte, Royal Botanic Gardens, Kew. UNKNOWN, hl seated, as an older man, neg, Royal Botanic Gardens.

EMERY, Samuel Anderson (1817-1881) actor.

PR Several theatrical prints, Harvard Theatre Collection, Cambridge, Mass, USA. G.GREATBACH, after a daguerreotype by Mayall, wl as Robin Roughhead in *Fortune's Frolics*, stipple and line, for Tallis's *Drawing Room Table Book*, BM, NPG.

PH ADOLPHE BEAU, two cartes, both in character, wl and tql seated, NPG. UNKNOWN, hs, carte, NPG.

EMLY, William Monsell, Baron (1812-1894) politician.

PR R.TAYLOR, after a photograph by London Stereoscopic Co, hs, woodcut, for *Illust London News*, 11 Feb 1871, NPG.

C 'FAUSTIN', wl, chromo-lith, a 'Figaro Cartoon', NPG. CARLO PELLEGRINI ('Ape'), wl, semi-profile, chromo-lith, for *Vanity Fair*, 11 Feb 1871, NPG.

EMMOTT, Alfred Emmott, 1st Baron (1858-1926) politician and cotton spinner.

C 'WHO', wl, Hentschel-Colourtype, for *Vanity Fair*, 19 Oct 1910, NPG.

EPPS, John (1805-1869) homeopathic physician.

PR W.B.SCOTT, hs, oval, etch, BM.

ERICHSEN, Sir John Eric (1818-1896) surgeon.

SC SIR WILLIAM HAMO THORNYCROFT, RA 1883, marble bust, University College, London; replica, Royal College of Surgeons, London.

PR C.BAUGNIET, tql, lith, 1853, BM.

PH CLAUDET STUDIO, 1880, hs, profile, cabinet, NPG.

ERNLE, Rowland Edmund Prothero, 1st Baron (1851-1937) administrator, author and minister of agriculture.

PH WALTER STONEMAN, 1920 and 1931, both hs, NPG (NPR).

ESHER, Reginald Baliol Brett, 2nd Viscount (1852-1930) government official.

D WILLIAM STRANG, 1907, hs, chalk, Royal Coll.

PH WALTER STONEMAN, 1923, hs, NPG (NPR).

ESHER, Sir William Baliol Brett, 1st Viscount (1815-1899) judge.

P UNKNOWN, Gonville and Caius College, Cambridge.

SC UNKNOWN, recumbent effigy on monument, Esher Family Vault, Esher Churchyard, Surrey.

PH LOCK & WHITFIELD, hs, oval, woodburytype, for *Men of Mark*, 1877, NPG. UNKNOWN, hs, carte, NPG (Album 38).

ESTCOURT, James Bucknall Bucknall (1802-1855) major-general.

PH ROGER FENTON, tql in uniform, print, NPG P141.

ESTCOURT, Thomas Henry Sutton Sotheron (1801-1876) statesman.

G JOHN PHILLIP, 'The House of Commons, 1860', oil, Palace of Westminster, London.

PR UNKNOWN, after a photograph by John Watkins, hs, oval, woodcut, for *Illust London News*, 27 March 1858, NPG. UNKNOWN, 1863, hl, mezz, NPG.

ETTRICK, Sir Francis Napier, 1st Baron, see 10th Baron Napier.

EUAN-SMITH, Sir Charles Bean (1842-1910) soldier and diplomatist.

PR UNKNOWN, hs, wood engr, for *Illust London News*, 12 Jan 1889, NPG.

EVANS, Sir Arthur John (1851-1941) archaeologist.

P SIR W.B.RICHMOND, RA 1907, tql in the ruins of the palace at Knossos with some of the excavated finds, Ashmolean Museum, Oxford.

D FRANCIS DODD, 1935, tql seated, pencil, NPG 3540. ROBIN GUTHRIE, 1937, crayon, Ashmolean Museum.

SC DAVID EVANS, 1936, marble bust, Ashmolean Museum. UNKNOWN, bronze bust, Knossos, Crete.

EVANS, Sir (Evan) Vincent (1851-1934) journalist.

P WILLIAM OLIVER, 1892, hs, National Museum of Wales 492, Cardiff.

SC SIR WILLIAM GOSCOMBE JOHN, c1910, bust, National Library of Wales, Aberystwyth.

PH WALTER STONEMAN, 1923, hs, NPG (NPR).

EVANS, Frederick Henry (1852-1943) photographer.

PH E.O.HOPPÉ, hs, profile, print, International Museum of Photography, George Eastman House, Rochester, NY, USA. UNKNOWN, hs, print, Royal Photographic Society, Bath.

EVANS, John (1823-1908) antiquary; trustee of the British Museum.

P SIR A.S.COPE, RA 1900, tql seated, Royal Society, London. JOHN COLLIER, 1905, Shire Hall, Hertford.

SC J.H.PINCHES, 1887, copper medal, NPG 5006. SIR WILLIAM RICHMOND, marble relief, St Lawrence the Martyr Church, Abbots Langley, Herts.

PR SIR HUBERT VON HERKOMER, head, monotype, Somerville College, Oxford.

EVANS, John (1840-1897) 'Eglwysbach'; Welsh Wesleyan divine.

P UNKNOWN, hl, National Museum of Wales 390, Cardiff.

EVANS, Mary Ann, see Cross.

EVANS, Sir Samuel Thomas (1859-1918) judge and politician.

P CHRISTOPHER WILLIAMS, wl seated in robes, Middle Temple, London.

D C.P.HAWKES, hs, profile, ink and wash, NPG 3991.

SC GEORGE FRAMPTON, 1921, marble bust, DoE (Law Courts, London).

c Sir Leslie Ward ('Spy'), wl, profile, mechanical repro, for *Vanity Fair*, 12 Feb 1908, NPG.

EVE, Sir Harry Trelawney (1856-1940) judge.
p Edward Clegg Wilkinson, tql seated, Exeter College, Oxford.
PH Walter Stoneman, 1930, hs, NPG (NPR).

EVERETT, Joseph David (1831-1904) scientist.
p W.R.Symonds, *c*1898, Queen's College, Belfast.

EVERSLEY, George John Shaw-Lefevre, Baron (1831-1928) statesman.
PH Unknown, hs, print, NPG.

EWING, Sir (James) Alfred (1855-1935) engineer.
p D.G.Shields, 1919, tql seated, Department of Engineering, University of Cambridge. Henry Lintott, 1929, tql seated, Edinburgh University.
PH Walter Stoneman, 1931, hs, NPG (NPR).

EYRE, Edward John (1815-1901) governor of Jamaica.
PR F.Joubert, hs, line, pub 1865, NPG. J.Brown, after a photograph by H.Hering, hs, stipple, pub 1867, NPG. Unknown, hs, woodcut, for *Illust London News*, 6 April 1867, NPG. C.A.Tomkins, after C.Mercier, hl, mezz, pub 1868, BM, NPG.
PH Julia Margaret Cameron, hs, print, NPG.

EYRE, Sir Vincent (1811-1881) general.
PR L.Dickinson, hl, lith, BM, NPG. Unknown, after a photograph, hs in uniform, woodcut, for *Illust London News*, 17 Oct 1857, NPG.

F

FABER, Frederick William (1814-1863) superior of the London Oratory.
P J.L.LOMAS, exhib 1868, hs, Brompton Oratory, London.
PR J.BROWN, hs, stipple, NPG.

FAED, James (1856-1920) artist.
P Self-portrait, SNPG 1590.

FAED, John (1819-1902) artist.
D THOMAS FAED (his brother), pencil drg of a bust, Carnegie Library, Stranraer, Scotland.
M Self-portrait, hs, oval, wash, Carnegie Library.

FAED, Thomas (1826-1900) artist.
P JOHN BALLANTYNE, SNPG 962. SIR WILLIAM FETTES DOUGLAS, head, profile, NPG 4840. SIR WILLIAM FETTES DOUGLAS, hl, SNPG 674. JOHN PETTIE, 1884, hs, oval, MacDonald Collection, Aberdeen Art Gallery. JOHN PETTIE, Royal Academy, London.
D GEORGE FAED, 1852, pencil, SNPG 1772. JOHN FAED, wl, w/c, SNPG 1591.
G JOHN FAED, hl with John Ballantyne and Sir William Fettes Douglas, wash, SNPG 1589. G.GRENVILLE MANTON, 'Conversazione at the Royal Academy, 1891', w/c, NPG 2820.
PH ERNEST EDWARDS, wl, print, for *Men of Eminence*, ed L.Reeve, vol II, 1864, NPG. DAVID WILKIE WYNFIELD, c1860s, hs, profile, print, NPG P73. LOCK & WHITFIELD, hs, oval, woodburytype, for *Men of Mark*, 1880, NPG. RALPH W.ROBINSON, tql seated, print, for *Members and Associates of the Royal Academy of Arts, 1891*, NPG x7362. Several cartes by ELLIOTT & FRY, HAY, LUCAS and MAULL & POLYBLANK, various dates and sizes, NPG.

FAGAN, Louis Alexander (1845-1903) etcher and writer on art.
P J.S.SARGENT, 1894, Arts Club, London.

FAIRBAIRN, Andrew Martin (1838-1912) congregational divine.
PR UNKNOWN, hl seated, stipple, NPG.

FAIRHOLT, Frederick William (1814-1866) antiquary.
PR A. S., hl, etch, 1847, BM, NPG. UNKNOWN, hs, etch, 1857, NPG.

FALCONER, Hugh (1808-1865) palaeontologist and botanist.
SC JOHN BELL, 1867, bust, Madras, India. TIMOTHY BUTLER, bust, Royal Society, London. UNKNOWN, bust, Asiatic Society of Bengal, Calcutta.
PH ERNEST EDWARDS, wl seated, print, for *Men of Eminence*, ed L.Reeve, vol III, 1865, NPG.

FALKENER, Edward (1814-1896) architect.
D CARL CHRISTIAN VOGEL, 1847, hs, profile, Staatliche Kunstsammlungen, Dresden.

FANE, Francis William Henry, see 12th Earl of Westmorland.

FANE, Julian Henry Charles (1827-1870) diplomat and poet.
PR C.HOLL & F.A.ROBERTS, hs, profile, oval, stipple, pub 1871, NPG.

FANSHAWE, Sir Edward Gennys (1814-1906) admiral.
M ANTHONY STEWART, hs, aged 8, NGS 1991.

FARGUS, Frederick John (1847-1885) 'Hugh Conway';
novelist.
PR UNKNOWN, head, woodcut, BM. UNKNOWN, hs, profile, woodcut, for *Illust London News*, 30 May 1885, NPG.

FARMER, John (1835-1901) musician.
P UNKNOWN, Harrow School, Middx.
PR UNKNOWN, after a photograph, hs, process block, BM.

FARNBOROUGH, Sir Thomas Erskine May, 1st Baron (1815-1886) jurist.
SC ALBERT BRUCE JOY, 1890, marble bust, Palace of Westminster, London.
C CARLO PELLEGRINI ('Ape'), wl, w/c study, for *Vanity Fair*, 6 May 1871, NPG 2712.

FARNELL, Lewis Richard (1856-1934) rector of Exeter College, Oxford.
P JOHN ST HELIER LANDER, 1921, hs, Exeter College, Oxford.
PH WALTER STONEMAN, 1925, hs, NPG (NPR).

FARNINGHAM, Marianne, see Mary Anne Hearn.

FARR, William (1807-1883) statistician.
PR UNKNOWN, hl, lith, NPG.
PH ERNEST EDWARDS, wl seated, print, for *Men of Eminence*, ed L.Reeve, vol III, 1865, NPG

FARRAR, Frederick William (1831-1903) dean of Canterbury and author of popular moral tales.
P B.S.MARKS, 1879, Marlborough College, Wilts. H.A.OLIVIER, 1902, hl, The Deanery, Canterbury.
SC UNKNOWN, marble medallion, Canterbury Cathedral.
PR Several prints and popular prints, NPG.
C HARRY FURNISS, pen and ink sketch, NPG 3447. SIR LESLIE WARD ('Spy'), wl, profile, chromo-lith, for *Vanity Fair*, 10 Oct 1891, NPG.
PH LOCK & WHITFIELD, hs, oval, woodburytype, for *Men of Mark*, 1876, NPG. BARRAUD, tql, semi-profile, print, for *Men and Women of the Day*, vol I, 1888, NPG AX5438. WALERY, tql, print, NPG. Several cartes by ELLIOTT & FRY, HILLS & SAUNDERS and SAMUEL A.WALKER, various sizes, NPG.

FARRAR, John (1802-1884) president of the Wesleyan methodist conference.
PR UNKNOWN, hs, woodcut, for *Illust London News*, 6 Aug 1870, NPG.

FARRE, Arthur (1811-1887) obstetrician.
P SAVERIO ALTAMURA, 1862?, tql seated, oval, Royal College of Physicians, London.

FARREN, Ellen (1848-1904) 'Nellie Farren', actress.
P WALFORD GRAHAM ROBERTSON, 1902, hl, NPG 3133.
D UNKNOWN, wl in character, w/c, NPG.
PR E.MATTHEWS & SONS, hs, oval, lith, NPG. Several theatrical prints, BM, NPG, and various prints, Harvard Theatre Collection, Cambridge, Mass, USA.
PH W.WALKER & SONS, tql seated, carte, NPG. UNKNOWN, hl, carte, NPG AX7728.

FARREN, William (1825-1908) actor.
PR T.SHERRATT, after a daguerreotype by Mayall, wl with William Hoskins, as Romeo and Mercutio, stipple and line, for Tallis's

Dramatic Magazine; and two prints by unknown artists, one after a photograph by Elliott & Fry, and the other after a daguerreotype by Mayall, both hs, Harvard Theatre Collection, Cambridge, Mass, USA.

PH ELLIOTT & FRY, *c*1872, two cartes, with Amy Fawsitt and John Clayton in *School for Scandal*, NPG x4334–5. UNKNOWN, *c*1875, hs, carte, NPG AX7638. ELLIOTT & FRY, 1878, in a group entitled 'Our Boys' at the Vaudeville Theatre, carte, NPG AX7682.

FARRER, Sir Thomas Henry Farrer, 1st Baron (1819–1899) civil servant.

PR R.TAYLOR, hs, woodcut, for *Illust London News*, 15 Sept 1883, NPG.

FARWELL, Sir George (1845–1915) judge.

C F.T.DALTON ('FTD'), hl, w/c study, for *Vanity Fair*, 15 Nov 1900, NPG 3273.

FAUCIT, Helena, Lady Martin, see Martin.

FAWCETT, Henry (1833–1884) political economist.

P FORD MADOX BROWN, 1872, tql seated, profile, with his wife, NPG 1603; chalk study, Wightwick Manor (NT), W Midlands. H.S.RATHBONE, exhib 1885, Trinity Hall, Cambridge. SIR HUBERT VON HERKOMER, 1886, tql seated, Fitzwilliam Museum, Cambridge. H.VON TROSH, tql seated, Salisbury Corporation.

SC MARY GRANT, 1886, medallion on monument, Victoria Embankment, London; related plaster medallion, NPG 1086. SIR ALFRED GILBERT, *c*1887, bronze medallion, Fawcett Memorial, Westminster Abbey, London. H.R.HOPE PINKER, *c*1887, statue, Salisbury Market Place. H.R.HOPE PINKER, plaster bust, NPG 1418. GEORGE TINWORTH, 1893, terracotta statue, seated, Vauxhall Park, London.

C UNKNOWN, wl, profile, chromo-lith, for *Vanity Fair*, 21 Dec 1872, NPG.

PH Several cartes by BARRAUD & JERRARD, BASSANO, H.N.KING of Bath and H.J.WHITLOCK, and two cabinets by BASSANO, various dates and sizes, NPG. LOCK & WHITFIELD, hs, oval, woodburytype, for *Men of Mark*, 1876, NPG.

FAWCETT, Dame Millicent, née Garrett (1847–1929) leader of the women's suffrage movement.

P FORD MADOX BROWN, 1872, tql seated with her husband, NPG 1603; chalk study, Wightwick Manor (NT), W Midlands. LIONEL ELLIS, 1927, Newnham College, Cambridge. ANNIE SWYNNERTON, exhib 1930, TATE 4545.

PH W. & D.DOWNEY, tql seated, woodburytype, for Cassell's *Cabinet Portrait Gallery*, vol I, 1890, NPG. ELLIOTT & FRY, hs, carte, NPG. WALERY, tql, print, NPG. UNKNOWN, hl seated at desk, print, NPG. Various photographs, and campaign photographs, Fawcett Library, London.

FAYRER, Sir Joseph, 1st Bart (1824–1907) surgeon-general and author.

PR UNKNOWN, hs, semi-profile, wood engr, for *Illust London News*, 15 Aug 1891, NPG.

FECHTER, Charles Albert (1824–1879) actor.

P UNKNOWN, wl as Ruy Blas, Garrick Club, London.

PR R.J.LANE, hl, lith, pub 1864, BM. Several theatrical prints, BM, NPG, and numerous prints, Harvard Theatre Collection, Cambridge, Mass, USA.

PH ASHFORD BROS, wl, carte, NPG. ADOLPHE BEAU, two cartes, wl and hl seated, both in character, NPG. SARONY & Co, tql in character, carte, NPG. SOUTHWELL BROS, wl in character, carte, NPG (Album 108).

FEILD, Edward (1801?–1876) bishop of Newfoundland.

D GEORGE RICHMOND, 1859, hs, profile, chalk, Queen's College, Oxford.

FELIX, N., see Nicholas Wanostrocht.

FENN, George Manville (1831–1909) novelist.

PH LONDON STEREOSCOPIC CO, hs, profile, print, NPG.

FENN, Joseph Finch (1820–1884) honorary canon of Gloucester.

PR UNKNOWN, hl, lith, NPG.

FERENS, Thomas Robinson (1847–1930) politician and philanthropist.

P SIR FRANK DICKSEE, 1913, tql, The Guildhall, Hull.

FERGUSON, Richard Saul (1837–1900) antiquary.

P G.H.SEPHTON, 1896, hl seated, Carlisle Museum and Art Gallery.

FERGUSON, Sir Samuel (1810–1886) poet and antiquary.

P SARAH PURSER, 1888, after a photograph, tql, Royal Irish Academy, Dublin.

D SIR F.W.BURTON, 1848, hs, chalk, NGI 2583.

FERGUSSON, James (1808–1886) writer on architecture.

PR C.G., tql, lith, 1838, BM.

PH ERNEST EDWARDS, wl seated, print, for *Men of Eminence*, ed L.Reeve, vol I, 1863, NPG. MCLEAN, MELHUISH, NAPPER & Co, wl, carte, NPG (Album 113).

FERGUSSON, Sir James, 6th Bart of Kilkerran (1832–1907) governor of Bombay.

SC SIR WILLIAM GOSCOMBE JOHN, 1910, bronze statue, Wellington Square, Ayr, Scotland.

C SIR LESLIE WARD ('Spy'), wl, chromo-lith, for *Vanity Fair*, 30 April 1892, NPG.

PH BARRAUD, hs, print, for *Our Conservative and Unionist Statesmen*, vol IV, NPG (Album 21).

FERGUSSON, Sir William, Bart (1808–1877) surgeon.

P RUDOLPH LEHMANN, 1874, wl, Royal College of Surgeons, London. SIR JOHN WATSON GORDON, SNPG 565.

PR UNKNOWN, after a photograph by J. & C.Watkins, hs, profile, woodcut, for *Illust London News*, 24 Feb 1866, NPG.

C CARLO PELLEGRINI ('Ape'), wl, chromo-lith, for *Vanity Fair*, 17 Dec 1870, NPG.

PH ERNEST EDWARDS, wl, print, for *Men of Eminence*, ed L.Reeve, vol I, 1863, NPG. C.R.FITT, hs, carte, NPG. LOCK & WHITFIELD, hs, profile, oval, woodburytype, for *Men of Mark*, 1877, NPG.

FERRERS, Norman Macleod (1829–1903) Master of Caius College, Cambridge.

P JOHN COLLIER, *c*1885, Caius College, Cambridge.

D T.C.WAGEMAN, w/c drg, Trinity College, Cambridge.

FERRIER, Sir David (1843–1928) physician.

PH WALTER STONEMAN, 1917, hs, NPG (NPR).

FERRIER, James Frederick (1808–1864) philosopher.

P SIR JOHN WATSON GORDON, tql seated, University of St Andrews.

PH T.RODGER, wl seated, carte, NPG.

FESTING, Sir Francis Worgan (1833–1886) major-general.

PR UNKNOWN, after a photograph by Elliott & Fry, hs in uniform, woodcut, for *Illust London News*, 25 April 1874, NPG.

FESTING, John Wogan (1837–1902) bishop of St Albans.

PR UNKNOWN, hs, lith, NPG.

PH UNKNOWN, two prints, hs and hl, NPG (Anglican Bishops).

FIELD, Sir (Arthur) Mostyn (1855–1950) admiral.

PH UNKNOWN, hs, print, Royal Society, London.

FIELD, Edwin Wilkins (1804–1871) law reformer and amateur artist.

SC THOMAS BROCK, 1875, plaster bust, Dr Williams's Library,

London. THOMAS WOOLNER, 1877, marble statue, DoE (Law Courts, London).
PR C.G.LEWIS, after Sir J.Watson Gordon of 1858, tql, mezz, NPG.

FIELD, William Ventris Field, Baron (1813-1907) judge.
PR UNKNOWN, after a photograph by Charles Watkins, hs, woodcut, for *Illust London News*, 20 Feb 1875, NPG.
C SIR LESLIE WARD ('Spy'), tql, w/c study, for *Vanity Fair*, 30 April 1887, NPG 2713.

FILDES, Sir (Samuel) Luke (1843/4-1927) painter.
P Self-portrait, 1883, hs, oval, MacDonald Collection, Aberdeen Art Gallery. P.A.DE LÁSZLÓ, 1914, hs, NPG 4960. Self-portrait, 1918, hl, Royal Academy, London.
G W.H.BARTLETT, 'Saturday Night at the Savage Club', oil, Savage Club, London.
C HARRY FURNISS, pen and ink sketch, NPG 3570. SIR LESLIE WARD ('Spy'), wl with palette, chromo-lith, for *Vanity Fair*, 24 Dec 1892, NPG.
PH LONDON STEREOSCOPIC CO, hs, as a young man, carte, NPG X11851. FREDERICK HOLLYER, 1884, print, V &A. RALPH W.ROBINSON, wl seated in studio, print, for *Members and Associates of the Royal Academy of Arts, 1891*, NPG X7363. W. & D.DOWNEY, hl, woodburytype, for Cassell's *Cabinet Portrait Gallery*, vol V, 1894, NPG. W. & D.DOWNEY, hs, cabinet, NPG X11852.

FINCH, Francis Oliver (1802-1862) water-colour painter.
PR A.ROFFE, hs, semi-profile, stipple, NPG.

FINCH-HATTON, George, see 11th Earl of Winchilsea.

FINDLAY, Sir George (1829-1893) railway manager.
P SIR HUBERT VON HERKOMER, 1889, hl, Museum of British Transport, York.
C SIR LESLIE WARD ('Spy'), wl, chromo-lith, for *Vanity Fair*, 29 Oct 1892, NPG.

FINLAY, Robert Bannatyne Finlay, 1st Viscount (1842-1929) lord chancellor.
P SIR HUBERT VON HERKOMER, 1908, hl seated, Edinburgh University. GEORGE FIDDES WATT, 1917, tql in lord chancellor's robes, Middle Temple, London. ANTOON VAN WELIE, c1925, Edinburgh University.
PR EDMOND KAPP, 1924, coloured lith, for the *Law Journal*, 21 March 1925, V &A. C.W.SHERBORN, after H.T.Wells, hs, etch, BM.
C SIR FRANCIS CARRUTHERS GOULD, sketch, NPG 2836. CARLO PELLEGRINI ('Ape'), wl, profile, chromo-lith, for *Vanity Fair*, 15 Dec 1888, NPG.
PH G.FERRARD, hl, cabinet, NPG. SIR BENJAMIN STONE, 1897, wl, print, NPG. WALTER STONEMAN, hs, NPG (NPR).

FINNIE, John (1829-1907) artist.
PH E.R.DIBDIN, hs, photogravure, BM (Engr Ports Coll).

FIRTH, Sir Charles Harding (1857-1936) historian.
D IRENE BURCH, hs, chalk, Oriel College, Oxford.
SC UNKNOWN, relief stone head over an alcove, Edgar Allen Library, University of Sheffield.
PH UNKNOWN, tql seated, print, NPG.

FIRTH, Mark (1819-1880) steel manufacturer and philanthropist.
SC ALBERT BRUCE JOY, RA 1879, bust, University of Sheffield.
PR UNKNOWN, hs, woodcut, for *Illust London News*, 28 Aug 1875, NPG.

FISHER, John Arbuthnot Fisher, 1st Baron (1841-1920) admiral.
P SIR A.S.COPE, 1902, tql in uniform, NMM, Greenwich. SIR

HUBERT VON HERKOMER, 1911, tql in uniform, NPG 2805. AUGUSTUS JOHN, c1916, tql in uniform, Lennoxlove, Lothian region, Scotland. AUGUSTUS JOHN, hs in uniform, Leicester Museum and Art Gallery. WILLIAM STRANG, hs in uniform, Glasgow Museum and Art Gallery.
D WILLIAM STRANG, 1908, hl, chalk, Royal Coll. FRANCIS DODD, charcoal drg, Manchester City Art Gallery.
SC SIR JACOB EPSTEIN, 1915, bronze head, study, IWM, London; 1916, related bronze bust, Lennoxlove.
PR WILLIAM NICHOLSON, c1905, hl in uniform, coloured woodcut, NPG. FRANCIS DODD, 1916, hl, etch, NPG 3080.
C SIR LESLIE WARD ('Spy'), wl in uniform, chromo-lith, for *Vanity Fair*, 6 Nov 1902, NPG.
PH G.C.BERESFORD, 1905, three negs, hs and hs, profile, NPG X6498-6500. G.C.BERESFORD, three prints, all hs, one in uniform, NPG.

FITZALAN of Derwent, Edmund Bernard Fitzalan-Howard, 1st Viscount (1855-1947) statesman.
P SIR OSWALD BIRLEY, 1932, tql seated in Garter robes, Arundel Castle, W Sussex.
PH WALTER STONEMAN, 1921 and 1943, hs and hl, NPG (NPR).

FITZALAN-HOWARD, Henry, see 15th Duke of Norfolk.

FITZGERALD, Edward (1809-1883) translator and poet.
D JAMES SPEDDING, c1830, hl seated, pencil, Fitzwilliam Museum, Cambridge.
M EVA, LADY RIVETT-CARNAC, after a photograph by Cade & Whiten of 1873, hl, NPG 1342.
PR UNKNOWN, after the photograph by Cade & Whiten on which NPG 1342 is also based, hs, stipple, NPG. UNKNOWN, after a slightly different photograph by Cade & Whiten of 1873, hs, stipple, pub 1895, NPG.
PH CADE & WHITEN, 1873, the photograph on which the engr pub 1895 is based, hs, print, Trinity College, Cambridge.

FITZGERALD, George Francis (1851-1901) professor and scientist.
PR UNKNOWN, Engineering School, Trinity College, Dublin.

FITZGERALD, John David Fitzgerald, Lord (1816-1889) Irish judge.
PR UNKNOWN, hs, wood engr, for *Illust London News*, 26 Oct 1889, NPG.

FITZGERALD, Sir William Robert Seymour Vesey (1818-1885) governor of Bombay.
PR UNKNOWN, hs, woodcut, for *Illust London News*, 2 Feb 1867, NPG.
C CARLO PELLEGRINI ('Ape'), wl, chromo-lith, for *Vanity Fair*, 2 May 1874, NPG.

FITZGIBBON, Gerald (1837-1909) lord justice of appeal in Ireland.
P MISS HARRISON, University Club, Dublin. SIR WILLIAM ORPEN, in robes, King's Inns, Dublin. WALTER OSBORNE, 1894, NGI 953.
SC ALBERT BRUCE JOY, statue, St Patrick's Cathedral, Dublin.

FITZMAURICE, Edmond George Petty-Fitzmaurice, Baron (1846-1935) statesman and historian.
C SIR LESLIE WARD ('Spy'), two portraits: wl, profile, chromo-lith, for *Vanity Fair*, 16 Feb 1878, NPG, and wl, mechanical repro, for *Vanity Fair*, 14 June 1906, NPG.

FITZMAURICE-KELLY, James, see Kelly.

FITZPATRICK, Sir Dennis (1837-1920) lieutenant-governor of the Punjab.
P J.D.COSTA, 1891, hs, NPG 4038.

FITZPATRICK, William John (1830-1895) Irish biographer.

P STEPHEN CATTERSON SMITH jun, 1899, after a portrait of 1891, tql seated with cross of Papal order of St Gregory, NGI 492.

FITZROY, Robert (1805-1865) vice-admiral.
P UNKNOWN, Royal Naval College, Greenwich.
D Two drgs by P.P.KING and P.G.KING, as a young man, Mitchell Library, State Library of New South Wales, Sydney, Australia.
PH ERNEST EDWARDS, wl seated, print, for *Men of Eminence*, ed L.Reeve, vol III, 1865, NPG. MAULL & POLYBLANK, wl seated, carte, NPG.

FITZWILLIAM, Frances Elizabeth, née Copeland (1801-1854) actress.
P JOHN PRESCOTT KNIGHT, RA 1850, hl, Garrick Club, London.
PR Various theatrical prints, BM, NPG, Harvard Theatre Collection, Cambridge, Mass, USA.

FLEETWOOD, Sir Peter Hesketh, 1st Bart (1801-1866) founder of the town of Fleetwood.
G SIR GEORGE HAYTER, 'The House of Commons, 1833', oil, NPG 54.
SC H.B.BURLOWE, bust, Fleetwood, Lancashire.

FLEMING, George (1833-1901) veterinary surgeon.
P B.HUDSON, 1883, wl, Royal College of Veterinary Surgeons, London.

FLEMING, James (1829-1908) canon of York and writer.
C SIR LESLIE WARD ('Spy'), wl, chromo-lith, for *Vanity Fair*, 29 June 1899, NPG.
PH W. & D.DOWNEY, hs, woodburytype, for Cassell's *Cabinet Portrait Gallery*, vol II, 1891, NPG.

FLEMING, Sir (John) Ambrose (1849-1945) electrical engineer and inventor of the wireless valve.
P SIR WILLIAM ORPEN, RA 1927, seated in robes, University College, London.
SC G.H.PAULIN, 1932, bust, University College.
PH WALTER STONEMAN, 1923, hs, NPG (NPR).

FLETCHER, James (1852-1908) naturalist.
P FRANKLYN BROWNELL, Ottawa Public Library, Canada.

FLETCHER, Joseph (1816-1876) congregational minister.
PR J.COCHRAN, tql seated, stipple, BM.

FLETCHER, Maria Jane, see Jewsbury.

FLEXMORE, Richard (1824-1860) dancer and clown.
PR C.BAUGNIET, wl with Mlle Auriol in the ballet *Esmeralda*, produced at Princess's Theatre, 1848, lith, BM. C.N.G., wl as a clown, dancing, lith, Harvard Theatre Collection, Cambridge, Mass, USA.

FLINT, Robert (1838-1910) philosopher and theologian.
P SIR GEORGE REID, 1903, hl, Edinburgh University. UNKNOWN, University of St Andrews.
PR W.HOLE, tql in armour, etch, for *Quasi Cursores*, 1884, NPG.

FLOWER, Sir William Henry (1831-1899) director of the Natural History Museum, London.
P C.SCHMID, 1868, hl, oval, Royal College of Surgeons, London.

FOAKES-JACKSON, Frederick John, see Jackson.

FOLEY, John Henry (1818-1874) sculptor.
P THOMAS MOGFORD, hs, NGI 518.
SC C.B.BIRCH, 1876, plaster medallion, NPG 1541; related wax relief, NGI 8157.
PR UNKNOWN, after a photograph by John Watkins, hs, oval, woodcut, for *Illust London News*, 2 May 1857, NPG. G.STODART, after a bust by Sir Thomas Brock of 1873, stipple, NPG. UNKNOWN, after a photograph by London Stereoscopic Co, hs, oval, woodcut, for *Illust London News*, 12 Sept 1874, NPG.

PH ERNEST EDWARDS, wl, print, for *Men of Eminence*, ed L.Reeve, vol I, 1863, NPG.

FOOTE, Lydia (1844?-1892) actress.
PH Five cartes by ALBUM PORTRAIT CO, ADOLPHE BEAU, LONDON STEREOSCOPIC CO, C.B.WALKER and an unknown photographer, various dates and sizes, one with Miss Raynham, NPG.

FORBES, Archibald (1838-1900) war correspondent.
P SIR HUBERT VON HERKOMER, 1881, tql, Kunsthalle, Hamburg, W Germany.
D FREDERICK VILLIERS, wl in Afghan dress, with villagers, pencil, NPG 2931.
SC UNKNOWN, medallion portrait on tablet, St Paul's Cathedral, London.
PR UNKNOWN, tql, woodcut, NPG.
C CARLO PELLEGRINI ('Ape'), wl in uniform, chromo-lith, for *Vanity Fair*, 5 Jan 1878, NPG.

FORBES, Edward (1815-1854) naturalist.
SC J.G.LOUGH, RA 1856, marble bust, Geological Museum, London. L.C.WYON, bronze medal, based on Lough's bust, NPG 1609. N.N.BURNARD, RA 1867, marble bust, Douglas, Isle of Man. SIR JOHN STEELL, plaster bust, SNPG 174; version, Linnean Society, London.
PR T.H.MAGUIRE, tql seated, lith, for *Ipswich Museum Portraits*, 1851, BM, NPG. C.COOK, after a daguerreotype by Claudet, tql, stipple, pub 1855, BM.
PH D.O.HILL, c1854, hl, print, SNPG.

FORBES, James David (1809-1868) scientist and principal of the University of Edinburgh.
D THOMAS FAED, hs, wash, SNPG 1079.

FORBES, James Staats (1823-1904) railway manager and art connoisseur.
P SIR WILLIAM ORPEN, 1900, tql seated, Manchester City Art Gallery.
C HARRY FURNISS, pen and ink sketch, NPG 3572. 'PET', chromo-lith, supplement to *The Monetary Gazette*, 24 Jan 1877 NPG. SIR LESLIE WARD ('Spy'), wl seated, chromo-lith, for *Vanity Fair*, 22 Feb 1900, NPG.
PH G.C.BERESFORD, 1902, hs, neg, NPG x6501. G.C.BERESFORD, two prints, both hs, NPG.

FORBES, Stanhope Alexander (1857-1947) painter.
P Self-portrait, 1891, hs, MacDonald Collection, Aberdeen Art Gallery.
SC UNKNOWN, bronze medallion, Passmore Edwards Art Gallery Newlyn, Cornwall.
PH UNKNOWN, tql, print, NPG.

FORBES-ROBERTSON, Sir Johnston (1853-1937) actor-manager.
P GEORGE COATES, exhib 1926?, hs, City Art Gallery, Birmingham. GEORGE HARCOURT, wl, Garrick Club, London G.V.MEREDITH FRAMPTON, 1920, tql seated, Royal Shakespeare Theatre Picture Gallery, Stratford-upon-Avon. Self-portrait SNPG 1981.
SC EMIL FUCHS, c1902, plaster bust, NPG 3642.
PR Several theatrical prints, Harvard Theatre Collection, Cambridge, Mass, USA.
C AUBREY BEARDSLEY, as Julian Beauclerc, in *Diplomacy*, pen and ink sketch, for *The Pall Mall Budget*, 23 Feb 1893, V&A. SIR LESLIE WARD ('Spy'), wl, w/c study, for *Vanity Fair*, 2 May 1895, NPG 3008. HARRY FURNISS, 1905, pen and ink sketch, for *The Garrick Gallery*, NPG 4095(4). ALICK P.F.RITCHIE, wl, profile, mechanical repro, for *Vanity Fair*, 4 June 1913, NPG. SIR BERNARD PARTRIDGE tql, ink, pencil and crayon study, for *Punch*, 1926, NPG.

PH BARRAUD, tql, print, for *Men and Women of the Day*, vol III, 1890, NPG AX5496. BASSANO, hs, cabinet, NPG X4174. Several prints by W. & D.DOWNEY, ALFRED ELLIS and unknown photographers, all hs or hs, profile, two in character, NPG. WALTER STONEMAN, 1930, hs, NPG (NPR).

FORD, Edward Onslow (1852-1901) sculptor.
P JOHN MCLURE HAMILTON, 1893, hl, profile, modelling statuette, NPG 1866; pencil study, NPG 4391. SIR CHARLES HOLROYD, hs, The Art Workers' Guild, London. J.M.SWAN, unfinished hl sketch, City of Bradford Art Gallery.
D S.P.HALL, two pencil sketches, NPG 2384-5.
G G.GRENVILLE MANTON, 'Conversazione at the Royal Academy, 1891', w/c, NPG 2820. S.P.HALL, 'The St John's Wood Arts Club, 1895', chalk and wash, NPG 4404.
SC A.C.LUCCHESI, relief bronze medallion on stone obelisk, Junction of Grove End Road and Abbey Road, London.
PH BROWN, BARNES & BELL, hs, cabinet, NPG. ELLIOTT & FRY, hs, profile, cabinet, NPG. RALPH W.ROBINSON, wl in studio, print, for *Members and Associates of the Royal Academy, 1891*, NPG X7364.

FORD, Sir Francis Clare (1828-1899) diplomat.
PR R.T. & CO, hs, oval, woodcut, for *Illust London News*, 30 Jan 1892, NPG.

FORDHAM, George (1837-1887) jockey.
PR STURGESS, wl equestrian on Sir Bevys, the winner of the 100th Derby, woodcut, for *Illust London News*, 7 June 1879, NPG.
C SIR LESLIE WARD ('Spy'), wl, w/c study, for *Vanity Fair*, 2 Sept 1882, NPG 2629.

FORESTIER-WALKER, Sir Frederick William Edward Forestier (1844-1910) general.
C SIR LESLIE WARD ('Spy'), wl, w/c study, for *Vanity Fair*, 25 Dec 1902, NPG 4716.

FORREST, John Forrest, 1st Baron (1847-1918) Australian explorer and conservative politician.
C 'IMP', wl, chromo-lith, for *Vanity Fair*, 7 Oct 1897, NPG.

FORRESTER, Alfred Henry ('Alfred Crowquill') (1804-1872) artist.
PR C.BAUGNIET, three liths: 1843, tql, BM, NPG; 1850, nearly wl, oval, BM; tql seated, BM. UNKNOWN, after a photograph by John Watkins, hs, woodcut, for *The Illust Review*, 15 June 1872, NPG.

FORSTER, Hugh Oakeley Arnold-, see ARNOLD-Forster.

FORSTER, John (1812-1876) historian and biographer.
P THOMAS WARRINGTON and DANIEL MACLISE, 1830, hs, V & A. E.M.WARD and E.M.DOWNARD, c1850, wl seated in his study, V & A.
D DANIEL MACLISE, 1840, two ink sketches, hs and tql seated, V & A.
G CLARKSON STANFIELD, 'The Logan Rock, Cornwall, climbed by Charles Dickens, John Forster, Daniel Maclise and the Artist', water-and-body-colour, c1842, V & A. DANIEL MACLISE, as Kitely in a scene from Ben Jonson's *Every Man in his Humour*, oil, RA 1848, V & A.
PR C.H.JEENS, tql seated, stipple and line, NPG.
C RICHARD DOYLE, three pen sketches, one with Dickens and one with Dickens and Jerrold, BM. UNKNOWN, with Dickens, Maclise and Stanfield in a carriage on their tour of Cornwall, pen and ink, 1842, V & A.
PH ELLIOTT & FRY, in late middle age, carte, V & A.

FORSTER, John Cooper (1823-1886) surgeon.
G HENRY JAMYN BROOKS, 'Council of the Royal College of Surgeons of England, 1884-85', oil, Royal College of Surgeons, London.

FORSTER, William Edward (1818-1886) under secretary for the Colonies.
P H.T.WELLS, 1875, wl seated, NPG 1917.
SC H.R.HOPE PINKER, 1889, statue, Victoria Embankment Gardens, London. JAMES HAVARD THOMAS, RA 1890, bronze statue, Forster Square, Bradford.
PR BURTON, tql seated, etch, NPG. Various popular prints, NPG.
C HARRY FURNISS, wl seated, pen and ink sketch, NPG 3358. CARLO PELLEGRINI ('Ape'), wl, w/c study, for *Vanity Fair*, 6 March 1869, NPG 5153.
PH APPLETON, hs, carte, NPG. M.BOWNESS, wl seated, carte, NPG (Album 136). ELLIOTT & FRY, two cartes, hs, and hl seated, profile, NPG (Album 99 and Album 102). LOCK & WHITFIELD, hs, oval, woodburytype, for *Men of Mark*, 1878, NPG. LONDON STEREOSCOPIC, CO, hs, carte, NPG.

FORSYTH, Andrew Russell (1858-1942) mathematician.
PH WALTER STONEMAN, 1917 and 1931, both hs, NPG (NPR).

FORSYTH, William (1812-1899) man of letters and politician.
PR UNKNOWN, hs, circle, woodcut, for *Illust London News*, 6 March 1875, NPG.
C FAUSTIN, wl, chromo-lith, a 'Figaro Cartoon', NPG.

FORTESCUE, Chichester Samuel, see Baron Carlingford.

FORTESCUE, Hugh Fortescue, 3rd Earl (1818-1905) politician.
SC E.B.STEPHENS, 1861, bust, Barnstaple Infirmary.
PR F.C.LEWIS, after G.Richmond, hs, stipple, one of 'Grillion's Club' series, BM, NPG.
C THÉOBALD CHARTRAN ('T'), wl seated, chromo-lith, for *Vanity Fair*, 17 Sept 1881, NPG.
PH BASSANO, 1895, four negs, various sizes, NPG X1654-57.

FORTESCUE, Hugh Fortescue, 4th Earl (1854-1932) sportsman and politician.
PR UNKNOWN, hs, as a young man, lith, NPG. JOSEPH BROWN, after a photograph by J.Mayall, hs, stipple, NPG.
C CARLO PELLEGRINI ('Ape'), wl, profile, w/c study, for *Vanity Fair*, 19 Feb 1887, NPG 3266.

FORTESCUE, Sir John William (1859-1933) military historian.
D ERIC GILL, 1927, pencil, Trinity College, Cambridge.
PR WILLIAM STRANG, 1909, hs, semi-profile, etch, NPG.

FORTNUM, Charles Drury Edward (1820-1899) collector.
P CHARLES ALEXANDER, 1893, hl seated in robes, Ashmolean Museum, Oxford. C.ALEXANDER, hl seated, holding piece of china, Ashmolean Museum.
D JULES JACQUEMART, 1878, hl seated, w/c sketch, Ashmolean Museum.
G HENRY JAMYN BROOKS, 'Private view of the Old Masters Exhibition, Royal Academy, 1888', oil, NPG 1833.
SC CIRILOTTI, cameo, oval, Ashmolean Museum.

FOSTER, Sir Michael (1836-1907) physiologist.
P SIR HUBERT VON HERKOMER, 1892, hl seated, Trinity College, Cambridge. JOHN COLLIER, 1907, tql, NPG 1869; hs replica, Royal Society, London.
PH Three prints by unknown photographers, two hs, one wl seated, NPG. SIR BENJAMIN STONE, three prints, NPG.

FOSTER, Myles Birket (1825-1899) water-colourist.
P Self-portrait, hs, oval, MacDonald Collection, Aberdeen Art Gallery.
D WALTER HODGSON, 1891, hl, pencil and w/c, NPG 4041(1).
PR UNKNOWN, tql seated, woodcut, for *The Family Friend*, 1875, BM.

PH ELLIOTT & FRY, hs, carte, NPG (Album 40). LOCK & WHITFIELD, hs, oval, woodburytype, for *Men of Mark*, 1880, NPG. MCLEAN & HAES, wl, carte, NPG AX7571. DAVID WILKIE WYNFIELD, *c*1860s, hs, print, NPG P99.

FOSTER, Vere Henry Lewis (1819-1900) philanthropist.
PH KILPATRICK, *c*1890, hs, print, NPG. UNKNOWN, wl, photogravure, NPG. UNKNOWN, Royal Victoria Hospital, Belfast.

FOWKE, Francis (1823-1865) captain of the Royal Engineers and architect.
SC MINTON & CO, after a plaster model by Thomas Woolner, terracotta bust, V & A.
PR UNKNOWN, hl seated, woodcut, for *Illust London News*, 3 May 1862, NPG.

FOWLE, Thomas Welbank (1835-1903) theologian and writer on the poor law.
PH UNKNOWN, Union Society Debating Hall, Oxford.

FOWLER, Henry Hartley, see 1st Viscount Wolverhampton.

FOWLER, Sir John, 1st Bart (1817-1898) civil engineer.
P SIR J.E.MILLAIS, 1868, tql seated, Institution of Civil Engineers, London.
SC D.W.STEVENSON, 1889, plaster bust, SNPG 612. H.C.FEHR, 1899, bust, Institution of Civil Engineers.
PH LOCK & WHITFIELD, hs, oval, woodburytype, for *Men of Mark*, 1882, NPG.

FOWLER, Sir Robert Nicholas, 1st Bart (1828-1891) banker and politician.
PR H.MANESSE, hs, etch, NPG. UNKNOWN, hs, wood engr, for *Illust London News*, 30 May 1891, NPG.
C THÉOBALD CHARTRAN ('T'), wl, w/c study, for *Vanity Fair*, 25 June 1881, NPG 2571.

FOWLER, Thomas (1832-1904) president of Corpus Christi College, Oxford.
C F.T.DALTON ('FTD'), wl, chromo-lith, for *Vanity Fair*, 2 Nov 1899, NPG.

FOWLER, William Warde (1847-1921) historian and ornithologist.
P ALEXANDER MACDONALD, 1908, tql seated, Lincoln College, Oxford.

FOWNES, George (1815-1849) chemist.
PR C.COOK, after a photograph by Collins, hl seated, profile, stipple and line, NPG.

FOX, Sir Charles (1810-1874) civil engineer.
G H.W.PHILLIPS, 'The Royal Commissioners for the Great Exhibition 1851', oil, V & A.
PR C.BAUGNIET, tql seated, lith, 1851, BM, NPG. UNKNOWN, after a photograph by Elliott & Fry, hs, profile, woodcut, for *Illust London News*, 27 June 1874, NPG.
PH MAULL & CO, hs, carte, NPG X11846.

FOX, Samson (1838-1903) inventor and benefactor.
SC UNKNOWN, marble bust, Royal College of Music, London.

FOX, Sir William (1812-1893) prime minister of New Zealand.
P UNKNOWN, hs, City Art Gallery, Auckland, New Zealand.
PR UNKNOWN, hs, woodcut, for *Illust London News*, 23 Nov 1861, NPG.

FOX, Wilson (1831-1887) physician.
P VAL PRINSEP, RA 1889, tql seated in gown, Royal College of Physicians, London.

FOX STRANGWAYS, Arthur Henry, see Strangways.

FOX TALBOT, William Henry, see Talbot.

FOXWELL, Herbert Somerton (1849-1936) economist and bibliographer.
P CHARLES HOPKINSON, Harvard Graduate College of Business Administration, Cambridge, Mass, USA. AGATHA SHORE, hs, St John's College, Cambridge.
PH WALTER STONEMAN, 1917, hs, NPG (NPR).

FRANCATELLI, Charles Elmé (1805-1876) cook.
PR UNKNOWN, hs, stipple, NPG.

FRANKLAND, Sir Edward (1825-1899) chemist.
SC JOHN ADAMS-ACTON, 1896, plaster medallion, NPG 4017.
PH LOCK & WHITFIELD, hs, profile, oval, woodburytype, for *Men of Mark*, 1880, NPG. UNKNOWN, prints, Chemical Society, London and Royal Institution, London.

FRANKLAND, Percy Faraday (1858-1946) chemist.
P BERNARD MUNNS, 1919, tql, University of Birmingham.

FRANKS, Sir Augustus Wollaston (1826-1897) antiquary.
SC C.J.PRAETORIUS, bronze plaque, NPG 1584; related plaque, Society of Antiquaries, London.
PR C.W.SHERBORN, hs, oval, etch, book-plate for his bequest to the Society of Antiquaries, BM, NPG. UNKNOWN, hs, semi-profile, stipple, NPG.

FRASER, Alexander (1827-1899) artist.
D THOMAS FAIRBAIRN, 1858, pencil and chalk, SNPG 1081.

FRASER, Alexander Campbell (1819-1914) philosopher.
P SIR GEORGE REID, tql seated, Edinburgh University.
PR W.HOLE, wl, etch, for *Quasi Cursores*, 1884, NPG.
PH D.O.HILL & ROBERT ADAMSON, *c*1843–7, with his students, print, NPG X7952. D.O.HILL & ROBERT ADAMSON, 1843–8, hl seated, profile, print, NPG P6(51).

FRASER, Sir Andrew Henderson Leith (1848-1919) Indian civil servant.
SC LEONARD JENNINGS, *c*1910, bust, Dundee City Art Gallery.

FRASER, Donald (1826-1892) presbyterian divine.
PR UNKNOWN, hs, profile, woodcut, NPG.

FRASER, James (1818-1885) bishop of Manchester.
P SIR J.E.MILLAIS, 1880, tql, Manchester City Art Gallery. W.WONTNER, hl seated, Oriel College, Oxford.
SC JAMES FORSYTH, 1887, recumbent effigy on monument, Manchester Cathedral. THOMAS WOOLNER, 1887, statue on monument, with relief scenes from his ministry on the base, Albert Square, Manchester.
PR J.GALLOWAY, after G.E.Tilson, tql, lith, BM. Several popular prints, NPG.
PH LOCK & WHITFIELD, hs, oval, woodburytype, for *Men of Mark*, 1878, NPG. UNKNOWN, hs, photogravure, NPG.

FRASER, James Keith (1832-1895) general.
C SIR LESLIE WARD ('Spy'), wl, w/c study, for *Vanity Fair*, 6 March 1880, NPG 2572.
PH T.H.VOIGT, 1885, tql in uniform, cabinet, NPG.

FRASER, Patrick Fraser, Lord (1819-1889) lawyer.
P J.H.LORIMER, probably exhib 1877, tql seated in robes, Faculty of Advocates, Parliament Hall, Edinburgh.

FRASER, Sir Thomas Richard (1841-1920) pharmacologist.
P ROBERT HOME, 1919, tql seated, Edinburgh University.
PR W.HOLE, tql with specimens, etch, for *Quasi Cursores*, 1884, NPG.

FRASER, Sir William (1816-1898) genealogist.
P WILLIAM CRABB, 1869, hl, Edinburgh University.
PR UNKNOWN, tql seated, mezz, BM.

PH DEBENHAM of Edinburgh, hs, cabinet, NPG.

FRASER, Sir William Augustus, 4th Bart (1826–1898) politician.

C CARLO PELLEGRINI ('Ape'), wl, profile, w/c study, for *Vanity Fair*, 9 Jan 1875, NPG 2573.

FRAZER, Sir James George (1854–1941) anthropologist.

P HENRY MACBETH RAEBURN, University of Liverpool.

D Two related drgs by LUCIEN H. MONOD, both 1907, Fitzwilliam Museum, Cambridge, and SNPG 1182. SIR WILLIAM ROTHENSTEIN, 1925, hs, sanguine, NPG L168(2).

SC E. A. BOURDELLE, 1922, bronze bust, NPG 2099; version, Trinity College, Cambridge.

PH WALTER STONEMAN, 1924 and 1936, two portraits, both hs, NPG (NPR).

FRÉCHETTE, Louis Honoré (1839–1908) Canadian poet and journalist.

SC LOUIS-PHILIPPE HÉBERT, c1895, bronze bust, National Gallery of Canada, Ottawa.

FREEMAN, Edward Augustus (1823–1892) historian.

P HUBERT VOS, 1889, hl seated, semi-profile, Trinity College, Oxford.

PR UNKNOWN, hl, woodcut, for *Illust London News*, 1892, NPG.

PH HILLS & SAUNDERS, hs, photogravure, NPG.

FREEMAN-MITFORD, Algernon Bertram, see 1st Baron Redesdale.

FREEMAN-MITFORD, John Thomas, see 1st Earl of Redesdale.

FREEMANTLE, Sir Edmund Robert (1836–1929) admiral.

C 'PAT', tql in uniform, chromo-lith, for *Vanity Fair*, 29 Nov 1894, NPG.

PH WALTER STONEMAN, 1917, hl seated, in uniform, NPG (NPR).

FRENCH, John Denton Pinkstone, see 1st Earl of Ypres.

FRERE, Sir Henry Bartle Edward, 1st Bart (1815–1884) statesman.

P SIR GEORGE REID, 1881, tql, profile, in uniform, NPG 2669.

G S. P. HALL, 'The Duke and Duchess of Teck receiving Officers of the Indian Contingent, 1882', oil, NPG 4441.

SC THOMAS WOOLNER, three sculptures: 1868, plaster bust, NPG 1670; 1872, marble statue, Bombay Town Hall; 1887, statue on monument, Victoria Embankment, London.

PR S. COUSINS, after H. W. Phillips, tql, mezz, pub 1859, BM, NPG. G. J. STODART, after W. E. Miller, hs, stipple, one of 'Grillion's Club' series, BM, NPG.

C SIR LESLIE WARD ('Spy'), tql, chromo-lith, for *Vanity Fair*, 20 Sept 1873, NPG.

PH JOHN WATKINS, hl in uniform, carte, NPG. LOCK & WHITFIELD, hs, profile, oval, woodburytype, for *Men of Mark*, 1876, NPG. UNKNOWN, hs, carte, NPG (Album 38). UNKNOWN, tql seated in uniform, print, NPG.

FRESHFIELD, Douglas William (1845–1934) mountain explorer and geographer.

PH Several prints in the Royal Geographical Society, London: HILLS & SAUNDERS, 1880, hs; JOHN THOMSON, 1903, hs; JOHNSTON & HOFFMAN, 1904, hs, semi-profile; several, c1930, all hs.

FREYER, Sir Peter Johnston (1851–1921) lieutenant colonel and surgeon.

P UNKNOWN, tql, St Peter's Hospital, London.

PH WALTER STONEMAN, 1917, hs in uniform, NPG (NPR).

FRITH, William Powell (1819–1909) painter.

P Self-portrait, 1838, hs, NPG 2139. AUGUSTUS EGG, c1847, hl seated, Harrogate Art Gallery. Self-portrait, 1867, wl seated with an unidentified model, NPG 1738. Self-portrait, 1883, hs, oval, MacDonald Collection, Aberdeen Art Gallery. HENRY NELSON O'NEIL, Castle Museum, Nottingham.

F D MABEL D. LAPTHORN, 1909, hs, chalk, NPG 5058. W. W. WARREN, c1850, w/c, V & A. UNKNOWN, hs, ink over pencil, BM.

G H. N. O'NEIL, 'The Billiard Room of the Garrick Club', oil, 1869, Garrick Club, London. NICAISE DE KEYSER, 'Les grands artistes, École du XIXme Siècle', oil, 1878, Musée des Beaux Arts Jules Chéret, Nice. HENRY JAMYN BROOKS, 'Private view of the Old Masters Exhibition, Royal Academy 1888', oil, NPG 1833. G. GRENVILLE MANTON, 'Conversazione at the Royal Academy, 1891', w/c, NPG 2820.

SC JOHN THOMAS, RA 1859, marble bust, TATE 2061. JOHN CASSIDY, c1909, bronze bust, Manchester City Art Gallery.

PR Several prints by C. BAUGNIET, J. M. JOHNSTONE, P. NAUMANN and others, some after self-portraits by Frith, BM, NPG.

C SIR LESLIE WARD ('Spy'), wl with palette, chromo-lith, for *Vanity Fair*, 10 May 1873, NPG.

PH BARRAUD, tql seated, print, for *Men and Women of the Day*, vol III, 1890, NPG AX5493. ELLIOTT & FRY, hs, carte, NPG (Album 106). LOCK & WHITFIELD, hs, oval, woodburytype, for *Men of Mark*, 1880, NPG. JOHN & CHARLES WATKINS, two cartes, both hs, one in Album 104, NPG. F. R. WINDOW, wl, carte, NPG AX7552. WINDOW & GROVE, tql seated, cabinet, NPG.

FROST, William Edward (1810–1877) painter.

D Self-portrait, 1839, hs, pencil and w/c, NPG 4303.

PR Three woodcuts by unknown artists, all hs, one after T. Scott, and one for *Art Journal*, 1849, BM. UNKNOWN, after a photograph by John Watkins, hs, profile, woodcut, for *Illust London News*, 21 Jan 1871, NPG.

PH ELLIOTT & FRY, hs, carte, NPG (Album 103). JOHN & CHARLES WATKINS, hs, carte, NPG (Album 104).

FROUDE, James Anthony (1818–1894) historian.

P SIR GEORGE REID, 1881, hs, NPG 4990.

D J. E. GOODALL, hs, chalk, NPG 1439.

PR UNKNOWN, hs, woodcut, supplement to *Illust London News*, BM. Several popular prints, NPG.

C HARRY FURNISS, two pen and ink sketches, NPG 3448–49. UNKNOWN, wl, profile, chromo-lith, for *Vanity Fair*, 27 Jan 1872, NPG.

PH JOHN & CHARLES WATKINS, wl, carte, NPG AX7536. LOCK & WHITFIELD, hs, oval, woodburytype, for *Men of Mark*, 1876, NPG. H. J. WHITLOCK, tql seated, carte, NPG.

FROUDE, William (1810–1879) engineer and naval architect.

PH UNKNOWN, hs, print, Royal Institution of Naval Architects, London.

FRY, Sir Edward (1827–1918) judge.

P FRANK HOLL, 1883, hl seated, NPG 2466. ROGER FRY, hl seated, Lincoln's Inn, London.

C SIR LESLIE WARD ('Spy'), tql in robes, chromo-lith, for *Vanity Fair*, 30 May 1891, NPG.

PH LAFAYETTE, hs, semi-profile, print, NPG. LOCK & WHITFIELD, hs, oval, woodburytype, for *Men of Mark*, 1881, NPG. BARRAUD, tql, print, for *Men and Women of the Day*, vol III, 1890, NPG AX5487. UNKNOWN, hs, profile, print, NPG.

FULFORD, Francis (1803–1868) first bishop of Montreal.

PR UNKNOWN, after a photograph by Kilburn, hl seated, woodcut, for *Illust London News*, 24 Aug 1850, NPG.

FULLER, Sir (Joseph) Bampfylde (1854–1935) Indian administrator.

P UNKNOWN, Government House, Shillong, Meghalaya, India.

FULLER-MAITLAND, John Alexander, see MAITLAND.

FULLEYLOVE, John (1845–1908) landscape-painter.
PH ELLIOTT & FRY, hs, cabinet, NPG.

FURNESS, Sir Christopher Furness, 1st Baron (1852–1912) shipowner and industrialist.
P UNKNOWN, tql, Furness Withy Ltd, London.
C SIR LESLIE WARD ('Spy'), wl, Hentschel-Colourtype, for *Vanity Fair*, 21 Oct 1908, NPG.
PH SIR BENJAMIN STONE, 1902, wl, print, NPG.

FURNISS, Harry (1854–1925) caricaturist.
D S.P.HALL, pencil sketch, NPG 2386. E.J.SULLIVAN, 1891, hs, pen and ink, NPG 2900. Self-portrait, wl, pen and ink, NPG 3039.
G W.H.BARTLETT, 'A Saturday Night at the Savage Club', oil, Savage Club, London.
PR UNKNOWN, sketching in court, woodcut, BM.
C SIR MAX BEERBOHM, exhib 1911, Princeton University Library, USA. Two pen and ink self-portrait drgs, NPG 3567 and 3599.
PH BASSANO, hs, print, NPG (Album 38). ELLIOTT & FRY, hs, cabinet, NPG. WALERY, tql, print, NPG.

FURNIVALL, Frederick James (1825–1910) English scholar and oarsman.
P SIR WILLIAM ROTHENSTEIN, tql seated as an older man, Trinity Hall, Cambridge. A.A.WOLMARK, Working Men's College, London.
D SIR WILLIAM ROTHENSTEIN, 1901, hl seated, pencil, NPG 3172. C.H.SHANNON, 1901, head, pencil and chalk, NPG 1577.
PR Three engravings after photographs: two platinotypes, hl seated, aged 64, and tql seated, aged 76; and one heliogravure, hl, aged 64, BM.
C HARRY FURNISS, pen and ink sketch, NPG 3450.
PH G.C.BERESFORD, hs, print, NPG. C.W.CAREY, two prints, hl, profile, and tql seated, NPG. ELLIOTT & FRY, tql seated, cabinet, NPG. UNKNOWN, with his family and members of his boating club, print, NPG.

FUST, Herbert Jenner-, see JENNER-Fust.

FYFE, William Baxter Collier (1836?–1882) painter.
PR UNKNOWN, hs, profile, woodcut, for *Illust London News*, 30 Sept 1882, NPG.

G

GAIRDNER, James (1828-1912) historian.
SC FRANK BAXTER, 1900, plaster bust, NPG 2021.

GAIRDNER, Sir William Tennant (1824-1907) professor of medicine at Glasgow.
P SIR GEORGE REID, before 1893, hs, University of Glasgow.

GALE, William (1823-1909) painter.
PH DAVID WILKIE WYNFIELD, c1860s, hs, print, NPG P100.

GALLENGA, Antonio Carlo Napoleone (1810-1895) author and journalist.
P ORAZIO MANARA, 1850, The Times Newspapers Ltd, London.

GALLOWAY, Alan Plantagenet Stewart, 10th Earl of (1835-1901) conservative politician.
C MELCHIORRE DELFICO, wl, w/c study, for *Vanity Fair*, 1 Feb 1873, NPG 3274.

GALT, Sir Alexander Tilloch (1817-1893) finance minister of Canada.
PR Two woodcuts by unknown artists, hl seated and hs, for *Illust London News*, 18 Feb 1860, and 12 Nov 1864, NPG.

GALTON, Sir Douglas Strutt (1822-1899) man of science, captain in Royal Engineers.
SC THOMAS BROCK, bust, Shire Hall, Worcester.

GALTON, Sir Francis (1822-1911) founder of the science of eugenics.
P GUSTAV GRAEF, 1882, hs, NPG 1997. C.W.FURSE, 1903, hl seated, NPG 3916.
D JANET C.FISHER, hl seated, chalk, NPG 3095. OCTAVIUS OAKLEY, 1840, tql seated, w/c, NPG 3923.
SC SIR GEORGE FRAMPTON, c1910, bronze bust, University College, London.
PH MAULL & POLYBLANK, c1856, tql seated, print, NPG. GRAHAM'S ART STUDIOS, hl, profile, cabinet, NPG. H.J.WHITLOCK, tql seated, carte, NPG (Album 40).

GARBETT, James (1802-1879) professor of poetry at Oxford.
PR UNKNOWN, hs, semi-profile, woodcut, for *Illust London News*, 19 April 1879, NPG.

GARCIA, Manuel (Patricio Rodriguez) (1805-1906) singer and teacher of singing.
P J.S.SARGENT, RA 1905, tql seated, Rhode Island School of Design, USA.

GARDINER, Samuel Rowson (1829-1902) historian.
PH JOHN RUSSELL & SONS, hs, print, NPG.

GARDNER, Alan Legge Gardner, 3rd Baron (1810-1883) sportsman.
D COUNT ALFRED D'ORSAY, 1841, hl, profile, chalk, NPG 4026 (27).
PR W.SHARP, after J.Slater, hl, lith, pub 1835, BM, NPG.
C SIR LESLIE WARD ('Spy'), wl, profile, with dog, w/c study, for *Vanity Fair*, 21 July 1883, NPG 3287.

GARDNER, Percy (1846-1937) classical archaeologist and numismatist.
PH DEW SMITH, Christ's College, Cambridge. WALTER STONEMAN, 1917, hs, NPG (NPR).

GARNETT, Richard (1835-1906) man of letters and keeper

of printed books in the British Museum.
PR WILLIAM STRANG, 1899, hs, etch, BM, NPG. M.MORRIS, hs, etch, BM.
C HARRY FURNISS, wl, pen and ink sketch, NPG 3451. SIR LESLIE WARD ('Spy'), wl seated, profile, chromo-lith, for *Vanity Fair*, 11 April 1895, NPG.
PH UNKNOWN, 1902, hl, profile, seated at desk, print, NPG.

GARRETT ANDERSON, Elizabeth, see Anderson.

GARROD, Sir Alfred Baring (1819-1907) physician.
P SIR HUBERT VON HERKOMER, 1882, tql seated, Royal College of Physicians, London.

GARROD, Alfred Henry (1846-1879) zoologist.
PR UNKNOWN, after a photograph by Elliott & Fry, hs, profile, woodcut, for *Illust London News*, 8 Nov 1879, NPG.

GARROD, Sir Archibald Edward (1857-1936) physician.
PH WALTER STONEMAN, 1918, hs, NPG (NPR).

GARTH, Sir Richard (1820-1903) chief-justice of Bengal.
P JOHN COLLIER, 1888, wl in chief justice's robes, High Court, Calcutta.

GASKELL, Elizabeth Cleghorn, née Stevenson (1810-1865) novelist.
D GEORGE RICHMOND, 1851, hs, chalk, NPG 1720.
M W.J.THOMSON, 1832, University of Manchester Library.
SC DAVID DUNBAR, c1831, bust, Mrs Gaskell Memorial Tower, Knutsford; marble copy by SIR W.H.THORNYCROFT of 1895, University of Manchester Library. CAVALIERE A.D'ORSI, posthumous bronze plaque, Mrs Gaskell Memorial Tower.
PH ALEXANDER MCGLASHON of Edinburgh, 1862-63, nearly wl seated, carte, NPG X5945.

GASKELL, Walter Holbrook (1847-1914) physiologist.
PH UNKNOWN, hs, print, NPG.

GASKELL, William (1805-1884) unitarian minister.
P ANNIE LOUISA SWYNNERTON, 1879, hl seated, Manchester City Art Gallery.
PH RUPERT POTTER, hl, Emery Walker copy neg, NPG.

GASQUET, Francis Neil (Dom Aidan) (1846-1929) cardinal and historian.
PH JOHN RUSSELL & SONS, hl, print, for *National Photographic Record*, vol I, NPG.

GASTER, Moses (1856-1939) scholar and rabbi.
P MOSES MAIMON, Spanish and Portuguese Synagogue, London.

GATACRE, Sir William Forbes (1843-1906) major-general.
PH Several prints, National Army Museum, London.

GATHORNE-HARDY, Gathorne, see 1st Earl of Cranbrook.

GATTY, Margaret, née Scott (1807-1873) writer for children.
PR UNKNOWN, after a photograph, hs, semi-profile, woodcut, for *Illust London News*, 18 Oct 1873, NPG.
PH ELLIOTT & FRY, hs, profile, carte, NPG.

GAUNTLETT, Henry John (1805-1876) organist and composer.

PH C.E.FRY & SONS, hs, print, NPG. MAULL & CO, 1875, tql seated, print, NPG. MAULL & CO, three cartes, two hs, one hl seated, NPG. VICTORIA PHOTOGRAPHIC CO, wl, carte, NPG.

GEDDES, Sir Patrick (1854-1932) sociologist and town planner.
P UNKNOWN, SNPG 2028.
D DESMOND CHUTE, 1930, pencil, SNPG 2044.
SC C.J.PIBWORTH, bronze head, SNPG 1305.

GEE, Samuel Jones (1839-1911) physician.
P CHARLES VIGOR, c1900, hl seated, Royal College of Physicians, London.
M UNKNOWN, hs, profile, Royal College of Physicians.

GEIKIE, Sir Archibald (1835-1924) geologist.
P R.G.EVES, c1915, Royal Society, London.
D R.G.EVES, pencil drg, SNPG 1422. WILLIAM STRANG, 1914, hs, chalk, Royal Coll.
SC EDOUARD LANTÉRI, c1916, marble bust, Geological Museum, London.
PH WALTER STONEMAN, 1917, hs, NPG (NPR).

GELL, Frederick (1820-1902) bishop of Calcutta.
D 'JEJ', 1885, wl, profile, w/c, NPG 4550.
PH UNKNOWN, hl, print, NPG (Anglican Bishops).

GENT-THARP, William Montagu (1837-1899) sportsman.
C SIR LESLIE WARD ('Spy'), wl, w/c study, for Vanity Fair, 21 June 1894, NPG 2990.

GEORGE, Sir Ernest (1839-1922) architect.
P SIR HUBERT VON HERKOMER, tql seated, RIBA, London.
PH UNKNOWN, hs, print, NPG X11859.

GEORGE William Frederick Charles, 2nd Duke of Cambridge, Earl of Tipperary and Baron Culloden, see Cambridge.

GIBBS, Henry Hucks, see 1st Baron Aldenham.

GIBBS, Vicary (1853-1932) genealogist.
P R.G.EVES, exhib 1925, National Provident Institution, London.

GIBBS, Mrs, née Graddon (1804-1854?) actress and singer.
PR Several theatrical prints, NPG, and various prints, Harvard Theatre Collection, Cambridge, Mass, USA.

GIBSON, Edward (1837-1913), see 1st Baron Ashbourne.

GIBSON, Thomas Milner-, see MILNER-Gibson.

GIFFARD, Sir George Markham (1813-1870) lord justice of appeal.
PR UNKNOWN, after a photograph by John Watkins, hl seated, woodcut, for Illust London News, 4 April 1868, NPG.
PH DISDERI, wl, carte, NPG (Album 120).

GIFFARD, Hardinge Stanley, see 1st Earl of Halsbury.

GIFFORD, Adam Gifford, Lord (1820-1887) lord of session.
PH JOHN MOFFAT of Edinburgh, hs, carte, NPG.

GIFFORD, Helen Selina Sheridan, Countess of, see Countess of DUFFERIN and Claneboye.

GIGLIUCCI, Countess, see Clara Anastasia NOVELLO.

GILBERT, Sir Alfred (1854-1934) sculptor.
D JOHN MCLURE HAMILTON, 1887, head, chalk, NPG 1865.
G W.H.BARTLETT, 'Saturday Night at the Savage Club', oil, Savage Club, London.
C SIR MAX BEERBOHM, c1896, drg, V & A. SIR BERNARD PARTRIDGE, tql, profile, pencil and chalk, for Punch, 8 May 1929, NPG 4076.
PH RALPH W.ROBINSON, wl seated in his studio, print, for Members and Associates of the Royal Academy of Arts, 1891, NPG X7365.

UNKNOWN, hs, profile, print, NPG.

GILBERT, Sir John (1817-1897) painter and illustrator.
G HENRY NELSON O'NEIL, 'The Billiard Room of the Garrick Club', oil, 1869, Garrick Club, London.
PR UNKNOWN, after a photograph by John Watkins, tql seated, semi-profile, oval, woodcut, for Illust London News, 16 March 1872, NPG. SMEETON & TILLY, after A.Gilbert, hs, semi-profile, oval, woodcut, for L'Art, 1875, BM. Several woodcuts, BM, NPG.
C HARRY FURNISS, pen and ink sketch, NPG 3573.
PH CUNDALL, DOWNES & CO, tql seated, carte, NPG AX7562. LOCK & WHITFIELD, hs, profile, oval, woodburytype, for Men of Mark, 1877, NPG. W.WALKER & SONS, hs, semi-profile, carte, NPG (Album 106). JOHN & CHARLES WATKINS, wl seated, carte, NPG (Album 104).

GILBERT, Sir John Thomas (1829-1898) Irish historian and antiquary.
P SIR JOHN LAVERY, NGI 637.

GILBERT, Sir Joseph Henry (1817-1901) agricultural chemist.
P JOSIAH GILBERT (his brother), c1840, hs, NPG 2472. FRANK SALISBURY, tql seated, Rothamsted Experimental Station, Harpenden, Herts, engr J.E.Clutterbuck, mezz, NPG.
PH UNKNOWN, hs, print, NPG.

GILBERT, Marie Dolores Eliza Rosanna, (Lola Montez) (1818-1861) adventuress, dancer and lecturer.
P JOSEPH STIELER, 1847, hl, Residenzmuseum (Bayerische Verwaltung der staatlichen Schlösser), Munich, W Germany.
PR Various theatrical prints, Harvard Theatre Collection, Cambridge, Mass, USA.
PH ANTOINE ADAM-SALOMON, c1860, tql, print, Bibliothèque Nationale, Paris.

GILBERT, Sir William Schwenk (1836-1911) poet, dramatist and librettist of the Savoy operas.
P FRANK HOLL, 1886, tql seated, NPG 2911.
D RUDOLPH LEHMANN, 1893, hs, BM.
SC SIR GEORGE FRAMPTON, 1913, bas-relief head on bronze tablet, Victoria Embankment, London.
C HARRY FURNISS, three pen and ink sketches, NPG 3452-3 and 3574. SIR LESLIE WARD ('Spy'), wl, profile, chromo-lith, for Vanity Fair, 21 May 1881, NPG.
PH BARRAUD, tql seated, print, for Men and Women of the Day, vol II, 1890, NPG AX5508. WALERY, tql, print, NPG.

GILES, John Allen (1808-1884) church historian.
PR J.D.MILLER, after G.Richmond, hs, mezz, BM.

GILFILLAN, George (1813-1878) writer.
P WILLIAM B.LAMOND, hs, profile, oval, Dundee City Art Gallery.
PR Two popular prints, NPG.
PH D.O.HILL & ROBERT ADAMSON, 1844, with Dr Samuel Brown, print, Gernsheim Collection, University of Texas, Austin, USA. JAMES VALENTINE, hs, carte, NPG (Album 102).

GILL, Sir David (1843-1914) astronomer.
P SIR GEORGE REID, c1883, wl, Royal Astronomical Society, London. GEORGE HENRY, RA 1912, hl seated, Royal Society, London.

GILL, William John (1843-1882) captain of Royal Engineers.
PR T.B.WIRGMAN, hs, oval, etch, NPG.

GILLIES, Duncan (1834-1903) premier of Victoria, Australia.
P PHILIP TENNYSON COLE, tql, National Gallery of Victoria, Melbourne.

GILLIS, James (1802-1864) Roman Catholic prelate.
PR J.LE CONTE, after J.Archer, tql, stipple, BM.

GINSBURG, Christian David (1831-1914) Old Testament scholar.
p A.CARRUTHERS GOULD, 1914, National Liberal Club, London.

GIRAUD, Herbert John (1817-1888) chemist and physician.
PR UNKNOWN, hs, wood engr, for *Illust London News*, 11 Feb 1888, NPG.

GISSING, George Robert (1857-1903) novelist.
PR W.ROTHENSTEIN, 1897, lith, BM, NPG.
PH UNKNOWN, *c*1860s, with his brothers Algernon and William, Wakefield Public Library, W Yorks. UNKNOWN, 1884, print, University of Yale, New Haven, USA.

GLADSTONE, Herbert John Gladstone, Viscount (1854-1930) statesman.
p PHILIP TENNYSON COLE, tql, Government House, South Africa; w/c replica, hs, Keble College, Oxford.
PR H.ADLARD, hs, stipple, BM. UNKNOWN, hs, oval, with oval portraits of W.E.Gladstone and W.H.Gladstone, lith, issued with *The West London Advertiser*, 9 Dec 1882, in commemoration of W.E.Gladstone's Parliamentary Jubilee, NPG.
c SIR LESLIE WARD ('Spy'), wl, w/c study, for *Vanity Fair*, 6 May 1882, NPG 3288. SIR MAX BEERBOHM, 1900, drg, The William Andrews Clark Memorial Library, University of California at Los Angeles, USA.
PH Two family groups, a cabinet by BARRAUD and a print by an unknown photographer, NPG X5979 and X7260. G.C.BERESFORD, hs, print, NPG. SIR BENJAMIN STONE, two prints, both wl, NPG. WALTER STONEMAN, 1918, hs, NPG (NPR). UNKNOWN, hs, print, NPG.

GLADSTONE, John Hall (1827-1902) chemist.
c SIR LESLIE WARD ('Spy'), wl, chromo-lith, for *Vanity Fair*, 14 Nov 1891, NPG.
PH LOCK & WHITFIELD, hs, oval, woodburytype, for *Men of Mark*, 1880, NPG. H.J.WHITLOCK, tql seated, carte, NPG (Album 40).

GLADSTONE, William Ewart (1809-1898) statesman and writer.
p JOSEPH SEVERN, *c*1833, hl seated, Reform Club, London. W.H.CUBLEY, *c*1840, hs, Museum and Art Gallery, Newark-on-Trent. WILLIAM BRADLEY, 1841, tql, Eton College, Berks. PHILIP WESTCOTT, RA 1855, wl in robes of the Chancellor of the Exchequer, National Liberal Club, London. G.F.WATTS, 1859, hs, NPG 1126. CHARLES LUCY, *c*1869, V & A. LOWES DICKINSON, RA 1875, Liverpool College. SIR J.E.MILLAIS, 1879, tql, NPG 3637. W.T.RODEN, 1879, City Art Gallery, Birmingham. FRANZ-SERAPH VON LENBACH, *c*1879, tql seated, SNPG 837. SIR J.E.MILLAIS, 1885, hl seated in DCL robes, Christ Church, Oxford. H.J.THADDEUS, *c*1888, tql, profile, Reform Club. A.E.EMSLIE, 1890, hl seated, NPG 3898. JOHN MCLURE HAMILTON, 1890, hl seated, Musée du Luxembourg, Paris. JOHN MCLURE HAMILTON, Philadelphia Museum and Art Gallery, USA. PERCY BIGLAND, 1890, hl seated, Walker Art Gallery, Liverpool. JOHN COLIN FORBES, *c*1892, wl, National Liberal Club, London. S.P.HALL, *c*1893, tql reading the lesson in Hawarden Church, NPG 3641. S.P.HALL, wl reclining, NPG 2227. PRINCE PIERRE TROUBETSKOY, 1893, hl seated, profile, NPG 2159. PRINCE PAUL TROUBETSKOY, hl, SNPG 670.
d HEINRICH MÜLLER, 1839, hs, chalk, NPG 4034. GEORGE RICHMOND, 1843, chalk, DoE (British Embassy, Athens). RUDOLPH LEHMANN, 1891, hs, BM. G.R.HALKETT, 1893, tql seated, pencil, NPG 3183. SIR W.B.RICHMOND, 1898, after death, head, profile, pencil, NPG 3319. SIR W.Q.ORCHARDSON, charcoal drg, SNPG 753. S.P.HALL, several pencil sketches, NPG 2308-12, 2319 and 2323-5.

g SIR GEORGE HAYTER, 'The House of Commons, 1833', oil, NPG 54. SIR JOHN GILBERT, 'The Coalition Ministry, 1854', pencil and wash, NPG 1125. JOHN PHILLIP, 'House of Commons, 1860', oil, Palace of Westminster, London. HENRY BARRAUD, 'Gladstone with his first cabinet, 1868', oil, 1870, National Liberal Club. L.C.DICKINSON, 'Gladstone's Cabinet of 1868', oil, 1869-74, NPG 5116. H.T.WELLS, 'Queen Victoria Opening the Royal Courts of Justice, 4 Dec 1882', oil, DoE (Law Courts). A.E.EMSLIE, 'Dinner at Haddo House, 1884', oil, NPG 3845. LIBERIO PROSPERI, 'The Lobby of the House of Commons, 1886', oil, NPG 5256. UNKNOWN, Gladstone speaking in the House of Commons, *c*1886, black and white gouache, Palace of Westminster, London. HENRY JAMYN BROOKS, 'Private view of the Old Masters Exhibition, Royal Academy, 1888', oil, NPG 1833.
SC THOMAS WOOLNER, 1866, marble bust, Ashmolean Museum, Oxford. JOHN ADAMS ACTON, RA 1869, statue, in robes of chancellor of the exchequer, St George's Hall, Liverpool. JOHN ADAMS ACTON, marble bust, National Liberal Club. WILLIAM THEED, 1878, statue, Manchester. THOMAS WOOLNER, 1882, bronze bust, NPG 2167. DANTE SOLDISI, 1894, bronze statuette, Balliol College, Oxford. EDWARD ONSLOW FORD, *c*1894, statue, National Liberal Club. F.W.POMEROY, 1900, marble statue, Palace of Westminster. THOMAS BROCK, RA 1902, statue, Westminster Abbey, London. SIR W.H.THORNYCROFT, *c*1905, statue on memorial, Aldwych, London. ALBERT BRUCE JOY, bronze statuette, National Liberal Club. MARY GRANT, marble bust, All Souls College, Oxford. MARIO RAGGI, statue on monument, Albert Square, Manchester. ALBERT TOFT, bust, National Liberal Club.
PR W.H.MOTE, after J.Severn, 1836, hl, octagon, stipple and line, BM, NPG. WILLIAM NICHOLSON, 1899, wl, coloured woodcut, NPG. Numerous prints and popular prints, BM, NPG.
c HONORÉ DAUMIER, wl with Richard Cobden and John Bright, lith, for *Le Charivari*, 14 April 1856, NPG. CARLO PELLEGRINI ('Ape'), wl, profile, w/c study, for *Vanity Fair*, 6 Feb 1869, NPG 1978. SIR LESLIE WARD ('Spy'), tql, profile, chromo-lith, for *Vanity Fair*, 1 July 1879, NPG. SIR LESLIE WARD, wl, profile, w/c study, for *Vanity Fair*, 5 Nov 1887, NPG 5057. PHIL MAY, 1893, wl seated, pen and ink, NPG 2819. Various drgs by HARRY FURNISS, NPG 3359-87 and 3575. SIR MAX BEERBOHM, 1898, eleven drgs, 'Mr Gladstone goes to Heaven', Carlton Club, London. Various political cartoons, BM, NPG, V & A.
PH EVELEEN MYERS, 1890s, hs, print, NPG P54. Numerous prints, by BARRAUD, NUMA BLANC, CALDESI, BLANFORD & CO, W.E.DEBENHAM, W. & D.DOWNEY, ELLIOTT & FRY, L.V.HARCOURT, LOMBARDI & CO, LONDON STEREOSCOPIC CO, MAULL & POLYBLANK, MAYALL, H.S.MENDELSSOHN, RUPERT POTTER, A. & C.TAYLOR, SAMUEL A.WALKER, W.WALKER & SONS, H.J.WHITLOCK and others, various dates and sizes, and several family groups, NPG.

GLADSTONE, William Henry (1840-1891) politician.
c SIR LESLIE WARD ('Spy'), wl, profile, w/c study, for *Vanity Fair*, 11 Feb 1882, NPG 3289.

GLAISHER, James (1809-1903) astronomer and meteorologist.
PH T.R.ANNAN, after J.E.Mayall, hs, photogravure, NPG. SAMUEL A.WALKER, tql seated, carte, NPG. H.J.WHITLOCK, hs, carte, NPG (Album 40), NEGRETTI & ZAMBRA, hl, with Henry Coxwell in a balloon, carte, NPG.

GLAISHER, James Whitbread Lee (1848-1928) mathematician, astronomer and collector.
d FRANCIS DODD, 1927, hs, pencil, Trinity College, Cambridge.

GLASS, Sir Richard Atwood (1820-1873) manufacturer of

telegraph cables.
PR UNKNOWN, after a photograph by Mayall, hs, oval, woodcut, for *Illust London News*, 8 Dec 1866, NPG.

GLAZEBROOK, Michael George (1853-1926) schoolmaster.
P HUGH DE T.GLAZEBROOK, hl, Dulwich College, London. UNKNOWN, after Richmond, Clifton College, Bristol.

GLAZEBROOK, Sir Richard Tetley (1854-1935) physicist.
P HUGH DE T.GLAZEBROOK, 1920, tql seated, profile, National Physical Laboratory, Teddington, Middx.
PH OLIVE EDIS, three prints, two hs and one tql seated, and one autochrome, hs, (X7182), NPG. WALTER STONEMAN, two portraits, 1919 and 1931, hs, and hl, NPG (NPR). UNKNOWN, hl seated, print, National Physical Laboratory.

GLEICHEN, Prince Victor Ferdinand Franz Eugen Gustaf Adolf Constantin Friedrich of Hohenlohe-Langenburg, Count (1833-1891) admiral and sculptor.
C CARLO PELLEGRINI, 1872, wl, profile, chromo-lith, for the 'Marlborough Club' series, NPG. 'GO', wl, profile, with bust, chromo-lith, for *Vanity Fair*, 5 July 1884, NPG.
PH UNKNOWN, wl, carte, NPG.

GLENALMOND, George Patton, Lord (1803-1869) lord justice clerk.
SC SIR JOHN STEELL, marble bust, Faculty of Advocates, Parliament Hall, Edinburgh.

GLENAVY, James Henry Mussen Campbell, 1st Baron (1851-1931) Irish lawyer and politician.
P SIR WILLIAM ORPEN, 1922, tql in robes, Gray's Inn, London.

GLENCORSE, John Inglis, Lord (1810-1891) lord justice general of Scotland.
P SIR JOHN WATSON GORDON, 1854, wl, University of Edinburgh. SIR DANIEL MACNEE, 1872, hl in robes of chancellor of the University of Edinburgh, Fettes College, Edinburgh. SIR GEORGE REID, 1882, wl seated in robes of lord justice general, Faculty of Advocates, Parliament Hall, Edinburgh; related ink drg, SNPG 1314.
D JOHN FAED, chalk, SNPG 1106.
SL ERNST LJUNGH, 1888, SNPG 1315.
SC WILLIAM BRODIE, marble bust, Faculty of Advocates, Parliament Hall.
PR W.HOLE, tql seated in robes, etch, for *Quasi Cursores*, 1884, NPG.

GLENESK, Sir Algernon Borthwick, 1st Baron (1830-1908) newspaper proprietor.
C HARRY FURNISS, wl, pen and ink, NPG 3454. CARLO PELLEGRINI ('Ape'), wl, chromo-lith, for *Vanity Fair*, 17 June 1871, NPG.
PH W. & D.DOWNEY, tql, woodburytype, for Cassell's *Cabinet Portrait Gallery*, vol II, 1891, NPG. SIR BENJAMIN STONE, wl, print, NPG. WALERY, tql seated, print, NPG.

GLYN, George Grenfell, see 2nd Baron Wolverton.

GLYN, Isabella Dallas, née Gearns (1823-1889) actress.
PR Various theatrical prints, BM, NPG, Harvard Theatre Collection, Cambridge, Mass, USA.

GLYNNE, Sir Stephen Richard, 9th Bart (1807-1874) antiquary.
D STEPHEN CATTERSON SMITH, chalk drg, V & A.
G SIR GEORGE HAYTER, 'The House of Commons, 1833', oil, NPG 54.
SC UNKNOWN, marble effigy, Hawarden Church, Clwyd.

GODFREY, Daniel (1831-1903) bandmaster.
C SIR LESLIE WARD ('Spy'), wl, conducting, chromo-lith, for *Vanity Fair*, 10 March 1888, NPG.

PH W. & D.DOWNEY, hl in uniform, woodburytype, for Cassell's *Cabinet Portrait Gallery*, vol V, 1894, NPG.

GODKIN, Edwin Lawrence (1831-1902) editor.
PH WILLIAM· M.HOLLINGER, tql seated, print, National Portrait Gallery, Smithsonian Institution, Washington DC, USA.

GODLEE, Sir Rickman John, Bart (1849-1925) surgeon.
P ALAN BACON, 1923, hl, Royal College of Surgeons, London.
PH WALTER STONEMAN, 1919, hl, NPG (NPR).

GODLEY, (John) Arthur, see 1st Baron Kilbracken.

GODLEY, John Robert (1814-1861) politician.
SC THOMAS WOOLNER, 1865, bronze statue, Christchurch, New Zealand.

GODWIN, George (1815-1888) architect.
PR E.MORTON, after S.Laurence, hs, lith, pub 1847, BM, NPG. UNKNOWN, hs, woodcut, for *Illust London News*, 11 Feb 1888, NPG.
PH ERNEST EDWARDS, wl, print, for *Men of Eminence*, ed L.Reeve, vol III, 1865, NPG.

GODWIN-AUSTEN, Henry Haversham (1834-1923) explorer and geologist.
PH MAULL & FOX, hl, print, Royal Society, London.

GOLDIE, Sir George Dashwood Taubman (1846-1925) founder of Nigeria.
P SIR HUBERT VON HERKOMER, 1899, tql seated, NPG 2512.
PH WALTER STONEMAN, 1917, hs, NPG (NPR).

GOLDSMID, Sir Francis Henry (1808-1878) lawyer and politician.
SC WILLIAM THEED, 1879, marble bust, Lincoln's Inn, London.
C UNKNOWN, wl, profile, chromo-lith, for *Vanity Fair*, 7 Dec 1872, NPG.
PH JOHN WATKINS, hs, profile, carte, NPG (Album 99).

GOLDSMID-MONTEFIORE, Claude Joseph, see Montefiore.

GOOCH, Sir Daniel (1816-1889) railway pioneer and inventor.
P LOUIS DESANGES, 1872, tql seated, Swindon Railway Museum. SIR FRANCIS GRANT, 1872, tql seated, NPG 5080.
SC E.W.WYON, 1862, marble bust, Swindon Railway Museum.
C SIR LESLIE WARD ('Spy'), wl, profile, chromo-lith, for *Vanity Fair*, 9 Dec 1882, NPG.
PH BARRAUD, tql seated, print, for *Men and Women of the Day*, vol I, 1888, NPG AX5429. UNKNOWN, print, Science Museum, London.

GOODALL, Frederick (1822-1904) painter.
P Self-portrait, hs, oval, MacDonald Collection, Aberdeen Art Gallery.
D J.B.DAVIS, wl, profile, pen and ink, NPG 3257.
PR GREEN, hs, woodcut, BM.
PH ELLIOTT & FRY, hs, carte, NPG (Album 106). LOCK & WHITFIELD, hs, semi-profile, oval, woodburytype, for *Men of Mark*, 1878, NPG. JOHN & CHARLES WATKINS, two cartes, wl, and wl seated, the first in Album 104, NPG.

GOODENOUGH, James Graham (1830-1875) commodore
SC COUNT GLEICHEN, c1878, marble bust, Painted Hall, Greenwich.
PR UNKNOWN, after a photograph by H.Lenthall, hs, oval, woodcut, for *Illust London News*, 11 Sept 1875, NPG. LIEUT HARRISON, sketch 'Murder of Commodore Goodenough RN, in the South Sea Islands', woodcut, for *Illust London News*, 4 Dec 1875, NPG

GOODFORD, Charles Old (1812-1884) provost of Eton.
PR 'RH', tql seated, mezz, pub 1869, NPG.
C SIR LESLIE WARD ('Spy'), wl, w/c study, for *Vanity Fair*, 22 Jan

1876, NPG 2716.

PH LOCK & WHITFIELD, hs, oval, woodburytype, for *Men of Mark*, 1878, NPG.

GOODSIR, John (1814-1867) professor of anatomy at Edinburgh University.

P W.D.DRUMMOND YOUNG, 1889, tql, Edinburgh University.

PR WILLIAM HOLE, hs, etch, for *Quasi Cursores*, 1884, NPG.

GOODWIN, Harvey (1818-1891) bishop of Carlisle.

P GEORGE RICHMOND, hs, Church House, London.

D T.C.WAGEMAN, w/c, Trinity College, Cambridge.

SC SIR W.H.THORNYCROFT, RA 1895, bronze recumbent effigy, Carlisle Cathedral.

PR T.L.ATKINSON, after G.Richmond, hl, mezz, BM.

C SIR LESLIE WARD ('Spy'), wl seated, chromo-lith, for *Vanity Fair*, 17 March 1888, NPG.

PH UNKNOWN, hl, print, NPG (Anglican Bishops).

GORDON, Arthur Charles Hamilton-, see 1st Baron Stanmore.

GORDON, Charles George (1833-1885) general.

P VAL PRINSEP, RA 1866, wl in mandarin costume, Royal Engineers HQ Mess, Chatham, Kent.

D EDWARD CLIFFORD, 1882, head, profile, pencil, NPG 1479. 'C.J.A.', 1887, hl, w/c, Royal Engineers, Chattenden Barracks. LADY ABERCROMBY, posthumous, replica, hs, w/c, NPG 1772.

SC SIR J.E.BOEHM, RA 1885, marble bust, Royal Coll; related plaster bust, NPG 864. W.F.WOODINGTON, 1885, terracotta bust, SNPG 1972. EDWARD ONSLOW FORD, RA 1888, bust, Royal Engineers, Chatham. SIR W.H.THORNYCROFT, 1888, bronze statue, Victoria Embankment, London. EDWARD ONSLOW FORD, RA 1890, bronze statue, on camel, Royal Engineers, Chatham. JOHN BROAD, statue, Gordon Gardens, Gravesend, Kent.

PR T.L.ATKINSON, after Lowes Dickinson, tql on terrace at Khartoum, mezz, BM. J.FAED, after Alexander Melville, tql in his palace at Khartoum writing his last despatch, 1884, mezz, pub 1886, NPG. Various popular prints, BM, NPG, National Army Museum.

C HARRY FURNISS, pen and ink sketch, NPG 3576. CARLO PELLEGRINI ('Ape'), wl, profile, w/c study, for *Vanity Fair*, 19 Feb 1881, NPG 2575.

PH Various prints, some in uniform, NPG, National Army Museum and Royal Engineers, Chatham.

GORDON, Edward Strathearn Gordon, Baron (1814-1879) lord of appeal.

C CARLO PELLEGRINI ('Ape'), wl, profile, chromo-lith, for *Vanity Fair*, 10 Oct 1874, NPG.

GORDON, Ishbel Maria, see Marchioness of ABERDEEN and Temair.

GORDON, John Campbell (1847-1934), see 1st Marquess of ABERDEEN and Temair.

GORDON, Sir (John) William (1814-1870) major-general.

P CHARLES LUTYENS, wl, Royal Engineers, Military College of Science, Shrivenham.

PH T.R.WILLIAMS, *c*1865, wl seated in uniform, carte, NPG x8351.

GORDON, Lady Lucy Duff-, see DUFF-Gordon.

GORDON, Osborne (1813-1883) divine.

PR UNKNOWN, hs, stipple, NPG.

PH C.L.DODGSON ('Lewis Carroll'), *c*1856, hl seated, print, NPG P7(5).

GORDON-CUMMING, Sir William Gordon, 4th Bart (1848-1930) soldier.

C CARLO PELLEGRINI ('Ape'), wl, profile, w/c study, for *Vanity Fair*,

5 June 1880, NPG 4631.

GORDON-LENNOX, Charles Henry, 6th Duke of Richmond and 1st Duke of Gordon, see Richmond.

GORDON-LENNOX, Lord Henry Charles George, see Lennox.

GORE, Charles (1853-1932) bishop successively of Worcester, Birmingham and Oxford.

P SIR JOHN LAVERY, Hartlebury Castle, Hereford and Worcester. GLYN PHILPOT, 1920, tql, Theological College, Cuddesdon, Oxon. A.U.SOORD, Community of the Resurrection, Mirfield, W Yorks.

D JOHN MANSBRIDGE, head, profile, pencil, NPG 2611.

SC THOMAS STIRLING LEE, statue, Birmingham Cathedral.

PH LONDON STEREOSCOPIC CO, hs, profile, postcard, NPG. UNKNOWN, hl, profile, print, NPG (Anglican Bishops).

GORELL of Brampton, John Gorell Barnes, 1st Baron (1848-1913) judge.

P SIR WILLIAM LLEWELLYN, RA 1896, wl in robes as President of Probate, Divorce and Admiralty, DoE (Law Courts, London). UNKNOWN, Peterhouse, Cambridge.

GORST, Sir John Eldon (1835-1916) solicitor-general.

C SIR FRANCIS CARRUTHERS GOULD, wl seated, pen, NPG 2839. SIR LESLIE WARD ('Spy'), wl, chromo-lith, for *Vanity Fair*, 31 July 1880, NPG.

PH W. & D.DOWNEY, hs, woodburytype, for Cassell's *Cabinet Portrait Gallery*, vol III, 1892, NPG. JOHN RUSSELL & SONS, hs, print, for *Our Conservative and Unionist Statesmen*, vol I, NPG (Album 18). SIR BENJAMIN STONE, five prints, all wl, NPG.

GOSCHEN, George Joachim Goschen, 1st Viscount (1831-1907) chancellor of the exchequer.

D S.P.HALL, pencil sketch, NPG 2307.

G LOWES CATO DICKINSON, 'Gladstone's Cabinet of 1868', oil, NPG 5116.

PR UNKNOWN, after a photograph by London Stereoscopic Co, hs, etch, NPG. Various popular prints, NPG.

C SIR MAX BEERBOHM, *c*1898, wl, profile, NPG 3854. Drgs by SIR FRANCIS CARRUTHERS GOULD and HARRY FURNISS, NPG 2838 and 3577. CARLO PELLEGRINI ('Ape'), wl, profile, chromo-lith, for *Vanity Fair*, 12 June 1869, NPG. SIR JOHN TENNIEL, 1892, 'April Showers, or a spoilt Easter Holiday', pencil, Fitzwilliam Museum, Cambridge.

PH LOCK & WHITFIELD, hs, profile, woodburytype, oval, for *Men of Mark*, 1877, NPG. LONDON STEREOSCOPIC CO, two prints, both hs, NPG. LONDON STEREOSCOPIC CO, hs, print, for *Our Conservative and Unionist Statesmen*, vol IV, NPG (Album 21). SIR BENJAMIN STONE, 1897, wl, print, NPG. JOHN WATKINS, hs, carte, NPG (Album 99).

GOSS, Sir John (1800-1880) composer.

P UNKNOWN, *c*1835, tql seated, NPG 3019.

SC SIR W.H.THORNYCROFT, bas-relief figure on tablet, St Paul's Cathedral, London.

GOSSE, Sir Edmund William (1849-1928) poet and man of letters.

P J.S.SARGENT, 1886, hs, NPG 2205. J.S.SARGENT, 1886, hs, profile, Brotherton Library, University of Leeds.

D SIR WILLIAM ROTHENSTEIN, 1928, head, profile, pencil, NPG 2359.

SC SIR WILLIAM GOSCOMBE JOHN, 1920, bronze bust, Palace of Westminster, London.

PR SYLVIA GOSSE, 1911, in his study, etch, V & A.

C SIR MAX BEERBOHM, several political cartoons: Savile Club, London; Harvard College Library, USA; University of Texas, Austin, USA; Ashmolean Museum, Oxford. DAVID LOW, hs,

profile, pencil, NPG 4529 (141).
PH WILLIAM BELLOWS, wl with Thomas Hardy, print, NPG. JOHN
RUSSELL & SONS, hs, profile, cabinet, NPG. JOHN RUSSELL & SONS,
hs, print, for *National Photographic Record*, vol I, NPG. SIR
BENJAMIN STONE, 1904, two wl prints, NPG. WALTER STONEMAN,
hs, NPG (NPR).

GOSSE, Philip Henry (1810-1888) zoologist.
M WILLIAM GOSSE (his brother), 1839, hs, NPG 2367.
PH MAULL & POLYBLANK, 1855, tql seated, NPG P120(51).

GOTCH, John Alfred (1852-1942) architect and author.
P T.C.GOTCH, tql seated, RIBA, London.

GOTT, John (1830-1906) bishop of Truro.
PR R.T. & CO, hs, profile, wood engr, for *Illust London News*, 13
June 1891, NPG.
PH UNKNOWN, c1894, tql, print, NPG (Anglican Bishops).

GOUGH, Sir Hugh Henry (1833-1909) general.
C SIR LESLIE WARD ('Spy'), wl, mechanical repro, for *Vanity Fair*,
15 Feb 1906, NPG.

GOUGH, John Ballantine (1817-1886) temperance lecturer.
D ROBERT CRUIKSHANK, 1853, hl, pencil, BM.
PR E.BURTON, after D.Macnee, wl, mezz, BM, NPG. A.HAEHNISCH,
after a daguerreotype by Ross & Thomson, hs, lith, NPG.
D.J.POUND, after a photograph by Mayall, tql seated, stipple and
line, NPG.

GOULBURN, Edward Meyrick (1818-1897) dean of
Norwich.
P UNKNOWN, tql seated, Norwich Cathedral.
PH LOCK & WHITFIELD, hs, woodburytype, oval, for *Men of Mark*,
1880, NPG. POULTON, wl, carte, NPG. UNKNOWN, hs, carte, NPG
(Album 38).

GOULBURN, Henry (1813-1843) barrister.
D T.C.WAGEMAN, 1835, w/c, Trinity College, Cambridge.

GOULD, Sir Francis Carruthers (1844-1925) cartoonist and
journalist.
P R.G.JENNINGS, National Liberal Club, London.
D EDMOND KAPP, 1919, hs, chalk, NPG 3315.
C LIBERIO PROSPERI ('Lib'), wl, profile, w/c study, for *Vanity Fair*,
22 Feb 1890, NPG 3278. SIR MAX BEERBOHM, c1908?, sketch,
University of Texas, Austin, USA.
PH G.C.BERESFORD, 1902, hs, neg, NPG X6508. OLIVE EDIS, tql seated,
print, NPG. OLIVE & KATHARINE EDIS, tql, print, NPG.

GOULD, John (1804-1881) ornithologist.
PR T.H.MAGUIRE, 1849, hl, lith, one of set of *Ipswich Museum
Portraits*, BM, NPG.
PH ERNEST EDWARDS, wl, print, for *Men of Eminence*, ed L.Reeve,
vol II, 1864, NPG.

GOULDING, Frederick (1842-1909) copper plate printer.
D JEAN-EDOUARD LACRETELLE, 1880, hl, pencil, BM.
PR WILLIAM STRANG, 1906, hs, drypoint, NPG.
PH Two photogravures by unknown artists, hl seated, and tql in his
workshop, BM.

GOWARD, Mary Ann, see Keeley.

GOWER, Edward Frederick Leveson-, see LEVESON-
Gower.

GOWER, Lord Ronald Sutherland (1845-1916) dilettante,
sculptor and writer.
P SIR J.E.MILLAIS, 1876, hs, profile, Royal Shakespeare Theatre,
Stratford-upon-Avon. HENRY SCOTT TUKE, 1897, hs, NPG 4841.
PR G.J.STODART, after a photograph by Negretti & Zambra of 1882,
hs, profile, stipple, NPG.

C SIR LESLIE WARD ('Spy'), wl, profile, chromo-lith, for *Vanity
Fair*, 18 Aug 1877, NPG.
PH WALERY, tql, print, NPG.

GRACE, William Gilbert (1848-1915) cricketer.
P ARCHIBALD STUART-WORTLEY, 1890, wl on cricket pitch, Mary-
lebone Cricket Club, London. UNKNOWN, hl, NPG 2112.
PR UNKNOWN, hs, stipple, for *Baily's Mag*, 1870, NPG.
C SIR MAX BEERBOHM, wl, pen and ink, Marylebone Cricket Club.
HARRY FURNISS, several drgs of Grace playing cricket, from *A
Century of Grace*, Marylebone Cricket Club. SIR LESLIE WARD
('Spy'), wl in cricket dress, chromo-lith, for *Vanity Fair*, 9 June
1877, NPG.
PH BARRAUD, tql with cricket bat, print, for *Men and Women of the
Day*, vol I, 1888, NPG AX5424.

GRADDON, Miss, see Mrs Gibbs.

GRAHAM, Douglas, see 5th Duke of Montrose.

GRAHAM, Sir Gerald (1831-1899) lieutenant-general.
P SIR E.J.POYNTER, RA 1886, hl in tropical dress, Royal Engineers,
The Conservatory, Brompton.
PR UNKNOWN, hs, semi-profile, woodcut, for *Illust London News*, 12
Aug 1882, NPG.

GRAHAM, Robert Bontine Cunninghame- (1852-1936)
writer, traveller, horseman and socialist.
P SIR JOHN LAVERY, 1893, wl, Glasgow Art Gallery and Museum.
SIR JOHN LAVERY, on his horse Pampa, Museo de Bellas Artes de
la Boca, Buenos Aires, Argentina. JAMES MCBEY, 1934, tql
seated, NPG 4626.
D FREDERICK PEGRAM, pencil sketch, made during the sessions of the
Parnell Special Commission, for *The Pictorial World*, 6 Dec 1888,
V & A. T.B.WIRGMAN, 1918, hs, chalk, NPG 2212. EDMOND KAPP,
1919, Barber Institute of Fine Arts, Birmingham University.
LESLIE HUNTER, wl equestrian in a riding group, crayon and
wash, SNPG 2124. GEORGE WASHINGTON LAMBERT, head, pencil,
NPG 4846.
SC ALBERT TOFT, 1891, bronze head, SNPG 1468. SIR JACOB EPSTEIN,
1923, bronze heads, NPG 4220, SNPG 1363, Aberdeen Art Gallery
and Manchester City Art Gallery.
PR SIR WILLIAM ROTHENSTEIN, 1898, hl, profile, lith, NPG. WILLIAM
STRANG, hs, semi-profile, etch, NPG.
C SIR MAX BEERBOHM, 1921, six studies, Dartmouth College,
Hanover, New Hampshire, USA. SIR MAX BEERBOHM,
'Twenty-One Prominent Men', oil, University of Texas, Austin,
USA. HARRY FURNISS, pen and ink sketch, NPG 3444. SIR LESLIE
WARD ('Spy'), wl, chromo-lith, for *Vanity Fair*, 25 Aug 1888,
NPG.
PH STUART, wl on horseback, print, NPG X1447.

GRAHAM, Thomas (1805-1869) chemist.
P WILHELM TRAUTSCHOLD, hl seated, NPG 2164. G.F.WATTS, hs,
Royal Society, London.
SC WILLIAM BRODIE, bronze statue, George Square, Glasgow.
PR S.BELLIN, tql, mezz, BM. W.BOSLEY, after a daguerreotype, hl
seated, lith, pub 1849, BM. C.COOK, after a photograph by
Claudet, hl seated, stipple, NPG.
PH MAULL & POLYBLANK, c1855, tql seated, print, NPG P106(9).
ERNEST EDWARDS, wl seated, print, for *Men of Eminence*, ed
L.Reeve, vol III, 1864, NPG.

GRAHAM, Thomas Alexander Ferguson (1840-1906)
artist.
P Self-portrait, 1882, hs, MacDonald Collection, Aberdeen Art
Gallery. JAMES ARCHER, SNPG 721. ROBERT WALKER MACBETH,
1883, hl, Royal Scottish Academy, Edinburgh. SIR
W.Q.ORCHARDSON, SNPG 827.

GRAHAME, Kenneth (1859-1932) author.
J.S.SARGENT, 1912, hs, charcoal, Bodleian Library, Oxford.

GRAIN, Richard Corney (1844-1895) entertainer and song writer.
P.NAUMANN, hs, profile, woodcut, for *Illust London News*, 23 March 1895, BM.
HARRY FURNISS, pen and ink sketch, NPG 3455. SIR LESLIE WARD ('Spy'), wl seated, profile, at piano, chromo-lith, for *Vanity Fair*, 22 Aug 1885, NPG.
BASSANO, hl, cabinet, NPG.

GRAINGER, Richard Dugard (1801-1865) anatomist and physiologist.
UNKNOWN, hl with skull, w/c, Royal College of Surgeons, London.

GRANDISON, Victor Albert George Child-Villiers, 10th Viscount, see 7th Earl of Jersey.

GRANT, Albert (1830-1899) known as Baron Grant, politician and company promoter.
CARLO PELLEGRINI ('Ape'), wl, chromo-lith, for *Vanity Fair*, 21 Feb 1874, NPG. 'PET', wl, chromo-lith, supplement to *The Monetary Gazette*, 31 Jan 1877, NPG.

GRANT, Sir Alexander, 8th Bart 'of Dalvey' (1826-1884) principal of Edinburgh University.
WILLIAM HOLE, tql in robes, etch, for *Quasi Cursores*, 1884, NPG.

GRANT, Sir Francis (1803-1878) portrait painter and president of the Royal Academy.
Self-portrait, *c*1845, hl, NPG 1286. Self-portrait, *c*1865, hs, Royal Academy, London. JOHN BALLANTYNE, 1866, wl in his studio, NPG 5239. J.P.KNIGHT, hs, SNPG 6.
C.B.BIRCH, *c*1870, wl with Sir Edwin Landseer, pencil, NPG 2521. DANIEL MACLISE, V & A.
JOHN FERNELEY, 1823, with his brothers on horseback at Melton Mowbray, Leicester Museum and Art Gallery.
MARY GRANT, 1866, marble bust, Royal Academy; related plaster bust, NPG 1088. MARY GRANT, small marble bust, Royal Academy. J.NOBLE, Parian-ware bust, Royal Coll.
T.FAIRLAND, after Sir J.W.Gordon (RA 1846), hl, lith, BM, NPG. CARLO PELLEGRINI ('Ape'), tql, semi-profile, chromo-lith, for *Vanity Fair*, 29 April 1871, NPG.
D.O.HILL & ROBERT ADAMSON, 1845, hl seated, print, NPG P6(25). ELLIOTT & FRY, hs, semi-profile, carte, NPG (Album 103). Two cartes by JOHN & CHARLES WATKINS, both hs, NPG (Album 104 and Album 106).

GRANT, George Monro (1835-1902) principal of Queen's University, Kingston, Canada.
ROBERT HARRIS, 1889, Queen's University, Kingston, Canada. HAMILTON MCCARTHY, 1891, bust, Queen's University.

GRANT, James (1802-1879) journalist.
UNKNOWN, hs, semi-profile, woodcut, for *Illust London News*, 14 June 1879, NPG.

GRANT, James Augustus (1827-1892) African traveller.
COLVIN SMITH, Nairn County Buildings.
S.HOLLYER, after a photograph by Urquhart, wl seated in travelling dress, stipple, NPG. UNKNOWN, hs, semi-profile, oval, stipple, NPG.

GRANT, Sir James Hope (1808-1875) general.
Several portraits by SIR FRANCIS GRANT: 1853, wl as Colonel of the 9th Lancers, SNPG 343; *c*1861?, wl seated with violoncello, NPG 783; *c*1861, before the Anting Gates of Pekin, with Major Grant and Major Anson, formerly United Service Club, London (c/o The Crown Commissioners); 1865, as commander-in-chief,

Madras, Lawrence Asylum, Madras.
H.H.CREALOCK, 1860, w/c, National Army Museum, London.
T.J.BARKER, after sketches by E.Lundgren, 'The Relief of Lucknow', oil, 1857, Corporation of Glasgow. C.G.LEWIS, after T.J.Barker, 'Intellect and Valour of Great Britain', engr, pub 1864, NPG.
J.NOBLE, Parian-ware bust, Royal Coll.
UNKNOWN, on horseback in winter costume, engr, pub 1862, Collection of 9th/12th Royal Lancers, Market Harborough.
UNKNOWN, wl seated with Lord Clyde and Lord Sandhurst, print, NPG X1588. Various prints by BASSANO, HILL & CO, RODGER of St Andrews and unknown photographers, Collection of 9th/12th Royal Lancers.

GRANT, Sir John Peter (1807-1893) Indian and colonial governor.
G.F.WATTS, after 1873, hl, NPG 1127.

GRANT, Sir Patrick (1804-1895) field-marshal.
E.J.TURNER, after a photograph by Maull & Fox of post 1883, tql in uniform, NPG 1454. MARY FRASER-TYTLER (later Mrs G.F.Watts), 1887, Royal Horse Guards, London.
CAPTAIN MARTIN, *c*1856-61, hl seated, profile, w/c, NPG 4251.
GEORGE WADE, statue, Royal Hospital, Chelsea.

GRANT, Thomas (1816-1870) Roman catholic bishop of Southwark.
UNKNOWN, English College at Rome.

GRANT-DUFF, Sir Mountstuart Elphinstone (1829-1906) statesman and author.
RUDOLPH LEHMANN, 1872, BM.
W.ROFFE, after H.T.Wells, hs, profile, stipple, NPG.
CARLO PELLEGRINI ('Ape'), wl, chromo-lith, for *Vanity Fair*, 2 Oct 1869, NPG.
JOHN WATKINS, hs, carte, NPG (Album 99).

GRANTHAM, Sir William (1835-1911) judge.
SIR LESLIE WARD ('Spy'), wl in robes, chromo-lith, for *Vanity Fair*, 15 March 1890, NPG.

GRANVILLE, Granville George Leveson-Gower, 2nd Earl (1815-1891) statesman.
GEORGE RICHMOND, 1876, tql seated in robes, University of London; related chalk drg, head, NPG 4900. D.A.WEHRSCHMIDT, *c*1890, National Liberal Club, London.
FREDERICK SARGENT, hl seated in uniform, pencil, NPG 3809.
JOHN GILBERT, 'The Coalition Ministry, 1854', pencil and wash, NPG 1125.
SIR W.H.THORNYCROFT, 1895, marble statue, Palace of Westminster, London.
W.WALKER, after R.Lehmann, hl, mezz, pub 1853, BM. J.BROWN, after a photograph, hs, stipple, for *Baily's Mag*, 1874, BM. J.BROWN, hs, stipple, pub 1875, BM. T.L.ATKINSON, after G.Richmond, hl with Garter, mezz, pub 1879, BM. DALZIEL, hs, circle, woodcut, BM. Various prints after photographs and various popular prints, NPG.
CARLO PELLEGRINI ('Ape'), wl, chromo-lith, for *Vanity Fair*, 13 March 1869, NPG. THÉOBALD CHARTRAN ('T'), 'Purse, Pussy, Piety and Prevarication', chromo-lith, for *Vanity Fair*, 5 July 1882, NPG. SIR MAX BEERBOHM, *c*1890, several sketches, Merton College, Oxford.
HILLS & SAUNDERS, 1863, with the house party group after the presentation of DCL to Edward VII and others at Christ Church, Oxford, print, NPG X4336. Various prints by J.BERRYMAN, CALDESI, BLANFORD & CO, DISDERI, ELLIOTT & FRY, LOCK & WHITFIELD, MAULL & CO, W.WALKER, and JOHN & CHARLES WATKINS, various dates and sizes, NPG.

GRAVES, Algernon (1845-1922) art-historian.
SC ALEXANDER ZEITLIN, 1901, plaster bust, NPG 1937.

GRAVES, Henry (1806-1892) printseller and publisher.
D FREDERICK SANDYS, hs, chalk, NPG 1774b.
PR After W.M.TWEEDIE (RA 1866), engr by twelve artists, tql seated, mixed engr, BM, NPG.
PH H.S.MENDELSSOHN of Newcastle-upon-Tyne, hs, cabinet, NPG X5572.

GRAY, Andrew (1805-1861) presbyterian divine.
PH D.O.HILL & ROBERT ADAMSON, hl seated, print, NPG P6(85).

GRAY, Edmund Dwyer (1845-1888) politician and journalist.
PR UNKNOWN, after a photograph by Lafayette of Dublin, hs, wood engr, for *Illust London News*, 14 April 1888, NPG.

GRAY, George Robert (1808-1872) assistant keeper of zoological department, British Museum.
PR MOORE, after B.Smith, head, profile, lith, BM.

GRAY, Sir John (1816-1875) Irish journalist and politician.
P STEPHEN CATTERSON SMITH jun, NGI 913.
SC SIR THOMAS FARRELL, 1879, marble statue, Sackville Street, Dublin.

GRAY, John Edward (1800-1875) keeper of zoological department, British Museum.
P MARGARET CARPENTER, hl seated, Royal Society, London.
PR T.H.MAGUIRE, tql, lith, one of set of *Ipswich Museum Portraits*, BM, NPG. B.SMITH, head, profile, etch, 1845, BM.
PH CALDESI, BLANFORD & CO, wl seated, carte, NPG (Album 114). ERNEST EDWARDS, wl seated, for *Men of Eminence*, ed L.Reeve, vol I, 1863, NPG. THE LONDON SCHOOL OF PHOTOGRAPHY, wl with his wife, Maria Emma, carte, NPG (Album 114). MAULL & POLYBLANK, 1855, tql seated, print, NPG P120(52).

GRAY, John Miller (1850-1895) art critic and first curator of the Scottish National Portrait Gallery.
P PATRICK WILLIAM ADAM, 1885, hl seated, profile, SNPG 1226.
D G.R.HALKETT, 1881, w/c, SNPG 2071. CHARLES MATTHEW, two pencil drgs, the first dated 1888, SNPG 1072 and 1077. W.G.BURN MURDOCH, 1889, pencil, SNPG 1729.
SC CHARLES MATTHEW, 1886, bronze medallion, SNPG 2070.

GRAY, Robert (1809-1872) bishop of Cape Town.
PR J.THOMSON, after G.Richmond, hs, stipple, pub 1848, BM.
PH H.N.KING, wl seated, carte, NPG AX7478.

GREAVES, Walter (1846-1930) painter.
P Self-portrait, c1880-90, wl with his sister Alice on the Embankment, TATE 4564. Self-portrait, c1910, hl, oil on paper, TATE 6246. SIR WILLIAM NICHOLSON, 1917, wl, Manchester City Art Gallery.
D POWYS EVANS, c1928, hs, pen and ink, NPG 4394. SIR WILLIAM ROTHENSTEIN, head, pencil, NPG 3179.

GREEN, John Richard (1837-1883) historian.
PR G.J.STODART, after F.Sandys, hs, stipple, BM, NPG.

GREEN, Mary Ann Everett, née Wood (1818-1895) historian.
D G.P.GREEN (her husband), head, chalk, NPG 1438.

GREEN, Richard (1803-1863) shipowner and philanthropist.
SC E.W.WYON, statue, East India Dock Road, London.
PR UNKNOWN, hs, woodcut, for *Illust London News*, 31 Jan 1863, NPG.

GREEN, Thomas Hill (1836-1882) philosopher.
PR C.W.SHERBORN, tql seated, etch, BM.

GREEN, Sir William Kirby Mackenzie (1836-189▌ diplomat.
PR UNKNOWN, after a photograph by Elliott & Fry, hs, wood eng for *Illust London News*, 14 March 1891, NPG.

GREENAWAY, Kate (1846-1901) artist.
PR UNKNOWN, hs, woodcut, one of a set, 'Our Artists – Past a Present', for *Illust London News*, 14 May 1892, BM, NPG.
PH ELLIOTT & FRY, tql seated, cabinet, NPG.

GREENE, Sir (William) Graham (1857-1950) civil serva
P R.E.FULLER-MAITLAND, c1921, hl, DoE (The Admiralty).
PH WALTER STONEMAN, 1917 and 1933, two portraits, both hs, N (NPR).

GREENHILL, William Alexander (1814-1894) writer a philanthropist.
SC A.E.L.ROSTI, bust, Trinity College, Oxford.

GREENWELL, William (1820-1918) archaeologist.
P SIR A.S.COPE, 1898, tql seated, Durham Cathedral Library.

GREENWOOD, Frederick (1830-1909) journalist.
PR R.T. & CO, hs, wood engr, for *Illust London News*, 14 May 18 NPG.
C CARLO PELLEGRINI ('Ape'), wl, profile, w/c study, for *Vanity F* 19 June 1880, NPG 2714.

GREENWOOD, Joseph Gouge (1821-1894) principal Owen's College, Manchester and vice-chancellor of Victo University, Manchester.
P J.H.E.PARTINGTON, 1883, hs, Manchester City Art Gallery.

GREGG, Robert Samuel (1834-1896) archbishop Armagh.
P STAPLES, Bishop's Palace, Armagh.
PH UNKNOWN, hl, print, NPG (Anglican Bishops).

GREGORY, Edward John (1850-1909) painter.
P Self-portrait, 1883, tql seated with palette, MacDonald Col tion, Aberdeen Art Gallery.
D Self-portrait, 1879, hs, semi-profile, w/c, NPG 2621.
G W.H.BARTLETT, 'Saturday Night at the Savage Club', Savage Club, London UNKNOWN, after T.B.Wirgman, ' Graphic Artists', woodcut, BM.
PH ELLIOTT & FRY, hs, profile, cabinet, NPG. RALPH W.ROBINS tql seated with palette, print, for *Members and Associates of Royal Academy of Arts, 1891*, NPG X7368.

GREGORY, Isabella Augusta, Lady (1852-19▌ playwright.
P J.B.YEATS, 1903, hs, NGI 1318. SIR GERALD KELLY, c1914, Ab Theatre, Dublin. ANTONIO MANCINI, hl, Municipal Galler Modern Art, Dublin.
D GEORGE RUSSELL ('A.E.'), drg?, Abbey Theatre, J.B.YEATS pencil sketch, in a copy of the December 1904 *Samhain*, N York Public Library. J.B.YEATS, Abbey Theatre.
SC JACOB EPSTEIN, bronze bust, Municipal Gallery of Modern Dublin. THEODORE SPICER-SIMSON, bronze medallion, NGI 8
PR FLORA LION, 1913, hs, lith, NPG 3950.
C SIR WILLIAM ORPEN, 1907, wl with Sir Hugh Lane, J.M.Sy and W.B.Yeats, pen and ink, NPG 4676.

GREGORY, Mary Ann Stirling, Lady, see Stirling.

GREGORY, Robert (1819-1911) dean of St Paul's.
P SIR WILLIAM RICHMOND, RA 1899, The Deanery, St P Cathedral.
PR UNKNOWN, after a photograph by Samuel A.Walker, hs, w engr, for *Illust London News*, 3 Jan 1891, NPG.
PH LOCK & WHITFIELD, hs, oval, woodburytype, for *Men of M* 1877, NPG.

GREGORY, William (1803-1858) chemist.
R C.COOK, hl, stipple and line, NPG. F.SCHENCK, after W.Stewart, hs, lith, NPG.

GREGORY, Sir William Henry (1817-1892) governor of Ceylon.
R W.ROFFE, after A.Clay, hs, stipple, one of 'Grillion's Club' series, BM, NPG.
C UNKNOWN, wl, chromo-lith, for *Vanity Fair*, 30 Dec 1871, NPG.
H WALKER & BOUTALL, after F.Hollyer, hs, photogravure, NPG.

GRENFELL, Francis Wallace Grenfell, 1st Baron (1841-1925) field-marshal.
C SIR LESLIE WARD ('Spy'), wl, profile, in uniform, chromo-lith, for *Vanity Fair*, 19 Oct 1889, NPG.
H BARRAUD, hl seated in uniform, print, for *Men and Women of the Day*, vol II, 1889, NPG AX5474. WALTER STONEMAN, 1919, hs in uniform, NPG (NPR). Several prints, National Army Museum, London.

GRENFELL, William Henry, see 1st Baron Desborough.

GRENVILLE, Richard Plantagenet Campbell Temple Nugent Brydges Chandos, see 3rd Duke of BUCKINGHAM and Chandos.

GRESLEY, William (1801-1876) divine, tried to popularise Tractarian teaching.
R R.SMITH, after Pardon, tql seated, line and stipple, NPG.

GRESWELL, Richard (c1801-1881) scholar and benefactor.
P J.BRIDGES, 1837, hs, Worcester College, Oxford.

GREVILLE, Algernon William Fulke Greville, 2nd Baron (1841-1910) landowner and politician.
R J.BROWN, after a photograph, hs, stipple, for *Baily's Mag*, 1884, BM.
C SIR LESLIE WARD ('Spy'), wl, profile, w/c study, for *Vanity Fair*, 31 Dec 1881, NPG 2576.

GREVILLE, Henry William (1801-1872) diarist.
P JOHN JACKSON, hl, Hardwick Hall (NT), Derbys. UNKNOWN, 1844, hs, Goodwood, W Sussex.

GREY, Albert Henry George Grey, 4th Earl (1851-1917) governor general of Canada.
P UNKNOWN, 1905, University of Newcastle-upon-Tyne.
C UNKNOWN, bronze bust, Royal Commonwealth Society, London.
C SIR LESLIE WARD ('Spy'), wl seated, chromo-lith, for *Vanity Fair*, 28 April 1898, NPG.

GREY, Charles (1804-1870) general.
C SIR J.E.BOEHM, RA 1871, bust, Royal Coll.
R J.BACON, after G.Thomas, hs, profile, lith, BM, NPG. UNKNOWN, after a photograph, hs, woodcut, for *Illust London News*, 23 April 1870, NPG. UNKNOWN, hl seated, semi-profile, stipple, NPG.

GREY, Sir George (1812-1898) colonial governor.
P SIR HUBERT VON HERKOMER, 1901, posthumous, hl, NPG 1290.
C W.C.MARSHALL, RA 1862, marble statue, Cape Town.
R W.W.ALAIS, after a photograph, wl seated, stipple, NPG. UNKNOWN, after a photograph by York, tql seated, oval, woodcut, for *Illust London News*, 17 Dec 1859, NPG.
H HEATH & BEAU, hs, carte, NPG. HANNA of New Zealand, 1867-8, hs, as an older man, print, NPG.

GREY, Sir Henry George Grey, 3rd Earl (1802-1894) secretary for colonies.
G SIR GEORGE HAYTER, 'The House of Commons, 1833', oil, NPG 54. SIR DAVID WILKIE, 'The Queen Presiding Over her First Council, 1837', oil, Royal Coll.

SC J.P.DANTAN, 1834, plaster statuette, Musée Carnavalet, Paris.
PR J.BACON, after G.Thomas, head, profile, lith, BM.
C Several drgs by JOHN DOYLE, political satires, BM. CARLO PELLEGRINI ('Ape'), wl, profile, chromo-lith, for *Vanity Fair*, 8 May 1869, NPG.
PH CAMILLE SILVY, 1861, two cartes, wl and wl seated, the first AX7430, the second in Album 3, NPG. UNKNOWN, hs, carte, NPG (Album 38).

GREY-EGERTON, Sir Philip de Malpas, Bart (1806-1881) palaeontologist.
PR F.C.LEWIS, after G.Richmond, hs, stipple, one of 'Grillion's Club' series, BM, NPG. S.W.REYNOLDS, after J.Bostock, tql, mezz, NPG.

GRIERSON, Sir James Moncrieff (1859-1914) lieutenant-general.
PH GALE & POLDEN, wl in uniform, on horseback, photogravure, NPG.

GRIEVE, William (1800-1844) scene-painter.
D COUNT ALFRED D'ORSAY, 1836, hl, profile, pencil and chalk, this portrait could be either William Grieve or his brother Thomas (1799–1882), NPG 4026(32). UNKNOWN, hl seated, w/c, Garrick Club, London.

GRIFFIN, Gerald (1803-1840) writer.
P RICHARD ROTHWELL, NGI 609.
PR DALZIEL, after E.Fitzpatrick, hs, circle, woodcut, for *Dublin Journal*, 1861, BM. DALZIEL, hs, woodcut, BM.

GRIFFIN, John Joseph (1802-1877) chemist.
SC DAVID DAVIS, RA 1882, marble bust, Chemical Society, London.

GRIFFITHS, Ernest Howard (1851-1932) physicist.
P GABRIEL THOMPSON, University College, Cardiff.
PH WALTER STONEMAN, 1918, hs, NPG (NPR).

GRIFFITHS, John (1806-1885) keeper of the archives at Oxford.
D G.F.WATTS, head, chalk, Wadham College, Oxford, engr by S.Cousins, mezz, BM, NPG.

GRIMSTON, Robert (1816-1884) sportsman.
PH BARRAUD, tql, print, NPG.

GRIMTHORPE, Sir Edmund Beckett, 1st Baron (1816-1905) lawyer, mechanician and controversialist.
C SIR LESLIE WARD ('Spy'), wl seated, profile, chromo-lith, for *Vanity Fair*, 2 Feb 1889, NPG.

GROOME, Robert Hindes (1810-1889) archdeacon of Suffolk.
P W.R.SYMONDS, hl, Christchurch Mansion, Ipswich.

GROSE, Thomas Hodge (1845-1906) registrar of Oxford University.
P R.E.MORRISON, 1903, tql seated, Queen's College, Oxford.

GROSSMITH, George (1847-1912) entertainer.
PR 'JACK', wl in character, chromo-lith, supplement to *Society*, 6 Jan 1883, NPG. J.W.KENT, hs, Music Sheet, 'The Society Clown Lancers', lith, Harvard Theatre Collection, Cambridge, Mass, USA.
C HARRY FURNISS, two pen and ink sketches, NPG 3456-57. SIR LESLIE WARD ('Spy'), wl, chromo-lith, for *Vanity Fair*, 21 Jan 1888, NPG.
PH LOCK & WHITFIELD, hs, woodburytype, for *The Theatre*, 1879?, NPG. BARRAUD, hs as 'Ko Ko' in *The Mikado*, woodburytype, for *The Theatre*, 1885, BM, NPG. ELLIS & WALERY, two postcards, tql and wl, both in character, NPG.

GROSSMITH, (Walter) Weedon (1854-1919) actor, artist

and author.
c HARRY FURNISS, pen and ink sketch, NPG 3458.
PH HILLS & SAUNDERS, wl as 'The New Boy', woodburytype, for *The Theatre*, August 1894, NPG. ALFRED ELLIS, tql with his wife, woodburytype, for *The Theatre*, Sept 1895, NPG. RADIO PHOTO Co, 1904, tql, postcard, NPG.

GROSVENOR, Hugh Lupus, see 1st Duke of Westminster.

GROSVENOR, Richard de Aquila, see 1st Baron Stalbridge.

GROSVENOR, Lord Robert, see 1st Baron Ebury.

GROTE, Arthur (1814-1886) botanist and entomologist.
p JOHN PRESCOTT KNIGHT, two portraits, RA 1869 and RA 1870, Asiatic Society Calcutta, and Horticultural Society of India.
PR UNKNOWN, hs, woodcut, for *Illust London News*, 18 Dec 1886, NPG.

GROVE, Sir Coleridge (1839-1920) major-general.
p FRED ROE, hs, NPG 2420.

GROVE, Sir George (1820-1900) writer on music.
p H.A.OLIVIER, c1894, The Athenaeum, London. C.W.FURSE, 1895, wl, Royal College of Music, London.
SC SIR ALFRED GILBERT, 1896, bronze bust, Royal College of Music.
c SIR LESLIE WARD ('Spy'), tql seated, profile, chromo-lith, for *Vanity Fair*, 31 Jan 1891, NPG.

GROVE, Sir William Robert (1811-1896) scientist and judge.
p HELEN DONALD-SMITH, posthumous, hs, NPG 1478.
SC JOSEPH DURHAM, c1876, marble bust, Royal Institution, London.
G SHAPPEN, after daguerreotypes by Mayall, 'Celebrated English Chemists', lith, pub 1850, BM.
PR BOSLEY, after a daguerreotype by Claudet, hl, lith, pub 1849, BM.
c SIR LESLIE WARD ('Spy'), hs, w/c study, for *Vanity Fair*, 8 Oct 1887, NPG 2717.
PH BASSANO, hl, print, NPG (Album 38). ERNEST EDWARDS, wl seated, print, for *Men of Eminence*, ed L.Reeve, vol III, 1865, NPG. LOCK & WHITFIELD, hs, woodburytype, oval, for *Men of Mark*, 1877, NPG. LONDON STEREOSCOPIC Co, hs in wig and robes, carte, NPG (Album 40).

GRUB, George (1812-1892) Scottish ecclesiastical historian.
p SIR GEORGE REID, 1892, hs, Marischal College, University of Aberdeen. SIR GEORGE REID, Advocates' Hall, Aberdeen.

GUEST, Edwin (1800-1880) historical writer.
p SIR JOHN WATSON GORDON, Caius College, Cambridge.

GUINNESS, Sir Arthur Edward, see 1st Baron Ardilaun.

GUINNESS, Edward Cecil, see 1st Earl of Iveagh.

GUINNESS, Henry Gratton (1835-1910) divine and author.
PH OLIVE EDIS, c1910, hs, print, NPG.

GULL, Sir William Withey, 1st Bart (1816-1890) physician.
D UNKNOWN, Guy's Hospital, London.
PR UNKNOWN, hs, woodcut, for *Illust London News*, 23 Dec 1871, NPG. UNKNOWN, hs, lith, NPG.
c CARLO PELLEGRINI ('Ape'), wl, profile, w/c study, for *Vanity Fair*, 18 Dec 1875, NPG 2909.
PH LOCK & WHITFIELD, hs, semi-profile, woodburytype, oval, for *Men of Mark*, 1878, NPG.

GULLY, James Manby (1808-1883) physician.
c SIR LESLIE WARD ('Spy'), wl, profile, chromo-lith, for *Vanity Fair*, 5 Aug 1876, NPG.

GULLY, William Court, see 1st Viscount Selby.

GÜNTHER, Albert Charles Lewis Gotthilf (1830-1914) zoologist.
D LUCY GEE, 1900, hl seated, w/c, NPG 4965.
SC FRANK BOWCHER, 1912, bronze portrait plaques, Linnea Society, London and BM (Natural History).

GURNEY, Henry Palin (1847-1904) scientist.
p A.H.MARSH, 1906, University of Newcastle-upon-Tyne.
SC C.NEUPER, bust, University of Newcastle-upon-Tyne.

GURNEY, Russell (1804-1878) recorder of London.
p G.F.WATTS, c1877, hs, Montreal Museum of Fine Arts, Canad study, TATE 1654. W.W.OULESS, RA 1877, hl, Fishmongers' Ha London.
SC H.P.MACCARTHY, marble bust, (copy), Corporation of Londo
PR UNKNOWN, hs, lith, NPG. UNKNOWN, hs, stipple, NPG.
c UNKNOWN, wl seated, chromo-lith, for *Vanity Fair*, 9 Sept 187 NPG.

GUTHRIE, Frederick (1833-1886) scientific writer.
PR UNKNOWN, hs, woodcut, for *Illust London News*, 13 Nov 188 NPG.

GUTHRIE, Sir James (1859-1930) portrait-painter and pre sident of the Royal Scottish Academy.
p Self-portrait, SNPG 1867.
D E.A.WALTON, 1888, pencil, SNPG 1150.
PH UNKNOWN, hs, as a young man, print, NPG. UNKNOWN, 191 sixteen prints, various sizes, NPG.

GUTHRIE, Thomas (1803-1873) Scottish minister ar philanthropist.
p SIR GEORGE HARVEY, 1855, SNPG 1502. UNKNOWN, SNPG 159
D KENNETH MACLEAY, w/c, SNPG 1845.
SC SIR WILLIAM BRODIE, bas-relief, St John's Free Church, Edi burgh. SIR JOHN STEELL, bronze bust, SNPG 805.
PR E.BURTON, after J.W.Gordon, tql seated, mezz, pub 1852, B JOHN LE CONTE, after James Edgar, wl with several childre engr, SNPG. Several popular prints and prints after photograph NPG.
c B.W.CROMBIE, 1841, wl, profile, coloured etch, for *Mode Athenians*, 1882, NPG.
PH ELLIOTT & FRY, hs, carte, NPG (Album 40). D.O.HILL & ROBE ADAMSON, hl seated, print, NPG P6 (29). D.O.HILL & ROBE ADAMSON, print, NPG P6(105). J.MAGILL, wl seated, carte, N AX7492. T.RODGER, hs, carte, NPG.

GUTHRIE, Thomas Anstey (1856-1934) humorous writ under pseudonym of F.Anstey.
D LAURA ANNING-BELL, hs, profile, chalk, NPG 4507.
PH UNKNOWN, hl with dog, print, NPG.

GUYON, Richard Debaufre (1803-1856) general in t Hungarian army.
PR G.STODART, after a daguerreotype, tql seated in uniform, stipp NPG.

GUYTON, Emma Jane, see Worboise.

GWYNN, John (1827-1917) scholar and divine.
p SARAH PURSER, Trinity College, Dublin.

GYE, Frederick (1810-1878) director of Italian opera.
SC COUNT GLEICHEN, c1880, marble statue, Royal Opera Hou Covent Garden, London.

GYE, Marie Louise Cécilie Emma, see Dame Albani.

H

HAAST, Sir John Francis Julius von (1824-1887) geologist and explorer.
R.T. & Co, hs, woodcut, for *Illust London News*, 7 Aug 1886, NPG.

HACKER, Arthur (1858-1919) painter.
S.P.HALL, 'The St John's Wood Arts Club, 1895', chalk and wash, NPG 4404; pencil and chalk study, hs, profile, NPG 4389.
JOHN RUSSELL & SONS, hs, profile, print, for *National Photographic Record*, vol I, NPG. UNKNOWN, hs, semi-profile, print, NPG.

HADDON, Alfred Cort (1855-1940) anthropologist.
P.A.DE LÁSZLÓ, two portraits, 1924. Christ's College, Cambridge, and 1925, tql seated, Museum of Archaeology and Ethnology, Cambridge.
WALTER STONEMAN, 1921, hs, NPG (NPR).

HADEN, Sir Francis Seymour (1818-1910) surgeon and engraver.
G.P.JACOMB-HOOD, 1892, two portraits, hs, profile, NPG 1826, and tql seated with etching needle and plate, Royal Society of Painter Etchers, London.
JAMES ABBOTT MCNEILL WHISTLER, c1858-59, wl playing cello, pen and ink, Freer Gallery of Art, Washington DC, USA SIR WILLIAM ROTHENSTEIN, c1897, hl seated, profile, pencil, NPG 3870; related lith, BM, NPG.
J.A.MCNEILL WHISTLER, 1859, with his wife and James Traer, 'The Music Room', etch, McCallum Collection, University of Glasgow. Self-portrait, 1862, hl seated, etch, BM, NPG.
L.FLAMENG, 1875, tql seated with print and magnifying glass, etch, BM. C.W.SHERBORN, 1880, head, profile, oval, etch, BM.
A.LEGROS, 1881, hs, profile, mezz, BM. W.ROTHENSTEIN, 1897, hl asleep in a chair, BM, NPG.

HADOW, Sir (William) Henry (1859-1937) scholar, educationist and critic and historian of music.
SIR WILLIAM ROTHENSTEIN, 1920, hs, sanguine and black, University of Sheffield.
WALTER STONEMAN, two portraits, 1918 and 1931, both hs, NPG (NPR).

HAGGARD, Sir Henry Rider (1856-1925) novelist.
LEON LITTLE, 1886, hl, profile, NPG 2350. JOHN PETTIE, 1889, hs, NPG 2801. MAURICE GREIFFENHAGEN, 1897, Castle Museum, Norwich.
W.STRANG, hs, etch, NPG. W.TITTLE, 1922, hs, lith, NPG.
HARRY FURNISS, three pen and ink sketches, NPG 3459-61. SIR LESLIE WARD ('Spy'), wl, profile, chromo-lith, for *Vanity Fair*, 21 May 1887, NPG.
BARRAUD, tql, print, for *Men and Women of the Day*, vol III, 1890, NPG AX5491. G.C.BERESFORD, 1902, hs, neg, NPG X6513.
G.C.BERESFORD, c1902, hs, print, NPG. JOHN RUSSELL & SONS, hs, print, for *National Photographic Record*, vol II, NPG. RUSSELL & SONS, hs, woodburytype, NPG. SIR BENJAMIN STONE, wl, print, Birmingham Reference Library. UNKNOWN, tql, semi-profile, print, NPG X4615.

HAGHE, Louis (1806-1885) lithographer and water-colour painter.
UNKNOWN, after a photograph by M.J.Ganz of Brussels, hs,

woodcut, for *Illust London News*, 28 March 1885, NPG.

HAIG BROWN, William, see Brown.

HAINES, Sir Frederick Paul (1819-1909) field-marshal.
PR UNKNOWN, after a photograph by Shepherd & Bourne of Calcutta, hl in uniform, woodcut, for *Illust London News*, 4 Jan 1879, NPG.
C 'JTC', tql with orders, chromo-lith, for *Vanity Fair*, 25 March 1876, NPG.

HAINES, Herbert (1826-1872) archaeologist.
P UNKNOWN, memorial brass with effigy, Gloucester Cathedral.

HAKE, Thomas Gordon (1809-1895) physician and poet.
PH W. & A.H.FRY, hs, carte mignonne, NPG.

HALDANE, Richard Burdon Haldane, Viscount (1856-1928) statesman and philosopher.
P SIR A.S.COPE, 1914, wl, DoE (Privy Council). P.A.DE LÁSZLÓ, 1928, hs, NPG 2364. GEORGE FIDDES WATT, hl, Lincoln's Inn, London. G.FIDDES WATT, SNPG 1401.
D SIR WILLIAM ROTHENSTEIN, 1916, hs, pencil, SNPG 877.
C SIR LESLIE WARD ('Spy'), wl, profile, w/c study, for *Vanity Fair*, 13 Feb 1896, NPG 5125. SIR MAX BEERBOHM, 1907, '8.30 pm Mr Haldane exercising a ministerial prerogative', Ashmolean Museum, Oxford. SIR MAX BEERBOHM, 1912, hl, w/c, NPG 3855. 'OWL', wl, mechanical repro, for *Vanity Fair*, 19 March 1913, NPG. SIR BERNARD PARTRIDGE, drg, for *Punch*, 1 Nov 1926, NPG. SIR FRANCIS CARRUTHERS GOULD, tql, pen and ink, NPG 2840.
PH G.C.BERESFORD, 1903, two negs, hs and hs, profile, (X6514-15), and one print, NPG. OLIVE EDIS, c1920, hs, print, NPG X7806. OLIVE EDIS, c1920, hs, autochrome, NPG X7185. LONDON STEREOSCOPIC CO, hs, semi-profile, cabinet, NPG. JOHN RUSSELL & SONS, hs in wig, print, for *National Photographic Record*, vol I, NPG. WALTER STONEMAN, hs, NPG (NPR).

HALE-WHITE, Sir William (1857-1949) physician.
D SIR WILLIAM ROTHENSTEIN, hs, sanguine and white, NPG L168(4).
PH WALTER STONEMAN, 1931, hl seated, NPG (NPR).

HALFORD, Sir Henry St John, 3rd Bart (1828-1897) rifleman.
P JOHN COLLIER, 1897, tql seated, Leicester Town Hall.

HALIFAX, Sir Charles Lindley Wood, 2nd Viscount (1839-1934) president of English Church Union; supporter of reunion of Anglicans and Roman Catholics.
D S.P.HALL, pencil sketch, NPG 2376.
PH JOHN RUSSELL & SONS, hs, print, for *National Photographic Record*, vol II, NPG. WALTER STONEMAN, hl seated, NPG (NPR).

HALIFAX, Sir Charles Wood, 1st Viscount (1800-1885) chancellor of the exchequer.
P GEORGE RICHMOND, c1873, tql seated with Bath star and sash, Oriel College, Oxford; copy by Anthony de Brie, NPG 1677.
G F.BROMLEY, after B.R.Haydon, 'The Reform Banquet, 1832', etch, pub 1835, NPG. SIR GEORGE HAYTER, 'The House of Commons, 1833', oil, NPG 54. SIR JOHN GILBERT, 'The Coalition Ministry, 1854', pencil and wash, NPG 1125. JOHN PHILLIP, 'The House of Commons, 1860', oil, Palace of Westminster, London. W.P.FRITH, 'The Marriage of the Prince of Wales, 1863', oil,

Royal Coll.

PR W.HOLL, after G.Richmond, hs, stipple, one of 'Grillion's Club'
series, BM, NPG. W.WALKER, tql seated, mezz, pub 1856, BM, NPG.

C Several drgs by JOHN DOYLE, BM. CARLO PELLEGRINI ('Ape'), wl,
profile, chromo-lith, for *Vanity Fair*, 6 Aug 1870, NPG.

PH CALDESI, BLANFORD & CO, wl, carte, NPG (Album 114).
W.WALKER & SONS, tql seated, carte, NPG X13324.

HALL, Anna Maria, née Fielding (1800-1881) writer.

P G.DE LATRE, 1851, NGI 851.

D CARL CHRISTIAN VOGEL, 1850, hs, pencil and chalk, Staatliche
Kunstsammlungen, Dresden.

PR JOHN KIRKWOOD, after H.MacManus, tql, profile, etch, NPG.
D.MACLISE, wl seated at piano, ljth, from a drg originally pub in
Fraser's Mag, for Maginn's *Gallery of Illustrious Literary Charac-
ters*, 1873, BM, NPG. D.J.POUND, after a photograph by John &
Charles Watkins, tql seated, mixed engr, for *Drawing Room
Portrait Gallery*, BM. C.E.WAGSTAFF, after J.Hayter, tql seated,
octagon, stipple, for *New Monthly Mag*, 1838, BM, NPG.
UNKNOWN, hl seated, oval, stipple, NPG.

PH JOHN & CHARLES WATKINS, wl seated with her husband, carte,
NPG.

HALL, Sir Benjamin, see 1st Baron Llanover.

HALL, Sir Charles (1814-1883) vice-chancellor.

PH LOCK & WHITFIELD, hs, oval, woodburytype, for *Men of Mark*,
1876, NPG.

HALL, Sir Charles (1843-1900) recorder of London.

P JOHN COLLIER, RA 1895, tql seated in robes, Lincoln's Inn,
London.

C SIR LESLIE WARD ('Spy'), wl, semi-profile, chromo-lith, for
Vanity Fair, 18 Feb 1888, NPG.

HALL, Christopher Newman (1816-1902) congregationalist
divine.

PR J.COCHRAN, after G.Sayer, hl seated, stipple, NPG. D.J.POUND,
after a photograph by John & Charles Watkins, tql, stipple and
line, BM, NPG.

PH BARRAUD, hs, profile, print, for *Men and Women of the Day*, vol III,
1890, NPG AX5490. MAULL & POLYBLANK, wl seated, carte, NPG.
JOHN & CHARLES WATKINS, wl, carte, NPG AX7500.

HALL, Sir Edward Marshall (1858-1929) advocate.

C HARRY FURNISS, pen and ink sketch, NPG 3462. SIR LESLIE WARD
('Spy'), wl seated, chromo-lith, for *Vanity Fair*, 24 Sept 1903,
NPG.

PH LONDON STEREOSCOPIC CO, hs, print, NPG. JOHN RUSSELL &
SONS, hs, print, for *National Photographic Record*, vol I, NPG.

HALL, Samuel Carter (1800-1889) author.

D CARL CHRISTIAN VOGEL, 1850, hs, pencil and chalk, Staatliche
Kunstsammlungen, Dresden.

SC H.B.BURLOWE, 1834, marble bust, Bethnal Green Museum,
London.

PR D.J.POUND, after a photograph by Mayall, tql seated, stipple, for
The Drawing Room Portrait Gallery, 1861, BM, NPG.

PH F.JOUBERT, hs, carte, NPG AX7516. JOHN & CHARLES WATKINS, wl
with his wife, carte, NPG.

HALL, Sir William King (1816-1886) admiral.

PR UNKNOWN, tql in uniform, woodcut, for *The British Workman*,
Sept 1877, NPG.

HALLAM, Arthur Henry (1811-1833) friend of Tennyson.

P Attrib SIR MARTIN ARCHER SHEE, hs, Eton College, Berks.

D JAMES SPEDDING, hs, Lincoln Museum and Art Gallery.

SC SIR FRANCIS CHANTREY, marble bust, Trinity College,
Cambridge.

HALLAM, Henry Fitzmaurice (1824-1850) scholar.

PR F.HOLL, after G.Richmond, hs, line, BM, NPG.

HALLÉ, Sir Charles (1819-1895) conductor and founder
the Hallé Orchestra.

P G.F.WATTS, *c*1870, hl seated, profile, NPG 1004.

G C.BAUGNIET, 'The Musical Union, 1851', lith, NPG.

SC EDWARD ONSLOW FORD, marble bust, Manchester City A
Gallery. UNKNOWN, death mask, Watts Gallery, Compto
Surrey.

PH BARRAUD, tql seated, print, for *Men and Women of the Day*, vol
1889, NPG AX5447. ELLIOTT & FRY, two cartes, both hs, profi
NPG. ELLIOTT & FRY, hs, carte, NPG (Album 99). UNKNOWN,
seated, carte, NPG (Album 108).

HALLÉ, Wilma Maria Francisca, Lady, forme
Madame Norman-Neruda (1839-1911) violinist.

PH BARRAUD, tql with violin, oval, print, for *Men and Women of*
Day, vol II, 1889, NPG AX5446.

HALLIDAY, Andrew (1830-1877) dramatist.

PR UNKNOWN, hs, woodcut, for *Entr'Acte* Supplement, 21 A
1877, Harvard Theatre Collection, Cambridge, Mass, US
UNKNOWN, after a photograph by London Stereoscopic Co,
woodcut, for *Illust London News*, 21 Aug 1877, NPG.

PH Three cartes by BERTIN of Brighton, ELLIOTT & FRY and LOND
STEREOSCOPIC CO, all hs, NPG.

HALLIWELL-PHILLIPPS, James Orchard (1820-18
biographer of Shakespeare.

SL UNKNOWN, 1839, wl, profile, NPG 3859.

PR UNKNOWN, hs, woodcut, for *Illust London News*, 1889,
W.L.WALTON, hl, lith, NPG.

PH ERNEST EDWARDS, wl, print, for *Men of Eminence*, ed L.Ree
vol I, 1863, NPG.

HALSBURY, Hardinge Stanley Giffard, 1st Earl of (18
1921) lord chancellor.

P JOHN COLLIER, 1897, tql in robes, Inner Temple, London; c
by W.Menzies, Merton College, Oxford.

D S.P.HALL, pencil sketch, NPG 2336.

C HARRY FURNISS, two pen and ink sketches, NPG 3393-4. JOS
SIMPSON, wl seated, ink, NPG 4547. SIR LESLIE WARD ('Spy'),
profile, w/c study, for *Vanity Fair*, 22 June 1878, NPG 3290.

PH OLIVE EDIS, tql seated, profile, print, NPG. FRY & SON, hs, pr
for *Our Conservative and Unionist Statesmen*, vol III, NPG (Alb
20).

HALSWELLE, Keeley (1832-1891) artist.

PR R.T. & CO, hs, semi-profile, wood engr, for *Illust London Ne*
18 April 1891, NPG.

HAMBLIN SMITH, James, see Smith.

HAMERTON, Philip Gilbert (1834-1894) writer on ar

PR UNKNOWN, after a photograph, hs, woodcut, BM.

HAMILTON, George Alexander (1802-1871) politician

PR J.POSSELWHITE, after W.J.Newton, hl seated, octagon, stip
for *Eminent Conservative Statesmen*, BM, NPG. UNKNOWN,
woodcut, for *Illust London News*, 11 Dec 1852, NPG.

HAMILTON, Lord George Francis (1845-1927) statesm

P SIR J.D.MACDONALD, The Admiralty (Plymouth Hospital)

C SIR LESLIE WARD ('Spy'), wl, profile, chromo-lith, for *Va*
Fair, 5 April 1879, NPG.

PH LOCK & WHITFIELD, hs, oval, woodburytype, for *Men of M*
1876, NPG. RUSSELL & SONS, hs, print, for *Our Conservative*
Unionist Statesmen, vol III, NPG (Album 20). WALTER STONEM
1920, hs, profile, NPG (NPR).

HAMILTON, Sir Ian Standish Monteith (1853-19

general.
P J.S.SARGENT, 1898, tql, TATE 5246. J.S.SARGENT, hs, SNPG 1406.
D I.SHELDON-WILLIAMS, 1900, hl, pencil and w/c, NPG 4039(3). SIR WILLIAM ROTHENSTEIN, 1916, hs, pencil, NPG 3871. SIR W.ROTHENSTEIN, 1916, pencil drg, IWM.
SC SIGISMUND DE STROBL, RA 1933, bust, National Army Museum, Sandhurst, Camberley, Surrey.
C SIR LESLIE WARD ('Spy'), wl, profile, in uniform, w/c study, for *Vanity Fair*, 2 May 1901, NPG 4609.
PH WALTER STONEMAN, 1917, hs in uniform, NPG (NPR).

HAMILTON, James (1811-1885), see 1st Duke of Abercorn.

HAMILTON, James (1814-1867) presbyterian minister.
PR C.BAUGNIET, wl in pulpit, lith, BM, NPG. G.B.SHAW, after Henry Anelay, hs, stipple, NPG. Several prints by unknown artists, NPG.

HAMILTON, James (1838-1913), see 2nd Duke of Abercorn.

HAMILTON, John Andrew, see Viscount Sumner.

HAMILTON, John McLure (1853-1936) artist.
P THOMAS EAKINS, 1895, wl, Wadsworth Athenaeum, Hartford, Conn, USA.

HAMILTON, Sir Richard Vesey (1829-1912) admiral.
P UNKNOWN, after 1895, tql in uniform with Bath ribbon and star and other medals, NMM, Greenwich.

HAMILTON, Sir Robert George Crookshank (1836-1895) governor of Tasmania.
PR UNKNOWN, after a photograph by Lombardi & Co, hs, semi-profile, woodcut, for *Illust London News*, 20 May 1882, NPG.

HAMILTON, Sir Robert North Collie, 6th Bart (1802-1887) Indian official.
P UNKNOWN, DoE (New Delhi).
PR W.SHARP, after G.Hayter, hl, lith, BM, NPG.

HAMILTON, Walter Kerr (1808-1869) bishop of Salisbury.
P GEORGE RICHMOND, 1858, hl seated, Bishop's Palace, Salisbury.
PR W.HOLL, after a drg by G.Richmond of 1858, hs, stipple, pub 1862, BM, NPG.
PH MAYALL, wl seated, carte, NPG AX7479.

HAMILTON, William Alexander Anthony Archibald Douglas, 11th Duke of (1811-1863) Knight-marischal of Scotland.
P UNKNOWN, hl as a boy, Brodick Castle, Strathclyde region, Scotland. RICHARD BUCKNER, two portraits, hs, and wl in Highland dress, Brodick Castle. Attrib R.BUCKNER, hl, Brodick Castle.
D JOHN HAYTER, 1835, hs, chalk, Brodick Castle. SIR THOMAS LAWRENCE, hl with Lady Susan, oval, chalk, Lennoxlove, Lothian region, Scotland.
G FILIPO PALIZZI, 1848, wl on horseback, with the Duchess of Hamilton and the Earl of Angus, oil, Brodick Castle. UNKNOWN, with Princess Marie of Baden, Susan, Countess of Lincoln, and others, at Brodick, oil, Brodick Castle.
PR W.HOLL, tql, profile, seated, mixed engr, pub 1864, BM.

HAMILTON, William Alexander Baillie (1803-1881) admiral.
G STEPHEN PEARCE, 'The Arctic Council planning a search for Sir John Franklin', oil, NPG 1208; oil study, 1850, hs, NPG 908.

HAMILTON, Sir William Rowan (1805-1865) mathematician.
SC THOMAS KIRK, 1830, marble bust, The Dunraven-Limerick Estates Co. J.H.FOLEY, 1867, after photographs and Kirk's bust, marble bust, Trinity College, Dublin.
PR J.KIRKWOOD, after C.Grey, hl seated with mace, lith, NPG.

E

HAMILTON-GORDON, Arthur Charles, see 1st Baron Stanmore.

HAMLEY, Sir Edward Bruce (1824-1893) general and writer.
P SIR JOHN WATSON GORDON, c1856, hl in uniform, Staff College, Camberley, Surrey.
PR UNKNOWN, after a photograph by Fradelle, hs in uniform, woodcut, for *Illust London News*, 12 Aug 1882, NPG. UNKNOWN, hs in uniform, chromo-lith, BM.
C CARLO PELLEGRINI ('Ape'), wl, profile, chromo-lith, for *Vanity Fair*, 2 April 1887, NPG.
PH UNKNOWN, hl in uniform with orders, print, NPG.

HAMMOND, Edmund Hammond, Baron (1802-1890) diplomat.
SC WILLIAM BEHNES, 1849, bust, Eton College, Berks. HENRY WEEKES, 1874, marble bust, DoE (Foreign Office, London).
PR UNKNOWN, hs, woodcut, for *Illust London News*, 1 Nov 1873, NPG.
C CARLO PELLEGRINI ('Ape'), wl, profile, chromo-lith, for *Vanity Fair*, 19 June 1875, NPG.

HAMPDEN, Sir Henry Bouverie William Brand, 1st Viscount (1814-1892) speaker of the House of Commons.
P FRANK HOLL, 1885, wl, Palace of Westminster, London.
PR F.SARGENT, tql, aged 69, etch, BM.
C J.J.TISSOT, wl in wig and gown, chromo-lith, for *Vanity Fair*, 16 Nov 1872, NPG.
PH LOCK & WHITFIELD, hs, oval, woodburytype, for *Men of Mark*, 1876, NPG. LOMBARDI, two cartes, hl seated, profile, and tql, NPG (Album 136). LONDON STEREOSCOPIC CO, hs, carte, NPG (Album 40).

HAMPDEN, Henry Robert Brand, 2nd Viscount (1841-1906) governor of New South Wales.
PR UNKNOWN, after a photograph by Russell & Sons, hs, wood engr, for *Illust London News*, 22 June 1895, NPG.
C SIR LESLIE WARD ('Spy'), wl, profile, chromo-lith, for *Vanity Fair*, 15 March 1884, NPG.

HANBURY, Daniel (1825-1875) chemist.
PR C.H.JEENS, after a photograph, hs, stipple, for his *Science Papers*, 1876, BM, NPG.

HANBURY, Robert William (1845-1903) president of the Board of Agriculture.
D S.P.HALL, pencil sketch, NPG 2327.
C SIR LESLIE WARD ('Spy'), wl, profile, chromo-lith, for *Vanity Fair*, 28 May 1896, NPG.
PH SIR BENJAMIN STONE, two prints, both wl, NPG.

HANKEY, Thomson (1805-1893) politician.
PR J.H.LYNCH, tql, lith, Bank of England, London. UNKNOWN, hl, woodcut, for *Illust London News*, 4 Feb 1854, NPG.

HANLAN or **HANLON, Edward (1855-1908)** Canadian oarsman.
PR UNKNOWN, hs, lith, NPG.

HANMER, John Hanmer, Baron (1809-1881) poet and politician.
D FREDERICK SARGENT, c1870-80, hl, profile, pencil, NPG 1834(n).
G SIR GEORGE HAYTER, 'The House of Commons, 1833', oil, NPG 54.
PR UNKNOWN, after a photograph by Maull & Co, hs, semi-profile, woodcut, for *Illust London News*, 12 Oct 1872, NPG.

HANNA, William (1808-1882) theological writer.
SC C.B.BIRCH, c1894, statue, in front of St Enoch's Church, Belfast.
PH T.RODGER of St Andrews, hs, carte, NPG.

HANNEN, Sir James Hannen, Baron (1821–1894) judge.
P THEODORE BLAKE WIRGMAN, RA 1890, tql seated in court dress, Middle Temple, London; related etch, BM.
D S.P.HALL, pencil sketches, NPG 2232, 2296 and 2305.
C SIR LESLIE WARD ('Spy'), hl seated at bench, chromo-lith, for *Vanity Fair*, 21 April 1888, NPG.

HANNINGTON, James (1847–1885) bishop of Eastern equatorial Africa.
PR UNKNOWN, after a photograph by Fradelle, hs, wood engr, for *Illust London News*, 20 Feb 1886, NPG.

HANSOM, Joseph Aloysius (1803–1882) architect and inventor of the Hansom cab.
PR R. & E.TAYLOR, hs, semi-profile, woodcut, for *Illust London News*, 15 July 1882, NPG.

HANSON, Sir Richard Davies (1805–1876) chief-justice of South Australia.
PR UNKNOWN, after a photograph by John Watkins, hs, in wig and gown, oval, woodcut, for *Illust London News*, 31 July 1869, NPG.

HARBEN, Sir Henry (1823–1911) pioneer of industrial life assurance.
P NORMAN MACBETH, 1872, Prudential Mutual Life Assurance Association, London. JOHN COLLIER, 1899, Hampstead Town Hall, London.

HARCOURT, Charles (1838–1880) actor.
PH UNKNOWN, hs, woodburytype, carte, NPG.

HARCOURT, Sir William George Granville Venables Vernon (1827–1904) statesman.
P LANCE CALKIN, after Sir A.S.Cope, National Liberal Club, London.
D S.P.HALL, pencil sketches, NPG 2307, 2315 and 2317.
G G.F.WATTS, 'The School of Legislation', fresco, c1860, (the figure of Justinian is a portrait of Harcourt), Lincoln's Inn, London.
SC WALDO STORY, 1899, plaster bust, NPG 1461. WALDO STORY, 1906, marble statue in robes of Chancellor of the Exchequer, Palace of Westminster, London.
PR Several popular prints, BM, NPG.
C ALFRED THOMPSON ('Atη'), wl, chromo-lith, for *Vanity Fair*, 4 June 1870, NPG. SIR LESLIE WARD ('Spy'), wl seated, 'Mixed Political Wares', chromo-lith, for *Vanity Fair*, 3 Dec 1892, NPG. Possibly (H.C.SEPPING) WRIGHT ('Stuff'), 'Empire Makers and Breakers', chromo-lith, for *Vanity Fair*, 25 Nov 1897, NPG. 'CLOISTER', wl, profile, in monk's robes, chromo-lith, for *Vanity Fair*, 11 May 1899, NPG. SIR MAX BEERBOHM, 1926, with Mr Loulou Harcourt in 1889, Sheffield City Art Galleries. Several drgs by HARRY FURNISS and SIR FRANCIS CARRUTHERS GOULD, NPG 3390–2, 2841–5.
PH BARRAUD, tql seated, print, for *Men and Women of the Day*, vol III, 1890, NPG AX5482. BARRAUD, hs, cabinet, NPG. LOCK & WHITFIELD, hs, semi-profile, oval, woodburytype, for *Men of Mark*, 1877, NPG. PALMER, hs, carte, NPG. SIR BENJAMIN STONE, six prints, all wl, NPG. H.J.WHITLOCK, hl, carte, NPG (Album 136).

HARCOURT-SMITH, Sir Cecil (1859–1944) archaeologist and director of the Victoria and Albert Museum.
SC LADY WELBY, bust, V & A.
C SIR MAX BEERBOHM, 'Sir Cecil Harcourt-Smith receives a deputation from a Northern Town that is meditating a Museum', 1924, V & A.
PH WALTER STONEMAN, two portraits, 1924 and 1934, hs and hl, NPG.

HARDIE, James Keir (1856–1915) Socialist leader.
P H.J.DOBSON, two portraits: 1892, hl, Palace of Westminster, London, and 1893, tql, SNPG 1580.
D SYLVIA PANKHURST, two drgs: c1910, hs, chalk, NPG 3978; before 1910, head, w/c, NPG 3979. COSMO ROWE, after a photograph, by G.C.Beresford, 1905, head, pencil, NPG 2542.
SC BENNO SCHOTZ, c1939, bust, Cumnock, Ayrshire; replica, Palace of Westminster, London.
C HARRY FURNISS, pen and ink sketch, NPG 3579. SIR FRANCIS CARRUTHERS GOULD, hs, profile, pen and ink, NPG 2846. SIR LESLIE WARD ('Spy'), wl, profile, w/c study, for *Vanity Fair*, Feb 1906, NPG 4456.
PH G.C.BERESFORD, 1905, hs, neg, NPG X6516. SIR BENJAMIN STONE, four prints, all wl, NPG. ARTHUR WESTON, tql, cabinet, NPG. Various prints, NPG (*Daily Herald*).

HARDING, John (1805–1874) bishop of Bombay.
P J.BRIDGES, 1851, tql seated, Worcester College, Oxford.
PR R.J.LANE, after F.Talfourd, hs, lith, BM, NPG.

HARDINGE, Sir Arthur Edward (1828–1892) general.
PR MORRIS & CO, photo-lith, The Convent, Gibraltar.
PH UNKNOWN, wl in uniform as colonel of the Coldstream Guards, photogravure, BM (Engr Ports Coll).

HARDINGE of Penshurst, Charles Hardinge, 1st Baron (1858–1944) diplomat and Viceroy of India.
P SIR WILLIAM ORPEN, 1919, hl, NPG 4179.
PH WALTER STONEMAN, 1939, tql seated, for NPR, NPG X1442.

HARDWICKE, Charles Philip Yorke, 5th Earl of (1836–1897) sportsman and comptroller of the household.
D FREDERICK SARGENT, 1876, tql seated, pencil, NPG 1834(o).
C CARLO PELLEGRINI ('Ape'), wl, profile, w/c study, for *Vanity Fair*, 9 May 1874, NPG 4717.

HARDY, Gathorne Gathorne-, see 1st Earl of Cranbrook.

HARDY, Herbert Hardy Cozens-, see 1st Baron COZENS-Hardy.

HARDY, Thomas (1840–1928) novelist and poet.
P WILLIAM STRANG, 1893, hs, NPG 2929. JACQUES-EMILE BLANCHE, 1906, two portraits, hl seated, TATE 3580, and tql seated, profile, Manchester City Art Gallery. SIR HUBERT VON HERKOMER, c1906, hs, Dorset County Museum, Dorchester. W.W.OULESS, 1922, hs, NPG 2181. Several portraits by R.G.EVES: 1923, hs, NPG 2498; 1923, two portraits, both hs, one in D Litt robes, Dorset County Museum; 1923, tql seated, University of Texas, Austin, USA; 1924, hl seated, TATE 4461; hl seated, Birmingham City Art Gallery. AUGUSTUS JOHN, 1923, hl seated, Fitzwilliam Museum, Cambridge; pencil study, Fitzwilliam Museum. R.E.FULLER MAITLAND, Magdalene College, Cambridge.
D SIR WILLIAM ROTHENSTEIN, 1903, hs, chalk, Dorset County Museum. WILLIAM STRANG, 1910, drgs, Royal Coll, Fitzwilliam Museum, Cambridge and Dorset County Museum. SIR WILLIAM ROTHENSTEIN, 1916, pencil drgs, Manchester City Art Gallery and The Athenaeum, London. WILLIAM STRANG, 1919, hs, profile, pencil, NPG 1922. WILLIAM STRANG, 1919, pencil, NGS. W.STRANG, hl, profile, pencil, BM.
SC SIR WILLIAM HAMO THORNYCROFT, 1917, bronze head, NPG 2156. SIR W.H.THORNYCROFT, marble head, Dorset County Museum. THEODORE SPICER-SIMSON, c1922, plasticine medallion, NPG 2050. MAGGIE RICHARDSON MITCHELL, 1923, bronze bust, Dorset County Museum. ERIC KENNINGTON, c1931, seated statue, Dorchester.
PR W.ROTHENSTEIN, 1897, tql, lith, BM, NPG. W.STRANG, c1919–20, several engrs, BM, NPG, NGS, Fitzwilliam Museum, Glasgow Art Gallery and University of Glasgow.
C SIR MAX BEERBOHM, 'Mr Hardy composing a lyric', Charterhouse School, Surrey; variant, Dorset County Museum.

HARRY FURNISS, several pen and ink drgs, NPG 3463–4 and 3580–3. SIR LESLIE WARD ('Spy'), wl, chromo-lith, for *Vanity Fair*, 4 June 1892, NPG.
PH Several prints, various dates and sizes, Dorset County Museum. BARRAUD, hl, print, for *Men and Women of the Day*, vol II, 1889, NPG AX5452. W. & D.DOWNEY, tql seated, woodburytype, for Cassell's *Cabinet Portrait Gallery*, vol V, 1894, NPG. SIR BENJAMIN STONE, 1908, wl, print, NPG. ALVIN LANGDON COBURN, 1913, hs, photogravure, for *More Men of Mark*, 1922, NPG AX7809. OLIVE EDIS, 1914, hs, profile, autochrome, NPG X7186. OLIVE EDIS, two prints, hl seated, profile, and hl seated, NPG. OLIVE EDIS, hs, profile, print, NPG. WILLIAM BELLOWS, wl with Edmund Gosse, print, NPG. CLIVE HOLLAND, two prints, both hl seated, NPG. FREDERICK HOLLYER, print, Gernsheim Collection, University of Texas. LONDON STEREOSCOPIC CO, hs, profile, print, NPG. RUSSELL & SONS, hs, profile, print, for *National Photographic Record*, vol II, NPG. UNKNOWN, hs, platinotype, NPG X4616. UNKNOWN, hs, photogravure, NPG.

HARDY, Sir Thomas Duffus (1804-1878) archivist.
PR UNKNOWN, hs, oval, woodcut, NPG.

HARE, Augustus John Cuthbert (1834-1903) author.
P GIUSEPPE DA POZZO, tql, University College, Oxford.
PH UNKNOWN, hl, woodburytype, NPG.

HARE, Sir John (Fairs) (1844-1921) actor.
P SIR J.E.MILLAIS, 1893, tql, Garrick Club, London. H.G.RIVIERE, 1908, tql seated as Lord Kildare in *A Quiet Rubber*, Garrick Club.
PR W.H.KENDAL, 1881, wl, back-view, as Baron Croodle in Pinero's *The Money Spinner*, process print, NPG. E.MATTHEWS & SONS, hs, oval, lith, NPG.
C SIR LESLIE WARD ('Spy'), wl, chromo-lith, for *Vanity Fair*, 1 March 1890, NPG. HARRY FURNISS, wl, pen and ink sketch, for *The Garrick Gallery*, 1905, NPG 4095(5). E.A.ABBEY, wl as Uncle Sam, pencil, Garrick Club.
PH BARRAUD, hs, print, for *Men and Women of the Day*, vol III, 1890, NPG AX5488. W. & D.DOWNEY, hl, woodburytype, for Cassell's *Cabinet Portrait Gallery*, vol V, 1894, NPG. LONDON STEREOSCOPIC CO, hs, carte, NPG. UNKNOWN, wl seated as Colonel Daunt in *The Queen's Shilling*, woodburytype, NPG AX7704. UNKNOWN, hs, woodburytype, carte, NPG AX7687.

HARE, Thomas (1806-1891) political reformer.
P LOWES DICKINSON, 1867, hs, NPG 1819.
D ALICE WESTLAKE (his daughter), c1885, hs, profile, pencil, NPG 1820.

HARGREAVES, John (1839-1895) sportsman.
PR UNKNOWN, hs, stipple, NPG. UNKNOWN, tql, lith, 1879, NPG.
C SIR LESLIE WARD ('Spy'), wl, profile, w/c study, for *Vanity Fair*, 11 June 1887, NPG 4718.

HARINGTON, Edward Charles (1804-1881) chancellor and sub-dean of Exeter Cathedral.
P UNKNOWN, The Deanery, Exeter.

HARKER, Alfred (1859-1939) petrologist.
D ROBIN GUTHRIE, 1939, two drgs: hs, pencil, and head, pen and ink, Department of Mineralogy and Petrology, University of Cambridge.

HARKNESS, Robert (1816-1878) geologist.
P J.B.BRENAN, 1854, tql, Department of Geology, University of Cambridge.
PR UNKNOWN, after a photograph by C.Voss Park, hs, woodcut, for *Illust London News*, 26 Oct 1878, NPG.

HARLEY, George (1829-1896) physician.
PR UNKNOWN, after a photograph by Jerrard, hs, semi-profile,

wood engr, for *Illust London News*, 7 Nov 1896, NPG.
PH UNKNOWN, tql seated in robes, photogravure, NPG.

HARMAN, Sir George Byng (1830-1892) general.
PR UNKNOWN, hs in uniform, lith, BM.

HARNESS, Sir Henry Drury (1804-1883) general, colonel-commandant Royal Engineers.
P UNKNOWN, hl, oval, Royal Engineers (Pasley House).

HARREL, Sir David (1841-1939) Irish administrator and public servant.
PH WALTER STONEMAN, 1918, hs, NPG (NPR).

HARRIS, Sir Augustus Henry Glossop (1852-1896) actor, impresario and dramatist.
SC UNKNOWN, bronze bust on drinking fountain, Drury Lane Theatre, London.
PR SIDNEY KENT, 1894, hs, semi-profile, lith, NPG.
C AUBREY BEARDSLEY, included in a design for the Frontispiece to John Davidson's *Plays*, 1894, pen and ink, TATE 4172. A.M.BROADLEY, wl as a baby in a pram, pen and ink sketch, NPG. 'HAY', wl seated, w/c, NPG. HARRY FURNISS, pen and ink sketch, NPG 3584. SIR LESLIE WARD ('Spy'), wl, chromo-lith, for *Vanity Fair*, 28 Sept 1889, NPG.
PH WALERY, tql print, NPG.

HARRIS, George Francis Robert Harris, 3rd Baron (1810-1872) governor of Madras.
P SIR FRANCIS GRANT, 1859, wl in uniform, Government House, Madras.
PH Studio of RICHARD BEARD, 1840s, hs, daguerreotype, NPG P117. Attrib HILLS & SAUNDERS, 1863, with the houseparty group after DCL presentation at Christ Church, Oxford, print, NPG X4336.

HARRIS, George Robert Canning Harris, 4th Baron (1851-1932) cricketer and administrator.
P ARTHUR HACKER, exhib 1919, hl seated, Marylebone Cricket Club, London. After SIR HUBERT VON HERKOMER, County Hall, Maidstone, Kent. WEBSTER HOARE, hl, Borough of Faversham, Kent.
PR JOSEPH BROWN, after a photograph by Downey, hs, stipple, for *Baily's Mag*, 1880, NPG.
C SIR LESLIE WARD ('Spy'), wl, profile, in cricket dress, chromo-lith, for *Vanity Fair*, 16 July 1881, NPG.
PH WALTER STONEMAN, two portraits, 1918 and 1931, both hs, the first in uniform, NPG (NPR).

HARRIS, James Howard, see 3rd Earl of Malmesbury.

HARRIS, James Rendel (1852-1941) biblical scholar, archaeologist and orientalist.
PH JOHN RUSSELL & SONS, hs, print, for *National Photographic Record*, vol I, NPG. WALTER STONEMAN, 1932, hs, NPG (NPR).

HARRIS, James Thomas ('Frank') (1856-1931) writer, editor and adventurer.
P SIR WILLIAM ROTHENSTEIN, 1895, hs, NPG L168(3).
C SIR MAX BEERBOHM, two drgs, c1898 and c1910, University of Texas, Austin, USA. JOHN DUNCAN FERGUSSON, 1911–13, head, brush and ink, NPG 4883. 'OWL', wl, mechanical repro, for *Vanity Fair*, 12 Nov 1913, NPG.
PH ALVIN LANGDON COBURN, 1913, hs, photogravure, for *More Men of Mark*, 1922, NPG X7815.

HARRIS, John (1802-1856) principal of New College, London; author of *Mammon*.
D Attrib GEORGE RICHMOND, hs, crayon, Dr Williams's Library, London.
PR R.WOODMAN, after H.Room, hl seated, line and stipple, pub 1837, BM, NPG. J.COCHRAN, hl, stipple and line, NPG.

HARRIS, Sir William Cornwallis (1807–1848) engineer and traveller.

P Attrib R.R.REINAGLE, c1823, hl in uniform, NPG 4098.

D OCTAVIUS OAKLEY, 1845, tql, w/c, Africana Museum, Johannesburg, South Africa.

HARRISON, Benjamin (1808–1887) archdeacon of Maidstone.

PR C.HOLL, after G.Richmond, hs, stipple, NPG.

C SIR LESLIE WARD ('Spy'), wl, profile, chromo-lith, for *Vanity Fair*, 6 June 1885, NPG.

HARRISON, Frederic (1831–1923) author and positivist.

P By his son, tql seated, Wadham College, Oxford.

D W.R.SICKERT, 1912, tql, profile, pencil, NPG 2214.

C CARLO PELLEGRINI ('Ape'), hl, w/c study, for *Vanity Fair*, 23 Jan 1886, NPG 2718.

PH G.C.BERESFORD, two prints, hs, and hs, profile, NPG. W. & D.DOWNEY, tql seated, woodburytype, for Cassell's *Cabinet Portrait Gallery*, vol II, 1891, NPG.

HARRISON, Jane Ellen (1850–1928) classical scholar.

P AUGUSTUS JOHN, 1909, wl reclining, Newnham College, Cambridge.

D THEO VAN RYSSELBERGHE, 1925, hs, pencil, NPG 5220.

HARRISON, Thomas Elliott (1808–1888) civil engineer.

P W.W.OULESS, replica, c1885–88, tql seated, Institution of Civil Engineers, London.

HARRISON, William (1812–1860) commander of the Great Eastern steamship

PR D.J.POUND, after a photograph by Mayall, tql seated, stipple and line, for *The Drawing Room Portrait Gallery of Eminent Personages*, NPG.

HARRISON, William (1813–1868) singer and operatic manager.

PR C.R.BONE, hs, lith, BM. D.J.POUND, after a photograph by Mayall, tql, stipple and line, BM, NPG.

HARROWBY, Dudley Francis Stuart Ryder, 3rd Earl of (1831–1900) educationalist.

P HERMAN HERKOMER, 1899. The British and Foreign Bible Society, London.

D GEORGE RICHMOND, 1860, hs, chalk, NPG 4226.

PR H.C.BALDING, after a photograph by H.Barraud, hl, stipple and line, NPG. (In vol II this was erroneously stated to be a portrait of 2nd Earl of Harrowby.)

C CARLO PELLEGRINI ('Ape'), wl, profile, w/c study, for *Vanity Fair*, 28 Nov 1885, NPG 2577.

PH LOCK & WHITFIELD, hs, oval, woodburytype, for *Men of Mark*, 1878, NPG.

HART, Sir Andrew Searle (1811–1890) vice-provost of Trinity College, Dublin.

P J.B.YEATS, tql seated, Trinity College, Dublin.

HART, Sir Robert, 1st Bart (1835–1911) inspector-general of customs in China.

P FRANK MCKELVEY, posthumous, hl seated, Queen's University, Belfast.

SC HENRY PEGRAM, c1914, statue, Shanghai.

C 'IMP', wl in Chinese dress, chromo-lith, for *Vanity Fair*, 27 Dec 1894, NPG.

PH SIR BENJAMIN STONE, 1908, wl, print, Birmingham Reference Library.

HART, Solomon Alexander (1806–1881) painter.

P Two self-portraits, hs, City Art Gallery, Exeter, and wl, Royal Academy, London.

D C.H.LEAR, 1845, hs, pencil, NPG 1456(9). C.B.BIRCH, two sketches, c1853, hl, pencil, NPG 2479, and c1858, head, pencil, NPG 2476. C.W.COPE, c1862, hs, profile, sketch, NPG 3182(3).

PR UNKNOWN, hs, woodcut, for *Illust London News*, 25 June 1881, NPG.

PH ERNEST EDWARDS, wl, print, for *Men of Eminence*, ed L.Reeve, vol I, 1863, NPG. JOHN & CHARLES WATKINS, wl, profile, carte, NPG (Album 104). UNKNOWN, hs, carte, NPG (Album 103).

HARTINGTON, Spencer Compton Cavendish, Marquess of, see 8th Duke of Devonshire.

HARVEY, Sir George (1806–1876) painter.

P JOHN BALLANTYNE, SNPG 277. ROBERT HERDMAN, 1874, hs, semi-profile, Royal Scottish Academy, Edinburgh; version, SNPG 848.

SC JOHN HUTCHISON, c1871, marble bust, Royal Scottish Academy.

PR UNKNOWN, woodcut, for *Art Journal*, 1850, BM. R. & E.T., after T.Scott, hs, as an old man, woodcut, BM. UNKNOWN, hs, woodcut, for *Illust London News*, 12 Feb 1876, BM.

PH JOHN MOFFAT, tql seated, carte, NPG (Album 102).

HARVEY, William Henry (1811–1866) botanist.

D SIR F.W.BURTON, head, chalk, NGI 2032.

PR T.H.MAGUIRE, tql seated, lith, one of set of *Ipswich Museum Portraits*, 1851, BM. UNKNOWN, hs, profile, line, NPG. UNKNOWN, hs, stipple, NPG.

HASTINGS, Lady Flora Elizabeth (1806–1839) lady-in-waiting to the Duchess of Kent.

SL UNKNOWN, hl, profile, pasted by Queen Victoria into an album, Royal Coll.

PR FINDEN, after E.Hawkins, tql seated, octagon, stipple, for Finden's *Female Aristocracy*, 1840, BM, NPG. UNKNOWN, hs, lith, NPG.

HATHERLEY, William Page Wood, Baron (1801–1881) lord chancellor.

P GEORGE RICHMOND, 1872, wl in chancellor's robes, NPG 646.

G L.C.DICKINSON, 'Gladstone's Cabinet of 1868', oil, NPG 5116. H.T.WELLS, 'The Lord Chancellor's Procession, 1868', oil, DoE (Law Courts, London).

PR W.HOLL, after G.Richmond, hs, stipple, one of 'Grillion's Club' series, BM. UNKNOWN, hs, profile, lith, NPG.

C CARLO PELLEGRINI ('Ape'), wl seated, chromo-lith, for *Vanity Fair*, 20 March 1869, NPG.

PH UNKNOWN, hs, carte, NPG (Album 120).

HATHERTON, Edward Littleton, 3rd Viscount (1842–1930) military secretary to governor-general of Canada.

C (Possibly H.C.SEPPING) WRIGHT ('Stuff'), wl seated, w/c study, for *Vanity Fair*, 23 May 1895, NPG 4605.

HATTON, John Liptrot (1809–1886) composer.

PR KNIEHUBER, hs, lith, BM. R.T., hs, semi-profile, woodcut, for *Illust London News*, 2 Oct 1886, NPG.

PH HERBERT WATKINS, wl seated, carte, NPG.

HATTON, Joseph (1841–1907) novelist and journalist.

PR P.NAUMANN & R.TAYLOR & Co, 'Our Literary Contributors – Past and Present', woodcut, for *Illust London News*, 14 May 1892, BM, NPG. UKNOWN, after a photograph by Vander Weyde, hs, wood engr, for *Harper's Mag*, 1888, NPG.

HAUGHTON, John Colpoys (1817–1887) lieutenant-general.

PR UNKNOWN, wl seated in oriental dress, lith, NPG.

HAUGHTON, Samuel (1821–1897) scientist.

P SARAH PURSER, 1883, tql seated, Trinity College, Dublin.

HAVELOCK–ALLAN, Sir Henry Marshman, 1st Bart (1839–1897) lieutenant-general.

c SIR LESLIE WARD ('Spy'), nearly wl, profile, chromo-lith, for *Vanity Fair*, 29 March 1879, NPG.

PH BASSANO, 1897, several negs, various sizes, in uniform and with orders, NPG X602–5 and X632.

HAVERS, Alice, see Alice Mary MORGAN.

HAWEIS, Hugh Reginald (1838–1901) preacher and writer on music.

p F.H.LEWIS, 1913, tql, NPG 4107.

PR G.J.STODART, hs, stipple, BM. UNKNOWN, after a photograph by Mayall, hs, woodcut, for *Harper's Mag*, 1888, NPG.

c CARLO PELLEGRINI ('Ape'), wl, w/c study, for *Vanity Fair*, 22 Sept 1888, NPG 2719.

PH BARRAUD, tql, print, for *Men and Women of the Day*, vol I, 1888, NPG AX5435. W. & D.DOWNEY, tql, woodburytype, for *Cassell's Cabinet Portrait Gallery*, vol IV, 1893, NPG.

HAWKER, Robert Stephen (1803–1875) poet and antiquary.

D W.WRIGHT, 1825, hs seated, pencil and w/c, Pembroke College, Oxford.

PR UNKNOWN, hl seated, stipple, NPG.

HAWKINS, Henry, see 1st Baron Brampton.

HAWKSHAW, Sir John (1811–1891) civil engineer.

p J.E.COLLINS, RA 1866, tql seated, Institution of Civil Engineers, London.

SC C.H.MABEY, 1899, after Wyon, 1860, marble bust, Science Museum, London.

PR G.B.BLACK, tql, lith, NPG. UNKNOWN, hs, woodcut, for *Illust London News*, 18 March 1865, NPG.

PH ERNEST EDWARDS, wl seated, print, for *Men of Eminence*, ed L.Reeve, vol III, 1864, NPG. LOCK & WHITFIELD, hs, oval, woodburytype, for *Men of Mark*, 1877, NPG.

HAWKSLEY, Thomas (1807–1893) civil engineer.

p SIR HUBERT VON HERKOMER, 1887, tql seated, NPG 4973.

HAWLEY, Sir Joseph Henry, 3rd Bart (1813–1875) race-horse owner.

PR J.BROWN, after a photograph by Southwell, hs, stipple, for *Baily's Mag*, 1861, BM, NPG.

c ALFRED THOMPSON (Atη), wl, semi-profile, chromo-lith, for *Vanity Fair*, 21 May 1870, NPG.

HAWTREY, Sir Charles Henry (1858–1923) actor.

PR Several theatrical prints, Harvard Theatre Collection, Cambridge, Mass, USA.

c SIR MAX BEERBOHM, tql, Harvard College Library, Cambridge, Mass, USA. SIR LESLIE WARD ('Spy'), tql, profile, chromo-lith, for *Vanity Fair*, 21 May 1892, NPG.

PH UNKNOWN, c1897, hs, woodburytype, NPG.

HAY, Arthur (1824–1878), see 9th Marquess of Tweeddale.

HAY, Sir John (1816–1892) Australian statesman.

SC UNKNOWN, 1889, marble bust, Legislative Council, Sydney, New South Wales, Australia.

HAY, Sir John Hay Drummond, see DRUMMOND-Hay.

HAY, William Montagu, see 10th Marquess of Tweeddale.

HAYES, Catherine, (Mrs Bushnell) (1825–1861) singer.

PR E.GRIMSTON, tql seated, lith, BM. UNKNOWN, tql, lith, BM. Several theatrical prints, BM, NPG, Harvard Theatre Collection, Cambridge, Mass, USA.

HAYNE, Charles Hayne Seale-, see SEALE-Hayne.

HAYTHORNE, Sir Edmund (1818–1888) general.

PR UNKNOWN, hs in uniform, wood engr, for *Illust London News*, 10 Nov 1888, NPG.

HAYWARD, Abraham (1801–1884) essayist.

c CARLO PELLEGRINI ('Ape'), wl, profile, w/c study, for *Vanity Fair*, 27 Nov 1875, NPG 4072.

HEAD, Sir Edmund Walker, Bart (1805–1868) governor-general of Canada.

p HENRY WEIGALL, RA 1866, tql seated, Merton College, Oxford.

PR W.HOLL, after G.Richmond, hs, stipple, one of 'Grillion's Club' series, BM.

HEADLAM, Thomas Emerson (1813–1875) politician.

PR UNKNOWN, after a photograph by Fradelle and Marshall, hs, woodcut, for *Illust London News*, 25 Dec 1875, NPG.

c SIR LESLIE WARD ('Spy'), wl, profile, chromo-lith, for *Vanity Fair*, 19 April 1873, NPG.

HEALY, James (1824–1894) Roman catholic divine and humorist.

SC LEON-JOSEPH CHAVALLIAUD, 1895, posthumous bronze bust, NGI 8189.

HEALY, Timothy Michael (1855–1931) Irish political leader.

p SIR JOHN LAVERY, exhib 1923, Municipal Gallery of Modern Art, Dublin. P.A.DE LÁSZLÓ, 1929?, tql seated, Gray's Inn, London.

D S.P.HALL, pencil sketch, NPG 2319. FREDERICK PEGRAM, pencil sketch, made during the session of the Parnell Special Commission, for *The Pictorial World*, 1888–9, V & A.

SC J.DAVIDSON, 1914, bronze bust, King's Inns, Dublin.

c SIR LESLIE WARD ('Spy'), wl, profile, chromo-lith, for *Vanity Fair*, 3 April 1886, NPG. HARRY FURNISS, with Justin McCarthy and Thomas Sexton, pen and ink sketch, NPG 3620.

PH SIR BENJAMIN STONE, 1898, wl, print, NPG.

HEAPHY, Thomas (Frank) (1813–1873) painter.

D Self-portrait, c1831, tql seated, w/c, NPG 4016.

PH BASSANO, tql seated, carte, NPG.

HEARN, Mary Anne, 'Marianne Farningham' (1834–1909) hymn-writer and author.

PR T.W.HUNT, tql seated, stipple and line, NPG.

HEATH, Christopher (1835–1905) surgeon.

G HENRY JAMYN BROOKS, 'Council of the Royal College of Surgeons of England, 1884–85', oil, Royal College of Surgeons, London.

SC H.R.HOPE PINKER, marble bas relief, University College Hospital, London.

HEATH, Douglas Denon (1811–1897) classical and mathematical scholar.

D T.C.WAGEMAN, 1836, w/c sketch, Trinity College, Cambridge.

HEATHCOTE-DRUMMOND-WILLOUGHBY, Gilbert Henry, see 1st Earl of Ancaster.

HEATON, Sir John Henniker, 1st Bart (1848–1914) postal reformer.

D WALTER CRANE, in the guise of Prospero, design for a decorative envelope, commemorating the extension of Imperial penny postage to Australia, 1905, pen and ink, V & A.

c SIR LESLIE WARD ('Spy'), wl, profile, chromo-lith, for *Vanity Fair*, 17 Sept 1887, NPG.

PH SIR BENJAMIN STONE, 1897, wl, print, NPG.

HEAVISIDE, Oliver (1850–1925) mathematical physicist and electrician.

p UNKNOWN, Institution of Electrical Engineers, London.

HECTOR, Annie, née French (1825–1902) novelist writing as Mrs Alexander.

PH W. & D.DOWNEY, tql seated, woodburytype, for *Cassell's Cabinet Portrait Gallery*, vol III, 1892, NPG.

HELENA, Augusta Victoria, Princess Christian of Schleswig-Holstein (1846-1923) daughter of Queen Victoria.
P HEINRICH VON ANGELI, hl, Royal Coll. F.X.WINTERHALTER, hl, Royal Coll.
D F.X.WINTERHALTER, 1849, wl seated in Scottish dress, Royal Coll. F.X.WINTERHALTER, 1850, tql with her attendant, Eliza Collins, w/c, Royal Coll. F.X.WINTERHALTER, tql with Prince Alfred, w/c, Royal Coll. Several drgs by QUEEN VICTORIA, as a child and with her brothers and sisters, Royal Coll.
M ANNIE DIXON, 1873, hs, Royal Coll. ANTON HÄHNISCH, hs, Royal Coll.
G F.X.WINTERHALTER, with Prince Alfred and Princess Alice, w/c, 1847, Royal Coll. F.X.WINTERHALTER, 'The Four Royal Princesses', oil, 1849, Royal Coll. Several family groups depicting royal occasions, Royal Coll. 'F.W.', 'The Opening of the Royal Albert Infirmary, 1865', oil, NPG 3083. CHRISTIAN MAGNUSSEN, 'The Marriage of Princess Helena', oil, 1866, Royal Coll.
SC MARY THORNYCROFT, marble bust, as a child, Royal Coll. M.THORNYCROFT, 1874, marble bust, Royal Coll. SUSAN DURANT, medallions, NPG 2023a(11, 12).
PR F.HOLL, after a miniature by R.Thorburn, 1847, engr, Royal Coll. Several popular prints, NPG.
PH L.CALDESI, 1857, with the Royal Family on the Terrace at Osborne House, print, NPG P26. W. & D.DOWNEY, tql, woodburytype, for Cassell's *Cabinet Portrait Gallery*, vol II, 1891, NPG. THEODOR PRÜMM, hs, profile, cabinet, NPG. Various cartes by W. & D.DOWNEY, GHÉMAR FRÈRES, HILLS & SAUNDERS, HUGHES, LEVITSKY, SOUTHWELL BROS and others, various dates and sizes, NPG. Royal Coll. Various family groups, NPG, Royal Coll.

HELE-SHAW, Henry Selby (1854-1941) engineer.
P HAROLD SPEED, exhib 1932, Institution of Mechanical Engineers, London.
PH WALTER STONEMAN, 1917, hs, NPG (NPR).

HELLMUTH, Isaac (1817-1901) bishop of Huron.
PR UNKNOWN, after a photograph by W.Williamson of Toronto, hs, woodcut, for *Illust London News*, 23 Nov 1878, NPG.

HELMORE, Thomas (1811-1890) musical writer and composer.
P UNKNOWN, hl seated, College of St Mark and St John, Chelsea, London.

HELPS, Sir Arthur (1813-1875) essayist and historian.
D GEORGE RICHMOND, 1858, hs, chalk, NPG 2027.
G 'F.W.', 'The Opening of the Royal Albert Infirmary, 1865', oil, NPG 3083.
PR C.G.LEWIS, after F.Williams, hl, line, oval, BM.
C CARLO PELLEGRINI ('Ape'), wl, profile, chromo-lith, for *Vanity Fair*, 15 Aug 1874, NPG.

HEMMING, George Wirgman (1821-1905) mathematician and law reporter.
D T.C.WAGEMAN, w/c drg, Trinity College, Cambridge.

HEMPHILL, Charles Hare Hemphill, 1st Baron (1822-1908) lawyer and politician.
C SIR LESLIE WARD ('Spy'), wl, profile, chromo-lith, for *Vanity Fair*, 11 Aug 1904, NPG.
PH SIR BENJAMIN STONE, 1898, three prints, all wl, NPG.

HENEAGE, Edward Heneage, 1st Baron (1840-1922) politician.
C SIR LESLIE WARD ('Spy'), wl, profile, w/c study, for *Vanity Fair*, 17 Dec 1887, NPG 4719.
PH WALTER STONEMAN, 1917, hs, NPG (NPR).

HENDERSON, Sir Edmund Yeamans Walcott (1821-
1896) lieutenant-colonel, Royal Engineers.
PR UNKNOWN, hs, woodcut, for *Illust London News*, 13 March 1869, NPG. UNKNOWN, after a photograph by Russell, hs, wood engr for *Illust London News*, 19 Dec 1896, NPG.
C CARLO PELLEGRINI ('Ape'), wl, chromo-lith, for *Vanity Fair*, March 1875, NPG.

HENDERSON, George Francis Robert (1854-1903) colonel and military writer.
P ARNOLD MOUNTFORT, tql in uniform, Staff College, Camberley, Surrey.

HENDERSON, William George (1819-1905) dean of Carlisle.
PR W.G.HENDERSON, after W.W.Ouless, tql seated in gown, mezz, pub 1888, BM.

HENFREY, Arthur (1819-1859) botanist.
PH MAULL & POLYBLANK, 1855, tql seated, print, NPG P120(49).

HENLEY, William Ernest (1849-1903) poet and man of letters.
P SIR WILLIAM NICHOLSON, 1901, hl, TATE 4087.
D FRANCIS DODD, 1900, hs, pastel, NPG 4420.
SC AUGUSTE RODIN, 1886, bronze busts, NPG 1697 and SNPG 838, related memorial bust, St Paul's Cathedral, London.
PR W.ROTHENSTEIN, hl, profile, at a window, lith, BM.
C HARRY FURNISS, hl, pen and ink sketch, NPG 3586. SIR LESLIE WARD ('Spy'), wl seated, chromo-lith, for *Vanity Fair*, 26 Nov 1892, NPG.
PH G.C.BERESFORD, hs, print, NPG. DEW SMITH, hs, print, NPG.

HENLEY, William Thomas (1813?-1882) telegraphic engineer.
P BASIL HOLMES, 1870, Institution of Electrical Engineers, London.

HENNESSY, Sir John Pope (1834-1891) colonial governor.
PR UNKNOWN, after a photograph by Elliott and Fry, hs, profile, wood engr, for *Illust London News*, 3 Jan 1891, NPG.
C CARLO PELLEGRINI ('Ape'), wl, profile, w/c study, for *Vanity Fair*, 27 March 1875, NPG 3267.

HENRY, Sir Edward Richard, Bart, of Campden House Court (1850-1931) Commissioner of Metropolitan Police.
C SIR LESLIE WARD ('Spy'), wl with dog, chromo-lith, for *Vanity Fair*, 5 Oct 1905, NPG.

HENRY Maurice of Battenberg, Prince, see Battenberg.

HENRY, Mitchell (1826-1910) Irish politician.
C SIR LESLIE WARD ('Spy'), wl, chromo-lith, for *Vanity Fair*, 19 April 1879, NPG.

HENRY, Sir Thomas (1807-1876) police magistrate.
PR UNKNOWN, hs, woodcut, for *Ilust London News*, 1 July 1876, NPG.

HENSCHEL, Sir George (1850-1934) musician; founder and conductor of London symphony concerts.
P P.A.DE LÁSZLÓ, 1917, hs, NPG 4935.
SC EDWARD ONSLOW FORD, 1895, bronze bust, SNPG 1474.
PH BARRAUD, tql with his wife, print, for *Men and Women of the Day*, vol IV, 1891, NPG AX5545. W. & D.DOWNEY, tql, woodburytype, for Cassell's *Cabinet Portrait Gallery*, vol II, 1891, NPG.

HENTY, George Alfred (1832-1902) author of books of adventure.
D UNKNOWN, 1897, hs, pencil, NPG.
G W.H.BARTLETT, 'Saturday Night at the Savage Club', oil, Savage Club, London.
C HARRY FURNISS, pen and ink sketch, NPG 3467.
PH UNKNOWN, hs, oval, print, NPG.

HERBERT, George Robert Charles, see 13th Earl of

Pembroke.

HERBERT, Henry Howard Molyneux, see 4th Earl of Carnarvon.

HERBERT, Henry John George, see 3rd Earl of Carnarvon.

HERBERT, John Rogers (1810-1890) history and portrait painter.
D C.H.LEAR, c1845, hs, profile, chalk, NPG 1456(10).
PR UNKNOWN, hs, wood engr, for *Illust London News*, 29 March 1890, NPG.

HERBERT, Sir Percy Egerton (1822-1876) lieutenant-general.
P SIR FRANCIS GRANT, 1857, tql in uniform, Powis Castle (NT), Welshpool, Powys, Wales.

HERBERT, Sir Robert George Wyndham (1831-1905) colonial official.
SC SIR GEORGE FRAMPTON, c1908, bust, DoE (Foreign Office, London).

HERBERT, St Leger Algernon (1850-1885) war correspondent.
PH HILLS & SAUNDERS, hs, carte, NPG.

HERBERT of Lea, Sidney Herbert, 1st Baron (1810-1861) secretary at war.
P SIR FRANCIS GRANT, 1847, tql, NPG 1639; related posthumous portrait, in his study, Wilton House, Wilts. UNKNOWN, The Admiralty, London.
D UNKNOWN, hs, oval, chalk, Oriel College, Oxford.
G SIR GEORGE HAYTER, 'The House of Commons, 1833', oil, NPG 54. SIR JOHN GILBERT, 'The Coalition Ministry, 1854', pencil and wash, NPG 1125.
SC BARON CARLO MAROCHETTI, c1863, bronze statue, Salisbury. J.B.PHILIP, 1864, recumbent marble effigy, Wilton Church, Wilts. J.H.FOLEY, 1865, marble bust, Harrow School, Middx. J.H.FOLEY, 1867, bronze statue in peers robes, Waterloo Place, London.
PR W.HOLL, after G.Richmond, hs, stipple, one of 'Grillion's Club' series, BM.
PH DISDERI, wl, carte, NPG.

HERDMAN, Robert (1829-1888) artist.
P Self-portrait, 1883, hs, MacDonald Collection, Aberdeen Art Gallery. ROBERT DUDDINGSTONE HERDMAN, 1886, tql seated, Royal Scottish Academy, Edinburgh, on loan to SNPG (L229).
PH NESBITT & LOTHIAN, hs, carte, NPG (Album 106).

HERDMAN, Sir William Abbott (1858-1924) marine naturalist.
P R.D.HERDMAN, University of Liverpool.
PH WALTER STONEMAN, 1917, hs, NPG (NPR).

HERDMAN, William Gawin (1805-1882) artist and author.
P H.E.KIDSON, 1895, hs, Walker Art Gallery, Liverpool.
M THOMAS HARGREAVES, c1826, Walker Art Gallery.

HERFORD, Charles Harold (1853-1931) scholar and critic.
P T.C.DUGDALE, University of Manchester.
D WILLIAM WEATHERBY, sketch, Manchester City Art Gallery.

HERFORD, William Henry (1820-1908) writer on education.
SC HELEN REED, 1887, medallion, Ladybarn House School, Manchester.

HERKOMER, Sir Hubert von (1849-1914) painter.
P ERNEST BOROUGH JOHNSON, posthumous portrait, Nottingham Castle Museum; 1892, hs, study, NPG 3175. Self-portrait, 1895, hs, Uffizi Gallery, Florence. GEORGE HARCOURT, c1915, Sout-

hampton City Museum and Art Gallery.
D RUDOLPH LEHMANN, 1891, BM. E.B.JOHNSON, 1892, tql seated, chalk study for the posthumous portrait, BM.
G G.GRENVILLE MANTON, 'Conversazione at the Royal Academy, 1891', w/c, NPG 2820. SIR HUBERT VON HERKOMER, 'The Council of the Royal Academy', oil, 1908, TATE 2481.
SC EDWARD ONSLOW FORD, c1897, bronze bust, NPG 2461.
PR Self-portrait, 1879, hs with a sketch of his children, etch, NPG.
C F.GOEDECKER ('F.G.'), wl, w/c study, for *Vanity Fair*, 26 Jan 1884, NPG 2720.
PH EMERY WALKER, after George Andrews, wl, photogravure, NPG. UNKNOWN, hs, cabinet, NPG.

HERRINGHAM, Sir Wilmot Parker (1855-1936) physician.
P SIR WILLIAM ROTHENSTEIN, 1935, Keble College, Oxford.

HERSCHEL, Alexander Stewart (1836-1907) astronomer.
PH UNKNOWN, Science Museum, London.

HERSCHELL, Farrer Herschell, 1st Baron (1837-1899) lord chancellor.
P UNKNOWN, Harvard Law Library, Cambridge, Mass, USA.
D S.P.HALL, pencil sketches, NPG 2343-45. RUDOLPH LEHMANN, 1893, hs, crayon, BM.
PR G.J.STODART, after H.T. Wells, hs, stipple, one of 'Grillion's Club' series, BM.
C SIR LESLIE WARD ('Spy'), wl, profile, w/c study, for *Vanity Fair*, 19 March 1881, NPG 2721.
PH W. & D.DOWNEY, hs, woodburytype, for Cassell's *Cabinet Portrait Gallery*, vol I, 1890, NPG.

HERSCHELL, Ridley Haim (1807-1864) dissenting minister.
PR T.FAIRLAND, tql, lith, pub 1850, BM, NPG.

HERVEY, Lord Arthur Charles (1808-1894) bishop of Bath and Wells.
P HENRY GRAVES, 1871, hl, The Athenaeum, Bury St Edmunds, Suffolk. SIR W.B.RICHMOND, tql seated, Wells Corporation; copy, Bishop's Palace, Wells.
PR UNKNOWN, after a photograph by John Watkins, hl seated, woodcut, for *Illust London News*, 8 Jan 1870, NPG.
PH LOCK & WHITFIELD, hs, oval, woodburytype, for *Men of Mark*, 1880, NPG.

HESKETH-FLEETWOOD, Sir Peter, see Fleetwood.

HESSE-DARMSTADT, Princess Alice Maud Mary, Grand Duchess of, see ALICE Maud Mary.

HESSEY, James Augustus (1814-1892) divine.
C CARLO PELLEGRINI ('Ape'), hs seated, chromo-lith, for *Vanity Fair*, 17 Oct 1874, NPG.

HEWETT, Sir John Prescott (1854-1941) Indian civil servant.
PH WALTER STONEMAN, 1918, hs, NPG (NPR).

HEWETT, Sir Prescott Gardner, 1st Bart (1812-1891) surgeon.
P W.W.OULESS, hl, St George's Hospital, London.

HEWETT, Sir William Nathan Wrighte (1834-1888) vice-admiral.
PH LOCK & WHITFIELD, hs, woodburytype, oval, for *Men of Mark*, 1882, NPG. BARRAUD, tql, print, for *Men and Women of the Day*, vol I, 1888, NPG AX5421. UNKNOWN, hl, print, NPG (Album 38).

HIBBERT, Sir John Tomlinson (1824-1908) politician.
P R.E.MORRISON, two portraits, Lancashire County Council Offices, Preston, and Royal Albert Hospital, Lancaster.

J.J.SHANNON, Oldham Art Gallery.
PR UNKNOWN, hs, wood engr, one of a series entitled 'The New Ministry: "Not in the Cabinet"', for *Illust London News*, 27 Aug 1892, NPG.

HICKS, Edward Lee (1843-1919) bishop of Lincoln.
PH UNKNOWN, hs, print, NPG (Anglican Bishops).

HICKS, William (1830-1883) 'Hicks Pasha', general in Egyptian army.
PR 'T.H.', hs, woodcut, for *Illust London News*, 1 Dec 1883, NPG. UNKNOWN, hs, chromo-lith, NPG.

HICKS BEACH, Sir Michael Edward, see 1st Earl St Aldwyn.

HIGGINS, Matthew James ('Jacob Omnium') (1810-1868) journalist.
P SIR FRANCIS GRANT, RA 1862, wl with dog, (the dog painted by Sir Edwin Landseer), The Times Newspapers Ltd, London.
D SAMUEL LAURENCE, hs, chalk, NPG 2433.
PR R.J.LANE, after R.Fidanza, 1844, hl, lith, BM, NPG. R.J.LANE, after A.D'Orsay, 1845, hl, profile, seated, lith, BM, NPG.
C RICHARD DOYLE, wl with Marshal Pelissier, pen and wash, BM.

HILL, Alexander Staveley (1825-1905) barrister and politician.
PH SIR BENJAMIN STONE, 1897, wl, print, NPG.

HILL, David Octavius (1802-1870) landscape and portrait painter; pioneer portrait photographer.
P ROBERT SCOTT LAUDER, 1829, hs, NPG 5049. ROBERT HERDMAN, 1870, hl, Royal Scottish Academy, Edinburgh. JOHN MACLAREN BARCLAY, SNPG 1954.
SC PATRIC PARK, marble bust, SNPG 969. AMELIA ROBERTSON HILL, 1868, marble bust, SNPG 620. AMELIA ROBERTSON HILL, two medallions, one in wax, the other in plaster, SNPG 2182 and 2067.
PR C.K.CHILDS, after A.R.Paton, hs, profile, woodcut, for *Art Journal*, 1850, BM.
PH THOMAS ANNAN, hl seated, carte, NPG (Album 106). Various prints by himself and ROBERT ADAMSON, various sizes, singly and in groups, NPG P6 (1, 2, 98, 100, 103, 141, 143, 155, 221, 227, 228, 237, 238), SNPG and Gernsheim Collection, University of Texas, Austin, USA.

HILL, George Birkbeck Norman (1835-1903) editor of Boswell's *Life of Johnson*.
D W.R.SYMONDS, 1895, hs, pastel, Pembroke College, Oxford.

HILL, Octavia (1838-1912) social reformer.
P J.S.SARGENT, exhib 1899, tql seated, NPG 1746.
D A member of the Barton family, c1864, head, semi-profile, pencil, NPG 3804.

HILL, Rowley (1836-1887) bishop of Sodor and Man.
PR UNKNOWN, after a photograph by Samuel A.Walker, hs, semi-profile, wood engr, for *Illust London News*, 18 June 1887, NPG.

HILLIER, Charles Parker, see Charles Harcourt.

HILTON, John (1804?-1878) surgeon.
P HENRY BARRAUD, hl seated, Royal College of Surgeons, London.
SC J.L.TUPPER, plaster relief medallion, Royal College of Surgeons.

HINCHCLIFF, Thomas Woodbine (1825-1882) president of the Alpine Club.
SC UNKNOWN, copy of memorial medallion, Alpine Club, London.

HINCKS, Thomas (1818-1899) zoologist.
PR W.J.EDWARDS, hl seated, oval, stipple and line, NPG.

HIND, Henry Youle (1823-1908) geologist and explorer.
PR UNKNOWN, hl seated, woodcut, for *Illust London News*, 2 Oct 1858, NPG.

HIND, John Russell (1823-1895) astronomer.
PR UNKNOWN, after a daguerreotype by Claudet, hs, woodcut, for *Illust London News*, 28 Aug 1852, NPG.
PH H.J.WHITLOCK, hl seated, carte, NPG (Album 40).

HINE, Henry George (1811-1895) landscape-painter.
PR UNKNOWN, hs, wood engr, one of a series entitled 'Our Artists – Past and Present', for *Illust London News*, 14 May 1892, NPG.

HINTON, James (1822-1875) surgeon and philosophical writer.
PR UNKNOWN, hs, stipple, NPG.

HIPKINS, Alfred James (1826-1903) musician and antiquary.
P EDITH J.HIPKINS (his daughter), 1898, tql seated, profile, NPG 2129.
PH HERBERT WATKINS, 1872, hs, profile, carte, NPG (Album 110).

HOBART-HAMPDEN, Augustus Charles, ('Hobart Pasha') (1822-1886) vice-admiral.
P IRVING MONTAGUE, tql in Turkish uniform, on loan to DoE (British Embassy, Istanbul).
C SIR LESLIE WARD ('Spy'), wl, profile, chromo-lith, for *Vanity Fair*, 1 June 1878, NPG.
PH ALEXANDER J.GROSSMANN, hl in uniform, carte, NPG. LOCK & WHITFIELD, hs, oval, woodburytype, for *Men of Mark*, 1882, NPG.

HOBHOUSE, Arthur Hobhouse, 1st Baron (1819-1904) judge.
D GEORGE RICHMOND, 1854, called 1st Baron Hobhouse, hs, chalk, Lincoln's Inn, London.
PH UNKNOWN, tql seated, print, NPG.

HOBHOUSE, Edmund (1817-1904) bishop of Nelson, New Zealand.
PR UNKNOWN, after a photograph by Maull & Polyblank, hl seated, oval, woodcut, for *Illust London News*, 26 Feb 1859, NPG.
PH UNKNOWN, tql seated, print, NPG (Anglican Bishops). UNKNOWN, tql seated, print, NPG.

HOBHOUSE, Henry (1854-1937) pioneer in local government.
PH WALTER STONEMAN, 1917, hs, NPG (NPR).

HOBSON, Ernest William (1856-1933) mathematician.
P KENNETH GREEN, 1925, Christ's College, Cambridge.
PH ELLIOTT & FRY, print, Christ's College, Cambridge. WALTER STONEMAN, 1926, hs, NPG (NPR).

HOBSON, William Robert (1831-1880) naval lieutenant.
P STEPHEN PEARCE, c1860, hs in uniform, NPG 910.
PR UNKNOWN, after a photograph, hl seated, woodcut, for *Illust London News*, 15 Oct 1859, NPG.

HOCKING, Silas Kitto (1850-1935) novelist and preacher.
PR W. & C.YATES, after a photograph by Allen & Co, hs, profile, stipple, NPG.
C SIR LESLIE WARD ('Spy'), wl, chromo-lith, for *Vanity Fair*, 1 Nov 1906, NPG.
PH OLIVE EDIS, hs, print, NPG. JOHN RUSSELL & SONS, hs, print, for *National Photographic Record*, vol I, NPG.

HODGE, John (1855-1937) labour leader.
PH WALTER STONEMAN, 1917, hs, NPG (NPR).

HODGKIN, Thomas (1831-1913) historian.
PH H.S.MENDELSSOHN, hs, carte, NPG.

HODGSON, Brian Houghton (1800-1894) orientalist.
P LOUISA STARR CANZIANI, 1872, hl, NPG 1707. MARGARET CARPENTER, 1817, Haileybury College, Herts. CHARLES ALEXANDER, tql seated, Indian Institute, Oxford.

sc Thomas Thornycroft, 1844, marble bust, Asiatic Society, Calcutta.

HODGSON, John Evan (1831-1895) painter.
p Self-portrait, 1882, hs, semi-profile, MacDonald Collection, Aberdeen Art Gallery. W.W.Ouless, ra 1884, Royal Academy, London.
g Henry Jamyn Brooks, 'Private view of the Old Masters Exhibition, Royal Academy, 1888', oil, npg 1833.
ph David Wilkie Wynfield, c1862–64, hs, print, npg P74. Ralph W.Robinson, wl with dog in his studio, print, for *Members and Associates of the Royal Academy of Arts, 1891*, npg x7369.

HODSON, Henrietta (afterwards Mrs Henry Labouchere) (1841-1910) actress.
pr F.G.Nethercliff, after a photograph, hl, 'The Ettie Valses', lith, Harvard Theatre Collection, Cambridge, Mass, USA.
ph London Stereoscopic Co, 1873, wl seated as Jack Sheppard, carte, npg (Album 109).

HOFMEYR, Jan Hendrick (1845-1909) South African politician.
sc C.Penstone, caricature wood carving in bas-relief, 'Cockfight between Mr Rhodes and Hofmeyr, with Kruger looking on', University of Cape Town, South Africa. Unknown, bronze bust, Parliament Buildings, Cape Town.
c Several political cartoons by Dennis Edwards ('Grip'), C. Penstone and an unknown artist, University of Cape Town.

HOGAN, John (1800-1858) sculptor.
d Charles Grey, wl, pencil drg for the etching in *Dublin University Magazine*, vol xxxv, 1858, ngi 2597. Bernard Mulrenin, hs, oval, indian ink, ngi 2197.
pr Unknown, hs, woodcut, for *Art Journal*, 1850, bm, npg.

HOGG, Sir James Macnaghten McGarel, see 1st Baron Magheramorne.

HOGG, Quintin (1845-1903) philanthropist.
p E.W.Appleby, Polytechnic of Central London.
sc Sir George Frampton, 1906, bronze group statue, Langham Place, London.
ph Several prints, Polytechnic of Central London.

HOHENLOHE-LANGENBURG, Prince Victor of, see Count Gleichen.

HOLDEN, Sir Isaac, 1st Bart (1807-1897) inventor.
p Samuel Sidley, City of Bradford Art Gallery.

HOLDEN, Luther (1815-1905) surgeon.
p T.Godart, hs, St Bartholomew's Hospital, London. Sir J.E.Millais, 1880, tql, semi-profile, St Bartholomew's Hospital.

HOLDERNESS, Sir Thomas William, 1st Bart (1849-1924) Indian civil servant.
ph Walter Stoneman, 1920, hs, npg (npr).

HOLDICH, Sir Thomas Hungerford (1843-1929) Anglo-Indian frontier surveyor.
ph Walter Stoneman, 1917, hs, profile, in uniform, npg (npr).

HOLE, Samuel Reynolds (1819-1904) dean of Rochester.
sc F.W.Pomeroy, ra 1906, marble recumbent effigy, Rochester Cathedral.
c F.T.Dalton ('Ftd'), tql, chromo-lith, for *Vanity Fair*, 18 July 1895, npg.
ph Dawsons, hl seated, profile, photogravure, npg.

HOLIDAY, Henry (1839-1927) painter and worker in stained glass.
ph Unknown, hs, cabinet, npg.

HOLKER, Sir John (1828-1882) lord justice.
pr Unknown, after a photograph by Beattie of Preston, hs, woodcut, for *Illust London News*, 23 May 1874, npg.
c Sir Leslie Ward ('Spy'), wl, profile, w/c study, for *Vanity Fair*, 9 Feb 1878, npg 2722.

HOLL, Francis (1815-1884) engraver.
p Frank Holl (his son), hl, npg 2530.

HOLL, Francis Montague, known as Frank Holl (1845-1888) painter.
p Self-portrait, 1863, hs, npg 2531. Self-portrait, ra 1889, hs, profile, oval, MacDonald Collection, Aberdeen Art Gallery.
c Henry Jamyn Brooks, 'Private view of the Old Masters Exhibition, Royal Academy, 1888', oil, npg 1833.
sc Sir Alfred Gilbert, 1890, bronze bust, The Crypt, St Paul's Cathedral, London.
pr Several woodcuts, bm, npg.
ph Lock & Whitfield, hs, oval, woodburytype, for *Men of Mark*, 1883, npg.

HOLL, William (1807-1871) engraver.
d T.W.Harland, 1830, hl seated, chalk, npg 2913.

HOLLAMS, Sir John (1820-1910) solicitor.
p John Collier, 1901, The Law Society, London.

HOLLAND, Henry Scott (1847-1918) theologian and preacher.
ph Elliott & Fry, hl seated, oval, print, npg.

HOLLAND, Sir Henry Thurstan, 2nd Bart, see 1st Viscount Knutsford.

HOLLAND, James (1800-1870) water-colour painter.
d William Holman Hunt, 1828, wl, v & a.

HOLLAND, Sir Sydney George, 3rd Bart, see 2nd Viscount Knutsford.

HOLLAND, Sir Thomas Erskine (1835-1926) jurist.
p Hugh Riviere, exhib 1915, The Athenaeum, London.
ph Walter Stoneman, 1917, hs, npg (npr).

HOLLINGSHEAD, John (1827-1904) journalist and theatrical manager.
c Several prints, npg, Harvard Theatre Collection, Cambridge, Mass, USA.
ph H.N.King, wl seated, carte, npg. Unknown, hs, woodburytype, npg.

HOLLINS, Peter (1800-1886) sculptor.
p W.T.Roden, exhib 1868, tql, City Museum and Art Gallery, Birmingham.

HOLLOND, Ellen Julia, née Teed (1822-1884) writer and philanthropist.
p Ary Scheffer, 1851, hl, oval, ng 1169.
pr L.Haghe, after drg, tql seated, profile, aged 19, lith, bm, npg.

HOLLOND, Robert (1808-1877) lawyer and aeronaut.
g John Hollins, 'A Consultation prior to the Aerial Voyage to Weilburg, 1836', oil, npg 4710.

HOLLOWAY, Thomas (1800-1883) patent medicine vendor, founder of Royal Holloway College.
p Ernest Gustave Girardot, 1882, Royal Holloway College, Egham, Surrey. W.Scott sen, tql in landscape, Royal Holloway College.

HOLLOWELL, James Hirst (1851-1909) advocate of unsectarian education.
sc John Cassidy, 1911, memorial bust, Congregational Church House, Manchester.

HOLMAN HUNT, William, see Hunt.

HOLMES, Alfred (1837-1876) violinist and composer.
PR UNKNOWN, hs, semi-profile, woodcut, for *Illust London News*, 1 April 1876, NPG.

HOLMES, John (1800-1854) antiquary.
SC R.C.LUCAS, wax relief portrait, Society of Antiquaries, London.

HOLMES, Sir Richard Rivington (1835-1911) librarian of Windsor Castle.
D WILLIAM STRANG, 1907, hs, profile, chalk, Royal Coll.
PH Two cartes by BINGHAM and A.S.WATSON, wl and tql seated, NPG (Album 114).

HOLMES, Thomas Rice Edward (1855-1933) historian and classical scholar.
PH WALTER STONEMAN, 1925, hs, NPG (NPR).

HOLMES, Timothy (1825-1907) surgeon.
P SIR W.B.RICHMOND, RA 1889, St George's Hospital, London.
G HENRY JAMYN BROOKS, 'Council of the Royal College of Surgeons of England, 1884-85', oil, Royal College of Surgeons, London.

HOLYOAKE, George Jacob (1817-1906) secularist, journalist and lecturer.
P WALTER RICHARD SICKERT, exhib 1892, hl seated, NPG 1810. ROWLAND HOLYOAKE, 1900, hl seated, Rationalist Press Association, London. WILLIAM HOLYOAKE, tql seated, profile, City Museum and Art Gallery, Birmingham. F.VON KAMPTZ, National Liberal Club, London.
PR C.CHABOT, after a medallion, hs, profile, circle, line, NPG.
PH W. & D.DOWNEY, hl, woodburytype, for Cassell's *Cabinet Portrait Gallery*, vol IV, 1893, NPG. REMBRANDT, after A.E.Praill, 1903, hs, photogravure, NPG.

HOME, Daniel Dunglas (1833-1886) spiritualist medium.
PR Several popular prints, NPG.

HOME, Robert (1837-1879) colonel of Royal Engineers.
PR UNKNOWN, after a photograph by A.Bassano, hs, in uniform, woodcut, for *Illust London News*, 22 Feb 1879, NPG.

HONEY, George (1822-1880) actor.
P RICHARD WALLER, 1880, hs, semi-profile, Garrick Club, London.
SC UNKNOWN, medallion on monument, Highgate Cemetery, London.
PR 'H.B.'?, wl in *Miriam's Crime*, lith, NPG. Several theatrical prints, Harvard Theatre Collection, Cambridge, Mass, USA.
PH FRADELLE & MARSHALL, hs, carte, NPG. UNKNOWN, hs, woodburytype, NPG.

HONEY, Laura, née Young (1816?-1843) actress.
PR Several theatrical prints, BM, NPG. Harvard Theatre Collection, Cambridge, Mass, USA.

HONNER, Maria, née Macarthy (1812-1870) actress.
PR Several theatrical prints, Harvard Theatre Collection, Cambridge, Mass, USA.

HONNER, Robert William (1809-1852) actor.
PR Several theatrical prints, Harvard Theatre Collection, Cambridge, Mass, USA.

HONYMAN, Sir George Essex, 4th Bart (1819-1875) judge.
PR UNKNOWN, after a photograph by London Stereoscopic Co, hs, semi-profile, woodcut, for *Illust London News*, 2 Oct 1875, NPG.

HOOD, Thomas (1835-1874) 'Tom Hood', writer and humorist.
PR UNKNOWN, after a photograph by Charles Watkins, hs, profile,

woodcut, for *Illust London News*, 28 Nov 1874, NPG.
PH ELLIOTT & FRY, hs, carte, NPG (Album 102). SAMUEL A.WALKER, tql seated, carte, NPG X11962. Two cartes by JOHN & CHARLES WATKINS, hs and wl seated, NPG X11960 and AX7543.

HOOD of Avalon, Arthur William Acland Hood, 1st Baron (1824-1901) admiral.
P J.SYDNEY HODGES, 1891, tql seated in admiral's uniform with Bath ribbon and star, NMM, Greenwich.

HOOK, James Clarke (1819-1907) painter.
P SIR GEORGE REID, 1881, MacDonald Collection, Aberdeen Art Gallery. Self-portrait, 1891, hl with palette, Uffizi Gallery, Florence. Self-portrait, 1895, hs, oval, MacDonald Collection, Aberdeen Art Gallery.
D C.H.LEAR, 1845, hs, profile, chalk, NPG 1456(13).
G REGINALD CLEAVER, 'Hanging Committee, Royal Academy, 1892', pen and ink, NPG 4245.
PR O.LEYDE, after Sir J.E.Millais (RA 1883), hl with palette, etch, pub 1884, BM, NPG.
PH ELLIOTT & FRY, hs, carte, NPG (Album 104). LOCK & WHITFIELD, hs, oval, woodburytype, for *Men of Mark*, 1880, NPG. RALPH W.ROBINSON, wl at easel, in garden, print, for *Members and Associates of the Royal Academy of Arts, 1891*, NPG X7370.

HOOKER, Sir Joseph Dalton (1817-1911) botanist.
P JOHN COLLIER, 1880?, hs, Royal Society, London. SIR HUBERT VON HERKOMER, 1889, tql seated, Linnean Society, London. E.COOK, 1909, hs, Royal Botanic Gardens, Kew.
D SIR WILLIAM ROTHENSTEIN, 1903, head, pencil, NPG 4199. COUNTESS FEODORA VON GLEICHEN, 1908, Royal Coll.
SC FRANK BOWCHER, several medallions: 1897, silvered copper, NPG 2276; 1897, Wedgwood, NPG 2033; Linnean Society, London; Royal Society, London.
PR C.H.JEENS, head, stipple, BM, NPG. T.H.MAGUIRE, tql seated, lith, one of set of *Ipswich Museum Portraits*, 1851, BM, NPG. W.WALKER, after Frank Stone, Dr Hooker in the Himalaya Mountains receiving specimens from hill villagers, mezz, pub 1854, India Office Library and Records, London.
PH MAULL & POLYBLANK, c1855, tql seated, print, NPG P106(12). ERNEST EDWARDS, wl seated, print, for *Men of Eminence*, ed. L.Reeve, vol II, 1864, NPG. LOCK & WHITFIELD, hs, oval, woodburytype, for *Men of Mark*, 1881, NPG. UNKNOWN, tql seated, aged 80, photogravure, BM. H.J.WHITLOCK, hs, carte, NPG (Album 40).

HOPE (afterwards BERESFORD-HOPE), Alexander James Beresford (1820-1887) politician and author.
P CHARLES MARTIN, tql seated, RIBA, London.
C CARLO PELLEGRINI ('Ape'), wl, profile, chromo-lith, for *Vanity Fair*, 10 Sept 1870, NPG.
PH ERNEST EDWARDS, wl, carte, NPG (Album 136).

HOPE, George (1811-1876) agriculturist.
P SIR GEORGE REID, hs, SNPG 1028.

HOPE, James (1801-1841) physician.
P THOMAS PHILLIPS, 1841, hl, Royal College of Physicians, London

HOPE Sir James (1808-1881) admiral.
P G.F.CLARKE, The Admiralty, Portsmouth. J.SYDNEY HODGES, c1857-8, tql in admiral's frock coat, NMM, Greenwich.

HOPE-SCOTT, James Robert (1812-1873) parliamentary barrister.
D GEORGE RICHMOND, 1842, hl, w/c, Abbotsford House, Border region, Scotland. GEORGE RICHMOND, hs, chalk, Abbotsford.
SC MATTHEW NOBLE, RA 1876, marble bust, Abbotsford.

HOPKINS, Gerard Manley (1845-1889) poet.
D ANNE ELEANOR HOPKINS (his aunt), 1859, two w/c drgs, both hs

NPG 4264 and Bodleian Library, Oxford. Self-portrait, 1864, sketch of himself reflected in a lake (the sketch shows his head and feet), Campion Hall, Oxford.

PH UNKNOWN, 1850s, tql seated, print, Oxford University Press. Several prints by his uncle (Judge) GEORGE GIBERNE: 1856, in fancy dress as a child cavalier; 1856, hs; c1858, wl; 1863, hs; 1874, hs, all at University of Texas, Austin, USA. Several group prints: 1863, a group at Balliol, Balliol College, Oxford; 1866, wl with A.W.Garrett and W.A.Comyn Macfarlane, Oxford University Press; 1879, the Oxford Catholic Club in front of St Aloysius's Church, Oxford, Crosby Library, Gonzaga University, Spokane, Washington, USA; 1883, a group at Clongowes Wood College, Clongowes Wood College.

HOPKINSON, Sir Alfred (1851-1939) lawyer, educationalist and politician.

D SIR WILLIAM ROTHENSTEIN, c1899, hl seated, lithographic chalk, NPG 4779.

PH LUCIA MOHOLY, 1937, hs, print, NPG P130.

HOPKINSON, John (1849-1898) electrical engineer.

P T.B.KENNINGTON, 1900, after a portrait of c1894 and photographs, tql seated, Department of Engineering, University of Cambridge. R.H.CAMPBELL, 1929, Institution of Electrical Engineers, London. R.H.CAMPBELL, The Athenaeum, London.

SC SIR WILLIAM HAMO THORNYCROFT, 1902, marble bust, Department of Engineering, University of Cambridge.

HOPLEY, Edward William John (1816-1869) painter.

PH ERNEST EDWARDS, wl, carte, NPG (Album 104).

HOPWOOD, Charles Henry (1829-1904) recorder of Liverpool.

P Attrib J.B.KENNING, hl seated, Middle Temple, London.

HORNBY, James John (1826-1909) provost of Eton.

P JOHN COLLIER, RA 1898, Eton College, Berks.

PR UNKNOWN, after a photograph by Hills & Saunders, hl seated, woodcut, for *Illust London News*, 25 Jan 1868, NPG.

C SIR LESLIE WARD ('Spy'), wl, profile, w/c study, for *Vanity Fair*, 31 Jan 1901, NPG 3105.

HORNE, Richard Henry or **Hengist (1803-1884)** writer.

P MARGARET GILLIES, c1840, tql, NPG 2168.

D MARGARET GILLIES, hs, profile, oval, wash, BM.

SC CHARLES SUMMERS, plaster medallions, NPG 2682 and Keats House, Hampstead.

PR UNKNOWN, after a daguerreotype by Paine of Islington, tql seated, stipple and line, NPG. W.J.LINTON, hs, woodcut, BM.

HORNIMAN, Frederick John (1835-1906) founder of the Horniman Museum.

P MALCOLM STEWART, 1891, tql, Horniman Museum, London.

D ELLIS ROBERTS, 1903, hs, pastel, Horniman Museum.

SC Possibly by J.WENLOCK ROLLINS, bronze bust, Horniman Museum.

PH Various prints singly and in family groups, Horniman Museum. SIR BENJAMIN STONE, 1897, wl, print, NPG.

HORRIDGE, Sir Thomas Gardner (1857-1938) judge.

P P.A.DE LÁSZLÓ, 1917, tql seated, Manchester City Art Gallery.

PH WALTER STONEMAN, 1930, hs, profile, in wig and gown, NPG (NPR).

HORSFORD, Sir Alfred Hastings (1818-1885) general.

C SIR LESLIE WARD ('Spy'), wl, profile, chromo-lith, for *Vanity Fair*, 3 Feb 1877, NPG.

HORSLEY, John Callcott (1817-1903) painter.

P Self-portrait, 1882, hs, oval, MacDonald Collection, Aberdeen Art Gallery. W.C.HORSLEY, RA 1902, hl, Royal Academy, London.

D C.W.COPE, c1862, hs, profile, pencil, NPG 3182(2). C.W.COPE, Horsley sketching at Padua, with others, pencil sketch, NPG.

G HENRY JAMYN BROOKS, 'Private view of the Old Masters Exhibition, Royal Academy, 1888', oil, NPG 1833. REGINALD CLEAVER, 'Hanging Committee, Royal Academy, 1892', pen and ink, NPG 4245.

PH ELLIOTT & FRY, hs, carte, NPG (Album 104). LOCK & WHITFIELD, hs, oval, woodburytype, for *Men of Mark*, 1882, NPG. RALPH W.ROBINSON, wl seated at easel, print, for *Members and Associates of the Royal Academy of Arts, 1891*, NPG X7371.

HORSLEY, Sir Victor Alexander Haden (1857-1916) physiologist and surgeon.

PH UNKNOWN, a group print of the medical staff of University College Hospital in 1897, University College, London.

HORSMAN, Edward (1807-1876) politician.

PR G.BÖHM, after a daguerreotype, hl seated, lith, NPG. UNKNOWN, after a photograph, hs, profile, oval, woodcut, for *Illust London News*, 16 May 1857, NPG. UNKNOWN, after a photograph by London Stereoscopic Co, hs, woodcut, for *Illust London News*, 16 Dec 1876, NPG.

C 'FAUSTIN', wl, chromo-lith, a 'Figaro' cartoon, NPG. UNKNOWN, wl, chromo-lith, for *Vanity Fair*, 10 Aug 1872, NPG.

PH SOUTHWELL BROS, wl seated, carte, NPG (Album 136).

HORT, Fenton John Anthony (1828-1892) scholar and divine.

P G.P.JACOMB HOOD, 1891, tql seated in academic robes, Emmanuel College, Cambridge; related hs portrait, Trinity College, Cambridge.

HORTON, Robert Forman (1855-1934) congregational divine and theological writer.

PH OLIVE EDIS, 1922, hs, profile, print, NPG.

HOSKINS, Sir Anthony Hiley (1828-1901) admiral.

C SIR LESLIE WARD ('Spy'), wl in uniform, profile, chromo-lith, for *Vanity Fair*, 28 April 1883, NPG.

PH WALERY, tql, print, NPG.

HOUGHTON, Richard Monckton Milnes, 1st Baron (1809-1885) politician and poet.

D GEORGE RICHMOND, c1844, hs, chalk, NPG 3824. RUDOLPH LEHMANN, 1871, BM.

SC W.W.STORY, c1886, marble bust, Trinity College, Cambridge.

PR R.J.LANE, after A.D'ORSAY, hl, profile, lith, pub 1839, BM, NPG. W.HOLL, after G.RICHMOND, hs, stipple, one of 'Grillion's Club' series, BM. UNKNOWN, hs, lith, NPG.

C CARLO PELLEGRINI ('Ape'), wl, w/c study, for *Vanity Fair*, 3 Sept 1870, NPG 2723.

PH LONDON STEREOSCOPIC Co, tql seated, carte, NPG (Album 99). JOHN & CHARLES WATKINS, c1870, tql seated, carte, NPG AX7429.

HOUGHTON, Robert Crewe-Milnes, 2nd Baron, see Marquess of Crewe.

HOUSMAN, Alfred Edward (1859-1936) poet and classical scholar.

D SIR WILLIAM ROTHENSTEIN, c1903, chalk, Manchester City Art Gallery. SIR WILLIAM ROTHENSTEIN, 1906, two chalk drgs, NPG 3873 and Trinity College, Cambridge. HENRY LAMB, 1909, pencil drg, Trinity College. FRANCIS DODD, 1926, hl seated, pencil, NPG 3075; related tql drg, University College, London. FRANCIS DODD, St John's College, Oxford. R.E.GLEADOWE, 1926, pencil, Trinity College.

SC THEODORE SPICER-SIMSON, c1922, plasticine medallion, NPG 2051.

PH E.O.HOPPÉ, c1911, hs, print, NPG X7765.

HOW, William Walsham (1823-1897) bishop of Wakefield.
P HUGH L.NORRIS, 1897, hs, Wadham College, Oxford.
SC J.NESFIELD FORSYTH, RA 1902, marble statue, Wakefield Cathedral.
PR C.BUTTERWORTH, hs, woodcut, BM.
PH UNKNOWN, hs, print, NPG (Anglican Bishops).

HOWARD, Sir Ebenezer (1850-1928) originator of the garden city movement and founder of Letchworth and Welwyn garden cities.
PH Various prints, singly and in groups, First Garden City Museum, Letchworth, Herts.

HOWARD, Edmund Bernard Fitzalan-, see 1st Viscount Fitzalan of Derwent.

HOWARD, Edward Henry (1829-1892) cardinal.
P JULIAN STORY, 1884, tql seated in robes, Arundel Castle, W Sussex. UNKNOWN, hs in robes, Chirk Castle, Clwyd. UNKNOWN, English College at Rome.

HOWARD, George   James, see 9th Earl of Carlisle.

HOWARD, George William Frederick, see 7th Earl of Carlisle.

HOWARD, Henry Fitzalan-, see 15th Duke of Norfolk.

HOWARD, Henry Granville Fitzalan-, see 14th Duke of Norfolk.

HOWARD, Rosalind Frances, see Countess of Carlisle.

HOWARD of Glossop, Edward George Fitzalan Howard, 1st Baron (1818-1883) politician and promoter of Roman Catholic Primary Education.
PR M.GAUCI, tql seated, lith, BM, NPG.

HOWE, Henry (real name Henry Howe Hutchinson) (1812-1896) actor.
PR Two theatrical prints, Harvard Theatre Collection, Cambridge, Mass, USA.

HOWELL, George (1833-1910) labour leader and writer.
P Two portraits by G.A.HOLMES and MRS HOWARD WHITE, Bishopsgate Foundation and Institute, London.

HOWITT, Alfred William (1830-1908) Australian anthropologist.
SC UNKNOWN, bas-relief portrait, The Burke and Wills Monument, Melbourne, Australia.

HOWLAND, Sir William Pearce (1811-1907) Canadian statesman.
P UNKNOWN, Government House, Ottawa, Canada. UNKNOWN, National Club, Toronto.

HOWORTH, Sir Henry Hoyle (1842-1923) historian and archaeologist.
C HARRY FURNISS, pen and ink sketch, NPG 3469. SIR LESLIE WARD ('Spy'), wl, profile, chromo-lith, for *Vanity Fair*, 11 July 1895, NPG.
PH SIR BENJAMIN STONE, 1897, wl, print, NPG. WALTER STONEMAN, 1921, hs, NPG (NPR).

HOWSON, John Saul (1816-1885) dean of Chester.
P GEORGE RICHMOND, RA 1878, Liverpool College.
PR R. & E.TAYLOR, after a photograph by Elliott & Fry, hs, oval, woodcut, for *The Day of Rest*, 7 June 1873, NPG. R.T., hs, wood engr, for *Illust London News*, 26 Dec 1885, NPG.
PH ELLIOTT & FRY, hs, carte, NPG. LOCK & WHITFIELD, hs, oval, woodburytype, for *Men of Mark*, 1882, NPG.

HUBBARD, John Gellibrand, see 1st Baron Addington.

HUDDLESTON, Sir John Walter (1815-1890) judge; last baron of the exchequer.
P FRANK HOLL, 1888, tql seated, NPG 1410. UNKNOWN, Harvard University Law Library, Cambridge, Mass, USA.
D SEBASTIAN EVANS, 1877, hs, profile, sketch, NPG 2173(9).
PR HORACE PETHERICK, 1884, hl, etch, NPG.
C CARLO PELLEGRINI ('Ape'), hl at bench, w/c study, for *Vanity Fair*, 28 Feb 1874, NPG 2724.
PH LOCK & WHITFIELD, hs, oval, woodburytype, for *Men of Mark*, 1876, NPG. WALERY, tql, print, NPG.

HUDSON, George (1800-1871) the 'Railway King'.
P SIR FRANCIS GRANT, 1846, wl as Lord Mayor of York, Mansion House, York.
C UNKNOWN, wl, 'The Man Wot Knows How to get up the Steam', lith, pub 1845, NPG.

HUDSON, Sir James (1810-1885) diplomat.
C CARLO PELLEGRINI ('Ape'), wl, chromo-lith, for *Vanity Fair*, 26 Sept 1874, NPG; w/c study, V & A.
PH UNKNOWN, hs, print, BM (Engr Ports Coll).

HUDSON, William Henry (1841-1922) ornithologist and writer.
P FRANK BROOKS, after a photograph, tql seated with binoculars, in landscape, Royal Society for the Protection of Birds, Sandy, Beds. SIR WILLIAM ROTHENSTEIN, hs, NPG 1965.
SC THEODORE SPICER-SIMSON, c1922, plasticine medallion, NPG 2052.

HUEFFER, Francis (Franz Hüffer) (1845-1889) musical critic.
PR R.T., hs, semi-profile, wood engr, for *Illust London News*, 2 Feb 1889, NPG.

HUGESSEN, Edward Hugessen Knatchbull-, see 1st Baron Brabourne.

HUGGINS, William (1820-1884) animal painter.
P Self-portrait, hs, Walker Art Gallery, Liverpool.

HUGGINS, Sir William (1824-1910) astronomer.
P JOHN COLLIER, 1905, hl seated, Royal Society, London; replica, NPG 1682.
C SIR LESLIE WARD ('Spy'), wl, chromo-lith, for *Vanity Fair*, 9 April 1903, NPG.
PH H.J.WHITLOCK, tql seated, carte, NPG (Album 40).

HUGHES, Arthur (1832-1915) painter.
P SAMUEL LANE, aged 4, TATE 4870. Self-portrait, c1849, wl reclining in landscape, City Museum and Art Gallery, Birmingham. Self-portrait, 1851, head, profile, NPG 2759.
D SIR J.E.MILLAIS, pencil study for the head of the cavalier in *The Proscribed Royalist*, 1853, Royal Academy, London.
PR F.DODD, tql seated at easel, drypoint, BM.
PH Possibly by W. & D.DOWNEY, 1860s, tql, print, NPG P30.

HUGHES, Hugh Price (1847-1902) Wesleyan minister and writer.
PH W. & D.DOWNEY, tql seated, woodburytype, for *Cassell's Cabinet Portrait Gallery*, vol I, 1890, NPG.

HUGHES, Joshua (1807-1889) bishop of St Asaph.
P UNKNOWN, St David's University College, Lampeter, Dyfed.
PR UNKNOWN, after a photograph by J.Brown of Rhyl, hs, woodcut, for *Illust London News*, 30 April 1870, NPG. R.T., hs, profile, wood engr, for *Illust London News*, 2 Feb 1889, NPG.

HUGHES, Sir Sam (1853-1921) Canadian soldier and politician.
PH JOHN RUSSELL & SONS, hs, print, for *National Photographic Record*, vol II, NPG.

HUGHES, Thomas (1822-1896) author of *Tom Brown's Schooldays*.

P LOWES DICKINSON, RA 1859, hl seated, Rugby School, Warwicks; replica, Oriel College, Oxford. G.F.WATTS, hs, Watts Gallery, Compton, Surrey. HENRY WEIGALL, hs, Inner Temple, London.

G WILLIAM HOLMAN HUNT, 'London Bridge on the Night of the Marriage of the Prince and Princess of Wales, 1863', oil, Ashmolean Museum, Oxford.

SC SIR J.E.BOEHM, 1871, plaster statuette, NPG L122. SIR THOMAS BROCK, memorial statue, Rugby School.

C ADRIANO CECIONI, wl, profile, chromo-lith, for *Vanity Fair*, 8 June 1872, NPG.

PH ELLIOTT & FRY, hs, carte, NPG (Album 40). W.JEFFREY, two cartes, wl and wl seated, NPG AX7540 and Album 136. LOCK & WHITFIELD, hs, oval, woodburytype, for *Men of Mark*, 1880, NPG. JOHN WATKINS, hs, profile, carte, NPG (Album 99).

HUGO, Thomas (1820-1876) historian.

PR 'J.S.'?, hs, profile, woodcut, BM.

HULKE, John Whitaker (1830-1895) surgeon.

G HENRY JAMYN BROOKS, 'Council of the Royal College of Surgeons of England of 1884-85', oil, Royal College of Surgeons, London.

HULLAH, John Pyke (1812-1884) musician.

D SIR W.B.RICHMOND, head, pencil, NPG 1348.

PR BUTTERWORTH & HEATH, hs, woodcut, for *Leisure Hour*, 1876, BM.

PH ERNEST EDWARDS, wl seated, print, for *Men of Eminence*, ed L.Reeve, vol III, 1865, NPG.

HUME, Abraham (1814-1884) antiquarian and social writer.

PR UNKNOWN, hs, profile, circle, stipple, NPG.

HUMPHRY, Sir George Murray (1820-1896) surgeon.

P W.W.OULESS, 1886, hs in academic robes, Fitzwilliam Museum, Cambridge. C.E.BROCK, 1891?, hs, Department of Pathology, University of Cambridge. MISS K.M.HUMPHRY, Town Hall, Sudbury, Suffolk.

SC HENRY WILES, 1891, marble bust, Addenbrooke's Hospital, Cambridge. H.R.HOPE PINKER, c1904, bronze bust, Department of Pathology, University of Cambridge.

PH UNKNOWN, Downing College, Cambridge.

HUMPHRY, William Gilson (1815-1886) divine and author.

P Attrib E.U.EDDIS, RA 1875?, tql, St Martin-in-the-Fields Church, London.

HUNGERFORD, Mrs Margaret Wolfe (1855?-1897) writer.

PR UNKNOWN, after a photograph by Guy & Co, hs, woodcut, for *Illust London News*, 30 Jan 1897, NPG.

HUNT, Alfred William (1830-1896) landscape painter.

D D.S.MACCOLL, 1890, hs, pencil drg, The Athenaeum, London. H.T.WELLS, 1896, hs, profile, on his deathbed, pencil, BM.

HUNT, George Ward (1825-1877) conservative statesman.

PR G.J.STODART, after a photograph by Maull & Fox, hl seated, stipple and line, NPG. UNKNOWN, hl, lith, for *Civil Service Review*, Feb 1877, NPG.

C 'FAUSTIN', wl, chromo-lith, June 1874, NPG. CARLO PELLEGRINI ('Ape'), tql seated, profile, chromo-lith, for *Vanity Fair*, 11 March 1871, NPG; w/c study, V & A. SIR JOHN TENNIEL, 'Fiat Experimentum –! Britannia introducing the torpedo to George Ward Hunt', pencil, for *Punch*, 9 June 1877, NPG.

PH LONDON STEREOSCOPIC CO, hs, carte, NPG (Album 40). UNKNOWN, hs, print, NPG.

HUNT, Robert (1807-1887) scientific writer.

PH ERNEST EDWARDS, wl seated, print, for *Men of Eminence*, ed L.Reeve, vol II, 1864, NPG.

HUNT, Thornton Leigh (1810-1873) journalist.

G W.M.THACKERAY, wl with Mr & Mrs George Henry Lewes, pencil, NPG 4686.

HUNT, William Holman (1827-1910) Pre-Raphaelite painter.

P Self-portrait, 1845, hs, City Museum and Art Gallery, Birmingham. JOHN BALLANTYNE, 1865, wl seated in studio, NPG 2555. Self-portrait, 1875, tql, Uffizi Gallery, Florence. SIR W.B.RICHMOND, c1877, hs, NPG 1901. SIR W.B.RICHMOND, c1897, hl, NPG 2803. HAROLD SPEED, 1909, tql seated, City Museum and Art Gallery, Birmingham.

D Self-portrait, 1853, hs, chalk, on loan to Wightwick Manor (NT), W Midlands. D.G.ROSSETTI, 1853, hs, oval, pencil, City Museum and Art Gallery, Birmingham. SIR J.E.MILLAIS, 1854, hs, profile, pencil and w/c, Ashmolean Museum, Oxford. ELINOR HALLÉ, 1907, Royal Coll.

G WILLIAM HOLMAN HUNT, 'London Bridge on the Night of the Marriage of the Prince and Princess of Wales, 1863', oil, Ashmolean Museum, Oxford. HENRY JAMYN BROOKS, 'Private view of the Old Masters Exhibition, Royal Academy, 1888', oil, NPG 1833.

C SIR LESLIE WARD ('Spy'), wl, profile, chromo-lith, for *Vanity Fair*, 19 July 1879, NPG.

PH JULIA MARGARET CAMERON, 1864, two prints, tql seated in Eastern dress and hs, NPG P18(11) and (23). DAVID WILKIE WYNFIELD, c1862-4, hs, print, NPG P75. BARRAUD, hl seated, print, for *Men and Women of the Day*, vol III, 1890, NPG AX5500. ELLIOTT & FRY, hs, cabinet, NPG. KINGSBURY & NOTCUTT, hs, cabinet, NPG X4179. Several cartes by ELLIOTT & FRY, W.JEFFREY and LONDON STEREOSCOPIC CO, various sizes, NPG.

HUNTER, Sir Archibald (1856-1936) general.

C SIR LESLIE WARD ('Spy'), wl in uniform, w/c study, for *Vanity Fair*, 27 April 1899, NPG 5126. SIR LESLIE WARD, 'A General Group', chromo-lith, for *Vanity Fair*, 29 Nov 1900, NPG.

PH BASSANO, The Convent, Gibraltar. WALTER STONEMAN, 1921, hs in uniform, NPG (NPR).

HUNTER, Colin (1841-1904) sea painter.

P Self-portrait 1882, hs, MacDonald Collection, Aberdeen Art Gallery.

PH RALPH W.ROBINSON, wl seated, print, for *Members and Associates of the Royal Academy of Arts, 1891*, NPG X7372.

HUNTER, Sir George Burton (1845-1937) shipbuilder.

PH WALTER STONEMAN, 1920, hs, NPG (NPR).

HUNTER, Sir Robert (1844-1913) solicitor, authority on commons and public rights and one of the founders of the National Trust.

PH UNKNOWN, hs, print, National Trust (Head Office), London.

HUNTER, Sir William Wilson (1840-1900) Indian civilian.

SC SIR WILLIAM HAMO THORNYCROFT, 1900, bronze bust, Indian Institute, Oxford.

HUTCHINSON, Henry Doveton (1847-1924) lieutenant-general and military historian.

C SIR LESLIE WARD ('Spy'), wl in uniform, w/c study, for *Vanity Fair*, 8 Sept 1904, NPG 4607.

HUTCHINSON, Horatio Gordon (Horace) (1859-1932) golfer and author.

P SIR OSWALD BIRLEY, 1909, tql with golf club, Royal and Ancient

Golf Club, St Andrews, Scotland.

c SIR LESLIE WARD ('Spy'), wl, profile, in golfing dress, chromo-lith, for *Vanity Fair*, 19 July 1890, NPG.

PH ELLIOTT & FRY, wl, photogravure, NPG. WALERY, wl with golf club, print, NPG.

HUTCHINSON, Sir Jonathan (1828-1913) surgeon.

G HENRY JAMYN BROOKS, 'Council of the Royal College of Surgeons of England of 1884–85', oil, Royal College of Surgeons, London.

c SIR LESLIE WARD ('Spy'), wl, profile, chromo-lith, for *Vanity Fair*, 27 Sept 1890, NPG.

HUTH, Henry (1815-1878) banker and book collector.

PR C.W.SHERBORN, hs, etch, NPG.

HUTT, Sir William (1801-1882) vice-president of the board of trade.

PR J.LIVESAY, wl, etch, BM.

HUTTON, Alfred (1839-1910) swordsman.

c 'JEST', wl in fencing dress, with rapier, chromo-lith, for *Vanity Fair*, 13 Aug 1903, NPG.

HUTTON, George Clark (1825-1908) presbyterian divine.

P SIR GEORGE REID, 1901, United Free Church Assembly Hall, Edinburgh.

HUXLEY, Thomas Henry (1825-1895) man of science and educationalist.

P JOHN COLLIER (his son-in-law), 1883, tql with skull, NPG 3168; replicas, Imperial College, London and Royal College of Surgeons, Down House, Kent. JOHN COLLIER, RA 1891, tql seated, on loan to Royal Society, London. ALPHONSE LEGROS, hs, V & A.

D MARIAN COLLIER (his daughter), two pencil drgs, head, semi-profile and head, profile, NPG 3145 and 3147. THEODORE BLAKE WIRGMAN, 1882, hl seated, pencil, NPG 1528. RUDOLPH LEHMANN, 1892, BM. UNKNOWN, hs, chalk, Department of Geology, University of Cambridge.

SC EDWARD ONSLOW FORD, plaster bust, NPG 1330. After JAMES FORSYTH, c1866?, plaster busts, Department of Zoology, University of Cambridge, and Royal College of Surgeons, London. UNKNOWN, medallion on decorative frieze, School of Science and Art, Stroud.

c CARLO PELLEGRINI ('Ape'), wl, profile, chromo-lith, for *Vanity Fair*, 28 Jan 1871, NPG.

PH WALKER & BOUTALL, after a daguerreotype of 1846, hl seated, photogravure, NPG. WALKER & COCKERELL, after Maull & Polyblank, 1857, tql seated, photogravure, NPG. ERNEST EDWARDS, wl, print, for *Men of Eminence*, ed L.Reeve, vol I, 1863, NPG. LOCK & WHITFIELD, hs, oval, woodburytype, for *Men of Mark*, 1880, NPG. W. & D.DOWNEY, tql, woodburytype, for Cassell's *Cabinet Portrait Gallery*, vol I, 1890, NPG. A.BASSANO, tql, cabinet, NPG. ELLIOTT & FRY, tql seated, cabinet, NPG. Several cartes by BARRAUD, ELLIOTT & FRY and LONDON STEREOSCOPIC Co, all hs, NPG.

HYLTON, Sir William George Hylton Jolliffe, 1st Baron (1800-1876) politician.

G SIR GEORGE HAYTER, 'The House of Commons, 1833', oil, NPG 54.

PR T.L.ATKINSON, after F.Grant, wl seated, mezz, pub 1865, BM, NPG. UNKNOWN, after a photograph by Herbert Watkins, hs, oval, woodcut, for *Illust London News*, 27 March 1858, NPG. UNKNOWN, hs, semi-profile, woodcut, for *Illust London News*, 7 Dec 1867, NPG.

HYNDMAN, Henry Mayers (1842-1921) Socialist leader.

D EDMOND KAPP, 1914, Barber Institute of Fine Arts, Birmingham.

SC E.H.LACEY, 1922, bronze bust, NPG 1947.

c SIR MAX BEERBOHM, 'Tout peut se rétablir', drg, 1920, Ashmolean Museum, Oxford.

PH G.C.BERESFORD, 1919, two negs, hs, profile and hs, NPG x6521–22.

I

IBBETSON, Sir Denzil Charles Jelf (1847-1908) lieutenant-governor of the Punjab.
P H.A.OLIVIER, exhib 1909, Lawrence Hall, Lahore, Pakistan.

IBBETSON, Sir Henry John Selwin-, 7th Bart, see Baron Rookwood.

IDDESLEIGH, Sir Stafford Henry Northcote, 1st Earl of (1818-1887) statesman.
P MARGARET CARPENTER, 1840?, hl, semi-profile, a leaving portrait, Eton College, Berks. A.S.LUMLEY, 1876, hs, profile, Hughenden (NT), Bucks. EDWIN LONG, 1882, tql, NPG 2944. E.LONG, 1883, tql with magnifying glass, University of Exeter; replica, 1889, NPG 820.
G HENRY GALES, 'The Derby Cabinet of 1867', w/c, NPG 4893.
SC SIR J.E.BOEHM, 1887, two statues, Palace of Westminster, London and Northernhay, Exeter, Devon; related plaster bust, NPG 861. WILLIAM TYLER, 1887, marble bust, Royal Coll; related plaster bust, Balliol College, Oxford.
PR UNKNOWN, hl, profile, lith, for *Civil Service Review*, Dec 1876, BM. WILLIAM HOLE, tql in academic robes, etch, for *Quasi Cursores*, 1884, NPG. W.HOLL, after G.Richmond, hs, semi-profile, stipple, one of 'Grillion's Club' series, BM. G.PILOTELL, hs profile, etch, BM. Various popular prints, NPG.
C HARRY FURNISS, pen and ink sketch, NPG 3396. CARLO PELLEGRINI ('Ape'), wl, chromo-lith, for *Vanity Fair*, 8 Oct 1870, NPG. THÉOBALD CHARTRAN ('T'), 'Birth, Behaviour and Business', chromo-lith, for *Vanity Fair*, 5 July 1881, NPG.
PH ADOLPHE BEAU, tql seated, carte, NPG X12112. ELLIOTT & FRY, hs, profile, carte, NPG X12113. LOCK & WHITFIELD, hs, oval, woodburytype, for *Men of Mark*, 1877, NPG. MAULL & POLYBLANK, wl seated, carte, NPG (Album 136). UNKNOWN, hs, profile, woodburytype, NPG X12115.

IGNATIUS, Father, see Joseph Leycester LYNE.

ILBERT, Sir Courtenay Peregrine (1841-1924) parliamentary draftsman.
D S.P.HALL, 1888-89, pencil drg, NPG 2245.
PH O.REJLANDER, tql seated, carte, NPG X12117.

IMAGE, Selwyn (1849-1930) artist.
SC W.S.FRITH, bust, The Art Workers' Guild, London.

INCE, William (1825-1910) regius professor of divinity at Oxford.
P UNKNOWN, tql seated, Christ Church, Oxford.

INCHBOLD, John William (1830-1888) landscape artist.
PR UNKNOWN, hs, wood engr, for *Illust London News*, 11 Feb 1888, NPG.

INCHCAPE, James Lyle Mackay, 1st Earl of (1852-1932) shipowner and company director.
P P.A.DE LÁSZLÓ, 1931, tql in robes of order of St Michael and St George, P & O Steam Navigation Company, London.
C HARRY FURNISS, pen and ink sketch, NPG 3470.

INDERWICK, Frederick Andrew (1836-1904) lawyer and antiquary.
SC SIR GEORGE FRAMPTON, 1906, marble bust, DoE (Law Courts, London).

C SIR LESLIE WARD ('Spy'), tql, profile, at bench, chromo-lith, for *Vanity Fair*, 30 July 1896, NPG.

INGELOW, Jean (1820-1897) poet.
PH ELLIOTT & FRY, two cartes, tql seated, semi-profile, and hs, profile, NPG. MAULL & POLYBLANK, wl seated, carte, NPG AX7546.

INGHAM, Sir James Taylor (1805-1890) police magistrate.
D S.P.HALL, 1888-89, hl seated, profile, pencil drg, NPG 2247.
PR UNKNOWN, after a photograph by J.C.Smallcombe, hs, profile, circle, woodcut, for *Illust London News*, 5 Aug 1876, NPG.
C SIR LESLIE WARD ('Spy'), wl, profile, chromo-lith, for *Vanity Fair*, 20 Feb 1886, NPG.

INGLEFIELD, Sir Edward Augustus (1820-1894) admiral.
P JOHN COLLIER, 1897, hl in uniform with medals, NPG 2500. STEPHEN PEARCE, c1853, hl in uniform, NPG 1223; replica, NPG 921.
PR UNKNOWN, after a photograph by Claudet, hs in uniform, woodcut, for *Illust London News*, 15 Oct 1853, NPG.
PH UNKNOWN, tql seated in uniform, cabinet, NPG X12125. UNKNOWN, Royal Geographical Society, London. FRADELLE & YOUNG, hs in uniform, cabinet, NPG X12124.

INGLIS, John (1810-1891), see Lord Glencorse.

INGLIS, Sir John Eardley Wilmot (1814-1862) general; the defender of Lucknow.
P WILLIAM GUSH, wl in uniform, Nova Scotia Legislative Library, Province House, Halifax, Canada.
PR D.J.POUND, after a photograph by Mayall, tql in uniform, mixed engr, supplement to *Illust News of the World*, BM, NPG. C.HOLL, after a photograph by Mayall, tql in uniform, stipple, NPG.

INGRAM, Arthur Foley Winnington-, see WINNINGTON-Ingram.

INGRAM, Herbert (1811-1860) politician; proprietor of the *Illustrated London News*.
SC ALEXANDER MUNRO, 1862, marble statue, Market Place, Boston, Lincs.
PR UNKNOWN, hl seated, for *Illust Family Paper*, 27 June 1857, NPG. SMYTH, after a photograph by John Watkins, tql seated, woodcut, for *Illust London News*, 6 Oct 1860, BM, NPG. R.TAYLOR & CO, tql seated, woodcut, for *Illust London News*, 14 May 1892, BM.

INGRAM, John Kells (1823-1907) scholar, economist and poet.
P SARAH PURSER, 1897, Royal Irish Academy, Dublin. SARAH PURSER, posthumous, after her pastel portrait, Trinity College, Dublin.
D SARAH PURSER, 1890, hs, pastel, Ulster Museum, Belfast.

INNES, Sir James Rose-, see ROSE-Innes.

INNES-KER, Lord Charles John (1842-1919) son of the Duke of Roxburghe.
C SIR LESLIE WARD ('Spy'), wl, profile, w/c study, for *Vanity Fair*, 20 March 1886, NPG 4721.

INVERARITY, Elizabeth, see Mrs Martyn.

IRVING, Sir Henry (1838-1905) actor, whose original name was John Henry Brodribb.

P JAMES ARCHER, two portraits: 1871–2, tql seated as Mathias in *The Bells*, Museum of London, and RA 1873, wl as Charles I, Russell-Cotes Art Gallery, Bournemouth. JAMES MCNEILL WHISTLER, 1876 (finished in 1885), wl as Philip II of Spain in Tennyson's Queen Mary, Metropolitan Museum of Art, New York, USA. J.B.LEPAGE, 1880, tql seated, NPG 1560. SIR J.E.MILLAIS, RA 1884, tql, profile, Garrick Club, London; copy by HARRY ALLEN, NPG 1453. W.H.MARGETSON, probably *c*1885, as Mephistopheles in the Scene of the Witches' Kitchen from Goethe's *Faust*, with Sir George Alexander as Faust, V & A. UNKNOWN, hs, oil sketch for a Jubilee picture 1887, Russell-Cotes Art Gallery. SIR BERNARD PARTRIDGE, *c*1903, wl at rehearsal, Museum of London. R.G.EVES, 1905–10, probably based on a photograph of 1904 by William Crooke, hs, Museum of London. POWER O'MALLEY, tql seated with King Edward VII, The Vancouver Club, Vancouver, Canada. UNKNOWN, tql as Robespierre, Russell-Cotes Art Gallery.

D E.H.GORDON CRAIG, sketch of Irving in *The Bells*, ink and w/c, V & A. ANDREW MACLAREN, drg, Garrick Club. MORTIMER L.MENPES, 1898, pencil, The Athenaeum, London. F.D.NIBLETT, as Hamlet, w/c, Museum of London. WALTER SEYMOUR, as Macbeth, wash, V & A. UNKNOWN, as Wolsey, Garrick Club.

SL SIR FRANCIS CARRUTHERS GOULD, wl, profile, with dog, NPG 3538.

G W.H.BARTLETT, 'Saturday Night at the Savage Club', oil, Savage Club, London. G.GRENVILLE MANTON, 'Conversazione at the Royal Academy, 1891', w/c, NPG 2820.

SC EDWARD ONSLOW FORD, 1883–5, marble statue, seated as Hamlet, Guildhall Art Gallery, London. E.O.FORD, plaster bust, Manchester City Art Gallery. E.O.FORD, small figure as Tamburlaine, part of the Marlowe memorial, Dane John Gardens, Canterbury. J.BLACKWELL, 1893, bronze medallion, Russell-Cotes Art Gallery. SIR THOMAS BROCK, 1910, bronze statue, in collegiate gown, in front of the north side of the National Portrait Gallery, Charing Cross Road. COURTENAY POLLOCK, bronze busts, Russell-Cotes Art Gallery and Garrick Club. SIR GEORGE FRAMPTON, death-mask, Museum of London.

PR W.NICHOLSON, 1899, tql, coloured woodcut, NPG. W.ROTHENSTEIN, liths, BM, NPG, Bradford City Art Gallery. Various theatrical and popular prints, BM, NPG, V & A (Theatre Museum), Harvard Theatre Collection, Cambridge, Mass, USA.

C SIR MAX BEERBOHM, several drgs including: 1895, speaking after dinner, Savage Club, London; 1900, wl, Harvard College Library, Cambridge, Mass, USA; 1903, wl, Garrick Club. HARRY FURNISS, various drgs including: 1905, pen and ink sketch,

for *The Garrick Gallery*, NPG 4095(6); hs, profile, pen, Garrick Club; pen and ink sketch, NPG 3471; with Sir Lawrence Alma Tadema, pen and ink, Museum of London. SIR FRANCIS CARRUTHERS GOULD, pen, ink and w/c sketch, for *The Struwwelpeter Alphabet*, by Harold Begbie, 1900, V & A. PHIL MAY, 1899, three pencil sketches, wl seated, profile, tql, profile, and wl seated, NPG 3679–81. PHIL MAY, wl, profile, pen and ink, NPG 1611. SIR BERNARD PARTRIDGE, several pencil drgs in character, V & A, and one wl drg, wash, Garrick Club. CARLO PELLEGRINI ('Ape'), wl, profile, in character in *The Bells*, chromo-lith, for *Vanity Fair*, 19 Dec 1874, NPG; w/c study, Garrick Club. CARLO PELLEGRINI, wl, profile, as Benedick, w/c, NPG 5073.

PH ELLIOTT & FRY, hs, profile, carte, NPG (Album 99). DICKINSON BROS & FOSTER, *c*1876, two cabinets, both hl, NPG X3676 and X12128. SAMUEL A.WALKER, 1882, tql seated, cabinet, NPG X12129. LOCK & WHITFIELD, hs, semi-profile, oval, woodburytype, for *Men of Mark*, 1883, NPG. BARRAUD, tql seated, print, for *Men and Women of the Day*, vol I, 1888, NPG AX 5413. WARWICK BROOKE, 1888, hl, print, NPG X12130. W. & D.DOWNEY, wl in character, woodburytype, for Cassell's *Cabinet Portrait Gallery*, vol IV, 1893, NPG. WINDOW & GROVE, hs in academic robes, woodburytype, for *The Theatre*, March 1895, NPG. HISTED, 1899, hs, print, NPG X12131. FRANK EUGENE, *c*1903, tql seated, print, Royal Photographic Society, Bath. BARRAUD, hs, profile, cabinet, NPG X12126. H.H.HAY CAMERON, as Thomas à Beckett, print, Gernsheim Collection, University of Texas, Austin, USA. Various prints and photogravures, some in character, various dates, NPG and Theatre Museum.

ISAACS, Sir Isaac Alfred (1855-1948) chief-justice and governor-general of Australia.

PH WALTER STONEMAN, 1921, hs, NPG (NPR).

ISMAY, Thomas Henry (1837-1899) shipowner.

C LIBERIO PROSPERI ('Lib'), wl, chromo-lith, for *Vanity Fair*, 15 Nov 1894, NPG.

IVEAGH, Edward Cecil Guinness, 1st Earl of (1847-1927) philanthropist.

P SIR WILLIAM ORPEN, 1904, Guinness & Co Ltd, London. H.M.PAGET, after Sir A.S.Cope of *c*1912, tql in uniform of an Honorary Lieutenant (Royal Naval Reserve), Kenwood House (GLC), London.

C SIR LESLIE WARD ('Spy'), wl, profile, chromo-lith, for *Vanity Fair*, 11 July 1891, NPG.

PH WALTER L.COLLS, after Wermer & Son, 1903, hs, photogravure, NPG. WALTER STONEMAN, 1926, hs, NPG (NPR).

J

JACKSON, Frederick John Foakes (1855-1941) divine.
P F.M.LUTYENS, Jesus College, Cambridge.

JACKSON, Henry (1831-1879) novelist.
PR T.W.HUFFAM, after Herbert, hl, mezz, BM.

JACKSON, Henry (1839-1921) classical scholar.
P C.W.FURSE, 1889, hl, NPG 5045. C.W.FURSE, 1890, tql seated, Trinity College, Cambridge. ORLANDO ROWLAND, tql seated in gown, Trinity College, Cambridge.
D SIR WILLIAM ROTHENSTEIN, 1904, hs, pastel, Trinity College, Cambridge. HENRY LAMB, 1906, hl seated, chalk, The Athenaeum, London. WILLIAM STRANG, 1909, hs, chalk, Royal Coll.
PH V.H.MOTTRAM, hl, print, NPG. DEW SMITH, tql seated, print, NPG.

JACKSON, Sir Henry Bradwardine (1855-1929) admiral.
D FRANCIS DODD, 1917, charcoal and w/c, IWM.
PH WALTER STONEMAN, 1918, hs, NPG (NPR).

JACKSON, John (1811-1885) bishop of London.
P W.W.OULESS, RA 1876, hs, semi-profile, Fulham Palace, London.
SC THOMAS WOOLNER, 1887, recumbent figure on monument, St Paul's Cathedral, London.
PR C.W.SHARPE, after G.Richmond, hs, semi-profile, stipple, pub 1854, BM. W.WALKER, after W.Cooper, hl, mezz, BM.
C CARLO PELLEGRINI ('Ape'), wl, profile, chromo-lith, for *Vanity Fair*, 12 Nov 1870, NPG.
PH H.HERING, tql seated, carte, NPG AX7458. LOCK & WHITFIELD, hs, oval, woodburytype, for *Men of Mark*, 1876, NPG. MAULL & POLYBLANK, wl, profile, carte, NPG (Album 114). UNKNOWN, hs, carte, NPG X1090.

JACKSON, John Hughlings (1835-1911) physician.
P LANCE CALKIN, c1894, hl, Royal College of Physicians, London.
SC HERBERT HAMPTON, bust, Institute of Neurology, London.

JACKSON, Samuel Phillips (1830-1904) water-colour artist.
PH JOHN WATKINS, tql seated, carte, NPG (Album 104).

JACKSON, Sir Thomas Graham, 1st Bart (1835-1924) architect.
P H.G.RIVIERE, 1900, hl seated, Wadham College, Oxford. SOLOMON J.SOLOMON, hl, The Art Workers' Guild, London.
G SIR HUBERT VON HERKOMER, 'The Council of the Royal Academy', oil, 1908, TATE 2481.
PH ELLIOTT & FRY, tql, print, NPG. JOHN RUSSELL & SONS, hl, print, for *National Photographic Record*, vol I, NPG.

JACKSON, William Lawies, see 1st Baron Allerton.

JACOB, Edgar (1844-1920) bishop of St Albans.
G S.P.HALL, 'The Bench of Bishops, 1902', w/c, NPG 2369.
PR UNKNOWN, after a photograph by Whitlock, hs, semi-profile, wood engr, for *Illust London News*, 30 Nov 1895, NPG.
C SIR LESLIE WARD ('Spy'), wl, profile, mechanical repro, for *Vanity Fair*, 26 Sept 1906, NPG.
PH WHITLOCK, hs, postcard, NPG. UNKNOWN, tql seated, print, NPG X1454. UNKNOWN, hl, print, NPG (Anglican Bishops).

JACOB, John (1812-1858) brigadier-general.
SC M.THOMAS, 1884, bust, Shire Hall, Taunton.

PR T.L.ATKINSON, after an unknown artist, tql seated, mezz, 1859, NPG 2186a.

JACOBSON, William (1803-1884) bishop of Chester.
P GEORGE RICHMOND, hs seated, oval, Hertford College, Oxford.
D GEORGE RICHMOND, 1853, hs, chalk, Christ Church, Oxford.
PR MISS TURNER, after E.U.Eddis, hs, lith, BM. UNKNOWN, after a photograph by J. & C.Watkins, hl seated, for *Illust London News*, 2 Sept 1865, NPG.
PH C.L.DODGSON ('Lewis Carroll'), c1856, tql seated, print, NPG P7(1).

JAMES, David (1839-1893) actor, whose real name was Belasco.
D S.P.HALL, pencil sketch, NPG 2374.
PR Several theatrical prints and caricatures, Harvard Theatre Collection, Cambridge, Mass, USA.
C 'FAUSTIN', wl, chromo-lith, a 'Figaro' cartoon, 12 Dec 1874, NPG.
PH ELLIOTT & FRY, hs, woodburytype, carte, NPG AX7637. Several prints, some in character, various sizes, NPG.

JAMES, Henry (1843-1916) American-born novelist.
P JACQUES-ÉMILE BLANCHE, 1908, tql seated, National Portrait Gallery, Smithsonian Institution, Washington DC, USA. J.S.SARGENT, 1913, hl seated, NPG 1767. JOHN LAFARGE, hs, The Century Association, New York, USA.
D RUDOLPH LEHMANN, hs, profile, BM. J.S.SARGENT, 1912, hs, charcoal, Royal Coll.
SC FRANCIS DERWENT WOOD, 1913, marble bust, TATE 2976.
PR SIR WILLIAM ROTHENSTEIN, 1898, hl, semi-profile, lith, NPG.
C SIR MAX BEERBOHM, several cartoons, drgs, various dates, Ashmolean Museum, Oxford, National Gallery of Victoria, Melbourne, Australia, and University of Texas, Austin, USA.
PH ALICE BOUGHTON, c1906, tql, profile, print, National Portrait Gallery, Smithsonian Institution. ALVIN LANGDON COBURN, 1906, hs, profile, photogravure, for *Men of Mark*, NPG AX7777. F.HILAIRE D'AROIS, three prints, hs and two, hs profile, NPG. UNKNOWN, hs with William James, print, NPG.

JAMES, Sir William Milbourne (1807-1881) lord justice of appeal.
G JOHN HOLLINS, 'A Consultation prior to the Aerial Voyage to Weilburg, 1836', oil, NPG 4710.
PR UNKNOWN, after a photograph by John Watkins, hs, woodcut, for *Illust London News*, 27 March 1869, NPG. UNKNOWN, hs, woodcut, for *Illust London News*, 18 June 1881, NPG.
PH LOCK & WHITFIELD, hs, profile, oval, woodburytype, for *Men of Mark*, 1880, NPG.

JAMES of Hereford, Henry James, 1st Baron (1828-1911) barrister and politician.
P JOHN ST HELIER LANDER, 1907, hs, profile, Middle Temple, London.
D S.P.HALL, several pencil sketches, NPG 2239, 2250, 2254, 2272 and 2307. RUDOLPH LEHMANN, 1892, BM. FREDERICK PEGRAM, pencil sketch, V & A.
G HENRY NELSON O'NEIL, 'The Billiard Room of the Garrick Club', oil, 1869, Garrick Club, London.
PR W.ROFFE, after a photograph by A.Bassano, hl seated, stipple, pub 1891, NPG.

c CARLO PELLEGRINI ('Ape'), hl, w/c study, for *Vanity Fair*, 7 March 1874, NPG 2725.

PH RUPERT POTTER, 1875, wl seated with John Bright and J.E.Millais, print, NPG x4324. Several negs by BASSANO, 1893, various sizes, NPG x6225–30. BASSANO, hs, semi-profile, print, for *Our Conservative and Unionist Statesmen*, vol I, NPG (Album 18).

JAMESON, James Sligo (1856-1888) naturalist and African traveller.

PR R.T., hs, wood engr, for *Illust London News*, 22 Nov 1890, NPG.

JAMESON, Sir Leander Starr, Bart (1853-1917) South African statesman.

P MIDDLETON JAMESON (his brother), hs, NPG 2804.

SC UNKNOWN, marble bust, Rhodes House, Oxford.

c Several political cartoons by D.C.BOONZAIER, A.S.BOYD and SIR FRANCIS CARRUTHERS GOULD, University of Cape Town, South Africa.

PH G.C.BERESFORD, 1914, hs, neg, NPG x6523. G.C.BERESFORD, hs, print, NPG. UNKNOWN, hs, print, NPG.

JARDINE, Sir Robert, 1st Bart (1825-1905) East India merchant and racehorse owner.

c SIR LESLIE WARD ('Spy'), wl, profile, chromo-lith, for *Vanity Fair*, 23 Aug 1890, NPG.

JARDINE, Sir William (1800-1874) naturalist.

P UNKNOWN, SNPG 2192.

D W.H.LIZARS, hs, pencil, SNPG 1683.

PR T.H.MAGUIRE, tql, lith, one of set of *Ipswich Museum Portraits*, 1851, BM, NPG. UNKNOWN, after a photograph by Maull & Co, hs, woodcut, for *Illust London News*, 26 Dec 1874, NPG.

JARMAN, Frances Eleanor, (Mrs Ternan) (1803?-1873) actress.

PR I.W.SLATER, hl, lith, pub 1829, BM, Harvard Theatre Collection, Cambridge, Mass, USA. Two theatrical prints, Harvard Theatre Collection.

JAYNE, Francis John (1845-1921) bishop of Chester.

P UNKNOWN, St David's University College, Lampeter.

G S.P.HALL, 'The Bench of Bishops, 1902', w/c, NPG 2369.

PR R.R., after a photograph by Heslop Woods of Leeds, hs, wood engr. for *Illust London News*, 6 Oct 1888, NPG.

PH UNKNOWN, hl, print, NPG (Anglican Bishops).

JEAFFRESON, John Cordy (1831-1901) author.

P MARY HECTOR, posthumous, tql seated, Ipswich Museum.

JEBB, Sir Richard Claverhouse (1841-1905) Greek scholar.

P SIR GEORGE REID, 1903, wl, Trinity College, Cambridge. UNKNOWN, The British Academy, London.

c SIR LESLIE WARD ('Spy'), wl, profile, chromo-lith, for *Vanity Fair*, 20 Oct 1904, NPG.

PH C.A.SHAW, *c*1905, tql seated, print, NPG. SIR BENJAMIN STONE, wl, print, NPG. WINDOW & GROVE, tql seated, print, NPG.

JEFFERIES, Richard (1848-1887) novelist and naturalist.

SC MARGARET THOMAS, 1892, marble bust on monument, Salisbury Cathedral; related plaster cast, NPG 1097. UNKNOWN, bust, Shire Hall, Taunton.

PR WILLIAM STRANG, hs, etch, NPG.

PH LONDON STEREOSCOPIC Co, hs, photo-mezzotype, NPG.

JEFFREYS, John Gwyn (1809-1885) conchologist.

PR UNKNOWN, hs, woodcut, for *Illust London News*, 7 Feb 1885, NPG.

JEKYLL, Gertrude (1843-1932) horticulturist and writer.

P SIR WILLIAM NICHOLSON, 1920, hl seated, NPG 3334.

JELLETT, John Hewitt (1817-1888) provost of Trinity College, Dublin.

P SARAH PURSER, 1889, tql seated, Trinity College, Dublin. UNKNOWN, after a photograph by Chancellor, tql seated, Trinity College, Dublin.

PR UNKNOWN, after a photograph by Chancellor of Dublin, hs, woodcut, for *Illust London News*, 7 May 1881, NPG.

JELLICOE, John Rushworth Jellicoe, 1st Earl (1859-1935) admiral.

P GLYN PHILPOT, 1918, IWM. SIR W.T.MONNINGTON, 1932–34, tql in uniform, NMM, Greenwich. R.G.EVES, 1935, hs, NPG 2799. R.G.EVES, hl, HMS Excellent, Portsmouth.

D FRANCIS DODD, 1917, charcoal and w/c, IWM. EDMOND KAPP, 1928, Barber Institute of Fine Arts, Birmingham.

G SIR A.S.COPE, 'Naval Officers of World War I, 1914–18', oil, NPG 1913.

SC WILLIAM MACMILLAN, bronze bust, Trafalgar Square, London. H.A.PEGRAM, 1928, plaster bust, IWM.

c DAVID LOW, pencil sketches, NPG 4529 (183–4). SIR LESLIE WARD ('Spy'), wl, for *Vanity Fair*, 26 Dec 1906, NPG.

PH MRS A.BROOM, hl, neg (x172), and print, NPG. WALTER STONEMAN, 1925, hs in uniform, NPG (NPR).

JENKIN, Henry Charles Fleeming (1833-1885) engineer and electrician.

PR W.HOLE, tql, etch, for *Quasi Cursores*, 1884, NPG.

PH WALKER & BOUTALL, hl seated, profile, photogravure, NPG.

JENKINS, Ebenezer Evans (1820-1905) Wesleyan minister and missionary.

PR UNKNOWN, after a photograph by Done and Co of Baker St, hs, circle, woodcut, for *Illust London News*, 31 July 1880, NPG.

JENKINS, John Edward (1838-1910) politician and writer.

PR UNKNOWN, after a photograph by Sarony, hs, profile, circle, woodcut, for *Illust London News*, 2 May 1874, NPG.

c SIR LESLIE WARD ('Spy'), wl, profile, w/c study, for *Vanity Fair*, 31 Aug 1878, NPG 2578.

JENKINS, Joseph John (1811-1885) engraver and water-colour artist.

PR UNKNOWN, after a photograph by H.S.Melville of East Grinstead, hs, woodcut, for *Illust London News*, 28 March 1885, NPG.

PH CUNDALL & FLEMING, tql seated, carte, NPG (Album 104).

JENKINS, Sir Lawrence Hugh (1857-1928) Indian judge.

P SIR WILLIAM ORCHARDSON, on loan to National Museum of Wales, Cardiff.

PH WALTER STONEMAN, 1918, hs, NPG (NPR).

JENKINSON, Francis John Henry (1853-1923) librarian.

P J.S.SARGENT, 1915, hl, University Library, University of Cambridge.

JENKINSON, Sir George Samuel, Bart (1817-1892) High Sheriff of Gloucestershire.

c CARLO PELLEGRINI ('Ape'), wl, w/c study, for *Vanity Fair*, 24 April 1875, NPG 2579.

JENNER, Sir William, 1st Bart (1815-1898) physician.

P VAL PRINSEP, after Frank Holl of 1888, tql seated in robes, Royal College of Physicians, London.

PR R.TAYLOR, after a photograph, hs, oval, woodcut, for *Illust London News*, 23 Dec 1871, NPG.

c SIR LESLIE WARD ('Spy'), wl, chromo-lith, for *Vanity Fair*, 26 April 1873, NPG.

PH UNKNOWN, hs, carte, NPG (Album 40).

JENNER-FUST, Herbert (1806-1904) cricketer.

P UNKNOWN, Lord's Cricket Ground, London.

JEPHSON, Arthur Jermy Mounteney (1858-1908) explorer.

PH UNKNOWN, wl with rifle, print, NPG X12642.

JEREMIE, James Amiraux (1802–1872) dean of Lincoln.
SC E.RICHARDSON, RA 1855, monumental marble relief, St Peter's Church, Guernsey.
PR R.E.TAYLOR, hs, woodcut, for *Illust London News*, 29 June 1872, NPG.

JEROME, Jerome Klapka (1859–1927) author.
P SOLOMON J.SOLOMON, c1889, hl, NPG 4492. P.A.DE LÁSZLÓ, 1921, tql seated, NPG 4491.
PH W. & D.DOWNEY, tql, woodburytype, for Cassell's *Cabinet Portrait Gallery*, vol IV, 1893, NPG. BASSANO, 1897, four negs, various sizes, NPG X599–601 and X661. JOHN RUSSELL & SONS, hl, print, for *National Photographic Record*, vol I, NPG. HAY WRIGHTSON, tql, print, NPG X11843. UNKNOWN, hl, print, NPG X11844.

JERRAM, Sir (Thomas Henry) Martyn (1858–1933) admiral.
P NEVILLE LYTTON, 1920, IWM.
PH WALTER STONEMAN, 1917, hs in uniform, NPG (NPR).

JERROLD, Douglas William (1803–1857) journalist and playwright.
P SIR DANIEL MACNEE, 1853, hl seated, NPG 292.
G DANIEL MACLISE, 'Dickens reading *The Chimes* to his friends, 1844', pencil, V & A.
SC E.H.BAILY, 1853, marble bust, NPG 942.
PR T.A.PRIOR, after a photograph by Beard, tql seated, line, NPG. UNKNOWN, after a photograph by London Stereoscopic Co, hs, woodcut, for *The Illustrated Review*, 15 May 1872, NPG. Several woodcuts, some after photographs, BM, NPG.
C RICHARD DOYLE, with Dickens and John Forster, pen sketch, BM.
PH HERBERT WATKINS, 1857, hl, print, NPG AX7917. UNITED ASSOCIATION OF PHOTOGRAPHY LTD, 1864–67, hs, wothlytype, carte, NPG AX7507. JOHN & CHARLES WATKINS, hs, semi-profile, carte, NPG.

JERROLD, William Blanchard (1826–1884) journalist and author.
PR UNKNOWN, after a photograph by Elliott & Fry, hs, woodcut, for *The Illust Review*, 13 March 1873, NPG. UNKNOWN, hs, profile, woodcut, for *Illust London News*, 22 March 1884, NPG.

JERSEY, Margaret Elizabeth Child-Villiers, Countess of, née Leigh (1849–1945) founder of the Victoria League; writer for children.
G HENRY JAMYN BROOKS, 'Private View of the Old Masters Exhibition, Royal Academy, 1888', oil, NPG 1833.
PR UNKNOWN, after Desanges, wl seated, lith, for *The Whitehall Review*, 25 Oct 1879, NPG.

JERSEY, Victor Albert George Child-Villiers, 7th Earl of (1845–1915) colonial governor.
P After W.W.OULESS of 1909, hl in robes, Oxfordshire County Council.
D FREDERICK SARGENT, hs, pencil, NPG 1834r.
G HENRY JAMYN BROOKS, 'Private View of the Old Masters Exhibition, Royal Academy, 1888', oil, NPG 1833.

JERVOIS, Sir William Francis Drummond (1821–1897) general.
PR D.J.POUND, after a photograph by John & Charles Watkins, tql seated in uniform, line, for *The Drawing Room Portrait Gallery of Eminent Personages*, BM. UNKNOWN, after a photograph by Elliott & Fry, hs, woodcut, for *Illust London News*, 10 April 1875, NPG.

JESSE, John Heneage (1815–1874) historical writer.
D COUNT ALFRED D'ORSAY, hl seated, profile, pencil and chalk,

NPG 4026(37).

JESSEL, Sir George (1824–1883) master of the rolls.
P JOHN COLLIER, 1885, (replica), hl seated in vice-chancellor's robes, University of London. MOUSSA AYOUB, posthumous, hs, profile, in robes, Lincoln's Inn, London.
SC W.R.INGRAM, 1888, marble bust, DoE (Law Courts, London).
PR MORRIS & CO, hl, lith, NPG.
C SIR LESLIE WARD ('Spy'), hs at bench, chromo-lith, for *Vanity Fair*, 1 March 1879, NPG.
PH LOCK & WHITFIELD, hs, profile, oval, woodburytype, for *Men of Mark*, 1881, NPG.

JESSOPP, Augustus (1823–1914) schoolmaster and historical writer.
PR P.NAUMANN & R.TAYLOR & CO, hs, one of a set, woodcut, 'Our Literary Contributors – Past and Present', for *Illust London News*, 14 May 1892, BM.

JEUNE, Francis (1806–1868) bishop of Peterborough.
P W.M.TWEEDIE, c1863, tql, Pembroke College, Oxford.
PR UNKNOWN, after a photograph by John & Charles Watkins, hs, woodcut, for *Illust London News*, 28 May 1864, NPG.
PH W.WALKER & SONS, tql seated, carte, NPG AX7463.

JEUNE, Francis Henry, see Baron St Helier.

JEVONS, William Stanley (1835–1882) economist and logician.
SC UNKNOWN, bust, University of Manchester.
PR UNKNOWN, 1858, hl seated, print, NPG. MAULL & CO, tql seated, print, NPG; related carte by Maull & Fox, hs, NPG.

JEWSBURY, Maria Jane (1800–1833) writer.
PR J.COCHRAN, after G.Freeman, hl seated, stipple, for W.Cooke-Taylor's *National Portrait Gallery*, vol III, 1846, NPG.

JEX-BLAKE, Sophia Louisa (1840–1912) physician.
P SAMUEL LAURENCE, 1865, hs, Royal Society of Medicine, London.

JEX-BLAKE, Thomas William (1832–1915) schoolmaster and dean of Wells.
P HERMAN G.HERKOMER, RA 1891, Rugby School, Warwicks.
PR UNKNOWN, after a photograph by A.G.Tod of Cheltenham, hs, woodcut, for *Illust London News*, 11 April 1874, NPG. R.T. & CO, after a photograph by E.H.Speight of Rugby, hs, profile, woodcut, for *Illust London News*, 28 Feb 1891, NPG.

JOACHIM, Joseph (1831–1907) violinist.
P E.J.F.BENDEMANN, 1870, tql with violin, Royal College of Music, London. JAMES ARCHER, 1876, hl seated playing violin, Corporation of London. SIR HUBERT VON HERKOMER, 1882, hs, Trinity College, Cambridge. FRIEDRICH HEYSER, 1888, tql seated with violin, Berlin Museum, W Germany. G.F.WATTS, hl playing violin, Watts Gallery, Compton, Surrey.
D RUDOLPH LEHMANN, 1851, hs, BM. ALICE E.DONKIN, 1880, pencil, Royal College of Music, London.
G L.LOWENSTAM, after Bruck-Lajos, 'The Quartett', etch, BM.
SC UNKNOWN, bronze bust, Corporation of London.
C SIR LESLIE WARD ('Spy'), wl seated, playing violin, profile, w/c study, for *Vanity Fair*, 5 Jan 1905, NPG 4930.
PH W. & D.DOWNEY, tql, print, for Cassell's *Cabinet Portrait Gallery*, vol I, 1890, NPG. KINGSBURY & NOTCUTT, tql, cabinet, NPG X4178. C.REUTLINGER, hs, carte, NPG. UNKNOWN, hl, oval, print, NPG X727.

JOBSON, Frederick James (1812–1881) Wesleyan minister.
PR UNKNOWN, after a photograph by John Watkins, hs, woodcut, for *Illust London News*, 14 Aug 1869, NPG.

JOCELYN, Robert, see 4th Earl of Roden.

JOHNS, Claude Hermann Walter (1857-1920) Assyriologist.
P KENNETH GREENE, 1932, tql seated in robes, St Catherine's College, Cambridge.
PH ELLIOTT & FRY, tql, print, NPG.

JOHNSON, Sir George (1818-1896) physician.
P FRANK HOLL, 1888, tql seated, Royal College of Physicians, London.

JOHNSON, George Henry Sacheverell (1808-1881) dean of Wells.
P BESSIE JOHNSON, after George Richmond of c1861, Queen's College, Oxford.

JOHNSON, Manuel John (1805-1859) astronomer.
D After GEORGE RICHMOND of c1850, hs, chalk and pencil, Radcliffe Observatory, Oxford.

JOHNSON, William Ernest (1858-1931) logician.
P DELMAR BANNER, 1927, King's College, Cambridge.
PH WALTER STONEMAN, 1930, hl, NPG (NPR).

JOHNSTON, Alexander Keith (1844-1879) African explorer and geographer.
PR UNKNOWN, after a photograph by C.Henwood, hs, semi-profile, woodcut, for *Illust London News*, 23 Aug 1879, NPG.

JOHNSTON, Sir Christopher Nicholson, see Lord Sands.

JOHNSTON, Sir Harry Hamilton (1858-1927) explorer and administrator.
D T.B.WIRGMAN, 1894, hs, pencil, NPG 2902.
C HARRY FURNISS, pen and ink sketch, NPG 3473.
PH JOHN RUSSELL & SONS, hl, print, for *National Photographic Record*, vol I, NPG.

JOHNSTON, Sir William (1802-1888) Lord Provost of Edinburgh.
P SIR JOHN WATSON GORDON, exhib 1852, wl in robes, Royal Scottish Academy, Edinburgh.

JOHNSTON, William (1829-1902) Orangeman.
PR UNKNOWN, hs, lith, pub 1902, BM.
PH SIR BENJAMIN STONE, 1898, wl, print, NPG.

JOHNSTONE, James (1806-1869) physician.
PR G.T.DOO, after W.Roden, hl seated, oval, line, BM.

JOHNSTONE, James (1815-1878) newspaper proprietor.
C CARLO PELLEGRINI ('Ape'), wl, w/c study, for *Vanity Fair*, 14 Feb 1874, NPG 2726.

JOHNSTONE, William Borthwick (1804-1868) landscape and historical painter.
P JOHN PHILLIP, two portraits: 1861, tql, NGS 565; 1865, hs, NGS 1004.

JOICEY, James Joicey, 1st Baron (1846-1936) colliery proprietor.
C SIR LESLIE WARD ('Spy'), wl, mechanical repro, for *Vanity Fair*, 19 Dec 1906, NPG.
PH SIR BENJAMIN STONE, 1905, four prints, three with Lady Joicey and Miss Joicey, NPG. WALTER STONEMAN, 1919 and 1933, two portraits, both hl, NPG (NPR).

JOLLIFFE, William George Hylton, see 1st Baron Hylton.

JOLY, John (1857-1933) engineer, geologist and physicist.
P After LEO WHELAN, Royal Dublin Society, Dublin, Eire.

JONES, Sir Alfred Lewis (1845-1909) businessman.
P F.S.BEAUMONT, tql seated, Walker Art Gallery, Liverpool.

JONES, Avonia, afterwards Mrs Brooke (1839?-1867) actress.
PR Several theatrical prints, Harvard Theatre Collection, Cambridge, Mass, USA.

JONES, Sir Edward Coley Burne-, see BURNE-Jones.

JONES, Sir Henry (1852-1922) philosopher.
P UNKNOWN, University College of North Wales, Bangor. UNKNOWN, University of Glasgow.

JONES, Henry Arthur (1851-1929) dramatist.
D ALFRED WOLMARK, 1928, hs, pen and ink, NPG 4482.
PR WALTER TITTLE, 1924, hs, lith, NPG 4239.
C HARRY FURNISS, wl, profile, pen and ink, NPG 3474. SIR LESLIE WARD ('Spy'), wl, chromo-lith, for *Vanity Fair*, 2 April 1892, NPG.
PH BARRAUD, hs, profile, woodburytype, for *The Theatre*, Sept 1886, NPG. W. & D.DOWNEY, hs, woodburytype, for Cassell's *Cabinet Portrait Gallery*, vol III, 1892. NPG. JOHN RUSSELL & SONS, hs, print, for *National Photographic Record*, vol I, NPG.

JONES, Henry Bence (1814-1873) physician and chemist.
D GEORGE RICHMOND, 1865, crayon, Royal Institution, London.
SC THOMAS WOOLNER, c1873, bust, Royal Institution.
PR C.HOLL, after G.Richmond, hs, stipple, pub 1873, BM.

JONES, Henry Cadman (1818-1902) law reporter.
D T.C.WAGEMAN, w/c, Trinity College, Cambridge.

JONES, Henry Festing (1851-1928) author.
P SIR GEORGE CLAUSEN, 1923, hs, Fitzwilliam Museum, Cambridge; related pencil drg, BM.
PR F.E.JACKSON, hs, lith, V & A.

JONES, Sir Horace (1819-1887) city of London architect.
P FRANK HOLL, hl seated, RIBA, London.
PR R.T., after a photograph by S.A.Walker, hs, semi-profile woodcut, for *Illust London News*, 4 June 1887, NPG.
PH SAMUEL A.WALKER, c1887, tql seated, cabinet, NPG X4962.

JONES, John Viriamu (1856-1901) physicist.
SC SIR WILLIAM GOSCOMBE, JOHN, RA 1906, marble statue, seated University College of South Wales, Cardiff.

JONES, John Winter (1805-1881) principal librarian of the British Museum.
SC R.C.LUCAS, 1856, wax portrait, BM.
PR UNKNOWN, hs, woodcut, for *Illust London News*, 3 Nov 1866 NPG.

JONES, Owen (1809-1874) architect.
P H.W.PHILLIPS, c1856, tql, RIBA, London.
PR C.BAUGNIET, tql, lith, BM. UNKNOWN, after T.Scott, hs, woodcut, BM. UNKNOWN, hs, semi-profile, circle, woodcut, for *Th Builder*, 11 Dec 1869, NPG. UNKNOWN, after a photograph by Watkins and Haigh, hs, oval, woodcut, for *Illust London News*, May 1874, NPG.

JONES, Sir Robert, 1st Bart (1857-1933) orthopaedi surgeon.
P FRANK COPNALL, hl, Royal College of Surgeons, London R.E.MORRISON, tql in uniform, Royal College of Surgeons.

JONES, Thomas (1810-1875) librarian of Chetham's Library Manchester.
P JOHN HANSON WALKER, c1875, hs, Chetham's Library Manchester.

JONES, Thomas Heron, see 7th Viscount Ranelagh.

JONES, William Basil (1822-1897) bishop of St David's.
PH UNKNOWN, hs, print, NPG (Anglican Bishops).

JONES, William West (1838-1908) archbishop of Cap Town.
P SIR WILLIAM ORPEN, 1909, hl seated, St John's College, Oxford

PHILIP TENNYSON COLE, Diocesan Library, Cape Town. C.H.THOMPSON, Diocesan College, Cape Town.

SC CHARLES HARTWELL, RA 1911, recumbent effigy, Cape Town Cathedral.

PH UNKNOWN, hl, print, NPG (Anglican Bishops).

JORDAN, Sir John Newell (1852–1925) diplomat.

D UNKNOWN, after a photograph, pencil sketch, Queen's College, Belfast.

PH WALTER STONEMAN, 1920, hs, NPG (NPR).

JOSI, Henry (1802–1845) keeper of department of prints and drawings, British Museum.

PR W.CARPENTER, head, etch, BM, NPG.

JOULE, James Prescott (1818–1889) physicist.

P GEORGE PATTEN, 1863, Manchester Literary and Philosophical Society. JOHN COLLIER, 1882, hl, Royal Society, London.

SC SIR ALFRED GILBERT, 1890–94, marble seated statue, Town Hall, Manchester.

PR DALZIEL, hs, circle, woodcut, BM. C.H.JEENS, hs, stipple, for *Nature*, vol 26, BM, NPG.

H LADY ROSCOE, c1876, tql seated, print, NPG.

JOWETT, Benjamin (1817–1893) master of Balliol College, Oxford.

P G.F.WATTS, 1889, hl, Balliol College, Oxford; copy by LADY ABERCROMBY, Balliol College.

D Several portraits at Balliol College: GEORGE RICHMOND, c1855, hs, pencil and chalk; GEORGE, 9TH EARL OF CARLISLE, 1871, hl seated with Giuseppe Mazzini, pencil; LADY ABERCROMBY, 1892,

hl seated, w/c; C.M.ROSS, hs, pastel. S.P.HALL, hl, profile, pencil, NPG 2389.

SC H.R.HOPE PINKER, 1896, marble bust, Balliol College. H.R.HOPE PINKER, bust, St Paul's School, London. EDWARD ONSLOW FORD, RA 1897, memorial effigy, Balliol College Chapel, Oxford.

C HARRY FURNISS, wl seated, pen and ink, NPG 3475. SIR LESLIE WARD ('Spy'), wl in gown, chromo-lith, for *Vanity Fair*, 26 Feb 1876, NPG.

PH ELLIOTT & FRY, hs, cabinet, NPG. HILLS & SAUNDERS, hs, carte, NPG (Album 40). T. & G.SHRIMPTON, hs, carte, NPG (Album 99). TAUNT & Co, c1890?, wl with Sir Henry Wentworth Dyke Acland, cabinet, NPG X5146.

JOYCE, Sir Matthew Ingle (1839–1930) judge.

C SIR LESLIE WARD ('Spy'), hs, profile, at bench, chromo-lith, for *Vanity Fair*, 23 Jan 1902, NPG.

JULIEN or JULLIEN, Louis Antoine (1812–1860) musical conductor.

SC J.P.DANTAN, 1836, caricature plaster statuette, Musée Carnavalet, Paris.

PR N.HANHART, hs, coloured lith, NPG. D.J.POUND, after a photograph by Mayall, tql, stipple and line, NPG. Several popular woodcuts, NPG. Several liths and woodcuts, Harvard Theatre Collection, Cambridge, Mass, USA.

PH MAYALL, wl, carte, NPG.

JUTSUM, Henry (1816–1869) landscape painter.

D UNKNOWN, hl, profile, w/c, BM (Engr Ports Coll).

PH JOHN WATKINS, tql seated, carte, NPG (Album 104).

K

KANE, Sir Robert John (1809-1890) president of the Queen's College, Cork.

PR H.MEYER, after C.Grey, hs, profile, stipple, pub 1849, NPG; pencil study, NGI 2599. S.FREEMAN, after G.F.Mulvany, hl seated, stipple, NPG.

KARSLAKE, Sir John Burgess (1821-1881) lawyer.

PR UNKNOWN, hs, woodcut, for *Illust London News*, 29 Dec 1866, NPG.

C W.VINE ('W.V.'), wl, profile, w/c study, for *Vanity Fair*, 22 Feb 1873, NPG 2581. 'FAUSTIN', wl, chromo-lith, a 'Figaro' cartoon, NPG.

KAVANAGH, Julia (1824-1877) novelist and biographical writer.

P HENRI CHANET, hl, oval, NGI 312.

KAY, Sir Edward Ebenezer (1822-1897) judge.

D SEBASTIAN EVANS, 1877, hs, profile, ink, NPG 2173(15).

C SIR LESLIE WARD('Spy'), hs at bench, w/c study, for *Vanity Fair*, 7 Jan 1888, NPG 2727.

PH LOCK & WHITFIELD, hs, oval, woodburytype, for *Men of Mark*, 1883, NPG.

KAYE, Sir John William (1814-1876) military historian.

SC ALEXANDER BRODIE, plaster bust, India Office Library and Records, London.

KEAN, Charles John (1811-1868) actor.

P S.J.STUMP, c1830, tql seated as Sir Edward Mortimer in George Colman's *The Iron Chest*, NPG 1249. RICHARD DADD, c1840, said to be Kean, wl with Mrs Kean as Gertrude, in *Hamlet*, Yale Center for British Art, New Haven, USA. WILLIAM ETTY, 1860, as King Lear, University of Bristol. WILLIAM DANIELS, as Hamlet, V & A. H.W.PHILLIPS, wl as Louis XI, Garrick Club, London.

D Attrib ROSE M.DRUMMOND, c1838, head, chalk, NPG 2524. A.E.CHALON, 1840, as Macbeth, w/c, The Athenaeum, London. UKNOWN (possibly L.S.Starkley), c1858, wl with Mrs Kean, as Benedick and Beatrice, w/c, V & A. E.G.LEWIS, hs, chalk, NPG 1307. JEMIMA WEDDERBURN, two drgs, both wl as Richard III, pencil and w/c, NPG 2772.

M S.J.STUMP, hl, Guildhall Art Gallery, London. 'P.M.B.', tql as Richard III, Royal Shakespeare Theatre, Stratford-upon-Avon.

R Various popular and theatrical prints, BM, NPG, Harvard Theatre Collection, Cambridge, Mass, USA.

H UNKNOWN, 1856, wl as Leontes with Ellen Terry as Mamillius in *The Winter's Tale*, print, NPG X7954. Several cartes by H.N.KING, MAULL & CO, SOUTHWELL BROS and unknown photographers, various sizes, NPG. Several prints in character, V & A.

KEAN, Ellen, née Tree (1805-1880) actress.

P RICHARD DADD, c1840, said to be Mrs Kean, wl, with Charles Kean as Hamlet, Yale Center for British Art, New Haven, USA. C.R.LESLIE, RA 1856, as Hermione in *The Winter's Tale*, Royal Shakespeare Theatre, Stratford-upon-Avon.

D UNKNOWN, c1840, hs, w/c, Garrick Club, London. UNKNOWN (possibly L.S.Starkley), c1858, wl with Charles Kean, as Beatrice and Benedick, w/c, V & A.

R Various theatrical prints, BM, NPG, Harvard Theatre Collection,

Cambridge, Mass. USA.

PH SOUTHWELL BROS, wl, carte, NPG. UNKNOWN, hs, carte, NPG (Album 102). Three cartes, all wl, NPG (Album 108).

KEARLEY, Hudson Ewbanke, see 1st Viscount Devonport.

KEATING, Sir Henry Singer (1804-1888) judge.

PR D.J.POUND, after a photograph by Mayall, tql seated, stipple and line, for *The Drawing Room Portrait Gallery of Eminent Personages*, NPG. UNKNOWN, after a photograph by London Stereoscopic Co, hs, woodcut, for *Illust London News*, 20 Feb 1875, NPG.

KEAY, John Seymour (1839-1909) Anglo-Indian politician.

C SIR LESLIE WARD ('Spy'), wl, profile, chromo-lith, for *Vanity Fair*, 8 Oct 1892, NPG.

KEELEY, Mary Ann, née Goward (1805?-1899) actress.

P WALTER GOODMAN, c1888, hl seated, Garrick Club, London. JULIA B.FOLKARD, 1898, hs, NPG 1558.

D T.H.WILSON, 1845, wl, w/c, Garrick Club. C.F.TOMKINS, as Lurline, sepia, BM.

PR Various theatrical prints, BM, NPG, Harvard Theatre Collection, Cambridge, Mass, USA.

PH FRADELLE & MARSHALL, tql, carte, NPG. WALKER & SONS, wl seated, carte, NPG. UNKNOWN, c1897, hs, oval, print, NPG.

KEENE, Charles Samuel (1823-1891) illustrator.

P Self-portrait, c1860, wl at easel, TATE 3644. SIR GEORGE REID, 1881, hs, semi-profile, MacDonald Collection, Aberdeen Art Gallery.

D A.W.COOPER, 1866, wl, pencil, NPG 2771. WALTON CORBOULD, wl, w/c, NPG 1337. Self-portrait, c1865, pen, ink and wash, Ashmolean Museum, Oxford. Self-portrait, c1885, tql, pen and ink, NPG 2817. Several self-portraits at the Tate Gallery: 1883, in officer's uniform, pencil, TATE 4371; 1884, pencil, TATE 4370; 1885?, wl seated, pencil, TATE T2088; pencil sketch, TATE 3022; tql with a gun, pen and ink, TATE 3611.

SC SIR GEORGE FRAMPTON, 1896, bronze memorial bas-reliefs, Shepherd's Bush Library, London and TATE 1954; plaster model, TATE 5998.

C HARRY FURNISS, pen and ink sketches, NPG 3476-77.

PH DAVID WILKIE WYNFIELD, c1862-4, hs, profile, print, NPG P92. UNKNOWN, tql, print, NPG.

KEITH-FALCONER, Algernon, see 9th Earl of Kintore.

KEITH-FALCONER, Ion Grant Neville (1856-1887) Arabic scholar and bicyclist.

PR UNKNOWN, 'Bicycle Match at Lillie-Bridge, West Brompton', woodcut, for *Illust London News*, 30 Jan 1875, NPG.

PH UNKNOWN, hs, photogravure, NPG.

KEKEWICH, Sir Arthur (1832-1907) judge.

C SIR LESLIE WARD ('Spy'), hs at bench, chromo-lith, for *Vanity Fair*, 24 Jan 1895, NPG.

PH BARRAUD, tql, print, for *Men and Women of the Day*, vol IV, 1891, NPG AX5541.

KELLAND, Philip (1808-1879) mathematician.

D J.W.SLATER, pencil and w/c, Queen's College, Cambridge. T.C.WAGEMAN, w/c, Trinity College, Cambridge.

PR WILLIAM HOLE, hs, etch, for *Quasi Cursores*, 1884, NPG.

KELLETT, Sir Henry (1806-1875) vice-admiral.
P STEPHEN PEARCE, 1856, hs, in uniform, NPG 1222; replica, NPG 915.
PR UNKNOWN, after a photograph by Kilburn, hs in uniform, woodcut, for *Illust London News*, 24 April 1852, NPG.

KELLY, James Fitzmaurice- (1857-1923) historian of Spanish literature.
P SIR JOHN LAVERY, 1898, tql seated, NPG 2018.
G UNKNOWN, a group of some members of the faculty of Arts of Liverpool University, oil, 1917, University of Liverpool.

KELLY-KENNY, Sir Thomas (1840-1914) general.
C SIR LESLIE WARD ('Spy'), wl, profile, chromo-lith, for *Vanity Fair*, 29 Aug 1901, NPG.

KELTIE, Sir John Scott (1840-1927) geographer.
PH JOHN RUSSELL & SONS, hl, print, for *National Photographic Record*, vol I, NPG.

KELVIN, William Thomson, 1st Baron (1824-1907) physicist.
P LOWES DICKINSON, RA 1869, Peterhouse, Cambridge. ELIZABETH T.KING (his sister), 1886-87, hl seated, profile, NPG 1708. E.T.KING, SNPG 926. SIR HUBERT VON HERKOMER, 1891, tql seated in doctoral robes, University of Glasgow. SIR W.Q.ORCHARDSON, RA 1899, tql seated, Royal Society, London. W.W.OULESS, RA 1902, hs, Clockmakers' Company, London. E.G.LEWIS, Institution of Electrical Engineers, London.
D ELIZABETH KING, 1840, hs, pencil, NPG 1708(f). ELIZABETH KING & AGNES GARDNER KING, sketch in an album of drgs of the Thomson family, NPG 1708(a). SIR W.Q.ORCHARDSON, charcoal drg, SNPG 884. SIR WILLIAM ROTHENSTEIN, 1904, pastel, SNPG 743.
SC ARCHIBALD MCFARLANE SHANNAN, 1896, bronze bust, SNPG 681. MARGARET M.GILES, wax medallion, NPG 1896. UNKNOWN, medallion on decorative frieze, School of Science and Art, Stroud. UNKNOWN, 1910, statue, Belfast.
PR C.H.JEENS, after a photograph, hs, line, for *Nature*, vol 14, 1876, BM, NPG. UNKNOWN, hs, lith, NPG.
C HARRY FURNISS, pen and ink sketch, NPG 3587. SIR LESLIE WARD ('Spy'), wl, w/c study, for *Vanity Fair*, 29 April 1897, NPG 3005.
PH BERLIN PHOTOGRAPHIC CO, hl, photogravure, NPG. DICKINSON, hs, photogravure, NPG. W. & D.DOWNEY, hs, woodburytype, for Cassell's *Cabinet Portrait Gallery*, vol III, 1892, NPG. ELLIOTT & FRY, 1900, hs, profile, print, NPG. ANNAN & SONS, after Elliott & Fry, hs, profile, photogravure, NPG. LONDON STEREOSCOPIC CO, two prints, hs and hs, profile, NPG. UNKNOWN, tql seated, woodburytype, NPG.

KEMBALL, Sir Arnold Burrowes (1820-1908) general.
PR UNKNOWN, wl at the battle of Jahnilar, woodcut, for *Illust London News*, 29 Sept 1877, NPG.
C CARLO PELLEGRINI ('Ape'), wl, profile, chromo-lith, for *Vanity Fair*, 8 June 1878, NPG.
PH CAMILLE SILVY, 1860, hl, print, NPG (Album 2).

KEMBLE, Adelaide, see Mrs Sartoris.

KEMBLE, Frances Anne, (Mrs Pierce Butler) (1809-1893) actress and writer.
P HENRY INMAN, hl seated, Brooklyn Museum, New York, USA. THOMAS SULLY, two portraits, 1833, hs as Beatrice and hs as Bianca in H.H.Milman's *Fazio*, Pennsylvania Academy of Fine Arts, Philadelphia, USA.
D After SIR THOMAS LAWRENCE of 1830, tql seated, pencil, Metropolitan Museum of Art, New York, USA, and pencil and w/c, University of London, Courtauld Institute of Art (Witt Collection). UNKNOWN, hl, oval, w/c, Garrick Club, London.
G HENRY ANDREWS, 'The Trial of Queen Katherine', oil, c1831,

Royal Shakespeare Theatre, Stratford-upon-Avon.
PR Various prints and theatrical prints, BM, NPG, Harvard Theatre Collection, Cambridge, Mass, USA.
C JOHN DOYLE, 1851, as Juliet, on her balcony, pencil, BM.

KEMBLE, Henry (1848-1907) comedian.
P HARRY ALLEN, 1908, posthumous, hs, Garrick Club, London.
C SIR LESLIE WARD ('Spy'), wl, mechanical repro, for *Vanity Fair*, 24 April 1907, NPG.

KEMBLE, John Mitchell (1807-1857) philologist and historian.
SC THOMAS WOOLNER, 1865, marble bust, Trinity College, Cambridge.

KENDAL, Dame Margaret Shafto, née Robertson (1848-1935) better known as Madge Kendal, actress.
P VAL PRINSEP, RA 1883, tql, profile, as Lady Giovanna in *The Falcon*, Garrick Club, London. SIR WILLIAM ORPEN, c1927-8, tql seated, TATE 4400.
G JOHN COLLIER, nearly wl as Mrs Ford, with Ellen Terry as Mrs Page and Herbert Tree as Falstaff in a scene from *The Merry Wives of Windsor*, oil, 1904, Garrick Club.
PR Various theatrical and popular prints, BM, NPG, Harvard Theatre Collection, Cambridge, Mass, USA.
PH BARRAUD, tql with her husband, William Hunter Kendal, in character, in *Clancarty*, print, for *Men and Women of the Day*, vol I, 1888, NPG AX5408. W. & D.DOWNEY, tql, profile, woodburytype, for Cassell's *Cabinet Portrait Gallery*, vol II, 1891, NPG. Various prints, some with her husband and some in character, BM, NPG.

KENDAL, William Hunter (1843-1917) actor-manager whose original name was Grimston.
P H.G.RIVIERE, 1918, tql, Garrick Club, London.
PR Several theatrical and popular prints, BM, NPG, Harvard Theatre Collection, Cambridge, Mass, USA.
C SIR LESLIE WARD ('Spy'), wl, profile, chromo-lith, for *Vanity Fair*, 20 April 1893, NPG.
PH BARRAUD, tql with his wife, Madge Kendal, in character, in *Clancarty*, print, for *Men and Women of the Day*, vol I, 1888, NPG AX5408. W. & D.DOWNEY, tql, woodburytype, for Cassell's *Cabinet Portrait Gallery*, vol IV, 1893, NPG. Various prints, some with his wife and some in character, BM, NPG.

KENEALY, Edward Vaughan Hyde (1819-1880) lawyer.
PR UNKNOWN, tql at the trial of the Tichborne claimant, woodcut, for *Illust London News*, 23 Aug 1873, NPG.
C SIR LESLIE WARD ('Spy'), wl, profile, w/c study, for *Vanity Fair*, Nov 1873, NPG 2685. UNKNOWN, wl with Mr Hawkins, chromo-lith, 'London Sketch-Book of Celebrities', NPG.
PH LONDON STEREOSCOPIC CO, hl, cabinet, NPG.

KENMARE, Valentine Augustus Browne, 4th Earl of (1825-1905) landowner.
C SIR LESLIE WARD ('Spy'), wl, w/c study, for *Vanity Fair*, 26 Feb 1881, NPG 4720.

KENNARD, Howard John (1829-1896) financier.
C LIBERIO PROSPERI ('Lib'), wl, profile, w/c study, for *Vanity Fair*, Dec 1890, NPG 2988.
PH HENNAH & KENT, tql seated, cabinet, NPG X4964.

KENNAWAY, Sir John Henry, 3rd Bart (1837-1919) politician.
C SIR LESLIE WARD ('Spy'), wl, w/c study, for *Vanity Fair*, 10 April 1886, NPG 2582.

KENNEDY, Sir Alexander Blackie William (1847-1928) engineer.

P H.G.Riviere, replica, tql seated, Institution of Civil Engineers, London.
D Unknown, tql seated, University College, London.
PH Walter Stoneman, 1917, hs, NPG (NPR).

KENNEDY, Benjamin Hall (1804-1889) regius professor of Greek at Cambridge.
P W.W.Ouless, RA 1885, tql seated, St John's College, Cambridge.
PR Unknown, after a photograph by Scott and Wilkinson, hs, wood engr, for *Illust London News*, 27 April 1889, NPG.

KENNEDY, Patrick (1801-1873) Irish writer and Dublin bookseller.
P Unknown, NGI 1120.

KENNEDY, William (1813-1890) sailor.
P Stephen Pearce, 1853, hs, NPG 1225; replica, NPG 917.

KENNEDY, Sir William Rann (1846-1915) judge.
P Sir George Richmond, tql seated, Lincoln's Inn, London.
C Sir Leslie Ward ('Spy'), hl, profile, at bench, chromo-lith, for *Vanity Fair*, 14 Dec 1893, NPG.

KENNY, Courtney Stanhope (1847-1930) legal scholar.
P Clegg Wilkinson, Downing College, Cambridge.
PH Unknown, print, Downing College.

KENNY, Sir Thomas Kelly-, see KELLY-Kenny.

KENYON, George Thomas (1840-1908) politician.
C Sir Leslie Ward ('Spy'), wl, profile, chromo-lith, for *Vanity Fair*, 29 Dec 1888, NPG.

KENYON-SLANEY, William Slaney (1847-1908) colonel and politician.
PR Unknown, after a photograph by Russell & Sons, hs, profile, wood engr, for *Illust London News*, 29 Nov 1890, NPG.

KEOGH, Sir Alfred (1857-1936) lieutenant-general.
P Arthur Hacker, RA 1919, hl in uniform, RAMC Mess, London; copy, Imperial College (Keogh Hall of Residence), London.
PH Walter Stoneman, hs in uniform, NPG (NPR).

KEOGH, William Nicholas (1817-1878) Irish judge.
P Louis Werner, King's Inns, Dublin.
PR Unknown, after a photograph by Chancellor of Dublin, hs, woodcut, for *Illust London News*, 12 Oct 1878, NPG.
C Harry Furniss, pen and ink sketch, NPG 3395.

KEPPEL, Sir Henry (1809-1904) admiral.
SC Count Gleichen, c1882, marble bust, formerly United Service Club, London (c/o The Crown Commissioners); related marble bust, Royal Coll.
PR D.J.Pound, after a photograph by Mayall, tql in uniform, stipple and line, for *The Drawing Room Portrait Gallery of Eminent Personages*, BM, NPG.
C Unknown, tql seated, chromo-lith, for *Vanity Fair*, 22 April 1876, NPG. 'Ao', wl, chromo-lith, for *Vanity Fair*, 15 Oct 1903, NPG.
PH W. & D.Downey, tql in uniform, woodburytype, for Cassell's *Cabinet Portrait Gallery*, vol IV, 1893, NPG.

KEPPEL, William Coutts, see 7th Earl of Albermarle.

KER, William Paton (1855-1923) scholar and writer.
P Philip Wilson Steer, c1923, hs, University College, London.
D Sir William Rothenstein, 1921, hs, sanguine and white, All Souls College, Oxford. Sir W.Rothenstein, 1923, head, chalk, NPG 4803.
SC John Tweed, bronze bust, University College, London. John Tweed, bust, All Souls College, Oxford; replica, University of Glasgow.

KERR, Schomberg Henry, see 9th Marquess of Lothian.

KERR, Lord Walter Talbot (1839-1927) admiral of the fleet.
P Miss A.J.Challin, tql in uniform, Melbourne Hall, Derbys.
C Sir Leslie Ward ('Spy'), wl, profile, chromo-lith, for *Vanity Fair*, 8 Nov 1900, NPG.
PH Camille Silvy, wl in uniform, carte, NPG AX7448.

KETTLE, Sir Rupert Alfred (1817-1894) judge, known as the 'Prince of Arbitrators'.
D Sebastian Evans, hs, pen and ink, NPG 2173(14).

KEYL, Frederick William (Friedrich Wilhelm) (1823-1873) animal painter.
PH Lucas & Groom, nearly wl seated, carte, NPG (Album 104).

KIALLMARK, George Frederick (1804-1887) musician.
SC E.H.Baily, RA 1843, marble bust, Royal College of Music, London.
PR I.W.Slater, after J.Slater, head, from a sketch, lith, for *Musical Keepsake*, 1834, BM, NPG.

KICKHAM, Charles Joseph (1826-1882) journalist.
SC Unknown, plaster death mask, NGI 8155.

KILBRACKEN, (John) Arthur Godley, 1st Baron (1847-1932) civil servant.
P R.E.Morrison, Rugby School, Warwicks.
SL Hubert Leslie, 1926, hs, profile, NPG.
PH G.C.Beresford, hs, print, NPG.

KIMBERLEY, John Gurdon Wodehouse, 1st Earl of (1826-1902) statesman.
P Stephen Catterson Smith, exhib 1866, Dublin Castle.
SC Sir William Hamo Thornycroft, 1907, marble bust, Palace of Westminster, London.
PR W.Holl, after G. Richmond, hs, stipple, one of 'Grillion's Club' series, BM, NPG. D.J.Pound, after a photograph by John Watkins, tql seated, stipple and line, for *The Drawing Room Portrait Gallery of Eminent Personages*, NPG. Unknown, after a photograph, wl in uniform, woodcut, for *Illust London News*, 13 May 1865, NPG.
C Carlo Pellegrini ('Ape'), wl, profile, chromo-lith, for *Vanity Fair*, 16 July 1869, NPG.
PH T.Cranfield, wl, carte, NPG AX7431. John Watkins, hs, carte, NPG (Album 99). Unknown, wl, carte, NPG (Album 136).

KINCARDINE, James Bruce, 12th Earl of, see 8th Earl of Elgin.

KINCARDINE, Victor Alexander Bruce, 13th Earl of, see 9th Earl of Elgin.

KING, Charles William (1818-1888) author of works on engraved gems.
P George Mason, 1846, hl seated, Trinity College, Cambridge.

KING, David (1806-1883) Scottish divine.
D Elizabeth King (his wife), 1842, hs, pencil, NPG 1708(g).
PR W.H.Egleton, after H.Anelay, hs, stipple, BM, NPG.

KING, Edward (1829-1910) bishop of Lincoln.
P George Richmond, before 1877, Cuddesdon College, Oxford. W.W.Ouless, RA 1899, hl, Old Palace, Lincoln.
SC Sir W.B.Richmond, bronze seated statue, in robes, Lincoln Cathedral.
C Sir Leslie Ward ('Spy'), tql, chromo-lith, for *Vanity Fair*, 13 Sept 1890, NPG.
PH Rotary Photo, tql seated, postcard, NPG. Unknown, tql, print, NPG (Anglican Bishops). Unknown, wl seated with several ministers, cabinet, NPG.

KING, Sir George (1840-1909) Indian botanist.
SC Frank Bowcher, 1899, bronze medallion, Zoological Garden,

F

Calcutta; copy, SNPG 748.

KING, Peter John Locke (1811-1885) politician.
PR D.J.POUND, after a photograph by Mayall, tql seated, stipple and line, for *Drawing Room Portrait Gallery of Eminent Personages*, NPG. UNKNOWN, tql seated, woodcut, for *Illust Times*, 12 June 1858, NPG.

KINGLAKE, Alexander William (1809-1891) historian.
P HARRIET M.HAVILAND, *c*1863, hs, NPG 1903.
C UNKNOWN, wl seated, chromo-lith, for *Vanity Fair*, 2 March 1872, NPG.
PH LONDON STEREOSCOPIC CO, hs, profile, carte, NPG. JOHN WATKINS, hs, profile, carte, NPG (Album 99). WEBBER & BLIZARD, wl seated, carte, NPG.

KINGSBURGH, John Hay Athole Macdonald, Lord (1836-1919) lord justice-clerk of Scotland.
P GEORGE FIDDES WATT, probably exhib 1917, tql seated in robes of lord justice-clerk, Faculty of Advocates, Parliament Hall, Edinburgh.
C SIR LESLIE WARD ('Spy'), wl seated, profile, chromo-lith, for *Vanity Fair*, 23 June 1888, NPG.
PH WALTER STONEMAN, 1917, hs, NPG (NPR).

KINGSCOTE, Sir Robert Nigel Fitzhardinge (1830-1908) agriculturalist.
PR W.ROFFE, after a photograph by Barraud, hs, stipple, for *Baily's Mag*, 1891, NPG.
C SIR LESLIE WARD ('Spy'), wl, profile, w/c study, for *Vanity Fair*, 14 Feb 1880, NPG 4723.

KINGSLEY, Charles (1819-1875) novelist and divine.
P LOWES DICKINSON, 1862, wl seated, NPG 2525. LOWES DICKINSON, Magdalene College, Cambridge.
D WILLIAM S.HUNT, after a photograph (*c*1874), hs, pen, NPG 1284.
SC R.C.BELT, marble bust, Chester Cathedral. THOMAS WOOLNER, 1876, marble bust, Westminster Abbey, London; 1875, original plaster cast, NPG 1666, and related medallion, St Mary's Church, Eversley, Hants. UNKNOWN, statue, Victoria Park, Bideford, Devon.
PR C.H.JEENS, after a photograph, hs, stipple and line, 1874, BM, NPG.
C ADRIANO CECIONI, wl, w/c study, for *Vanity Fair*, 30 March 1872, NPG 1939.
PH Various prints by CUNDALL & DOWNES, ELLIOTT & FRY, LONDON STEREOSCOPIC CO, MAYALL, R.W.THRUPP and J. & C.WATKINS, various dates and sizes, some cartes, some cabinets, NPG.

KINGSLEY, Henry (1830-1876) novelist.
D WILLIAM S.HUNT, after a photograph (*c*1874), hs, pen, NPG 1285. Attrib JULIA JACQUES, 1834, tql as a child, w/c, Worcester College, Oxford.
PR UNKNOWN, after a photograph by London Stereoscopic Co, hs, semi-profile, woodcut, for *Illust London News*, 3 June 1876, NPG.
PH MASON & CO, tql seated, carte, NPG.

KINLOCH, William Penney, Lord (1801-1872) Scottish judge.
PR UNKNOWN, after a photograph by Claudet, hs, oval, woodcut, for *Illust London News*, 9 Nov 1872, NPG.

KINNAIRD, Arthur Fitzgerald Kinnaird, 10th Baron (1814-1887) politician and philanthropist.
C CARLO PELLEGRINI ('Ape'), wl, chromo-lith, for *Vanity Fair*, 15 Jan 1876, NPG.

KINNAIRD, George William Fox Kinnaird, 9th Baron (1807-1878) lord-lieutenant of Perthshire and agricultural reformer.
P JAMES ARCHER, tql, semi-profile, Dundee City Art Gallery.

Attrib J.R.SWINTON, hl, Winton House, Lothian region Scotland.
G S.BELLIN, after J.R.Herbert, 'Meeting of the Council of the Anti Corn Law League', mixed engr, pub 1850, BM, NPG.
SC WILLIAM BRODIE, marble bust, Dundee City Art Gallery.
PH J.VALENTINE, wl, carte, NPG AX7434.

KINROSS, John Blair Balfour, 1st Baron (1837-1905) Scottish judge and politician.
P SIR GEORGE REID, SNPG 1396.
PH SIR BENJAMIN STONE, 1898, wl, print, NPG X1098.

KINTORE, Algernon Keith-Falconer, 9th Earl of (1852-1930) governor of South Australia.
C SIR LESLIE WARD ('Spy'), wl, profile, w/c study, for *Vanity Fair* 27 March 1880, NPG 4722.

KIRK, Sir John (1832-1922) naturalist and administrator.
D A.H.KIRK (his nephew), 1915, hs, w/c, NPG 1936.

KITCHENER of Khartoum and of Broome, Horatic Herbert Kitchener, 1st Earl (1850-1916) field-marshal.
P SIR HUBERT VON HERKOMER and FREDERICK GOODALL, 1890, tq in uniform, NPG 1782. HEINRICH VON ANGELI, 1899, in uniform Royal Engineers, Chattenden Barracks. HEINRICH VON ANGELI hl in uniform, Royal Coll. SIR A.S.COPE, 1900, wl, Roya Engineers, Brompton. JOHN COLLIER, 1916, replica of portrait o 1910, wl in uniform on mountain pass, Oriental Club, London
D C.M.HORSFALL, 1899, hs, pastel, NPG 1780. WILLIAM STRANG 1910, hs, chalk, Royal Coll. 'G.R.H.', wl equestrian, chalk and wash, NPG 4549.
G SIR JAMES GUTHRIE, 'Statesmen of World War I, 1914-18', oil 1924-30, NPG 2463.
SC R.C.BELT, 1916, bronze bust, DoE (War Office). SIR WILLIAM GOSCOMBE JOHN, RA 1917, bronze bust, Gordon Memoria College, Khartoum. SIR W.GOSCOMBE JOHN, plaster bust, IWM SIR WILLIAM REID DICK, 1923, recumbent effigy in memoria chapel, St Paul's Cathedral, London. JOHN TWEED, 1926, bronz statue in field marshal's uniform, Horse Guards Parade, London
PR ALFRED LEETE, hs, recruiting poster, IWM.
C SIR LESLIE WARD ('Spy'), wl, w/c study, for *Vanity Fair*, 23 Fe 1899, NPG 2684. SIR LESLIE WARD ('Spy'), 'A General Group' chromo-lith, for *Vanity Fair*, 29 Nov 1900, NPG.
PH UNKNOWN, 1898, tql, print, NPG. Various prints, IWM an National Army Museum, London.

KITCHIN, George William (1827-1912) dean of Winchester
P H.M.PAGET, hl seated, Non-Collegiate Building, Library Oxford. J.W.SCHOFIELD, wl, University College, Durham UNKNOWN, hl, semi-profile, Christ Church, Oxford.
PH C.L.DODGSON ('Lewis Carroll'), *c*1856, hl seated, print, NP P7(14).

KITSON, James, see 1st Baron Airedale.

KNATCHBULL-HUGESSEN, Edward Hugessen, see 1s Baron Brabourne.

KNIBB, William (1803-1845) missionary and abolitionist.
G B.R.HAYDON, 'The Anti-Slavery Society Convention, 1840' oil, NPG 599.
SC UNKNOWN, 1838, medallion, Falmouth Church, West Indies.
PR UNKNOWN, 1838, hs, lith, NPG. BELL SMITH, tql seated, lith, pu 1845, NPG. GEORGE BAXTER, 1847, tql seated, colour print, NP 4957. J.COCHRAN, after a daguerreotype, tql seated, stipple an line, NPG.

KNIGHT, John Prescott (1803-1881) portrait painter.
P Self-portrait, probably RA 1829, hs, oval, Stafford Art Gallery related engr, *c*1830, hl, mezz, Stafford Art Gallery.

D Daniel Maclise, c1860, chalk sketch, V & A.
G Unknown, one of a series of woodcuts, ovals, 'Members of the Royal Academy in 1857', for *Illust London News*, 2 May 1857, NPG.
PR C.Baugniet, tql with palette and brushes, lith, 1844, BM. Unknown, hl seated, woodcut, for *Art Journal*, 1849, BM, NPG. Unknown, tql with fishing rod, mezz, BM. R. & E.Taylor, hs, semi-profile, as an old man, woodcut, for *Illust London News*, 9 April 1881, BM, NPG.
PH Maull & Polyblank, wl, carte, NPG (Album 104). Unknown, hs, carte, NPG (Album 103).

KNIGHT, Joseph (1829-1907) drama critic.
P Margaret Grose, posthumous, hs seated, Garrick Club, London.
M 'M.W.', 1901, hs, Garrick Club.
C Harry Furniss, two pen and ink sketches, NPG 3479-80.
PH Walker & Boutall, tql seated, photogravure, NPG.

KNIGHT, Joseph Philip (1812-1887) composer.
PR Unknown, hs, lith, BM.

KNIGHT-BRUCE, George Wyndham Hamilton (1852-1896) first bishop of Mashonaland.
PR Unknown, after a photograph by Ball, hs, profile, wood engr, for *Illust London News*, 26 Dec 1896, NPG.
PH Unknown, hs, print, NPG (Anglican Bishops).

KNOLLYS, Sir Francis Knollys, 1st Viscount (1837-1924) private secretary to King Edward VII.
C Carlo Pellegrini, 1870, wl with the Prince of Wales, on ice-skates, gouache, Royal Coll. Sir Leslie Ward ('Spy'), wl, profile, chromo-lith, for *Vanity Fair*, 14 March 1891, NPG.

KNOX, Edmund Arbuthnott (1847-1937) bishop of Manchester.
PH Rotary Photo, hs, postcard, NPG. Walter Stoneman, 1917, hs,

NPG (NPR). Unknown, hs, print, NPG (Anglican Bishops).

KNOX, Robert Bent (1808-1893) archbishop of Armagh.
P Unknown, Bishop's Palace, Armagh, N Ireland.
PR Two wood engrs, the first after a photograph by Chancellor of Dublin, hs, for *Illust London News*, 29 May 1886, the second, hs, profile, for *Illust London News*, 25 June 1892, NPG.

KNUTSFORD, Sir Henry Thurstan Holland, 2nd Bart, 1st Viscount (1825-1914) secretary of state for colonies.
P Sir A.S.Cope, 1906, tql seated, NPG 2947.
PR J.Brown, after H.T.Wells, hs, stipple, one of 'Grillion's Club' series, BM.
C A.S.Boyd, 'The Future of South Africa. Dr Jameson's Lecture at the Imperial Institute', University of Cape Town, South Africa. Carlo Pellegrini ('Ape'), wl, profile, chromo-lith, for *Vanity Fair*, 29 Jan 1887, NPG.
PH Russell & Sons, hs, print, for *Our Conservative and Unionist Statesmen*, vol V, NPG (Album 22). Walery, tql seated, print, NPG.

KNUTSFORD, Sir Sydney George Holland, 3rd Bart, 2nd Viscount (1855-1931) hospital administrator and reformer.
P Sir Oswald Birley, 1914, hl seated, The London Hospital, London. Sir Oswald Birley, 1930, hl seated, Commercial Union, London.
C Sir Leslie Ward ('Spy'), wl, chromo-lith, for *Vanity Fair*, 25 Aug 1904, NPG.
PH Walter Stoneman, 1917, hs, NPG (NPR).

KUPER, Sir Augustus Leopold (1809-1885) admiral.
PR Unknown, hs, woodcut, for *Illust London News*, 20 Feb 1864, NPG.

KYNASTON, Herbert (1809-1878) high master of St Paul's school.
SC George Halse, 1860, marble bust, St Paul's School, London.
PR W.Walker, after Miss Walker, tql, mezz, pub 1856, BM.

L

LABOUCHERE, Henry du Pré (1831-1912) journalist and politician.
P E.A.WARD, tql seated, Reform Club, London.
D S.P.HALL, pencil sketches, NPG 2248 and 2283-4. FREDERICK PEGRAM, pencil sketch made during the sessions of the Parnell Special Commission, for vol 14 of *The Pictorial World*, 7 March 1889, V & A.
C HARRY FURNESS, tql pen and ink sketch, NPG 3589. SIR FRANCIS CARRUTHERS GOULD, two drgs, NPG 2848 and 2867. CARLO PELLEGRINI ('Ape'), wl, chromo-lith, for *Vanity Fair*, 7 Nov 1874. NPG. (Possibly H.C.SEPPING) WRIGHT ('Stuff'), 'Empire Makers and Breakers', chromo-lith, for *Vanity Fair*, 25 Nov 1897, NPG.
PH G.BROGI of Florence, tql seated, print, NPG X12143. SIR BENJAMIN STONE, 1897, wl, print, NPG. WALERY, tql, print, NPG.

LACAITA, Sir James Philip (1813-1895) Italian scholar and politician.
SC GEORGIO MATARRESE, 1894, bronze seated statuette, NPG 5272.

LACY, Harriette Deborah, née Taylor (1807-1874) actress.
PR R.J.LANE, wl as Rosalind, lith, pub 1838, NPG. R.J.LANE, hs with Priscilla Horton and Jane Shirreff as the 'Singing Witches', in a scene from *Macbeth*, lith, pub 1838, NPG. Several theatrical prints, Harvard Theatre Collection, Cambridge, Mass, USA.

LACY, Maria Anne, (Mrs G.W.Lovell) (1803-1877) actress.
PR Several theatrical prints, BM. Harvard Theatre Collection, Cambridge, Mass, USA.

LACY, Walter (1809-1898) actor.
P SIR A.S.COPE, 1886, hl, Garrick Club, London.
PR J.W.GEAR, wl as Narciss Boss in *Single Life*, lith, BM, Harvard Theatre Collection, Cambridge, Mass, USA.

LAFFAN, Sir Robert Michael (1821-1882) governor of Bermuda.
PH GRILLET & Co of Naples, 1869, tql seated, carte, NPG X8359.

LAING, Samuel (1812-1897) politician and author.
C SIR LESLIE WARD ('Spy'), wl, profile, chromo-lith, for *Vanity Fair*, 16 Aug 1873, NPG.

LAIRD, John (1805-1874) shipbuilder.
D C.S.KEENE, c1872, three pencil sketches, hl, head and wl, NPG 2686.
SC JOHN MACBRIDE, 1863, bust, Birkenhead Hospital, Cheshire. ALBERT BRUCE JOY, c1877, bronze statue, Hamilton Square, Birkenhead.
C SIR LESLIE WARD ('Spy'), wl, profile, chromo-lith, for *Vanity Fair*, 17 May 1873, NPG.
PH JOHN & CHARLES WATKINS, hs, carte, NPG (Album 136).

LAKE, Sir Henry Atwell (1808-1881) chief engineer at Kars 1854.
PR C.BAUGNIET, hl in uniform, lith, pub 1857, BM. UNKNOWN, hs in uniform, stipple, NPG.

LAKE, Sir Percy Henry Noel (1855-1940) lieutenant-general.
PH WALTER STONEMAN, 1917, hs in uniform, NPG (NPR).

LAMB, Sir Horace (1849-1934) mathematician.
P HENRY LAMB (his son), before 1913, University of Manchester.

D HENRY LAMB, 1927, hs, pencil, Trinity College, Cambridge.
PH WALTER STONEMAN, 1922, hs, NPG (NPR).

LAMBERT, Brooke (1834-1901) vicar of Greenwich.
SC ALBERT BRUCE JOY, marble bust, Roan Schools, Greenwich.

LAMBERT, Sir John (1815-1892) civil servant and mayor of Salisbury.
PR UNKNOWN, Salisbury Corporation. UNKNOWN, hs, wood engr, for *Illust London News*, 6 Feb 1892, NPG.
PH UNKNOWN, print, Salisbury Corporation.

LAMBOURNE, Amelius Mark Richard Lockwood, 1st Baron (1847-1928) politician and horticulturist.
P W.G.de GLEHN, 1926, tql, Royal Horticultural Society, London.
SC SIR WILLIAM REID DICK, bas-relief plaque, Royal Horticultural Society.
C SIR LESLIE WARD ('Spy'), wl, profile, chromo-lith, for *Vanity Fair*, 6 Sept 1894, NPG.

LAMINGTON, Alexander Dundas Ross Wishart Cochrane-Baillie, 1st Baron (1816-1890) author and politician.
PR R.J.LANE, after A.D'Orsay, 1846, hl, profile, lith, BM, NPG. UNKNOWN, hs, lith, pub 1871, BM, NPG.
C J.J.J.TISSOT, wl seated, chromo-lith, for *Vanity Fair*, 2 Dec 1871, NPG.

LAMPSON, Sir Curtis Miranda, 1st Bart (1806-1885) advocate of the Atlantic cable.
PR UNKNOWN, after a photograph by Mayall, hs, oval, woodcut, for *Illust London News*, 8 Dec 1866, NPG.

LANCE, George (1802-1864) painter of still-life.
P Self-portrait, c1830, V & A.
D Two self-portrait drgs: head, pencil, NPG 1713, and head, w/c, BM.
PR J.SMYTH, after G.Clint, hl, line, for the *Art Union*, 1847, BM, NPG. UNKNOWN, hs, profile, woodcut, for *Illust London News*, 21 Dec 1861, NPG. UNKNOWN, after a drg by J.Gilbert, hl, woodcut, BM. UNKNOWN, hs, aquatint, BM.
PH MAULL & Co, wl seated at easel, carte, NPG X12144. MAULL & POLYBLANK, two cartes, both wl with palette, NPG AX11930 and (Album 104).

LANDELLS, Robert Thomas (1833-1877) artist and war correspondent.
G UNKNOWN, hs, one of a series of woodcuts, 'Our Artists – Past and Present', for *Illust London News*, 14 May 1892, BM, NPG.
PR UNKNOWN, after a photograph by Fradelle and Marshall, hs, woodcut, for *Illust London News*, 20 Jan 1877, NPG.

LANDER, John (1807-1839) African traveller.
D WILLIAM BROCKEDON, 1834, hs, chalk, NPG 2515 (64).
SC WILLIAM BROCKEDON, plaster bust, Royal Geographical Society, London.
PR UNKNOWN, hs, line, for R. and J.Lander, *Travels into the Interior of Africa for the Discovery of the Course of the River Niger*, 1836, NPG.

LANDER, Richard Lemon (1804-1834) African traveller.
P Two portraits by WILLIAM BROCKEDON, both based on the NPG drg: c1835, hs in African dress, NPG 2442; in conventional dress,

Royal Geographical Society, London.
D WILLIAM BROCKEDON, 1831, hs, chalk, NPG 2515(47).
SC WILLIAM BROCKEDON, plaster bust, Royal Geographical Society; related marble bust, DoE (Foreign and Commonwealth Office Library, London). N.N.BURNARD, c1852, posthumous statue on column (based on the Brockedon bust in the Royal Geographical Society), Lemon St, Truro, Cornwall.
PR UNKNOWN, hs, line, for R. and J.Lander, *Journal of an Expedition to Explore the Course and Termination of the Niger*, 1832, NPG. UNKNOWN, hs in Arab dress, stipple, NPG.

LANDON, Letitia Elizabeth (Mrs Maclean) (1802-1838) poet and novelist.
D DANIEL MACLISE, wl seated, w/c drg, for *Fraser's Mag*, VIII, Oct 1833, BM. D.MACLISE, 1830-35, hl seated, pencil, NPG 1953. D.MACLISE, standing by a horse, V & A.
PR FINDEN, after D.Maclise, tql, stipple, for her *Poetical Works*, 1835, BM, NPG. E.FINDEN, after a drg by Maclise, tql seated, octagon, stipple, BM. S.FREEMAN, after J.Wright, hl, stipple, for *New Monthly Mag*, 1837, BM. UNKNOWN, tql, lith, pub 1839, BM. H.ROBINSON, after H.Pickersgill, hl seated, stipple, for vol III of *Autobiography of W.Jerdan*, 1852, BM, NPG. D.MACLISE, wl on horseback, riding, lith, BM.

LANDSEER, Sir Edwin Henry (1802-1873) animal-painter.
P SIR FRANCIS GRANT, c1852, several related portraits: 1852, tql with dog, NPG 834 (oil sketch, Russell-Cotes Art Gallery, Bournemouth); hl with palette, brushes and dog, NPG 1018 (pencil study, NPG 436); tql in hunting clothes with telescope, in landscape, unfinished, Royal Academy, London. JOHN BALLANTYNE, c1865, wl, modelling the lions for the base of Nelson's column, NPG 835. Self-portrait, RA 1865, tql seated with two dogs, 'The Connoisseurs', Royal Coll.
D Self-portrait, 1818, hs, profile, pencil, NPG 4267. Self-portrait, wl lying face downwards, a recumbent lion has its paws on him, pen, ink and wash, Hatfield House, Herts. Self-portrait, boxing with Count D'Orsay, chalk, BM. C.B.BIRCH, c1870, wl with Sir Francis Grant, pencil, NPG 2521. COUNT A.D'ORSAY, hl, pencil, DoE. SIR FRANCIS GRANT, pen sketch, The Athenaeum, London. SIR GEORGE HAYTER, two drgs: 1825, head, pen and ink, BM; wl seated, pencil, BM. J.F.LEWIS, hs, pencil, Royal Academy. Drgs by DANIEL MACLISE and W.M.THACKERAY, V & A. G.S.NEWTON, NGS. CARL CHRISTIAN VOGEL, 1834, hl, chalk, Kupferstichkabinett, Staatliche Kunstsammlungen, Dresden.
C JOHN HAYTER, hl seated with Sir George Hayter, Charles Hayter and another unidentified artist, oil, 1823, Shipley Art Gallery, Gateshead.
SC BARON CARLO MAROCHETTI, RA 1867, marble bust, Royal Academy, London. THOMAS WOOLNER, 1882, marble medallion on memorial, St Paul's Cathedral, London.
PR UNKNOWN, after a drg by J.Hayter (1813), hs, profile, stipple, for his *Works*, BM. UNKNOWN, after A.D'Orsay of 1843, wl, lith, pub 1843, NPG; related hl lith, NPG. Various prints after photographs, BM, NPG. UNKNOWN, wl in his studio, woodcut, for *Illust London News*, 19 Sept 1874, BM.
C GEORGES GOURSAT ('Sem'), head, w/c and pencil, V & A. 'H.H.', wl, for 'The Mask's Album', woodcut, NPG.
PH JOHN WATKINS, tql seated, sketching, print, NPG AX7328. UNKNOWN, hs, carte, NPG X12146.

LANDSFELD, Marie Dolores Eliza Rosanna Gilbert, Countess of, see Gilbert.

LANE, Edward William (1801-1876) Arabic scholar.
D CLARA S.LANE (his niece), 1850, wl seated, profile, w/c, NPG 3099.
SC R.J.LANE (his brother), 1829, plaster statue, seated in the 'memlook' dress of an Egyptian gentleman, NPG 940. R.J.LANE,

1833, plaster bust, Bodleian Library, Oxford.
PR R.J.LANE, wl seated in the dress of a Bedouin Arab, lith, BM. UNKNOWN, after R.J.Lane of c1835, wl seated in Egyptian dress, woodcut, for *Illust London News*, 2 Sept 1876, NPG.

LANE, Richard James (1800-1872) engraver and lithographer.
D EDWARD HODGES, 1839, hs, profile, pencil, NPG.
G UNKNOWN, one of a series of woodcuts, oval, 'Members of the Royal Academy in 1857', for *Illust London News*, 2 May 1857, BM, NPG.
PR UNKNOWN, after a photograph by Charles Watkins, hs, woodcut, for *Illust London News*, 7 Dec 1872, NPG.
PH ELLIOTT & FRY, two cartes, hs, and hs, profile, NPG (Albums 103 and 106). MAYALL, c1863, wl, profile, carte, NPG (Album 105).

LANE, Sir (William) Arbuthnot, 1st Bart (1856-1943) surgeon.
P EDWARD NEWLING, Guy's Hospital, London.
D ALFRED WOLMARK, 1926, hs, pen and ink, NPG 4484.
C DAVID LOW, pencil sketch, NPG 4529 (109). EIANLEY COCK, wl, mechanical repro, for *Vanity Fair*, 21 May 1913, NPG.

LANE POOLE, Reginald, see Poole.

LANG, Andrew (1844-1912) scholar, folk-lorist, poet and man of letters.
P SIR W.B.RICHMOND, exhib 1885, tql seated, SNPG 1206.
G P.NAUMANN & R.TAYLOR & Co, one of a series of woodcuts, 'Our Literary Contributors – Past and Present', for *Illust London News*, 14 May 1892, BM, NPG.
SC PERCY PORTSMOUTH, relief portrait, Selkirk Free Library, Scotland.
C SIR MAX BEERBOHM, two drgs, 1896, wl, Newberry Library, Chicago, USA, and 1926, tql, University of California at Los Angeles, USA. HARRY FURNISS, two pen and ink sketches, NPG 3482-3.
PH ALVIN LANGDON COBURN, 1904, hs, photogravure, for *Men of Mark*, 1913, NPG AX7770. CROWDY & LOUD, after Elliott & Fry, hl seated, photogravure, NPG X12149. ELLIOTT & FRY, hs, cabinet, NPG X12148. FRADELLE & YOUNG, hl seated, cabinet, NPG X12150; detail, hs, carte, NPG X12151. FREDERICK HOLLYER, hl, print, V & A (Hollyer Albums).

LANG, John Marshall (1834-1909) principal of the University of Aberdeen.
P E.R.CALTERNS, Barony Church, Glasgow.
SC UNKNOWN, 1911, bronze memorial medallion, Barony Church.

LANGFORD, John Alfred (1823-1903) Birmingham antiquary and journalist.
PR W.HOLL, after a photograph, tql seated, stipple, NPG.

LANGTRY, Emily Charlotte, ('Lily'), née Le Breton, afterwards Lady de Bathe (1853-1929) actress and famous beauty.
P SIR J.E.MILLAIS, 1878, tql with lily, The Jersey Museum, St Helier, Jersey. SIR EDWARD POYNTER, c1878, hl with rose, The Jersey Museum. G.F.WATTS, 1880, hs, profile, Watts Gallery, Compton, Surrey.
SC SIR EDWARD POYNTER, 1882, bronze medal, BM.
PR G.PILOTELL, two drypoint engrs, hs, and hs, profile, BM. Several popular and theatrical prints, NPG, and various prints, Harvard Theatre Collection, Cambridge, Mass, USA.
PH SIR CECIL BEATON, hl with lily, print, NPG. W. & D.DOWNEY, hl, woodburytype, for Cassell's *Cabinet Portrait Gallery*, vol I, 1890, NPG. W. & D.DOWNEY, hs wearing tiara, postcard, NPG. LAFAYETTE, c1888, wl, print, University of Texas, Austin, USA. VANDER WEYDE, tql, back-view, face in profile, cabinet, NPG. WINDOW & GROVE, hl, woodburytype, for *The Theatre*, NPG.

LANKESTER, Edwin (1814-1874) man of science.

PR T.H.MAGUIRE, tql, lith, one of set of *Ipswich Museum Portraits*, 1852, BM. UNKNOWN, hl, woodcut, for *Illust London News*, 26 July 1862, NPG.

H A.CLAUDET, wl, carte, NPG (Album 114). ERNEST EDWARDS, wl seated, print, for *Men of Eminence*, ed L.Reeve, vol III, 1865, NPG.

LANKESTER, Sir Edwin Ray (1847-1929) zoologist.

P JOHN COLLIER, 1904, tql, Exeter College, Oxford. SIR WILLIAM ORPEN, 1929, hs, City Art Gallery, Birmingham. G.P.JACOMB HOOD, tql seated, Ipswich Museum.

D SIR WILLIAM ROTHENSTEIN, two drgs: 1922, hs, chalk, NPG 4378; 1925, head, sanguine, NPG 4781.

C SIR LESLIE WARD ('Spy'), wl, w/c study, for *Vanity Fair*, 12 Jan 1905, NPG 3006. SIR MAX BEERBOHM, 1907, drg, Merton College, Oxford.

H ELLIOTT & FRY, hl, as a young man, carte, NPG. G.C.BERESFORD, 1902, hs, neg (x6529), and print, NPG. WALTER STONEMAN, 1921, hs, NPG (NPR).

LANSBURY, George (1859-1940) labour leader and pacifist.

P SYLVIA GOSSE, 1939, hs, NPG 3775.

D EDMOND KAPP, 1929, two studies, hs, and hs, profile, Barber Institute of Fine Arts, Birmingham.

H BASSANO, hs, print, NPG. LAFAYETTE, tql seated with his wife, print, NPG. UNKNOWN, c1901, tql seated, print, NPG (*Daily Herald*). SIR BENJAMIN STONE, 1911, three prints, all wl, NPG. UNKNOWN, 1921, wl seated with his wife and family, print, NPG (*Daily Herald*). WALTER STONEMAN, two portraits, 1929 and 1940, both hs, NPG (NPR). FELIX H.MAN, 1934, tql seated, print, NPG X1153. HOWARD COSTER, 1935, two prints, wl and hs, NPG X10662-3. HOWARD COSTER, c1935, six negs, NPG.

LANSDOWNE, Henry Charles Keith Petty-Fitzmaurice, 5th Marquess of (1845-1927) Viceroy of India and foreign secretary.

P GEORGE FIDDES WATT, before 1914, tql seated in uniform with Garter ribbon and star, Balliol College, Oxford. P.A.DE LÁSZLÓ, 1920, hl, profile, in Garter robes, NPG 2180. P.A.DE LÁSZLÓ, hl in uniform with sword, Bowood, Wilts; copy by S.P.KENDRICK, Oriental Club, London.

C HARRY BATES, equestrian statue, Calcutta.

C CARLO PELLEGRINI ('Ape'), wl, profile, w/c study, for *Vanity Fair*, 4 April 1874, NPG 2625. HARRY FURNISS, c1880-1910, pen and ink sketch, NPG 3590. SIR BERNARD PARTRIDGE, pen and ink drg, for *Punch*, 1 March 1911, NPG. SIR MAX BEERBOHM, 1913, 'Lord Lansdowne embarrassed by the unwisdom of Lord Willoughby de Broke', drg, Merton College, Oxford.

H COWELL, c1894, hl, panel, NPG x4100. RUSSELL & SONS, hs, semi-profile, print, for *Our Conservative and Unionist Statesmen*, vol V, NPG (Album 22). WALTER STONEMAN, 1917, hs, profile, NPG (NPR).

LANSDOWNE, Henry Thomas Petty-Fitzmaurice, 4th Marquess of (1816-1866) statesman.

P JOHN LINNELL, 1839, tql seated, Bowood, Wilts.

R C.BAUGNIET, tql, lith, BM.

LANYON, Sir Charles (1813-1889) civil engineer.

R UNKNOWN, after a photograph by James Magill of Belfast, hs, wood engr, for *Illust London News*, 22 June 1889, NPG.

LARKING, Cuthbert (b1842) sportsman and royal official.

C CARLO PELLEGRINI ('Ape'), wl, profile, w/c study, for *Vanity Fair*, 11 Aug 1888, NPG 4724.

LARMOR, Sir Joseph (1857-1942) physicist.

P FRANK McKELVEY, tql seated, Queen's University, Belfast.

H WALTER STONEMAN, 1920, hs, NPG (NPR).

LASCELLES, Sir Frank Cavendish (1841-1920) diplomat.

PR P.NAUMANN, tql seated, woodcut, for *Illust London News*, 28 Sept 1895, NPG.

C SIR LESLIE WARD ('Spy'), wl, profile, chromo-lith, for *Vanity Fair*, 27 March 1902, NPG. UNKNOWN ('K'), wl, w/c study, for *Vanity Fair*, 23 Oct 1912, NPG 5083.

LATEY, John (1842-1902) journalist.

G R.T. & CO, hs, one of a series of woodcuts, 'Our Literary Contributors – Past and Present', for *Illust London News*, 14 May 1892, NPG.

LATHAM, Henry (1821-1902) master of Trinity Hall, Cambridge.

P Portraits by LOWES DICKINSON, and two by FRANK HOLL (the first in 1884 and the second after 1888 as Master of Trinity Hall), Trinity Hall, Cambridge.

LATHAM, Robert Gordon (1812-1888) ethnologist and philologist.

PH ERNEST EDWARDS, wl seated, print, for *Men of Eminence*, ed L.Reeve, vol I, 1863, NPG.

LATROBE, Charles Joseph (1801-1875) governor of Victoria.

P SIR FRANCIS GRANT, c1851-54, tql in uniform, Town Hall, Melbourne, Australia.

D WILLIAM BROCKEDON, 1835, hs, chalk, NPG 2515 (45).

SC THOMAS WOOLNER, 1853-4, bronze medal, NPG 1672.

LAUDER, James Eckford (1811-1869) artist.

P ROBERT INNES, SNPG 675. CHARLES LEES, exhib 1849, hs, Royal Scottish Academy, Edinburgh. Self-portrait, SNPG 2027.

LAUDER, Robert Scott (1803-1869) artist.

P Self-portrait, hs, SNPG 593. THOMAS DUNCAN, SNPG 1425.

D Called a self-portrait, 1823, pencil and chalk, SNPG 2301.

SC JOHN HUTCHISON, 1861, marble bust, SNPG 970.

PR GREEN, after a drg, hs, woodcut, for the *Art Journal*, 1850, BM. UNKNOWN, after J.Hutchison, hs, circular medallion, for *Illust London News*, 13 Jan 1872, BM, NPG.

LAUDERDALE, Thomas Maitland, 11th Earl of (1803-1878) admiral of the fleet.

SC SIR FRANCIS CHANTREY, marble bust, Wellington Museum, Apsley House, London.

LAURIE, Simon Somerville (1829-1909) educational reformer.

P GEORGE FIDDES WATT, 1904, tql, Edinburgh University.

PR WILLIAM HOLE, tql, etch, for *Quasi Cursores*, 1884, NPG.

LAURIER, Sir Wilfred (1841-1919) Canadian statesman.

D S.P.HALL, pencil sketch, NPG 2382.

C SIR LESLIE WARD ('Spy'), wl, profile, chromo-lith, for *Vanity Fair*, 19 Aug 1897, NPG.

LAVERY, Sir John (1856-1941) portrait painter.

P Self-portraits: 1896-7, nearly wl seated with his daughter, Musée National d'Art Moderne, Paris; 1906, tql, Uffizi Gallery, Florence; 1906-11, tql, Uffizi Gallery, Florence, and related hl portrait, 1928, Ulster Museum, Belfast. LADY HAZEL LAVERY, Municipal Gallery of Modern Art, Dublin. JAMES KERR-LAWSON, hs painting the portrait of George V and his family at Buckingham Palace (1913), Ferens Art Gallery, Hull. HARRINGTON MANN, 1936, tql seated, Glasgow City Art Gallery.

D SIR JAMES GUNN, c1924, chalk, Glasgow City Art Gallery. JAMES KERR-LAWSON, pencil, SNPG 1436.

SC G.H.PAULIN, RA 1935, bronze head, Glasgow City Art Gallery.

C 'GAL', wl painting, ink and wash, NPG. SIR BERNARD PARTRIDGE, tql, pencil and chalk, for *Punch*, 30 March 1927, NPG 3671. ALICK P.F.RITCHIE, wl, mechanical repro, for *Vanity Fair*, 7 May 1913,

NPG. DAVID WILSON, drg, Municipal Gallery of Modern Art.
PH UNKNOWN, 1909, hl, print, NPG. WALTER STONEMAN, 1918, hs, NPG (NPR).

LAW, Andrew Bonar (1858-1923) prime-minister.
P J.B.ANDERSON, Conservative Club, Glasgow. RENÉ DE L'HÔPITAL, Carlton Club, London. SIR JAMES GUTHRIE and J.B.ANDERSON, Constitutional Club, London.
D MINNIE AGNES COHEN, 1890, hs, pencil, NPG 2358.
G SIR JAMES GUTHRIE, 'Statesmen of World War I, 1914–18', oil, NPG 2463; oil sketch, SNPG 1466 and hl study, SNPG 1127. SIR WILLIAM ORPEN, 'A Peace Conference at the Quai D'Orsay', and 'The Signing of Peace in the Hall of Mirrors, Versailles, 28th June, 1919', both oil, both IWM.
C SIR LESLIE WARD ('Spy'), wl, chromo-lith, for *Vanity Fair*, 2 March 1905, NPG. STRICKLAND, tql seated, chromo-lith, for *Vanity Fair*, 10 April 1912, NPG. SIR BERNARD PARTRIDGE, two pen and ink drgs for *Punch*, 18 Sept 1912 and 9 Feb 1921, NPG. SIR MAX BEERBOHM, 1923, 'The Glasgow School', drg, Columbus Gallery of Fine Arts, Ohio, USA. SIR FRANCIS CARRUTHERS GOULD, wl, profile, ink, NPG 2847.
PH WALTER STONEMAN, 1923, hs, NPG (NPR).

LAW, David (1831-1901) engraver and etcher.
P GEORGE PAUL CHALMERS, 1878, paper mounted on canvas, SNPG 1440.

LAWES (afterwards Lawes-Wittewronge), Sir Charles Bennet, 2nd Bart (1843-1911) sculptor and athlete.
D VERHEYDEN, 1883, tql, pencil, pen and wash, Rothamsted Experimental Station, Herts.
C SIR LESLIE WARD ('Spy'), wl, chromo-lith, for *Vanity Fair*, 12 May 1883, NPG.

LAWES, Sir John Bennet, 1st Bart (1814-1900) agriculturalist.
P SIR HUBERT VON HERKOMER, c1893, tql, Rothamsted Experimental Station, Herts.
SC VERHEYDEN, 1901, marble bust, Rothamsted.
PR UNKNOWN, hs, woodcut, for *Illust London News*, 10 June 1882, NPG.
C THÉOBALD CHARTRAN ('T'), wl, w/c study, for *Vanity Fair*, 8 July 1882, NPG 2643.

LAWLESS, Matthew James (1837-1864) artist.
PH UNKNOWN, hs, carte, NPG (Album 104).

LAWLEY, Beilby, see 3rd Baron Wenlock.

LAWRENCE, Sir Alfred Tristram, see 1st Baron Trevethin.

LAWRENCE, Sir George St Patrick (1804-1884) general.
G F.C.LEWIS, 'A Durbar at Udaipur, 1855', oil, India Office Library and Records, London.
PR UNKNOWN, hs in uniform, wood engr, for *Illust London News*, 29 Nov 1884, NPG.
PH A.MURANO, hs, profile, cabinet, NPG.

LAWRENCE, Sir Henry Montgomery (1806-1857) general.
P UNKNOWN, c1827, hs, NPG 1990. H.W.PHILLIPS, RA 1862, Lawrence Asylum, India. J.R.DICKSEE, tql seated with Bath ribbon and star, NGI 135.
M UNKNOWN, c1847, hl, India Office Library and Records, London; version, NPG 727. UNKNOWN, Lahore Art Gallery, India.
G UNKNOWN, 'The Second Lahore Durbar, 26 Dec 1846', BM. F.C.LEWIS, 'A Durbar at Udaipur, 1855', oil, India Office Library and Records. C.G.LEWIS, after T.J.Barker, 'The Intellect and Valour of Great Britain', mixed engr, pub 1864, NPG.
SC THOMAS CAMPBELL, 1849, marble bust, NPG 1989. J.G.LOUGH,

1862, marble statue, with bas-relief of Lawrence on the plinth, S Paul's Cathedral, London. J.G.LOUGH, statue, Lahore J.G.LOUGH, statue, exterior of old India Office building J.H.FOLEY, medallion, St Paul's Cathedral, Calcutta. UNKNOWN bust, India Office Library and Records, London.
PR W.J.EDWARDS, after a photograph, hl seated, stipple, NPG. M. & N.HANHART, two liths, India Office Library and Records UNKNOWN, wl equestrian, lith, c1857, V & A.
PH AHMED ALI KHAN ('Chotay Meah'), 1857, tql seated, copy print NPG. AHMED ALI KHAN, tql seated with George Lawrence and Si Herbert Edwardes, copy print, NPG.

LAWRENCE, John Laird Mair Lawrence, 1st Baron (1811-1879) governor-general of India.
P G.F.WATTS, 1862, hs, NPG 1005. J.R.DICKSEE, c1865, hl, City o London School. VAL PRINSEP, 1876, Government House, Calcu tta. JOHN COLLIER, two portraits, 1911 and 1914, probabl replicas of a portrait of 1881, Oriental Club, London an Victoria Memorial Hall, Calcutta.
D E.G.LEWIS, 1872, hs, chalk, NPG 2610.
G C.G.LEWIS, after T.J.Barker, 'The Intellect and Valour of Grea Britain', mixed engr, pub 1864, NPG.
SC R.THEED, 1861, marble bust, Grocers Company, Londor HENRY WEEKES, 1867, bust, St Bartholomew's Hospita London. THOMAS WOOLNER, c1871, bronze bust, Commor wealth Relations Office, London. THOMAS WOOLNER, 187 bronze statue, Government House, Calcutta. THOMA WOOLNER, 1881, memorial marble bust, Westminster Abbe London; replica, 1882, NPG 2111. SIR J.E.BOEHM, c1882, bronz statue, Waterloo Place, London; related plaster bust, NPG 786
PR T.W.KNIGHT, after a photograph by Mayall, tql, stipple, NP D.J.POUND, after a photograph by Mayall, tql seated, stipple an line, for *The Drawing Room Portrait Gallery of Eminent Personage* NPG.
C CARLO PELLEGRINI ('Ape'), wl, chromo-lith, for *Vanity Fair*, 2 Jan 1871, NPG.
PH ELLIOTT & FRY, hs, profile, cabinet, NPG. Several cartes b CALDESI, BLANFORD & CO, DEBENHAM, ELLIOTT & FRY and JOH & CHARLES WATKINS, various sizes, NPG. MAULL & POLYBLAN tql, print, NPG AX7280.

LAWRENCE, Sir Walter Roper, 1st Bart (1857-194(Indian civil servant.
C SIR LESLIE WARD ('Spy'), wl, chromo-lith, for *Vanity Fair*, June 1905, NPG.
PH WALTER STONEMAN, 1918, hs in uniform, NPG (NPR).

LAWS, Robert (1851-1934) pioneer missionary.
SC UNKNOWN, 1936, plaster cast, Christ's College, Aberdeen.

LAWSON, Cecil Gordon (1849-1882) landscape painter.
D SIR HUBERT VON HERKOMER, 1877, hs, w/c, NPG 388 F.W.LAWSON (his brother), hs, profile, pencil, NPG 2797.

LAWSON, Edward Levy-, see 1st Baron Burnham.

LAWSON, George Anderson (1832-1904) sculptor.
P JAMES ARCHER, SNPG 724. TOM GRAHAM, 1882, hs, MacDona Collection, Aberdeen Art Gallery.
PR UNKNOWN, after T.B.Wirgman, wl in his studio, woodcut, f *Century Mag*, 1883, BM.
PH BROWN, BARNES & BELL, c1890, hs, pofile, cabinet, NPG.

LAWSON, Malcolm Leonard (1847-1918) composer.
D F.W.LAWSON (his brother), c1865, hs, pencil, NPG 2798.

LAWSON, Sir Wilfrid, 2nd Bart (1829-1906) politician.
SC DAVID McGILL, bronze statue, Victoria Embankment Garde London. ROSELIEB, medallion portrait on drinking founta Aspatria, Cumbria.

PR M.KLINKICHT, after a photograph, hl, woodcut, for *Illust London News*, 23 March 1889, BM, NPG. Several popular liths, NPG.

C THOMAS NAST, wl, w/c study, for *Vanity Fair*, 11 May 1872, NPG 2728.

PH LOCK & WHITFIELD, hs, oval, woodburytype, for *Men of Mark*, 1882, NPG. SIR BENJAMIN STONE, 1897, wl, print, Birmingham Reference Library, NPG. LAFAYETTE, 1906, hs, circle, print, NPG.

LAYARD, Sir Austen Henry (1817-1894) diplomat and archaeologist.

P UNKNOWN, *c*1890, hs, DoE (Southbridge).

D WILLIAM BROCKEDON, hs, chalk, NPG 2515 (103). G.F.WATTS, 1848, head, chalk, NPG 3787. G.F.WATTS, *c*1851, head, semi-profile, pencil, NPG 1006. L.J.PASSINI, 1891, hl seated, w/c, NPG 1797.

SC PATRIC PARK, 1855, marble bust, BM. SIR J.E.BOEHM, *c*1891, marble bust, BM. ENID LAYARD, bronze plaque, DoE.

PR S.W.REYNOLDS jun, after H.W.Phillips, tql, mezz, pub 1850, BM, NPG. UNKNOWN, tql, lith, for *The Whitehall Review*, 27 July 1878, NPG. Several popular prints, NPG.

C CARLO PELLEGRINI ('Ape'), wl, chromo-lith, for *Vanity Fair*, 28 Aug 1869, NPG.

PH LOCK & WHITFIELD, hs, oval, woodburytype, for *Men of Mark*, 1877, NPG. MAULL & POLYBLANK, tql, print, NPG AX7282. Several cartes by CALDESI, BLANFORD & CO, W. & D.DOWNEY, G. & L.FRATELLI and MAULL & POLYBLANK, various sizes, NPG.

LEACH, Sir George Archibald (1820-1913) secretary to the Board of Agriculture.

C F.T.DALTON ('FTD'), wl, w/c study, for *Vanity Fair*, 21 Dec 1896, NPG 2974.

LEADER, Benjamin Williams (1831-1923) landscape painter.

P Self-portrait, 1884, hs, profile, MacDonald Collection, Aberdeen Art Gallery.

PR R.TAYLOR, after photographs, at four different ages, woodcut, BM.

G SIR HUBERT VON HERKOMER, 'The Council of the Royal Academy', oil, 1908, TATE 2481.

PH UNKNOWN, hs, profile, print, NPG.

LEADER, John Temple (1810-1903) connoisseur and author.

SC UNKNOWN, 1895, bronze medallion portrait, Reform Club, London.

PR W.H.MOTE, after B.E.Duppa, hl, semi-profile, stipple, for Saunders's *Political Reformers*, 1840, BM, NPG. UNKNOWN, nearly tql, stipple, NPG.

C JOHN DOYLE, 'An Irish Wake', pen and pencil, 1839, BM. JOHN DOYLE, 'Good Training', pen and pencil, 1842, BM.

LEAF, Walter (1852-1927) classical scholar and banker.

D SIR WILLIAM ROTHENSTEIN, 1910, head, crayon, NPG 4782. RANDOLPH SCHWABE, 1927, pencil, Trinity College, Cambridge.

LEAHY, Arthur (1830-1878) colonel, Royal Engineers.

PH DISDERI, *c*1863, carte, NPG x8364.

LEAR, Edward (1812-1888) artist and author of the *Book of Nonsense*.

D W.N.MARSTRAND, 1840, hl seated, pencil, NPG 3055. WILLIAM HOLMAN HUNT, 1857, hs, chalk, Walker Art Gallery, Liverpool.

SL UNKNOWN, hs, profile, NPG 1759.

C Self-portrait, 1862-3, wl, pen and ink, NPG 4351. Several self-portrait drgs, Harvard College Library, Cambridge, Mass, USA, and University of Texas, Austin, USA.

PH McLEAN, MELHUISH & HAES, wl, carte, NPG (Album 99). SCHIER & SCHOEFFT, *c*1863, carte, NPG x8360.

LEARED, Arthur (1822-1879) traveller.

SC GEORGE SIMONDS, 1881?, marble bust, Royal College of Physicians, London.

LEASK, William (1812-1884) divine.

PR UNKNOWN, hl seated, stipple, NPG.

LECHMERE, Sir Edmund Anthony Harley, 3rd Bart (1826-1894) pioneer of Red Cross.

C THÉOBALD CHARTRAN ('T'), wl, w/c study, for *Vanity Fair*, 23 June 1883, NPG 4628.

LECKY, William Edward Hartpole (1838-1903) historian and essayist.

P SIR JOHN LAVERY, hl, NGI 574. G.F.WATTS, 1878, hs, profile, NPG 1350.

D MARIAN COLLIER, 1877, head, pencil, NPG 3146. H.T.WELLS, Royal Coll.

SC SIR J.E.BOEHM, 1890, bronze bust, NGI 8148. SIR J.E.BOEHM, terracotta bust, NPG 1360. SIR WILLIAM GOSCOMBE JOHN, *c*1905, seated bronze statue, Trinity College, Dublin.

PR W.ROTHENSTEIN, 1897, tql seated, lith, NPG. W.ROTHENSTEIN, liths, BM and Bradford City Art Gallery. G.J.STODART, after H.T.Wells, hs, semi-profile, stipple, NPG.

C SIR LESLIE WARD ('Spy'), tql, w/c study, for *Vanity Fair*, 27 May 1882, NPG 5165.

PH ELLIOTT & FRY, tql seated, carte, NPG. BARRAUD, tql, print, for *Men and Women of the Day*, vol III, 1890, NPG AX5505. RUSSELL & SONS, *c*1891, hs, woodburytype, NPG. SIR BENJAMIN STONE, 1897, wl, print, NPG.

LECLERCQ, Carlotta (1840?-1893) actress.

PR W.W.ALAIS, after a photograph, tql, line, NPG, Harvard Theatre Collection, Cambridge, Mass, USA. Two portraits by J.E.BAKER and H.A.THOMAS, both hs, liths, Harvard Theatre Collection.

PH SOUTHWELL BROS, wl in character, carte, NPG.

LECLERCQ, Rose (1845?-1899) actress.

PR Two woodcuts, in character by M.KLINKICHT and an unknown artist, both hs, Harvard Theatre Collection, Cambridge, Mass, USA.

PH ELLIOTT & FRY, nearly tql seated, carte, NPG (Album 102). UNKNOWN, hl, semi-profile, woodburytype, carte, NPG AX7711.

LEE, James Prince (1804-1869) bishop of Manchester.

PR H.ROBINSON, after G.Richmond, hs, stipple, NPG. D.J.POUND, after a photograph, tql, stipple and line, for *Drawing Room Portrait Gallery of Eminent Personages*, NPG.

PH DUVAL & CO, tql seated, carte, NPG (Album 114). JOHN EASTHAM, tql seated, print, NPG.

LEE, Robert (1804-1868) professor of biblical criticism at Edinburgh.

P JAMES EDGAR, 1853, tql seated, SNPG 285.

PR W.HOLE, hs, etch, for *Quasi Cursores*, 1884, NPG.

PH MOFFAT, hs, carte, NPG (Album 102).

LEE, Sir Sidney (1859-1926) Shakespearian scholar.

D FRANCIS DODD, hl seated, chalk, NPG 4423.

LEE, Vernon, see Violet Paget.

LEECH, John (1817-1864) illustrator and caricaturist.

D SIR J.E.MILLAIS, 1854, hs, w/c, NPG 899. Self-portrait, hs, pencil and sanguine, Garrick Club, London.

SC SIR J.E.BOEHM, *c*1865, plaster bust, NPG 866.

PR BUTTERWORTH & HEATH, hs, circle, woodcut, BM. M.JACKSON, hs, woodcut, BM, NPG. D.TODD, hs, etch, NPG. UNKNOWN, hs, woodcut, for *The Illust Review*, 15 Nov 1872, NPG.

C RICHARD DOYLE, hs with Tom Taylor, pen and ink, BM.

PH Several cartes by LUCAS & TUCK, McLEAN, MELHUISH & HAES, CAMILLE SILVY and an unknown photographer, all wl, NPG.

LEESON, Edward Nugent, see 6th Earl of Milltown.

LE FANU, Joseph Thomas Sheridan (1814-1873) novelist and journalist.
D UNKNOWN, 1842, hl seated, w/c, NPG 4864.

LEFROY, William (1836-1909) dean of Norwich and writer.
P BLACKDEN, hl, Norwich Cathedral.
PR UNKNOWN, after a photograph by Russell & Sons, hs, profile, wood engr, for *Illust London News*, 22 June 1889, NPG.
PH BASSANO, 1894, five negs, various sizes, NPG x7153-7.

LEGH, Thomas Wodehouse, see 2nd Baron Newton.

LEGROS, Alphonse (1837-1911) painter, sculptor and etcher.
P SIR CHARLES HOLROYD, hs, profile, TATE 3398. C.H.SHANNON, 1899, hl, NPG 2551.
D RUDOLPH LEHMANN, 1880, BM. Self-portrait, 1903, hs, pencil, Uffizi Gallery, Florence.
SC JULES DALOU, c1876, bronze heads, National Museum of Wales, Cardiff, and Cleveland Museum of Art, Ohio, USA; plaster cast, V & A. AUGUSTE RODIN, c1881, bronze bust, Manchester City Art Gallery, EDOUARD LANTERI, bust, University College, London.
PR Self-portrait, 1895, hs, goldpoint, Fitzwilliam Museum, Cambridge. Several self-portrait etchings, Bradford City Art Gallery, Carlisle City Art Gallery and Municipal Gallery of Modern Art, Dublin. J.BENWELL CLARK, 1880, hs, etch, NPG. FELIX BRACQUEMOND, hs, etch, BM, NPG. C.J.DURHAM, hs, profile, etch, NPG. C.HOLROYD, hs, etch, NPG. C.HOLROYD, hs, semi-profile, etch, BM. E.R.HUGHES, hs, etch, NPG. FREDERIC REGAMEY, hs, etch, NPG. W.ROTHENSTEIN, 1896, hs, lith, BM, NPG. W.ROTHENSTEIN, two liths, wearing top hat, tql and tql seated, the first dated 1897, NPG. W.ROTHENSTEIN, 1899, hl seated, back view, head in profile, lith, NPG. C.H.SHANNON, tql seated, lith, BM, NPG. W.STRANG, wl seated at desk, etch, NPG. G.F.WATTS, c1879, hs, profile, etch, NPG.
PH G.C.BERESFORD, 1902, two negs (x6532-3), and prints, hs and hs, profile, NPG. UNKNOWN, wl seated at work, print, University College, London.

LEHMANN, Rudolph (1819-1905) painter.
P? Self-portrait, Uffizi Gallery, Florence.

LEICESTER, Thomas William Coke, 2nd Earl of (1822-1909) agriculturist.
P SAMUEL LANE, RA 1832, hl with Edward Keppel Coke, Shugborough (NT), Staffs. GEORGE RICHMOND, RA 1858, wl in landscape, Holkham Hall, Norfolk, engr F.Joubert, mixed engr, BM, NPG.
SC UNKNOWN, as a young man on bas-relief ('Granting a Lease'), on monument to his father, Holkham Hall. UNKNOWN, 1871, terracotta bust, Holkham.
C SIR LESLIE WARD ('Spy'), tql, profile, chromo-lith, for *Vanity Fair*, 4 Aug 1883, NPG.

LEIGH, Augustus Austen (1840-1905) provost of King's College, Cambridge.
P JOHN COLLIER, 1897, King's College, Cambridge.

LEIGH, Egerton (1815-1876) writer on dialect.
PR UNKNOWN, hs, woodcut, for *Illust London News*, 15 July 1876, NPG.

LEIGH, Evan (1811-1876) inventor.
PR J.SMITH, hs, oval, stipple, NPG.

LEIGH, Henry Sambrook (1837-1883) dramatist.
PR R.TAYLOR, after a sketch from memory by Wallis Mackay, 20 June 1883, tql seated, woodcut, for *Illust London News*, 30 June 1883, NPG.

LEIGHTON, Frederic Leighton, Baron (1830-1896) painter and President of the Royal Academy.
P Self-portrait, 1852, hs with palette, Städelsches Kunstinstitut, Frankfurt. Self-portrait, 1880, hl in DCL robes and chain, Uffizi Gallery, Florence. FELIX DUPUIS, 1880, hs, profile, Leighton House, London. G.F.WATTS, two related portraits, 1881, hl seated, profile, NPG 1049 (related w/c, Leighton House), and RA 1881, but worked on until 1888, tql seated in DCL robes and chain, Royal Academy, London. Self-portrait, 1882, hs, MacDonald Collection, Aberdeen Art Gallery.
D Self-portrait, c1848-50, hs, pencil, NPG 2141. HEINRICH HASSELHORST, c1850, hs, pencil, Städelsches Kunstinstitut, Frankfurt. EDWARD VON STEINLE, two portraits, 1852, hl with Count Enrico Gamba, chalk and wash, Sammlung der Zeichnungen, Staatliche Museen zu Berlin, and c1852, hs, profile, pencil and chalk, BM. RUDOLPH LEHMANN, 1889, hs, BM. S.P.HALL, 1889, hl with Clifford Lloyd, at the Parnell Commission, pencil, NPG 2262. FREDERICK PEGRAM, 1889, with others at the Parnell Commission, V & A.
M ROSA CARTER, 1895-6, hl seated, profile, NPG 2016.
G HENRY NELSON O'NEIL, 'Forty-three Members in the Billiard Room of the Garrick Club', oil, 1869, Garrick Club, London. HENRY JAMYN BROOKS, 'Private view of the Old Master Exhibition, Royal Academy, 1888', oil, NPG 1833. G.GRENVILLE MANTON, 'Conversazione at the Royal Academy, 1891', w/c NPG 2820. REGINALD CLEAVER, 'Hanging Committee, Royal Academy, 1892', pen and ink, NPG 4245.
SC SIR THOMAS BROCK, 1892, bronze bust, Royal Academy, London; related plaster cast, NPG 1957 and bronze cast from NPG 1957, NPG 1957a. SIR THOMAS BROCK, c1901, recumbent bronze effigy, St Paul's Cathedral, London. SIDNEY BOYES, 1909, stone statue, South Front, V & A. UNKNOWN, stone medallion on decorative frieze, Stroud School of Science and Art.
PR A.HENDSCHEL, 'Students at the Städelsches Kunstinstitut', etch, c1850-52, Städelsches Kunstinstitut, Frankfurt, A.LEGROS, c1880, hs, profile, etch, BM. J.BROWN, after H.T.Wells of c1881, hs, semi-profile, stipple, one of 'Grillion's Club' series, BM. After w/c by S.P.HALL, wl, chromo-lith, for *Society*, 5 May 1883, NPG. Various prints after photographs.
C Self-portrait drgs by himself and Steinle, 1852, hs, profile, pencil, Royal Academy notebook no XXVII, Royal Academy. J.J.TISSOT, wl, profile, chromo-lith, for *Vanity Fair*, 29 June 1872, NPG. 'F.W.', wl, profile, with palette, woodcut, for *Hornet*, 9 Jan 1878, NPG. E.L.SAMBOURNE, wl with Sir Robert Peel, woodcut, for *Punch*, 10 May 1884, NPG. HARRY FURNISS, pen and ink sketch, NPG 3484.
PR DAVID WILKIE WYNFIELD, c1864, hs, print, NPG P77. CAMILLE SILVY, early 1860s, wl, V & A. LOCK & WHITFIELD, hs, profile, oval, woodburytype, for *Men of Mark*, 1877, NPG. W. & D.DOWNEY, tql seated, woodburytype, for Cassell's *Cabinet Portrait Gallery*, vol I, 1890, NPG. RALPH W.ROBINSON, wl seated in his studio, print, for *Members and Associates of the Royal Academy of Arts, 1891*, NPG x7373. ELLIOTT & FRY, hl, print, NPG x6153. ELLIOTT & FRY, hs, carte, NPG (Album 103). KINGSBURY & NOTCUTT, hs, profile, cabinet, NPG x6151. LONDON STEREOSCOPIC Co, hl, cabinet, NPG x6152. LONDON STEREOSCOPIC Co, tql seated, carte, NPG x6149. LONDON STEREOSCOPIC Co, hs, profile, carte, NPG (Album 99). J. & C.WATKINS, hs, carte, NPG (Album 104). WALERY, tql, print, NPG x6148.

LEIGHTON, Stanley (1837-1901) politician and antiquary.
PR UNKNOWN, after a photograph by Maull & Fox, hs, profile, wood engr, for *Illust London News*, 5 Oct 1895, NPG.

LEININGEN, Prince Ernest Leopold Victor Charles Auguste Joseph Emich (1830-1904) admiral.
P FRANÇOIS D'ALBERT DURADE, 1847, head, Royal Coll. J. (or F

R.SAY, 1857, with his cousin Prince Victor, in naval uniform, Royal Coll.

LEISHMAN, Thomas (1825–1904) Scottish divine and liturgiologist.
PH UNKNOWN, Church of Scotland Assembly Hall, Edinburgh.

LEITCH, William Leighton (1804–1883) water-colour painter.
D E.F.BRIDELL-FOX, 1861, head, chalk, SNPG 650.
PR Two woodcuts by unknown artists, both hs, BM.
PH ELLIOTT & FRY, hs, carte, NPG (Album 106). UNKNOWN, tql seated, carte, NPG (Album 104).

LEITH, John Farley (1808–1887) lawyer and politician.
C SIR LESLIE WARD ('Spy'), wl, profile, w/c study, for *Vanity Fair*, 21 June 1879, NPG 4725.

LE JEUNE, Henry (1819–1904) painter.
PR UNKNOWN, hl, woodcut, for *Illust London News*, 25 July 1863. NPG.
PH ELLIOTT & FRY, hs, carte, NPG. LOCK & WHITFIELD, wl seated, carte, NPG (Album 104). MAULL & POLYBLANK, wl, carte, NPG AX7572.

LE KEUX, John Henry (1812–1896) architectural engraver and draughtsman.
PH HILLS & SAUNDERS, hs, carte, NPG.

LEMMENS-SHERRINGTON, Helen (1834–1906) soprano singer.
PR E.MATTHEWS & SONS, hs, oval, lith, NPG.
PH MOIRA & HAIGH, wl, carte, NPG. HERBERT WATKINS, wl, carte, NPG. UNKNOWN, tql, woodburytype, carte, NPG AX7693.

LEMON, Mark (1809–1870) first editor of *Punch*.
PR A.E.DOWNING, hs, etch, NPG. SWAIN, after J.Tenniel, wl as Falstaff, woodcut, BM. SWAIN, wl seated, oval, woodcut, BM. UNKNOWN, after a photograph by H.J.Whitlock, hs, woodcut, for *Illust London News*, 4 June 1870, NPG. UNKNOWN, after a photograph by London Stereoscopic Co, hs, woodcut, for *The Illust Review*, 15 Feb 1872, NPG.
C RICHARD DOYLE, tql as Robert Macaire, pen and ink, BM. GEORGE GOURSAT ('Sem'), wl, w/c, NPG.
PH Various cartes by H.N.KING, LONDON STEREOSCOPIC & PHOTO-GRAPHIC CO, JOHN & CHARLES WATKINS and others, various sizes, NPG.

LEMPRIERE, Charles (1818–1901) writer and politician.
P UNKNOWN, St John's College, Oxford.

LENG, Sir John (1828–1906) newspaper proprietor.
P SIR W.Q.ORCHARDSON, RA 1902, tql, Dundee City Art Gallery.
PH SIR BENJAMIN STONE, 1898–99, three prints, all wl, NPG.

LENG, Sir William Christopher (1825–1902) journalist.
C SIR LESLIE WARD ('Spy'), wl, chromo-lith, for *Vanity Fair*, 8 March 1890, NPG.

LENNOX, Charles Henry Gordon-, see 6th Duke of Richmond.

LENNOX, Lord Henry Charles George Gordon- (1821–1886) statesman.
C H.R.GRAVES, wl, pen and ink, 1848, NPG. 'FAUSTIN', wl, chromo-lith, NPG. CARLO PELLEGRINI ('Ape'), wl, profile, chromo-lith, for *Vanity Fair*, 30 July 1870, NPG.
PH GRILLET JNE, tql seated, carte, NPG X1568. CAMILLE SILVY, 1860, wl seated, carte, NPG (Album 2).

LENNOX, Sir Wilbraham Oates (1830–1897) general, Royal Engineers.
PR UNKNOWN, after a photograph by Russell & Sons, hs in uniform,

wood engr, for *Illust London News*, 20 Feb 1897, NPG.
PH CAMILLE SILVY, 1861, wl, carte, NPG (Album 2).

LEOPOLD, Prince (1853–1884), see 1st Duke of Albany.

LE SAGE, Sir John Merry (1837–1926) journalist and managing editor of *Daily Telegraph*.
C 'OWL', tql seated, profile, mechanical repro, for *Vanity Fair*, 20 Aug 1913, NPG.

LESLIE, Frederick (1855–1892) actor.
PR Several theatrical prints, Harvard Theatre Collection, Cambridge, Mass, USA.
C Several woodcuts, Harvard Theatre Collection.
PH ST JAMES PHOTOGRAPHIC CO, hs, profile, woodburytype, for *The Theatre*, June 1884, NPG.

LESLIE, George Dunlop (1835–1921) painter and writer.
P C.R.LESLIE (his father), 1840, V & A. Self-portrait, 1882, MacDonald Collection, Aberdeen Art Gallery.
D C.B.BIRCH, c1858, hs, pencil, NPG 2477.
PH LOCK & WHITFIELD, hs, oval, woodburytype, for *Men of Mark*, 1882, NPG. JOHN WATKINS, two cartes, both hs, NPG (Albums 104 and 106).

LESLIE, Henry David (1822–1896) conductor and composer.
P JULIA B.FOLKARD, 1878, hs, Royal College of Music, London.
D T.G.COOPER, c1868–72, hs, pen and ink, NPG 2522.

LESLIE-MELVILLE, Alexander, see 12th Earl of LEVEN and Melville.

LETHABY, William Richard (1857–1931) writer and architect.
SC GILBERT BAYES, c1923, bronze bust, The Art Workers' Guild, London. GILBERT BAYES, c1924, bronze plaque, RIBA, London.

LETHEBY, Henry (1816–1876) analytical chemist.
PR UNKNOWN, hs, profile, woodcut, NPG. UNKNOWN, after a photograph by Barraud and Jerrard, hs, woodcut, for *Illust London News*, 15 April 1876, NPG.

LEVEN and MELVILLE, Alexander Leslie-Melville, 12th Earl of (1817–1889) banker.
C SIR LESLIE WARD ('Spy'), wl, profile, w/c study, for *Vanity Fair*, 17 Dec 1881, NPG 4726.

LEVER, Charles James (1806–1872) novelist.
D STEPHEN PEARCE, 1849, hs, chalk, NGI 2229.
PR DALZIEL, hs, woodcut, BM. R.TAYLOR, after a photograph by C.Watkins, hs, profile, woodcut, for *The Illust Review*, 1 July 1871. NPG. UNKNOWN, after a photograph by Charles Watkins, hs, oval, woodcut, for *Illust London News*, 15 June 1872, NPG. H.T.RYALL, after S.Louer, hs, oval, stipple, NPG.
PH MAYALL, tql seated, carte, NPG.

LEVER, William Heskith, see 1st Viscount Leverhulme.

LEVERHULME, William Hesketh Lever, 1st Viscount (1851–1925) soap manufacturer and art collector.
P GEORGE HALL NEALE, 1916, wl in court dress, Lady Lever Art Gallery, Port Sunlight. P.A.DE LÁSZLÓ, 1924, wl in peer's robes, Lady Lever Art Gallery. WILLIAM STRANG, University of Liverpool.
SC EDWARD ONSLOW FORD, 1900, marble bust, Lady Lever Art Gallery. SIR WILLIAM GOSCOMBE JOHN, c1926, bronze recumbent effigy, Christ Church, Port Sunlight.
PH SIR BENJAMIN STONE, 1909, wl, print, NPG. WALTER STONEMAN, two portraits, 1921 and 1922, both hs, NPG (NPR).

LEVESON-GOWER, (Edward) Frederick (1819–1907) politician.
P ORAZIO MANARA, Hardwick Hall (NT), Derbys.

PR C.HOLL & A.ROBERTS, after H.T.Wells, hs, stipple, one of 'Grillion's Club' series, BM.

LEVESON-GOWER, Lord Francis, see 1st Earl of Ellesmere.

LEVESON-GOWER, George Granville William Suther-land, see 3rd Duke of Sutherland.

LEVESON-GOWER, Granville George, see 2nd Earl Granville.

LEVESON-GOWER, Harriet Elizabeth Georgiana, see Duchess of Sutherland.

LEVI, Leone (1821-1888) jurist and statistician.
PR UNKNOWN, after a daguerreotype by Beard, hs, woodcut, NPG.
PH ELLIOTT & FRY, 1873, tql, carte, NPG. ELLIOTT & FRY, 1873, hs, cabinet, NPG.

LEVY, Joseph Moses (1812-1888) founder of the *Daily Telegraph.*
P SIR HUBERT VON HERKOMER, exhib 1888, tql seated, NPG 4760.
PR UNKNOWN, hs, semi-profile, wood engr, for *Illust London News*, 27 Oct 1888, NPG.

LEVY-LAWSON, Edward, see 1st Baron Burnham.

LEWES, George Henry (1817-1878) writer.
D ANNE GLIDDON, 1840, tql, pencil, NPG 1373. RUDOLPH LEHMANN, 1867, hs, BM.
G W.M.THACKERAY, wl with his wife and Thornton Leigh Hunt, pencil, NPG 4686.
PR UNKNOWN, after a photograph by Elliott & Fry, hs, woodcut, for *Illust London News*, 14 Dec 1878, NPG.
PH SWAN ELECTRIC ENGRAVING CO, after Elliott & Fry, hs photo-gravure, NPG. Several cartes by JOHN & CHARLES WATKINS, various sizes, NPG.

LEWIS, Agnes (1843-1926) discoverer of the *Sinai Palimpsest.*
P 'J.P.', 1920, tql, Westminster College, Cambridge.
PH Several prints, Westminster College.

LEWIS, Charles George (1808-1880) engraver.
D MARSHALL CLAXTON, 1864, wl, w/c, NPG 890.
PR C.G.LEWIS, after J.H.Lewis, hs, stipple, BM.
PH JOHN WATKINS, hl, carte, NPG (Album 105).

LEWIS, Sir George Cornewall, 2nd Bart (1806-1863) chancellor of the exchequer.
P SIR JOHN WATSON GORDON, hs, DoE (Somerset House, London). HENRY WEIGALL, RA 1863, wl seated, National Museum of Wales, Cardiff.
D GEORGE RICHMOND, head, chalk, NPG 1063.
G JOHN PHILLIP, 'The House of Commons, 1860', oil, Palace of Westminster, London.
SC BARON CARLO MAROCHETTI, c1864, bronze statue, Hereford. HENRY WEEKES, RA 1864, bust, Westminster Abbey, London.
PR D.J.POUND, after a photograph by J.Watkins, tql seated, stipple and line, for *The Drawing Room Portrait Gallery of Eminent Personages*, NPG.
PH L.CALDESI, wl, carte, NPG. HERBERT WATKINS, 1858, hs, oval, print, NPG AX7910. Attrib JOHN WATKINS, hs, oval, print, NPG AX7326. JOHN WATKINS, hs, carte, NPG (Album 99).

LEWIS, Sir George Henry, 1st Bart (1833-1911) solicitor.
D S.P.HALL, several pencil drgs, three at the Parnell Commission, NPG 2243, 2244, 2250, 2258, 2282, 2292 and 2299. FREDERICK PEGRAM, three pencil sketches, at the Parnell Commission, V & A.
C SIR LESLIE WARD ('Spy'), wl, profile, chromo-lith, for *Vanity Fair*, 2 Sept 1876, NPG. SIR MAX BEERBOHM, two drgs, c1896, wl, profile, Garrick Club, London, and c1908, sketch, University of

Texas, Austin, USA.
PH WALERY, wl, print, NPG.

LEWIS, John Frederick (1805-1876) painter.
P SIR WILLIAM BOXALL, 1832, hl, profile, NPG 1470. SIR JOHN WATSON GORDON, RA 1854, hs, Royal Scottish Academy, Edinburgh.
D Self-portrait, hs, pencil, Royal Academy Album no 137, Royal Academy, London.
PR C.G.LEWIS, after a photograph by J. & C.Watkins, hs, stipple and line, NPG; similar photograph, as a woodcut, for *Illust London News*, 25 March 1865, NPG.
C GEORGE GOURSAT ('Sem'), wl, w/c, Ashmolean Museum, Oxford.
PH ELLIOTT & FRY, three cartes, hs and hs, profile, two in Albums (104 and 106). NPG.

LEWIS, John Travers (1825-1901) archbishop of Ontario.
PH UNKNOWN, hs, print, NPG (Anglican Bishops).

LEWIS, Lady Maria Theresa, née Villiers (1803-1865) writer.
D SIR EDWIN LANDSEER, 1836, sepia and wash, sketch for the portrait known as 'The Mantilla', Chatsworth (NT), Derbys.
PR R.J.LANE, after a drg by G.S.Newton, wl seated, lith, pub 1828, NPG. S.COUSINS, after G.S.Newton, hl, mezz, pub 1834, BM, NPG. J.H.ROBINSON, after E.Landseer, tql, 'The Mantilla' portrait, line, pub 1838, BM. G.H.PHILLIPS, after G.S.Newton, tql seated, mezz, for Murray's *Gems of G.S.Newton*, 1842, BM, NPG. FINDEN, after J.Hayter, tql in evening dress, octagon, stipple, BM, NPG.

LEWIS, Richard (1821-1905) bishop of Llandaff.
P SIR A.S.COPE, c1904, Bishop's Palace, Llandaff.
SC SIR WILLIAM GOSCOMBE JOHN, c1908, bronze memorial statue, in robes, Llandaff Cathedral.
PH UNKNOWN, tql, print, NPG (Anglican Bishops).

LEWIS, Samuel Savage (1836-1891) librarian of Corpus Christi College, Cambridge.
P? BROCK, Corpus Christi College, Cambridge.

LEWIS, William Thomas, see 1st Baron Merthyr.

LIBERTY, Sir Arthur Lasenby (1843-1917) fabric manufacturer.
P ARTHUR HACKER, RA 1913, tql seated, Liberty & Co Ltd, London.
SC SIR GEORGE FRAMPTON, RA 1914, marble bust, Liberty & Co Ltd.
PH Several prints, Liberty & Co Ltd.

LIDDELL, Henry George (1811-1898) dean of Christ Church.
P G.F.WATTS, 1875, hl seated, semi-profile, Christ Church, Oxford. SIR HUBERT VON HERKOMER, 1891, tql seated, Ash-molean Museum, Oxford.
SC H.R.HOPE-PINKER, 1888, marble bust, NPG 1871; version, West-minster Abbey, London. UNKNOWN, stone statue, Deanery Tower, Christ Church.
PR W.HOLL, after G.Richmond, hs, stipple, NPG.
C CARLO PELLEGRINI ('Ape'), wl, chromo-lith, for *Vanity Fair*, 30 Jan 1875, NPG.
PH HILLS & SAUNDERS, hs, profile, oval, carte, NPG (Album 40). Attrib HILLS & SAUNDERS, 1863, in a house party group after a degree presentation ceremony, print, NPG X4336. JULIA MARGARET CAMERON, c1870, hl, profile, print, NPG P153.

LIDDERDALE, William (1832-1902) governor of the Bank of England.
PR UNKNOWN, after a photograph by Walery, hs, woodcut, for *Illust London News*, 9 May 1891, NPG.

LIDDON, Henry Parry (1829-1890) canon of St Paul's.

P GEORGE RICHMOND, 1870–72, hl, Keble College, Oxford, SIR HUBERT VON HERKOMER, posthumous, tql seated, profile, Christ Church, Oxford.

D GEORGE RICHMOND, 1866, hl, chalk, NPG 1060.

C SIR LESLIE WARD ('Spy'), wl, profile, chromo-lith, for *Vanity Fair*, 16 Sept 1876, NPG.

PH C.L.DODGSON ('Lewis Carroll'), c1856, hl seated, print, NPG P7 (22). LOCK & WHITFIELD, hs, oval, woodburytype, for *Men of Mark*, 1881, NPG.

LIGHTFOOT, Joseph Barber (1828-1889) bishop of Durham.

P SIR W.B.RICHMOND, tql seated, semi-profile, Trinity College, Cambridge. UNKNOWN, tql seated, profile, Durham Cathedral.

D LOWES DICKINSON, 1891, after a photograph, wl seated, chalk, Trinity College, Cambridge.

PR UNKNOWN, after a photograph, hs, woodcut, for *The Graphic*, BM.

PH LOCK & WHITFIELD, hs, profile, oval, woodburytype, for *Men of Mark*, 1880, NPG. ROTARY PHOTO, hs, profile, postcard, NPG X12441.

LINCOLNSHIRE, Charles Robert Wynn-Carrington, 1st Marquess of (1843-1928) governor of New South Wales.

P SIR A.S.COPE, National Liberal Club, London. D.A.WEHRSCHMIDT, National Liberal Club.

D HAROLD SPEED, 1907, chalk, National Liberal Club. UNKNOWN, oval, National Liberal Club.

C CARLO PELLEGRINI ('Ape'), 1868–69, tql seated, w/c, Royal Coll; a preparatory sketch for this drg and a different chalk sketch are also in the Royal Coll. SIR LESLIE WARD ('Spy'), wl, profile, w/c study, for *Vanity Fair*, 11 Sept 1907, NPG 3111. SIR MAX BEERBOHM, 'The Old and the Young Self', 1924, and 'Always Admired', drgs, Ashmolean Museum, Oxford.

LIND, Johanna Maria (Jenny) (1820-1887) singer.

P EDUARD MAGNUS, 1846, tql seated, Staatliche Museen zu Berlin; replica, NPG 3801. COUNT ALFRED D'ORSAY, 1847, hl, NPG 2204.

D DANIEL MACLISE, V & A.

SC KARL RADNITZKY, medal, Barcelona Museum, Spain.

PR Various theatrical and popular prints, BM, NPG, Harvard Theatre Collection, Cambridge, Mass, USA.

PH E.BIEBER, wl, carte, NPG. KILBURN, 1848, wl, daguerreotype, Royal Coll. UNKNOWN, 1848, nearly wl, daguerreotype, Royal Coll. H.MURRAY, tql seated with her husband, carte, NPG.

LINDLEY, Nathaniel Lindley, Baron (1828-1921) judge.

P SIR GEORGE REID, 1907, tql seated in robes, Middle Temple, London.

PR W.STRANG, tql seated in judicial robes, etch, BM.

C SIR LESLIE WARD ('Spy'), hs at bench, chromo-lith, for *Vanity Fair*, 8 Feb 1890, NPG.

LINDSAY, Alexander William Crawford, see 25th Earl of Crawford.

LINDSAY, Sir Coutts, 2nd Bart (1824-1913) artist.

C JOSEPH MIDDLETON JOPLING, wl, w/c study, for *Vanity Fair*, 3 Feb 1883, NPG 2729.

PH THOMAS BUIST, wl with his wife, carte, NPG X8474. JULIA MARGARET CAMERON, c1865, hs, print, NPG P52. Attrib J.M.CAMERON, hl seated, profile, print, NPG X8473. DAVID WILKIE WYNFIELD, hs, print, Royal Academy, London.

LINDSAY, James Ludovic, see 26th Earl of Crawford.

LINDSAY, afterwards LOYD-LINDSAY, Robert James, see Baron Wantage.

LINDSAY, Thomas Martin (1843-1914) historian.

PH OLIVE EDIS, two prints: 1914, hs, NPG X12446, and tql seated, profile, NPG X12445.

LINDSAY, Wallace Martin (1858-1937) classical scholar.

PH WALTER STONEMAN, 1919, hs, NPG (NPR).

LINGEN, Ralph Robert Wheeler Lingen, Baron (1819-1905) civil servant.

P G.P.JACOMB-HOOD, 1896, tql seated with Bath ribbon and star, Trinity College, Oxford.

LINTON, Eliza, née Lynn (1822-1898) writer.

P JOHN COLLIER, 1900, hs, Fitz Park Museum and Art Gallery, Keswick.

PH BARRAUD, tql, print, for *Men and Women of the Day*, vol III, 1890, NPG AX5483. W. & D.DOWNEY, tql seated, woodburytype, for Cassell's *Cabinet Portrait Gallery*, vol I, 1890, NPG.

LINTON, Sir William (1801-1880) army physician.

G JERRY BARRETT, sketch for Florence Nightingale at Scutari, NPG 4305; study, NPG 2939a.

LINTON, William James (1812-1898) wood engraver and poet.

PR DALZIEL, after W.J.Linton, hs, woodcut, for *Frank Leslie's Illustrated Newspaper*, 1867, BM. UNKNOWN, hs, woodcut, for *Illust London News*, 14 May 1892, NPG.

LIPTON, Sir Thomas Johnstone, Bart (1850-1931) grocer and yachtsman.

P SIR HUBERT VON HERKOMER, 1896, Glasgow City Art Gallery.

D T.ROBINSON, 1898, hs, profile, NPG. EDOUARD PIZZELLA, Lipton Ltd, London.

C SIR LESLIE WARD ('Spy'), wl, chromo-lith, for *Vanity Fair*, 19 Sept 1901, NPG.

PH HOWARD COSTER, 1930, various negs and sizes, NPG X3576–85 and 3587–88, and one print, NPG AX2311.

LISGAR, Sir John Young, Baron (1807-1876) governor-general of Canada.

D J.HOLMES, 1850, wl seated, w/c and gouache, Royal Ontario Museum, Toronto, Canada.

G SIR GEORGE HAYTER, 'The House of Commons, 1833', oil, NPG 54.

LISTER, Joseph Lister, Baron (1827-1912) founder of antiseptic surgery.

P J.H.LORIMER, 1895, tql seated, University of Edinburgh. W.W.OULESS, RA 1897, tql seated, Royal College of Surgeons, London.

G HENRY JAMYN BROOKS, 'Council of the Royal College of Surgeons of England of 1884–85', oil, Royal College of Surgeons.

SC E.B.STEPHENS, 1873, bust, St Thomas's Hospital, London. MARGARET M.JENKIN, 1898, wax medallion, NPG 1897. SIR THOMAS BROCK, 1912, marble bust, Royal College of Surgeons, London; related plaster cast, NPG 1958. SIR T.BROCK, c1922, bronze bust, Portland Place, London. SIR T.BROCK, marble medallion, Westminster Abbey, London. J.H.THOMAS, memorial medallions, University College, London and University College Hospital, London.

PR H.M.PAGET, from sketches by A.Cox, at the British Association Meeting at Liverpool, process print, for *The Graphic*, 26 Sept 1896, NPG. S.BEGG, hl as President of the Royal Society, process print, for *Illust London News*, 9 Jan 1897, NPG.

PG BARRAUD, hs, cabinet, NPG X4965. EMERY WALKER, after Moffat, tql seated, profile, photogravure, NPG X12429. WALKER & BOUTALL, after Barraud, hs, photogravure, NPG. UNKNOWN, 1850s, tql seated, glass positive, NPG X7962.

LISTER, Samuel Cunliffe, see 1st Baron Masham.

LISTER, Thomas Henry (1800-1842) novelist.
PR I.W.SLATER, after J.Slater, hs, lith, pub 1834, BM. FINDEN, after Wright, hs, stipple, for his *Granby*, 1836, BM.

LITTLER, Sir Ralph Daniel Makinson (1835-1908) barrister.
P Two portraits, one by SIR HUBERT VON HERKOMER, the other by MISS B.O.OFFER, Middlesex Guildhall, London.

LITTLETON, Edward (1842-1930), see 3rd Viscount Hatherton.

LITTON, Marie (1847-1884) actress.
PR E.MATTHEWS, hs, profile, lith, NPG; related tql, lith, for *Touchstone*; or *The New Era*, 8 June 1878, NPG.
PH UNKNOWN, *c*1880, hl in character, woodburytype, NPG AX 7598.

LIVEING, George Downing (1827-1924) chemist.
P SIR GEORGE REID, St John's College, Cambridge.
SC EDITH BATESON, 1901-2, bronze bust, Department of Organic and Inorganic Chemistry, University of Cambridge.
PH OLIVE EDIS, 1923, hs, print, NPG.

LIVERSEEGE, Henry (1803-1832) painter.
PR H.COUSINS, after W.Bradley, tql seated, mezz, for his *Works*, BM, NPG. PARRY, after C.Hawthorn, hs, stipple, for *Library of the Fine Arts*, 1832, BM, NPG.

LIVESEY, Sir George Thomas (1834-1908) promoter of labour co-partnership.
P W.M.PALIN, *c*1890, South Eastern Gas Co, London.
SC SYDNEY MARCH, 1909, bronze bust, Ferens Art Gallery, Hull. F.W.POMEROY, 1910, bronze statue, South Eastern Gas Co, Old Kent Road, London.

LIVINGSTONE, Charles (1821-1873) missionary and traveller.
PR UNKNOWN, after Charles Gow, hs, chromo-lith, NPG.

LIVINGSTONE, David (1813-1873) missionary and explorer.
P FREDERICK HAVILL, posthumous, tql seated, NPG 1040. MALCOLM STEWART, 1876, posthumous, Glasgow Art Gallery and Museum.
D JOSEPH BONOMI, 1857, hs, profile, pencil, NPG 386. EDWARD GRIMSTONE, RA 1857, hl, chalk, SNPG 1500.
M SARAH NEWELL, 1840, hs, London Missionary Society.
G C.G.LEWIS, after T.J.Barker, 'The Intellect and Valour of Great Britain', mixed engr, pub 1864, NPG. UNKNOWN, the meeting of Stanley and Livingstone, line, pub 1872, NPG.
SC AMELIA ROBERTSON HILL, *c*1869, bronze statue, Edinburgh; 1868, plaster statuette, probably related to the bronze, SNPG 844. JOHN MOSSMAN, 1876, posthumous statue, Glasgow. A.B.WYON, RA 1875, medal, Royal Geographical Society, London. WILLIAM BRODIE, *c*1878, marble bust, Dundee City Art Gallery. SIR WILLIAM REID DICK, statue, Victoria Falls. THOMAS HUXLEY-JONES, *c*1954, bronze statue, Royal Geographical Society.
PR D.J.POUND, after a photograph by Mayall, tql, for *Drawing Room Portrait Gallery of Eminent Personages*, 1859, NPG. Several woodcuts after photographs, NPG. Two anonymous engrs, NPG.
PH CAMERON, 1851, two daguerreotypes, hl and tql, London Missionary Society. ANNAN & SONS, hs, oval, print, NPG AX7278. MAULL & POLYBLANK, tql seated, print, NPG AX7279. UNKNOWN, tql seated, print, NPG. Several cartes by H.N.KING, LONDON STEREOSCOPIC CO, MAYALL and URIE, various dates and sizes, NPG.

LLANDAFF, Henry Matthews, Viscount (1826-1913) lawyer and politician.

PR UNKNOWN, after a photograph by J.Collier of Birmingham, hs, woodcut, for *Illust London News*, 14 Aug 1886, NPG. UNKNOWN, after a photograph by London Stereoscopic Co, hs, etch, NPG.
C SIR LESLIE WARD ('Spy'), wl, profile, chromo-lith, for *Vanity Fair*, 10 Sept 1887, NPG.
PH LONDON STEREOSCOPIC CO, hs, print, for *Our Conservative and Unionist Statesmen*, vol IV, NPG (Album 21). SIR BENJAMIN STONE, 1895, wl, print, NPG.

LLANOVER, Sir Benjamin Hall, 1st Baron (1802-1867) politician.
G PLOSZCZYNSKI, after C.Compton, 'Banquet given by the Reformers of Marylebone, 1st Dec 1847', lith, BM.
PR G.ZOBEL, after T.Hurlstone, hl, mezz, BM, NPG. UNKNOWN, hl seated, profile, woodcut, for *Illustrated Times*, 9 Jan 1858, NPG.

LLEWELLYN, Sir William (1858-1941) artist and President of the Royal Academy.
D SIR BERNARD PARTRIDGE, tql, profile, chalk drg, for *Punch*, 19 Dec 1928, NPG 5064.
SC SIR WILLIAM GOSCOMBE JOHN, RA 1932, bronze bust, Royal Academy, London.
PH ELLIOTT & FRY, hs, cabinet, NPG X12454. HOWARD COSTER, 1937, hl seated, print, NPG X1981.

LLOYD, Charles Dalton Clifford (1844-1891) servant of the crown.
D S.P.HALL, 1888-89, hl with Lord Leighton, at the sessions of the Parnell Commission, pencil, NPG 2262.
PR UNKNOWN, after a photograph by Lafayette of Dublin, hs, woodcut, for *Illust London News*, 6 Oct 1883, NPG.

LLOYD, Humphrey (1800-1881) provost of Trinity College, Dublin.
SC ALBERT BRUCE JOY, marble bust, Trinity College, Dublin.
PR UNKNOWN, after a photograph by Chancellor & Son of Dublin, hs, semi-profile, woodcut, for *Illust London News*, 5 Feb 1881, NPG.

LLOYD, William Watkiss (1813-1893) classical and Shakespearian scholar.
P MISS E.M.BUSH, hs, Society of Dilettanti, Brooks's Club, London.
PH HERBERT WATKINS, wl, carte, NPG (Album 114). UNKNOWN, tql seated, carte, NPG (Album 114).

LOCK, Walter (1846-1933) warden of Keble College, Oxford.
P C.W.FURSE, 1895, hl seated, Keble College, Oxford.
PH WALTER STONEMAN, 1920, hs, NPG (NPR).

LOCKE, John (1805-1880) legal writer and politician.
PR UNKNOWN, after a photograph by John Watkins, hl, woodcut for *Illust London News*, 16 May 1857, NPG.
C UNKNOWN, wl, chromo-lith, for *Vanity Fair*, 12 Aug 1871, NPG.

LOCKE, Joseph (1805-1860) civil engineer.
P SIR FRANCIS GRANT, 1845, wl in landscape, Institution of Civil Engineers, London.
G JOHN LUCAS, 'Conference of Engineers at Britannia Bridge', oil, Institution of Civil Engineers.
SC BARON CARLO MAROCHETTI, *c*1866, statue, Locke Park, Barnsley. C.H.MABEY, 1897, after E.W.Wyon of 1862, marble bust, Science Museum, London.
PR JOSEPH BROWN, after a photograph by J.E.Mayall, tql seated, stipple and line, pub 1862, NPG.

LOCKER, Arthur (1828-1893) novelist and journalist.
PR R.T. & CO, hs, wood engr, for *Illust London News*, 19 Dec 1891, NPG. UNKNOWN, after a photograph by Elliott & Fry, hs, wood engr, NPG.

LOCKER-LAMPSON, Frederick (1821–1895) poet.
PR C.W.SHERBORN, after G.du Maurier, head, profile, etch, BM. UNKNOWN, after J.E.Millais?, hs, profile, etch, NPG.
PH JULIA MARGARET CAMERON, c1867, tql seated, print, NPG P102.

LOCKHART, William Ewart (1846–1900) painter.
P Self-portrait, hs, MacDonald Collection, Aberdeen Art Gallery. JAMES ARCHER, SNPG 723.

LOCKHART, Sir William Stephen Alexander (1841–1900) general.
PR UNKNOWN, hs, semi-profile, in uniform, wood engr, for *Illust London News*, 20 Nov 1886, NPG.
C SIR LESLIE WARD ('Spy'), tql, semi-profile, colortype, for *Vanity Fair*, 8 Sept 1898, NPG.
PH BASSANO, c1898, several negs, various sizes, in uniform, NPG X4762–69. UNKNOWN, c1900, tql, print, National Army Museum, London.

LOCKWOOD, Amelius Mark Richard, see 1st Baron Lambourne.

LOCKWOOD, Sir Frank (1846–1897) solicitor-general.
P SIR A.S.COPE, tql, Lincoln's Inn, London.
D S.P.HALL, several pencil drgs, the first made at the Parnell Commission, NPG 2253, 2298, 2306 and 2307. FREDERICK PEGRAM, pencil sketch, made during the sessions of the Parnell Commission, V & A.
C HARRY FURNISS, tql seated, pen and ink sketch, NPG 3487.
PH W. & D.DOWNEY, tql, woodburytype, for Cassell's *Cabinet Portrait Gallery*, vol I, 1890, NPG. BARRAUD, tql, print, for *Men and Women of the Day*, vol IV, 1891, NPG AX5536. SIR BENJAMIN STONE, 1897, wl, print, Birmingham Reference Library, NPG. J.RUSSELL & SONS, tql seated, cabinet, NPG X12468. WALKER & BOUTALL, after a photograph by his daughter, hl seated, profile, photogravure, NPG.

LOCKYER, Sir (Joseph) Norman (1836–1920) astronomer.
SC UNKNOWN, portrait medallion, Salcombe Regis Observatory, Devon.
PH MISS LOCKYER, 1917, tql seated, print, NPG X12472. WALERY, tql, print, NPG.

LODGE, Sir Oliver Joseph (1851–1940) scientist.
P JOHN BERNARD MUNNS, Birmingham City Art Gallery. SIR GEORGE REID, two related portraits, hs, NPG 3952, and tql in robes, University of Birmingham. THOMSON, hs, Royal Institution, London. UNKNOWN, Institution of Electrical Engineers, London.
D SIR WILLIAM ROTHENSTEIN, 1916, head, chalk, NPG 3875. EDMOND KAPP, two portraits, 1919 and 1931, Barber Institute of Fine Arts, Birmingham.
SC C.J.ALLEN, marble bust, University Library, Liverpool.
C SIR LESLIE WARD ('Spy'), wl, chromo-lith, for *Vanity Fair*, 4 Feb 1904, NPG. SIR MAX BEERBOHM, 1932, nearly wl, profile, w/c, NPG 3856. SIR BERNARD PARTRIDGE, tql seated, chalk, NPG 4077.
PH BARRAUD, hl seated, profile, cabinet, NPG. WALTER STONEMAN, before 1917, hs, semi-profile, cabinet, NPG (NPR). OLIVE EDIS, c1926, hs, autochrome, NPG X7194. OLIVE EDIS, hs, print, NPG. UNKNOWN, c1927, tql with John Logie Baird, print, NPG X11615. HOWARD COSTER, 1931, head, print, NPG AX3422. HOWARD COSTER, hs, profile, print, NPG X1990. JOHN RUSSELL & SONS, hs, semi-profile, print, for *National Photographic Record*, vol I, NPG.

LODGE, Sir Richard (1855–1936) historian and teacher.
P SIR WILLIAM NICHOLSON, replica, 1925, wl, University of Edinburgh.
PH A.SWAN WATSON, hl, print, NPG.

LOFFT, Capell (1806–1873) classical scholar, poet and miscellaneous writer.

P LAURA LOFFT (his sister), hl in landscape, King's College, Cambridge.

LOFTUS, Lord Augustus William Frederick Spencer (1817–1904) diplomat.
PR UNKNOWN, after a photograph by C.Roesch, hs, semi-profile, oval, chromo-lith, NPG.
PH UNKNOWN, after Freeman & Co, tql, photogravure, NPG. LOCK & WHITFIELD, hs, semi-profile, oval, woodburytype, for *Men of Mark*, 1880, NPG.

LOFTUS, William Kennett (1821?–1858) archaeologist and traveller.
PH UNKNOWN, tql seated, print, Newcastle Literary and Philosophical Society.

LOGUE, Michael (1840–1924) cardinal.
P SIR JOHN LAVERY, 1920, hl, Ulster Museum.
PH LONDON STEREOSCOPIC CO, hl, oval, print, NPG.

LOLA MONTEZ, see Marie Dolores Eliza Rosanna GILBERT.

LONDESBOROUGH, Albert Denison, 1st Baron (1805–1860) politician and antiquary.
PR J.FAED, after F.Grant, tql, mezz, BM.

LONDONDERRY, Charles Stewart Vane-Tempest-Stewart, 6th Marquess of (1852–1915) politician, Viceroy of Ireland.
P SIR T.A.JONES, Dublin Castle, Eire.
D W.W.HODGSON, wl seated, w/c, NPG 4545.
PR J.BROWN, after a photograph, hs, stipple, for *Baily's Mag*, 1875, BM. UNKNOWN, after a photograph by London Stereoscopic Co, hs, woodcut, for *Illust London News*, 28 Aug 1886, NPG.
C SIR LESLIE WARD ('Spy'), wl, profile, chromo-lith, for *Vanity Fair*, 7 June 1879, NPG. F.T.DALTON ('FTD'), hs, w/c study, for *Vanity Fair*, 6 Feb 1896, NPG 2964.
PH OLIVE EDIS, hs, print, NPG. ELLIOTT & FRY, hs, print, for *Our Conservative Statesmen*, vol I, NPG (Album 24).

LONDONDERRY, George Henry Robert Charles William Vane-Tempest, 5th Marquess of (1821–1884) landowner and politician.
D THOMAS MOGFORD, after Sir Thomas Lawrence of c1824, 1831, pencil sketch, V & A.
PR J.BROWN, after a photograph, hl with telescope, stipple for *Baily's Mag*, 1868, BM. UNKNOWN, after a photograph by Barraud, hs, semi-profile, wood engr, for *Illust London News*, 22 Nov 1884, NPG.
C SIR LESLIE WARD ('Spy'), wl, profile, w/c study, for *Vanity Fair*, 11 Nov 1876, NPG 4429.
PH DISDERI, wl, carte, NPG (Album 114).

LONG, Edwin Longsden (1829–1891) painter.
D C.B.BIRCH, 1858, tql, profile, pencil, NPG 2474.
PR Two woodcuts, after photographs by Charles Watkins, both hs, one for *Illust London News*, 6 May 1876, the other for *Year-book of Celebrities*, NPG.
PH RALPH W.ROBINSON, tql, print, for *Members and Associates of the Royal Academy of Arts*, 1891, NPG X7374.

LONG of Wraxall, Walter Hume Long, 1st Viscount (1854–1924) statesman.
P A.H.COLLINS, replica of portrait of 1918, Harrow War Memorial Hall, Middx.
PR JOSEPH BROWN, after a photograph by Downey, hs, stipple, for *Baily's Mag*, 1882, NPG.
C SIR LESLIE WARD ('Spy'), wl in riding dress, chromo-lith, for *Vanity Fair*, 16 Oct 1886, NPG.

PH ELLIOTT & FRY, hs, print, for *Our Conservative and Unionist Statesmen*, vol V, NPG (Album 22). SIR BENJAMIN STONE, 1897, wl, print, NPG.

LONSDALE, Hugh Cecil Lowther, 5th Earl of (1857-1944) sportsman.

P SIR JOHN LAVERY, 1930, wl in Garter robes, Mansion House, Dublin.

PR JOSEPH BROWN, after a photograph by John Mayall, hs, stipple, for *Baily's Mag*, 1884, NPG.

C SIR MAX BEERBOHM, *c*1894, University of Texas, Austin, USA. SIR BERNARD PARTRIDGE, pen and ink sketch, for *Punch*, 21 May 1928, NPG. JOSEPH SIMPSON, head, chalk, BM. Several prints for *Vanity Fair*: SIR LESLIE WARD ('Spy'), wl, profile, chromo-lith, (10 July 1886); SIR LESLIE WARD, 'At Cowes', chromo-lith, (6 Dec 1894); SIR LESLIE WARD, 'A Master's Meet', chromo-lith, (28 Nov 1895); 'BEDE', 'A Fox Hunting Constellation', mechanical repro, (7 Dec 1905); 'WH', wl, chromo-lith, (19 June 1912), NPG.

PH HOWARD COSTER, one print, 1929, hs, (X1991), and one neg, NPG.

LONSDALE, James Gylby (1816-1892) professor of classical literature.

P JAMES LONSDALE, hs, a leaving portrait, Eton College, Berks.

LOPES, Henry Charles, see 1st Baron Ludlow.

LOPES, Sir Lopes Massey, 3rd Bart (1818-1908) politician and agriculturist.

C CARLO PELLEGRINI ('Ape'), wl, profile, chromo-lith, for *Vanity Fair*, 15 May 1875, NPG.

PH MAULL & POLYBLANK, wl, carte, NPG (Album 136).

LOREBURN, Robert Threshie Reid, 1st Earl (1846-1923) lord chancellor.

P SIR GEORGE REID, 1907, tql, DoE (Privy Council). HENRY HARRIS BROWN, 1911, hl seated, Inner Temple, London. GEORGE FIDDES WATT, RA 1912, tql seated in lord chancellor's gown, Balliol College, Oxford. RUTH GARNETT, Cheltenham College, Gloucs.

C SIR LESLIE WARD ('Spy'), tql, profile, chromo-lith, for *Vanity Fair*, 10 Jan 1895, NPG. 'OWL', hs, mechanical repro, for *Vanity Fair*, 24 Sept 1913, NPG.

PH SIR BENJAMIN STONE, 1897, wl, print, NPG.

LORIMER, James (1818-1890) jurist and political philosopher.

P J.H.LORIMER (his son), two portraits, 1878, tql seated, University of Edinburgh, and 1890, SNPG 1347.

PR WILLIAM HOLE, hl, etch, for *Quasi Cursores*, 1884, NPG.

LOTHIAN, Schomberg Henry Kerr, 9th Marquess of (1833-1900) diplomat and secretary of state for Scotland.

D W.GRAHAM BOSS, pencil, SNPG 1714.

PR R.T., hs, wood engr, for *Illust London News*, 19 March 1887, NPG.

PH RUSSELL & SONS, hs, print, for *Our Conservative and Unionist Statesmen*, vol I, NPG (Album 18).

LOUISE Caroline Alberta, Princess, Duchess of Argyll (1848-1939) daughter of Queen Victoria.

P F.X.WINTERHALTER, 1865, tql, profile, Royal Coll. HEINRICH VON ANGELI, exhib 1892, hs, Royal Coll. Attrib J.M.BARCLAY, wl, Inveraray Castle, Strathclyde region, Scotland.

D LOUIS BEROUD, pencil, SNPG 1738.

G QUEEN VICTORIA, 1850–53, three drgs, in groups with her brothers and sisters, Queen Victoria's sketchbooks, Royal Coll. F.X.WINTERHALTER, 'The Four Royal Princesses', oil, 1849, Royal Coll. F.X.WINTERHALTER, 1856, with Prince Arthur and Prince Leopold, Royal Coll. F.W., 'The Opening of the Royal Albert Infirmary, 1865', oil, NPG 3083. S.P.HALL, 'The Marriage of Princess Louise to the Marquess of Lorne, 1871', oil, Royal

Coll.

SC MARY THORNYCROFT, statuette, as a child, as 'Plenty', Royal Coll. MARY THORNYCROFT, 1870, marble bust, Royal Coll. P.F.CONNELLY, 1874, marble bust, Inveraray. P.F.CONNELLY, 1879, marble bust, Royal Coll. Attrib to herself, terracotta bust, NPG 4455.

PR T.FAIRLAND, after F.X.Winterhalter, hs, aged 3, circle, lith, BM. NPG. C.MAYER, hl, line, for *Almanach de Gotha*, 1870, BM. W.H.SIMMONS, after W.Holyoake, tql, stipple, pub 1872, NPG. Various prints and various woodcuts for *Illust London News*, BM, NPG.

PH L.CALDESI, 1857, with the royal family on the terrace at Osborne House, print, NPG P26. BASSANO, tql, cabinet, NPG AX5559. W. & D.DOWNEY, 1868, wl with Prince Leopold, print, NPG P22(7). W. & D.DOWNEY, wl in her wedding dress, woodburytype, BM. OLIVE EDIS, *c*1927, tql seated, print, NPG. Various cartes by DISDERI, W. & D.DOWNEY, ELLIOTT & FRY, HILLS & SAUNDERS, JABEZ HUGHES, LONDON STEREOSCOPIC CO, MAYALL, SOUTHWELL BROS, JOHN WATKINS and others, singly and in groups, NPG, Royal Coll.

LOVE, William Edward (1806-1867) the polyphonist.

PR C.BAUGNIET, tql, lith, BM. UNKNOWN, as Mr Tranquillus Calm in his *The London Season*, woodcut, BM.

LOVELL, Maria Anne, Mrs, see Lacy.

LOVETT, William (1800-1877) chartist.

PR ALFRED HARRAL, after H.Anelay, hs, woodcut, for *Howitt's Journal*, 8 May 1847, NPG.

PH UNKNOWN, tql seated, print, NPG X1599.

LOW, Alexander Low, Lord (1845-1910) Scottish judge.

P GEORGE FIDDES WATT, probably exhib 1908, hl seated, Faculty of Advocates, Parliament Hall, Edinburgh.

LOWDER, Charles Fuge (1820-1880) vicar of St Peter's, London Docks.

PR G.COOK, hs, oval, stipple, NPG.

LOWE, Sir Drury Curzon Drury-, see DRURY-Lowe.

LOWE, Robert, see 1st Viscount Sherbrooke.

LOWER, Mark Anthony (1813-1876) antiquary.

PR DALZIEL, after H.Weir, hs, woodcut, BM.

LOWTHER, Hugh Cecil, see 5th Earl of Lonsdale.

LOWTHER, James (1840-1904) politician and sportsman.

PR W.ROFFE, after a photograph by W.T. & R.Cowland, hl seated, stipple and line, NPG. UNKNOWN, hs, stipple, NPG. UNKNOWN, hs, woodcut, for *Illust London News*, 18 May 1878, NPG.

C HARRY FURNISS, wl seated, pen and ink, NPG 3615. SIR LESLIE WARD ('Spy'), two chromo-liths, wl, profile, on horseback, for *Vanity Fair*, 8 Dec 1877, and wl, profile, for *Vanity Fair*, 1 March 1900, NPG.

PH LONDON STEREOSCOPIC CO, hs, print, for *Our Conservative and Unionist Statesmen*, vol II, NPG (Album 19). MAULL & FOX, tql seated, cabinet, NPG X4098.

LOWTHER, James William, see 1st Viscount Ullswater.

LOYD-LINDSAY, Robert James, see Baron Wantage.

LUARD, Henry Richards (1825-1891) registrar of the university of Cambridge.

P LOWES DICKINSON, 1897, hs, Trinity College, Cambridge.

LUBBOCK, Sir John, see 1st Baron Avebury.

LUBBOCK, Sir John William, 3rd Bart (1803-1865) astronomer and mathematician.

P THOMAS PHILLIPS, 1843, hl seated, Senate House, University of

London.

LUCAN, George Charles Bingham, 3rd Earl of (1800-1888) field-marshal.
P SIR FRANCIS GRANT, 1855, wl in uniform, on loan to DoE (Ministry of Defence).
D UNKNOWN, wl in uniform, oval, w/c, NGI 2332.
PR M. & N.HANHART, tql in uniform, lith, NPG. T.W.HUNT, after a daguerreotype, hl seated, stipple and line, NPG. D.J.POUND, after a photograph by John Watkins, tql seated in uniform, stipple and line, for *The Drawing Room Portrait Gallery of Eminent Personages*, NPG. UNKNOWN, after a photograph, hl seated, stipple and line, for Nolan's *History of the war against Russia*, 1878, BM.
C CARLO PELLEGRINI ('Ape'), wl, chromo-lith, for *Vanity Fair*, 23 April 1881, NPG.
PH UNKNOWN, hl, profile, carte, NPG (Album 38).

LUCAS, Sir Charles Prestwood (1853-1931) civil servant and historian.
SC A.G.WYON, *c*1933, marble bust, DoE (Foreign and Commonwealth Office).
PH WALTER STONEMAN, 1917, hs, NPG (NPR).

LUCAS, David (1802-1881) engraver.
D THOMAS H.HUNN, 1902, after John Lucas, head, profile, chalk, NPG 1353.
M Attrib R.W.SATCHWELL, *c*1820, hs, profile, NPG 3070.

LUCAS, John (1807-1874) painter.
PR UNKNOWN, hs, woodcut, for *Illust London News*, 16 May 1874, NPG.
PH LUCAS BROS, wl, carte, NPG (Album 104).

LUCAS, John Seymour (1849-1923) painter.
P J.S.SARGENT, 1905, hl seated, NPG 5219.
D Self-portrait, 1887, hs, pencil, NPG 3040.
G G.GRENVILLE MANTON, 'Conversazione at the Royal Academy, 1891', w/c, NPG 2820. SIR HUBERT VON HERKOMER, 'The Council of the Royal Academy', oil, 1908, TATE 2481.
PR UNKNOWN, hs, oval, woodcut, BM.
C UNKNOWN, wl with palette, chromo-lith, for *Vanity Fair*, 14 Dec 1899, NPG.
PH UNKNOWN, 1914, hs, print, NPG.

LUCAS, Richard Cockle (1800-1883) sculptor.
SC Self-portrait, 1868, plaster bust, NPG 1783.
PR Self-portrait, at work on his statue of Isaac Watts, 1858, etch, pen and wash, NPG 1651b.
PH UNKNOWN, print, BM.

LUCKOCK, Herbert Mortimer (1833-1909) dean of Lichfield.
PR UNKNOWN, hs, wood engr, for *Illust London News*, 22 Oct 1892, NPG.

LUCY, Charles (1814-1873) painter.
PR R. & E.TAYLOR, after a photograph by John Watkins, hs, semi-profile, woodcut, for *Illust London News*, 7 June 1873, NPG.
PH ROLFE, wl with palette, carte, NPG (Album 104).

LUCY, Sir Henry William (1845-1924) journalist.
P J.S.SARGENT, 1905, hs, NPG 2930.
D S.P.HALL, two pencil drgs, NPG 2333-34.
C SIR LESLIE WARD ('Spy'), wl, profile, chromo-lith, for *Vanity Fair*, 31 Aug 1905, NPG.
PH JOHN RUSSELL & SONS, hs, print, for *National Photographic Record*, vol II, NPG.

LUDLOW, Henry Charles Lopes, 1st Baron (1828-1899) judge.
D SEBASTIAN EVANS, 1877, hs, pen and ink, NPG 2173(7).

C 'QUIZ', hs at bench, chromo-lith, for *Vanity Fair*, 25 March 1893, NPG.
PH LOCK & WHITFIELD, hs, oval, woodburytype, for *Men of Mark*, 1881, NPG.

LUGARD, Frederick John Dealtry Lugard, Baron (1858-1945) soldier, administrator and author.
P ANDRÉ CLUYSENAAR, 1915, University of Hong Kong. W.J.CARROW, 1936, after a photograph of 1929, hs in uniform, NPG 3306.
M CHARLOTTE E.LUGARD (his sister-in-law), 1893, hs, NPG 3305.
SC CHARLES D'ORVILLE PILKINGTON JACKSON, plaster bust, NPG 4289, and bronze bust, University of Hong Kong.
C SIR LESLIE WARD ('Spy'), wl in khaki dress, chromo-lith, for *Vanity Fair*, 19 Dec 1895, NPG.
PH W. & D.DOWNEY, hl, woodburytype, for Cassell's *Cabinet Portrait Gallery*, vol V, 1894, NPG. WALTER STONEMAN, two portraits, 1924 and 1936, hs and hl seated (x4648), NPG (NPR).

LUMBY, Joseph Rawson (1831-1895) author and divine.
PR UNKNOWN, after a photograph by Russell, hs, wood engr, for *Illust London News*, 30 Nov 1895, NPG.

LUMLEY, Benjamin (1811-1875) author and manager of the opera in London.
PR UNKNOWN after A.D'Orsay, hl, profile, lith, 1847, NPG.

LUMSDEN, Sir Harry Burnett (1821-1896) lieutenant-general.
PR R J LANE, 1865, hs, lith, NPG. UNKNOWN, hs in uniform, lith, BM.

LUNDGREN, Egron Sellif (1815-1875) water-colour painter.
PR UNKNOWN, after a photograph of 1874, hs, woodcut, for *Illust London News*, 8 Jan 1876, NPG. Two woodcuts by unknown artists, both hs, BM.

LUNN, Sir Henry Simpson (1859-1939) founder of the Lunn travel agency.
C 'ELF', wl playing at curling, Hentschel-Colourtype, for *Vanity Fair*, 6 Oct 1909, NPG.

LUSH, Sir Charles Montague (1853-1930) judge.
C 'APE' Junior, tql seated, Hentschel-Colourtype, for *Vanity Fair*, 18 Jan 1911, NPG.

LUSH, Sir Robert (1807-1881) judge.
P UNKNOWN, hs, Gray's Inn, London.
PR UNKNOWN, after a photograph by J. & C.Watkins, hs, woodcut, for *Illust London News*, 25 Nov 1865, NPG.
C SIR LESLIE WARD ('Spy'), hs, w/c study, for *Vanity Fair*, 31 May 1873, NPG 2730. UNKNOWN, hl at bench, chromo-lith, a 'Figaro Cartoon', NPG.
PH LOCK & WHITFIELD, hs, oval, woodburytype, for *Men of Mark*, 1881, NPG. MAULL & POLYBLANK, wl, carte, NPG.

LUSHINGTON, Edmund Law (1811-1893) Greek scholar.
SC THOMAS WOOLNER, RA 1877, bust, University of Glasgow; replica, Maidstone Museum.

LUSK, Sir Andrew, 1st Bart (1810-1909) lord mayor of London.
PR UNKNOWN, after a photograph by Disderi, hs, circle, woodcut, for *Illust London News*, 15 Nov 1873, NPG.
C 'FAUSTIN', wl in mayor's robes, chromo-lith, for 'The London Sketch Book', NPG, V & A. UNKNOWN, wl, chromo-lith, for *Vanity Fair*, 7 Oct 1871, NPG.
PH MAULL & CO, wl, carte, NPG (Album 136).

LYALL, Sir Alfred Comyn (1835-1911) Indian civil servant and writer.

P J.J.SHANNON, 1890, wl, University of Allahabad, India; copy by H.J.HUDSON, hs (cut down), NPG 2170. CHRISTOPHER WILLIAMS, 1908, Dulwich College, London.

PR VIOLET, DUCHESS OF RUTLAND, 1892, hs, profile, lith, NPG. C.W.SHERBORN, after J.J.Shannon, hs, etch, one of 'Grillion's Club' series, BM.

LYGON, Frederick, see 6th Earl of Beauchamp.

LYNE, Joseph Leycester (Father Ignatius) (1837-1908) preacher.

D Two drgs, both hl profile, 1867, w/c and 1897, pencil, NPG.

C CARLO PELLEGRINI ('Ape'), wl, profile, in monk's robes, chromo-lith, for Vanity Fair, 9 April 1887, NPG.

PH W. & D.DOWNEY, hs, woodburytype, for Cassell's Cabinet Portrait Gallery, vol II, 1891, NPG. MASON & CO, two cartes, wl and wl seated, NPG AX7504 and X12118. SAMUEL A.WALKER, hs, profile, carte, NPG (Album 40).

LYON, Claude George Bowes-, see 14th and 1st Earl of STRATHMORE and Kinghorne.

LYONS, Richard Bickerton Pemell Lyons, 1st Earl (1817-1887) diplomat.

PR UNKNOWN, tql seated, lith, for The Whitehall Review, 23 March 1878, NPG. UNKNOWN, after a photograph by Maull & Co, hs, woodcut, for Illust London News, 18 May 1878, NPG.

C CARLO PELLEGRINI ('Ape'), wl, w/c study, for Vanity Fair, 6 April 1878, NPG 1995.

LYSONS, Sir Daniel (1816-1898) major-general.

PR R.T., after a photograph by Done and Ball, hs in uniform, wood engr, for Illust London News, 15 March 1890, NPG.

C SIR LESLIE WARD ('Spy'), wl, profile, chromo-lith, for Vanity Fair, 13 April 1878, NPG.

PH LOCK & WHITFIELD, hs, oval, woodburytype, for Men of Mark, 1882, NPG.

LYTE, Sir Henry Churchill Maxwell (1848-1940) deputy keeper of the public records and historian.

P S.M.FISHER, 1933, hl, NPG 3937.

PH WALTER STONEMAN, 1930, hs, profile, NPG (NPR).

LYTTELTON, Alfred (1857-1913) lawyer, statesman and sportsman.

P P.A.DE LÁSZLÓ, tql, Eton College, Berks.

SC SIR WILLIAM GOSCOMBE JOHN, RA 1915, marble tablet, St Margaret's Church, Westminster.

PR W.ALLINGHAM, after a photograph by Smartt & Sons, tql seated, stipple and line, for Baily's Mag, 1898, NPG.

C CARLO PELLEGRINI ('Ape'), wl, playing cricket, chromo-lith, for Vanity Fair, 20 Sept 1884, NPG. SIR MAX BEERBOHM, 1908, drg, Ashmolean Museum, Oxford.

PH ELLIOTT & FRY, hs, print, for Our Conservative and Unionist Statesmen, vol I, NPG (Album 24). SIR BENJAMIN STONE, 1904, wl, print, NPG.

LYTTELTON, Arthur Temple (1852-1903) suffragan bishop of Southampton.

PH UNKNOWN, hs, print, NPG (Anglican Bishops).

LYTTELTON, Edward (1855-1942) schoolmaster, divine and cricketer.

P HENRY HARRIS BROWN, 1905, Haileybury College, Herts. THOMAS BINNEY GIBBS, tql, Lady Margaret School, Parsons Green, London.

D SIR WILLIAM ROTHENSTEIN, 1923, head, profile, sanguine, NPG 4783. SIR WILLIAM ROTHENSTEIN, Eton College, Berks.

C SIR LESLIE WARD ('Spy'), wl, chromo-lith, for Vanity Fair, 9 May 1901, NPG.

PH JOHN RUSSELL & SONS, hs, print, for National Photographic Record, vol I, NPG.

LYTTELTON, Sir Neville Gerald (1845-1931) general.

P ARCHIBALD STUART-WORTLEY, 1893, hl in uniform, Royal Hospital, Chelsea. HENRY HARRIS BROWN, c1912-13, seated in uniform, Royal Hospital, Chelsea. HENRY HARRIS BROWN, in general's uniform, Hagley Hall, W Midlands.

C SIR LESLIE WARD ('Spy'), tql in uniform, chromo-lith, for Vanity Fair, 5 Sept 1901, NPG.

LYTTELTON, William Henry (1820-1884) canon of Gloucester.

P JOHN JACKSON, as a child with his mother Sarah Spencer (Lady Lyttelton), Althorp, Northants. A.R.VENABLES, hs as a child, circle, Hagley Hall, W Midlands.

LYTTELTON of Frankley, George William Lyttelton, 4th Baron (1817-1876) lord-lieutenant of Worcestershire and under-secretary of state for the colonies.

P GEORGE RICHMOND, 1876, hl, Hagley Hall, W Midlands.

D GEORGE RICHMOND, c1844, head, crayon, Hagley Hall.

PR F.C.LEWIS, after a drg by G.Richmond, hs, stipple, one of 'Grillion's Club' series, BM, NPG. UNKNOWN, after a photograph by R.W.Thrupp, hs, woodcut, for Illust London News, 29 April 1876, NPG.

C CARLO PELLEGRINI ('Ape'), wl seated, chromo-lith, for Vanity Fair, 1 April 1871, NPG.

PH ERNEST EDWARDS, wl, print, for Men of Eminence, ed L.Reeve, vol III, 1865, NPG. F.R.WINDOW, wl, carte, NPG AX7441.

LYTTON, Edward George Earle Lytton Bulwer-Lytton, 1st Baron (1803-1873) novelist.

P T.M.VON HOLST, wl as a youth, Knebworth, Herts. H.W.PICKERSGILL, c1831, tql seated, NPG 1277. DANIEL MACLISE, 1850, wl, Knebworth; copies, Trinity College, Cambridge and Hughenden (NT), Bucks. E.M.WARD, 1851, wl seated in his study, Knebworth.

D A.E.CHALON, 1828, tql seated, w/c, Knebworth. SIR LESLIE WARD & T.MACQUOID, 1873, in the great hall at Knebworth, w/c, Knebworth. M.B.FOSTER, hs, pencil, V & A. DANIEL MACLISE, wl seated, ink, V & A.

G F.BROMLEY, after B.R.Haydon, 'The Reform Banquet, 1832', etch, pub 1835, NPG. JOHN PHILLIP, 'The House of Commons, 1860', oil, Palace of Westminster, London. C.G.LEWIS, after T.J.Barker, 'The Intellect and Valour of Great Britain', mixed engr, pub 1864, NPG.

SC FRANÇOIS LÉQUINE, called Lytton, parian-ware bust, Knebworth. UNKNOWN, marble medallion, inset into a mantlepiece, Knebworth.

PR J.THOMSON, after F.R.Say, hl seated, profile, stipple, for New Monthly Mag, 1831, BM, NPG. D.MACLISE, wl standing before a cheval glass, no 27 of his 'Gallery of Illustrious Literary Characters', for Fraser's Mag, 1832, BM, NPG. COUNT A.D'ORSAY, 1837, hl seated, profile, lith, NPG. SIR E.LANDSEER, with Count A.D'Orsay and Lady Blessington, lith, 1840, Royal Coll. A.D'ORSAY, 1845, hl seated, profile, lith, NPG. G.COOK, after R.J.Lane, hs, stipple, pub 1848, NPG.

C JOHN DOYLE, c1839, wl with Disraeli, pencil, BM. CARLO PELLEGRINI ('Ape'), wl, chromo-lith, for Vanity Fair, 29 Oct 1870, NPG.

PH MAYALL, three cartes, two wl seated, one hs, NPG.

LYTTON, Edward Robert Bulwer-Lytton, 1st Earl of (1831-1891) Viceroy of India.

P SIR J.E.MILLAIS, 1876, tql, V & A. G.F.WATTS, 1884, hl, NPG 1007; related sketch, Knebworth, Herts.

M UNKNOWN, tql with his mother, Knebworth.
G VAL PRINSEP, 'Imperial Assemblage held at Delhi by the Viceroy', oil, RA 1880, Royal Coll.
SC SIR ALFRED GILBERT, marble roundel, Knebworth.
PR J.BROWN, after Baron Legrange, hl seated, stipple, NPG. G.PILOTELL, hs, drypoint, BM. E.STODART, after a photograph by Bassano, hl, stipple and line, NPG.
C HARRY FURNISS, pen and ink sketch, NPG 3488.
PH LOCK & WHITFIELD, hs, woodburytype, for *Men of Mark*, 1876, NPG. UNKNOWN, hs, profile, print, NPG. UNKNOWN, hs, woodburytype, NPG.

LYTTON, Rosina Bulwer-Lytton, Lady, née Wheeler
(1802–1882) novelist.
M UNKNOWN, hl with her son Teddy, later 1st Earl of Lytton, Knebworth, Herts.
PR J.JEWELL PENSTONE, after a drg of 1852 by A.E.Chalon, head, stipple, NPG.

LYVEDEN, Robert Vernon Smith, 1st Baron (1800–1873)
president of Board of Control.
G SIR GEORGE HAYTER, 'The House of Commons, 1833', oil, NPG 54.
SC MATTHEW NOBLE, 1876, marble recumbent effigy, St Andrew's Church, Brigstock, Northants.

M

MAAS, Joseph (1847-1886) singer.
PR UNKNOWN, hs, wood engr, for *Illust London News*, 6 Feb 1886, NPG.

MABERLY, Catherine Charlotte, née Prittie (1805-1875) novelist.
PR W.H.MOTE, after A.E.Chalon, tql seated playing harp, stipple, octagon, for Heath's *Book of Beauty*, 1839, BM, NPG. T.LANDSEER, after F.Grant, wl on horseback, mezz, pub 1840, BM, NPG. A.D'ORSAY, tql, profile, lith, BM. J.THOMSON, after W.C.Ross, tql, octagon, stipple, BM, NPG.

MacALISTER, Sir Donald, 1st Bart (1854-1934) physician.
P MAURICE GREIFFENHAGEN, 1924, General Medical Council, London. GEORGE HENRY, *c*1924, University of Glasgow.
PH OLIVE EDIS, tql seated, print, NPG. WALTER STONEMAN, 1924, hs, NPG (NPR).

MACARA, Sir Charles Wright, 1st Bart (1845-1929) cotton manufacturer and philanthropist.
C ALICK P.F.RITCHIE, wl, profile, chromo-lith, for *Vanity Fair*, 13 March 1912, NPG.

McARTHUR, Sir William (1809-1887) lord mayor of London.
PR UNKNOWN, hs, woodcut, NPG.
C SIR LESLIE WARD ('Spy'), wl with mayor's chain of office, chromo-lith, for *Vanity Fair*, 8 Oct 1881, NPG.
PH UNKNOWN, Guildhall Library and Art Gallery, London.

MACAULAY, Thomas Babington Macaulay, 1st Baron (1800-1859) historian, poet and statesman.
P HENRY INMAN, 1844–45, hs, Pennsylvania Academy of Fine Arts, Philadelphia, USA. JOHN PARTRIDGE, 1849–53, hl seated, profile, (study for NPG 342,3), NPG 1564. SIR JOHN WATSON GORDON, 1850, tql seated, University of Glasgow; related portrait, SNPG 1585. SIR FRANCIS GRANT, 1853, hl seated, NPG 453. E.M.WARD, 1853, wl seated in his study, NPG 4882. JAMES ARCHER, 1880, after a photograph by Claudet of *c*1856, Reform Club, London.
G F.BROMLEY, after B.R.Haydon, 'The Reform Banquet, 1832', etch, pub 1835, NPG. S.W.REYNOLDS, 'The Reform Bill Receiving the King's Assent', oil, 1832, Palace of Westminster, London. SIR GEORGE HAYTER, 'The House of Commons, 1833', oil, NPG 54. JOHN PARTRIDGE, 'The Fine Arts Commissioners, 1846', NPG 342,3. SIR GEORGE SCHARF, 'The Funeral of Lord Macaulay', pen and ink, 1860, NPG 2689. T.J.BARKER, after C.G.Lewis, 'The Intellect and Valour of Great Britain', mixed engr, pub 1864, NPG.
C PATRIC PARK, 1846, plaster bust, Wallington (NT), Northumberland. BARON CARLO MAROCHETTI, 1848, bronze medallions, NPG 257, SNPG 559, and National Liberal Club, London. GEORGE BURNARD, 1866, marble bust, Westminster Abbey, London. THOMAS WOOLNER, 1868, marble statue, seated, Trinity College, Cambridge.
PR INCHBOLD, after I.Atkinson, lith, pub 1832, Trinity College, Cambridge. L.HAGHE, after J.N.Rhodes, hl, lith, *c*1832, BM. S.W.REYNOLDS sen, after S.W.Reynolds jun, hl, mezz, pub 1833, BM, NPG. W.HOLL, after G.Richmond, hs, stipple, *c*1850, BM. J.BROWN, after E.U.Eddis, hs, stipple, for *Bentley's Mis-*

cellany, 1852, BM, NPG. W.GREATBACH, after E.U.Eddis, hl seated, line, for *Critical and Historical Essays*, 1857, NPG. Several prints after photographs by Claudet and Maull and Polyblank, NPG.
C JOHN DOYLE, two political cartoons, drgs, BM.
PH UNKNOWN, after Claudet, hl, photogravure, NPG. MAULL & CO, hs, carte, NPG. MAULL & POLYBLANK, 1856, tql, print, NPG AX7926.

McAVOY, Margaret (1800-1820) blind girl who was said to be able to distinguish colours by touch.
PR UNKNOWN, hl, stipple, pub 1819, NPG.

MACBETH, Robert Walker (1848-1910) painter.
P Self-portrait, 1883, hs, semi-profile, MacDonald Collection, Aberdeen Art Gallery.
G G.Grenville MANTON, 'Conversazione at the Royal Academy, 1891', w/c, NPG 2820.
PR UNKNOWN, hs, profile, woodcut, for *Illust London News*, 12 May 1883, NPG. Self-portrait, hl standing with F.Goulding over copperplate press, etch, headpiece to private view card of Messrs Agnew, Liverpool, 1886, BM.
PH RALPH W.ROBINSON, wl, print, for *Members and Associates of the Royal Academy of Arts, 1891*, NPG X7375.

M'CABE, Edward (1816-1885) cardinal.
SC SIR THOMAS FARRELL, recumbent figure on tomb, Glasnevin Cemetery.
PR JUDD & CO, tql, lith, for *The Whitehall Review*, 22 Nov 1879, NPG. UNKNOWN, hs, wood engr, for *Illust London News*, 22 April 1882, NPG.
PH FRATELLI D'ALESSANDRI, hs, carte, NPG.

MACCALL, William (1812-1888) unitarian minister; writer on ethics.
PR UNKNOWN, tql, mezz, BM.

MacCALLUM, Andrew (1821-1902) landscape painter.
PH UNKNOWN, hs, carte, NPG (Album 103).

MACCARTHY, Denis Florence (1817-1882) poet.
P UNKNOWN, NGI 1295.

McCARTHY, Dame (Emma) Maud (1858-1949) Army matron-in-chief.
D AUSTIN O.SPARE, pastel, IWM.

McCARTHY, Justin (1830-1912) politician and writer.
P HAROLD WAITE, *c*1907, NGI 1210.
D S.P.HALL, three pencil sketches, NPG 2284 and 2387–88. FREDERICK PEGRAM, pencil sketch made at the sessions of the Parnell Commission, V & A.
C HARRY FURNISS, two pen and ink sketches, NPG 3591 and 3620. SIR LESLIE WARD ('Spy'), wl seated, chromo-lith, for *Vanity Fair*, 23 May 1885, NPG.
PH LONDON STEREOSCOPIC CO, *c*1881, hs, semi-profile, carte, NPG. BARRAUD, hs, print, for *Men and Women of the Day*, vol IV, 1891, NPG AX5542. W. & D.DOWNEY, tql seated, woodburytype, for Cassell's *Cabinet Portrait Gallery*, vol IV, 1893, NPG. WALERY, tql, print, NPG.

McCHEYNE, Robert Murray (1813-1843) minister of St Peter's, Dundee.

PR J. LE CONTE, after H.J.Stewart, hl, profile, aged 21, stipple, NPG.

MACCLESFIELD, Thomas Augustus Wolstenholme Parker, 9th Earl of (1811-1896) landowner.
PR J.BROWN, after a photograph, hs, stipple, for *Baily's Mag*, 1867, BM, NPG.
C SIR LESLIE WARD ('Spy'), wl, profile, w/c study, for *Vanity Fair*, 22 Oct 1881, NPG 4727.

McCLINTOCK, Sir Francis Leopold (1819-1907) admiral.
P STEPHEN PEARCE, 1856, hl in uniform, NPG 1226; replica, NPG 919, and version, 1859, tql, NPG 1211.
SC J.R.KIRK, exhib 1862, marble bust, Royal Dublin Society.
PR UNKNOWN, after a photograph by Beard, hl seated, 'The Arctic Searching Squadron', woodcut, for *Illust London News*, 1 May 1852, NPG. UNKNOWN, after a photograph by Beard, hl, woodcut, for *Illust London News*, 8 Oct 1859, NPG. D.J.POUND, after a photograph by Cheyne, tql in uniform, stipple and line, for *Drawing Room Portrait Gallery of Eminent Personages*, NPG. W.H.MOTE, hs, stipple, NPG. UNKNOWN, hs in uniform, chromo-lith, NPG.
PH LOCK & WHITFIELD, hs, oval, woodburytype, for *Men of Mark*, 1878, NPG. UNKNOWN, wl, carte, NPG. UNKNOWN, hs in uniform, print, NPG (Album 38).

McCLURE, Sir Robert John Le Mesurier (1807-1873) vice-admiral and arctic explorer.
P STEPHEN PEARCE, 1855, tql in arctic dress, NPG 1210.
PR UNKNOWN, wl in uniform, profile, lith, pub 1854, NPG.

MacCOLL, Dugald Sutherland (1859-1948) painter, critic and gallery director.
P D.G.MacLaren, c1906, hs, TATE 5778.
D ALPHONSE LEGROS, 1897, hs, silverpoint, NPG 4857. POWYS EVANS, 1922, pen sketch, The Athenaeum, London. FRANCIS DODD, 1939, hl seated, chalk, NPG 4424. PHILIP WILSON STEER, w/c sketch, The Athenaeum.
G SIR WILLIAM ORPEN, 'The Selecting Jury of the New English Art Club', 1909, oil, NPG 2556. SIR WILLIAM ORPEN, 'Homage to Manet', oil, 1909, Manchester City Art Gallery.
C SIR MAX BEERBOHM, 'A quiet morning at the Tate Gallery', drg, 1907, TATE. D.G.MacLaren, 'Some Members of the New English Art Club', w/c, NPG 2663. HENRY TONKS, as Don Quixote, with William Rothenstein as Sancho Panza, w/c over pencil, BM.
PH G.C.BERESFORD, 1906, hs, profile, neg, NPG x6625. JOHN RUSSELL & SONS, hs, print, for *National Photographic Record*, vol II, NPG.

MacCOLL, Norman (1843-1904) editor of the *Athenaeum* and Spanish scholar.
P CLEGG WILKINSON, replica, Downing College, Cambridge.

MacCORMAC, Sir William, 1st Bart (1836-1901) surgeon.
P PRINCE PIERRE TROUBETZKOY, 1891, tql seated, Royal College of Surgeons, London. HENRY HARRIS BROWN, 1897, tql seated in robes, Queen's University, Belfast. UNKNOWN, St Thomas's Hospital, London.
SC ALFRED DRURY, marble bust, St Thomas's Hospital; replica, Royal College of Surgeons.
C SIR LESLIE WARD ('Spy'), tql, chromo-lith, for *Vanity Fair*, 1 Oct 1896, NPG.
PH W. & D.DOWNEY, hl, woodburytype, for Cassell's *Cabinet Portrait Gallery*, vol V, 1894, NPG.

McCORMICK, Robert (1800-1890) naval surgeon and naturalist.
P STEPHEN PEARCE, c1856, hs in uniform, NPG 1216.

McCORMICK, Sir William Symington (1859-1930)

scholar and administrator.
P SIR WILLIAM ORPEN, 1920, wl, TATE 3628.

McCULLAGH, James (1809-1847) mathematician.
D SIR F.W.BURTON, four pencil sketches, heads, NGI 2031.
SC CHRISTOPHER MOORE, RA 1849, marble bust, Trinity College, Dublin.

McCULLOCH, Horatio (1805-1867) landscape painter.
P SIR DANIEL MACNEE, 1858, hs, NGS 610. SIR DANIEL MACNEE, SNPG 233.
D T.F.HEAPHY, with William Borthwick Johnstone, ink, SNPG 1783. SIR DANIEL MACNEE, 1828, chalk, SNPG 356.
SC PATRIC PARK, exhib 1849, marble bust, Royal Scottish Academy, Edinburgh.
PR J.SMYTH, after D.Macnee, tql seated with canvas and brush, line, for *Art Union Journal*, 1847, BM, NPG.
PH J.G.TUNNY, wl, carte, NPG (Album 106).

MacDERMOT, Hugh Hyacinth O'Rorke, 'The MacDermot' (1834-1904) attorney-general for Ireland.
PR UNKNOWN, hs, sketch, woodcut, for *Illust London News*, 3 Dec 1887, NPG.

MACDERMOTT, Gilbert Hastings (1845-1901) music-hall singer.
PR Various theatrical prints, Harvard Theatre Collection, Cambridge, Mass, USA.

MACDONA, John Cumming (1836-1907) president of the Kennel Club.
C SIR LESLIE WARD ('Spy'), wl, w/c study, for *Vanity Fair*, 8 Feb 1894, NPG 2973.
PH SIR BENJAMIN STONE, 1902, wl with his two nieces, print, NPG.

MACDONALD, Sir Claude Maxwell (1852-1915) soldier and diplomat.
C SIR LESLIE WARD ('Spy'), wl, chromo-lith, for *Vanity Fair*, 1 Oct 1901, NPG.

MacDONALD, George (1824-1905) poet and novelist.
P SIR GEORGE REID, 1868, two related portraits, both hs, NPG 201 and Marischall College, Aberdeen. CECILIA HARRISON, 1897, SNPG 665.
SC GEORGE ANDERSON LAWSON, 187(3), copper bust, Royal Scottish Academy, Edinburgh, on loan to SNPG (L108). ALEXANDER MUNRO, bronze medallion, SNPG 972.
PR UNKNOWN, hs, profile, chromo-lith, BM. GEORGE COOK, after photograph by Elliott & Fry, hs, profile, stipple, NPG.
PH Attrib C.L.DODGSON, hl seated, print, NPG P36. ELLIOTT & FRY, hs, carte, NPG (Album 99). ELLIOTT & FRY, tql seated, cabinet, NPG. ELLIOTT & FRY, hs, profile, carte, NPG. DR WALLICH, hl profile, carte, NPG. H.J.WHITLOCK, hs, carte, NPG (Album 102).

MACDONALD, Sir Hector Archibald (1853-1903) major-general.
C SIR LESLIE WARD ('Spy'), 'A General Group', chromo-lith, for *Vanity Fair*, 29 Nov 1900, NPG.

MACDONALD, Hugh (1817-1860) writer.
P A.S.MACKAY, Glasgow City Art Gallery.

MACDONALD, Sir John Alexander (1815-1891) prime minister of Canada.
P A.D.PATTERSON (copy), hl, Public Archives of Canada, Ottawa.
SC C.B.BIRCH, plaster statuette, NPG 1550. W.M.REYNOLDS STEPHENS, bronze bust, DoE (Ottawa). G.E.WADE, marble bust, St Paul's Cathedral, London, and bronze statue, Montreal.
PR UNKNOWN, hs, chromo-lith, NPG.
PH BASSANO, two cabinets, hs, and hs, profile, NPG. UNKNOWN, seated, photogravure, NPG.

McDONALD, John Blake (1829-1901) artist.
D J.R.ABERCROMBY, wash, SNPG 1743.

MACDONALD, John Hay Athole, see Lord Kingsburgh.

MACDONALD, Sir Reginald John (1820-1899) admiral.
C SIR LESLIE WARD ('Spy'), wl, w/c study, for *Vanity Fair*, 7 Feb 1880, NPG 2583.

MACDONELL, Arthur Anthony (1854-1930) Sanskrit scholar.
PH WALTER STONEMAN, 1918, hs, NPG (NPR).

MACDONELL, Sir John (1845-1921) jurist.
PH JOHN RUSSELL & SONS, hl seated, print, for *National Photographic Record*, vol I, NPG.

MACDONNELL, John J. (1825-1900) general.
C SIR LESLIE WARD ('Spy'), wl, w/c study, for *Vanity Fair*, 7 Oct 1882, NPG 2584.

MacDONNELL, Antony Patrick MacDonnell, Baron (1844-1925) statesman.
P SIR WILLIAM ORPEN, c1905-6, hl seated with ribbon and star, Municipal Gallery of Modern Art, Dublin. J.B.YEATS, Municipal Gallery of Modern Art.
SC SIR GEORGE FRAMPTON, c1905, statue, Lucknow.
C SIR LESLIE WARD ('Spy'), wl, chromo-lith, for *Vanity Fair*, 3 Aug 1905, NPG.
PH WALTER STONEMAN, 1920, hs, NPG (NPR). W.H.WARBURTON, wl seated with others, print, NPG.

MACDONNELL, Sir Richard Graves (1814-1881) colonial governor.
PR UNKNOWN, hs, wood engr, for *Illust London News*, 5 March 1881, NPG.

MACE, James (Jem Mace) (1831-1910) pugilist.
PH HAINES, hs, print, NPG.

MACEWEN, Sir William (1848-1924) surgeon.
P C.R.DOWELL, hs, Royal College of Surgeons, Edinburgh.
SC GEORGE PAULIN, 1925, marble bust, SNPG 1101.
PH T. & R.ANNAN & SONS, hl seated, print, NPG.

MACFARLANE, John (1807-1874) Scottish divine.
PR E.BURTON, after N.Macbeth, tql seated, mezz, pub 1858, BM.

MACFARREN, Sir George Alexander (1813-1887) musical composer.
PR UNKNOWN, after a photograph by Herbert Watkins, hs, profile, oval, woodcut, for *Illust London News*, 24 April 1875, NPG.
PH LOCK & WHITFIELD, hs, oval, woodburytype, for *Men of Mark*, 1881, NPG.

McGEE, Thomas d'Arcy (1825-1868) Irish-Canadian statesman and poet.
P D.J.HURLEY, 1867, nearly tql, Public Archives of Canada, Ottawa.

MACGREGOR, Sir Charles Metcalfe (1840-1887) general.
PR UNKNOWN, after a photograph by Suscipi of Rome, hs in uniform, wood engr, for *Illust London News*, 20 Sept 1879, NPG.

MACGREGOR, John ('Rob Roy') (1825-1892) traveller and philanthropist.
PR BUTTERWORTH & HEATH, hl seated, circle, woodcut, for *Reformatory and Refuge Journal*, 1874, BM.
PH ELLIOTT & FRY, hs, carte, NPG. ELLIOTT & FRY, two prints, hs and hl, NPG. MAULL & FOX, hs, cabinet, NPG. HENRY WAYLAND, with his family, cabinet, NPG. WINDOW & GROVE, hs, photogravure, NPG.

MACHELL, James Octavius (1837-1902) captain.

C SIR LESLIE WARD ('Spy'), wl, profile, chromo-lith, for *Vanity Fair*, 3 Dec 1887, NPG.

MACHRAY, Robert (1831-1904) archbishop of Rupert's Land and primate of all Canada.
PH UNKNOWN, wl, print, NPG (Anglican Bishops).

McIAN, Robert Ranald or Ronald (1803-1856) artist.
P JOHN STONE, SNPG 2033.
D FANNY McIAN, chalk, SNPG 2034.

McILWRAITH, Sir Thomas (1835-1900) premier of Queensland.
PR UNKNOWN, hs, wood engr, for *Illust London News*, 30 Dec 1882, NPG.

McINTOSH, William Carmichael (1838-1931) zoologist.
P JAMES CAW, c1880, Linnean Society, London. J.LESSELS, oil?, University of St Andrews. M.ROSS, oil?, University of St Andrews.
PH WALTER STONEMAN, 1919, hs, NPG (NPR). UNKNOWN, hl seated, photogravure, NPG X1684.

MACKAIL, John William (1859-1945) classical scholar.
PH ELLIOTT & FRY, hs, print, NPG.

MACKARNESS, John Fielder (1820-1889) bishop of Oxford.
P W.W.OULESS, 1881, hl seated, Cuddesdon College, Oxford.
SC UNKNOWN, bronze plaque with portrait medallion, Christ Church, Oxford.
PR UNKNOWN, after a photograph by W.T. & R.Gowland, hs, woodcut, for *Illust London News*, 1 Jan 1870, NPG.

MACKAY, Aeneas James George (1839-1911) historian.
D J.H.LORIMER, 1890, pencil, SNPG 1354. W.GRAHAM BOSS, pencil, SNPG 1698.

MACKAY, Alexander (1808-1852) journalist.
PR C.S.HERVÉ, hl, lith, BM.

MACKAY, Charles (1814-1889) poet and journalist.
G P.NAUMANN, & R.TAYLOR & Co, hs, one of a series of woodcuts, 'Our Literary Contributors – Past and Present', for *Illust London News*, 14 May 1892, BM, NPG.
PR W.ROFFE, after a photograph by C.Watkins, hl seated, stipple, NPG. CHARLES COOK, after J.O.Murray, hs, stipple, NPG.

MACKAY, Donald James, see 11th Baron Reay.

MACKAY, James Lyle, see 1st Earl of Inchcape.

MACKAY, Mary ('Marie Corelli') (1855-1924) novelist.
P HELEN DONALD-SMITH, 1897, tql, NPG 4891.
PH G.GABELL, 1906, tql, photogravure, NPG X6820.

MACKENNAL, Alexander (1835-1904) Congregational minister.
PR UNKNOWN, after a photograph by Martin and Sallnow, hs, profile, wood engr, for *Illust London News*, 31 Oct 1891, NPG.

MACKENZIE, Alexander (1822-1892) first liberal premier of the Canadian Dominion.
PR UNKNOWN, hs, chromo-lith, NPG.

MACKENZIE, Sir Alexander Campbell (1847-1935) composer and principal of the Royal Academy of Music.
P RENÉ DE L'HÔPITAL, 1923, Royal Academy of Music, London.
D FLORA LION, head, pencil, NPG 3972.
C HARRY FURNISS, pen and ink sketch, NPG 3490. SIR LESLIE WARD ('Spy'), wl, profile, chromo-lith, for *Vanity Fair*, 14 Jan 1904, NPG.
PH W. & D.DOWNEY, hl, profile, woodburytype, for *Cassell's Cabinet Portrait Gallery*, vol V, 1894, NPG. JOHN RUSSELL & SONS,

hl, print, for *National Photographic Record*, vol II, NPG. WALTER STONEMAN, 1922, hs, NPG (NPR). VANDYK, tql with Sir Edward German, print, NPG. WALERY, tql, print, NPG.

MACKENZIE, Charles (1805-1877), see Henry Compton.

MACKENZIE, Charles Frederick (1825-1862) missionary bishop of Central Africa.
P UNKNOWN, Caius College, Cambridge.
PR DALZIEL, hs, circle, woodcut, BM.

MACKENZIE, Colin (1806-1881) lieutenant-general.
PR UNKNOWN, after a photograph by Bassano, hs, profile, wood engr, for *Illust London News*, 12 Nov 1881, NPG.

MACKENZIE, Sir George Sutherland (1844-1910) explorer and administrator.
PR UNKNOWN, hs, wood engr, for *Illust London News*, 24 Aug 1889, NPG.

MACKENZIE, Henry (1808-1878) bishop of Nottingham.
PR UNKNOWN, after a photograph by John Watkins, hs, woodcut, for *Illust London News*, 5 March 1870, NPG. UNKNOWN, after a photograph by Maull & Co, hs, wood engr, for *Illust London News*, 26 Oct 1878, NPG.

MACKENZIE, Sir Morell (1837-1892) physician.
P UNKNOWN, hl, Royal College of Physicians, London. UNKNOWN, hl, Royal Society of Medicine, London.
PR UNKNOWN, hs, wood engr, for *Illust London News*, 24 Sept 1887, NPG. UNKNOWN, after a photograph by Elliott & Fry, hs, profile, wood engr, for *Illust London News*, 13 Feb 1892, NPG.
C CARLO PELLEGRINI ('Ape'), wl, profile, chromo-lith, for *Vanity Fair*, 15 Oct 1887, NPG.

MACKENZIE, Sir Stephen (1844-1909) physician.
PH OLIVE EDIS, tql seated, print, NPG.

MACKENZIE, William Bell (1806-1870) incumbent of St James' Holloway; writer.
PR T.H.MAGUIRE, after L.Stocks, hl, lith, BM.

MACKENZIE, William Forbes (1807-1862) politician.
SL AUGUSTIN EDOUART, 1830, SNPG 833.

MacKINLAY, Antoinette, née Sterling (1843?-1904) singer.
P J.D.PENROSE, 1891, tql, Royal Society of Musicians, London.
D LOUISE V.BLANDY, 1880, head, profile, chalk, NPG 2774.
PR UNKNOWN, after a photograph by Fradelle & Marshall, hs, woodcut, for *Illust London News*, 24 April 1875, NPG. UNKNOWN, tql, lith, BM. Several theatrical prints, Harvard Theatre Collection, Cambridge, Mass, USA.
PH BARRAUD, tql, print, for *Men and Women of the Day*, vol I, 1888, NPG AX5431. WALERY, hl, profile, cabinet, NPG.

McKINLAY, John (1819-1872) Australian explorer.
PR UNKNOWN, hs, woodcut, for *Illust London News*, 14 Jan 1865, NPG.

MACKINNON, Sir William, 1st Bart (1823-1893) founder of British East Africa Company.
PR UNKNOWN, hs, wood engr, for *Illust London News*, 24 Aug 1889, NPG.

MACKINNON, Sir William Henry (1852-1929) general.
C SIR LESLIE WARD ('Spy'), wl in uniform, chromo-lith, for *Vanity Fair*, 7 Feb 1901, NPG.
PH WALTER STONEMAN, 1917, hs in uniform, NPG (NPR).

MACKONOCHIE, Alexander Heriot (1825-1887) divine.
D UNKNOWN, 1867, hl, profile, in pulpit, sketch, NPG.
PR 'R.T.', hs, wood engr, for *Illust London News*, 31 Dec 1887, NPG.
C CARLO PELLEGRINI ('Ape'), wl, chromo-lith, for *Vanity Fair*, 31

Dec 1870, NPG.
PH SAMUEL A.WALKER, tql, carte, NPG (Album 40).

MACLAGAN, William Dalrymple (1826-1910) archbishop of York.
P SIR HUBERT VON HERKOMER, RA 1892, tql seated in robes, Diocese of Lichfield; replica, Bishopthorpe Palace, York. A.U.SOORD, 1903, wl wearing cope, St William's College, York. E.A.ABBEY, a study for the Coronation of Edward VII, 1904, Yale University, New Haven, USA. JOHN COLLIER, 1909, Peterhouse, Cambridge.
G S.P.HALL, 'The Bench of Bishops, 1902', w/c, NPG 2369. E.A.ABBEY, 'The Coronation of King Edward VII, 1902', oil, 1904, Royal Coll.
C SIR LESLIE WARD ('Spy'), wl, chromo-lith, for *Vanity Fair*, 5 Sept 1891, NPG.
PH LOCK & WHITFIELD, hs, oval, woodburytype, for *Men of Mark*, 1881, NPG. ROTARY PHOTO, hs, postcard, NPG. UNKNOWN, hl, print, NPG (Anglican Bishops).

MACLAREN, Alexander (1826-1910) pastor at the Union Chapel, Manchester.
P SIR GEORGE REID, tql, Manchester City Art Gallery.

McLAREN, Charles Benjamin Bright, see 1st Baron Aberconway.

McLAREN, Duncan (1800-1886) lord provost of Edinburgh.
P EDWARD JOHN GREGORY, hs, SNPG 333.
D SIR GEORGE REID, ink, SNPG 303.

MACLAREN, Ian (pseudonym), see John Watson.

McLAREN, John McLaren, Lord (1831-1910) Scottish judge.
SC OTTILIE WALLACE (his daughter), 1920, marble bust, Faculty of Advocates, Parliament Hall, Edinburgh.

MACLEAN, Sir Harry Aubrey de Vere (1848-1920) military adviser in Morocco.
D UNKNOWN, wl, profile, pencil, SNPG 2196.
C SIR LESLIE WARD ('Spy'), wl in Moroccan dress, chromo-lith, for *Vanity Fair*, 25 Feb 1904, NPG.

MACLEAN, Letitia Elizabeth, see Landon.

MACLEAR, George Frederick (1833-1902) theological writer.
P S.P.HALL, *c*1902, King's College School, Wimbledon, London.

MACLEAY, Kenneth (1802-1878) miniature painter.
P JOHN GIBSON, SNPG 1427.
PH D.O.HILL & ROBERT ADAMSON, 1843-8, wl, print, NPG P6 (101).

McLENNAN, John Ferguson (1827-1881) sociologist.
SC JOHN HUTCHISON, 1892, marble bust, Trinity College Cambridge.

MACLEOD, Sir Donald Friell (1810-1872) Indian administrator.
PR UNKNOWN, hs, woodcut, for *Illust London News*, 14 Dec 1872 NPG.

MACLEOD, Fiona (pseudonym), see William Sharp.

MACLEOD, Sir George Husband Baird (1828-1892) surgeon.
PH UNKNOWN, tql seated in academic robes, print, NPG.

MACLEOD, Norman (1812-1872) divine and author.
P TAVERNOR KNOTT, 1848, tql, SNPG 633.
SC JOHN MOSSMAN, 1881, statue, Glasgow.
PR UNKNOWN, after a photograph by Elliott & Fry, hs, profile, oval woodcut, for *Illust London News*, 29 June 1872, NPG. R. &

E.TAYLOR, after Ralston & Sons, hs, semi–profile, woodcut, for *The Illust Review*, 15 July 1872, NPG. UNKNOWN, hs, woodcut, for *Great Thoughts*, 1887, BM. UNKNOWN, hs, profile, stipple, NPG.
H W. & D.DOWNEY, hs, profile, carte, NPG (Album 40). ELLIOTT & FRY, hs, profile, carte, NPG. T.RODGER, hs, carte, NPG AX7498.

MACLISE, Daniel (1806–1870) history and portrait painter.
P E.M.WARD, 1846, tql seated, NPG 616.
D Self–portrait, 1829, hs, w/c, NGI 2179. THOMAS BRIDGFORD, 1844, pencil drg, NGI 2025. Several self–portrait sketches, V & A. C.H.LEAR, 1845, two chalk sketches, hs and hs, profile, NPG 1456 (19, 20). C.W.COPE, c1846–9, painting a fresco in the House of Lords, pencil, Palace of Westminster, London. C.B.BIRCH, c1858, hs, back–view, pencil, NPG 2476.
G CLARKSON STANFIELD, 1842, with Forster, Dickens and the artist in Cornwall, w/c and body colour, V & A. Self–portrait, 1844, with others, listening to Dickens reading *The Chimes*, pencil, V & A C.G.LEWIS, after T.J.Barker, 'The Intellect and Valour of Great Britain', mixed engr, pub 1864, NPG.
C JOHN THOMAS, c1859, marble bust, NGI 8113; replica, NGI 8184. EDWARD DAVIS, 1871, marble bust, Royal Academy, London. A.B.WYON, 1878, medal, NPG, for the Art Union.
PR C.BAUGNIET, hs, lith, pub 1857, BM, NPG. M.JACKSON, after T.Scott, hl, woodcut, BM. M.L.MENPES, head, profile, drypoint, BM, NPG. D.J.POUND, after a photograph by Mayall, tql seated, stipple and line, for *Drawing Room Portrait Gallery of Eminent Personages*, BM, NPG. UNKNOWN, tql seated with canvas and brush, lith, from a drg originally pub in *Fraser's Mag*, for *Maginn's Gallery of Illustrious Literary Characters*, 1873, BM.
H ELLIOTT & FRY, hs, profile, carte, NPG (Album 99). ELLIOTT & FRY, hs, profile, carte, NPG (Album 103). LUCAS, tql, carte, NPG (Album 104). MAULL & POLYBLANK, wl, carte, NPG (Album 104). Attrib MAULL & POLYBLANK, tql, print, NPG AX7302. J. & C.WATKINS, tql seated, carte, NPG AX7558.

MACLURE, Edward Craig (1833–1906) dean of Manchester.
P MYRA E.LUXMORE, 1895, tql seated, Manchester City Art Gallery.
PR W.ROTHENSTEIN, tql seated, lith, BM. 'R.T.', after a photograph by Russell & Sons, hs, semi–profile, wood–engr for *Illust London News*, 26 July 1890, NPG.

MACLURE, Sir John William, 1st Bart (1835–1901) politician.
P UNKNOWN, hs, Museum of British Transport, York.
C SIR LESLIE WARD ('Spy'), wl, chromo–lith, for *Vanity Fair*, 22 Oct 1892, NPG.
H SIR BENJAMIN STONE, 1897, two prints, both wl, NPG.

MacMAHON, Percy Alexander (1854–1929) mathematician.
H WALTER STONEMAN, 1926, hl, NPG (NPR).

MACMILLAN, Daniel (1813–1857) publisher.
PR C.H.JEENS, after L.Dickinson, hs, stipple, for his *Life*, 1882, BM.

MACMILLAN, Sir Frederick Orridge (1851–1936) publisher.
PR F.E.JACKSON, hs, lith, BM.

McMURRICH, James Playfair (1859–1939) Canadian anatomist.
P KENNETH FORBES, University of Toronto, Canada.

MACNAGHTEN, Sir Edward Macnaghten, 4th Bart, Baron (1830–1913) judge.
P HUGH DE GLAZEBROOK, 1913, hl seated with Bath ribbon and star, Lincoln's Inn, London; replica, DoE (Privy Council).
C C.L.HARTWELL, marble bust, Lincoln's Inn.

G

C SIR LESLIE WARD ('Spy'), wl, profile, chromo–lith, for *Vanity Fair*, 31 Oct 1895, NPG.

MACNEE, Sir Daniel (1806–1882) artist.
P JAMES ARCHER, exhib 1877, tql seated, Royal Scottish Academy, Edinburgh. JAMES MACBETH, SNPG 741.
PR UNKNOWN, after a photograph by John Fergus, hs, woodcut, for *The Graphic*, NPG. UNKNOWN, hs, woodcut, for *Illust London News*, 6 May 1876, NPG.
PH MAULL & POLYBLANK, wl, carte, NPG (Album 104).

McNEILL, Sir John Carstairs (1831–1904) major–general.
PR UNKNOWN, after a photograph by W.Notman of Montreal, hs, woodcut, for *Illust London News*, 6 Dec 1873, NPG.

MacNEILL, John Gordon Swift (1849–1926) Irish politician and jurist.
C SIR LESLIE WARD ('Spy'), tql, profile, chromo–lith, for *Vanity Fair*, 13 March 1902, NPG.
PH SIR BENJAMIN STONE, 1897–1901, three prints, all wl, NPG.

MACNISH, Robert (1802–1837) physician and author.
PR D.MACLISE, wl seated, lith, for *Fraser's Mag*, 1835, BM. T.DOBBIE, after J.Ritchie, from a marble bust, line, for his *Modern Pythagorean*, 1838, BM.

MACPHERSON, Sir Herbert Taylor (1827–1886) general.
PR UNKNOWN, after a photograph by P.Vucino & Co, hs in uniform, chromo–lith, for *The Pictorial World*, 4 Nov 1882, NPG. UNKNOWN, hs in uniform, wood engr, for *Illust London News*, 30 Oct 1886, NPG.

MACPHERSON, Samuel Charters (1806–1860) political agent in India.
PR UNKNOWN, after a photograph, hs, stipple, pub 1865, NPG.

MACRORIE, William Kenneth (1831–1905) bishop of Maritzburg.
PH UNKNOWN, hl, print, NPG (Anglican Bishops).

McTAGGART, William (1835–1910) painter.
P Self–portrait, 1892, hl, SNPG L308 (on loan from NGS). SIR GEORGE REID, hs, profile, MacDonald Collection, Aberdeen Art Gallery.
D WALKER HODGSON, 1892, hs, pencil and w/c, NPG 4041(2).
PH NESBITT & LOTHIAN, hs, carte, NPG (Album 106). OLIVE EDIS, hs, profile, print, NPG.

MacWHIRTER, John (1839–1911) landscape painter.
P JAMES ARCHER, SNPG 722. JOHN PETTIE, 1882, head, MacDonald Collection, Aberdeen Art Gallery.
D SIR HUBERT VON HERKOMER, 1892, hs, w/c, SNPG 1511.
PR UNKNOWN, hs, woodcut, for *Illust London News*, 3 May 1879, NPG.
PH LONDON STEREOSCOPIC Co, hs, cabinet, NPG. J.E.MAYALL, hs, profile, oval, woodburytype, for *Men of Mark*, 1883, NPG. J.P.MAYALL, wl in studio, photogravure, NPG. RALPH W.ROBINSON, wl seated, print, for *Members and Associates of the Royal Academy of Arts*, 1891, NPG X7376.

McWILLIAM, James Ormiston (1808–1862) medical officer to the Niger expedition.
P UNKNOWN, tql seated, Wellcome Institute, London.
SC T.BUTLER, 1864, plaster medallion, Royal College of Physicians, London.

MADDEN, Sir Frederic (1801–1873) antiquary and palaeographer.
P WILLIAM DRUMMOND, hl seated, BM; lith, *Athenaeum Portraits*, no 53, pub 1837, BM, NPG.
SC R.C.LUCAS, 1849, wax medallion, NPG 1979.
PH UNKNOWN, wl, print, Portsmouth City Record Office.

MAGEE, William Connor (1821-1891) bishop of Peterborough, archbishop of York.

P FRANK HOLL, 1885, Bishop's Palace, Peterborough; copy, 1891, Bishopthorpe Palace, York.

SC JOSEPH WATKINS, 1869, marble bust, Trinity College, Dublin.

PR C.J.TOMKINS, after F.Holl, tql seated, mezz, pub 1886, BM, NPG. UNKNOWN, hs, chromo-lith, NPG.

C CARLO PELLEGRINI ('Ape'), wl, w/c study, for *Vanity Fair*, 3 July 1869, NPG 1994.

PH LOCK & WHITFIELD, hs, oval, woodburytype, for *Men of Mark*, 1877, NPG. J.ROBINSON, hl seated, carte, NPG (Album 99). JOHN & CHARLES WATKINS, hs, carte, NPG. UNKNOWN, hs, print, NPG (Anglican Bishops).

MAGHERAMORNE, Sir James Macnaghten McGarel Hogg, 1st Baron (1823-1890) politician.

PR UNKNOWN, hs, woodcut, for *Illust London News*, 7 Dec 1867, NPG. UNKNOWN, hs, woodcut, for *Illust London News*, 10 Dec 1870, NPG.

C SIR LESLIE WARD ('Spy'), wl, profile, chromo-lith, for *Vanity Fair*, 15 Nov 1873, NPG.

PH LOCK & WHITFIELD, hs, oval, woodburytype, for *Men of Mark*, 1876, NPG.

MAGRATH, John Richard (1839-1930) provost of Queen's College, Oxford.

P WILLIAM CARTER, RA 1894, tql seated, Queen's College, Oxford. JOHN COLLIER, 1898, tql, Queen's College.

MAGUIRE, James Rochfort (1855-1925) president of British South Africa Company.

C SIR LESLIE WARD ('Spy'), wl, chromo-lith, for *Vanity Fair*, 1 March 1894, NPG.

MAGUIRE, John Francis (1815-1872) Irish politician.

C UNKNOWN, wl, profile, chromo-lith, for *Vanity Fair*, 23 March 1872, NPG.

MAGUIRE, Rochford (d1867) naval lieutenant. Correction of Information in vol II.

P STEPHEN PEARCE, 1860, hs in uniform, NPG 1214. (In vol II the information given about NPG 1214 was confused with details of the Pearce group (NPG 1208) in which Maguire does not appear.)

MAHAFFY, Sir John Pentland (1839-1919) provost of Trinity College, Dublin.

P Attrib SARAH CECILIA HARRISON, NGI 1767. SIR WILLIAM ORPEN, 1907, Municipal Gallery of Modern Art, Dublin. JAMES WILCOX, Trinity College, Dublin.

SC CARRE, bas-relief, Trinity College Chapel. MISS SHAW, bronze bust, Philosophical Society, Trinity College.

PH FRADELLE & YOUNG, c1887, hl seated, cabinet, NPG.

MAHON, Charles James Patrick (1880-1891) Irish politician, 'The O'Gorman Mahon'.

D Attrib THOMAS BRIDGFORD, hl, w/c, NPG 4584. DANIEL MACLISE, pencil, NGI 2180.

SC JOHN ADAMS ACTON, 1877, terracotta bust, NGI 8109.

C SIR LESLIE WARD ('Spy'), wl, chromo-lith, for *Vanity Fair*, 17 Jan 1885, NPG.

MAHON, Philip Henry Stanhope, Viscount, see 5th Earl Stanhope.

MAHONY, Francis Sylvester ('Father Prout') (1804-1866) humorous author.

D DANIEL MACLISE, wl seated, pencil study, V & A.

G D.MACLISE, 'The Fraserians', lith, for *Fraser's Mag*, 1835, BM.

PR UNKNOWN, after a photograph by Lesage, hs, lith, NPG. UNKNOWN, hl seated, woodcut, for *Illust London News*, 11 Aug

1866, NPG.

MAINE, Sir Henry James Sumner (1822-1888) jurist.

P LOWES DICKINSON, 1888, hl seated, Trinity Hall, Cambridge. LOWES DICKINSON, Pembroke College, Cambridge.

SC SIR J.E.BOEHM, marble memorial medallion, oval, Westminster Abbey, London; related plaster plaque, Fitzwilliam Museum, Cambridge.

PR R.T., hs, wood engr, for *Illust London News*, 11 Feb 1888, NPG.

MAINZER, Joseph (1801-1851) teacher of music.

PR WILLIAM ESSEX jun, 1843, hs, profile, lith, NPG.

MAIR, William (1830-1920) Scottish divine.

P SIR GEORGE REID, 1896, Church of Scotland Assembly Hall, Edinburgh.

MAITLAND, Agnes Catherine (1850-1906) principal of Somerville College, Oxford.

D WILLIAM STRANG, 1905, hs, chalk, Somerville College, Oxford. WILLIAM STRANG, crayon, Girton College, Cambridge.

MAITLAND, Edward Francis, see Lord Barcaple.

MAITLAND, Frederic William (1850-1906) historian of Law.

P BEATRICE LOCK, 1906, hs, profile, NPG 1966; replica, Downing College, Cambridge.

SC S.N.BABB, 1908, bronze bust, Squire Law Library, Cambridge. S.N.BABB, marble bust, Lincoln's Inn, London.

PH CAMERON STUDIO, hs, print, NPG.

MAITLAND, John Alexander Fuller (1856-1936) music critic.

D WILLIAM STRANG, 1905, chalk, Royal College of Music, London.

MAITLAND, Thomas, see 11th Earl of Lauderdale.

MAJOR, Richard Henry (1818-1891) geographer.

SC R.C.LUCAS, 1850, wax portrait, BM.

MALCOLM, Sir George (1818-1897) general.

PR UNKNOWN, after a photograph by Maull & Fox, hs in uniform, wood engr, for *Illust London News*, 17 April 1897, NPG.

MALDEN, Henry (1800-1876) classical scholar.

SC ALBERT BRUCE JOY, RA 1878, bust?, University College, London.

MALET, Sir Edward Baldwin, 4th Bart (1837-1908) diplomat.

PR UNKNOWN, hs, wood engr, for *Illust London News*, 21 Oct 1882, NPG. R.T., after a photograph by W. & D.Downey, hs, wood engr, for *Illust London News*, 5 July 1890, NPG. P.NAUMANN, after a photograph, wl in his study at the embassy, Berlin, woodcut, for *Illust London News*, 1893, BM, NPG.

C SIR LESLIE WARD ('Spy'), wl, profile, chromo-lith, for *Vanity Fair*, 12 Jan 1884, NPG.

MALINS, Sir Richard (1805-1882) judge.

PR UNKNOWN, hs, wood engr, for *Illust London News*, 28 Jan 1882, NPG.

C 'FAUSTIN', hs, chromo-lith, a 'Figaro' cartoon, NPG.

PH LOCK & WHITFIELD, hs, oval, woodburytype, for *Men of Mark*, 1882, NPG. UNKNOWN, wl, carte, NPG (Album 120).

MALLET, Sir Louis (1823-1890) civil servant and economist.

PR UNKNOWN, after a photograph by Hill & Saunders, hs, wood engr, for *Illust London News*, 1 March 1890, NPG.

MALLOCK, William Hurrell (1849-1923) author.

PR UNKNOWN, after a photograph by Elliott & Fry, hs, profile, process print, NPG.

C SIR LESLIE WARD ('Spy'), wl, profile, chromo-lith, for *Vanity Fair*, 30 Dec 1882, NPG.

MALMESBURY, James Howard Harris, 3rd Earl of (1807-1889) statesman.

P J.G.MIDDLETON, 1852, tql, Hughenden (NT), Bucks; version, DoE (Foreign Office, London).

G HENRY GALES, 'The Derby Cabinet of 1867', w/c, NPG 4893.

PR R.J.LANE, after A.D'ORSAY, 1840, hl, profile, lith, BM, NPG. W.ROFFE, after a photograph by H.R.BARRAUD, hl seated, stipple and line, NPG.

C CARLO PELLEGRINI ('Ape'), wl seated, profile, chromo-lith, for *Vanity Fair*, 25 July 1874, NPG.

MANCHESTER, William Montagu, 7th Duke of (1823-1890) landowner.

C SIR LESLIE WARD ('Spy'), wl, w/c study, for *Vanity Fair*, 28 Dec 1878, NPG 2585.

PH W. & D.DOWNEY, hl seated, carte, NPG AX7413. CAMILLE SILVY, wl, carte, NPG (Album 115).

MANGAN, James (Clarence) (1803-1849) Irish poet.

D SIR FREDERICK BURTON, 1849, hs, chalk, drawn after his death in Meath hospital, NGI 2033.

MANGLES, Ross Donnelly (1801-1877) chairman of East India Company.

PR UNKNOWN, hs, one of a series of woodcuts, 'The New East India Council', for *Illust London News*, 9 Oct 1858, NPG.

MANISTY, Sir Henry (1808-1890) judge.

P W.W.OULESS, 1891, replica, tql seated, Gray's Inn, London.

PR UNKNOWN, after a photograph by Elliott & Fry, hs, woodcut, for *Illust London News*, 4 Nov 1876, NPG.

C 'QUIZ', hl seated at bench, chromo-lith, for *Vanity Fair*, 30 Nov 1889, NPG.

PH LOCK & WHITFIELD, hs, oval, woodburytype, for *Men of Mark*, 1880, NPG.

MANNERS, Charles Cecil John, see 6th Duke of Rutland.

MANNERS, Lord John James Robert, see 7th Duke of Rutland.

MANNERS-SUTTON, John Henry Thomas, see 3rd Viscount Canterbury.

MANNING, Henry Edward (1808-1892) Cardinal Archbishop of Westminster.

P G.F.WATTS, 1882, tql seated, NPG 1008. CHARLES GOLDSBOROUGH ANDERSON, 1892, tql seated, Balliol College, Oxford.

D RUDOLPH LEHMANN, 1890, two chalk portraits, both hs, Harrow School, Middx and BM.

G GEORGE RICHMOND, wl with C.J.Blomfield and Sir John Gurney, ink, pencil and wash, 1840–45, NPG 4166.

SC JAMES HARVARD THOMAS, 1876–86, bronze bust, TATE 3674. J.HARVARD THOMAS, marble bust, Archbishop's House, Westminster Cathedral, London. JOHN ADAMS ACTON, c1884, plaster bust, NPG 1589. BASIL GOTTO, c1929, bronze bust, Harrow School. ALPHONSE LEGROS, bronze portrait medallion, Manchester City Art Gallery. UNKNOWN, death mask, Watts Gallery, Compton, Surrey.

PR F.HOLL, after G.Richmond, head, stipple, pub 1851, BM, NPG. A.LEGROS, hl, etch, BM. MORTIMER MENPES, tql seated, profile, etch, NPG. G.PILOTELL, head, semi-profile, etch, BM. UNKNOWN, after a photograph by J. & C.WATKINS, hs, profile, woodcut, for *Illust London News*, 10 June 1865, NPG. Several popular prints, NPG.

C CARLO PELLEGRINI ('Ape'), wl, w/c study, for *Vanity Fair*, 25 Feb 1871, NPG 3628.

PH BARRAUD, hl seated, print, for *Men and Women of the Day*, vol III, 1890, NPG AX5476. Various cartes by ELLIOTT & FRY, W. &

D.DOWNEY, H.J.WHITLOCK and unknown photographers, various sizes, some in robes, NPG. LOCK & WHITFIELD, hs, profile, oval, woodburytype, for *Men of Mark*, 1876, NPG. NEGRETTI & ZAMBRA, two cabinets, wl and tql seated, NPG X4966–67. WALERY, tql, print, NPG.

MANNS, Sir August (1825-1907) conductor of the Crystal Palace concerts from 1855 to 1901.

C SIR LESLIE WARD ('Spy'), tql with baton, chromo-lith, for *Vanity Fair*, 13 June 1895, NPG.

MANSEL, Henry Longueville (1820-1871) metaphysician.

P UNKNOWN, hl seated, St John's College, Oxford.

G MISS CLARA PUSEY, c1856, with various other figures at a lunch or dinner party, pencil, pen and ink, NPG 4541 (9, verso).

SC E.W.WYON, 1872, marble bust, St John's College.

PR R.TAYLOR, after a photograph by John Watkins, hs, woodcut, for *Illust London News*, 12 Aug 1871, NPG.

PH UNKNOWN, tql seated, print, NPG AX7323. UNKNOWN, tql seated, profile, photogravure, NPG.

MANSERGH, James (1834-1905) civil engineer.

P W.M.PALIN, 1900, tql seated, Institution of Civil Engineers, London. W.M.PALIN, Lancaster Museum and Art Gallery.

MANSFIELD, Sir William Rose, see 1st Baron Sandhurst.

MANSON, Sir Patrick (1844-1922) pioneer of tropical medicine.

P E.WEBSTER, c1921, tql seated, London School of Hygiene and Tropical Medicine.

D M.LUCY GEE, w/c, London School of Hygiene and Tropical Medicine.

SC J.R.PINCHES, 1922, bronze medal, NPG 4058 and Molteno Institute of Biology and Parasitology, Cambridge University. UNKNOWN, 1934, bronze bas-relief portrait, London School of Hygiene and Tropical Medicine.

PH OLIVE EDIS, c1905, hs, print, NPG.

MAPLE, Sir John Blundell, Bart (1845-1903) merchant and sportsman.

PR UNKNOWN, hs, wood engr, for *Illust London News*, 24 Dec 1887, NPG.

C SIR LESLIE WARD ('Spy'), wl, profile, chromo-lith, for *Vanity Fair*, 6 June 1891, NPG.

PH SIR BENJAMIN STONE, 1901, three prints, all wl, NPG. WALERY, tql, print, NPG.

MAPLESON, James Henry (1830-1901) operatic manager.

PH UNKNOWN, hl, woodburytype, carte, NPG (Album 108).

MAPPIN, Sir Frederick Thorpe, 1st Bart (1821-1910) benefactor to Sheffield.

P W.W.OULESS, 1892, Mappin Art Gallery, Sheffield. ERNEST MOORE, Sheffield Court House. UNKNOWN, University of Sheffield.

D WILLIS EADON, 1903, w/c, Mappin Art Gallery.

SC UNKNOWN, c1903, bronze bust, Botanic Gardens, Sheffield.

MARGARY, Augustus Raymond (1846-1875) traveller.

PR C.H.JEENS, after a photograph, hs, stipple, for his *Journey from Shanghai to Bhamo*, 1876, BM. UNKNOWN, after a photograph by Elliott & Fry, hs, woodcut, for *Illust London News*, 13 March 1875, NPG.

MARGOLIOUTH, David Samuel (1858-1940) classical scholar and orientalist.

P HARRIET HALHED, exhib 1897, Griffith Institute, Oxford.

PH WALTER STONEMAN, 1917, hs, NPG (NPR).

MARJORIBANKS, Edward, see 2nd Baron Tweedmouth.

MARKHAM, Sir Albert Hastings (1841-1918) admiral and Arctic explorer.
PR UNKNOWN, after a photograph by Elliott & Fry, hs, profile, woodcut, for *Illust London News*, 29 May 1875, NPG.

MARKHAM, Sir Clements Robert (1830-1916) geographer and historical writer.
P UNKNOWN, *c*1914, hs, Scott Polar Research Institute, Cambridge.
D UNKNOWN, *c*1855, hs, chalk, Scott Polar Research Institute.
SC F.W.POMEROY, 1921, bronze bust, Royal Geographical Society, London.

MARKS, David Woolf (1811-1909) professor of Hebrew at University College, London.
P JULIA GOODMAN, *c*1877, West London Synagogue.

MARKS, Henry Stacy (1829-1898) painter.
P Self-portrait, 1882, hs, MacDonald Collection, Aberdeen Art Gallery.
G G.GRENVILLE MANTON, 'Conversazione at the Royal Academy, 1891', w/c, NPG 2820. REGINALD CLEAVER, 'Hanging Committee, Royal Academy, 1892', pen and ink, NPG 4245.
PR B.L.A.DAMMAN, after W.W.Ouless of 1875, tql seated, etch, NPG. UNKNOWN, after a photograph by Elliott & Fry, hs, woodcut, for *Illust London News*, 8 May 1875, NPG.
PH DAVID WILKIE WYNFIELD, *c*1862-4, hs, print, NPG P94. RALPH W.ROBINSON, wl in studio, print, for *Members and Associates of the Royal Academy of Arts, 1891*, NPG X7377.

MARLBOROUGH, John Winston Spencer Churchill, 7th Duke of (1822-1883) politician.
P H.R.GRAVES, wl seated, Blenheim Palace, Oxon. SIR T.A.JONES, Dublin Castle.
G HENRY GALES, 'The Derby Cabinet of 1867', w/c, NPG 4893.
SC SIR J.E.BOEHM, marble bust, Radcliffe Infirmary, Oxford.
PH LOCK & WHITFIELD, hs, oval, woodburytype, for *Men of Mark*, 1881, NPG. MAULL & POLYBLANK, wl carte, NPG AX7414.

MARNOCK, Robert (1800-1889) landscape gardener.
P THEODORE BLAKE WIRGMAN, RA 1879, hl seated, Royal Horticultural Society, London.

MAROCHETTI, Carlo, Baron (1805-1867) sculptor.
G W.MURDEN, 'Associates of the Royal Academy in 1861', woodcut, for *Illust London News*, 23 Feb 1861, BM, NPG.
SC GABRIELE AMBROSIO, 1888, bronze statuette, NPG 1038.
PR V.BROOKS, after J.Ballantyne, wl in his studio, chromo-lith, NPG.
PH CAMILLE SILVY, 1861, wl, carte, NPG AX11923. JOHN & CHARLES WATKINS, hs, carte, NPG (Album 103).

MARR, John Edward (1857-1933) geologist.
P KENNETH GREEN, 1925, tql seated, Department of Geology, University of Cambridge.

MARRIOTT, Charles (1811-1858) sub-dean of Oriel College, Oxford.
P JULIAN DRUMMOND, hs, oval, Oriel College, Oxford, engr J.Posselwhite, stipple, pub 1853, BM.

MARRIOTT, Sir John Arthur Ransome (1859-1945) historian, educationist and politician.
PH WALTER STONEMAN, hs, NPG (NPR).

MARRIOTT, Sir William Thackeray (1834-1903) lawyer and politician.
C THÉOBALD CHARTRAN ('T'), wl, w/c study, for *Vanity Fair*, 24 March 1883, NPG 2586.

MARRYAT, Florence, successively Mrs Church and Mrs Lean (1838-1899) novelist.
PR A.WEGER, hl, stipple, NPG.

PH UNKNOWN, hs, print, NPG.

MARSH, Catherine (1818-1912) evangelical philanthropist.
D L.G.FAWKES, 1895, hs, w/c, NPG 2365.
PH F.R.WINDOW, hl seated, carte, NPG.

MARSHALL, Alfred (1842-1924) economist.
P SIR WILLIAM ROTHENSTEIN, 1908, hl seated, St John's College, Cambridge; version, Marshall Library of Economics, Cambridge.
PH WALTER STONEMAN, 1917, hs, NPG (NPR).

MARSHALL, Sir Frederick (1829-1900) lieutenant-general.
C CARLO PELLEGRINI ('Ape'), wl, w/c study, for *Vanity Fair*, 16 March 1878, NPG 2587. SIR LESLIE WARD ('Spy'), wl, chromolith, for *Vanity Fair*, 24 Dec 1896, NPG.
PR W.ROFFE, after a photograph by G.Jerrard, hs, stipple, for *Baily's Mag*, 1891, NPG.

MARSHALL, John (1818-1891) anatomist and surgeon.
P ALPHONSE LEGROS, hs, V & A.
G HENRY JAMYN BROOKS, two portraits, 'Council of the Royal College of Surgeons of England of 1884-85', and 'Court of Examiners, 1894', both oil, Royal College of Surgeons, London.
SC SIR THOMAS BROCK, 1891, marble bust, Royal College of Surgeons.
PR UNKNOWN, after a photograph by Claudet, hs, wood engr, for *Illust London News*, 28 July 1883, NPG.

MARSHALL, William Calder (1813-1894) sculptor.
P JOHN PETTIE, 1883, hs, profile, MacDonald Collection, Aberdeen Art Gallery.
SC Self-portrait, plaster bust, SNPG 1170.
PH DONE & BALL, hs, cabinet, NPG. ELLIOTT & FRY, hs, carte, NPG (Album 103). LOCK & WHITFIELD, hs, oval, woodburytype, for *Men of Mark*, 1878, NPG. RALPH W.ROBINSON, wl seated, print, for *Members and Associates of the Royal Academy of Arts, 1891*, NPG X7378. JOHN & CHARLES WATKINS, wl seated, carte, NPG (Album 104).

MARSHALL HALL, Sir Edward, see Hall.

MARSTON, John Westland (1819-1890) dramatist and poet.
PR H.LINTON, after E.Morin, hl, oval, woodcut, BM, NPG.
C UNKNOWN, wl holding umbrella, woodcut, BM.

MARSTON, Philip Bourke (1850-1887) poet.
PR 'R.T.', hs, semi-profile, wood engr, for *Illust London News*, 26 Feb 1887, NPG.

MARTIN, Alexander (1857-1946) chaplain to the King in Scotland.
P H.W.KERR, New College, Edinburgh.
D DAVID FOGGIE, 1934, pencil, SNPG 1794.

MARTIN, George William (1828-1881) musical composer.
PR UNKNOWN, hs, woodcut, NPG.

MARTIN, Helena Saville, née Faucit, Lady (1817-1898) actress.
D THOMAS WAGEMAN, *c*1838, wl, w/c, NPG 4998. KENNETH MACLEAY, 1844, wl, w/c, Royal Scottish Academy, Edinburgh. KENNETH MACLEAY, hs, w/c sketch, SNPG 649. SIR F.W.BURTON, 1845, wl, 'The Greek Muse', w/c, SNPG 695; replica, NGI 2359. SIR F.W.BURTON, 1849, wl in character, w/c, Manchester City Art Gallery. SIR F.W.BURTON, numerous sketches, as Antigone and possibly as Iphigenia, Harvard Theatre Collection, Cambridge Mass, USA. UNKNOWN, tql, profile, w/c, NPG 3908.
SC J.H.FOLEY, 1843, marble bust, NPG 1554. SIR F.W.BURTON, 1845, gold fibula, kneeling figure as Antigone, National Museum of Ireland.
PR Various theatrical prints, BM, NPG, Harvard Theatre Collection.

PH CAMILLE SILVY, wl, carte, NPG (Album 102). CAMILLE SILVY, wl seated, carte, NPG.

MARTIN, John (1812-1875) Irish nationalist.
PR H.O'NEILL, after a daguerreotype, hs, oval, lith, BM.

MARTIN, Sir Samuel (1801-1883) baron of the exchequer.
PR W.WALKER, after H.W.Phillips, tql, mezz, pub 1853, BM. UNKNOWN, after a photograph by London Stereoscopic Co, hs, circle, woodcut, for *Illust London News*, 20 Jan 1883, NPG.

MARTIN, Samuel (1817-1878) minister of Westminster congregational chapel.
PR C.BAUGNIET, tql, lith, BM. J.COCHRAN, after H.Room, hl, stipple, BM, NPG. D.J.POUND, after a photograph by W.G.Smith, tql seated, stipple and line, NPG.
PH ELLIOTT & FRY, hs, carte, NPG (Album 40).

MARTIN, Sir Theodore (1816-1909) man of letters and politician.
P THOMAS DUNCAN, tql seated, aged 10, SNPG 694. ROBERT HERDMAN, 1876, hs, NPG 3100. JAMES ARCHER, 1881, tql seated, SNPG L283. F.M.BENNETT, 1908, head, NPG 1555. REGINALD CHOLMONDELEY, SNPG 955.
D RUDOLPH LEHMANN, 1873, hs, crayon, BM.
C SIR LESLIE WARD ('Spy'), wl, w/c study, for *Vanity Fair*, 7 July 1877, NPG 2731.
PH LOCK & WHITFIELD, hs, semi-profile, oval, woodburytype, for *Men of Mark*, 1881, NPG. WALERY, tql, print, NPG. JOHN & CHARLES WATKINS, two cartes, wl and wl seated, the first in Album 102, NPG. UNKNOWN, hs, print, NPG.

MARTIN, Sir William (1807-1880) chief justice of New Zealand.
PR J.DICKSON, after J.Carpenter, tql seated, lith, pub 1842, BM.

MARTINEAU, Harriet (1802-1876) social philosopher and miscellaneous writer.
P RICHARD EVANS, 1833-34, tql seated, NPG 1085. Attrib CHARLES OSGOOD, Essex Institute, Salem, Mass, USA.
D GEORGE RICHMOND, 1849, hs, chalk, NPG 1796.
SC UNKNOWN, death mask, Armitt Library, Ambleside, Cumbria.
PR FINDEN, after M.Gillies, hl, stipple, pub 1833, BM, NPG. D.MACLISE, wl seated, lith, for *Fraser's Mag*, 1833, BM, NPG; pencil study, V & A.
PH M.BOWNESS of Ambleside, tql seated, carte, NPG, and woodcut after this photograph, NPG. UNKNOWN, wl seated, print, NPG P33.

MARTINEAU, James (1805-1900) unitarian divine.
P C.AGAR, 1846, hl, Manchester College, Oxford. G.F.WATTS, 1873, hs, Manchester College; replica, NPG 1251.
D CLARA MARTINEAU (his daughter-in-law), 1887, hs, profile, pencil, NPG 2526; related silverpoint drg, Dr Williams's Library, London. HELEN ALLINGHAM, 1891, Manchester College. S.P.HALL, 1893, tql, pencil, NPG 2348. CLARA MARTINEAU, 1899, hs, profile, pastel, Dr Williams's Library. EDITH MARTINEAU, hs, w/c, Dr Williams's Library.
SL UNKNOWN, 1813, Manchester College.
G EDWARD ARMITAGE, fresco, Dr Williams's Library; pencil study, 1870, hs, profile, Dr Williams's Library.
SC UNKNOWN, c1845, bust, Manchester College. E.R.MULLINS, 1877, terracotta bust, Dr Williams's Library. H.R.HOPE PINKER, 1897, marble statue, Manchester College; plaster model, statuette, NPG 2080, and related statuettes, Dr Williams's Library, Unitarian Headquarters, London and Unitarian College, Manchester. PIETRO PIERACCINI, plaster bust, Dr Williams's Library. UNKNOWN, relief bust on memorial, Rochdale.
PR UNKNOWN, hs, chromo-lith, NPG.
PH ELLIOTT & FRY, hs, profile, carte, NPG (Album 40).

MARTINEAU, Robert Braithwaite (1826-1869) painter.
D WILLIAM HOLMAN HUNT, 1860, hs, chalk, Walker Art Gallery, Liverpool.
G FORD MADOX BROWN, 'Work', 1852-65, oil, Manchester City Art Gallery. WILLIAM HOLMAN HUNT, 'London Bridge at Night; Rejoicings in Honour of the Marriage of the Prince and Princess of Wales, 10th March 1863', oil, Ashmolean Museum, Oxford.

MARTYN, Elizabeth, née Inverarity (1813-1846) actress and singer.
PR H.ROBINSON, after A.E.Chalon, tql in evening dress with spaniel, octagon, stipple, for Heath's *Book of Beauty*, 1840, BM, NPG. W.SHARP, after W.Booth, hl seated, lith, pub 1832, NPG. Several theatrical prints, NPG, Harvard Theatre Collection, Cambridge, Mass, USA.

MARWICK, Sir James David (1826-1908) legal and historical writer.
SC G.S.TEMPLETON, 1905, marble bust, Glasgow City Art Gallery.

MASHAM, Samuel Cunliffe Lister, 1st Baron (1815-1906) inventor.
P JOHN COLLIER, 1901, Bradford Museum and Art Gallery.
SC MATTHEW NOBLE, 1873, statue, Lister Park, Bradford. ALFRED DRURY, c1904, marble bust, Bradford Museum and Art Gallery. H.C.FEHR, marble bust, Bradford Museum and Art Gallery.

MASON, Arthur James (1851-1928) theological scholar and preacher.
P ARTHUR HAYWARD, Pembroke College, Cambridge. GEORGE HENRY, c1914, Pembroke College.

MASON, George Heming (1818-1872) painter.
P VAL PRINSEP, hs, NPG 1295.
PR UNKNOWN, head, semi-profile, woodcut, for *Illust London News*, 8 May 1869, NPG.
PH JOHN WATKINS, hl, carte, NPG (Album 104).

MASON, Thomas Monck (1803-1889) musician, writer and aeronaut.
G JOHN HOLLINS, 'A Consultation prior to the Aerial Voyage to Weilburg, 1836', oil, NPG 4710.

MASSEY, Gerald (1828-1907) poet.
PR R. & E.TAYLOR, hs, oval, woodcut, for *The Illustrated Review*, 4 Sept 1873, NPG.
PH JOHN & CHARLES WATKINS, two cartes, tql seated and wl seated (AX7531), NPG.

MASSEY, William Ferguson (1856-1925) prime minister of New Zealand.
P SIR JAMES GUTHRIE, hs, study for NPG 2463, SNPG 1135. SIR WILLIAM ORPEN, 1919, hl, NPG 2639.
G SIR JAMES GUTHRIE, 'Statesmen of World War I, 1914-18', oil, NPG 2463.
PH WALTER STONEMAN, before 1917, hs, NPG (NPR). UNKNOWN, print, Alexander Turnbull Library, Wellington, New Zealand.

MASSEY, William Nathaniel (1809-1881) politician and historian.
PR UNKNOWN, hl, woodcut, for *Illust London News*, 11 March 1865, NPG.

MASSON, David (1822-1907) biographer and editor.
P SIR GEORGE REID, 1896, SNPG 678. SIR GEORGE REID, exhib 1899, tql seated, Edinburgh University.
SC J.P.MACGILLIVRAY, exhib 1896, plaster bust, Aberdeen Art Gallery; marble (probably related), Edinburgh University.
PR UNKNOWN, after a photograph by John & Charles Watkins, hl, woodcut, for *Illust London News*, 2 Dec 1865, NPG. W.HOLE, wl seated, etch, for *Quasi Cursores*, 1884, NPG.

PH JOHN & CHARLES WATKINS, hs, profile, carte, NPG.

MASSON, Sir David Orme (1858-1937) chemist.
P W.B.McINNES, University of Melbourne, Australia.

MASSY, William Godfrey Dunham (1838-1906) lieutenant-general.
PR S.MARKS, tql resting on crutches, mezz, BM. UNKNOWN, after a photograph by Sawyer and Bird, hs in uniform, woodcut, for *Illust London News*, 11 Oct 1879, NPG.

MASTERS, Maxwell Tylden (1833-1907) botanist.
PH UNKNOWN, 1877, hs, print, Royal Botanic Gardens, Kew. UNKNOWN, as an older man, Royal Botanic Gardens.

MATHESON, George (1842-1906) theologian and hymn writer.
P OTTO LEYDE, St Bernard's Parish Church, Edinburgh.

MATHEW, Sir James Charles (1830-1908) judge.
C SIR LESLIE WARD ('Spy'), hl seated at bench, chromo-lith, for *Vanity Fair*, 12 March 1896, NPG.
PH LOCK & WHITFIELD, hs, oval, woodburytype, for *Men of Mark*, 1883, NPG. BARRAUD, tql, print, for *Men and Women of the Day*, vol IV, 1891, NPG AX5532.

MATHEWS, Charles James (1803-1878) actor and dramatist.
P UNKNOWN, after a drg by Samuel de Wilde of 1807, as a 'little parson', Garrick Club, London. R.W.BUSS, wl as George Rattleton in *The Hump-Backed Lover*, Garrick Club.
D J.F.LEWIS, 1827, wl, pencil and chalk, NPG 1636. J.W.CHILDE, 1835-45, 116 w/cs, in various roles, Garrick Club. QUEEN VICTORIA, 1837, two drgs, in character, Royal Coll.
PR Various theatrical and popular prints, BM, NPG, Harvard Theatre Collection, Cambridge, Mass, USA.
C Various prints, Harvard Theatre Collection. CARLO PELLEGRINI ('Ape'), wl, profile, chromo-lith, for *Vanity Fair*, 2 Oct 1875, NPG.
PH Various cartes by HENNAH & KENT, MAYALL, HERBERT WATKINS and others, various dates and sizes, NPG.

MATHEWS, Sir Charles Willie, Bart (1850-1920) director of Public Prosecutions.
C HARRY FURNISS, two pen and ink sketches, NPG 3491-2. SIR LESLIE WARD ('Spy'), hl at bench, chromo-lith, for *Vanity Fair*, 6 Feb 1892, NPG.
PH WALTER STONEMAN, 1917, hs, NPG (NPR).

MATTHEWS, Henry, see Viscount Llandaff.

MATTHEWS, Sir William (1844-1922) civil engineer.
P STANHOPE A.FORBES, 1908, tql seated, Institution of Civil Engineers, London.

MAURICE, Frederick Denison (1805-1872) progressive writer and divine.
P JANE M.HAYWARD, 1854, hl, NPG 354. SAMUEL LAURENCE, c1871, tql seated, NPG 1042. LOWES DICKINSON, 1886, representing him as if in c1860, tql, Queen's College, London.
D S.LAURENCE, c1846, head, chalk, NPG 1709. UNKNOWN, 1859, drg, Queen's College.
G FORD MADOX BROWN, 'Work', oil, 1852-65, Manchester City Art Gallery; wl pencil study, Manchester City Art Gallery.
SC THOMAS WOOLNER, 1872, bust, Westminster Abbey, London; 1873, replica, Old Schools, Cambridge. THOMAS WOOLNER, plaster cast of death mask, NPG 1397. E. & M.GILLICK, modern bronze memorial plaque, Cambridge.
PH ERNEST EDWARDS, wl, print, for *Men of Eminence*, vol I, 1863, NPG. UNKNOWN, tql seated, print, NPG AX7324. Various cartes by ELLIOTT & FRY, W.JEFFREY, KILBURN, MASON & CO and POULTON, various dates and sizes, NPG.

MAURICE, Sir John Frederick (1841-1912) major-general.
PH W. & D.DOWNEY, tql seated, woodburytype, for Cassell's *Cabinet Portrait Gallery*, vol I, 1890, NPG.

MAXIM, Sir Hiram Stevens (1840-1916) engineer and inventor.
SL FRANK SMYTH BADEN-POWELL, 1894, hs, profile, NPG.
C SIR LESLIE WARD ('Spy'), wl, chromo-lith, for *Vanity Fair*, 15 Dec 1904, NPG.
PH JOHN RUSSELL & SONS, hs, print, for *National Photographic Record*, vol I, NPG.

MAX-MÜLLER, Friedrich (1823-1900) orientalist and philologist.
P SIR HUBERT VON HERKOMER, hl seated, All Souls College, Oxford. G.F.WATTS, 1894, hl seated, NPG 1276.
D RUDOLPH LEHMANN, 1894, hs, crayon, BM.
PR W.ROTHENSTEIN, hl, profile, lith, BM.
PH BARRAUD, hs, print, for *Men and Women of the Day*, vol III, 1890, NPG AX5506. C.L.DODGSON, tql seated, print, NPG P7 (25). W. & D.DOWNEY, hl, profile, woodburytype, for Cassell's *Cabinet Portrait Gallery*, vol IV, 1893, NPG. HILLS & SAUNDERS, wl seated, profile, carte, NPG AX7527. Three photogravures, two after HILLS & SAUNDERS, hs, profile, and seated in his study, and the third, after an unknown photographer, hs, profile, NPG. HILLS & SAUNDERS, hl, carte, NPG (Album 40). LOCK & WHITFIELD, hs, profile, oval, woodburytype, for *Men of Mark*, 1878, NPG. H.J.WHITLOCK, tql seated, carte, NPG (Album 40).

MAXSE, Sir Henry Berkeley Fitzhardinge (1832-1883) governor of Newfoundland.
PR UNKNOWN, after a photograph by G.Friederichs, hs, semi-profile, in uniform, woodcut, for *Illust London News*, 6 Oct 1883, NPG.

MAXWELL, Lady Caroline Stirling-, see STIRLING-Maxwell.

MAXWELL, Sir Herbert Eustace, 7th Bart, of Monreith (1845-1937) country gentleman, politician and writer.
D W.GRAHAM BOSS, pencil, SNPG 1713. WILLIAM STRANG, 1917, pastel, SNPG 1451.
C SIR LESLIE WARD ('Spy'), wl, chromo-lith, for *Vanity Fair*, 28 Sept 1893, NPG.
PH JOHN RUSSELL & SONS, hs in uniform, print, for *National Photographic Record*, vol I, NPG. WALTER STONEMAN, 1933, hs, profile, NPG (NPR).

MAXWELL, James Clerk-, see CLERK-Maxwell.

MAXWELL, John Hall (1812-1866) agriculturalist.
PR HÄHNISCH, hs, lith, BM. J.B.HUNT, after a photograph, tql, stipple and line, pub 1858, NPG.

MAXWELL, Mary Elizabeth, née Braddon (1837-1915) novelist.
P W.P.FRITH, 1865, tql, NPG 4478.
SC JOHN E.HYETT, RA 1917, bronze relief memorial, Richmond Parish Church.
PR UNKNOWN, hs, oval, lith, NPG.
C H.HARCAL, 'Miss Braddon in her daring flight', for 'The Mask's Album', NPG.

MAXWELL, Sir William Stirling-, see STIRLING-Maxwell.

MAXWELL LYTE, Sir Henry Churchill, see Lyte.

MAY, Sir Thomas Erskine, see 1st Baron Farnborough.

MAY, Sir William Henry (1849-1930) admiral of the fleet.
C SIR LESLIE WARD ('Spy'), wl, profile, in uniform, chromo-lith,

for *Vanity Fair*, 26 March 1903, NPG.
PH WALTER STONEMAN, 1917, hs in uniform, NPG (NPR).

MAYER, Joseph (1803-1886) collector.
P WILLIAM DANIELS, 1843, wl seated in his library, Art Gallery, Liverpool.
SC G.G.FONTANA, several portraits: 1856, marble relief medallion; 1868, marble bust; marble bust; marble statue, all at the Walker Art Gallery, Liverpool.

MAYHEW, Henry (1812-1887) author.
PR UNKNOWN, after a daguerreotype by Beard, tql seated, woodcut, pub 1851, NPG. 'R.T.', after a photograph by Bedford Lemere & Co, hs, profile, wood engr, for *Illust London News*, 6 Aug 1887, NPG.

MAYHEW, Horace (1816-1872) author.
PR R. & E.TAYLOR, after a photograph by Bassano, hs, woodcut, for *The Illustrated Review*, 1 June 1872, NPG.

MAYNE, Richard Charles (1835-1892) admiral.
PR 'R.T. & Co', after a photograph by Russell & Sons, hs in uniform, wood engr, for *Illust London News*, 4 June 1892, NPG.

MAYNE, William (1818-1855) colonel.
PR G.S.SHURY, after K.Hartmann, tql seated in uniform, mezz, pub 1856, NPG.

MAYO, Richard Southwell Bourke, 6th Earl of (1822-1872) viceroy and governor-general of India.
P JOHN COLLIER, after a photograph, in Garter robes, Oriental Club, London. UNKNOWN, 1873, after a photograph, wl seated, India Office Library and Records, London.
G HENRY GALES, 'The Derby Cabinet of 1867', w/c, NPG 4893.
SC SIR W.H.THORNYCROFT, c1875, bronze equestrian statue, Calcutta. W. & T.WILLS, marble statue on monument, Cockermouth, Cumbria.
PR J.BROWN, after a photograph, hs, stipple, for *Baily's Mag*, 1866, BM. E.STODART, after a photograph by S.A.Walker, hl seated, stipple and line, NPG.
PH JOHN WATKINS, hs, carte, NPG.

MAYOR, John Eyton Bickersteth (1825-1910) classical scholar and divine.
P SIR HUBERT VON HERKOMER, 1891, St John's College, Cambridge.

MEADE, Richard James, see 4th Earl of Clanwilliam.

MEADE, Sir Robert Henry (1835-1898) civil servant.
PH Attrib HILLS & SAUNDERS, 1863, with the houseparty group after the presentation of the DCL to Edward VII and others, print, NPG X4336.

MEAGHER, Thomas Francis (1823-1867) Irish nationalist.
P GEORGE MULVANY, NGI 1284.
D JOSEPH HAYES, with William Smith O'Brien, in Clonmel jail, 1848, w/c, Aras an Uachtarain (President's Residence), Dublin.
PR H.O'NEILL, after a daguerreotype, hl, oval, lith, BM.

MEATH, Reginald Brabazon, 12th Earl of (1841-1929) diplomat and philanthropist.
P SIR WILLIAM ORPEN, exhib 1929, hl seated, in uniform, NPG 2624.
SC UNKNOWN, relief medallion on memorial, Lancaster Gate, London. UNKNOWN, bronze bust, Royal Commonwealth Society, London. UNKNOWN, hs, profile, memorial plaque, Ottershaw Church, Surrey.
PH BASSANO, 1895, two negs, tql seated, and tql, NPG X489 and X490. WALTER STONEMAN, 1924, hs, NPG (NPR). JOHN RUSSELL & SONS, hl seated, print, for *National Photographic Record*, vol I, NPG.

MECHI, John Joseph (1802-1880) cutler and agriculturist.

PR UNKNOWN, hl, oval, lith, BM. UNKNOWN, hs, stipple, pub 1877, NPG. UNKNOWN, after a photograph by London Stereoscopic Co, hl, woodcut, for *Illust London News*, 11 April 1857, NPG.

MEDLEY, John (1804-1892) first bishop of Fredericton, New Brunswick.
P JOHN BRIDGES, 1848, tql seated, Wadham College, Oxford.

MELDOLA, Raphael (1849-1915) chemist.
P SOLOMON J.SOLOMON, hs, NPG 2529.
SC FRANK BOWCHER, posthumous bronze plaque, NPG 1943.

MELLISH, Sir George (1814-1877) judge.
PR UNKNOWN, after a photograph by John Watkins, hs, woodcut, for *Illust London News*, 5 Nov 1870, NPG.
C SIR LESLIE WARD ('Spy'), hl, w/c study, for *Vanity Fair*, 30 Dec 1876, NPG 2732.

MELLON, Alfred (1820-1867) musician.
PR C.BAUGNIET, tql, lith, 1854, BM. UNKNOWN, after a photograph, hl, woodcut, for *Illust London News*, 13 April 1867, NPG.
C UNKNOWN, wl, woodcut, for *Entr'acte* supplement, 30 June 1877, Harvard Theatre Collection, Cambridge, Mass, USA.

MELLON, Sarah Jane, née Woolgar (1824-1909) actress.
PR G.GREATBACH, after a daguerreotype, wl as Rosalind in *As You Like It*, stipple and line, for Tallis's *Drawing Room Table Book*, BM, NPG. T.H.WILSON, 1849, hs, lith, NPG. Several theatrical prints, Harvard Theatre Collection, Cambridge, Mass, USA.
PH FRADELLE & MARSHALL, hl, woodburytype, carte, NPG AX7675. J.T.WIGNEY, wl in character, carte, NPG.

MELLOR, Sir John (1809-1887) judge.
P JOHN NAPIER, wl seated in robes, Leicester Museum.
SC E.G.PAPWORTH, 1870, marble bust, DoE (Law Courts, London).
C 'FAUSTIN', tql at bench, chromo-lith, a 'Figaro' cartoon, NPG. SIR LESLIE WARD ('Spy'), hl, w/c study, for *Vanity Fair*, 24 May 1873, NPG 2733.
PH LOCK & WHITFIELD, hs, oval, woodburytype, for *Men of Mark*, 1880, NPG.

MELVILLE, George John Whyte-, see WHYTE-Melville.

MENKEN, Adah Isaacs, formerly Adelaide McCord (1835-1868) actress and writer.
PR UNKNOWN, as Mazeppa at Astley's, 3 Oct 1864, lith, V & A. Various theatrical prints, Harvard Theatre Collection, Cambridge, Mass, USA.
C Several prints, Harvard Theatre Collection.
PH C.REUTLINGER, wl as Mazeppa, carte, NPG. SARONY & CO, tql seated, carte, NPG.

MEREDITH, George (1828-1909) novelist and poet.
P G.F.WATTS, 1893, hl, profile, NPG 1543. WILLIAM STRANG, 1908, hs, profile, NPG 1908.
D J.S.SARGENT, 1896, hs, charcoal, Fitzwilliam Museum, Cambridge. WILLIAM STRANG, 1908, hs, profile, chalk, Royal Coll. VIOLET, DUCHESS OF RUTLAND, pencil drg, SNPG 1018.
SC SIR CHARLES HOLROYD, bronze medals, NPG 1981 and TATE 3638. THEODORE SPICER-SIMSON, bronze medallion, NPG 1583.
C SIR MAX BEERBOHM, wl, profile, drg, for *Vanity Fair*, 24 Sept 1896, Ashmolean Museum, Oxford. SIR MAX BEERBOHM, sketch for 'The Nobel Award, 1907', with Kipling, Hall Caine and Swinburne, Berg Collection, New York Public Library, USA.
PH FREDERICK HOLLYER, c1891, hs, profile, cabinet, NPG X3699. A.L.COBURN, 1904, hs, profile, photogravure, for *Men of Mark*, 1913, NPG AX7772. UNKNOWN, hs, semi-profile, print, University College Medical School, London.

MEREWETHER, Sir William Lockyer (1825-1880) Indian military officer and administrator.

PR UNKNOWN, hs, profile, with medals, woodcut, for *Illust London News*, 5 Sept 1868, NPG.

MERIVALE, Herman (1806-1874) under-secretary for India.
PR UNKNOWN, after a photograph by Dickinson, hs, woodcut, for *Illust London News*, 21 Feb 1874, NPG.

MERRIVALE, Henry Edward Duke, 1st Baron (1855-1939) judge and politician.
P SIR WILLIAM ORPEN, 1925, tql seated in robes, Gray's Inn, London.
PH WALTER STONEMAN, two, both hs, 1922 and 1932, NPG (NPR).

MERRY, William Walter (1835-1918) classical scholar.
P CYRUS JOHNSON, RA 1898, tql seated, semi-profile, in robes, Lincoln College, Oxford.

MERSEY, John Charles Bigham, 1st Viscount (1840-1929) judge.
C SIR LESLIE WARD ('Spy'), hs, profile, at bench, chromo-lith, for *Vanity Fair*, 3 Feb 1898, NPG.
PH WALTER STONEMAN, hs, NPG (NPR).

MERTHYR, William Thomas Lewis, 1st Baron (1837-1914) engineer and coal-owner.
SC SIR THOMAS BROCK, RA 1899, bronze statue, Merthyr Tydfil, S Wales.
PR UNKNOWN, hs, wood engr, for *Illust London News*, 14 Feb 1891, NPG.

METHUEN, Sir Algernon Methuen Marshall, 1st Bart (1856-1924) publisher, whose original name was Algernon Stedman.
SC UNKNOWN, bronze bas-relief portrait, Essex Street, London.

METHUEN, Paul Sanford Methuen, 3rd Baron (1845-1932) field-marshal.
P WILLIAM CARTER, 1904, tql in uniform, Corsham Court, Wilts. PAUL AYSHFORD METHUEN (his son), 1920, hs, NPG 5017.
PR 'R.T.', hs, in uniform, wood engr, for *Illust London News*, 6 Dec 1884, NPG.
C SIR LESLIE WARD ('Spy'), wl, profile, in uniform, chromo-lith, for *Vanity Fair*, 17 Dec 1892, NPG.

MEUX (formerly Lambton), Sir Hedworth (1856-1929) admiral of the fleet.
C SIR LESLIE WARD ('Spy'), wl, profile, in uniform, chromo-lith, for *Vanity Fair*, 28 June 1900, NPG.

MEYER, Frederick Brotherton (1847-1929) Baptist divine.
P JOHN COLLIER, 1907?, The Baptist Union, London.

MEYNELL, Alice Christiana Gertrude, née Thompson (1847-1922) poet and critic.
D J.S.SARGENT, 1894, tql, pencil, NPG 2221.
PR W.ROTHENSTEIN, 1897, hs, lith, BM, NPG.
PH JOHN RUSSELL & SONS, tql seated, print, for *National Photographic Record*, vol I, NPG. UNKNOWN, tql, print, NPG X12511.

MEYRICK, Edward (1854-1938) entomologist.
PH WALTER STONEMAN, 1921, hs, NPG (NPR).

MEYRICK, Frederick (1827-1906) divine.
PH THE ART REPRO CO, hs, semi-profile, photogravure, NPG X12512.

MIALL, Edward (1809-1881) politician.
G P.NAUMANN & R.TAYLOR & Co, 'Our Literary Contributors – Past and Present', hs, one of a series of woodcuts, for *Illust London News*, 14 May 1892, BM, NPG.
PR UNKNOWN, after a photograph by Mayall, hl seated, woodcut, for Cassell's *Illustrated Family Paper*, 2 April 1859, NPG. UNKNOWN, hs, woodcut, for *Illust London News*, 7 May 1881,

NPG.
C CARLO PELLEGRINI ('Ape'), wl, chromo-lith, for *Vanity Fair*, 2 July 1871, NPG.
PH MAYALL, wl, carte, NPG X12513. H.J.WHITLOCK, hs, carte, NP (Album 40).

MICHELL, Nicholas (1807-1880) miscellaneous writer.
PR H.ADLARD, hs, stipple, BM, NPG.

MICHELL, Richard (1805-1877) first principal of Hertfor College, Oxford.
P UNKNOWN, hs, oval, Hertford College, Oxford. UNKNOWN, tc seated, Hertford College.

MICKLETHWAITE, John Thomas (1843-1906) architect
PH G.C.BERESFORD, hs, profile, print, NPG X12514.

MIDDLETON, John (1827-1856) artist.
PH UNKNOWN, hs, print, BM (Engr Ports Coll).

MIDLETON, (William) St John (Fremantle) Brodrick, 9th Viscount and 1st Earl of (1856-1942) statesman.
P WILLIAM CARTER, County Hall, Kingston upon Thames, Surrey
C SIR LESLIE WARD ('Spy'), wl, chromo-lith, for *Vanity Fair*, 1 July 1901, NPG. SIR BERNARD PARTRIDGE, pen and ink cartoon, fo *Punch*, 29 Jan 1902, NPG.
PH SIR BENJAMIN STONE, 1902, wl, print, NPG. RUSSELL, 1911, h photogravure, NPG X12517. Attrib RUSSELL, tql seated, print, NP X12516. WALTER STONEMAN, 1921, hs, for NPR, NPG X6978.

MIERS, Sir Henry Alexander (1858-1942) mineralogist administrator and scholar.
D SIR WILLIAM ROTHENSTEIN, 1917, head, pencil, NPG 4787.
PH WALTER STONEMAN, 1933, hl seated, NPG (NPR).

MILFORD HAVEN, Louis Alexander Mountbatten, 1s Marquess of (1854-1921) admiral of the fleet.
P P.A. DE LÁSZLÓ, 1914, hs, Broadlands, Hants.
G SIR A.S.COPE, 'Naval Officers of World War I, 1914–1918', oi NPG 1913.
C SIR LESLIE WARD ('Spy'), wl, chromo-lith, for *Vanity Fair*, 16 Fel 1905, NPG.
PH WALTER STONEMAN, 1921, hs, for NPR, NPG X4668.

MILL, John Stuart (1806-1873) philosopher.
P G.F.WATTS, 1873, hs, City of Westminster, London; replica NPG 1009 and Watts Gallery, Compton, Surrey.
SC THOMAS WOOLNER, c1878, bronze statue, seated, Victoria Em bankment Gardens, London, ALPHONSE LEGROS, posthumo bronze medallion, Manchester City Art Gallery.
C SIR LESLIE WARD ('Spy'), tql, profile, chromo-lith, for *Vanit Fair*, 29 March 1873, NPG; w/c and pencil study of the head, NPG
PH JOHN & CHARLES WATKINS, 1865, tql seated, print, NPG P46. J. & C.WATKINS, 1865, hs, profile, cabinet, NPG X12522. JOH WATKINS, two related cartes, both hs, NPG X3685 and X12518

MILLAIS, Sir John Everett, Bart (1829-1896) painter an president of the Royal Academy.
P C.R.LESLIE, 1852, hs, NPG 1859. G.F.WATTS, 1871, hs, profil NPG 3552. Self-portrait, 1878, hs, profile, Wightwick Manc (NT), W Midlands. Self-portrait, 1880, hl with palette, Uffi: Gallery, Florence. SIR GEORGE REID, 1880, MacDonald Collec tion, Aberdeen Art Gallery. Self-portrait, 1883, hs, MacDona Collection, Aberdeen Art Gallery. FRANK HOLL, RA 1886, tc profile, with palette, Royal Academy, London.
D C.A.COLLINS, 1850, hs, pencil, ink and wash, Ashmolea Museum, Oxford. Self-portrait, 1853, two pen and ink sketche both wl in fancy dress, The Athenaeum, London. Self-portrai 1854, with his mother, showing his drawings to Sir Marti Archer Shee (a recollection of a visit made in 1838), chal

Ashmolean Museum. WILLIAM HOLMAN HUNT, c1860, hs, chalk, NPG 2914. RUDOLPH LEHMANN, 1868, hs, crayon, BM. T.B.WIRGMAN, 1896, hs, profile, pencil, NPG 1711. C.W.COPE, hs, profile, study, Fitzwilliam Museum, Cambridge. C.S.KEENE, wl seated, pencil, NPG 1117.

G Self-portrait, c1851, in a group at a party 'Miss Sm-th's Party', pen and ink, Winnipeg Art Gallery, Manitoba, Canada. HENRY NELSON O'NEIL, 'The Billiard Room of the Garrick Club', oil, 1869, Garrick Club, London. NICAISE DE KEYSER, 'Les grands artistes, École du XIXme siècle', oil, 1878, Musée Chéret, Nice. HENRY JAMYN BROOKS, 'Private view of the Old Masters Exhibition, Royal Academy, 1888', oil, NPG 1833. G.GRENVILLE MANTON, 'Conversazione at the Royal Academy, 1891', w/c, NPG 2820. REGINALD CLEAVER, 'Hanging Committee, Royal Academy, 1892', pen and ink, NPG 4245.

SC ALEXANDER MUNRO, c1854, plaster plaques, NPG 4959 and Ashmolean Museum. SIR J.E.BOEHM, 1863, plaster statuette, NPG 1516. SIR J.E.BOEHM, 1882, plaster bust, V & A; RA 1883, related bronze bust, Royal Academy, London. EDWARD ONSLOW FORD, 1895, bronze bust, Royal Academy, London; related plaster bust, NPG 1329, and bronze cast, NPG 1329a. SIR THOMAS BROCK, bronze statue, Tate Gallery, London.

PR G.PILOTELL, hs, drypoint, BM, NPG.

C CARLO PELLEGRINI ('Ape'), tql, profile, w/c study, for Vanity Fair, 13 May 1871, NPG 2626. SIR LESLIE WARD, hl, semi-profile, with palette, pencil, for The Graphic, 22 Aug 1896, Garrick Club.

PH Various prints by ELLIOTT & FRY, FRADELLE & MARSHALL, LOCK & WHITFIELD, A.F.MACKENZIE, RUPERT POTTER, RALPH W.ROBINSON, HERBERT WATKINS, JOHN & CHARLES WATKINS, WINDOW & GROVE, DAVID WILKIE WYNFIELD and others, various dates and sizes, prints, cartes, cabinets and photogravures, NPG.

MILLER, Hugh (1802-1856) geologist and writer.
SC WILLIAM BRODIE, marble bust, SNPG 255. A.H.RITCHIE, 1858, statue, Cromarty.
PR F.CROLL, hl, line, for Hogg's Instructor, BM, NPG. J.SARTAIN, after W.Bonnar, tql seated, mezz, for Eclectic Mag, NPG.
PH ALEXANDER RAE, hs, carte, NPG (Album 102). J.G.TUNNY, tql seated, carte, NPG.

MILLER, James (1812-1864) professor of surgery at Edinburgh University.
P THOMAS DUNCAN, exhib 1845, tql seated, Royal College of Surgeons, Edinburgh. JOHN HARRIS, 1855, tql, Royal College of Surgeons, Edinburgh.
PR D.J.POUND, after a photograph by Moffat, tql seated, stipple and line, NPG.
PH D.O.HILL & ROBERT ADAMSON, hl, print, NPG P6 (58). D.O.HILL & ROBERT ADAMSON, wl profile with D.O.Hill, print, NPG P6 (155).

MILLER, John Cale (1814-1880) vicar of Greenwich and Canon of Rochester.
PR C.BAUGNIET, in pulpit preaching, 1846, lith, BM. D.J.POUND, after a photograph by Mayall, tql, stipple and line, for The Drawing Room Portrait Gallery of Eminent Personages, NPG.
PH H.J.WHITLOCK, hs, profile, carte, NPG AX7499. H.J.WHITLOCK, hl seated, carte, NPG (Album 40).

MILLER, William Allen (1817-1870) chemist.
G SHAPPEN, after daguerreotypes by Mayall, 'Celebrated English Chemists', lith, pub 1850, BM.
SC TIMOTHY BUTLER, RA 1875, marble bust, King's College, London.
PH ERNEST EDWARDS, wl seated, print, for Men of Eminence, vol II, 1864, NPG. H.J.WHITLOCK, hl seated, carte, NPG (Album 40).

MILLIGAN, William (1821-1893) Scottish divine.
P SIR GEORGE REID, University of Aberdeen.

MILLS, Sir Charles (1825-1895) first agent-general for Cape Colony.
PR 'R.T.', hs, wood engr, for Illust London News, 31 July 1886, NPG.

MILLTOWN, Edward Nugent Leeson, 6th Earl of (1835-1890) landowner.
P SIR FRANCIS GRANT, 1875, wl, NGI 1036.
SC SIR WILLIAM HAMO THORNYCROFT, 1879, marble bust, NGI 8205. SIR W.HAMO THORNYCROFT, plaster bust, NGI 8098.
PR UNKNOWN, after a photograph by Fradelle and Young, hs, wood engr, for Illust London News, 14 June 1890, NPG.
C SIR LESLIE WARD ('Spy'), wl, profile, w/c study, for Vanity Fair, 24 Nov 1883, NPG 4728.

MILMAN, Robert (1816-1876) bishop of Calcutta.
PR UNKNOWN, hs, semi-profile, woodcut, for Illust London News, 30 March 1867, NPG.

MILNE, Sir Alexander, 1st Bart (1806-1896) admiral.
P W.W.OULESS, 1879, tql in uniform with Bath ribbon and star, NMM, Greenwich.
C THÉOBALD CHARTRAN ('T'), wl, profile, in uniform, chromolith, for Vanity Fair, 29 July 1882, NPG.
PH LONDON STEREOSCOPIC CO, tql in uniform, cabinet, NPG X4968.

MILNE, Sir (Archibald) Berkeley, 2nd Bart (1855-1938) admiral.
PH WALTER STONEMAN, 1917, hl in uniform, NPG (NPR).

MILNE, William Charles (1815-1863) Chinese missionary.
PR J.COCHRAN, after H.Room, hl, engr, NPG.

MILNER, Alfred Milner, Viscount (1854-1925) High Commissioner for South Africa.
P HUGH DE GLAZEBROOK, 1901, tql seated, NPG 2135. HERBERT OLIVIER, 1919, tql seated, DoE (Paris Chancery). SIR JAMES GUTHRIE, c1919–21, hl seated, study for NPG 2463, SNPG 1138. SIR WILLIAM ORPEN, 1923, hs, South African National Gallery, Cape Town. MAX BALFOUR, tql seated, New College, Oxford. UNKNOWN, tql, Balliol College, Oxford.
D J.S.SARGENT, 1909, hs, pencil, Municipal Gallery of Modern Art, Johannesburg.
G SIR JAMES GUTHRIE, 'Statesmen of World War I, 1914–18', oil, 1924–30, NPG 2463.
SC KATHLEEN, LADY KENNET, posthumous marble bust, Rhodes House, Oxford. FRANÇOIS SICARD, bronze bust, Doullens, France. UNKNOWN, portrait plaque, Westminster Abbey, London; replica, Toynbee Hall, Whitechapel, London.
C SIR LESLIE WARD ('Spy'), wl, profile, chromo-lith, for Vanity Fair, 15 April 1897, NPG. SIR MAX BEERBOHM, 'Lord Milner awaiting the fulfilment of his worst fears about the South African Constitution', drg, 1913, New College, Oxford.
PH ELLIOTT & FRY, 1901, hl, print, NPG. LONDON STEREOSCOPIC CO, hs, print, NPG. JOHN RUSSELL & SONS, hs, print, for National Photographic Record, vol I, NPG.

MILNER, Sir Frederick George, 7th Bart (1849-1931) politician.
PR UNKNOWN, hs, wood engr, for Illust London News, 27 Dec 1890, NPG.
C CARLO PELLEGRINI ('Ape'), wl, profile, w/c study, for Vanity Fair, 27 June 1885, NPG 4729.

MILNER-GIBSON, Thomas (1806-1884) statesman.
D C.A.DUVAL, 1843, hl, w/c, NPG 1930, engr S.W.Reynolds, mezz, BM, NPG.
G S.BELLIN, after J.R.Herbert of 1847, 'The Anti Corn Law

League', mixed engr, pub 1850, BM, NPG. JOHN PHILLIP, 'The House of Commons, 1860', oil, Palace of Westminster, London.

PR W.HOLL, after J.Holmes, hl, stipple, pub 1842, NPG.

C HONORE DAUMIER, wl with Richard Cobden and John Bright, lith, for *Le Charivari*, 25 Feb 1856, NPG.

PH MAYALL, wl seated, carte, NPG. W.WALKER & SONS, hl seated, NPG.

MILNES, Richard Monckton, see 1st Baron Houghton.

MILNES, Robert Offley Ashburton Crewe-, see 1st Marquess of Crewe.

MINTO, Gilbert John Murray Kynynmond Elliot, 4th Earl of (1845-1914) governor-general of Canada and viceroy of India.

P P.A.DE LÁSZLÓ, Victoria Memorial Hall, Calcutta. UNKNOWN, wl in uniform, Public Archives of Canada, Ottawa.

SC SIR WILLIAM GOSCOMBE JOHN, RA 1913, bronze equestrian statue, Calcutta.

C SIR LESLIE WARD ('Spy'), wl in riding dress, chromo-lith, for *Vanity Fair*, 29 June 1905, NPG.

PH UNKNOWN, 1909, with his wife and their staff during a visit to Rajputana, print, National Army Museum, London.

MINTO, William (1845-1893) critic.

PR UNKNOWN, hs, wood engr, for *Illust London News*, 11 March 1893, NPG.

MITCHEL, John (1815-1875) Irish agitator.

G UNKNOWN, 'The Illustrious Sons of Ireland', chromo-lith, NPG.

SC THOMAS FARRELL, plaster death mask, NGI 8133.

PR C.BAUGNIET, after a photograph, hl, lith, BM. UNKNOWN, after a daguerreotype, hl, oval, lith, NPG.

MITCHELL, Alexander Ferrier (1822-1899) Scottish ecclesiastical historian.

P SIR GEORGE REID, RA 1897, tql, University of St Andrews.

MITCHELL, Sir Arthur (1826-1909) writer on insanity and antiquary.

P SIR GEORGE REID, SNPG 1464.

D W.GRAHAM BOSS, pencil drg, SNPG 1692. JOHN HENRY LORIMER, 1891, pencil, SNPG 769.

MITCHELL, Sir Henry (1823-1898) mayor of Bradford.

C SIR LESLIE WARD ('Spy'), wl, w/c study, for *Vanity Fair*, 5 July 1890, NPG 2989.

MITCHELL, John Murray (1815-1904) presbyterian missionary and orientalist.

P W.E.LOCKHART, *c*1898, United Free Church Assembly Hall, Edinburgh.

MITFORD, Algernon Bertram Freeman-, see 1st Baron Redesdale.

MITFORD, John Thomas Freeman-, see 1st Earl of Redesdale.

MIVART, St George Jackson (1827-1900) biologist.

P MISS SOLOMON, hs, Linnean Society, London. UNKNOWN, hs, as an older man, oval, Linnean Society.

MOBERLY, George (1803-1885) bishop of Salisbury.

P SIR FRANCIS GRANT, 1852, tql seated, Winchester College, Hants. LOWES CATO DICKINSON, 1876, tql seated, Winchester College.

PR L.LOWENSTAM, after W.B.Richmond, etch, Salisbury Corporation. UNKNOWN, after a photograph by John Watkins, hs, woodcut, for *Illust London News*, 30 Oct 1869, NPG.

PH LOCK & WHITFIELD, hs, oval, woodburytype, for *Men of Mark*, 1877, NPG.

MOCATTA, Frederic David (1828-1905) Jewish philanthropist.

PH NADAR, tql, cabinet, NPG X4126.

MOLE, John Henry (1814-1886) water-colour painter.

PH McLEAN & HAES, wl, carte, NPG (Album 104).

MOLESWORTH, Mary Louisa (1839-1921) author of books for children.

D WALKER HODGSON, 1895, tql seated, profile, pencil and w/c, NPG 4041 (3).

MOLESWORTH, Sir William, Bart (1810-1855) radical politician.

P SIR JOHN WATSON GORDON, 1854, tql seated, NPG 810.

G SIR GEORGE HAYTER, 'The House of Commons, 1833', oil, NPG 54. SIR JOHN GILBERT, 'The Coalition Ministry, 1854', pencil and wash, NPG 1125.

SC WILLIAM BEHNES, 1842, marble bust, Reform Club, London; version, National Gallery of Canada, Ottawa.

PR UNKNOWN, after a photograph by Kilburn, hl, woodcut, for *Illust London News*, 1851, NPG. E.LANDELLS, after a photograph by B.E.Duppa, tql seated, woodcut, for *Illust London News*, 27 Oct 1855, NPG. D.MACLISE, wl seated, originally pub in *Fraser's Mag*, lith, for Maginn's *Gallery of Illustrious Literary Characters*, 1873 BM, NPG. UNKNOWN, hl, profile, stipple, NPG.

C JOHN DOYLE, various political cartoons, BM.

MOLESWORTH, William Nassau (1816-1890) historian.

PR UNKNOWN, after a photograph by E.Debenham, hs, wood engr for *Illust London News*, 3 Jan 1891, NPG.

MOLTENO, Sir John Charles (1814-1886) South African statesman.

PH UNKNOWN, hs, print, Houses of Parliament, Cape Town, South Africa.

MOLYNEUX, Sir Robert Henry More-, see MORE Molyneux.

MOMERIE, Alfred Williams (1848-1900) divine.

PH BARRAUD, tql, print, for *Men and Women of the Day*, vol IV, 1891 NPG AX5527.

MONAHAN, James Henry (1804-1878) judge.

P UNKNOWN, King's Inns, Dublin.

PR UNKNOWN, hs, sketch, woodcut, one of a set, 'The Dublin State Trials. Counsel for the Traversers', for *Illust London News*, 2 Dec 1843, NPG.

MONCK, Sir Charles Stanley Monck, 4th Viscount and 1st Baron (1819-1894) governor-general of Canada.

PR Two woodcuts by unknown artists, both hs, for *Illust London News*, 3 Feb 1867 and 6 March 1869, NPG.

MONCREIFF of Tulliebole, James Moncreiff, 1st Baron (1811-1895) lord justice clerk of Scotland.

P SIR GEORGE REID, exhib 1887, wl in robes, Faculty of Advocates Parliament Hall, Edinburgh.

D JAMES ARCHER, oval, pastel, Dundee City Art Gallery.

PR T.ATKINSON, after D.Macnee, tql, mezz, pub 1872, NPG. W.HOLL, after G.Richmond, hs, stipple, one of 'Grillion's Club' series, BM, NPG. UNKNOWN, hs, woodcut, for *Illust London News* 17 April 1869, NPG.

PH CALDESI, BLANFORD & CO, wl, carte, NPG (Album 102).

MONCRIEFF, Sir Alexander (1829-1906) engineer.

D JOHN HENRY LORIMER, 1891, pencil, SNPG 1076.

MOND, Ludwig (1839-1909) chemist and art collector.

P SOLOMON J.SOLOMON, RA 1909, tql seated, NPG 3053.

SC EDOUARD LANTERI, 1909, bronze plaques, NPG 4511 and Department of Physics, Cambridge University. H.GLICENSTEIN, bronze bust, Department of Physics.

PH UNKNOWN, hs, photogravure, for *Cat of Mond Collection*, 1910, BM (Engr Ports Coll).

MONIER-WILLIAMS, Sir Monier (1819-1899) orientalist.
P W.W.OULESS, 1882, tql in gown, Indian Institute, Oxford.
PH HILLS & SAUNDERS, wl seated, carte, NPG (Album 40).

MONK, William Henry (1823-1889) composer.
PH W. & A.H.FRY, tql seated, carte, NPG.

MONKBRETTON, John George Dodson (1825-1897) politician.
P FRANK TOPHAM, 1896, replica, East Sussex County Council.
C UNKNOWN, hs seated at desk, chromo-lith, for *Vanity Fair*, 16 Dec 1871, NPG. SIR LESLIE WARD ('Spy'), wl, profile, chromo-lith, for *Vanity Fair*, 25 Jan 1894, NPG.
PH JOHN & CHARLES WATKINS, hs, carte, NPG (Album 136).

MONKHOUSE, William Cosmo (1840-1901) poet and critic.
P JOHN McLURE HAMILTON, RA 1899, hl seated, profile, NPG 1868.
PR WILLIAM STRANG, 1892, hl seated, etch, NPG 1884. W.STRANG, hl, etch, BM.
C HARRY FURNISS, pen and ink sketch, NPG 3592.

MONKSWELL, Robert Porrett Collier, 1st Baron (1817-1886) judge.
P SIR WILLIAM BOXALL, hs, semi-profile, Inner Temple, London.
PR UNKNOWN, hl, woodcut, for *Illust London News*, 17 Oct 1863, NPG.
C ALFRED THOMPSON (ΛΤή), wl, w/c study, for *Vanity Fair*, 19 Feb 1870, NPG 2734.
PH LOCK & WHITFIELD, hs, woodburytype, oval, for *Men of Mark*, 1880, NPG. JOHN & CHARLES WATKINS, two cartes, hs, NPG (Album 136), and wl seated, NPG x6314.

MONRO, David Binning (1836-1905) classical scholar.
P SIR W.Q.ORCHARDSON, RA 1897, hl seated, Oriel College, Oxford.

MONRO, Henry (1817-1891) physician and philanthropist.
P Self-portrait, c1870, hs, Royal College of Physicians, London.

MONSELL, William, see Baron Emly.

MONTAGU, Lord Robert (1825-1902) politician and controversialist.
C CARLO PELLEGRINI ('Ape'), wl, chromo-lith, for *Vanity Fair*, 1 Oct 1870, NPG.

MONTAGU, Samuel, see 1st Baron Swaythling.

MONTAGU, William, see 7th Duke of Manchester.

MONTAGU-WORTLEY-MACKENZIE, Edward, see 1st Earl of Wharncliffe.

MONTAGUE, Henry James (1843?-1878) actor.
PR Several theatrical prints, Harvard Theatre Collection, Cambridge, Mass, USA.
PH ELLIOTT & FRY, hs, carte, NPG. UNKNOWN, hs, woodburytype, carte, NPG.

MONTEFIORE, Claude Joseph Goldsmid- (1858-1938) biblical scholar and philanthropist.
P G.F.WATTS, 1903, hs, Watts Gallery, Compton, Surrey. SIR OSWALD BIRLEY, 1925, tql seated, The Liberal Jewish Synagogue, London.
D SIR WILLIAM ROTHENSTEIN, hl, sanguine, NPG 4789.
SC BENNO ELKAN, 1934, bronze bust, University of Southampton.
PH UNKNOWN, tql seated, print, NPG.

MONTEZ, Lola, see Marie Dolores Eliza Rosanna GILBERT.

MONTGOMERIE, Archibald William, see 13th Earl of Eglinton.

MONTGOMERY, George Robert Charles Herbert, 9th Earl of, see 13th Earl of Pembroke.

MONTGOMERY, Robert (1807-1855) poet.
M Self-portrait, hl, Holburne of Menstrie Museum, Bath.
PR C.BAUGNIET, tql in pulpit, lith, BM. THOMSON, after Derby, hl, stipple, pub 1828, NPG. THOMSON, after Hobday, hl seated, stipple, pub 1828, NPG. J.ROMNEY, after C.Grant, hs, line, NPG. Several popular prints, NPG. UNKNOWN, hs, woodcut, for *Illust London News*, 24 March 1855, NPG.

MONTGOMERY, Sir Robert (1809-1887) Indian administrator.
P ARTHUR RENDALL, after Sir Francis Grant of 1865, tql with Bath ribbon and star, India Office Library and Records, London.
SC ALBERT BRUCE JOY, RA 1893, marble bust, India Office. ALBERT BRUCE JOY, medallion, St Paul's Cathedral, London.

MONTROSE, Douglas Graham, 5th Duke of (1852-1925) soldier.
PR JOSEPH BROWN, after a photograph by Numa Blanc, hs, stipple, for *Baily's Mag*, 1880, NPG.
C SIR LESLIE WARD ('Spy'), wl, w/c study, for *Vanity Fair*, 18 March 1882, NPG 2588.

MOORE, Albert Joseph (1841-1893) painter.
D S.P.HALL, two pencil sketches, NPG 2375 and 2379.
PR R.TAYLOR, after a photograph, hl with palette, woodcut, for *Mag of Art*, 1885, NPG.

MOORE, Arthur William (1853-1909) Manx antiquary.
P R.E.MORRISON, House of Keys, Douglas, Isle of Man.
SC F.M.TAUBMAN, 1911, bust, House of Keys.
PH Several prints, Manx Museum, Library and Art Gallery, Douglas.

MOORE, Aubrey Lackington (1848-1890) writer on theology.
P C.W.FURSE, 1892, posthumous, hl, Keble College, Oxford.

MOORE, Edward (1835-1916) principal of St Edmund Hall, Oxford and Dante scholar.
P UNKNOWN, hs, St Edmund Hall, Oxford.

MOORE, George (1806-1876) philanthropist.
PR P.ANDERSON, after a photograph by V.Blanchard, hs, profile, stipple, NPG. UNKNOWN, after a photograph by Maull & Co, hs, woodcut, for *Illust London News*, 2 Dec 1876, NPG.

MOORE, George Augustus (1852-1933) novelist.
P EDOUARD MANET, c1879, wl seated in the artist's garden, Mellon Collection, USA. EDOUARD MANET, hl seated, oil sketch, Metropolitan Museum of Art, New York, USA. J.E.BLANCHE, 1887, hs, Musée des Beaux Arts, Rouen. W.R.SICKERT, 1890-1, head, TATE 3181. J.B.YEATS, 1905, hl, NGI 873. F.L.HARRIS, 1920, hl seated, semi-profile, Fitzwilliam Museum, Cambridge. PHILIP WILSON STEER, oval, University of Texas, Austin, USA.
D SIR WILLIAM ROTHENSTEIN, 1896, hs, chalk, NGI 2968. GEORGE RUSSELL ('AE'), 1900, pastel, University of Texas, USA. HENRY TONKS, 1901, hl seated, pencil, NPG 4154. HENRY TONKS, c1920, wl seated, pastel, NPG 2807. FRANCIS DODD, 1932, hs, pencil, NPG 2673. EDMOND KAPP, 1933, Barber Institute of Fine Arts, Birmingham. EDOUARD MANET, hs, pastel, Metropolitan Museum of Art, New York. SIR WILLIAM ORPEN, tql seated, pencil, NPG 2565.
G SIR WILLIAM ORPEN, 'Homage to Manet', oil, 1909, Manchester City Art Gallery. SIR WILLIAM ORPEN, group in the Café Royal, oil, 1911-12, Nicols Bar, Café Royal, London; Copy, Musée

d'Art Moderne, Paris. HENRY TONKS, 'Saturday Night in the Vale', oil, 1928–9, TATE 4614.

SC UNKNOWN, plaster death masks, NPG 2622 and NGI 8129.

C SIR MAX BEERBOHM, there are various drgs, various dates, including those at Ashmolean Museum, Oxford, Municipal Gallery of Modern Art, Dublin, Savile Club, London, Harvard College Library, Cambridge, Mass, USA, University of California at Los Angeles, USA and University of Texas, USA. 'SIC', wl, chromo-lith, for *Vanity Fair*, 21 Jan 1897, NPG.

PH A.L.COBURN, 1908, wl, profile, photogravure, for *Men of Mark*, 1913, NPG AX7785.

MOORE, Henry (1831-1896) marine painter.

PR G.PILOTELL, hs, drypoint, BM. UNKNOWN, hs, oval, woodcut, for *Illust London News*, 4 July 1885, NPG.

PH RALPH W.ROBINSON, hl seated with palette, print, for *Members and Associates of the Royal Academy of Arts, 1891*, NPG X7380.

MOORE, John Bramley, see BRAMLEY-Moore.

MOORE, Joseph (1817-1892) medallist.

P W.T.RODEN, Birmingham City Art Gallery.

MOORE, Thomas Edward Laws (1819-1872) rear-admiral, governor of the Falkland Islands.

P STEPHEN PEARCE, 1860, hl in uniform, NPG 1215.

MOORHOUSE, James (1826-1915) bishop of Melbourne and afterwards of Manchester.

P SIR GEORGE REID, tql seated, Manchester City Art Gallery.

PH BARRAUD, hs, print, for *Men and Women of the Day*, vol III, 1890, NPG AX5503. UNKNOWN, hs, print, NPG (Anglican Bishops).

MORAY, Edmund Archibald Stuart, 15th Earl of (1840-1901) landowner.

C SIR LESLIE WARD ('Spy'), wl seated, w/c study, for *Vanity Fair*, 9 June 1898, NPG 2966.

MORDAUNT, Miss (1812?-1858), see Nisbett.

MORE-MOLYNEUX, Sir Robert Henry (1838-1904) admiral.

PR 'RT', hs, wood engr, for *Illust London News*, 2 Jan 1886, NPG.

MORELL, John Daniel (1816-1891) philosopher and inspector of schools.

PR R.T. & CO, hs, wood engr, for *Illust London News*, 4 April 1891, NPG.

MORETON, Henry George Francis Reynolds-, see 2nd Earl of Ducie.

MORFILL, William Richard (1834-1909) Slavonic scholar.

PH UNKNOWN, British Academy, London.

MORGAN, Alice Mary, née Havers (1850-1890) painter.

PR UNKNOWN, after a photograph by H.S.Mendelssohn, hs, profile, wood engr, for *Illust London News*, 6 Sept 1890, NPG.

MORGAN, Augustus De, see DE Morgan.

MORGAN, Conwy Lloyd (1852-1936) comparative psychologist and philosopher.

P ROBERT ANNING BELL, 1921, University of Bristol.

PH WALTER STONEMAN, 1921, hs, NPG (NPR).

MORGAN, Frederic Courtenay (1834-1909) politician.

C SIR LESLIE WARD ('Spy'), wl, w/c study, for *Vanity Fair*, 2 Nov 1893, NPG 2976.

PH SIR BENJAMIN STONE, 1897, wl, print, Birmingham Reference Library, NPG.

MORGAN, Sir George Osborne, 1st Bart (1826-1897) lawyer and politician.

C SIR LESLIE WARD ('Spy'), wl, chromo-lith, for *Vanity Fair*, 17

May 1879, NPG.

PH LOCK & WHITFIELD, hs, oval, woodburytype, for *Men of Mark*, 1883, NPG.

MORIARTY, David (1814-1877) bishop of Kerry.

PH FRATELLI D'ALESSANDRI, hs, carte, NPG.

MORIARTY, Henry Augustus (1815-1906) captain in the navy.

PR UNKNOWN, after a photograph by Mayall, hs, semi-profile, woodcut, for *Illust London News*, 12 Jan 1867, NPG.

MORIER, Sir Robert Burnett David (1826-1893) diplomat

P FRANZ VON LENBACH, 1874, tql seated, Balliol College, Oxford

PR 'RT', hs, semi-profile, wood engr, for *Illust London News*, 19 Jan 1889, NPG.

PH WALERY, c1890, tql, print, NPG.

MORLEY, Albert Edmund Parker, 3rd Earl of (1843-1905) chairman of committees of the House of Lords.

P ELLIS ROBERTS, hs, Saltram (NT), Devon; copy, hs, Devon County Council, Exeter.

PR UNKNOWN, hs in uniform, woodcut, for *Illust London News*, Feb 1866, NPG. UNKNOWN, after a photograph by Elliott & Fry, hs, wood engr, for *Illust London News*, 20 April 1889, NPG.

MORLEY, Edmund Parker, 2nd Earl of (1810-1864) lord in-waiting to Queen Victoria.

PR R.J:LANE, after F.Talfourd of c1851, hs, lith, NPG.

MORLEY, Henry (1822-1894) professor of literature at University College.

P IDA R.MORLEY, tql seated, Apothecaries Hall, London.

PH W. & D.DOWNEY, hl, woodburytype, for Cassell's *Cabinet Portrait Gallery*, vol III, 1892, NPG.

MORLEY, Samuel (1809-1886) politician and philanthropist

P H.T.WELLS, RA 1874, Congregational Memorial Hall, London

SC J.H.THOMAS, c1885, plaster statuette, NPG 1303. J.H.THOMAS, two statues, Bristol and Nottingham.

PR UNKNOWN, hs, chromo-lith, NPG. R.TAYLOR, hs, woodcut, for *Illust London News*, 18 Feb 1871, NPG.

C UNKNOWN, wl, profile, chromo-lith, for *Vanity Fair*, 15 June 1872, NPG. 'PET', wl, chromo-lith, for *The Monetary Gazette*, 21 July 1877, NPG.

PH ELLIOTT & FRY, two cabinets, both tql seated, NPG X4969–70. ELLIOTT & FRY, hs, profile, carte, NPG. ELLIOTT & FRY, tql seated, carte, NPG (Album 136). F.GUTEKUNST, hs, cabinet, NPG X497. LOCK & WHITFIELD, hs, oval, woodburytype, for *Men of Mark*, 1882, NPG. LONDON STEREOSCOPIC CO, hs, carte, NPG (Album 40).

MORLEY of Blackburn, John Morley, 1st Viscount (1838-1923) statesman.

P W.W.OULESS, 1891, hs, NPG 3051. JOHN COLLIER, 1913, tql seated in gown with Order of Merit, Lincoln College, Oxford; replica 1924, National Liberal Club, London.

D S.P.HALL, four pencil sketches, NPG 2248, 2307 and 2316–17. EDMOND KAPP, 1914, Barber Institute of Fine Arts, Birmingham

PR W.ROTHENSTEIN, 1903, hs, lith, NPG. R.TAYLOR, after a photograph by Bassano, hs, wood engr, for *Illust London News*, 20 Feb 1886, NPG.

C HARRY FURNISS, three pen and ink sketches, NPG 3399, 3400 and 3593. SIR FRANCIS CARRUTHERS GOULD, hl, profile, pen sketch, NPG 2849. CARLO PELLEGRINI ('Ape'), wl, profile, chromo-lith, for *Vanity Fair*, 30 Nov 1878, NPG.

PH BARRAUD, tql, print, for *Men and Women of the Day*, vol I, 1888, NPG AX5436. ALEXANDER BASSANO, 1886, hs, carte, NPG X12495. G.C.BERESFORD, 1902, two negs, both hs, NPG X6547–8. G.C.BERESFORD, two prints, hs and hs, profile, NPG X12492–3. W. & D.DOWNEY, tql seated, woodburytype, for Cassell's

Cabinet Portrait Gallery, vol I, 1890, NPG. LONDON STEREOSCOPIC Co, hs, print, NPG. RUSSELL & SONS, *c*1891, hs, woodburytype, NPG X12498.

MORPHETT, Sir John (1809-1892) pioneer and politician of South Australia.
PR UNKNOWN, hs, woodcut, NPG.

MORRIS, Edward Patrick Morris, Baron (1859-1935) prime minister of Newfoundland.
P SIR JAMES GUTHRIE, hl study for NPG 2463, SNPG 1141.
G SIR JAMES GUTHRIE, 'Statesmen of World War I, 1914-18', oil, NPG 2463; sketch, SNPG 1466.
PH WALTER STONEMAN, 1917, hs, profile, NPG (NPR).

MORRIS, Francis Orpen (1810-1893) naturalist.
PH SWAN ELECTRIC ENGRAVING Co, tql, profile, photogravure, NPG.

MORRIS, Jane, née Burden (1839?-1914) wife of William Morris; model for numerous Pre-Raphaelite paintings.
P WILLIAM MORRIS, 1858, wl, 'Queen Guinevere', TATE 4999. D.G.ROSSETTI, 1866–68, tql seated, 'The Blue Silk Dress', Kelmscott Manor (Society of Antiquaries), Oxon. D.G.ROSSETTI and FORD MADOX BROWN, hs, circle, Wightwick Manor (NT), W Midlands. Jane Morris sat as model for numerous paintings by ROSSETTI, including: 1858–64, as the Virgin in 'The Seed of David', Llandaff Cathedral; 1859, 'The Salutation of Beatrice', National Gallery of Canada, Ottawa; 1868–80, tql seated, 'La Pia de' Tolomei', Museum of Art, University of Kansas, Lawrence, USA; 1870, tql seated, 'Mariana', Aberdeen Art Gallery; 1871, hs 'Water Willow', Bancroft Collection, Wilmington Society of Fine Arts, Delaware, USA; 1877, tql, 'Astarte Syriaca', Manchester City Art Gallery; 1879, hl, 'La Donna della Finestra', Fogg Museum of Art, Harvard University, Cambridge, Mass, USA; 1880, wl seated, 'The Day Dream', V & A; 1880–81, tql, 'The Salutation of Beatrice', Toledo Museum of Art, Ohio, USA.
D WILLIAM MORRIS, hs, pencil, pen and ink, BM. WILLIAM MORRIS, wl as Iseult, William Morris Gallery, Walthamstow. D.G.ROSSETTI, various portrait drgs, *c*1857–1875, various sizes and media, Kelmscott Manor; NGI 2259; Fitzwilliam Museum, Cambridge; Fogg Museum of Art; Galleria Nazionale d'Arte Moderna, Rome; Art Institute of Chicago, USA; Museum of Fine Arts, Boston, USA; BM; William Morris Gallery; Whitworth Art Gallery, Manchester University; Walker Art Gallery, Liverpool; Birmingham City Museum and Art Gallery; Cincinnati Art Museum; National Gallery of South Australia, Adelaide; Wightwick Manor. Various drgs by D.G.ROSSETTI for which Jane Morris sat as a model, including: 1856, 'Dante's Dream at the Time of the Death of Beatrice', w/c, TATE 5229; 1857, wl, 'Sir Launcelot in the Queen's Chamber', pen and ink, Birmingham City Art Gallery; 1867, 'Sir Tristram and La Belle Yseult drinking the love potion', w/c, Cecil Higgins Art Gallery, Bedford; *c*1868, hl seated, 'Aurea Catena', pencil, Fogg Museum of Art; 1869, head, study for 'Pandora', oval, chalks, Manchester City Art Gallery; 1870, tql seated, 'Silence', chalk, Brooklyn Museum, New York, USA; 1870, hs, profile, 'The Roseleaf', pencil, National Gallery of Canada, Ottawa; 1870, tql seated, 'La Donna della Fiamma', chalks, Manchester City Art Gallery; 1871, hs, profile, 'Perlascura', pastel, Ashmolean Museum, Oxford; 1879, tql, 'Pandora', crayons, Fogg Art Museum. CHARLES GERE, *c*1900, head, pencil and body colour, BM.
C D.G.ROSSETTI, several pen and ink drgs, some with her husband, BM, Birmingham City Art Gallery.
PH Various prints by PAOLO LOMBARDI, HARRY F.PHILLIPS and other photographers, singly and in groups with family and friends, NPG. Various prints, NPG, V & A, William Morris Gallery,

Kelmscott. EMERY WALKER, several negs, various sizes, as an old woman, NPG.

MORRIS, Sir Lewis (1833-1907) poet.
P H.FOULGER, finished by B.A.LEWIS, University College of Wales, Aberystwyth.
SC J.MILO GRIFFITH, 1897, finished by P.R.MONTFORD in 1900, plaster bust, National Museum of Wales 1188, Cardiff. SIR WILLIAM GOSCOMBE JOHN, RA 1899, plaster bust, University College, Aberystwyth.
PH W. & D.DOWNEY, hl, woodburytype, for Cassell's *Cabinet Portrait Gallery*, vol I, 1890, NPG.

MORRIS, Sir Michael, see Lord MORRIS and Killanin.

MORRIS, Philip Richard (1836-1902) painter.
P Self-portrait, MacDonald Collection, Aberdeen Art Gallery.
PR UNKNOWN, hs, woodcut, for *Illust London News*, 14 July 1877, NPG.
PH RALPH W.ROBINSON, wl seated, print, for *Members and Associates of the Royal Academy of Arts, 1891*, NPG X7381.

MORRIS, Richard (1833-1894) philologist.
PR 'P.N.', hs, wood engr, for *Illust London News*, 26 May 1894, NPG.

MORRIS, Tom (1821-1908) golfer.
P SIR GEORGE REID, 1903, tql, Royal and Ancient Golf Club of St Andrews, Scotland.
SC UNKNOWN, figure on monument, St Andrews' Cathedral burying ground.

MORRIS, William (1834-1896) poet, draftsman and socialist.
P G.F.WATTS, 1870, hs, NPG 1078. SIR W.B.RICHMOND, exhib 1882, hs, NPG 1938.
D Self-portrait, hs, before he grew his beard, pencil, V & A. D.G.ROSSETTI, 1861, head, pencil study for head of David in Llandaff Cathedral, Birmingham City Art Gallery. GEORGE HOWARD, 9th EARL OF CARLISLE, with Thomas Carlyle, Carlisle Art Gallery. UNKNOWN, hs, profile, w/c, NPG 3652. CHARLES FAIRFAX-MURRAY, 1896, two studies of Morris on his death bed, pencil, NPG 3021 and TATE 5001.
G D.G.ROSSETTI, 'The Seed of David', oil, 1858–64, Morris was the model for the figure of David, Llandaff Cathedral. SIR EDWARD BURNE-JONES, 'The Adoration of the Magi', oil, 1861, Morris was the model for the figure of the foremost king, TATE 4743.
SC ARTHUR WALKER, 1909, West Front, V & A.
C WALTER CRANE, 'Homage to Morris', with his friends in Elysium, William Morris Gallery, Walthamstow. Various drgs by SIR EDWARD BURNE-JONES and D.G.ROSSETTI, BM, Birmingham City Art Gallery, Fogg Art Museum, Cambridge, Mass, USA and William Morris Gallery. SIR MAX BEERBOHM, 1916, posthumous drg, wl settled on the Settle in Red Lion Square with Sir Edward Burne-Jones, pencil and w/c, TATE 5391 (xii).
PH Numerous prints by ELLIOTT & FRY, ELLIS & GREEN, FREDERICK HOLLYER, ABEL LEWIS, LONDON STEREOSCOPIC Co, EMERY WALKER and others, various dates and sizes, singly and in groups with family and friends, NPG, V & A, Kelmscott Manor (Society of Antiquaries), Oxon, and William Morris Gallery.

MORRIS, William O'Connor (1824-1904) Irish county court judge and historian.
PH FARRINGDON, after a photograph by Chancellor & Son, tql seated, profile, photogravure, NPG.

MORRIS and KILLANIN, Sir Michael Morris, Baron (1826-1901) lord chief justice of Ireland.
C SIR LESLIE WARD ('Spy'), wl, profile, chromo-lith, for *Vanity Fair*, 14 Sept 1893, NPG.

PH UNKNOWN, King's Inns, Dublin.

MORRISON, Alfred (1821–1897) collector.
G HENRY JAMYN BROOKS, 'Private view of the Old Masters Exhibition, Royal Academy, 1888', oil, NPG 1833.

MORTIMER, Mrs Favell Lee, née Bevan (1802–1878) author of *Peep of Day* etc.
PR UNKNOWN, wl seated, writing, woodcut, for *Christmas Bookseller*, 1878, BM.

MORTIMER, George Ferris Whidborne (1805–1871) schoolmaster.
SC CHARLES BACON, RA 1866, bust, City of London School.

MORTON, Sir Alpheus Cleophas (1840–1923) architect and politician.
C SIR LESLIE WARD ('Spy'), wl, w/c study, for *Vanity Fair*, 15 June 1893, NPG 2977.
PH SIR BENJAMIN STONE, 1907, two prints, both wl, NPG.

MORTON, Thomas (1814–1849) surgeon.
P ANDREW MORTON, tql, Royal College of Surgeons, London.

MOSELEY, Henry Nottidge (1844–1891) naturalist.
PR UNKNOWN, hs, wood engr, for *Illust London News*, 28 Nov 1891, NPG.
PH UNKNOWN, hl seated, photogravure, NPG.

MOSTYN, George Charles, see 6th Baron VAUX of Harrowden.

MOTT, Sir Basil, 1st Bart (1859–1938) civil engineer.
P STANHOPE A.FORBES, 1925, tql seated, Institution of Civil Engineers, London.
PH WALTER STONEMAN, 1936, hl, NPG (NPR).

MOTT, Charles Grey (1833–1905) civil engineer.
C SIR LESLIE WARD ('Spy'), wl, w/c study, for *Vanity Fair*, 14 June 1894, NPG 2456.

MOTT, Sir Frederick Walker (1853–1926) neuropathologist.
PH WALTER STONEMAN, 1917, hs in uniform, NPG (NPR).

MOULE, George Evans (1828–1912) missionary Bishop in mid-China.
PH UNKNOWN, hl, print, NPG (Anglican Bishops).

MOULE, Handley Carr Glyn (1841–1920) bishop of Durham.
P H.G.RIVIERE, 1914, tql seated, Bishop Auckland Palace, Durham.

MOULTON, John Fletcher Moulton, Baron (1844–1921) lord of appeal in ordinary.
PH ELLIOTT & FRY, hl seated, cabinet, NPG. WALTER STONEMAN, 1917, hs, NPG (NPR).

MOULTON, William Fiddian (1835–1898) biblical scholar.
PR UNKNOWN, hl seated, stipple, NPG. H.PRATER, hs, wood engr, for *Illust London News*, 2 Aug 1890, NPG.

MOUNTBATTEN, Louis Alexander (1854–1921), see 1st Marquess of Milford Haven.

MOUNT STEPHEN, George Stephen, 1st Baron (1829–1921) financier and philanthropist.
P SIR GEORGE REID, 1894, Canadian Pacific Company, Toronto, Canada.

MOUNT-TEMPLE, William Francis Cowper-Temple, Baron (1811–1888) statesman.
PR R.J.LANE, after A.D'Orsay, 1842, hl, profile, lith, BM, NPG.
PH W.WALKER & SONS, 1860s, tql, carte, NPG X6912. LOCK &

WHITFIELD, hs, woodburytype, oval, for *Men of Mark*, 1876, NPG. BRADNEE, hl seated with his wife, cabinet, NPG. UNKNOWN, tql in uniform, carte, NPG (Album 113).

MOWAT, Sir Oliver (1820–1903) Canadian statesman.
P ROBERT HARRIS, Ontario Legislative Buildings, Canada. DIXON PATTERSON, Government House, Toronto.

MOWATT, Sir Francis (1837–1919) civil servant.
P C.W.FURSE, RA 1904, tql, DoE (Southbridge).
PH BASSANO, 1898, seven negs, various sizes, NPG X4213–19. WALTER STONEMAN, 1918, hl, NPG (NPR).

MOWBRAY (formerly CORNISH), Sir John Robert, 1st Bart (1815–1899) judge, 'father of the House of Commons'.
P After W.W.OULESS, 1886, Oxford and Cambridge University Club, London.
SC CONRAD DRESSLER, 1900, bronze bust, Palace of Westminster, London.
C SIR LESLIE WARD ('Spy'), wl, profile, w/c study, for *Vanity Fair*, 8 April 1882, NPG 2591.
PH MAULL & POLYBLANK, wl, carte, NPG (Album 136). BASSANO, 1898, four negs, various sizes, NPG X4251–54. SIR BENJAMIN STONE, 1898, two prints, both wl, NPG.

MOZLEY, James Bowling (1813–1878) regius professor of divinity at Oxford.
PR UNKNOWN, after a photograph by Clement Rogers, hs, woodcut, for *Illust London News*, 2 Feb 1878, NPG.

MUDIE, Charles Edward (1818–1890) founder of 'Mudie's' library.
PR R.TAYLOR, after a photograph by Maull & Polyblank, hs, woodcut, for *Illust London News*, 8 Nov 1890, BM, NPG.

MUIR, John (1810–1882) orientalist.
P J.H.LORIMER, tql seated, Edinburgh University.
PR UNKNOWN, hs, woodcut, NPG.

MUIR, Sir William (1819–1905) Indian administrator and principal of Edinburgh University.
SC GEORGE SIMONDS, RA 1880, bust?, University of Allahabad. UNKNOWN, bust, Edinburgh University.

MUIRHEAD, James (1831–1889) jurist.
PR W.HOLE, hl seated, etch, for *Quasi Cursores*, 1884, NPG.

MUIRHEAD, John Henry (1855–1940) philosopher.
PH WALTER STONEMAN, 1932, hl, NPG (NPR).

MULLENS, Joseph (1820–1879) missionary.
PR UNKNOWN, hl seated, stipple, NPG.

MÜLLER, Friedrich Max, see MAX Müller.

MÜLLER, William James (1812–1845) landscape painter.
M NATHAN BRANWHITE, TATE 2388. Self-portrait, hl seated, NPG 1304.
SC NATHAN BRANWHITE, 1845, bust, Bristol Cathedral, engr C.K.Childs, woodcut, for *Art Journal*, 1850, BM, NPG.

MULVANY, George F. (1809–1869) painter.
P Self-portrait, hs, NGI 926.
SC JOSEPH WATKINS, 1866, plaster, NGI 8190.

MUNDELLA, Anthony John (1825–1897) statesman.
P SIR A.S.COPE, RA 1894, tql, Sheffield Town Hall.
SC SIR J.E.BOEHM, plaster bust, Mappin Art Gallery, Sheffield.
PR UNKNOWN, hs, woodcut, NPG.
C UNKNOWN, tql, chromo-lith, for *Vanity Fair*, 9 Dec 1871, NPG
PH LONDON STEREOSCOPIC CO, hs, carte, NPG. SIR BENJAMIN STONE 1897, wl, print, Birmingham Reference Library.

MUNDY, Sir George Rodney (1805–1884) admiral of the fleet.

P G.F.CLARKE, The Admiralty, Portsmouth.

MUNK, William (1816-1898) physician.

P JOHN COLLIER, 1898, hl seated, Royal College of Physicians, London.

MUNRO, Alexander (1825-1871) sculptor.

D SIR J.E.MILLAIS, 1853, hs, pencil, William Morris Gallery, Walthamstow.

PR UNKNOWN, after a photograph, hs, semi-profile, woodcut, for *Illust London News*, 28 Jan 1871, BM.

MUNRO, Hugh Andrew Johnstone (1819-1885) classical scholar.

P F.TUTTLE, 1865, tql seated, Trinity College, Cambridge.

SC THOMAS WOOLNER, 1886, marble bust, Trinity College. HENRY WILES, marble bust, posthumous, Fitzwilliam Museum, Cambridge.

PH UNKNOWN, hl, print, BM (Engr Ports Coll).

MUNTZ, Sir Philip Albert, Bart (1839-1908) politician.

C SIR LESLIE WARD ('Spy'), wl, profile, w/c study, for *Vanity Fair*, 23 July 1892, NPG 2978.

MURCHISON, Charles (1830-1879) physician.

D H.J.FRADELLE, hs, oval, chalk and wash, Royal College of Physicians, London.

SC E.ROSCOE MULLINS, RA 1881, marble bust, St Thomas's Hospital, London.

MURPHY, Sir Francis (1809-1891) first speaker of the legislative assembly of Victoria.

SC CHARLES SUMMERS, marble bust, State Library of Victoria, Australia.

MURPHY, Francis Stack (1810?-1860) serjeant-at-law; essayist.

G D.MACLISE, 'The Fraserians', lith, for *Fraser's Mag*, 1835, BM.

MURPHY, Robert (1806-1843) mathematician.

P Dr WOODHOUSE, Caius College, Cambridge.

MURRAY, Andrew Graham, see Viscount Dunedin.

MURRAY, Charles Adolphus, see 7th Earl of Dunmore.

MURRAY, Sir Charles Augustus (1806-1895) diplomat.

PR G.ZOBEL, after W.Maddox, tql seated with Egyptian servant, mezz, pub 1853, BM, NPG, SNPG.

MURRAY, Sir David (1849-1933) artist.

P JAMES ARCHER, SNPG 1149. J.COUTTS MICHIE, 1897, MacDonald Collection, Aberdeen Art Gallery. R.G.JENNINGS, 1914, SNPG 1234. JOHN PETTIE, SNPG 1233. Self-portrait, 1915, tql with brush and palette, Uffizi Gallery, Florence.

G SIR HUBERT VON HERKOMER, 'The Council of the Royal Academy', oil, 1908, TATE 2481.

PR H.F.DAVEY, after a photograph, hs, woodcut, BM.

PH WALTER STONEMAN, 1919, hs, NPG (NPR). UNKNOWN, hl seated, print, NPG. UNKNOWN, wl in studio, postcard, NPG.

MURRAY, David Christie (1847-1907) novelist and journalist.

G W.H.BARTLETT, 'Saturday Night at the Savage Club', oil, Savage Club, London.

PR UNKNOWN, after a photograph by J.Ganz of Brussels, hs, woodcut, for *Harper's Mag*, June 1888, NPG.

MURRAY, Mrs Elizabeth Leigh (d 1892) singer.

PR C.LOCKINGTON, wl as Aemilia in *The Magician*, woodcut, for *Theatrical Times*, 2 Sept 1848, Harvard Theatre Collection, Cambridge, Mass, USA.

PH WINDOW & BRIDGE, wl, carte, NPG.

MURRAY, Henry Leigh (1820-1870) actor.

D STEPHEN PEARCE, 1851, hs, chalk, Garrick Club, London.

PR J.H.BAKER, after S.Pearce, hl, stipple, BM. UNKNOWN, after a daguerreotype, tql seated, stipple and line, for Tallis's *Dramatic Mag*, BM, NPG. UNKNOWN, after a daguerreotype, wl with Mrs Stirling, as Orlando and Rosalind in *As You Like It*, stipple and line, for same work, BM, NPG, Harvard Theatre Collection, Cambridge, Mass, USA.

MURRAY, Sir James Augustus Henry (1837-1915) editor of the *Oxford English Dictionary*.

PR W.ROTHENSTEIN, hl, lith, BM.

MURRAY, Sir James Wolfe (1853-1919) lieutenant-general.

C SIR LESLIE WARD ('Spy'), wl in uniform, chromo-lith, for *Vanity Fair*, 4 May 1905, NPG.

PH WALTER STONEMAN, 1917, hs in uniform, NPG (NPR).

MURRAY, John (1808-1892) publisher.

P C.W.FURSE, c1881, tql seated, NPG 1885.

PR UNKNOWN, after a photograph by Maull & Fox, woodcut, NPG. R.T. & Co, hs, oval, woodcut, for *Illust London News*, 9 April 1892, NPG.

PH D.O.HILL & ROBERT ADAMSON, 1843-8, hl seated, print, NPG P6 (27).

MURRAY, Sir John (1841-1914) marine biologist.

P SIR GEORGE REID, SNPG L221.

MUSGRAVE, Sir Anthony (1828-1888) administrator.

D L.G.FAWKES, w/c, DoE.

MUSGRAVE, Sir James, 1st Bart (1826-1904) benefactor of Belfast.

P W.F.OSBORNE, Belfast Harbour Office.

SC ARCHIBALD McFARLANE SHANNAN, marble bust, Belfast Harbour Office.

MUSPRATT, James Sheridan (1821-1871) chemist.

PR W.HOLL, after a photograph, tql seated, semi-profile, stipple, for his *Dict of Chemistry*, pub W.Mackenzie, BM, NPG. JOHN LE CONTE, after a photograph by Foard & Beard, hl seated, stipple and line, NPG.

MUTRIE, Annie Feray (1826-1893) artist.

PH MAULL & CO, wl with her sister, carte, NPG (Album 104).

MUTRIE, Martha Darley (1824-1885) artist.

PH MAULL & CO, wl with her sister, carte, NPG (Album 104).

MUYBRIDGE, Eadweard (1830-1904) investigator of animal locomotion.

PR R.TAYLOR, after Walter Wilson, tql showing his instantaneous photographs of animal motion at the Royal Society, woodcut, for *Illust London News*, 25 May 1889, NPG.

MYERS, Frederic William Henry (1834-1901) poet and essayist; one of the founders of the Society of Psychical Research.

P W.C.WONTNER, c1895, hs, NPG 2928.

SC H.A.PROTHERO, plaque with relief portrait, Cheltenham College Chapel.

PH MRS EVELEEN MYERS, c1892, two photogravures, hs, semi-profile, and hs with his son Leo, NPG.

MYNN, Alfred (1807-1861) cricketer.

P W.BROMLEY, c1840, wl, Marylebone Cricket Club, London.

G N.PLOSZCZYNSKI, after a w/c by N.Felix, 'The Eleven of England', pub 1847, and G.H.PHILLIPS, after portraits by W.Drummond and C.J.Basebe, 'A Cricket Match Between Sussex and Kent', pub 1849, both chromo-liths, both Marylebone Cricket Club.

PR G.F.WATTS, wl, bowling, lith, BM; original drg, Marylebone Cricket Club.

N

NAAS, Richard Southwell Bourke, Baron, see 6th Earl of Mayo.

NAFTEL, Paul Jacob (1817-1891) painter.
PH JOHN & CHARLES WATKINS, tql seated, carte, NPG (Album 104).

NAIRNE, Sir Charles Edward (1836-1899) general.
P C.W.FURSE, wl on horseback, riding, with Indian retinue, Royal Artillery Mess, Woolwich, engr W.Strang, mezz, BM.

NAPIER, Sir Francis Napier, 10th Baron and 1st Baron Ettrick of Ettrick (1819-1898) diplomat and governor of Madras.
P G.F.WATTS, 1866, SNPG 811.

NAPIER, Sir Joseph, 1st Bart (1804-1882) lord chancellor of Ireland.
P THOMAS BRIDGFORD, King's Inns, Dublin. STEPHEN CATTERSON SMITH, exhib 1860, tql seated in chancellor's robes, Trinity College, Dublin.
PR UNKNOWN, after C.Grey, wl, etch, pub 1853, NPG. UNKNOWN, hs, woodcut, for *Illust London News*, 23 Oct 1858, NPG. UNKNOWN, hs, stipple, NPG.

NAPIER of Magdala, Robert Cornelis Napier, 1st Baron (1810-1890) field-marshal.
P SIR FRANCIS GRANT, 1868, wl, Royal Engineers HQ Mess, Chatham, Kent. MICHAEL ANGELO PITTATORE, 1869, hs, semi-profile, SNPG 566. LOWES DICKINSON, tql seated, in uniform, Royal Engineers HQ Mess.
D T.B.WIRGMAN, 1886, pencil, SNPG 1977.
SC SIR J.E.BOEHM, 1880, equestrian statue, Calcutta; replica, bronze, Queen's Gate, Kensington. SIR J.E.BOEHM, plaster bust, NPG 863.
PR UNKNOWN, hs in uniform, woodcut, for *Illust London News*, 28 Sept 1867, NPG. JUDD & CO, tql, lith, for *The Whitehall Review*, 4 May 1878, NPG. UNKNOWN, hs in uniform, chromo-lith, NPG.
C SIR LESLIE WARD ('Spy'), tql, chromo-lith, for *Vanity Fair*, 20 April 1878, NPG.
PH Various cartes by W. & D.DOWNEY, ELLIOTT & FRY, MAULL & CO, EDWIN SUTTON and JOHN WATKINS, various dates and sizes, some in uniform, NPG. ELLIOTT & FRY, tql, cabinet, NPG X11982. LOCK & WHITFIELD, hs, oval, woodburytype, for *Men of Mark*, 1878, NPG.

NARES, Sir George Strong (1831-1915) vice-admiral.
P STEPHEN PEARCE, 1877, tql in arctic dress, NPG 1212.
PR Three woodcuts by unknown artists for *Illust London News*, one hs in uniform (29 May 1875), and two in groups related to the Arctic Expedition (20 May 1875 and 5 June 1875), NPG. E.WHYMPER, hs, oval, woodcut, for *Leisure Hour*, 1876, BM.
PH LOCK & WHITFIELD, hs, oval, woodburytype, for *Men of Mark*, 1878, NPG.

NASH, Joseph (1809-1878) painter.
PR UNKNOWN, hs, woodcut, for *Illust London News*, 4 Jan 1879, NPG.
PH JOHN WATKINS, tql seated, carte, NPG (Album 104).

NASMYTH, Charles (1826-1861) major, 'defender of Silistria'.
PR UNKNOWN, after a photograph by Lock & Whitfield, hl, woodcut, for *Illust London News*, 13 July 1861, NPG.

NASMYTH, James (1808-1890) engineer, inventor of steam hammer.
P G.B.O'NEILL, 1874, hs, NPG 1582.
D Self-portrait, 1881, pastel, SNPG 1547.
PH D.O.HILL & ROBERT ADAMSON, c1844, hl seated, profile, print, NPG P6 (28). UNKNOWN, 1855, wl with steam hammer, print, Manchester Public Libraries. LOCK & WHITFIELD, hs, oval, woodburytype, for *Men of Mark*, 1877, NPG.

NEAVES, Charles Neaves, Lord (1800-1876) Scottish judge.
PR UNKNOWN, after a photograph by John Horsburgh, hs, woodcut, for *Illust London News*, 6 Jan 1877, NPG.

NEILL, James George Smith (1810-1857) brigadier-general.
SC UNKNOWN, statue, Ayr, Scotland.
PR G.STODART, after a photograph by Kilburn, tql seated, stipple, BM, NPG.

NEILSON, Lilian Adelaide (1848-1880) actress; real name Elizabeth Ann Brown.
D T.E.GAUNT, after a photograph by Napoleon Sarony, 1880, hs, as Juliet, oval, chalk, NPG 1781b.
PR Various theatrical prints, Harvard Theatre Collection, Cambridge, Mass, USA.
PH LOCK & WHITFIELD, hl, woodburytype, for *The Theatre*, NPG. UNKNOWN, hs, woodburytype, carte, NPG AX7605. UNKNOWN, hl, woodburytype, NPG AX7671. several cartes, NPG.

NELSON, Horatio Nelson, 3rd Earl (1823-1913) commissioner of the Royal Patriotic Fund.
C SIR LESLIE WARD ('Spy'), wl, w/c study, for *Vanity Fair*, 16 April 1881, NPG 2592.

NELSON, Thomas (1822-1892) publisher.
PR UNKNOWN, hs, wood engr, for *Illust London News*, 29 Oct 1892, NPG.

NELSON, William (1816-1887) publisher and philanthropist.
SC WILLIAM BRODIE, 1880, marble bust, SNPG 1435.

NESBIT, John Collis (1818-1862) agricultural chemist.
PR UNKNOWN, hs, woodcut, for *Illust London News*, 19 April 1862, NPG.

NESBITT, Louisa Cranstoun, see Nisbett.

NESFIELD, William Eden (1835-1888) architect.
D J.E.E.BRANDON, 1858, hs, pencil, NPG 1193. SIR W.B.RICHMOND, 1858, hs, pencil and chalk, NPG 4354.

NETTLESHIP, Henry (1839-1893) Latin scholar.
PR UNKNOWN, after a photograph by Elliott & Fry, hs, profile, wood engr, NPG.

NETTLESHIP, Richard Lewis (1846-1892) fellow and tutor of Balliol College, Oxford.
P GUSTAVE GIRARDOT, 1893, hs, Balliol College, Oxford.

NEUBAUER, Adolf (1832-1907) orientalist.
P LEONARD CAMPBELL TAYLOR, 1900, tql seated, Bodleian Library, Oxford.

NEVILL, Lady Dorothy, née Walpole (1826-1913) writer of memoirs.
G HENRY JAMYN BROOKS, 'Private view of the Old Masters

Exhibition, Royal Academy, 1888', oil, NPG 1833.

c 'K', tql seated, chromo-lith, for *Vanity Fair*, 6 Nov 1912, NPG.

NEVILLE, Henry Garside or **Gartside (1837-1910)** actor.

p J.W.WALTON, 1874, wl as Count Almaviva in Mortimer's *The School for Intrigue*, Garrick Club, London.

PR E.MATTHEWS & SONS, hs, lith, NPG.

c Various woodcuts and liths, some in character, Harvard Theatre Collection, Cambridge, Mass, USA.

PH LOCK & WHITFIELD, hs, woodburytype, for *The Theatre*, NPG. Several cartes by C.R.FITT, LONDON STEREOSCOPIC CO and others, some in character, NPG. ROTARY PHOTO CO, hs, postcard, NPG. UNKNOWN, hs, profile, woodburytype, carte, NPG AX7714.

NEVILLE, Richard Cornwallis, see 4th Baron Braybrooke.

NEVINSON, Henry Woodd (1856-1941) journalist and war correspondent.

p JOSEPH SOUTHALL, Christ Church, Oxford.

d SIR WILLIAM ROTHENSTEIN, 1919, head, chalk, NPG 3316. SIR W.ROTHENSTEIN, 1924, hs, sanguine, NPG 5193.

PH T.R.ANNAN, hs, semi-profile, print, NPG. WALTER STONEMAN, 1939, hs, for NPR, NPG X4649.

NEWALL, Hugh Frank (1857-1944) astrophysicist.

p GEORGE FIDDES WATT, 1929, tql seated, Observatories Syndicate, Cambridge University.

d SIR GEORGE CLAUSEN, 1928, pencil, Trinity College, Cambridge.

PH WALTER STONEMAN, 1917, hs, NPG (NPR). OLIVE EDIS, 1925, nearly tql, print, NPG.

NEWALL, Robert Stirling (1812-1889) engineer and astronomer.

sc After GEORGE SIMONDS, 1868, bronzed plaster relief plaque, Observatories Syndicate, Cambridge University.

NEWBOLD, Thomas John (1807-1850) traveller.

PR UNKNOWN, tql seated, profile, lith, BM.

NEWCASTLE-under-Lyme, Henry Pelham Fiennes Pelham Clinton, 5th Duke of (1811-1864) statesman.

p F.R.SAY, 1848, tql, NPG 4576. A.W.COX, Castle Art Gallery, Nottingham.

d GEORGE RICHMOND, 1856, head, chalk, NPG 4023.

G SIR GEORGE HAYTER, 'The House of Commons, 1833', oil, NPG 54. JOHN PARTRIDGE, 'The Fine Arts Commissioners, 1846', NPG 342,3. SIR JOHN GILBERT, 'The Coalition Ministry, 1854', pencil and wash, NPG 1125.

sc FRANK THEED, after Alexander Munro, 1887, marble bust, National Gallery of Canada, Ottawa.

PR JOSEPH BROWN, hs, stipple, pub 1866, NPG. G.ZOBEL, after J.W.Gordon, tql, mezz, BM, NPG.

c JOHN DOYLE, two drgs, political cartoons, BM.

PH CALDESI, BLANFORD & CO, wl, carte, NPG (Album 115).

NEWDEGATE, Charles Newdigate (1816-1887) politician.

PR 'R.T.', hs, wood engr, for *Illust London News*, 23 April 1887, NPG.

c CARLO PELLEGRINI ('Ape'), tql, profile, chromo-lith, for *Vanity Fair*, 13 Aug 1870, NPG.

NEWMAN, Francis William (1805-1897) scholar and man of letters.

PH J.BANKS, hs, print, NPG. HERBERT WATKINS, 1858, hs, oval, print, NPG AX7916.

NEWMAN, John Henry (1801-1890) cardinal; the chief founder of the Oxford movement.

p MISS MARIA GIBERNE, 1846, with Ambrose St John in Rome, Birmingham Oratory. MISS M.GIBERNE, 1851, 'Newman Lecturing', Birmingham Oratory. W.T.RODEN, *c*1874, tql seated, Keble College, Oxford. W.W.OULESS, *c*1880, hs, semi-profile,

Oriel College, Oxford. SIR J.E.MILLAIS, 1881, tql seated, NPG 5295. E.JENNINGS, *c*1881, after a photograph of 1879, hs, profile, Magdalen College, Oxford. MISS EMMELINE DEANE, 1887-9, hl seated, Birmingham Oratory. EMMELINE DEANE, 1889, tql seated, NPG 1022.

d GEORGE RICHMOND, 1844, hs, chalk, Oriel College; chalk study, NPG 1065. SIR W.C.ROSS, 1845, tql seated, w/c study, Keble College. MISS E.DEANE, 1884, hl seated, charcoal, English College, Rome. MISS ELINOR HALLÉ, 1885, Royal Coll. Drgs by H.DOYLE and R.DOYLE, Birmingham oratory.

sc THOMAS WOOLNER, 1866, marble bust, Keble College, Oxford; related plaster, NPG 1668. SIR THOMAS FARRELL, 1892, bust, University Chapel, Dublin. L.J.CHAVALLIAUD, 1896, marble statue, Brompton Oratory, London. H.A.PEGRAM, *c*1912, statue, Oriel College, Oxford. A.BROADBENT, *c*1915, bronze bust (part of a memorial), Trinity College, Oxford.

PR W.HUMPHREYS, after a drg by J.Bridges from a bust by R.Westmacott, line, pub 1844, NPG. R.WOODMAN, after a miniature by W.C.Ross of *c*1845, tql seated, stipple, BM, NPG. J.A.VINTER, after a drg by M.Giberne, hs, lith, pub 1850, BM, NPG. S.COUSINS, after J.Coleridge, hs in cassock, mezz, pub 1880, BM, NPG.

c J.R.GREEN, 1841, hs, profile, when vicar of St Mary's, drg, Truro Cathedral; anonymous etch, BM, NPG. UNKNOWN, 1850, hs, profile, engr, NPG. SIR LESLIE WARD ('Spy'), wl, profile, chromo-lith, for *Vanity Fair*, 20 Jan 1877, NPG. RICHARD DOYLE, hs, pen and ink, BM.

PH BARRAUD, hl, print, for *Men and Women of the Day*, 1888, NPG AX5406. H.J.WHITLOCK, hl, cabinet, NPG. Several cartes by MCLEAN & HAES, R.W.THRUPP and H.J.WHITLOCK, NPG.

NEWMARCH, Rosa Harriet, née Jefferson (1857-1940) writer on music.

PH HOWARD COSTER, 1931, three negs, with Feodor Chaliapin, NPG X10648-50.

NEWNES, Sir George, 1st Bart (1851-1910) newspaper and magazine projector.

sc OLIVER WHEATLEY, 1911, bronze relief portrait, Putney Library, London.

c SIR LESLIE WARD ('Spy'), wl, profile, chromo-lith, for *Vanity Fair*, 31 May 1894, NPG.

PH SIR BENJAMIN STONE, two prints, both wl, NPG.

NEWSHOLME, Sir Arthur (1857-1943) expert in public health.

PH WALTER STONEMAN, 1919, hl, NPG (NPR).

NEWTH, Samuel (1821-1898) principal of New College, London.

p UNKNOWN, hl, Dr Williams's Library, London.

PR J.COCHRAN, after a photograph by Mayall, hl seated, stipple and line, NPG.

PH ELLIOTT & FRY, hs, carte, NPG (Album 40).

NEWTON, Alfred (1829-1907) zoologist.

p LOWES DICKINSON, Magdalene College, Cambridge. C.W.FURSE, 1890, tql, Department of Zoology, Cambridge University.

NEWTON, Alfred Pizzi (1830-1883) artist.

PR UNKNOWN, after a photograph by Elliott & Fry, hs, semi-profile, woodcut, for *Illust London News*, 27 Oct 1883, NPG.

NEWTON, Ann Mary, née Severn (1832-1866) portrait painter.

p Self-portrait, hl, NPG 977.

d Self-portrait, pencil, Keats Memorial Library, Hampstead.

NEWTON, Sir Charles Thomas (1816-1894) archaeologist.

P H.W.PHILLIPS, hs, BM.

SC SIR J.E.BOEHM, 1863, plaster bust, NPG 973. WALDO STORY, 1888, marble relief portrait, Ashmolean Museum, Oxford.

PR P.NAUMANN, hs, woodcut, for *Illust London News*, 8 Dec 1894, BM, NPG.

PH LOCK & WHITFIELD, hs, oval, woodburytype, for *Men of Mark*, 1883, NPG.

NEWTON, Ernest (1856-1922) architect.

P ARTHUR HACKER, c1916, tql seated, RIBA, London.

PH ELLIOTT & FRY, hs, cabinet, NPG.

NEWTON, Thomas Wodehouse Legh, 2nd Baron (1857-1942) diplomat and politician.

P A.T.NOWELL, c1908, Lyme Park (NT), Cheshire.

C SIR LESLIE WARD ('Spy'), wl, profile, Hentschel-Colourtype, for *Vanity Fair*, 14 Oct 1908, NPG.

PH WALTER STONEMAN, 1917, hs, NPG (NPR). WALTER STONEMAN, hs, for NPR, NPG X5895.

NICHOL, John (1833-1894) man of letters.

P SIR W.Q.ORCHARDSON, hl, University of Glasgow.

NICHOLSON, Sir Charles, 1st Bart (1808-1903) speaker of the legislative council of New South Wales.

P H.W.PHILLIPS, University of Sydney, Australia.

PR J.R.JACKSON, after H.W.Phillips, wl in robes, with mace, mezz, BM. UNKNOWN, hs in robes, woodcut, for *Illust London News*, 3 Sept 1859, NPG.

NICHOLSON, John (1821-1857) soldier and administrator.

P J.R.DICKSEE, posthumous, hl in uniform, County Museum, Armagh; copy by C.Vivian, East India and Sports Club, London.

D WILLIAM CARPENTER, 1854, hs, chalk, NPG 3922.

SC J.H.FOLEY, 1862, monument, Lisburn Church, County Wicklow. SIR THOMAS FARRELL, after J.H.Foley, bust, East India and Sports Club. SIR THOMAS BROCK, c1904, bronze statue, Nicholson Garden, Delhi.

PR UNKNOWN, after a daguerreotype by Kilburn, hl seated, stipple, BM, NPG. UNKNOWN, after a photograph by Savory, hs, woodcut, for *Illust London News*, 31 Oct 1857, NPG.

NICHOLSON, Joseph Shield (1850-1927) economist.

R W.HOLE, hl seated, etch, for *Quasi Cursores*, 1884, NPG.

H WALTER STONEMAN, 1919, hs, NPG (NPR).

NICHOLSON, Sir Lothian (1828-1893) general.

P UNKNOWN, hl in uniform, oval, Royal Engineers HQ Mess, Chatham, Kent.

R UNKNOWN, after a photograph by Fry & Son, hs in uniform, wood engr, for *Illust London News*, 8 July 1893, NPG.

NICHOLSON, Renton (1809-1861) known as the Lord Chief Baron, president of the Judge and Jury Society.

P ARCHIBALD HENNING, c1841-61, wl, with allegorical scenes and figures, Museum of London.

R UNKNOWN, wl seated in the Queen's Bench prison, when editor of *The Town*, lith, BM.

NICHOLSON of Roundhay, William Gustavus Nicholson, Baron (1845-1918) field-marshal.

P GEORGE HALL NEALE, hl in uniform, Royal Engineers, Chatham, Kent.

H BASSANO, c1898, four negs, in uniform, various sizes, NPG X4770-3.

NICOL, Erskine (1825-1904) painter.

P SIR WILLIAM FETTES DOUGLAS, exhib 1862, Royal Scottish Academy.

D Self-portrait, oval, charcoal, SNPG 1160. Self-portrait, 1892, pencil, SNPG 1723. THOMAS FAED, wash, SNPG 1145.

SC CLARK STANTON, plaster bust, SNPG 1103.

PR UNKNOWN, hs, woodcut, for *Illust London News*, 30 June 1866, NPG.

PH LOCK & WHITFIELD, hs, profile, oval, woodburytype, for *Men of Mark*, 1880, NPG. J.G.TUNNY, wl, carte, NPG (Album 104).

NICOLL, Sir William Robertson (1851-1923) writer and editor of *Bookman* and *British Weekly*.

PH E.O.HOPPÉ, hl, print, NPG X6156.

NICOLSON, Arthur, see 1st Baron Carnock.

NIEMANN, Edmund John (1813-1876) landscape painter.

P E.H.CORBOULD, Castle Museum, Nottingham.

NIGHTINGALE, Florence (1820-1910) reformer of hospital nursing.

P SIR W.B.RICHMOND, c1886-7, hl, Claydon House (NT), Bucks.

D A.E.CHALON, as a child, with her mother and sister, Claydon House. WILLIAM WHITE, c1836, wl seated with her sister, Frances Parthenope, afterwards Lady Verney, w/c, NPG 3246. ELIZABETH, LADY EASTLAKE, 1846, hs, pencil, NPG 3254. JERRY BARRETT, 1856, hs, w/c study, for NPG 4305, NPG 2939. Probably JERRY BARRETT, 1856, three sketches, heads, profile, pencil and w/c, NPG 3303. GEORGE SCHARF, 1857, hl, pencil, NPG 1784. FEODORA, COUNTESS VON GLEICHEN, 1908, chalks, Royal Coll.

G JERRY BARRETT, sketch for a group at the entrance to the hospital at Scutari, oil, 1856?, NPG 4305; study, NPG 2939a.

SC H.BONHAM CARTER, c1856, plaster statuette, St Thomas's Hospital, London. SIR JOHN STEELL, 1859, marble bust, National Army Museum, London. SIR JOHN STEELL, 1862, bust, Derby Art Gallery; bronze cast, NPG 1748. FEODORA, COUNTESS VON GLEICHEN, statue, London Road, Derby. UNKNOWN, relief tablet, hl nursing a wounded soldier, St Paul's Cathedral, London. A.G.WALKER, 1915, statue, with relief scenes by J.H.Foley, Waterloo Place, London.

PR R.J.LANE, after H.Bonham Carter, hl seated, chromo-lith, pub 1854, BM, NPG. UNKNOWN, wl with lamp in the hospital at Scutari, woodcut for *Illust London News*, 24 Feb 1855, NPG. C.H.JEENS, after a statue by H.Bonham Carter, stipple, vignette on title to C.Yonge's *Book of Golden Deeds*, 1864, BM. T.PACKER, tql, lith, BM.

PH Various cartes by ASHFORD BROS, A.W.BENNETT, H.HERING, FREDERIC JONES, KILBURN and H.LENTHALL, various sizes, NPG. GOODMAN, 1858, wl, print, Claydon House. Two prints taken on her return from the Crimea, Claydon.

NISBETT, Louisa Cranstoun, née Macnamara (1812?-1858) actress.

P J.G.MIDDLETON, RA 1838, tql seated as Constance in *The Love Chase*, Worthing Museum and Art Gallery. W Sussex.

PR Several theatrical prints, BM, NPG.

NIXON, Francis Russell (1803-1879) bishop of Tasmania.

PR H.ROBINSON, after G.Richmond, hs, stipple, pub 1850, BM, NPG.

PH UNKNOWN, wl seated, carte, NPG (Album 46).

NOBLE, Matthew (1818-1876) sculptor.

PR UNKNOWN, after a photograph by Charles Watkins, head, woodcut, for *Illust London News*, 8 July 1876, BM, NPG.

PH W.WALKER & SONS, tql with bust, carte, NPG AX7565. JOHN & CHARLES WATKINS, wl seated, carte, NPG AX11932.

NOBLE, William Henry (1834-1892) major-general.

PR R.T. & Co, hs in uniform, woodcut, for *Illust London News*, 28 May 1892, NPG.

NORFOLK, Henry Fitzalan-Howard, 15th Duke of (1847-1917) politician.

P ERNEST MOORE, 1897, hl seated in lord mayor's chain, Arundel,

W Sussex. P.A.DE LÁSZLÓ, 1908, tql seated, Arundel.

SC EDWARD ONSLOW FORD, 1900, statue, City Hall, Sheffield.

C SIR LESLIE WARD ('Spy'), wl, chromo-lith, for *Vanity Fair*, 1 Oct 1881, NPG.

PH ELLIOTT & FRY, hs, print, for *Our Conservative and Unionist Statesmen*, vol II, NPG (Album 19). JOHN RUSSELL & SONS, hs, print, for *National Photographic Record*, vol II, NPG. WALERY, tql, print, NPG.

NORFOLK, Henry Granville, Fitzalan-Howard, 14th Duke of (1815-1860) politician.

P H.SMITH, tql seated with dog and hare, Arundel Castle, W Sussex. UNKNOWN, wl in robes, Arundel Castle.

M SIR W.C.ROSS, hs in uniform, Arundel Castle.

SC JOHN FRANCIS, 1845, marble bust, Arundel Castle.

NORMAN, Conolly (1853-1908) medical officer for the insane.

P MISS HARRISON, Royal College of Physicians of Ireland, Dublin.

SC J.M.S.CARRÉ, 1910, memorial with medallion, St Patrick's Cathedral, Dublin.

NORMAN, Sir Henry Wylie (1826-1904) field marshal.

P LOWES DICKINSON, RA 1879, City of Calcutta.

C SIR LESLIE WARD ('Spy'), wl in uniform, chromo-lith, for *Vanity Fair*, 25 June 1903, NPG.

PH W. & D.DOWNEY, hl in uniform, woodburytype, for Cassell's *Cabinet Portrait Gallery*, vol V, 1894, NPG. UNKNOWN, tql seated in uniform, coloured print, NPG.

NORMAN-NERUDA, Wilma Maria Francisca, see Lady Hallé.

NORMANBY, George Augustus Constantine Phipps, 2nd Marquess of (1819-1890) statesman.

PR Two woodcuts: one after a photograph by Mayall, hs, for *Illust London News*, 20 Feb 1858, and one after a photograph by John & Charles Watkins, hs in uniform, for *Illust London News*, 10 Feb 1866, NPG.

NORMANDY, Alphonse René Le Mire de (1809-1864) chemist.

PR UNKNOWN, hl seated, woodcut, for *Illust London News*, 23 July 1864, NPG.

NORRIS, John Pilkington (1823-1891) canon of Bristol.

PR UNKNOWN, hs, profile, woodcut, for *Illust London News*, 9 Jan 1892, NPG.

NORTH, Brownlow (1810-1875) lay preacher.

PH CALDESI, BLANFORD & CO, wl seated, carte, NPG (Album 101). J.MOFFAT, hs, cabinet, NPG X6863.

NORTH, Sir Ford (1830-1913) judge.

C SIR LESLIE WARD ('Spy'), wl, profile, w/c study, for *Vanity Fair*, 29 Oct 1887, NPG 3291.

NORTH, Marianne (1830-1890) artist and botanist.

D WILLIAMS, *c*1864, head, profile, w/c, Somerville College, Oxford.

SC UNKNOWN, bust, Royal Botanic Gardens, Kew.

PR UNKNOWN, hs, woodcut, for *Illust London News*, 24 June 1882, NPG.

NORTHBROOK, Thomas George Baring, 1st Earl of (1826-1904) statesman.

PR C.HOLL, after H.T.Wells, hs, stipple, one of 'Grillion's Club' series, BM, NPG. C.W.WALTON, hs, lith, NPG.

C SIR LESLIE WARD ('Spy'), wl, chromo-lith, for *Vanity Fair*, 9 Dec 1876, NPG. 'T', *'Purse, Pussy, Piety, and Prevarication'*, chromo-lith, for *Vanity Fair*, 5 July 1882, NPG.

NORTHCOTE, Henry Stafford Northcote, Baron (1846-1911) governor-general of Australia.

D S.P.HALL, pencil sketch, NPG 2289.

C SIR LESLIE WARD ('Spy'), wl, chromo-lith, for *Vanity Fair*, 3 March 1904, NPG.

PH LONDON STEREOSCOPIC CO, hs, profile, cabinet, NPG X6854. SIR BENJAMIN STONE, 1898, wl, print, NPG.

NORTHCOTE, Sir Stafford Henry, see 1st Earl of Iddesleigh.

NORTON, Caroline, see Lady Stirling-MAXWELL.

NORTON, Charles Bowyer Adderley, 1st Baron (1814-1905) statesman.

P HENRY WEIGALL, City Art Gallery, Birmingham.

PR W.HOLL, after G.Richmond, hs, stipple, one of 'Grillion's Club' series, BM, NPG.

C SIR LESLIE WARD ('Spy'), wl, profile, chromo-lith, for *Vanity Fair*, 17 Sept 1892, NPG.

PH UNKNOWN, wl seated, carte, NPG (Album 38).

NOVELLO, Clara Anastasia (Countess Gigliucci) (1818-1908) oratorio and operatic prima donna.

PR Several theatrical prints, BM, NPG, Harvard Theatre Collection, Cambridge, Mass, USA.

NUNBURNHOLME, Charles Henry Wilson, 1st Baron (1833-1907) shipowner and politician.

SC FRANCIS DERWENT WOOD, marble statue, Lowgate, Hull.

NUTTALL, Enos (1842-1916) bishop of Jamaica.

P UNKNOWN, Bishop's Lodge, Kingston, Jamaica.

PH JOHN RUSSELL & SONS, hs, print, for *National Photographic Record*, vol I, NPG. UNKNOWN, hl, print, NPG (Anglican Bishops).

OAKELEY, Sir Herbert Stanley (1830-1903) musical composer.
P C.K.ROBERTSON, tql in robes, Edinburgh University.
PR W.HOLE, wl seated at pianola, etch, for *Quasi Cursores*, 1884, NPG.
PH UNKNOWN, hs, print, NPG (Album 38).

OAKES, John Wright (1820-1887) landscape painter.
PR UNKNOWN, after a photograph, hs, woodcut, for *Illust London News*, 13 May 1876, NPG. UNKNOWN, hs, woodcut, NPG.

OAKLEY, John (1834-1890) dean of Manchester.
PR R.T., after a photograph by Russell & Sons, hs, woodcut, for *Illust London News*, 21 June 1890, NPG.

O'BRIEN, Cornelius (1843-1906) catholic archbishop of Halifax, Nova Scotia.
P UNKNOWN, Bishop's Palace, Halifax, Nova Scotia, Canada.

O'BRIEN, Henry (1808-1835) Irish antiquary; author of *Round Towers of Ireland*.
PR D.MACLISE, wl seated, lith, for *Fraser's Mag*, 1835, BM, NPG; pencil study, V & A.

O'BRIEN, Ignatius John, see Baron Shandon.

O'BRIEN, James (Bronterre) (1805-1864) chartist.
PR UNKNOWN, hl seated, stipple, NPG.

O'BRIEN, James Francis Xavier (1828-1905) Irish politician.
PH SIR BENJAMIN STONE, 1898, wl, print, NPG.

O'BRIEN, Matthew (1814-1855) mathematician.
D T.C.WAGEMAN, w/c, Trinity College, Cambridge.

O'BRIEN, William (1852-1928) Irish nationalist leader.
P SIR WILLIAM ORPEN, 1905, Municipal Gallery of Modern Art, Dublin.
D SIR WILLIAM ORPEN, 1905, hs, chalk, Crawford Art Gallery, Cork. SIR WILLIAM ORPEN, chalk, NGI 2932. FREDERICK PEGRAM, at the Parnell Special Commission, pencil, for *The Pictorial World*, 16 May 1889, NPG.
C SIR LESLIE WARD ('Spy'), wl, w/c study, for *Vanity Fair*, 15 May 1907, NPG 2979.
H SIR BENJAMIN STONE, 1908, four prints, all wl, NPG.

O'BRIEN, William Smith (1803-1864) Irish nationalist and rebel.
P STEPHEN CATTERSON SMITH sen, NGI 1127.
D JOSEPH HAYES, 1848, with Thomas Francis Meagher in Clonmel Jail, w/c, Aras an Uachtarain (President's Residence), Dublin.
G UNKNOWN, 'The Illustrious Sons of Ireland', chromo-lith, NPG.
C SIR THOMAS FARRELL, 1870, statue, South Side of Carlisle Bridge, Dublin.
PR H.O'NEILL, after a daguerreotype, hl, lith, BM.
C JOHN DOYLE, two political cartoons, drgs, BM.

O'CALLAGHAN, John Cornelius (1805-1883) Irish historical writer.
P HENRY O'NEILL, 1874, hl, NGI 313.

O'CONNELL, John (1810-1858) Irish politician.
G W.J.LINTON, aftr H.Anelay, 'The State Trial Portraits', 1844, a broadside, woodcut, BM.

O'CONNELL, Morgan (1804-1885) politician.
C JOHN DOYLE, 1839, wl, 'A Leaf from Nicholas Nickleby', chalk, BM.

O'CONNOR, Charles Yelverton (1843-1902) civil engineer.
SC PIETRO PORCELLI, 1911, bronze statue, Fremantle, Australia.

O'CONNOR, James (1836-1910) Irish journalist and politician.
PH SIR BENJAMIN STONE, two prints, both wl, NPG.

O'CONNOR, John (1830-1889) artist.
PR UNKNOWN, after a photograph by A.Bassano, hs, woodcut, for *Illust London News*, 8 June 1889, BM.

O'CONNOR, Thomas Power (1848-1929) journalist and politician.
P J.H.F.BACON, RA 1904, tql seated, Walker Art Gallery, Liverpool. SIR JOHN LAVERY, NGI 923.
D S.P.HALL, pencil sketch, NPG 2297.
SC UNKNOWN, bronze bust, Fleet Street, London.
C HARRY FURNISS, pen and ink sketch, NPG 3401. SIR LESLIE WARD ('Spy'), wl, profile, w/c study, for *Vanity Fair*, 25 Feb 1888, NPG 3127.
PH ERNEST H.MILLS, tql, postcard, NPG x12610. JOHN RUSSELL & SONS, hl, print, for *National Photographic Record*, vol I, NPG. SIR BENJAMIN STONE, two prints, both wl, NPG.

O'CONOR, Sir Nicholas Roderick (1843-1908) diplomat.
C SIR LESLIE WARD ('Spy'), wl, mechanical repro, for *Vanity Fair*, 1 May 1907, NPG.

ODGER, George (1820-1877) trade unionist.
C 'FAUSTIN', wl in a boat, chromo-lith, for 'The London Sketch Book', NPG.

O'DONOVAN, Edmund (1844-1883) newspaper correspondent.
PR UNKNOWN, hs, profile, in Arab headdress, stipple, NPG. UNKNOWN, after a photograph, hs in travelling dress, wood engr, for *Illust London News*, 27 Jan 1883, NPG.

O'DONOVAN, John (1809-1861?) Irish scholar.
P CHARLES GREY, hl, NGI 585.

OGLE, Charles Chaloner (1851-1878) *The Times* correspondent in Montenegro and Thessaly.
PR UNKNOWN, after a photograph by P.Moraites of Athens, hs, woodcut, for *Illust London News*, 13 April 1878, NPG.

O'GORMAN MAHON, The, see Charles James Patrick Mahon.

O'HAGAN, Thomas O'Hagan, 1st Baron (1812-1885) lord chancellor of Ireland.
P JOHN HANSON WALKER, King's Inns, Dublin.
D GEORGE RICHMOND, 1879, head, chalk, NGI 2250.
SC SIR THOMAS FARRELL, c1888, statue, Four Courts, Dublin. JOSEPH WATKINS, bust, National Museum of Ireland, Dublin.
PR UNKNOWN, tql seated in robes, woodcut, for *Illust London News*, 1 April 1865, NPG.
PH W. & D.DOWNEY, nearly wl seated, carte, NPG x12611. JOHN WATKINS, hs, carte, NPG (Album 99).

O'LEARY, John (1830-1907) Fenian journalist and leader.
P Two portraits by J.B.YEATS sen, the first dated 1904, NGI 869 and 595.
SC OLIVER SHEPPARD, two busts (?), bronze and plaster, Municipal Gallery of Modern Art, Dublin.

OLIPHANT, Laurence (1829-1888) novelist, war correspondent and mystic.
PR R.TAYLOR, after a photograph by the Autotype Company, hs, woodcut, for *Illust London News*, 5 Jan 1889, NPG.
PH T.RODGER, hs, carte, NPG X12612.

OLIPHANT, Margaret Oliphant, née Wilson (1828-1897) novelist and historical writer.
D JANET MARY OLIPHANT, 1895, pencil and chalk, SNPG 1788.
PR UNKNOWN, after a photograph by H.S.Mendelssohn, hs, woodcut, for *Harper's Mag*, June 1888, NPG.

OLIVER, Emma Sophia (1819-1885) painter.
PH UNKNOWN, hs, carte, NPG (Album 104).

OLIVER, Sir Thomas (1853-1942) physician and authority on industrial hygiene.
P T.B.GARVIE, c1930, University of Newcastle-upon-Tyne.

OLIVIER, Sydney Haldane Olivier, Baron (1859-1943) civil servant and statesman.
PH WALTER STONEMAN, 1924, hs, NPG (NPR).

O'LOGHLEN, Sir Colman Michael, 2nd Bart (1819-1877) Irish lawyer and politician.
C ADRIANO CECIONI, wl, w/c study, for *Vanity Fair*, 28 Sept 1872, NPG 2735.

OMMANNEY, Sir Erasmus (1814-1904) admiral.
P STEPHEN PEARCE, exhib 1861, hl in uniform, NPG 1219.

O'NEIL, Henry Nelson (1817-1880) historical painter.
P Self-portrait, 1873, tql, profile, Garrick Club, London.
G HENRY NELSON O'NEIL, 'The Billiard Room of the Garrick Club', oil, 1869, Garrick Club, London.
PH WINDOW & BRIDGE, wl seated, carte, NPG AX7576.

ONSLOW, William Hillier Onslow, 4th Earl of (1853-1911) governor of New Zealand.
P JOHN COLLIER, 1903, Clandon Park (NT), Surrey.
PR J.BROWN, after a photograph, hs, stipple, for *Baily's Mag*, 1882, BM, NPG.
C SIR LESLIE WARD ('Spy'), wl, profile, chromo-lith, for *Vanity Fair*, 18 Aug 1883, NPG.
PH LAFAYETTE, hs, print, for *Our Conservative and Unionist Statesmen*, vol I, NPG (Album 24).

ORCHARDSON, Sir William Quiller (1832-1910) painter.
P HENRY WEIGALL, c1878-81, hs, profile, NPG 2117. Self-portrait, hs, profile, oval, MacDonald Collection, Aberdeen Art Gallery. Self-portrait, 1890, tql with palette and brushes, Uffizi Gallery, Florence. Self-portrait, Castle Museum, Nottingham. JAMES ARCHER, SNPG 726. T.A.F.GRAHAM, exhib 1890, hl seated, profile, Royal Scottish Academy, Edinburgh. T.A.F.GRAHAM, Aberdeen Art Gallery. JOHN PETTIE, two portraits, SNPG 828 and 875.
D Self-portrait, charcoal, Aberdeen Art Gallery. J.H.LORIMER, 1892, pencil, SNPG 771.
G HENRY JAMYN BROOKS, 'Private view of the Old Masters Exhibition, Royal Academy, 1888', oil, NPG 1833. G.GRENVILLE MANTON, 'Conversazione at the Royal Academy, 1891', w/c, NPG 2820. REGINALD CLEAVER, 'Hanging Committee, Royal Academy, 1892', pen and ink, NPG 4245.
SC JOHN HUTCHISON, plaster bust, NPG 1093. EDWARD ONSLOW FORD, bronze busts, 1891, SNPG 1092 and 189-, SNPG 915.

EDWARD ONSLOW FORD, RA 1895, bronze bust, TATE 2971.
PR A.MONGIN, tql, etch, for *L'Art*, 1882, BM, NPG. Several woodcuts after self-portraits and photographs, BM, NPG.
C SIR LESLIE WARD ('Spy'), wl, w/c study, for *Vanity Fair*, 24 March 1898, NPG 5005.
PH ELLIOTT & FRY, two cartes, both hs, NPG (Albums 103 and 104). ELLIOTT & FRY, hs, cabinet, NPG X12617. LOCK & WHITFIELD, hs, oval, woodburytype, for *Men of Mark*, 1882, NPG. E.K.MILLS, hl, print, NPG X12618. RALPH W.ROBINSON, wl seated, print, for *Members and Associates of the Royal Academy of Arts, 1891*, NPG X7382.

ORD, William Miller (1834?-1902) physician.
PR UNKNOWN, hs, woodcut, for *Illust London News*, 27 March 1886, NPG.

ORDE-POWLETT, William Henry, see 3rd Baron Bolton.

O'REILLY, John Boyle (1844-1890) Irish nationalist and author.
SC D.C.FRENCH, 1896, bronze monument, Back Bay Fens, Boston, Mass, USA; related bust, Art Institute of Chicago, USA.

O'RELL, Max, see Léon Paul Blouet.

ORMEROD, Eleanor Anne (1828-1901) entomologist.
P UNKNOWN, c1900, hl in academic dress, Edinburgh University

ORR, Alexandra Sutherland, née Leighton (1828-1903) biographer of Browning.
P FREDERIC, LORD LEIGHTON (her brother), c1889, copy of portrait of c1860, Victoria Art Gallery, Bath.
D FREDERIC, LORD LEIGHTON, c1845-50, hs, chalk and body colour, NPG 2141(a).

ORTON, Arthur (1834-1898) The Tichborne claimant.
D SEBASTIAN EVANS, 1855, hs, pen and ink, NPG 2173 (39).
C 'FAUSTIN', chromo-lith, for *The London Sketch Book*, 1874-75 V & A. HARRY FURNISS, wl seated, pen and ink, NPG 3495. CARLO PELLEGRINI ('Ape'), wl, chromo-lith, for *Vanity Fair*, 10 June 1871, NPG.
PH LONDON STEREOSCOPIC CO, tql seated, carte, NPG X12623. UNKNOWN, tql seated, carte, NPG X12624.

OSBORN, George (1808-1891) president of Wesleyan conference.
PR UNKNOWN, after a photograph by Appleton & Co, hs, oval woodcut, for *Illust London News*, 6 Aug 1881, NPG.

OSBORN, Sherard (1822-1875) rear-admiral and author.
P STEPHEN PEARCE, 1857, hs in uniform, NPG 1224; replica, NPG 916
PR R. & E.TAYLOR, hs, woodcut, for *Illust London News*, 22 May 1875, NPG.

OSBORNE, Ralph Bernal (1808-1882) politician.
PR A.D'ORSAY, hl, profile, lith, BM.
C ALFRED THOMPSON (Atn̄), wl, chromo-lith, for *Vanity Fair*, 2 May 1870, NPG.

OSBORNE, Lord Sidney Godolphin (1808-1889) philanthropist.
PR UNKNOWN, after a photograph by John & Charles Watkins, h woodcut, for *Illust London News*, 25 May 1889, BM.
PH JOHN WATKINS, hs, profile, carte, NPG (Album 40). JOHN & CHARLES WATKINS, tql seated, carte, NPG AX7490.

OSBORNE, Walter Frederick (1859-1903) painter.
P Self-portrait, 1894, hs, NGI 555.
D NATHANIEL HILL, pencil sketch, NGI 2690.

O'SHEA, William Henry (1840-1905) Irish politician.
D S.P.HALL, 1888-89, pencil sketch, at the Parnell Commission NPG 2251. FREDERICK PEGRAM, pencil sketch, at the Parne

Commission, for *The Pictorial World*, 8 Nov 1888, NPG.

OSLER, Sir William, Bart (1849-1919) regius professor of medicine at Oxford.

P J.S.SARGENT, RA 1906, wl, 'Four Doctors', Johns Hopkins University, Baltimore, USA. STEPHEN SEYMOUR THOMAS, 1908, tql seated, Christ Church, Oxford.

PH JOHN RUSSELL & SONS, hs, print, for *National Photographic Record*, vol I, NPG.

OSSINGTON, John Evelyn Denison, 1st Viscount (1800-1873) speaker of the House of Commons.

P UNKNOWN, hl, a leaving portrait, Eton College, Berks. JANE HAWKINS, after Sir Francis Grant of 1862, wl, Palace of Westminster, London. After SIR FRANCIS GRANT, hs, Hughenden (NT), Bucks.

G SIR GEORGE HAYTER, 'The House of Commons, 1833', oil, NPG 54. JOHN PHILLIP, 'The House of Commons, 1860', oil, Palace of Westminster, London. W.P.FRITH, 'Marriage of the Prince of Wales, 1863', oil, Royal Coll.

PR F.C.LEWIS, after J.Slater, hs, stipple, one of 'Grillion's Club' series, BM. UNKNOWN, wl in speaker's robes, woodcut, BM.

C ALFRED THOMPSON ('Atη'), wl seated in speaker's chair, chromo-lith, for *Vanity Fair*, 12 March 1870, NPG.

H Four cartes: CALDESI, BLANFORD & CO, wl, NPG (Album 115); W. & D.DOWNEY, tql seated, NPG (Album 136); JOHN & CHARLES WATKINS, hs, NPG (Album 136); JOHN & CHARLES WATKINS, wl seated in robes, NPG (Album 115).

OUIDA, (pseudonym), see Marie Louise DE La Ramée.

OULESS, Walter William (1848-1933) painter.

P Self-portrait, 1883, hs, MacDonald Collection, Aberdeen Art Gallery. Self-portrait, 1918, tql with palette and brushes, Uffizi Gallery, Florence; replica, Barreau Art Gallery, Jersey Museum, St Helier, Jersey.

G G.GRENVILLE MANTON, 'Conversazione at the Royal Academy, 1891', w/c, NPG 2820. SIR HUBERT VON HERKOMER, 'The Council of the Royal Academy', oil, 1908, TATE 2481.

H LOCK & WHITFIELD, hs, oval, woodburytype, for *Men of Mark*, 1880, NPG. RALPH W.ROBINSON, wl in studio, for *Members and Associates of the Royal Academy of Arts, 1891*, NPG X7383. ELLIOTT & FRY, 1914, tql seated, cabinet, NPG X12626. JOHN RUSSELL & SONS, hl seated, print, for *National Photographic Record*, vol II, NPG. OLIVE EDIS, tql, print, NPG X12625. WALTER STONEMAN, 1933, hs, NPG (NPR).

OUSELEY, Sir Frederick Arthur Gore, 2nd Bart (1825-1889) musician and composer.

P ARTHUR FOSTER, 1893, from memory and a photograph, hl, Faculty of Music, Oxford.

H C.L.DODGSON ('Lewis Carroll'), c1856, hl, print, NPG P7(10). LOCK & WHITFIELD, hs, oval, woodburytype, for *Men of Mark*, 1883, NPG. UNKNOWN, wl, print, NPG P37. UNKNOWN, tql seated, print, NPG X4083. UNKNOWN, hs, print, NPG (Album 38).

OUTRAM, Sir James, 1st Bart (1803-1863) lieutenant-general.

P H.BAXTER, 1861, hl, formerly United Services and Royal Aero Club (c/o Crown Commissioners), London. THOMAS BRIGSTOCKE, RA 1863, wl in uniform, Oriental Club, London; hs, study, NPG 661. GENERAL A.Y.SHORTT, East India and Sports Club, London. UNKNOWN, hl seated, SNPG 1480; copy by J.E.Breun, East India and Sports Club.

G C.G.LEWIS, after T.J.Barker, 'The Relief of Lucknow', engr, pub 1863, NPG. UNKNOWN, 'The Durbar of the Rajah of Travencore: Reception of General Outram and Staff', coloured engr, NPG.

SC J.H.FOLEY, RA 1861, marble bust, Victoria Memorial Hall, Calcutta. MATTHEW NOBLE, 1866, marble bust, part of monument with a relief sculpture showing the meeting of Outram, Clyde and Havelock at Lucknow, Westminster Abbey, London. M.NOBLE, c1871, bronze statue, Victoria Embankment Gardens, London. J.H.FOLEY, 1873, equestrian statue, Calcutta.

PR C.BAUGNIET, hl, lith, pub 1858, NPG. R.J.LANE, hl in uniform, lith, BM. Several engrs after photographs, NPG, National Army Museum, London.

PH KILBURN, wl, carte, NPG X12628. P.PETIT of Nice, 1862, hl seated, print, National Army Museum. UNKNOWN, tql seated, print, NPG AX7327.

OUVRY, Frederic (1814-1881) president of Society of Antiquaries.

SC MARSHALL WOOD, 1869, marble bust, Society of Antiquaries, London.

OVERTOUN, John Campbell White, 1st Baron (1843-1908) Scottish churchman and philanthropist.

P GEORGE FIDDES WATT, 1909, Assembly Buildings, Edinburgh.

OWEN, Sir Francis Philip Cunliffe-, see CUNLIFFE-Owen.

OWEN, Sir Hugh (1804-1881) promoter of Welsh education and philanthropist.

SC W.DAVIS?, plaster head, University College of Wales, Aberystwyth. J.MILO GRIFFITH, c1888, statue, Carnarvon. J.MILO GRIFFITH, plaster, National Museum of Wales 1376, Cardiff.

OWEN, John (1854-1926) bishop of St David's.

P? UNKNOWN, St David's University College, Lampeter.

SC UNKNOWN, recumbent effigy, St David's Cathedral, Dyfed, Wales.

PH UNKNOWN, hs, print, NPG (Anglican Bishops).

OWEN, Sir Richard (1804-1892) naturalist.

P H.W.PICKERSGILL, c1845, tql, NPG 938. H.W.PICKERSGILL, c1852, hl, St Bartholomew's Hospital, London. WILLIAM HOLMAN HUNT, 1881, tql seated, BM (Natural History). W.H.GILBERT, as an old man, Lancaster Museum and Art Gallery (Storey Institute). H.J.THADDEUS, as an old man, Lancaster Town Hall. Two portraits, one as a young man, Lancaster Museum and Art Gallery.

D WILLIAM BROCKEDON, 1847, hs, chalk, NPG 2515(98). Attrib WILLIAM ETTY, based on a portrait by Pickersgill, hl, w/c, Royal College of Surgeons, London. CHARLES HOPLEY, RA 1869, hs, profile, pastel, Royal College of Surgeons. RUDOLPH LEHMANN, 1890, BM.

SC SIR WILLIAM HAMO THORNYCROFT, 1880, plaster bust, Royal College of Surgeons. SIR ALFRED GILBERT, 1895, bronze bust, Royal College of Surgeons. SIR THOMAS BROCK, c1895, bronze statue, BM (Natural History). UNKNOWN, stone bust, Lancaster Museum and Art Gallery (Storey Institute).

PR T.H.MAGUIRE, tql seated, lith, for *Ipswich Museum Portraits*, 1850, BM. H.J.THADDEUS, tql in academic robes, aged 85, mezz, BM, NPG. Several engravings after photographs, BM, NPG.

C ERNEST GRISET, c1873, with Mr Bryce-Wright, pen and w/c, V & A. UNKNOWN, wl, profile, chromo-lith, for *Vanity Fair*, 1 March 1873, NPG.

PH MAULL & POLYBLANK, c1855, tql, print, NPG P106(15). ERNEST EDWARDS, wl seated, print, for *Men of Eminence*, vol I, 1863, NPG. LOCK & WHITFIELD, hs, oval, woodburytype, for *Men of Mark*, 1878, NPG. BARRAUD, hs, print, for *Men and Women of the Day*, vol I, 1888, NPG AX5414. Various cartes by ERNEST EDWARDS, ELLIOTT & FRY, MASON & CO, MAULL & POLYBLANK and JOHN & CHARLES WATKINS, various sizes, NPG.

OXENFORD, John (1812-1877) dramatist.

PR UNKNOWN, after a photograph by London Stereoscopic Co, hs, oval, woodcut, for *Illust London News*, 10 March 1877, NPG.

PH UNKNOWN, hs, woodburytype, NPG X12635.

OXFORD and ASQUITH, Herbert Henry Asquith, 1st Earl of (1852-1928) statesman.

P SIR WILLIAM ORPEN, 1909, tql in chancellor's robes, Lincoln's Inn, London. SOLOMON J.SOLOMON, RA 1909, tql, National Liberal Club, London. GEORGE FIDDES WATT, RA 1912, tql, Balliol College, Oxford. SIR JOHN LAVERY, RA 1918, wl, Reform Club, London. ANDRÉ CLUYSENAAR, 1919, tql seated, NPG 2361. SIR JAMES GUTHRIE, *c*1920, hl seated, semi-profile, study for NPG 2463, SNPG 1128; related sketch, head, NPG 3544.

D FRANK DOBSON, 1920, head, profile, pencil, NPG 4387. S.P.HALL, three pencil sketches, hs and hl, NPG 2302-3 and 2307. JAMES KERR-LAWSON, head, taking a mask from his face, pencil, Ashmolean Museum, Oxford. FREDERICK PEGRAM, three pencil sketches, V & A.

G SIR JAMES GUTHRIE, 'Statesmen of World War I, 1914-18', oil, NPG 2463.

SC KATHLEEN, LADY KENNET, *c*1913, bronze bust, TATE 4467. FRANK DOBSON, 1921, head, TATE 4550. CLAIRE SHERIDAN, bust, Oxford Union. CLAIRE SHERIDAN, bronze bust, IWM, London. LEONARD MERRIFIELD and GILBERT BAYES, *c*1939-48, marble statue, in robes of chancellor of the exchequer, Palace of Westminster, London.

PR HENRIK LUND, lith, IWM. VIOLET, DUCHESS OF RUTLAND, hs, lith, NPG. UNKNOWN, head, lith, V & A. Several popular prints, NPG.

C SIR LESLIE WARD ('Spy'), wl, profile, w/c study, for *Vanity Fair*, 14 July 1904, NPG 4945. 'XIT', wl, profile, Hentschel-Colourtype, for *Vanity Fair*, 17 March 1910, NPG. SIR MAX BEERBOHM, 'The Old and the Young Self in Balliol', drg, 1924, National Liberal Club. SIR FRANCIS CARRUTHERS GOULD, tql seated, pen and ink, NPG 2866a. HARRY FURNISS, hl, pen and ink, NPG 3402. DAVID LOW, hs and tql, both in profile, pencil, NPG 4529(2). Several pen and ink drgs by SIR BERNARD PARTRIDGE, for *Punch*, NPG.

PH G.C.BERESFORD, print, National Liberal Club. ALVIN LANGDON COBURN, 1914, hs, profile, photogravure, for *More Men of Mark*, 1922, NPG AX7821. WALTER STONEMAN, 1917, hl, profile, for NPR, NPG X497.

P

PAGE, Thomas Ethelbert (1850-1936) classical scholar, teacher, editor and political critic.
P JOHN COLLIER, 1911, Charterhouse School, Godalming, Surrey. CLIVE GARDNER, 1927, Reform Club, London.
C SIR MAX BEERBOHM, 'Some Masters of Forty Years Ago', drg, 1928, Charterhouse School.
PH WALTER STONEMAN, 1934, hl seated, NPG (NPR).

PAGET, Lord Alfred Henry (1816-1888) general; royal equerry.
G RICHARD BARRETT DAVIS, Queen Victoria and her suite riding in Windsor Great Park, oil, 1837, Plas Newydd (NT), Gwynedd.
PR R.J.LANE, after A.D'Orsay, hl, profile, lith, BM, NPG.
C CARLO PELLEGRINI ('Ape'), wl, chromo-lith, for *Vanity Fair*, 3 July 1875, NPG.
PH UNKNOWN, with 7th Earl of Carlisle, Brunel, Mr Yates and the harbour master, print, NPG X4994.

PAGET, Sir Augustus Berkeley (1823-1896) diplomat.
C THÉOBALD CHARTRAN ('T'), wl, profile, chromo-lith, for *Vanity Fair*, 26 June 1880, NPG.
PH L.SUSCIPI of Rome, hs, oval, carte, NPG X12639.

PAGET, Lord Clarence Edward (1811-1895) admiral.
P UNKNOWN 1866, hl, DoE (Admiralty House).
PR D.J.POUND, after a photograph by John Watkins, tql seated in uniform, stipple and line, supplement to *Illust News of the World*, BM.
C CARLO PELLEGRINI ('Ape'), wl, profile, chromo-lith, for *Vanity Fair*, 25 Dec 1875, NPG.
PH W. & D.DOWNEY, tql seated, carte, NPG X12640.

PAGET, Francis (1851-1911) bishop of Oxford.
P SIR W.Q.ORCHARDSON, 1904, tql seated, Christ Church, Oxford.
C SIR LESLIE WARD ('Spy'), wl, profile, w/c study, for *Vanity Fair*, 22 Nov 1894, NPG 3002.
PH UNKNOWN, hs, print, NPG (Anglican Bishops).

PAGET, Lord George Augustus Frederick (1818-1880) general.
PR UNKNOWN, after a photograph by John Watkins, hl seated, woodcut, for *Illust London News*, 8 May 1858, NPG.
C SIR LESLIE WARD ('Spy'), wl, profile, chromo-lith, for *Vanity Fair*, 13 Oct 1877, NPG.

PAGET, Sir George Edward (1809-1892) physician.
P UNKNOWN, Caius College, Cambridge.
SC HENRY WILES, 1885, marble bust, Addenbrooke's Hospital, Cambridge.

PAGET, Sir James, 1st Bart (1814-1899) surgeon.
P SIR J.E.MILLAIS, 1872, tql, St Bartholomew's Hospital, London.
D W.H.N.?, 1838, hl, profile, pencil, Royal College of Surgeons, London. GEORGE RICHMOND, 1867, hs, chalk, NPG 1635.
G HENRY JAMYN BROOKS, 'Council of the Royal College of Surgeons of England, 1884-85', oil, Royal College of Surgeons.
SC SIR J.E.BOEHM, RA 1886, marble bust, Royal College of Surgeons; replica, 1887, St Bartholomew's Hospital.
PR T.H.MAGUIRE, 1849, hl, lith, NPG.
C SIR LESLIE WARD ('Spy'), wl, profile, chromo-lith, for *Vanity*

Fair, 12 Feb 1876, NPG.

PAGET, Dame (Mary) Rosalind (1855-1948) social reformer, nurse and midwife.
P STELLA CANZINI, Royal College of Midwives, London.

PAGET, Stephen (1855-1926) biographer and essayist.
PH JOHN RUSSELL & SONS, hs, print, for *National Photographic Record*, vol I, NPG.

PAGET, Violet ('Vernon Lee') (1856-1935) writer.
P J.S.SARGENT, 1881, hs, TATE 4787.
D J.S.SARGENT, 1889, hs, pencil, Ashmolean Museum, Oxford.

PALGRAVE, Francis Turner (1824-1897) poet and critic.
D SAMUEL LAURENCE, 1872, hs, profile, chalk, NPG 2070.
PR R.T., hs, wood engr, for *Illust London News*, 26 Dec 1885, NPG.

PALGRAVE, Sir Reginald Francis Douce (1829-1904) clerk of the House of Commons.
PH SIR BENJAMIN STONE, 1897, wl, print, Birmingham Reference Library. BASSANO, c1898, three negs, various sizes, NPG X4774-6.

PALGRAVE, William Gifford (1826-1888) Jesuit and diplomat.
SC THOMAS WOOLNER, 1864, plaster medallion, NPG 2071, engr C.H.Jeens, line, for his *Journey through Arabia*, 1865, BM, NPG.
PH ABDULLAH FRÈRES, tql, carte, NPG X8358. JULIA MARGARET CAMERON, 1868, print, Gernsheim Collection, University of Texas, Austin, USA. ERNEST EDWARDS, wl in oriental dress, carte, NPG X12647. LOCK & WHITFIELD, hs, oval, woodburytype, for *Men of Mark*, 1880, NPG. UNKNOWN, wl seated in cloak, carte, NPG X12648.

PALLES, Christopher (1831-1920) lord chief baron of the Exchequer in Ireland.
D J.B.YEATS, chalk, King's Inns, Dublin.

PALLISER, Sir William (1830-1882) inventor of 'Palliser shot'.
PR UNKNOWN, after a photograph by Bassano, hs, woodcut, for *Illust London News*, 22 Feb 1873, NPG.

PALMER, Charles John (1805-1882) topographer.
P UNKNOWN, Tolhouse Museum, Great Yarmouth.
PR W.HOLL, tql seated, octagon, stipple, BM.

PALMER, Sir Charles Mark, 1st Bart (1822-1907) shipowner and ironmaster.
PR UNKNOWN, after a photograph by W. & D.Downey, hs, profile, woodcut, for *Illust London News*, 7 March 1874, NPG.
C CARLO PELLEGRINI ('Ape'), wl, profile, w/c study, for *Vanity Fair*, 18 Oct 1884, NPG 4730.
PH SIR BENJAMIN STONE, 1899, wl, print, NPG.

PALMER, Edward Henry (1840-1882) oriental scholar.
P JOHN COLLIER, 1884, hl in Arab costume, St John's College, Cambridge.
PR UNKNOWN, hs, wood engr, for *Illust London News*, 4 Nov 1882, NPG.

PALMER, George (1818-1897) biscuit manufacturer.
SC UNKNOWN, statue, Palmer Park, Reading, Berks.
PR UNKNOWN, hs, semi-profile, woodcut, for *Illust London News*, 1

June 1878, NPG.

PH Two prints by unknown photographers, both hs, University of Reading.

PALMER, George William (1851-1913) biscuit manufacturer.

P UNKNOWN, tql seated, University of Reading.

PALMER, John Hinde (1808-1884) politician.

C SIR LESLIE WARD ('Spy'), wl, profile, w/c study, for *Vanity Fair*, 28 July 1883, NPG 4731.

PALMER, Sir Roundell, see 1st Earl of Selborne.

PALMER, Samuel (1805-1881) painter and etcher.

D HENRY WALTER, 1819, hs, pencil and wash, BM. Self-portrait, c1824–28, hs, chalk, Ashmolean Museum, Oxford. GEORGE RICHMOND, various drgs: 1828, hl assuming a character, pen, ink and chalk, Yale Center for British Art, New Haven, USA; 1829, wl seated, pencil, ink and w/c, Ashmolean Museum; c1829, hs, pencil, pen and wash, NPG 2154; two sketches c1828 and 1829, head and hl, ink, V & A; 1830, Graves Art Gallery, Sheffield; two sketches, head, profile, pen and ink, Walsall Museum and Art Gallery. C.W.COPE, hs, as an old man, pencil, NPG 2155.

M GEORGE RICHMOND, 1829, hs, profile, w/c and body-colour, NPG 2223.

C GEORGE RICHMOND, 1825, wl, back-view, pencil, V & A. HENRY WALTER, 1835, wl seated, w/c and ink, BM.

PH CUNDALL, DOWNES & CO, tql seated, carte, NPG (Album 104); woodcut after this photograph, hs, NPG. UNKNOWN, tql seated, print, V & A.

PALMER, William Waldegrave, see 2nd Earl of Selborne.

PANKHURST, Emmeline, née Goulden (1858-1928) leader of the militant movement for women's suffrage.

P GEORGINA BRACKENBURY, 1927, hl, NPG 2360; version, Museum of London.

SC A.G.WALKER, 1929, statue, Victoria Tower Gardens, London.

PH MRS ALBERT BROOM, hl, print, NPG x6194. OLIVE EDIS, two prints, tql seated, and tql, NPG x6195 and x4332.

PANMURE, Fox Maule Ramsay, Lord, see 11th Earl of Dalhousie.

PAPWORTH, Wyatt Angelicus Van Sandau (1822-1894) architect and antiquary.

PR UNKNOWN, after a photograph by Elliott & Fry, hs, wood engr, for *Illust London News*, 25 Aug 1894, NPG.

PARDOE, Julia (1806-1862) writer.

PR J.THOMSON, after H.Room, tql seated in evening dress, stipple, BM, NPG.

PAREPA-ROSA, Euphrosyne Parepa de Boyesku (1836-1874) operatic singer.

PR UNKNOWN, hs, woodcut, for *Illust London News*, 7 Feb 1874, NPG. Various theatrical and popular prints, Harvard Theatre Collection, Cambridge, Mass, USA.

PH HERBERT WATKINS, hs, carte, NPG x12667.

PARK, Patric (1811-1855) sculptor.

D KENNETH MACLEAY, 1859, hl, w/c, SNPG 654.

SC UNKNOWN, marble bust, Wallington Hall (NT), Northumberland.

PARKE, Thomas Heazle (1857-1893) surgeon and explorer.

PH BARRAUD, tql seated, print, for *Men and Women of the Day*, vol III, 1890, NPG AX5494. UNKNOWN, tql seated with gun, print, NPG x12643.

PARKER, Albert Edmund, see 3rd Earl of Morley.

PARKER, Charles Stuart (1829-1910) politician.

SC UNKNOWN, plaster medallion, SNPG 913.

PARKER, Edmund, see 2nd Earl of Morley.

PARKER, John Henry (1806-1884) writer on architecture.

PR UNKNOWN, hs, wood engr, for *Illust London News*, 16 Feb 1884, NPG.

PARKER, Joseph (1830-1902) congregationalist divine.

SC C.B.BIRCH, 1883, plaster bust, NPG 2073.

PR UNKNOWN, hl seated, stipple and line, NPG.

C HARRY FURNISS, three pen and ink sketches, NPG 3496, 3497 and 3595. CARLO PELLEGRINI ('Ape'), hl, chromo-lith, for *Vanity Fair*, 19 April 1884, NPG.

PARKER, Louis Napoleon (1852-1944) musician, playwright and inventor.

P SIR PHILIP BURNE-JONES, hl seated, Garrick Club, London.

C HARRY FURNISS, pen and ink sketch, NPG 3499.

PARKER, Thomas Augustus Wolstenholme, see 9th Earl of Macclesfield.

PARKER of Waddington, Robert John Parker, Baron (1857-1918) judge.

P GEORGE FIDDES WATT, RA 1913, King's College, Cambridge.

PARKES, Edmund Alexander (1819-1876) professor of hygiene and physician.

SC EDWARD DAVIS, 1862, marble bust, University College, London.

PR UNKNOWN, hs, woodcut, for *Illust London News*, 1 April 1876, NPG.

PARKES, Sir Harry Smith (1828-1885) diplomat.

PR UNKNOWN, after a photograph by Negretti & Zambra, tql, woodcut, for *Illust London News*, 1860, NPG.

PARKES, Sir Henry (1815-1896) Australian statesman.

P J.R.ASHTON, tql, Art Gallery of New South Wales, Sydney, Australia.

D J.R.ASHTON, 1891, hs, pencil, NPG 1480.

PARKIN, Sir George Robert (1846-1922) educationist and imperialist.

SC E.WHITNEY SMITH, RA 1928, marble bust, Rhodes House, Oxford.

PH WALTER STONEMAN, 1920, hs, NPG (NPR).

PARMOOR, Charles Alfred Cripps, 1st Baron (1852-1941) judge.

P SIR JOHN LAVERY, c1924, hs, Church House, Westminster.

C SIR LESLIE WARD ('Spy'), tql, profile, chromo-lith, for *Vanity Fair*, 10 April 1902, NPG.

PH WALTER STONEMAN, 1917, hs, NPG (NPR).

PARNELL, Charles Stewart (1846-1891) Irish patriot and politician.

P S.P.HALL, 1892, tql, NGI 481. H.C., oil?, Magdalene College, Cambridge.

D S.P.HALL, 1888–89, several drgs, some made at the sessions of the Parnell Commission, pencil, NPG 2229, 2242–4, 2250, 2293. FREDERICK PEGRAM, at the sessions of the Parnell Commission, pencil sketches, V & A.

G LIBERIO PROSPERI, 'The Lobby of the House of Commons, 1886' oil, NPG 5256.

SC RICHARD BARTER, 1893, bronze sculpture, NGI 8086. MARY GRANT, posthumous bronze bust, NPG 1087. MARY GRANT bronze bust (?), Municipal Gallery of Modern Art, Dublin.

PR R.TAYLOR, after W.Wilson, in the witness box before the special commission, woodcut, for *Illust London News*, 11 May 1889, BM. C.LAURIE, hs, etch, NPG.

c Sir Francis Carruthers Gould, hl, ink sketch, NPG 2850. Théobald Chartran ('T'), wl, profile, chromo-lith, for *Vanity Fair*, 11 Sept 1880, NPG.
PH William Lawrence, 1881, hs, profile, carte, NPG x12655.

PARR, George (1826-1891) cricketer.
P W. Bromley, c1850, Marylebone Cricket Club, London.
PR J. Brown, after a photograph by Kilburn, wl at wicket, holding bat, stipple, for *Baily's Mag*, 1860, BM, NPG.

PARRATT, Sir Walter (1841-1924) composer and organist.
P Gerald Moira, 1892, hl seated, Magdalen College, Oxford.
D E.M.Ellison, c1890, hl, pastel, NPG 4944. Sir William Rothenstein, c1921, head, sanguine and white, NPG 4791. Kate A.Coward, w/c, Royal College of Music, London.

PARRY, Sir Charles Hubert Hastings, Bart (1848-1918) composer.
D Sir William Rothenstein, 1897, tql seated, chalk, NPG 3877.
SC Courtenay Pollock, c1910, bronze bust, Royal College of Music, London.
PH W. & D.Downey, tql seated, woodburytype, for Cassell's *Cabinet Portrait Gallery*, vol IV, 1893, NPG. E.O.Hoppé, hs, print, Royal College of Music, London.

PARRY, Edward (1839-1890) bishop suffragan of Dover.
PR Unknown, after a photograph by Mason & Co, hs, woodcut, for *Illust London News*, 9 April 1870, NPG. R.T., hs, wood engr, for *Illust London News*, 19 April 1890, NPG

PARRY, John Humffreys (1816-1880) serjeant-at-law.
c Sir Leslie Ward ('Spy'), wl, w/c study, for *Vanity Fair*, 13 Dec 1873, NPG 2737.

PARRY, John Orlando (1810-1879) singer, actor and entertainer.
P Daniel Maclise, hl, oval, National Museum of Wales 455, Cardiff.
PR C.Baugniet, tql seated at piano, lith, BM. Unknown, after a photograph by Samuel Fry & Co, hs, woodcut, for *Illust London News*, 17 March 1877, NPG. Several theatrical prints, Harvard Theatre Collection, Cambridge, Mass, USA.
PH Nelson, wl with harp, carte, NPG x12670. Herbert Watkins, wl seated, carte, NPG x12669.

PARSONS, Alfred William (1847-1920) painter and illustrator.
D Self-portrait, hs, profile, pencil, NPG 2674.
PH Elliott & Fry, 1915, hl, cabinet, NPG x12668.

PARSONS, Sir Charles Algernon (1854-1931) engineer and scientist.
P Maurice Codner, Institution of Mechanical Engineers, London. Sir William Orpen, 1921, tql seated, Laing Art Gallery, Newcastle-upon-Tyne.
PH Walter Stoneman, 1919, hs, NPG (NPR).

PARSONS, Laurence, see 4th Earl of Rosse.

PARSONS, William, see 3rd Earl of Rosse.

PARTRIDGE, Richard (1805-1873) professor of anatomy.
PR Unknown, after a photograph by Barraud and Jerrard, hs, woodcut, for *Illust London News*, 5 April 1873, NPG.
PH Ernest Edwards, wl seated, print, for *Men of Eminence*, ed L.Reeve, vol III, 1865, NPG. Mayer & Pierson, tql, carte, NPG x12661. E.Moira, hs, carte, NPG x12664.

PASSFIELD, (Martha) Beatrice Webb, Lady, née Potter (1858-1943) social reformer and historian.
P George Coates, exhib 1924, tql seated, London School of Economics and Political Science, London. Sir William Nichol-son, wl seated with her husband, London School of Economics. E.S.Swinson, 1934, head, profile, NPG 4066.
D Jessie Holliday, c1909, hs, chalk, Beatrice Webb House, Dorking, Surrey.
PH George Bernard Shaw, wl seated as a young woman, photogravure, NPG x12675. Allan G.Chappelow, 1942, two prints, with her husband, and tql in her garden, NPG x12673-4. Unknown, tql with her husband, print, NPG x12672.

PASSFIELD, Sidney James Webb, Baron (1859-1947) social reformer and historian.
P Sir William Nicholson, wl with his wife, London School of Economics and Political Science, London.
D Jessie Holliday, c1909, hs, chalk, Beatrice Webb House, Dorking, Surrey. Eric Gill, 1927, hs, profile, pencil, NPG 5203.
M Winifred Cécile Dongworth, 1920-30, hl seated, NPG 5027. Lilian M.Mayer, hs, NPG 2068.
c Sir Max Beerbohm, several drgs, Ashmolean Museum, Oxford, Cornell University, Ithaca, New York, USA, and London School of Economics.
PH W. & D.Downey, hs, woodburytype, for Cassell's *Cabinet Portrait Gallery*, vol IV, 1893, NPG. Walter Scott, tql, postcard, NPG x12671. Walter Stoneman, 1924, hs, profile, NPG (NPR). Allan G.Chappelow, 1942, wl with his wife, print, NPG x12673. Unknown, tql with his wife, print, NPG x12672.

PATER, Walter Horatio (1839-1894) critic and humanist.
P A.A.McEvoy, posthumous, based on sketches and photographs, tql seated, Brasenose College, Oxford.
PR W.Rothenstein, 1894, hs, lith, BM.
c Unknown, Queen's College, Oxford.
PH Unknown, head, photogravure, for his *Greek Studies*, 1895, BM (Engr Ports Coll).

PATEY, Janet Monach, née Whytock (1842-1894) singer.
PR Unknown, after a photograph by Fradelle and Marshall, hs, woodcut, for *Illust London News*, 24 April 1875, NPG. J.M.B., 1888, hs, profile, lith, NPG.

PATMORE, Coventry Kersey Dighton (1823-1896) poet.
P J.S.Sargent, 1894, hl, NPG 1079.
G R.Taylor & Co, 'Modern Poets', hs, one of a series of woodcuts, for *Illust London News*, 15 Oct 1892, NPG.
c Sir Max Beerbohm, 1917, posthumous drg, 'Spring Cottage, Hampstead, 1860', drg, TATE 5391 (viii).
PH Barraud, hs, print, for *Men and Women of the Day*, vol IV, 1891, NPG AX5520.

PATON, John Brown (1830-1911) nonconformist divine and philanthropist.
P Sir J.A.Brown, Castle Museum, Nottingham.
PR Unknown, hl seated, stipple, NPG.

PATON, Sir Joseph Noel (1821-1901) painter.
P John Ballantyne, 1867, wl in his studio, SNPG 1453. Sir George Reid, 1882, hs, semi-profile, MacDonald Collection, Aberdeen Art Gallery.
D W.Graham Boss, pencil, SNPG 1701. Ranald Noel Paton, 1890, pencil, SNPG 605.
SC Amelia Robertson Hill, 1872, marble bust, SNPG 619. Amelia Robertson Hill, two medallions, the first in plaster, the second in wax, SNPG 2068 and 2181.
PR M.Klinkicht, hs, woodcut, for *Mag of Art*, 1880, NPG.
PH Thomas Annan, tql seated, carte, NPG AX7561. Kingsbury & Notcutt, hs, photogravure, NPG x12693. McGlashon & Walker, hs, carte, NPG (Album 104). Unknown, hs, print, NPG (Album 38).

PATON, Mary Ann, see Wood.

PATON, Waller Hugh (1828-1895) artist.
P GEORGE PAUL CHALMERS, 1867, SNPG 1235.
PH NESBITT & LOTHIAN, hs, semi-profile, carte, NPG (Album 106).

PATTEN, John Wilson-, see 1st Baron Winmarleigh.

PATTERSON, Robert (1802-1872) naturalist.
PR T.H.MAGUIRE, tql seated, lith, one of set of *Ipswich Museum Portraits*, 1851, BM, NPG.

PATTESON, John Coleridge (1827-1871) bishop of Melanesia.
SC THOMAS WOOLNER, 1875, marble relief tablet, Merton College, Oxford.
PR C.H.JEENS, after G.Richmond, hs, stipple, for vol I of his *Life* by C.M.Yonge, pub 1874, BM, NPG.

PATTI, Adelina (Baroness Cederström) (1843-1919) singer.
P JAMES SANT, tql seated, NPG 3625.
PR G.PILOTELL, hs, etch, BM. JMB, tql, lith, for *The Magazine of Music*, 1887, BM. Various theatrical and popular prints, BM, NPG, Harvard Theatre Collection, Cambridge, Mass, USA.
PH BARRAUD, tql seated, print, for *Men and Women of the Day*, vol II, 1889, NPG AX5451. LONDON STEREOSCOPIC CO, tql, cabinet, NPG AX5570. Various cartes by NELSON & MARSHALL, C.REUTLINGER, CAMILLE SILVY and unknown photographers, various dates and sizes, some in character, NPG.

PATTI, Carlotta (1835-1889) singer.
PR Various theatrical and popular prints, Harvard Theatre Collection, Cambridge, Mass, USA.
PH CHARLES REUTLINGER, tql, carte, NPG (Album 102). Two woodburytypes by unknown photographers, hs and hl seated, NPG X12689-90. Three cartes, hs, wl seated and tql, NPG (Album 108).

PATTISON, Dorothy Wyndlow (Sister Dora) (1832-1878) nurse.
SC F.J.WILLIAMSON, 1886, marble statue, Walsall, W Midlands.

PATTISON, Mark (1813-1884) writer; rector of Lincoln College, Oxford.
P ALEXANDER MACDONALD, 1900, hl seated, Lincoln College, Oxford.
PR R.T., hs, wood engr, for *Illust London News*, 23 Aug 1884, NPG.

PATTON, George, see Lord Glenalmond.

PAUL, Herbert Woodfield (1853-1935) author and politician.
PH SIR BENJAMIN STONE, 1906, two prints, both wl, NPG.

PAUL, Isabella Howard, née Featherstone (1833?-1879) singer and actress.
PR Various theatrical prints, BM, NPG, Harvard Theatre Collection, Cambridge, Mass, USA.
PH SOUTHWELL BROS, two cartes, both tql, the first with her husband, NPG X12695-6. UNKNOWN, hs, woodburytype, NPG X12697.

PAUL, Sir John Dean, 2nd Bart (1802-1868) banker.
PR L.HAGHE, wl, profile, in oriental dress, lith, BM.

PAULET, Lord William (1804-1893) field-marshal.
PR UNKNOWN, hs in uniform, woodcut, for *Illust London News*, 20 May 1893, NPG.
PH CAMILLE SILVY, wl in uniform, on horseback, carte, NPG X12698.

PAUNCEFOTE, Sir Julian Pauncefote, 1st Baron (1828-1902) British ambassador to USA.
P After BENJAMIN CONSTANT of c1896, Marlborough College, Wilts.

C THÉOBALD CHARTRAN ('T'), wl, chromo-lith, for *Vanity Fair*, 7 April 1883, NPG.

PAVY, Frederick William (1829-1911) physician.
P PERCY BIGLAND, hl seated, Guy's Hospital, London.
D WILLIAM STRANG, 1908, two drgs, Royal Society of Medicine, London, and Guy's Hospital (Medical School), London.

PAXTON, Sir Joseph (1801-1865) gardener and architect.
P H.P.BRIGGS, hl seated, Chatsworth, Derbys.
D OCTAVIUS OAKLEY, tql, w/c, Chatsworth, engr S.W.Reynolds, mixed engr, pub 1851, BM.
G H.W.PHILLIPS, 'The Royal Commissioners for the Great Exhibition, 1851', oil, V & A.
SC EDWARD WYON, 1864, bust, Royal Horticultural Society, London.
PR J.JENKINS, after a photograph by Kilburn, tql, profile, stipple, BM, NPG. UNKNOWN, hs, oval, woodcut, for *Illust London News*, 24 June 1865, NPG.
PH UNKNOWN, wl, carte, NPG (Album 38).

PAYN, James (1830-1898) author.
G R.TAYLOR & P.NAUMANN, 'Our Literary Contributors – Past and Present', one of a series of woodcuts, for *Illust London News*, 14 May 1892, BM.
C CARLO PELLEGRINI ('Ape'), wl, profile, chromo-lith, for *Vanity Fair*, 8 Sept 1888, NPG.
PH BARRAUD, tql, print, for *Men and Women of the Day*, vol III, 1890, NPG AX5511. W. & D.DOWNEY, tql seated, woodburytype, for Cassell's *Cabinet Portrait Gallery*, vol I, 1890, NPG.

PAYNE, George (1803-1878) patron of the turf.
P G.THOMPSON, tql, profile, with Admiral Rous, NPG 2957.
PR T.C.WILSON, wl, profile, holding whip, lith, for Wildrake's *Cracks of the Day*, 1841, BM.
C CARLO PELLEGRINI ('Ape'), wl, profile, w/c study, for *Vanity Fair*, 18 Sept 1875, NPG 4732.

PAYNE, Joseph (1808-1876) librarian.
PR C.W.SHERBORN, 1877, hs, semi-profile, etch, NPG.

PAYNE, Joseph Frank (1840-1910) physician.
D J.S.SARGENT, hs, charcoal, Royal College of Physicians, London.

PAYNE, William Henry Schofield (1804-1878) actor and pantomimist.
PR R.J.LANE, hs with George J.Bennett and Drinkwater Meadows as the three witches in *Macbeth*, lith, pub 1838, NPG.

PEACOCK, Sir Barnes (1810-1890) judge.
PR UNKNOWN, after a photograph by Sarony & Co, hs, wood engr, for *Illust London News*, 20 Dec 1890, NPG.

PEACOCKE, Joseph Ferguson (1835-1916) archbishop of Dublin.
P P.A.DE LÁSZLÓ, Bishop's Palace, Dublin.
PH UNKNOWN, hs, print, NPG (Anglican Bishops).

PEARCE, Stephen (1819-1904) painter.
P Self-portrait, hs, profile, NPG 1381.
PH UNKNOWN, hs, semi-profile, carte, NPG (Album 104).

PEARD, John Whitehead (1811-1880) 'Garibaldi's Englishman'.
PR T.NAST, hl, oval, sketch, woodcut, for *Illust London News*, 11 Aug 1860, NPG. G.J.STODART, after a photograph, hs, oval, stipple, NPG.
PH H.HERING, wl, carte, NPG X5105.

PEARS, Steuart Adolphus (1815-1875) schoolmaster and author.
P SIR FRANCIS GRANT, RA 1859, Repton School, Derby.

PEARSON, Charles Henry (1830-1894) historian.
PR P.N., after a photograph by Foster & Martin, hs, profile, wood engr, for *Illust London News*, 9 June 1894, NPG.

PEARSON, Hugh (1817-1882) canon of Windsor.
SC FREDERICK THRUPP, 1883, recumbent effigy, St Andrew's Church, Sonning, Berks.

PEARSON, John Loughborough (1817-1897) architect.
P JOHN PETTIE, MacDonald Collection, Aberdeen Art Gallery.
PR UNKNOWN, hs, woodcut, NPG.
PH ABEL LEWIS, hs, carte, NPG X4974. RALPH W.ROBINSON, hl seated, print, for *Members and Associates of the Royal Academy of Arts, 1891*, NPG X7384.

PEARSON, Karl (1857-1936) mathematician and biologist.
D F.A.DE BIDEN FOOTNER, 1924, hs, pencil, University College, London.
SC H.R.HOPE-PINKER, bust, University College, London.
PH CRELLIN, wl, as a child, carte, NPG X12706. ELLIOTT & FRY, 1890, two cabinets, both tql seated, NPG X12707-8. UNKNOWN, c1897, tql seated with his wife and children, print, NPG. UNKNOWN, 1910, two photogravures, tql and hl seated, NPG X12709-10. UNKNOWN, 1928, wl with his daughter, print, NPG.

PEARSON, Weetman Dickinson, see 1st Viscount Cowdray.

PEASE, Sir Joseph Whitwell, 1st Bart (1828-1903) director of mercantile enterprise.
C SIR LESLIE WARD ('Spy'), wl, chromo-lith, for *Vanity Fair*, 1 Oct 1887, NPG.

PEEL, Arthur Wellesley Peel, 1st Viscount (1829-1912) politician.
P SIR HUBERT VON HERKOMER, 1888, tql seated, Balliol College, Oxford. SIR W.Q.ORCHARDSON, 1898, wl seated in Speaker's chair, Palace of Westminster, London. LANCE CALKIN, hl, NPG 4085.
D S.P.HALL, 1886, hl seated, pencil, NPG 2326. SIR W.Q.ORCHARDSON, charcoal, NGS.
PR VIOLET, DUCHESS OF RUTLAND, 1891, hs, lith, NPG.
C HARRY FURNISS, pen and ink sketch, NPG 3403. SIR FRANCIS CARRUTHERS GOULD, two ink sketches, hl, profile, and tql seated, profile, NPG 2851-2. SIR LESLIE WARD ('Spy'), wl, profile, w/c study, for *Vanity Fair*, 2 July 1887, NPG 4733.
PH W. & D.DOWNEY, tql seated, woodburytype, for Cassell's *Cabinet Portrait Gallery*, vol III, 1892, NPG. ELLIOTT & FRY, tql in robes, cabinet, NPG X12579. LONDON STEREOSCOPIC CO, hl in robes, cabinet, NPG X12701.

PEEL, Sir Frederick (1823-1906) politician.
C SIR LESLIE WARD ('Spy'), wl, w/c study, for *Vanity Fair*, 17 Dec 1903, NPG 2980.
PH W. & D.DOWNEY, tql seated, carte, NPG AX8682.

PEEL, Sir Robert, 3rd Bart (1822-1895) politician.
PR UNKNOWN, after a photograph, tql, woodcut, for *Illust Times*, 25 Feb 1860, NPG.
C ALFRED THOMPSON ('Atη'), wl, chromo-lith, for *Vanity Fair*, 19 March 1870, NPG.
PH DISDERI & CIE, wl, carte, NPG X12711. JOHN & CHARLES WATKINS, tql, carte, NPG X12712. UNKNOWN, wl, carte, NPG AX8592.

PEEL, Sir William (1824-1858) captain in the navy.
P JOHN LUCAS, posthumous, wl, NMM, Greenwich.
SC WILLIAM THEED, three statues: 1860, Greenwich; 1861, St Swithun's Church, Sandy, Beds; 1863, Calcutta.
PR J.H.LYNCH, tql in uniform, lith, pub 1859, BM.

PEILE, John (1837-1910) master of Christ's College, Cambridge.
P SIR GEORGE REID, Christ's College, Cambridge; replica, Newnham College, Cambridge.
PH ELLIOTT & FRY, hl, profile, cabinet, NPG X12715. UNKNOWN, print, British Academy, London.

PELHAM, Henry Francis (1846-1907) Camden professor of ancient history, Oxford.
P SIR HUBERT VON HERKOMER, 1893, tql seated, Trinity College, Oxford.

PELHAM, Henry Thomas (1804-1886), see 3rd Earl of Chichester.

PELHAM, John Thomas (1811-1894) bishop of Norwich.
PR UNKNOWN, after a photographd by Mason, hl seated, woodcut, for *Illust London News*, 14 Oct 1865, NPG. J.FAED, after W.W.Ouless, tql seated, mezz, c1885, NPG.
PH CUNDALL & DOWNES, tql seated, carte, NPG X1474.

PELLEGRINI, Carlo (1839-1889) 'Ape'; caricaturist.
P JULES BASTIEN-LEPAGE, 1879, hl, NGI 583. SIR HENRY THOMPSON, hs, NPG 3947.
D EDGAR DEGAS, c1876-7, wl, w/c with oil and pastel, TATE 3157. Attrib to himself, 1877, tql, profile, w/c, NPG 2933.
C HARRY FURNISS, two pen and ink sketches, wl and hs, NPG 3500-1. A.J.MARKS, wl, chromo-lith, for *Vanity Fair*, 27 April 1889, NPG.

PELLY, Sir Lewis (1825-1892) Indian official.
PR UNKNOWN, at the trial of the Guicowar by the Special Commission at Baroda, woodcut, sketch, for *Illust London News*, 3 April 1875, NPG. R.T., after a photograph by Russell & Sons, hs, wood engr, for *Illust London News*, 30 April 1892, NPG.

PEMBER, Edward Henry (1833-1911) lawyer.
P SIR E.J.POYNTER, 1909, tql making an after dinner speech, Society of Dilettanti, Brooks's Club, London.

PEMBROKE, George Robert Charles Herbert, 13th Earl of (1850-1895).
P SIR W.B.RICHMOND, tql seated, Wilton House, Wilts.
SC SIR ALFRED GILBERT, 1900, bronze statue, Wilton House.
C CARLO PELLEGRINI ('Ape'), wl, profile, chromo-lith, for *Vanity Fair*, 14 July 1888, NPG.

PENDER, Sir John (1815-1896) pioneer of submarine telegraphy.
G HENRY JAMYN BROOKS, 'Private view of the Old Masters Exhibition, Royal Academy, 1888', oil, NPG 1833.
PR H.ADLARD, hs, circle, stipple, NPG. R.JOSEY, hs, stipple, NPG. UNKNOWN, hl seated, woodcut, for *Illust London News*, 21 Feb 1863, NPG. R.T., hs, profile, wood engr, for *Illust London News*, 5 May 1888, NPG.
C J.J.TISSOT, wl, w/c study, for *Vanity Fair*, 28 Oct 1871, NPG 2738. 'PET', wl, chromo-lith, for *The Monetary Gazette*, 21 March 1877, NPG.

PENGELLY, William (1812-1894) geologist.
P SIR A.S.COPE, RA 1882, tql, Torquay Natural History Society, Devon.
PR P.N., after a photograph by H.J.Whitlock, hs, wood engr, for *Illust London News*, 31 March 1894, NPG.

PENLEY, Aaron Edwin (1807-1870) water-colour painter.
PH Attrib F.F.COTTON, 1860, with John Callow, print, NPG X5013. UNKNOWN, tql seated, print, NPG X12717.

PENLEY, William Sydney (1852-1912) actor-manager.
PR UNKNOWN, after a photograph by Bertin of Brighton, hl, aged

26, woodcut, Harvard Theatre Collection, Cambridge, Mass, USA.

c SIR LESLIE WARD ('Spy'), wl, chromo-lith, for *Vanity Fair*, 22 June 1893, NPG.

PENNANT, Edward Douglas, see 1st Baron Penrhyn.

PENNANT, George Sholto Gordon Douglas-, see 2nd Baron Penrhyn.

PENNEFATHER, Catherine, née King (1818-1893) hymn-writer.

PR P.N., hs, wood engr, for *Illust London News*, 21 Jan 1893, NPG.

PENNEY, William (1801-1872), see Lord Kinloch.

PENNY, William (1809-1892) seaman and explorer.

P STEPHEN PEARCE, 1853, tql, NPG 1209.

PENRHYN, Edward Douglas-Pennant, 1st Baron (1800-1886) politician and landowner.

P E.U.EDDIS, 1845, wl, Penrhyn Castle (NT), Gwynedd, Wales. SIR HUBERT VON HERKOMER, 1881, hl, Penrhyn.

c SIR LESLIE WARD ('Spy'), wl, w/c study for *Vanity Fair*, 25 March 1882, NPG 3292.

PENRHYN, George Sholto Gordon Douglas-Pennant, 2nd Baron (1836-1907) landowner.

PR G.J.STODART, after a photograph by R.Faulkner & Co, hs, stipple, for *Baily's Mag*, 1888, NPG. UNKNOWN, hs, woodcut, for *Illust London News*, 23 Feb 1889, NPG.

PENROSE, Dame Emily (1858-1942) college principal.

P P.A.DE LÁSZLÓ, c1907, Royal Holloway College, London. FRANCIS HELPS, 1922, tql seated, Somerville College, Oxford.

PH UNKNOWN, tql, profile, print, NPG X12718.

PENROSE, Francis Cranmer (1817-1903) architect, archaeologist and astronomer.

P J.S.SARGENT, 1898, tql seated, RIBA, London; copy, Magdalene College, Cambridge.

PENSHURST, George Augustus Frederick Percy Sydney Smythe, 2nd Baron, see 7th Viscount Strangford.

PENSHURST, Percy Ellen Frederick William Smythe, 3rd Baron, see 8th Viscount Strangford.

PENZANCE, James Wilde, Baron (1816-1899) judge.

PR UNKNOWN, hl, woodcut, for *Illust London News*, 19 May 1860, NPG. UNKNOWN, after a photograph by J. & C.Watkins, hs, woodcut, for *Illust London News*, 26 Sept 1863, NPG.

c CARLO PELLEGRINI ('Ape'), hs, w/c study, for *Vanity Fair*, 18 Dec 1869, NPG 2739.

PH UNKNOWN, 1860s, tql seated, carte, NPG X12721. LOCK & WHITFIELD, hs, oval, woodburytype, for *Men of Mark*, 1880, NPG.

PERCIVAL, John (1834-1918) schoolmaster and bishop.

P SIR HUBERT VON HERKOMER, Queen's College, Oxford. MRS BASIL JOHNSON (his daughter), hs, Somerville College, Oxford. H.G.RIVIERE, RA 1899, tql, Trinity College, Oxford.

PH BASSANO, c1898, four negs, various sizes, NPG X4811-14. A.H.FRY, hl, postcard, NPG X12724. UNKNOWN, hs, print, NPG (Anglican Bishops).

PERCY, Lord Henry Hugh Manvers (1817-1877) general.

P GUSTAV POPE, 1878, wl in uniform, Alnwick Castle, Northumberland.

PH NOTMAN, c1863, hs, carte, NPG X8363.

PEREIRA, Jonathan (1804-1853) pharmacologist.

SC After PATRICK MACDOWELL of c1854, bust, Linnean Society, London.

PR D.POUND, after a daguerreotype by Mayall, hl, stipple and line, NPG.

PERIGAL, Arthur (1816-1884) landscape painter.

P SIR DANIEL MACNEE, 1881, hl, SNPG 1360.

PERKIN, Sir William Henry (1838-1907) chemist.

P HENRY GRANT, 1898, in robes, Leathersellers' Hall, London. SIR A.S.COPE, 1906, tql, NPG 1892.

SC F.W.POMEROY, marble bust, Chemical Society, London.

PERKS, Sir Robert William, 1st Bart (1849-1934) Methodist, industrialist and politician.

P After A.T.NOWELL, Westminster Central Hall, London.

PEROWNE, Edward Henry (1826-1906) master of Corpus Christi College, Cambridge.

P RUDOLPH LEHMANN, 1885, Corpus Christi College, Cambridge.

PEROWNE, John James Stewart (1823-1904) bishop of Worcester.

P JOHN COLLIER, 1892, seated in robes, Corpus Christi College, Cambridge. HENRY WEIGALL, Hartlebury Castle, Worcs.

PH UNKNOWN, hs, print, NPG (Anglican Bishops).

PERRY, Charles (1807-1891) bishop of Melbourne.

P HENRY WEIGALL, Ridley Hall, Cambridge.

SC CHARLES SUMMERS, 1876, marble busts, Harrow School, Middx and State Library of Victoria, Australia.

PR G.T.PAYNE, after S.Laurence, hl, mezz, BM.

PERRY, Sir Thomas Erskine (1806-1882) judge in India.

D JOHN LINNELL, head, pencil and chalk, NPG 1817.

PETIT, Sir Dinshaw Manockjee, 1st Bart (1823-1901) Parsi merchant and philanthropist.

SC SIR THOMAS BROCK, c1916, marble seated statue, Bombay.

PETO, Sir Samuel Morton, 1st Bart (1809-1889) contractor and politician.

P HENRY WEIGALL, wl, Regent's Park College, Oxford.

PR G.R.BLACK, after a photograph by Mayall, tql, lith, NPG. W.H.MOTE, after A.Wivell, hs, stipple, pub 1848, NPG. UNKNOWN, hs, stipple, NPG. Several popular prints, NPG.

PH JOHN BEATTIE, tql seated, carte, NPG AX8670.

PETRE, Sir George Glynn (1822-1905) diplomat.

PR UNKNOWN, after a photograph by A.Bobone of Lisbon, hs, wood engr, for *Illust London News*, 15 April 1893, NPG.

PETRIE, Sir (William Matthew) Flinders (1853-1942) archaeologist and egyptologist.

P G.F.WATTS, 1900, hs, NPG 3959. P.A.DE LÁSZLÓ, 1934, hl seated, NPG 4007. P.A.DE LÁSZLÓ, University College, London.

D WINIFRED BRUNTON, 1912, hs profile, w/c, University College, London.

PH WALTER STONEMAN, 1917, hs, profile, NPG (NPR). UNKNOWN, 1921, hl with some of University College's Egyptological collection, print, University College, London.

PETTIE, John (1839-1893) painter.

P Self-portrait, 1881, hs, profile, MacDonald Collection, Aberdeen Art Gallery. Self-portrait, 1882, TATE 2434. JAMES ARCHER, SNPG 720. GEORGE PAUL CHALMERS, hs, SNPG 1423.

G G.Grenville Manton, 'Conversazione at the Royal Academy, 1891', w/c, NPG 2820. REGINALD CLEAVER, 'Hanging Committee, Royal Academy, 1892', pen and ink, NPG 4245.

SC GEORGE ANDERSON LAWSON, bronze busts, SNPG 1091 and Glasgow Art Gallery.

PR Several popular woodcuts, after photographs, BM, NPG.

PH ELLIOTT & FRY, hs, profile, carte, NPG (Album 104). LOCK & WHITFIELD, hs, oval, woodburytype, for *Men of Mark*, 1882, NPG. RALPH W.ROBINSON, tql seated with palette, for *Members and Associates of the Royal Academy of Arts, 1891*, NPG X7385.

PETTIGREW, James Bell (1834-1908) professor of medicine at the University of St Andrews.

P W.W.OULESS, 1902, tql, Edinburgh University.

PETTY-FITZMAURICE, Edmond George, see Baron Fitzmaurice.

PETTY-FITZMAURICE, Henry Charles Keith, see 5th Marquess of Lansdowne.

PETTY-FITZMAURICE, Henry Thomas, see 4th Marquess of Lansdowne.

PHAYRE, Sir Arthur Purves (1812-1885) first commissioner of British Burma.

SC THOMAS NELSON MACLEAN, RA 1890, bronze statue, Rangoon, Burma.

PR UNKNOWN, hs, semi-profile, woodcut, NPG.

PHAYRE, Sir Robert (1820-1897) general.

PR Three woodcuts, all hs, NPG.

PHELPS, Lancelot Ridley (1853-1936) provost of Oriel College, Oxford.

P BRITON RIVIERE, 1916, tql seated, Oriel College, Oxford.

PHELPS, Samuel (1804-1878) actor.

P N.J.CROWLEY, wl as Hamlet, Royal Shakespeare Memorial Theatre Picture Gallery, Stratford-upon-Avon. SIR JOHNSTON FORBES-ROBERTSON, 1878, nearly wl, as Cardinal Wolsey, Garrick Club, London. RICHARD WALLER, hl, semi-profile, Garrick Club.

PR C.BAUGNIET, tql seated, oval, lith, BM. Various theatrical and popular prints, BM, NPG, Harvard Theatre Collection, Cambridge, Mass, USA. Several woodcuts and engravings after photographs, NPG.

C ALFRED BRYAN, wl, sepia, NPG 3015. HARRY FURNISS, two pen and ink sketches, hs and wl, NPG 3503 and 3596.

PH LONDON STEREOSCOPIC CO, tql seated, carte, NPG X12729. UNKNOWN, hs, woodburytype, carte, NPG X12730.

PHILIP, John Birnie (1824-1875) sculptor.

PR Two woodcuts after photographs, both hs, one for *Illust London News*, 13 March 1875, BM.

PHILIP, Sir Robert William (1857-1939) physician and founder of tuberculosis dispensaries.

P SIR JAMES GUTHRIE, Royal College of Physicians, Edinburgh.

PHILIPS, Frederick Charles (1849-1921) novelist and dramatist.

C CARLO PELLEGRINI ('Ape'), wl, profile, w/c study, for *Vanity Fair*, 7 July 1888, NPG 4632.

PHILLIMORE, Sir Robert Joseph, 1st Bart (1810-1885) civilian and judge.

PR UNKNOWN, hs, woodcut, for *Illust London News*, 14 Feb 1885, NPG.

PH Studio of RICHARD BEARD, c1845, hs, daguerreotype, NPG P118. LOCK & WHITFIELD, hs, oval, woodburytype, for *Men of Mark*, 1877, NPG. UNKNOWN, hs, carte, NPG (Album 38).

PHILLIMORE, Sir Walter George Frank Phillimore, 2nd Bart, 1st Baron (1845-1929) judge.

P GEORGE HENRY, Kensington Town Hall.

C SIR LESLIE WARD ('Spy'), hs, chromo-lith, for *Vanity Fair*, 24 Nov 1898, NPG.

PH MAULL & FOX, hs in wig and robes, print, NPG X12736. WALTER STONEMAN, 1917, hs in wig and robes, NPG (NPR).

PHILLIP, John (1817-1867) portrait and subject painter.

P Several self-portraits: four at the Aberdeen Art Gallery (one is dated 1840, one is with his wife); hs, NGS 1663; hl seated, SNPG

1473; hs, Glasgow Art Gallery. Attrib to himself, tql seated with palette, NPG 3335. JOHN BALLANTYNE, RA 1867, wl seated in his studio, SNPG 626. C.E.CUNDALL, hs, semi-profile, Garrick Club, London. J.A.HOUSTON, 1867, hs, semi-profile, Royal Scottish Academy, Edinburgh. UNKNOWN (B.N.D.?), tql seated with palette, Royal Scottish Academy.

D RICHARD DADD, 1839, hs, as 'Glorious Jock', chalk, BM. Attrib DANIEL MACNEE, hs, w/c, gouache and oil, NPG 2446.

SC JOHN HUTCHISON, c1861, plaster bust, SNPG 679. WILLIAM BRODIE, RA 1868, marble bust, Aberdeen Art Gallery.

PR Various engravings and woodcuts, BM, NPG.

PH ELLIOTT & FRY, two cartes, hs, semi-profile, and hs, NPG (Album 104 and Album 106). DAVID WILKIE WYNFIELD, c1862-4, hs, print, NPG P80.

PHILLIPS, Sir Claude (1846-1924) art critic.

D ALPHONSE LEGROS, 1890, two drgs, hs and hs, profile, both silverpoint, NPG 2431-2.

PHILLIPS, George (1804-1892) oriental scholar.

P SIR HUBERT VON HERKOMER, 1885, hl, Queen's College, Cambridge.

PHILLIPS, Henry (1801-1876) singer.

D A.E.CHALON, 1828, wl, pencil, pen and ink, NPG 1962(f).

PR C.TURNER, after J.Wright, wl as Uberto in the opera *The Freebooters*, mezz, pub 1829, BM. C.BAUGNIET, tql, lith, 1846, BM, NPG. Various theatrical prints, BM, NPG, Harvard Theatre Collection, Cambridge, Mass, USA.

PHILLIPS, Henry Wyndham (1820-1868) painter.

PH NADAR, tql, carte, NPG (Album 104). DAVID WILKIE WYNFIELD, c1862-4, hs, profile, print, NPG P81.

PHILLIPS, John (1800-1874) geologist.

SC MATTHEW NOBLE, 1849, marble bust, University Museum, Oxford.

PR T.H.MAGUIRE, tql, lith for *Ipswich Museum Portraits*, 1851, BM, NPG. UNKNOWN, after a photograph by Guggenheim, hl seated, woodcut, for *Illust London News*, 23 Sept 1865, NPG. R. & E.TAYLOR, after a photograph by Elliott & Fry, hs, oval, woodcut, for *Illust London News*, 16 May 1874, NPG.

PH UNKNOWN, tql, print, NPG X12733.

PHILLIPS, Sir Thomas (1801-1867) mayor of Newport during the chartist riots 1839.

PR W.GILLER, after F.Williams, tql, mezz, pub 1840, BM, NPG.

PH A.G.TOD, tql seated, carte, NPG X12731.

PHILLIPS, Watts (1825-1874) dramatist and designer.

PR UNKNOWN, after a photograph by S.Walker, hs, semi-profile, woodcut, for *Illust London News*, 19 Dec 1874, NPG.

PHILPOTT, Henry (1807-1892) bishop of Worcester.

P SIR JOHN WATSON GORDON, 1859, tql, St Catherine's College, Cambridge.

SC SIR THOMAS BROCK, 1896, marble seated statue, Worcester Cathedral.

PH MAULL & POLYBLANK, wl, carte, NPG AX7475. S.A.WALKER, c1889, tql, print, NPG.

PHIPPS, Sir Charles Beaumont (1801-1866) court official.

PR UNKNOWN, after a photograph by John & Charles Watkins, hs, profile, woodcut, for *Illust London News*, 11 April 1863, NPG.

PH CAMILLE SILVY, wl seated, carte, NPG (Album 116).

PHIPPS, Charles John (1835-1897) architect.

PR UNKNOWN, after a photograph by Vernon Haye, hs, wood engr, NPG.

PHIPPS, Edmund (1808-1857) writer and barrister.

D COUNT ALFRED D'ORSAY, 1848, hs, profile, pencil and chalk, NPG 4026 (45).

PHIPPS, Sir George Augustus Constantine, see 2nd Marquess of Normanby.

PHIZ (pseudonym), see Hablot Knight BROWNE.

PIATTI, Alfredo Carlo (1822-1901) violoncellist and composer.
G C.BAUGNIET, 'The Musical Union, 1851', lith, BM.
PH W. & D.DOWNEY, wl seated, playing, woodburytype, for Cassell's *Cabinet Portrait Gallery*, vol I, 1890, NPG. DEW SMITH, hl, print, NPG.

PICKARD, Benjamin (1842-1904) trade-union leader.
PH SIR BENJAMIN STONE, 1897, wl, print, NPG.

PICKERSGILL, Frederick Richard (1820-1900) historical painter.
P Self-portrait, *c*1850, tql, NPG 5183. Self-portrait, 1889, hs, semi-profile, MacDonald Collection, Aberdeen Art Gallery.
PR UNKNOWN, hs, woodcut, for *Art Journal*, 1850, BM, NPG.
PH LOCK & WHITFIELD, hs, oval, woodburytype, for *Men of Mark*, 1882, NPG. MAULL & POLYBLANK, wl, carte, NPG AX7574. JOHN & CHARLES WATKINS, hs, profile, carte, NPG (Album 104). DAVID WILKIE WYNFIELD, *c*1862–4, hs, print, NPG P82.

PICKFORD, William, see Baron Sterndale.

PICTON, Sir James Allanson (1805-1889) antiquary and architect.
P WILLIAM BARNES BOADLE, tql seated, Walker Art Gallery, Liverpool.

PIERSON (originally PEARSON), Henry Hugo (1815-1873) musician and composer.
SC G.A.KIETZ, 1873, plaster bust, Royal College of Music, London.
PH UNKNOWN, tql seated, carte, NPG X12745.

PIGOTT, Sir Gillery (1813-1875) baron of the exchequer.
PR UNKNOWN, hl, woodcut, for *Illust London News*, 31 Dec 1863. NPG.

PIGOTT, Richard (1828?-1889) Irish journalist and forger.
D S.P.HALL, 1888–89, at the sessions of the Parnell Commission, pencil sketch, NPG 2234.
PR UNKNOWN, two sketches, hs and hl, profile, for *Illust London News*, 2 March 1889, NPG.
C SIR LESLIE WARD ('Spy'), tql, profile, chromo-lith, for *Vanity Fair*, 9 March 1889, NPG.

PILCH, Fuller (1803-1870) cricketer.
G N.PLOSZCZYNSKI, 'The Eleven of England selected to contend in the Great Cricket Matches of the North for the year 1847', chromo-lith, Marylebone Cricket Club, London.
SC UNKNOWN, wl figure on bronze tablet on monument, St Gregory's Churchyard, Canterbury.
PR G.F.WATTS, wl with bat, lith, Marylebone Cricket Club, London. UNKNOWN, wl with bat, woodcut, for *Illust London News*, 15 July 1843, NPG.

PIM, Bedford Clapperton Trevelyan (1826-1886) admiral.
PH LOCK & WHITFIELD, hs, oval, woodburytype, for *Men of Mark*, 1883, NPG.

PINERO, Sir Arthur Wing (1855-1934) playwright.
P JOSEPH MORDECAI, RA 1891, tql seated, NPG 2761. WALFORD GRAHAM ROBERTSON, hl seated, V & A (Theatre Museum).
D PHIL MAY, wl, w/c, Garrick Club, London. A.J.MUNNINGS, 1928, seated at table, pencil, Garrick Club.
G W.H.BARTLETT, 'A Saturday Night at the Savage Club', oil, Savage Club, London.

SC UNKNOWN, bust, Garrick Club.
PR W.ROTHENSTEIN, tql seated, profile, lith, BM, NPG.
C SIR LESLIE WARD ('Spy'), wl, profile, chromo-lith, for *Vanity Fair*, 7 March 1891, NPG. SIR MAX BEERBOHM, several drgs: 1903, wl, Garrick Club; hs, Princeton University Library, USA; for *Vanity Fair*, 1 Feb 1906, University of Texas, Austin, USA; 1912, wl, Ashmolean Museum, Oxford; wl, profile, Lilly Library, Indiana University, Bloomington, USA; wl, profile, Berg Collection, New York Public Library, USA. HARRY FURNISS, 1905, pen and ink sketch, for *The Garrick Club*, NPG 4095(9). SIR BERNARD PARTRIDGE, tql, sketch, for *Punch*, 28 Sept 1927, NPG 3675.
PH W. & D.DOWNEY, hl, woodburytype, for Cassell's *Cabinet Portrait Gallery*, vol V, 1894, NPG. ALFRED ELLIS, tql seated, print for *The Theatre*, July 1893, NPG X12458. FREDERICK HOLLYER, 1895, hl, profile, print, NPG X12457. E.H.MILLS, hl, photogravure, NPG X12460. JOHN RUSSELL & SONS, hs, print, for *National Photographic Record*, vol I, NPG.

PINWELL, George John (1842-1875) water-colourist and illustrator.
D EYRE CROWE, hs, pencil and crayon, NPG 4496. THOMAS HENRY WHITE, 1862, wl seated, pencil and ink, V & A.
PR Two woodcuts after photographs, hs and hl, profile, the second for *Illust London News*, 18 Sept 1875, BM.

PIRBRIGHT, Henry de Worms, 1st Baron (1840-1903) politician.
P LIERON MAYER, tql seated, DoE.
C CARLO PELLEGRINI ('Ape'), wl, profile, chromo-lith, for *Vanity Fair*, 22 May 1880, NPG.
PH BROWN, BARNES & BELL, hs, print, for *Our Conservative and Unionist Statesmen*, vol VI, NPG (Album 23). RUSSELL & SONS, hl print, for *Our Conservative Statesmen*, vol I, NPG (Album 16). SIR BENJAMIN STONE, 1897, wl, print, NPG.

PIRRIE, William James Pirrie, Viscount (1847-1924) ship builder.
P SIR HUBERT VON HERKOMER, 1905, wl, Belfast Corporation.
C SIR LESLIE WARD ('Spy'), wl, profile, chromo-lith, for *Vanity Fair*, 8 Jan 1903, NPG.
PH ELLIOTT & FRY, 1906, hs, photogravure, NPG X12728.

PITMAN, Sir Henry Alfred (1808-1908) physician centenarian.
P W.W.OULESS, 1885, hl seated, Royal College of Physicians, London.
PR UNKNOWN, hs, woodcut, for *Illust London News*, 27 March 1886, NPG.

PITMAN, Sir Isaac (1813-1897) inventor of Pitman shorthand.
P SIR A.S.COPE, posthumous, tql seated, NPG 1509.
PR R.T., after a photograph by F.C.Bird, hs, wood engr, for *Illust London News*, 1 Oct 1887, NPG.

PLAYFAIR, William Smoult (1835-1903) obstetric physician.
P SUSANNE VAN NATHUSIUS, 1882, hs, Royal College of Physicians, London.
PH A.J.MELHUISH, tql seated, print, NPG.

PLAYFAIR of St Andrews, Sir Lyon Playfair, Baron (1818-1898) chemist.
P JOHN LORIMER, University of St Andrews. H.W.PICKERSGILL, *c*1857, tql, Edinburgh University.
M JOHN HASLEM, 1854, hs, enamel, NPG 5216.
SC MATTHEW NOBLE, 1848, bust, Geological Museum, London.
PR T.H.MAGUIRE, 1851, tql seated, lith, one of set of *Ipswich Museum*

Portraits, BM, NPG. W.HOLE, hl, etch, for *Quasi Cursores*, 1884, NPG. Several engravings and woodcuts after photographs by A.Bassano, Caldesi and Claudet, some for *Illust London News*, NPG.

C CARLO PELLEGRINI ('Ape'), wl, profile, chromo-lith, for *Vanity Fair*, 20 Feb 1875, NPG.

PH MAULL & POLYBLANK, 1855, tql, print, NPG P120(7). LOCK & WHITFIELD, hs, oval, woodburytype, for *Men of Mark*, 1877, NPG. BARRAUD, hs, print, for *Men and Women of the Day*, vol IV, 1891, NPG AX5518. W. & D.DOWNEY, hl, woodburytype, for Cassell's *Cabinet Portrait Gallery*, vol III, 1892, NPG.

PLEYDELL-BOUVERIE, Edward, see Bouverie.

PLIMSOLL, Samuel (1824-1898) champion of seamen's rights.
P R.H.CAMPBELL, posthumous, probably after a photograph, tql seated, NMM, Greenwich.
SC UNKNOWN, bust, Bristol Portway.
PR G.PILOTELL, hs, profile, drypoint, BM, NPG. Several popular prints, NPG.
C W.VINE ('WV'), wl, profile, w/c study, for *Vanity Fair*, 15 March 1873, NPG 4734.
PH BARRAUD, tql seated, print, for *Men and Women of the Day*, vol IV, 1891, NPG AX5517. LOCK & WHITFIELD, hs, profile, oval, woodburytype, for *Men of Mark*, 1876, NPG. LONDON STEREOSCOPIC CO, hs, carte, NPG (Album 40). UNKNOWN, hs, profile, woodburytype, carte, NPG AX7656.

PLOWDEN, Alfred Chichele (1844-1914) magistrate.
C A.G.WITHERBY ('Wag'), hl, w/c study, for *Vanity Fair*, 11 April 1901, NPG 2993. SIR LESLIE WARD ('Spy'), wl, w/c study, for *Vanity Fair*, 16 Dec 1908, NPG 2994.

PLUMER, Herbert Charles Onslow Plumer, 1st Viscount (1857-1932) field-marshal.
P SIR WILLIAM ORPEN, 1918, hl, IWM, London. UNKNOWN, tql seated in uniform, formerly United Services and Royal Aero Club, London (c/o The Crown Commissioners). UNKNOWN, hl in uniform, Staff College, Camberley, Surrey.
D FRANCIS DODD, 1917, charcoal and w/c, IWM. EDMOND KAPP, 1919, Barber Institute of Fine Arts, Birmingham.
G J.S.SARGENT, 'General Officers of World War I, 1914–18', oil, NPG 1954.
C SIR LESLIE WARD ('Spy'), 'A General Group', chromo–lith, for *Vanity Fair*, 29 Nov 1900, NPG. SIR LESLIE WARD ('Spy'), wl, w/c study, for *Vanity Fair*, 13 Nov 1902, NPG 3000.
PH WALTER STONEMAN, 1918, hs in uniform, NPG (NPR).

PLUMPTRE, Edward Hayes (1821-1891) dean of Wells.
PR UNKNOWN, hs, wood engr, for *Illust London News*, 3 Dec 1881, NPG. R.T., after a photograph by Elliott & Fry, hs, wood engr, for *Illust London News*, 7 Feb 1891, NPG.
PH LOCK & WHITFIELD, hs, oval, woodburytype, for *Men of Mark*, 1883, NPG.

PLUNKET, William Conyngham Plunket, 4th Baron (1828-1897) archbishop of Dublin.
SC SIR WILLIAM HAMO THORNYCROFT, 1901, statue, Dublin.
PR R.T., after a photograph by Chancellor of Dublin, hs, wood engr, for *Illust London News*, 3 Jan 1885, NPG.

PLUNKETT, Sir Horace Curzon (1854-1932) Irish statesman.
P SIR JOHN LAVERY, Municipal Gallery of Modern Art, Dublin. DERMOD O'BRIEN, Irish Agricultural Organization Society, Dublin. J.B.YEATS, Municipal Gallery of Modern Art.
D SIR WILLIAM ROTHENSTEIN, head, chalk, NPG 3878. SIR W.ROTHENSTEIN, drg, Municipal Gallery of Modern Art.

SC FRANCIS DERWENT WOOD, 1923, bronze bust, Irish Agricultural Organization Society, Dublin.
PH G.C.BERESFORD, 1903, hs, semi-profile, neg, NPG X6561.

POCOCK, Lewis (1808-1882) founder and secretary of the Art Union of London.
PR C.BAUGNIET, hl, lith, BM. E.MORTON, after S.Laurence, hs, semi-profile, lith, pub 1847, BM.

POEL, William (1852-1934) actor and author.
P HENRY TONKS, 1932, wl as Father Keegan, NPG 2762.
D HENRY TONKS, pencil studies, NPG 3072 (8–10, 11, 12–18).

POLAND, Sir Harry Bodkin (1829-1928) lawyer.
C HARRY FURNISS, pen and ink sketch, NPG 3505. SIR LESLIE WARD ('Spy'), hl, profile, in court, chromo-lith, for *Vanity Fair*, 13 March 1886, NPG.

POLE, William (1814-1900) engineer, musician and authority on whist.
SC UNKNOWN, bronze medallion, Institution of Civil Engineers, London.

POLLARD, Alfred William (1859-1944) librarian, bibliographer and English scholar.
P FRANK BROOKS, hl, British Library, London.

POLLOCK, Sir Charles Edward (1823-1897) judge.
D F.P., 1881, called Pollock, chalk, Trinity College, Cambridge.
C HARRY FURNISS, pen and ink sketch, NPG 3598. 'QUIZ', tql seated, profile, chromo-lith, for *Vanity Fair*, 9 Aug 1890, NPG.
PH LOCK & WHITFIELD, hs, oval, woodburytype, for *Men of Mark*, 1881, BM.

POLLOCK, Sir Frederick, 3rd Bart (1845-1937) legal writer and professor of jurisprudence at Oxford.
P R.G.EVES, 1926, tql seated, Lincoln's Inn, London; hs, version, NPG 3835.
D R.RAY JONES, 1927, pencil, Trinity College, Cambridge.
PR W.ROTHENSTEIN, hl, lith, BM, NPG.
C HARRY FURNISS, pen and ink sketch, NPG 3599.
PH WALTER STONEMAN, two portraits, 1917 and 1936, NPG (NPR).

POLLOCK, Sir William Frederick, 2nd Bart (1815-1888) queen's remembrancer and author.
P W.W.OULESS, 1873, The Equitable Life Assurance Society, London.

PONSONBY, Frederick George Brabazon, see 6th Earl of Bessborough.

PONSONBY, Sir Henry Frederick (1825-1895) general; private secretary to Queen Victoria.
SC FEODORA, COUNTESS VON GLEICHEN, 1897, bust, in uniform, Royal Coll.
C THÉOBALD CHARTRAN ('T'), wl, chromo–lith, for *Vanity Fair*, 17 March 1883, NPG.
PH W. & D.DOWNEY, hs, woodburytype, for Cassell's *Cabinet Portrait Gallery*, vol I, 1890, NPG. WALERY, wl, print, NPG.

PONSONBY, John (1809-1880), see 5th Earl of Bessborough.

PONTON, Mungo (1802-1880) photographic inventor.
PH KLÍC of Vienna, *c*1879, hl, photogravure, Gernsheim Collection, University of Texas, Austin, USA.

POOLE, Paul Falconer (1807-1879) history painter.
P FRANK HOLL, 1879, head, NPG 2532.
PR Two woodcuts after photographs, BM, NPG. UNKNOWN, after a photograph by John Watkins, hs, woodcut, for *Illust London News*, 23 Feb 1861, NPG.
PH UNKNOWN, hs, semi-profile, carte, NPG (Album 103).

POOLE, Reginald Lane (1857-1939) historian.

D WILLIAM STRANG, 1909, chalk, Magdalen College, Oxford.
PH J.RUSSELL & SONS, c1904, hs, print, NPG X12760.

POOLE, Reginald Stuart (1832-1895) archaeologist and orientalist.
PR P.N., after a photograph by Elliott & Fry, hs, wood engr, for *Illust London News*, 16 Feb 1895, NPG.

POPE, George Uglow (1820-1908) missionary and Tamil scholar.
P A.A.WOLMARK, 1903, tql seated in academic gown, Indian Institute, Oxford.

POPE, Samuel (1826-1901) barrister.
P SIR HUBERT VON HERKOMER, hs, Middle Temple, London.
C SIR LESLIE WARD ('Spy'), hl, profile, chromo-lith, for *Vanity Fair*, 12 Dec 1885, NPG.

POPE, William Burt (1822-1903) Wesleyan divine.
P A.T.NOWELL, Didsbury College, Manchester.

POPE HENNESSY, Sir John, see Hennessy.

PORCH, Mrs Montagu, see Lady Jennie Churchill.

PORCHESTER, Henry John George Herbert, 3rd Viscount, see 3rd Earl of Carnarvon.

PORTAL, Sir Gerald Herbert (1858-1894) diplomat.
PR VIOLET, DUCHESS OF RUTLAND, 1894, hs, lith, NPG.

PORTAL, Melville (1819-1904) politician.
P ARCHIBALD STUART-WORTLEY, c1890, The Great Hall, Winchester.

PORTER, Sir George Hornidge, 1st Bart (1822-1895) surgeon.
PR R.T., after a photograph by Chancellor of Dublin, hs, wood engr, for *Illust London News*, 8 June 1889, NPG.

PORTSMOUTH, Isaac Newton Wallop, 5th Earl of (1825-1891) landowner.
D FREDERICK SARGENT, hs, pencil, NPG 1834x.
PR JOSEPH BROWN, after a photograph by J.E.Mayall, tql, stipple, for *Baily's Mag*, 1861, NPG. UNKNOWN, hl, lith, NPG.
C SIR LESLIE WARD ('Spy'), wl, profile, chromo-lith, for *Vanity Fair*, 1 July 1876, NPG 4735.

POSTGATE, John Percival (1853-1926) classical scholar.
PH WALTER STONEMAN, 1917, hs, NPG (NPR).

POTTER, John Phillips (1818-1847) anatomist.
SC THOMAS CAMPBELL, 1847, bust, University College, London, engr T.H.Maguire, lith, NPG.

POTTER, Thomas Bayley (1817-1898) politician.
SC MATTHEW NOBLE, 1860, marble bust, Rochdale Town Hall.
C SIR LESLIE WARD ('Spy'), wl, chromo-lith, for *Vanity Fair*, 2 June 1877, NPG.
PH ELLIOTT & FRY, hs, carte, NPG AX8625.

POTTINGER, Eldred (1811-1841) soldier and diplomat.
P After GEORGE BEECHEY, c1840, hs in Indian dress, National Army Museum, London.
PR VINCENT EYRE, c1842, chromo-lith, for *Portraits of the Kabul Prisoners*, National Army Museum.

POULTON, Sir Edward Bagnall (1856-1943) zoologist.
D SIR WILLIAM ROTHENSTEIN, Jesus College, Oxford.

POWELL, Frederick York (1850-1904) professor of modern history at Oxford.
P J(?)B.YEATS, 1892, hs, Oriel College, Oxford.
PR W.ROTHENSTEIN, hl seated, lith, BM, NPG.
C SIR LESLIE WARD ('Spy'), wl, chromo-lith, for *Vanity Fair*, 21 March 1895, NPG.

POWELL, Sir George Baden-, see BADEN-Powell.

POWELL, Sir Richard Douglas, 1st Bart (1842-1925) physician.
P SPENCER WATSON (replica), tql seated, Royal College of Physicians, London.
C SIR LESLIE WARD ('Spy'), wl, semi-profile, chromo-lith, for *Vanity Fair*, 28 April 1904, NPG.
PH OLIVE EDIS, c1905, hs, print, NPG. WALTER STONEMAN, 1917, hs, NPG (NPR).

POWELL, Robert Baden-Powell, 1st Baron Baden-, see BADEN-Powell.

POWER, Sir D'Arcy (1855-1941) surgeon and historian.
P SIR MATTHEW THOMPSON, 1934, tql seated in gown, with cross of the order of the British Empire, Royal College of Surgeons, London.
G MOUSSA AYOUB, 'Council of the Royal College of Surgeons of England of 1926-27', oil, Royal College of Surgeons.
PH WALTER STONEMAN, 1917, hs, NPG (NPR).

POWER, Marguerite A. (1815?-1867) writer.
PR W.H.EGLETON, after W.Drummond, tql in evening dress, stipple, for Heath's *Book of Beauty*, 1842, BM, NPG. W.H.EGLETON, after W.Drummond, hl, stipple, pub 1842, BM.

POYNTER, Sir Edward John, 1st Bart (1836-1919) painter.
P Self-portrait, 1882, hs, profile, oval, MacDonald Collection, Aberdeen Art Gallery. Self-portrait, RA 1888, hl seated with brush and palette, Uffizi Gallery, Florence. SIR PHILIP BURNE-JONES, 1909, wl seated, profile, in studio, NPG 1951. SIR A.S.COPE, 1911, tql seated, Royal Academy, London. SEYMOUR LUCAS, 1911, hs, Royal Academy.
G HENRY JAMYN BROOKS, 'Private view of the Old Masters Exhibition, Royal Academy, 1888', oil, NPG 1833. SIR HUBERT VON HERKOMER, 'The Council of the Royal Academy', oil, 1908, TATE 2481.
PR A.LEGROS, hs, etch, for *The Portfolio*, 1877, BM, NPG.
C SIR LESLIE WARD ('Spy'), wl seated with brushes and palette, chromo-lith, for *Vanity Fair*, 4 March 1897, NPG.
PH ELLIOTT & FRY, hs, cabinet, NPG X12764. LOCK & WHITFIELD, hs, oval, woodburytype, for *Men of Mark*, 1880, NPG. RALPH W.ROBINSON, wl in studio, print, for *Members and Associates of the Royal Academy of Arts*, 1891, NPG X7386. JOHN RUSSELL & SONS, hl seated, print, for *National Photographic Record*, vol II, NPG. WALTER STONEMAN, hs, NPG (NPR). JOHN WATKINS, hs, semi-profile, carte, NPG (Album 104).

PRAED, Winthrop Mackworth (1802-1839) poet.
D DANIEL MACLISE, wl, w/c, NPG 3030.
G HENRY NELSON O'NEIL, 'The Billiard Room of the Garrick Club', oil, 1869, Garrick Club, London.
SC RAYMOND SMITH, medallion on tomb, Kensal Green Cemetery, London.
PR W.DRUMMOND, after A.Mayer, hs, lith, for 'Athenaeum Portraits', pub 1837, NPG.

PRAIN, Sir David (1857-1944) botanist and administrator.
P MISS F.A.DE BIDEN FOOTNER, Royal Botanic Gardens, Kew.
PH WALTER STONEMAN, 1917, hs, NPG (NPR).

PRATT, Hodgson (1824-1907) advocate of peace.
P FELIX MOSCHELES, 1891, hl seated, NPG 2032.

PRATTEN, Robert Sidney (1824-1868) flautist.
PH HERBERT WATKINS, wl, carte, NPG (Album 110). UNKNOWN, tql print, BM (Engr Ports Coll).

PREECE, Sir William Henry (1834-1913) electrical engineer.

P BEATRICE BRIGHT, 1899, tql, Science Museum, London.

PRENDERGAST, Sir Harry North Dalrymple (1834-1913) general.

P F.C.ELLIS, tql, Royal Engineers Headquarters Mess, Chatham, Kent. JOHN GARMAER, wl, Royal Engineers.

PR UNKNOWN, hs in uniform, wood engr, for *Illust London News*, 14 Nov 1885, NPG.

PH UNKNOWN, *c*1860, tql, print, National Army Museum, London.

PRESTWICH, Sir Joseph (1812-1896) geologist.

SC H.R.HOPE PINKER, RA 1901, posthumous marble bust, University Museum, Oxford; related bronze medallion, University Museum, Oxford.

PR P.N., after a photograph by Elliott & Fry, hs, wood engr, for *Illust London News*, 11 Jan 1896, NPG.

PRICE, Bartholomew (1818-1898) master of Pembroke College, Oxford.

P MARMADUKE C.W.FLOWER, 1896, tql seated, Pembroke College, Oxford.

PRICE, Bonamy (1807-1888) economist.

D UNKNOWN, hs, pencil on porcelain, Worcester College, Oxford.

PR UNKNOWN, hs, wood engr, for *Illust London News*, 21 Jan 1888, NPG.

PRICE, Thomas (1852-1909) premier of South Australia.

P C.D.MACKENZIE, hs, Walker Art Gallery, Liverpool.

PRICE, William Lake (1810-after 1896) water-colourist.

D A.E.CHALON, *c*1844, head, profile, chalk study for 'John Knox Reproving the Ladies of Queen Mary's Court' (RA 1844), NPG 2538.

G W.T.RODEN, after A.E.Chalon, 'John Knox Reproving the Ladies of Queen Mary's Court', engr, pub 1851, Witt Library, London.

PRIDEAUX, Walter (1806-1889) lawyer and poet.

G JOHN HOLLINS, 'A Consultation prior to the Aerial Voyage to Weilburg, 1836', oil, NPG 4710.

PRIESTLEY, Sir William Overend (1829-1900) physician.

P RUDOLPH LEHMANN, *c*1901 (replica of portrait exhib RA 1885), hs, Royal College of Physicians, London.

PH SIR BENJAMIN STONE, two prints, both wl, NPG.

PRIMROSE, Archibald Philip, see 5th Earl of Rosebery.

PRIMROSE, Sir Henry William (1846-1923) civil servant.

SC E.E.GOSTOWSKI, 1891, plaster bust, DoE (Somerset House, London).

PH UNKNOWN, hs, print, NPG x12767.

PRINSEP, Valentine Cameron (1838-1904) artist.

P Self-portrait, 1883, hs, oval, MacDonald Collection, Aberdeen Art Gallery.

G HENRY NELSON O'NEIL, 'The Billiard Room of the Garrick Club', oil, 1869, Garrick Club, London.

PR ALPHONSE LEGROS, hl, semi-profile, etch, University of Hull. UNKNOWN, hs, woodcut, for *Illust London News*, 3 May 1879, NPG.

C SIR LESLIE WARD ('Spy'), wl, chromo-lith, for *Vanity Fair*, 13 Jan 1877, NPG.

PH DAVID WILKIE WYNFIELD, *c*1862-4, hs, profile, print, NPG P83. RALPH W.ROBINSON, wl seated, print, for *Members and Associates of the Royal Academy of Arts, 1891*, NPG x7387. LONDON STEREOSCOPIC CO, tql seated, cabinet, NPG x12768.

PRIOR, Melton (1845-1910) war artist.

P FREDERICK WHITING, Savage Club, London.

PR Several self-portrait sketches, woodcuts, for *Illust London News*, 3

Feb 1877, 28 July 1877 and 18 Oct 1879, NPG.

PRIOR, Thomas Abiel (1809-1886) line-engraver.

PR R.T., hs, wood engr, for *Illust London News*, 27 Nov 1886, NPG.

PH E.CARPOT, hs, carte, NPG x12770.

PRITCHARD, Charles (1808-1893) astronomer.

PR UNKNOWN, after a photograph by Taunt & Co of Oxford, hs, wood engr, for *Illust London News*, 3 June 1893, NPG.

PROBERT, Lewis (1841-1908) Welsh divine.

P WILLIAM WILLIAMS, 1886, tql, National Museum of Wales 171, Cardiff.

PROCTER, Adelaide Ann (1825-1864) poet and hymn writer.

P EMMA GAGGIOTTI RICHARDS, hl, oval, NPG 789.

PH HERBERT WATKINS, wl, carte, NPG x12772.

PROCTER, Francis (1812-1905) divine.

P B.ROGERS, 1891, hs, St Catherine's College, Cambridge.

PROCTOR, Richard Anthony (1837-1888) astronomer.

PR R. & E.TAYLOR, hs, oval, woodcut, for *The Illust Review*, 28 Aug 1873, NPG. R.T., hs, wood engr, for *Illust London News*, 29 Sept 1888, NPG.

C SIR LESLIE WARD ('Spy'), wl, semi-profile, chromo-lith, for *Vanity Fair*, 3 March 1883, NPG.

PH W.NOTMAN, hs, carte, NPG (Album 40).

PROTHERO, Sir George Walter (1848-1922) historian.

PR W.ROTHENSTEIN, 1904, hs, lith, NPG, King's College, Cambridge.

PROTHERO, Rowland Edmund, see 1st Baron Ernle.

PROUT, Father (pseudonym), see Francis Sylvester MAHONY.

PROUT, Ebenezer (1835-1909) musical composer, organist and theorist.

P E.BENT WALKER, 1904, Incorporated Society of Musicians, London.

PROUT, John Skinner (1806-1876) artist.

PR UNKNOWN, hs, woodcut, for *Illust London News*, 9 Sept 1876, NPG.

PROWSE, William Jeffery (1836-1870) humorist.

PR DALZIEL, hs, circle, woodcut, BM.

PUGIN, Augustus Welby Northmore (1812-1852) architect.

P UNKNOWN, *c*1840, hs, NPG 1404. J.R.HERBERT, RA 1845, hl seated, RIBA, London.

SC UNKNOWN, effigy on monument, St Augustine's, Ramsgate. J.B.PHILIP, wl figure, podium relief, Albert Memorial, London.

PULESTON, Sir John Henry (1830-1908) politician.

PR UNKNOWN, after a photograph by London Stereoscopic Co, hs, circle, woodcut, for *Illust London News*, 1 Aug 1874, NPG.

C SIR LESLIE WARD ('Spy'), wl, w/c study, for *Vanity Fair*, 14 Oct 1882, NPG 2593.

PULLEN, Henry William (1836-1903) pamphleteer.

PH W.T. & R.GOWLAND of York, wl, carte, NPG x12773. E.ROGERS of Salisbury, wl with dog, carte, NPG x12774.

PULMAN, George Philip Rigney (1819-1880) antiquary; used pseudonym 'Trotandot'.

PR DALZIEL, hs, woodcut, BM.

PUNSHON, William Morley (1824-1881) Wesleyan preacher and lecturer.

PR H.C.BALDING, hs, etch, NPG. W.HOLL, after a photograph, hl seated, stipple and line, NPG. D.J.POUND, after a photograph by

Mayall, tql seated, stipple and line, for *Drawing Room Portrait Gallery of Eminent Personages*, NPG. UNKNOWN, hs, chromo-lith, NPG. UNKNOWN, after a photograph by Notman & Fraser of Toronto and Montreal, hs, oval, woodcut, for *Illust London News*, 8 Aug 1874, NPG.

PH APPLETON & CO, hl seated, carte, NPG X12775. MAULL & CO, hs, carte, NPG (Album 40).

PURCHAS, John (1823-1872) divine and author.

PH W. & A.H.FRY, two cartes, tql and hs, NPG (Album 40).

PURSER, Louis Claude (1854-1932) classical scholar.

P LEO WHELAN, 1926, Trinity College, Dublin.

PH WALTER STONEMAN, 1930, hs, NPG (NPR).

PUSEY, Edward Bouverie (1800-1882) a leader of the Oxford Movement.

P MISS ROSA CORDER, hs, profile, Pusey House, Oxford; copies, Christ Church, Oxford, and Keble College, Oxford. GEORGE RICHMOND, 1890, hs, oval, Christ Church, Oxford; chalk study, NPG 1059. UNKNOWN, hs, Christ Church.

D UNKNOWN, hl, profile, as an undergraduate, pen and ink, Christ Church. CLARA PUSEY, *c*1856, three sketches: with his family at breakfast; hl, profile; hl in pulpit, pencil, pen and ink, NPG 454 (4,7,9).

SC GEORGE RICHMOND, 1883, marble bust, based on a death-mask taken by Dr Acland, and various prints and sketches, Pusey House; plaster cast, Keble College, Oxford.

PR UNKNOWN, hl, profile, etch, for 'Oxford Theologians', BM, NPG. Several engrs, NPG.

C 'TOUCHSTONE', 1850–51, several liths, alone, with S. Wilberforce and Cardinal Wiseman, NPG. CARLO PELLEGRINI ('Ape'), wl, w/c study, for *Vanity Fair*, 2 Jan 1875, NPG 2594.

PYNE, James Baker (1800-1870) landscape painter.

PR UNKNOWN, after J.J.Hill, hs, woodcut, for *Art Journal*, 1849, BM, NPG. UNKNOWN, after a photograph by J.B.Pyne jun, hl, woodcut, for *Illust London News*, 20 Aug 1870, BM, NPG.

PH JOHN WATKINS, tql seated, carte, NPG (Album 104).

PYNE, Louisa Fanny, (Madame Bodda) (1832-1904) singer

PR C.BAUGNIET, tql in evening dress, lith, BM. Several theatrical prints, BM, NPG, Harvard Theatre Collection, Cambridge, Mass, USA.

PH SOUTHWELL BROS, wl, carte, NPG X12777.

Q

QUAIN, Sir John Richard (1816-1876) judge.
SC THOMAS WOOLNER, bust, Middle Temple, London.

QUAIN, Richard (1800-1887) surgeon.
P GEORGE RICHMOND, RA 1872, hl seated, Royal College of Surgeons, London.
SC THOMAS WOOLNER, 1884, marble bust, Royal College of Surgeons.
PR R.T., hs, wood engr, for *Illust London News*, 24 Sept 1887, NPG.

QUAIN, Sir Richard, 1st Bart (1816-1898) physician.
P SIR J.E.MILLAIS, 1896, tql, profile, Royal College of Physicians, London.
PR T.BARLOW, after D.Maclise of *c*1866, hl seated, mezz, pub 1883, NPG. R.T., hs, woodcut, for *Illust London News*, 17 Jan 1891, NPG.
C SIR LESLIE WARD ('Spy'), wl, profile, chromo-lith, for *Vanity Fair*, 15 Dec 1883, NPG.

QUARITCH, Bernard (1819-1899) bookseller.
PR J.BROWN, hs, stipple, BM.

QUEENSBERRY, Sir John Sholto Douglas, 8th Marquess of (1844-1900) patron of boxing.
SL PHIL MAY, 1889, wl, profile, NPG 3174.

C SIR LESLIE WARD ('Spy'), wl, chromo-lith, for *Vanity Fair*, 10 Nov 1877, NPG.

QUEKETT, John Thomas (1815-1861) histologist.
PR W.WALKER, after E.Walker, tql seated with microscope, mezz, BM.

QUEKETT, William (1802-1888) divine.
SC JOHN WARRINGTON WOOD, 1882, marble bust, Gawsworth Hall, Cheshire.

QUICK, Sir John (1852-1932) lawyer, politician and judge of the Commonwealth Arbitration Court.
P W.B.MCINNES, Bendigo Art Gallery, Victoria, Australia.

QUILTER, Sir William Cuthbert, 1st Bart (1841-1911) art collector and politician.
C LIBERIO PROSPERI ('Lib'), wl, chromo-lith, for *Vanity Fair*, 9 Feb 1889, NPG.
PH SIR BENJAMIN STONE, 1901, wl, Birmingham Reference Library, NPG.

QUIN, Windham Thomas Wyndham-, see 4th Earl of DUNRAVEN and Mount-Earl.

R

RAE, John (1813-1893) Arctic explorer.
P STEPHEN PEARCE, *c*1853, hl, NPG 1213; replica, SNPG 1488. UNKNOWN, Stromness Town Hall, Orkney.
PR UNKNOWN, after a daguerreotype by Beard, hl seated, woodcut, for *Illust London News*, 28 Oct 1854, NPG
PH E.W.DALLAS, wl, carte, NPG AX7539.

RAIKES, Henry Cecil (1838-1891) postmaster-general.
PR UNKNOWN, after a photograph by Fradelle, hs, woodcut, for *Illust London News*, 16 Dec 1882, NPG.
C CARLO PELLEGRINI ('Ape'), tql, w/c study, for *Vanity Fair*, 17 April 1875, NPG 2596.

RAILTON, Herbert (1858-1910) artist.
G UNKNOWN, 'Our Artists – Past and Present', hs, one of a series of woodcuts, for *Illust London news*, 14 May 1892, NPG.

RAINFORTH, Elizabeth (1814-1877) operatic singer.
PR Several theatrical prints, BM, NPG, Harvard Theatre Collection, Cambridge, Mass, USA.

RAINY, Robert (1826-1906) principal of New College, Edinburgh.
P JOHN BOWIE, SNPG 984. SIR GEORGE REID, hs, SNPG 1485.

RALEIGH, Alexander (1817-1880) nonconformist divine.
PR J.COCHRAN, after a photograph by Maull & Polyblank, hl seated, stipple and line, NPG.

RAMAGE, Craufurd Tait (1803-1878) miscellaneous writer.
PR H.ADLARD, hs, stipple, NPG.

RAMÉE, Marie Louise de la, see DE La Ramée.

RAMSAY, Sir Andrew Crombie (1814-1891) geologist.
SC WILLIAM DAVIS, RA 1864, bust, Geological Society, London.

RAMSAY, Fox Maule, see 11th Earl of Dalhousie.

RAMSAY, Sir James Andrew Broun, see 1st Marquess of Dalhousie.

RAMSAY, John William, see 13th Earl of Dalhousie.

RAMSAY, William (1806-1865) classical scholar.
SL AUGUSTIN EDOUART, SNPG 792.

RAMSAY, Sir William (1852-1916) chemist.
P MARK MILBANKE, 1913, tql, Science Museum, London.
SC C.L.HARTWELL, *c*1922, relief memorial tablet, Westminster Abbey, London.
C SIR LESLIE WARD ('Spy'), wl, Hentschel-Colourtype, for *Vanity Fair*, 2 Dec 1908, NPG.
PH UNKNOWN, tql seated, photogravure, NPG X12886. UNKNOWN, wl in laboratory, print, University College, London.

RAMSAY, Sir William Mitchell (1851-1939) classical scholar and archaeologist.
PH JOHN RUSSELL & SONS, hs, print, for *National Photographic Record*, vol I, NPG.

RANDALL, Richard William (1824-1906) dean of Chichester.
PR UNKNOWN, hs, wood engr, for *Illust London News*, 13 Feb 1892, NPG.

RANDEGGER, Alberto (1832-1911) musical composer and

conductor.
PR P.NAUMANN, after a photograph, hs, woodcut, BM.

RANDLES, Marshall (1826-1904) Wesleyan divine.
P ARTHUR NOWELL, Didsbury College, Manchester.
PR P.N., after a photograph by Ball, hs, wood engr, for *Illust London News*, 1 Aug 1896, NPG.

RANELAGH, Thomas Heron Jones, 7th Viscount (1812-1885) rake.
PR D.J.POUND, after a photograph by J. & C.Watkins, tql seated in uniform, stipple and line, for *The Drawing Room Portrait Gallery of Eminent Personages*, BM, NPG.
C CARLO PELLEGRINI ('Ape'), wl, w/c study, for *Vanity Fair*, 25 June 1870, NPG 4736.
PH MAYALL, wl in uniform, carte, NPG (Album 116).

RANKINE, William John Macquorn (1820-1872) civil engineer.
PH THOMAS ANNAN, hl, carte, NPG (Album 102).

RANSFORD, Edwin (1805-1876) singer.
PR J.BACON, hs, lith, BM.

RANSOME, James Allen (1806-1875) agricultural implement maker.
PR S.REYNOLDS jun & G.SHURY, after R.Ansdell, wl in landscape, mixed engr, pub 1844, BM, NPG.

RAPER, Robert William (1842-1915) classical scholar.
P BRYAN HATTON, 1914, head, sketch, Trinity College, Oxford.
D G.P.JACOMB-HOOD, *c*1916, from memory and snapshots etc, tql, chalk, Trinity College.

RASHDALL, Hastings (1858-1924) moral philosopher, theologian and historian of universities.
PH WALTER STONEMAN, 1918, hs, NPG (NPR).

RASSAM, Hormuzd (1826-1910) Assyrian explorer.
P ARTHUR ACKLAND HUNT, RA 1869, BM.
PH LOCK & WHITFIELD, hs, oval, woodburytype, for *Men of Mark*, 1881, NPG.

RATHBONE, William (1819-1902) pioneer organiser of nursing services.
SC HARGREAVES BOND, 1889, bust, Liverpool Reform Club. C.J.ALLEN, 1899, bronze medallion, NPG 4018. SIR GEORGE FRAMPTON, *c*1899, bronze statue, St John's Gardens, Liverpool. UNKNOWN, marble relief bust, Unitarian Church, Ullet Road, Liverpool.
PH ELLIOTT & FRY, 1883, hl, carte, NPG X12794.

RAWLINSON, George (1812-1902) canon of Canterbury, writer on ancient history.
P J.WILSON FORSTER, 1897, hl seated, Trinity College, Oxford.

RAWLINSON, Sir Henry Creswicke, 1st Bart (1810-1895) soldier, diplomat and Assyriologist.
P FRANK HOLL, 1881, tql seated, Corsham Court, Wilts.
SC R.C.LUCAS, 1850, wax medallion, NPG 1714.
PR S.COUSINS, after H.W.Phillips, hl seated, mezz, pub 1860, NPG. UNKNOWN, after a photograph by Elliott & Fry, hs, woodcut, for *Illust London News*, 12 July 1873, NPG.
C SIR LESLIE WARD ('Spy'), wl, w/c study, for *Vanity Fair*, 12 July

1873, NPG 4737.

PH ERNEST EDWARDS, wl seated, print, for *Men of Eminence*, vol II, 1864, NPG. LOCK & WHITFIELD, hs, profile, oval, woodburytype, for *Men of Mark*, 1882, NPG. UNKNOWN, tql seated, carte, NPG (Album 38).

RAWLINSON, Sir Robert (1810-1898) civil engineer.
P PHILIP MORRIS, 1892, tql seated, Institution of Civil Engineers, London.
PR T.O.BARLOW, after P.Westcott, hs, mezz, NPG, Institution of Civil Engineers.
PH THOMAS FALL and H.S.MENDELSSOHN, two cabinets, wl and hs, NPG AX5564 and AX5563. ROGER FENTON, 1855, with Dr John Sutherland, Gernsheim Collection, University of Texas, USA. Two prints by unknown photographers, c1855, the second with Dr Lemon, NPG X12536-37.

RAWSON, Sir Harry Holdsworth (1843-1910) admiral.
C SIR LESLIE WARD ('Spy'), wl in uniform, chromo-lith, for *Vanity Fair*, 25 April 1901, NPG.

RAY, Thomas Matthew (1801-1881) secretary of the Loyal National Repeal Association.
G W.J.LINTON, after H.Anelay, 'The State Trial Portraits', 1844, woodcut, a broadside, BM. UNKNOWN, 'The Traversers', woodcut, for *Illust London News*, 25 Nov 1843, NPG.

RAYLEIGH, John William Strutt, 3rd Baron (1842-1919) mathematician and physicist.
P SIR PHILIP BURNE-JONES, replicas of portrait of 1888, wl, profile, in laboratory, Trinity College, Cambridge and Royal Institution, London. SIR HUBERT VON HERKOMER, 1911?, wl seated in chancellor's robes, Examination School, Cambridge. SIR GEORGE REID, RA 1911, tql seated, Royal Society, London.
D SIR WILLIAM ROTHENSTEIN, 1916, head, profile, crayon and pencil, NPG 3879.
C F.T.DALTON ('FTD'), hl at laboratory bench, chromo-lith, for *Vanity Fair*, 21 Dec 1899, NPG.
PH ETHEL GLAZEBROOK, hs, profile, print, NPG X12793. WALTER STONEMAN, 1917, hs, NPG (NPR).

READ, Sir Charles Hercules (1857-1929) antiquary and art connoisseur.
PH WALTER STONEMAN, 1919, hs, NPG (NPR).

READ, Clare Sewell (1826-1905) agriculturist.
P J.J.SHANNON, 1897, tql, Castle Museum, Norwich.
PR J.B.HUNT, after a photograph by C.Hunt, hs, stipple, pub 1868, NPG.
C CARLO PELLEGRINI ('Ape'), wl, w/c study, for *Vanity Fair*, 5 June 1875, NPG 2597.

READ, Samuel (1815?-1883) artist.
G UNKNOWN, 'Our Artists – Past and Present', hs, one of a series of woodcuts, for *Illust London News*, 14 May 1892, BM, NPG.
PR UNKNOWN, after a photograph by R.Cade of Ipswich, hs, woodcut, for *Illust London News*, 19 May 1883, NPG.
PH CUNDALL, DOWNES & Co, tql seated, carte, NPG (Album 104).

READ, Walter William (1855-1907) Surrey cricketer.
C LIBERIO PROSPERI ('Lib'), wl, with cricket bat, chromo-lith, for *Vanity Fair*, 28 July 1888, NPG.

READE, Charles (1814-1884) novelist and dramatist.
P Attrib CHARLES MERCIER, wl seated, profile, NPG 2281.
D RUDOLPH LEHMANN, 1869, crayon, BM.
G HENRY NELSON O'NEIL, 'The Billiard Room of the Garrick Club', oil, 1869, Garrick Club, London.
SC PERCY FITZGERALD, bronze bust, Magdalen College, Oxford. PERCY FITZGERALD, bronzed plaster bust, NPG 1633.

PR UNKNOWN, hs, stipple and line, BM, NPG. Several prints, Harvard Theatre Collection, Cambridge, Mass, USA.
C UNKNOWN, wl, flying on a winged pen, woodcut, BM.

REAY, Donald James Mackay, 11th Baron (1839-1921) governor of Bombay and first president of the British Academy.
P A.A.VAN ANROOY, hs, British Academy, London.
SC SIR ALFRED GILBERT, bust, Bombay. H.R.HOPE PINKER, c1895, statue, Bombay.
PR UNKNOWN, after a photograph by Elliott & Fry, hs, profile, wood engr, for *Illust London News*, 17 Feb 1883, NPG.
PH JOHN RUSSELL & SONS, hs, print, for *National Photographic Record*, vol II, NPG.

REDESDALE, Algernon Bertram Freeman-Mitford, 1st Baron (1837-1916) diplomat and writer.
C CARLO PELLEGRINI, 1872, wl, profile, lith, NPG. SIR LESLIE WARD ('Spy'), wl, w/c study, for *Vanity Fair*, 16 June 1904, NPG 3860.

REDESDALE, John Thomas Freeman-Mitford, 1st Earl of (1805-1886) politician.
C CARLO PELLEGRINI ('Ape'), wl, chromo-lith, for *Vanity Fair*, 27 Feb 1875, NPG.
PH LOCK & WHITFIELD, hs, oval, woodburytype, for *Men of Mark*, 1876, NPG.

REDGRAVE, Richard (1804-1888) pioneer organiser of art education.
P Self-portrait, hl, NPG 2464. Self-portrait, hs, oval, Yale Center for British Art, New Haven, USA. SIR A.S.COPE, 1884, hs, MacDonald Collection, Aberdeen Art Gallery.
D SIR FRANCIS GRANT, 1872, hl, wash, NPG 4486.
PR UNKNOWN, hs, woodcut, for *Art Journal*, 1850, BM.
PH ELLIOTT & FRY, hs, carte, NPG (Album 104). LOCK & WHITFIELD, hs, oval, woodburytype, for *Men of Mark*, 1878, NPG.

REDMOND, John Edward (1856-1918) Irish political leader.
P SIR JOHN LAVERY, hl, Municipal Gallery of Modern Art, Dublin. H.J.THADDEUS, NGI 889.
D HAROLD SPEED, 1907, hs, sanguine, NPG 5123.
SC F.W.DOYLE-JONES, 1910, bronze busts, Palace of Westminster, London and NGI 8003.
PR J.G.DAY, hs, etch, NPG 2916a.
C SIR FRANCIS CARRUTHERS GOULD, sketch, NPG 2855. SIR BERNARD PARTRIDGE, two pen and ink cartoons, for *Punch*, 6 May 1903 and 5 April 1911, NPG. SIR LESLIE WARD ('Spy'), two w/c studies, both wl, for *Vanity Fair*, 12 Nov 1892 and 7 July 1904, NPG 2982-83.
PH G.C.BERESFORD, 1902, hs, neg, NPG X6567. SIR BENJAMIN STONE, two prints, both wl, NPG.

REECE, Robert (1838-1891) dramatist.
PR R.T., hs, wood engr, for *Illust London News*, 18 July 1891, NPG.

REED, Sir Charles (1819-1881) chairman of the London school board.
PR G.J.STODART, hs, semi-profile, stipple, NPG. UNKNOWN, hs, chromo-lith, NPG. UNKNOWN, hs, woodcut, for *Illust London News*, 20 Dec 1873, NPG. R. & E.TAYLOR, hs, woodcut, for *Illust London News*, 2 April 1881, NPG.
PH LOCK & WHITFIELD, hs, oval, woodburytype, for *Men of Mark*, 1880, NPG. LONDON STEREOSCOPIC Co, hs, carte, NPG AX8597.

REED, Sir Edward James (1830-1906) naval constructor.
SC SIR GEORGE FRAMPTON, RA 1917, memorial relief, Town Hall, Cardiff.
PR W.H.MOTE, after a photograph, hs, oval, stipple, BM. UNKNOWN, after a photograph by John & Charles Watkins, hl, woodcut, for *Illust London News*, 6 Jan 1866, NPG.
C CARLO PELLEGRINI ('Ape'), wl, semi-profile, chromo-lith, for

Vanity Fair, 20 March 1875, NPG.

PH SIR BENJAMIN STONE, wl, print, Birmingham Reference Library, NPG.

REED, Priscilla, née Horton (1818-1895) actress.

PR Various theatrical and popular prints, BM, NPG, Harvard Theatre Collection, Cambridge, Mass, USA.

REED, Thomas German (1817-1888) musician.

PR R.TAYLOR, after a photograph by John Watkins, hs, woodcut, for *Illust London News*, 7 April 1888, BM. UNKNOWN, after a photogtraph by John Watkins, hs, woodcut, Harvard Theatre Collection, Cambridge, Mass, USA.

REES, David (1801-1869) independent minister and editor.

PR J.COCHRAN, after W.Gush, hs, stipple, NPG.

REES, George Owen (1813-1889) physician.

P SIDNEY BUCK, tql seated, Royal College of Physicians, London.

REES, Thomas (1815-1885) independent minister at Swansea.

PR J.COCHRAN, tql seated, stipple, for *Evangelical Mag*, BM.

REES, William (1802-1883) Welsh minister and author.

P J.D.MERCIER, 1877, University College of Wales, Aberystwyth.

REEVE, Henry (1813-1895) journalist and man of letters.

D COUNT ALFRED D'ORSAY, 1839, hl seated, profile, pencil and wash, NPG 4372.

PR P.N., hs, wood engr, for *Illust London News*, 26 Oct 1895, NPG.

REEVE, Lovell Augustus (1814-1865) conchologist.

PR T.H.MAGUIRE, hl, lith, one of set of *Ipswich Museum Portraits*, BM, NPG.

REEVES, John Sims (1818-1900) singer.

P ALESSANDRO OSSANI, 1863, wl, NPG 2764.

D A.E.CHALON, wl, pencil and w/c, NPG 1962(g).

PR C.BAUGNIET, tql, oval, lith, 1850, BM. 'ALFRED CROWQUILL', wl, lith, pub 1850, NPG. Various popular prints, BM, NPG, Harvard Theatre Collection, Cambridge, Mass, USA.

C SIR LESLIE WARD ('Spy'), wl, chromo-lith, for *Vanity Fair*, 10 May 1890, NPG.

PH BARRAUD, tql, print, for *Men and Women of the Day*, vol I, 1888, NPG AX5428. KINGSBURY & NOTCUTT, hs, cabinet, NPG X4181. Various cartes by BURTON & CO, MARCUS WARD & CO, HERBERT WATKINS, H.J.WHITLOCK and unknown photographers, various sizes, NPG.

REGONDI, Giulio (1822-1872) performer on the guitar and concertina.

PR Three liths, as a child, playing the guitar, BM.

REID, Archibald David (1844-1908) painter.

P Self-portrait, MacDonald Collection, Aberdeen Art Gallery.

REID, David Boswell (1805-1863) inventor.

PR UNKNOWN, after a daguerreotype by Beard, hl, woodcut, for *Illust London News*, 20 March 1852, NPG.

REID, Sir George (1841-1913) portrait-painter.

P JOHN BOWIE, SNPG 2046. Self-portraits, 1882 and 1894, Mac-Donald Collection, Aberdeen Art Gallery. Self-portrait, hs, semi-profile, Royal Scottish Academy, Edinburgh.

SC JAMES PITTENDRIGH MACGILLIVRAY, 1894, bronze bust, Royal Scottish Academy; casts, SNPG 854 and Aberdeen Art Gallery.

PH ELLIOTT & FRY, hs, cabinet, NPG X12795. W.E.GRAY, 1911, hl, print, NPG X12796.

REID, Sir George Houstoun (1845-1918) colonial politician.

PR P.N., after a photograph by Kerry, hs, wood engr, for *Illust London News*, 15 Sept 1894, NPG.

PH LONDON STEREOSCOPIC CO, two prints, tql seated, profile, and hl, NPG X12797-8.

REID, John (1809-1849) anatomist.

P? UNKNOWN, University of St Andrews.

REID, Robert Threshie, see 1st Earl Loreburn.

REID, (Thomas) Mayne (1818-1883) novelist.

PR UNKNOWN, hs, woodcut, for *Illust London News*, 3 Nov 1883, NPG.

C UNKNOWN, tql, chromo-lith, for *Vanity Fair*, 8 March 1873, NPG.

REID, Sir Thomas Wemyss (1842-1905) journalist and biographer.

D S.P.HALL, 1888-9, pencil sketch, made at the sessions of the Parnell Commission, NPG 2257.

RENNELL, James Rennell Rodd, 1st Baron (1858-1941) diplomat and scholar.

P SIMON ELWES, Haileybury College, Herts.

C SIR LESLIE WARD ('Spy'), wl, w/c study, for *Vanity Fair*, 7 Jan 1897, NPG 5127.

REPINGTON, Charles à Court (1858-1925) soldier and military writer.

D SIR WILLIAM ROTHENSTEIN, 1916, hs, pencil, Manchester City Art Gallery.

C SIR MAX BEERBOHM, 1920, 'A Chiel', Manchester City Art Gallery.

REUTER, Paul Julius, Baron (1816-1899) founder of Reuter's Telegraph Agency.

PR T.O.BARLOW, after R.Lehmann, tql seated, mixed engr, BM, NPG.

C MELCHIORRE DELFICO, wl, w/c study, for *Vanity Fair*, 14 Dec 1872, NPG 3275. 'PET', wl, chromo-lith, NPG.

PH LONDON STEREOSCOPIC & PHOTOGRAPHIC CO, tql, carte, NPG (Album 40).

REYNOLDS, George William MacArthur (1814-1879) radical politician and journalist.

PR F.MANSELL, hl, profile, stipple, NPG.

REYNOLDS, Henry Robert (1825-1896) congregational divine.

PR J.COCHRAN, after W.Gush, hl, semi-profile, stipple, NPG. UNKNOWN, after a photograph by Thomas, hs, wood engr, for *Illust London News*, 19 Sept 1896, NPG.

REYNOLDS, James Emerson (1844-1920) chemist.

PR UNKNOWN, hs, profile, wood engr, NPG.

REYNOLDS, Sir John Russell, 1st Bart (1828-1896) physician.

P SYDNEY HODGES, 1882, tql seated, Royal College of Physicians, London.

REYNOLDS, Osborne (1842-1912) engineer and physicist.

P JOHN COLLIER, 1904, Manchester University.

REYNOLDS, Samuel Harvey (1831-1897) divine and journalist.

PR P.N., after a photograph by Leigh, hs, wood engr, for *Illust London News*, 20 Feb 1897, NPG.

REYNOLDS-MORETON, Henry George Francis, see 2nd Earl of Ducie.

RHODES, Cecil John (1853-1902) Imperialist and statesman in South Africa.

P SIR OSWALD BIRLEY, Hertford County Hall. PHILIP TENNYSON COLE, several portraits, including those at Oriel College, Oxford, Constitutional Club, London, Government House, Lusaka. 'FELIX', hl, Rhodes Trust Office, Oxford. SIR JAMES GUNN, 1949, posthumous, wl in landscape, Rhodes House, Oxford. SIR HUBERT VON HERKOMER, RA 1895, tql seated.

Kimberley Club, South Africa. SIR HUBERT VON HERKOMER, 1896, hs, Rhodes House, Oxford. SYDNEY KENDRICK, tql, Rhodes House. EDWARD ROWORTH, tql seated, University of Cape Town; copy, Rhodes House. G.F.WATTS, 1898, hl, NPG 1407.

D MORTIMER MENPES, several portraits, various sizes, pencil, pencil and crayon, chalk, etc, Rhodes Trust Office, Royal Coll, Oriel College and Central African Archives.

M MARY HELEN CARLISLE, hs, oval, oil, Rhodes House. M.H.CARLISLE, 1896, wl seated, Oriel College, Oxford.

SC JOHN TWEED, 1897–1902, statue, Bulawayo, Zimbabwe. SYDNEY MARCH, 1901, several bronze busts, Africana Museum, Johannesburg, Rhodes House, British South Africa Company, London, and NPG 4151. SYDNEY MARCH, bronze bust, Oriel College. JOHN TWEED, plaster cast of death mask, NPG 1730. FRANCIS DERWENT WOOD, 1902, bronze bust, Africana Museum, Johannesburg. H.A.PEGRAM, 1903, marble bust, Rhodes House. H.A.PEGRAM, 1903, bronze bust, City Club, Cape Town. H.A.PEGRAM, posthumous plaster bust, NPG 2545. H.A.PEGRAM, 1910, statue, Cape Town Botanical Gardens. H.A.PEGRAM, posthumous stone statue, High Street facade of Oriel College. G.F.WATTS, 1904, equestrian statue, Burlington House, London. SIR W.H.THORNYCROFT, 1907, equestrian statue, Kimberley. SIR W.H.THORNYCROFT, 1906, bronze modello, Rhodes Trust Office. SIR W.H.THORNYCROFT, 1904, plaster model of statue, TATE 4217. JOHN TWEED, 1928, statue, Salisbury, Zimbabwe. JOHN TWEED, c1932, statue, Mafeking, South Africa. JOHN TWEED, busts, Rhodes House and Parliament Buildings, Cape Town.

PR M.MENPES, hl, (with two smaller full-face studies), etch, BM. VIOLET, DUCHESS OF RUTLAND, 1898, hs, semi-profile, lith, NPG.

C SIR ROBERT BADEN-POWELL, 1897, head, pencil, Durham University. HARRY FURNISS, wl seated, pen and ink, NPG 3404. SIR FRANCIS CARRUTHERS GOULD, several pen sketches, hs, NPG 2853–54. Various drgs and political cartoons by D.C.BOONZAIER, A.S.BOYD, DENNIS EDWARDS ('Grip'), MISS F.P.FULLER, PHIL MAY, C.PENSTONE, W.H.SCHRÖDER, SIR JOHN TENNIEL, T.B.WIRGMAN and others, various dates, sizes and media, Africana Museum, Johannesburg, South Africa, Rhodes House and University of Cape Town. SIR LESLIE WARD ('Spy'), wl, profile, chromo-lith, for *Vanity Fair*, 28 March 1891, NPG. (Possibly H.C.SEPPING) WRIGHT ('Stuff'), 'Empire Makers and Breakers', chromo-lith, for *Vanity Fair*, 25 Nov 1897, NPG.

PH RUSSELL & SONS, hs, cabinet, NPG X12453.

RHODES, Francis William (1851-1905) colonel.
C SIR LESLIE WARD ('Spy'), wl in uniform, chromo-lith, for *Vanity Fair*, 8 June 1899, NPG.

RHONDDA, David Alfred Thomas, Viscount (1856-1918) statesman, colliery proprietor and financier.
P SOLOMON J.SOLOMON, hs, National Museum of Wales 676, Cardiff.

RHYS, Ernest Percival (1859-1946) author and editor.
PH LUCIA MOHOLY, 1938, hs, profile, print, NPG P131.

RHYS, Sir John (1840-1915) Celtic scholar.
P CHRISTOPHER WILLIAMS, 1913, tql, National Museum of Wales 318, Cardiff. SOLOMON J.SOLOMON, RA 1915, tql seated, Jesus College Oxford; study, NPG 4697. UNKNOWN, hs in robes, British Academy, London.
SC SIR WILLIAM GOSCOMBE JOHN, RA 1909, marble bust, National Library of Wales, Aberystwyth.
PH JOHN RUSSELL & SONS, hs, print, for *National Photographic Record*, vol II, NPG.

RICE, James (1843-1882) novelist.
P ARCHIBALD STUART WORTLEY, 1882, hl seated with Sir Walter Besant, NPG 2280.
PR UNKNOWN, after a photograph by London Stereoscopic Co, hs, woodcut, for *Illust London News*, 13 May 1882, NPG.

RICH, Alfred William (1856-1922) water-colourist.
D SIR WILLIAM ORPEN, 1911, 'The Model', w/c, TATE 3530. HENRY TONKS, 1917, wl seated, pastel, NPG 4200.
G SIR WILLIAM ORPEN, 'The Selecting Jury of the New English Art Club, 1909', oil, NPG 2556.

RICHARD, Henry (1812-1888) politician, congregationalist minister.
P FELIX S.MOSCHELES, 1883, hl, National Museum of Wales 145, Cardiff.
SC WILLIAM DAVIS, plaster bust, University College of Wales, Aberystwyth.
PR J.COCHRAN, after a photograph, hl seated, stipple, NPG.
PH ELLIOTT & FRY, wl seated, carte, NPG AX8581.

RICHARDS, Sir Frederick William (1833-1912) admiral.
P SIR A.S.COPE, RA 1901, tql in uniform, NMM, Greenwich.

RICHARDS, Sir George Henry (1820-1896) vice-admiral.
P STEPHEN PEARCE, 1865, hs in uniform, NPG 923.
G UNKNOWN, after photographs by Beard, 'Departure of the Arctic Searching Expedition', woodcut, for *Illust London News*, 1 May 1852, NPG.

RICHARDSON, Sir Benjamin Ward (1828-1896) physician.
G GEORGE CRUIKSHANK, 'Lecture at the Charterhouse on Stephen Gray's discoveries in electricity', woodcut, for *Illust London News*, 21 Feb 1874, NPG.
PH LOCK & WHITFIELD, hs, oval, woodburytype, for *Men of Mark*, 1883, NPG.

RICHMOND, Charles Henry Gordon-Lennox, 6th Duke of, and 1st Duke of Gordon (1818-1903) statesman.
P WILLIAM WEBB, 1825, wl with horse, Goodwood, W Sussex. SIR FRANCIS GRANT, c1876, wl with Garter, Goodwood. SIR GEORGE REID, c1885, tql seated, Goodwood.
G HENRY GALES, 'The Derby Cabinet of 1867', w/c, NPG 4893.
PR JOSEPH BROWN, after a photograph by Maull & Polyblank, tql, stipple, pub 1861, NPG. G.J.STODART, after a photograph by W.N.Malby, hl seated, stipple and line, NPG. Several popular prints, NPG.
C ALFRED THOMPSON ('Atη'), wl, chromo-lith, for *Vanity Fair*, 26 March 1870, NPG.
PH LOCK & WHITFIELD, hs, profile, oval, woodburytype, for *Men of Mark*, 1882, NPG. RUSSELL & SONS, hs, profile, cabinet, NPG X12805. RUSSELL & SONS, hs, print, for *Our Conservative and Unionist Statesmen*, vol I, NPG (Album 18). SOUTHWELL BROS, two cartes, wl and wl seated, NPG.

RICHMOND, George (1809-1896) portrait painter and draughtsman.
P Several self-portraits, including: 1840, hs, Fitzwilliam Museum, Cambridge; 1853, hs, NPG 2509; 1853, hs, Stanford University Art Museum, California, USA; 1854, hs, semi-profile, in black Renaissance cap, City Museum and Art Gallery, Birmingham; 1868, hl in DCL cap and gown, Uffizi Gallery, Florence.
D Self-portrait, c1840, Ashmolean Museum, Oxford. Self-portrait?, called Richmond and probably rightly named, NPG.
G HENRY JAMYN BROOKS, 'Private view of the Old Masters Exhibition, Royal Academy, 1888', oil, NPG 1833.
SC JOSEPH DENHAM, c1834, plaster cast of bust, NPG 2157; bronze cast, NPG 2157a.

PR STEPHENSON & ROYSTON, after W.Lovatt of 1842, hl, line, NPG. W.HOLL, after G.Richmond of 1863, hl, stipple, one of 'Grillion's Club' series, BM, NPG.

PH ELLIOTT & FRY, hs, profile, carte, NPG (Album 104). UNKNOWN, c1883, tql seated, print, NPG X12812.

RICHMOND, Sir William Blake (1842-1921) painter.

D GEORGE PHOENIX, 1893, hs, chalk, NPG 2065.

PR R.T., hs, woodcut, for *Illust London News*, 5 May 1888, NPG.

PH ELLIOTT & FRY, hl seated, cabinet, NPG X12811. MOFFAT, hs, semi-profile, cabinet, NPG X12809. RALPH W.ROBINSON, wl seated, print, for *Members and Associates of the Royal Academy of Arts, 1891*, NPG X7388.

RIDDING, George (1828-1904) bishop of Southwell.

P W.W.OULESS, 1879, hl seated, Winchester College, Hants.

G S.P.HALL, 'The Bench of Bishops, 1902', w/c, NPG 2369.

SC T.B.CARTER, 1907, wl memorial brass, Winchester College Chapel. F.W.POMEROY, bronze statue, kneeling, Southwell Cathedral, Notts.

PR UNKNOWN, hs, lith, BM. UNKNOWN, after a photograph by Schemboche, hs, profile, woodcut, for *Illust London News*, 8 March 1884, NPG.

C SIR LESLIE WARD ('Spy'), wl, profile, chromo-lith, for *Vanity Fair*, 15 Aug 1901, NPG.

PH HILLS & SAUNDERS, tql, profile, carte, NPG X12816. SCHEMBOCHE, with his second wife, Lady Laura, cabinet, NPG X4975. UNKNOWN, hl, print, NPG (Anglican Bishops).

RIDGEWAY, Sir Joseph West (1844-1930) soldier and administrator.

PR R.T., hs in uniform, woodcut, for *Illust London News*, 20 Aug 1887, NPG.

RIDGEWAY, Sir William (1853-1926) classical scholar.

P RICHARD JACK, 1921, tql seated in robes, Gonville and Caius College, Cambridge.

D D.G.LILLIE, 1909, tql, w/c, NPG.

PH J.PALMER CLARKE, hs, photogravure, NPG X12814. V.H.MOTTRAM, c1909, hl, print, NPG X12815.

RIDLEY, Sir Matthew White Ridley, 5th Bart, 1st Viscount (1842-1904) statesman.

PR J.BROWN, after H.T.Wells, hs, stipple, one of 'Grillion's Club' series, BM. UNKNOWN, after a photograph by R.E.Ruddock, hs, etch, NPG.UNKNOWN, hs, woodcut, for *Illust London News*, 12 Feb 1876, NPG.

C CARLO PELLEGRINI ('Ape'), wl, profile, chromo-lith, for *Vanity Fair*, 23 July 1881, NPG.

PH SIR BENJAMIN STONE, 1897, wl, print, NPG.

RIEL, Louis (1844-1885) Canadian insurgent leader.

PR UNKNOWN, after a sketch by Captain H.de H.Haig, hs, woodcut, for *Illust London News*, 27 June 1885, NPG.

RIGAUD, Stephen Jordan (1816-1859) bishop of Antigua.

PR T.H.MAGUIRE, tql, lith, one of set of *Ipswich Museum Portraits*, BM.

RIGBY, Edward (1804-1860) obstetrician.

P UNKNOWN, hs, Royal Society of Medicine, London.

RIGBY, Elizabeth, see Lady Eastlake.

RIGBY, Sir John (1834-1903) solicitor-general.

P ARTHUR TREVELYAN, hl, Lincoln's Inn, London.

C (Possibly H.C.SEPPING) WRIGHT ('Stuff'), wl, profile, w/c study, for *Vanity Fair*, 31 Aug 1893, NPG 2995. SIR LESLIE WARD ('Spy'), hs at bench, chromo-lith, for *Vanity Fair*, 28 March 1901, NPG.

RIGG, James Harrison (1821-1909) Wesleyan divine.

PR UNKNOWN, after a photograph by Appleton & Co, hs, semi-profile, oval, woodcut, for *Illust London News*, 10 Aug 1878, NPG.

RIPON, George Frederick Samuel Robinson, 1st Marquess of (1827-1909) statesman.

P S.ROSENTHAL, 1872, United Grand Lodge of England. SIR E.J.POYNTER, RA 1886, Government House, Calcutta. G.F.WATTS, 1895, hs, NPG 1553. SIR HUBERT VON HERKOMER, RA 1910, tql seated, Leeds University.

G LOWES CATO DICKINSON, 'Gladstone's Cabinet of 1868', oil, NPG 5116.

SC FRANCIS DERWENT WOOD, statue, Spa Gardens, Ripon, Yorks.

PR E.VAUTHEY, 1870, hl, lith, NPG.

C 'FAUSTIN', wl, chromo-lith, a 'Figaro' cartoon, NPG. HARRY FURNISS, pen and ink sketch, NPG 3405. SIR FRANCIS CARRUTHERS GOULD, two pen sketches, wl seated and wl, NPG 2856-57. CARLO PELLEGRINI ('Ape'), wl, profile, chromo-lith, for *Vanity Fair*, 22 May 1869, NPG. SIR LESLIE WARD ('Spy'), 'Mixed Political Wares', chromo-lith, for *Vanity Fair*, 3 Dec 1892, NPG.

PH J.T.WIGNEY, wl seated, carte, NPG AX8546.

RITCHIE, Alexander Handyside (1804-1870) sculptor.

PH D.O.HILL & ROBERT ADAMSON, 1843-8, hl seated, print, NPG P6 (33). D.O.HILL & R.ADAMSON, 1843-8, hl with John Henning, print, NPG P6 (24), and with John Henning and David Octavius Hill, print, NPG P6 (98).

RITCHIE, Anne Isabella Ritchie, Lady, née Thackeray (1837-1919) novelist.

PH JULIA MARGARET CAMERON, c1867, tql seated, print, NPG P53.

RITCHIE, David George (1853-1903) philosopher.

PR P.N., after a photograph by E.Pannell, hs, wood engr, for *Illust London News*, 6 Oct 1894, NPG.

RITCHIE of Dundee, Charles Thomson Ritchie, 1st Baron (1838-1906) chancellor of the exchequer.

PR R.TAYLOR, after W.Wilson, tql, addressing the House of Commons, woodcut, for *Illust London News*, 31 March 1888, BM, NPG. UNKNOWN, after a photograph by London Stereoscopic Co, hs, etch, NPG.

C CARLO PELLEGRINI ('Ape'), wl, profile, chromo-lith, for *Vanity Fair*, 31 Oct 1885, NPG.

PH BARRAUD, hs, print, for *Our Conservative and Unionist Statesmen*, vol I, NPG (Album 16). G.C.BERESFORD, c1902-3, hs, print, NPG X12889. G.C.BERESFORD, 1903, hs, neg, NPG X6568. WALERY, tql, print, NPG X12887. SIR BENJAMIN STONE, 1897, wl, print, NPG, Birmingham Reference Library.

RIVIERE, Briton (1840-1920) painter.

P P.H.CALDERON, 1882, hs, semi-profile, oval, MacDonald Collection, Aberdeen Art Gallery. SIR HUBERT VON HERKOMER, 1887, Royal Academy, London.

G G.GRENVILLE MANTON, 'Conversazione at the Royal Academy, 1891', w/c, NPG 2820. SIR HUBERT VON HERKOMER, 'The Council of the Royal Academy', oil, 1908, TATE 2481.

SC EDWARD ONSLOW FORD, RA 1895, bronze head, Oriel College, Oxford.

PR UNKNOWN, hs, woodcut, for *Illust London News*, 9 Feb 1878, NPG.

PH LOCK & WHITFIELD, hs, oval, woodburytype, for *Men of Mark*, 1882, NPG. W. & D.DOWNEY, tql, woodburytype, for *Cassell's Cabinet Portrait Gallery*, vol II, 1891, NPG. RALPH W.ROBINSON, wl seated in studio, print, for *Members and Associates of the Royal Academy of Arts, 1891*, NPG X7389. JOHN RUSSELL & SONS, hs, print, for *National Photographic Record*, vol II, NPG. UNKNOWN, hs, print, NPG X12478.

RIVIERE, Henry Parsons (1811-1888) water-colour painter.

PH JOHN WATKINS, tql, carte, NPG (Album 104).

ROBERTS, Arthur (1852-1933) comedian.
D AUGUSTUS JOHN, 1895, hs, pencil, NPG 2362.

ROBERTS, Frederick Sleigh Roberts, 1st Earl (1832-1914) field-marshal.
P FRANK HOLL, RA 1882, Royal Coll. W.W.OULESS, 1882, Royal Artillery Regimental Museum, Woolwich. C.W.FURSE, 1893-5, TATE 4611. C.W.FURSE, c1893-1900, wl on his charger 'Vonolel,' TATE T615. G.F.WATTS, 1898, hs in uniform, NPG 1744. J.S.SARGENT, 1904, tql in uniform, with medals and orders, NPG 3927. P.A.DE LÁSZLÓ, 1911, tql in uniform, Eton College, Berks. D I.SHELDON WILLIAMS, 1900, hl seated, pencil and w/c, NPG 4039 (5). FEODORA, COUNTESS VON GLEICHEN, 1909, Royal Coll.
C HARRY BATES, 1894, equestrian statue, Calcutta; copies, Horse Guards Parade, London, and Glasgow. JOHN TWEED, bust, St Paul's Cathedral, London.
R H.HERKOMER, hs, Herkomergravure, BM, NPG. WILLIAM NICHOLSON, 1899, wl, coloured woodcut, NPG. C.ROBERTS, after F.Holl, hl in uniform, woodcut, BM. UNKNOWN, tql in uniform, etch, BM.
C 'GWR' (?), wl, w/c study, for Vanity Fair, 10 April 1880, NPG 1996. SIR LESLIE WARD ('Spy'), wl in uniform, chromo-lith, for Vanity Fair, 21 June 1900, NPG.
PH Various prints and negs by ALEXANDER BASSANO, Mrs A.BROOM, JOHN BURKE, JAMES CRADDOCK, LAFAYETTE, LONDON STEREOSCOPIC CO, MAULL & FOX, J.RUSSELL & SONS and C.VANDYCK, various dates and sizes, postcards, cabinets, photogravures, some in uniform, NPG.

ROBERTS, Sir Henry Gee (1800-1860) major-general.
P UNKNOWN, c1840, hl in uniform, DoE (Foreign Office, London).

ROBERTS, Sir William (1830-1899) physician.
P G.F.WATTS, c1880, hs, Royal College of Physicians, London.

ROBERTS, William Prowting (1806-1871) trades unionist.
R UNKNOWN, tql seated, line, BM.

ROBERTSON, Archibald (1853-1931) bishop of Exeter.
P MISS ROBERTSON, tql, Bishop's Palace, Exeter.
PH UNKNOWN, tql, print, NPG (Anglican Bishops). ROTARY PHOTO, tql, postcard, NPG.

ROBERTSON, Douglas Moray Cooper Lamb Argyll (1837-1909) ophthalmic surgeon.
P SIR GEORGE REID (replica), wl, Royal College of Surgeons, Edinburgh.
R W.HOLE, tql with Thomas Smith Clouston, etch, for Quasi Cursores, 1884, NPG.

ROBERTSON, Eben William (1815-1874) historian.
P SIR W.C.ROSS, tql in highland dress, SNPG 1027.

ROBERTSON, Frederick William (1816-1853) divine.
SC W.PEPPER, marble bust, Bodleian Library, Oxford. E.W.WYON, 1853, bronze plaque, Brighton Cemetery. UNKNOWN, model of face and hands taken after death, Bodleian Library.
R J.C.ARMYTAGE, hl, stipple, NPG. T.H.MAGUIRE, after a picture done from memory by C.J.Basebe, hl, lith, pub 1849, NPG. UNKNOWN, hs, semi-profile, oval, stipple, NPG.
PH KILBURN, hl, oval, daguerreotype, NPG P1.

ROBERTSON, James (1803-1860) professor of divinity in the University of Edinburgh.
R E.BURTON, after J.P.Edgar, hs, oval, mezz, BM.
PH J.MOFFAT, hs, profile, carte, NPG (Album 102).

ROBERTSON, James Patrick Bannerman Robertson, Baron (1845-1909) judge.
R R.T. & Co, hs, semi-profile, wood engr, for Illust London News, 3 Oct 1891, NPG.

ROBERTSON, John Mackinnon (1856-1933) writer and politician.
PH SIR BENJAMIN STONE, 1909, two prints, both wl, NPG. WALTER STONEMAN, before 1917, hl, NPG (NPR).

ROBERTSON, Sir Johnston Forbes-, see FORBES-Robertson.

ROBERTSON, Thomas William (1829-1871) actor and dramatist.
PR UNKNOWN, after a photograph by Charles Watkins, hs, profile, woodcut, for The Illust Review, 1 March 1871, NPG.
PH SAMUEL A.WALKER, tql seated, carte, NPG.

ROBERTSON, Sir William Tindal (1825-1889) physician and politician.
PR R.T., hs, wood engr, for Illust London News, 12 Oct 1889, NPG.
C SIR LESLIE WARD ('Spy'), wl, chromo-lith, for Vanity Fair, 16 Feb 1889, NPG.

ROBINS, Arthur (1834-1899) clergyman.
C SIR LESLIE WARD ('Spy'), wl, w/c study, for Vanity Fair, 23 Dec 1897, NPG 3003.

ROBINSON, Frederick William (1830-1901) novelist.
PR UNKNOWN, after a photograph by C.N.Wheeler, hs, woodcut, for Harper's Mag, June 1888, NPG.

ROBINSON, George Frederick Samuel, see 1st Marquess of Ripon.

ROBINSON, Sir Hercules George Robert, see 1st Baron Rosmead.

ROBINSON, Sir John (1839-1903) first prime minister of Natal.
SC UNKNOWN, statue, Town Gardens, Durban.

ROBINSON, Sir John Charles (1824-1913) connoisseur and collector.
P J.J.NAPIER, hs, NPG 2543.
G HENRY JAMYN BROOKS, 'Private view of the Old Masters Exhibition, Royal Academy, 1888', oil, NPG 1833.
PR G.ROBINSON, hs, etch, BM.

ROBINSON, Sir John Richard (1828-1903) journalist.
PR P.N., after a photograph by Walery, hs, wood engr, for Illust London News, 10 June 1893, NPG.

ROBINSON, Joseph Armitage (1858-1933) dean of Westminster Abbey and of Wells Cathedral.
P H.RIVIERE, 1902, tql seated in robes, The Deanery, Westminster.
PH RUSSELL, print, Christ's College, Cambridge. SIR BENJAMIN STONE, wl in a group, Birmingham Reference Library.

ROBSON, Thomas Frederick (1822?-1864) actor.
D ARTHUR MILES, 1861, hs, chalk, NPG 1877.
PR UNKNOWN, wl as Samson Burr in The Porter's Knot, woodcut, for Illust London News, 1858, BM. UNKNOWN, after a photograph by Herbert Watkins, hl, woodcut, for Illust London News, 27 Aug 1864, NPG.
PH UNKNOWN, hl, print, NPG. Several cartes by ADOLPHE BEAU, CALDESI, BLANFORD & CO, MAYALL, CAMILLE SILVY, HERBERT WATKINS and others, various dates and sizes, some in character, NPG.

ROBSON, William Snowdon Robson, Baron (1852-1918) attorney-general.
C SIR LESLIE WARD ('Spy'), wl, w/c study, for Vanity Fair, 25 Jan 1906, NPG 2996.
PH SIR BENJAMIN STONE, 1902, two prints, both wl, NPG.

RODD, James Rennell, see 1st Baron Rennell.

RODEN, Robert Jocelyn, 4th Earl of (1846-1880) soldier

and courtier.

c SIR LESLIE WARD ('Spy'), tql seated, profile, w/c study, for *Vanity Fair*, 20 May 1876, NPG 4738.

RODEN, William Thomas (1817-1892) engraver and portrait-painter.

P HENRY STANIER, possibly a portrait of Roden, Herbert Art Gallery and Museum, Coventry.

RODNEY, George Rodney, 7th Baron (1857-1909) soldier.

c LIBERIO PROSPERI ('Lib'), wl, profile, seated, w/c study, for *Vanity Fair*, 10 Nov 1888, NPG 4739.

RODWELL, George Herbert Buonaparte (1800-1852) musical composer.

PR C.BAUGNIET, two liths, tql and wl seated, BM.

ROEBUCK, John Arthur (1801-1879) politician.

P JAMES GREEN, RA 1833, hl, semi-profile, Guildhall, Bath; version, National Gallery of Canada, Ottawa. H.W.PICKERSGILL, RA 1860, tql seated, Corporation of Sheffield. UNKNOWN, hl seated, NPG 1777.

D G.F.WATTS, Watts Gallery, Compton, Surrey.

G SIR GEORGE HAYTER, 'The House of Commons, 1833', oil, NPG 54.

SC WILLIAM BEHNES, 1842, marble bust, National Gallery of Canada, Ottawa. THEOPHILUS SMITH, marble bust, Mappin Art Gallery, Sheffield.

PR BUTTERWORTH & HEATH, after a photograph by Mayall, hl, woodcut, BM. D.J.POUND, after a photograph by Mayall, tql seated, line, supplement to *Illust News of the World*, NPG. H.ROBINSON, as after J.Watts (in fact after G.F.Watts), hl, stipple, for Saunders's *Political Reformers*, 1840, BM, NPG. Several engrs after photographs, BM, NPG.

c JOHN DOYLE, ten political drgs, BM. 'FAUSTIN', wl, lith, a 'Figaro' cartoon, NPG. CARLO PELLEGRINI ('Ape'), wl, profile, w/c study, for *Vanity Fair*, 11 April 1874, NPG 2695.

PH W. & D.DOWNEY, three cartes, various sizes, NPG AX8664 and X12860–1. LONDON STEREOSCOPIC CO, hs, profile, carte, NPG (Album 40). MAULL & POLYBLANK, 1856, tql seated, print, NPG AX7927.

ROGERS, Annie Mary Anne Henley (1856-1937) educationist.

D LESLIE BROOKE, St Hugh's College, Oxford.

ROGERS, Benjamin Bickley (1828-1919) barrister and translator of Aristophanes.

D UNKNOWN, pencil, Oxford Union.

ROGERS, Frederic, see Baron Blachford.

ROGERS, James Edwin Thorold (1823-1890) professor of Political Economy.

P MARGARET FLETCHER, 1891, hs, Worcester College, Oxford.

PR R.T., hs, wood engr, for *Illust London News*, 18 Oct 1890, NPG.

c SIR LESLIE WARD ('Spy'), wl, profile, chromo-lith, for *Vanity Fair*, 29 March 1884, NPG.

ROGERS, William (1819-1896) educational reformer.

P SIR A.S.COPE, RA 1895, tql seated, Dulwich College, London; copy by Sir C.Holroyd, Balliol College, Oxford.

ROGERSON, John Bolton (1809-1859) poet and bookseller.

PR UNKNOWN, hl, line, NPG.

ROLLESTON, George (1829-1881) physician.

D W.E.MILLER, 1877, hs, pencil, NPG 1933; similar portraits, Pembroke College, Oxford and Merton College, Oxford.

SC H.R.HOPE PINKER, RA 1884, marble bust, University Museum, Oxford.

PR UNKNOWN, after a photograph by Barraud and Jerrard, hs, wood

engr, for *Illust London News*, 2 July 1881, NPG.

ROLLIT, Sir Albert Kaye (1842-1922) politician.

P SIR HUBERT VON HERKOMER, RA 1905, tql seated, Guildhall, Hull.

G W.H.BARTLETT, 'Saturday Night at the Savage Club', oil, Savage Club, London.

c SIR LESLIE WARD ('Spy'), wl, profile, w/c study, for *Vanity Fair*, 9 Oct 1886, NPG 2694.

ROLT, Sir John (1804-1871) lord justice of appeal.

PR W.HOLL, tql seated, stipple, BM. UNKNOWN, hs, woodcut, for *Illust London News*, 29 Dec 1866, NPG.

PH A.J.MELHUISH, tql seated, carte, NPG (Album 120).

ROMAINE, William Govett (1815-1893) lawyer.

PH UNKNOWN, hl, print, NPG X12864.

ROMANES, George John (1848-1894) scientist.

PH WALKER & COCKERELL, after a photograph by Elliott & Fry, tq seated, photogravure, NPG X12822. A.J.MELHUISH, hs, cabinet NPG X12865.

ROMER, Emma (Mrs Almond) (1814-1868) singer.

PR W.T.PAGE, hl as Amina in *La Sonnambula*, stipple, BM. Two theatrical prints, Harvard Theatre Collection, Cambridge, Mass, USA.

ROMER, Sir Robert (1840-1918) judge.

P LOWES DICKINSON, Trinity Hall, Cambridge.

c (Possibly H.C.SEPPING) WRIGHT ('Stuff'), hl seated, chromo-lith for *Vanity Fair*, 12 Dec 1891, NPG.

ROMILLY, Sir John Romilly, 1st Baron (1802-1874 master of the rolls.

SC JOSEPH DURHAM, RA 1867, marble bust, Public Record Office London.

PR R. & E.TAYLOR, hs, woodcut, for *Illust London News*, 26 Apr 1873, NPG.

RONAN, Stephen (1848-1925) lord justice of appeal i Ireland.

D FREDERICK PEGRAM, pencil sketch, made during the sessions of th Parnell Special Commission, V & A.

ROOKWOOD, Sir Henry John Selwin-Ibbetson, 7t Bart, Baron (1826-1902) politician.

PR JOSEPH BROWN, after a photograph by J.Mayall, hs, stipple, fc *Baily's Mag*, 1882, NPG. R.T. & CO, after a photograph b G.Jerrard, hs, wood engr, for *Illust London News*, 4 June 189 NPG.

ROOSE, Edward Charles Robson (1848-1905) physician

PH W. & D.DOWNEY, hl, woodburytype, for Cassell's *Cabin Portrait Gallery*, vol III, 1892, NPG.

ROSA, Carl August Nicholas (1843-1889) musician.

PR UNKNOWN, after a photograph by Robinson and Thompson Liverpool, hs, woodcut, for *Illust London News*, 9 Oct 1875, NP

ROSCOE, Sir Henry Enfield (1833-1915) chemist.

PR C.H.JEENS, head, stipple, BM, NPG.

PH W. & D.DOWNEY, tql, woodburytype, for Cassell's *Cabin Portrait Gallery*, vol II, 1891, NPG. ANNAN & SWAN, aft A.Brothers, hs, photogravure, NPG X12874. OLIVE EDIS, c191 three autochromes, NPG X7202–4. OLIVE EDIS, tql seated, prii NPG X12876.

ROSE, George (1817-1882) dramatist and humorous e tertainer; wrote under pseudonym 'Arthur Sketchley'.

PR DALZIEL, hs, woodcut, for his book *The Brown Papers*, 1864, E UNKNOWN, after a photograph by Herbert Barraud, hs, wo engr, for *Illust London News*, 25 Nov 1882, NPG.

PH UNKNOWN, hs, carte, NPG.

ROSE, Hugh Henry, see 1st Baron Strathnairn.

ROSE, John Holland (1855-1942) historian.
H OLIVE EDIS, 1923, hs, profile, print, NPG X12877. UNKNOWN, with others at Rhodes memorial, March 26th 1933, print, Christ's College, Cambridge. WALTER STONEMAN, 1933, hs, NPG (NPR).

ROSE-INNES, Sir James (1855-1942) chief justice of South Africa.
P GEORGE CROSLAND ROBINSON, Houses of Parliament, Cape Town, South Africa. NEVILLE LEWIS, Appeal Court Building, Bloemfontein, South Africa.
H WALTER STONEMAN, 1919, hs, NPG (NPR).

ROSEBERY, Archibald Philip Primrose, 5th Earl of (1847-1929) statesman and author.
P HENRY WEIGALL, 1866, hs, Christ Church, Oxford. J.H.LORIMER, after J.E.Millais of 1886, tql, Eton College, Berks.
D UNKNOWN, ink, SNPG 1120.
G A.E.EMSLIE, 'Dinner at Haddo House, 1884', oil, NPG 3845.
C SIR MAX BEERBOHM, several drgs, c1901-12, various sizes, Ashmolean Museum, Oxford, V & A, Lilly Library, Indiana University, Bloomington, USA, University of Texas, Austin, USA. SIR FRANCIS CARRUTHERS GOULD, three pencil, pen and ink sketches, various sizes, NPG 2858-60. HARRY FURNISS, pen and ink sketches, NPG 3406, 3406a and 3600. SIR BERNARD PARTRIDGE, two cartoon drgs, for *Punch*, NPG. SIR LESLIE WARD ('Spy'), two chromo-liths, both wl, for *Vanity Fair*, 3 June 1876 and 14 March 1901, NPG.
H UNKNOWN, hs, woodburytype, for *University Mag*, 1878, NPG X12745. G.JERRARD, c1884, hs, print, NPG X12890. ELLIOTT & FRY, 1890s, hs, cabinet, NPG X12551.

ROSEN, Friedrich August (1805-1837) Sanskrit scholar.
C RICHARD WESTMACOTT jun, RA 1839, marble bust, BM.

ROSMEAD, Sir Hercules George Robert Robinson, 1st Baron (1824-1897) colonial governor.
R UNKNOWN, after a photograph by Elliott & Fry, hs, profile, wood engr, for *Illust London News*, 10 Jan 1891, NPG.

ROSS, George (1814-1863) legal writer.
C SIR JOHN STEELL, marble bust, Faculty of Advocates, Parliament Hall, Edinburgh.

ROSS, Horatio (1801-1886) sportsman.
R E.BURTON, after E.Landseer, wl stalking deer, with title 'Stealing a March', mixed engr, pub 1845, BM. J.BROWN, after a photograph by J.E.Mayall, tql with gun, stipple, NPG.

ROSS, Sir James Clarke (1800-1862) rear-admiral and arctic explorer.
P UNKNOWN, 1833, Royal Geographical Society, London. J.R.WILDMAN, 1833-4, tql in uniform, NMM, Greenwich. H.W.PICKERSGILL, RA 1848, hl in uniform, NMM. STEPHEN PEARCE, 1850, hl, study for NPG 1208, NPG 913. S.PEARCE, 1870, tql, NMM.
D WILLIAM BROCKEDON, 1848, hs, chalk, NPG 2515(99). UNKNOWN, w/c, Royal Geographical Society, London.
G S.PEARCE, 'The Arctic Council, 1851', oil, NPG 1208.
C BERNHARD SMITH, 1843, plaster medallion, NPG 887; versions, Scott Polar Research Institute, Cambridge, and Royal Geographical Society; related marble medallion, 1844, Linnean Society, London.
R F.HOLL of 1860, after G.Richmond (1849), Royal Geographical Society. T.H.MAGUIRE, 1851, tql in uniform, lith, one of set of *Ipswich Museum Portraits*, NPG. J.NEGELEN, hs, lith, NPG.

ROSS, Sir Ronald (1857-1932) discoverer of the mosquito

cycle in malaria.
SC FRANK BOWCHER, 1929, bronze plaque, NPG 3646; 1930, related? silver plaque, London School of Hygiene and Tropical Medicine. LADY WELBY, bronze bust, London School of Hygiene and Tropical Medicine.
PH Various prints, Ross Institute of Tropical Hygiene, London. WALTER STONEMAN, 1917 and 1928, two portraits, both hs, the first in uniform, NPG (NPR).

ROSSE, Laurence Parsons, 4th Earl of (1840-1908) astronomer.
D FREDERICK SARGENT, tql, pencil, NPG 1834(z).
PR UNKNOWN, after a photograph by Jabez Hughes, hs, woodcut, for *Illust London News*, 7 Feb 1880, NPG.

ROSSE, William Parsons, 3rd Earl of (1800-1867) constructor of the Rosse telescope.
P STEPHEN CATTERSON SMITH, tql seated, The Royal Society, London.
SC J.H.FOLEY, 1874-6, statue, St John's Place, Birr, Eire.
PR BOSLEY, after a daguerreotype, hl, lith, pub 1849, BM.
PH MAULL & POLYBLANK, tql seated, print, NPG AX7274.

ROSSETTI, Christina Georgina (1830-1894) poet.
P WILLIAM HOLMAN HUNT, 1853, wl, 'The Light of the World', (Christina Rossetti posed as a model for the head of Christ), Keble College, Oxford.
D Several drgs by DANTE GABRIEL ROSSETTI: 1847, head, profile, pencil, V & A; 1848, head, chalk, BM; 1852, tql seated, oval, pencil, Wightwick Manor (NT), W Midlands; 1865, head, profile, pencil, Wightwick Manor; c1866, head, semi-profile, chalks, Fitzwilliam Museum, Cambridge; 1877, hs, semi-profile, with her mother, chalk, NPG 990.
G Christina Rossetti posed as model for several paintings by D.G.Rossetti, eg: 'The Girlhood of Mary Virgin', oil, 1849, (she sat as a model for the Virgin), TATE 4872, and 'Ecce Ancilla Domini!', oil, 1850, (as model for Virgin), TATE 1210; 1849, pencil study, wl seated, TATE T287.
PR W.B.SCOTT, after a miniature by Pistrucci, head, oval, aged about 7, etch, BM. S.J.B.HAYDON, wl seated, etch and mezz, BM.
C DANTE GABRIEL ROSSETTI, 1862, wl in a tantrum, pen and ink, Wightwick Manor.
PH C.L.DODGSON ('Lewis Carroll'), 1863, 'The Rossetti Family', print, NPG P56.

ROSSETTI, Dante Gabriel (1828-1882) painter and poet.
P G.F.WATTS, c1871, hs, NPG 1011. WILLIAM HOLMAN HUNT, 1882, after pastel drg of 1853, hs, Birmingham City Art Gallery. HENRY TREFFRY DUNN, 1882, based on a photograph of c1864, hs, Uffizi Gallery, Florence.
D WILLIAM HOLMAN HUNT, 1848, hs, pen and ink, Fitzwilliam Museum, Cambridge. WILLIAM HOLMAN HUNT, 1853, hs, oval, pastel, Manchester City Art Gallery. Various self-portrait drgs: 1847, hs, pencil, NPG 857; 1853, wl, sitting to Elizabeth Siddal, pen and ink, Birmingham City Art Gallery; 1853-62, wl with Elizabeth Siddal, pen and sepia, Fondazione Horne, Florence; 1855, hs, pen and ink, Fitzwilliam Museum; c1860, head, pencil, Ashmolean Museum, Oxford; 1861, hs, pencil, Birmingham City Art Gallery. FREDERIC SHIELDS, 1880, at work on the 'Day Dream', pencil, Ashmolean Museum. H.T.DUNN, 1882, wl seated with Theodore Watts-Dunton, w/c, NPG 3022. CHARLES KEENE, hl, charcoal, Ashmolean Museum.
SC D.BRUCCIANI & Co, 1882, plaster cast of death mask, NPG 1699. UNKNOWN, medallion on decorative frieze, Stroud School of Science and Art.
PR W.B.SCOTT, hs, aged 25, etch, BM. F.COURBOIN, hs, etch, BM. Self-portrait, 1870, hs, etch, NPG 3033.

C Self-portrait, hs, pencil, NPG 3048. Self-portrait, 1869, wl kneeling, weeping at the death of a wombat, pen and ink, BM.

PH C.L.DODGSON ('Lewis Carroll'), 1863, tql seated, print, NPG P29. C.L.DODGSON, 1863, 'The Rossetti Family', print, NPG P56. W. & D.DOWNEY, 1863, wl with W.Bell Scott and John Ruskin, carte, NPG (Album 110). W. & D.DOWNEY, hl, carte, NPG x6424.

ROSSETTI, Elizabeth Eleanor, see Siddal.

ROSSETTI, Lucy Madox, née Brown (1843–1894) painter, daughter of Ford Madox Brown and wife of W.M.Rossetti.

D FORD MADOX BROWN, as a child, charcoal, Wightwick Manor (NT), W Midlands.

ROSSETTI, William Michael (1829–1919) critic and writer.

P FORD MADOX BROWN, 1856, hs, Wightwick Manor (NT), W Midlands. H.H.GILCHRIST, c1900, tql seated, Wightwick Manor. SIR WILLIAM ROTHENSTEIN, c1909, hs, NPG 2485.

D WILLIAM HOLMAN HUNT, hs, profile, ink, Fitzwilliam Museum, Cambridge. DANTE GABRIEL ROSSETTI, 1853, 'The First Anniversary of the Death of Beatrice', w/c, (W.M.Rossetti was the model for the head of Dante), Ashmolean Museum, Oxford.

G WILLIAM HOLMAN HUNT, 'A Converted British Family sheltering a Christian Priest from the Persecution of the Druids', oil, 1850, (W.M.Rossetti was the model for the priest), Ashmolean Museum.

C SIR MAX BEERBOHM, 'The small hours in the 'sixties at 16 Cheyne Walk – Algernon Swinburne reading 'Anactoria' to Gabriel and William', 1916, TATE 5391(xi).

PH C.L.DODGSON ('Lewis Carroll'), 1863, 'The Rossetti Family', print, NPG P56. JULIA MARGARET CAMERON, c1866, hs, print, NPG P126. RUSSELL & SONS, c1907, tql seated with his daughter Mary, cabinet, NPG x8022.

ROTHSCHILD, Alfred Charles de (1842–1918) banker.

G HENRY JAMYN BROOKS, 'Private view of the Old Masters Exhibition, Royal Academy, 1888', oil, NPG 1833.

C SIR MAX BEERBOHM, several cartoons: 1895, V & A; University of Texas, Austin, USA; TATE 4165. SIR LESLIE WARD ('Spy'), wl, profile, chromo-lith, for *Vanity Fair*, 31 May 1884, NPG.

ROTHSCHILD, Sir Anthony de, 1st Bart (1810–1876) Austrian consul-general.

PR UNKNOWN, hs, woodcut, for *Illust London News,* 22 Jan 1876, NPG.

ROTHSCHILD, Ferdinand James de (1839–1898) art collector.

P UNKNOWN, hs, Waddesdon Manor (NT), Bucks.

G HENRY JAMYN BROOKS, 'Private view of the Old Masters Exhibition, Royal Academy, 1888', oil, NPG 1833.

ROTHSCHILD, Lionel Nathan de (1808–1879) banker and philanthropist.

P M.D.OPPENHEIM, 1835, tql seated, NPG 3838. SIR FRANCIS GRANT, 1841, wl equestrian, hunting with his three brothers, Ascott (NT), Bucks.

G HENRY BARRAUD, 'Baron Lionel de Rothschild Introduced into the House of Commons, 1858', oil, Ascott.

PR W.RICHARDSON, wl, profile, lith, NPG. UNKNOWN, after a photograph by O.Rejlander, hs, semi-profile, lith, for Cassell's *National Portrait Gallery*, 1877, NPG. UNKNOWN, hl, woodcut, NPG.

C CARLO PELLEGRINI ('Ape'), tql seated, chromo-lith, for *Vanity Fair*, 22 Sept 1877, NPG.

PH MAULL & CO, wl seated, carte, NPG AX8601.

ROTHSCHILD, Meyer Amschel de (1818–1874) politician, sportsman and collector of art treasures.

PR UNKNOWN, after a photograph by Barraud and Jerrard, hs,

woodcut, for *Illust London News,* 21 Feb 1874, NPG.

C CARLO PELLEGRINI ('Ape'), wl, profile, chromo-lith, for *Vanity Fair*, 27 May 1871, NPG.

ROTHSCHILD, Sir Nathan Meyer Rothschild, 2nd Bart, 1st Baron (1840–1915) banker and philanthropist.

P LOUISE JOPLING, 1878, hl in uniform, Hughenden (NT), Bucks.

PR R.T., hs, woodcut, for *Illust London News,* 11 July 1885, NPG.

C LIBERIO PROSPERI ('Lib'), wl, profile, chromo-lith, for *Vanity Fair*, 9 June 1888, NPG.

ROTHWELL, Richard (1800–1868) painter.

P Self-portraits, both hl, NGI 265 and Ulster Museum, Belfast.

D C.W.COPE, c1862, head, pen, ink and chalk, NPG 3182 (8).

ROUSBY, Clara Marion Jessie (1852?–1879) actress.

PR R.T., hs, oval, woodcut, for *The Illust Review*, 15 Nov 1873, NPG. UNKNOWN, wl as Joan of Arc, woodcut, for *Illust London News*, 22 April 1871, NPG. Various theatrical prints, Harvard Theatre Collection, Cambridge, Mass, USA.

PH LONDON STEREOSCOPIC CO, hs, carte, NPG (Album 102). Various cartes, some in character, NPG. UNKNOWN, hs, woodburytype, carte, NPG AX7606.

ROUTH, Edward John (1831–1907) mathematician.

P SIR HUBERT VON HERKOMER, 1890, Peterhouse, Cambridge.

ROUTLEDGE, George (1812–1888) publisher.

PR R.T., hs, wood engr, for *Illust London News*, 12 Jan 1889, NPG.

ROWBOTHAM, Thomas Charles Leeson (1823–1875) painter.

PH McLEAN & HAES, hs, carte, NPG (Album 104).

ROWE, Joshua Brooking (1837–1908) antiquary and naturalist.

PH UNKNOWN, print, Exeter public library.

ROWTON, Montagu William Lowry Corry, Baron (1838–1903) politician and philanthropist.

P HEINRICH VON ANGELI, hs, Hughenden (NT), Bucks.

C SIR LESLIE WARD ('Spy'), wl, profile, chromo-lith, for *Vanity Fair*, 3 March 1877, NPG. SIR LESLIE WARD ('Spy'), wl with Lord Beaconsfield, chromo-lith, dated 16 Dec 1879, for *Vanity Fair* Winter Number, NPG.

RUGGLES-BRISE, Sir Evelyn John (1857–1935) prison reformer.

C SIR LESLIE WARD ('Spy'), wl, mechanical repro, for *Vanity Fair*, 10 Feb 1910, NPG.

PH BASSANO, hs, print, NPG. WALTER STONEMAN, 1918, hs, NPG (NPR).

RUMBOLD, Sir Horace, 8th Bart (1829–1913) diplomat.

PR P.N., hs, wood engr, NPG.

RUNCIMAN, Walter Runciman, 1st Baron (1847–1937) shipowner.

C HARRY FURNISS, pen and ink sketch, NPG 3407.

RUNDLE, Sir (Henry Macleod) Leslie (1856–1934) general.

PR UNKNOWN, hs in uniform, wood engr, NPG.

PH WALTER STONEMAN, hs, NPG (NPR).

RUSKIN, John (1819–1900) author, artist and social reformer.

P GEORGE RICHMOND, 1842, wl seated, Ruskin Galleries, Bembridge School, Isle of Wight.

D GEORGE RICHMOND, c1843, head, chalk, NPG 1058. SIR J.E.MILLAIS, 1853, several sketches: wl, for portrait of 1854, pencil, Ashmolean Museum, Oxford; with William Millais wading in a stream in Scotland, pencil, pen and sepia ink, Bolton Museum and Art Gallery; hs, semi-profile, pencil and w/c, Bembridge School. DANTE GABRIEL ROSSETTI, 1861, hs, chalk, Ashmolean Museum. WILLIAM BELL SCOTT, 1864, hl seated, teaching Miss Mackenzie to draw at Wallington, w/c, Wallington (NT), Northumberland. Self-portrait, 1873, hs, Pierpont Morgan Library, New York, USA. Self-portrait, 1873–4, hs, pencil, The Brantwood Trust, Coniston, Lancashire. Self-portrait, 1874, hs, w/c, Wellesley College Library, Mass, USA. SIR HUBERT VON HERKOMER, 1879, hs, w/c, NPG 1336. T.B.WIRGMAN, c1886, hl seated, pencil, NPG 3035.

G HENRY JAMYN BROOKS, 'Private view of the Old Masters Exhibition, Royal Academy, 1888', oil, NPG 1833.

SC SIR J.E.BOEHM, c1880–1, marble bust, Ashmolean Museum. SIR J.E.BOEHM, 1881, plaster cast, NPG 1053. CONRAD DRESSLER, 1885, terracotta bust, TATE 2242. CONRAD DRESSLER, 1888, bronze bust, NPG 2030. CONRAD DRESSLER, 1903, bronze bust, Ruskin Hall, Bournville School of Art and Crafts, Birmingham. H.C.FEHR, marble bust, South London Art Gallery. EDWARD ONSLOW FORD, memorial bust, Westminster Abbey, London. A.C.LUCCHESI, plaster medallion, Corpus Christi College, Oxford.

PR W.BURTON, tql seated, etch, BM. G.PILOTELL, hs, profile, drypoint, BM. Various prints, BM, NPG.

C ADRIANO CECIONI, wl, profile, w/c study, for *Vanity Fair*, 17 Feb 1872, South London Art Gallery; chromo-lith, NPG and preliminary studies, Gabinetto dei disegni e delle stampe degli Uffizi, Florence.

PH C.L.DODGSON ('Lewis Carroll'), c1875, hl seated, carte, NPG P50. LOCK & WHITFIELD, hs, oval, woodburytype, for *Men of Mark*, 1882, NPG. BARRAUD, wl seated, print, for *Men and Women of the Day*, vol I, 1888, NPG AX5407. ELLIOTT & FRY, 1891, hs, woodburytype, NPG. UNKNOWN, after a photograph by Miss Acland, 1893, wl seated with Sir Henry Acland, photogravure, NPG. BARRAUD, two cabinets, both hs, NPG X1372 and X1513. UNKNOWN, hl, cabinet, NPG. W. & D.DOWNEY, wl with W.B.Scott and D.G.Rossetti, carte, NPG (Album 110). FREDERICK HOLLYER, hl, profile, seated, print, V & A. JAMES MCCLELAND, 1895, various negs, various sizes, in later life, NPG. Various cartes by L.CALDESI & CO, W. & D.DOWNEY, ELLIOTT & FRY, various dates and sizes, NPG. Various prints, Bembridge School.

RUSSEL, Alexander (1814–1876) journalist.

SC WILLIAM BRODIE, marble bust, SNPG 557.

PR UNKNOWN, after a photograph by Truefitt Brothers, hl seated, woodcut, for *Illust London News*, 10 March 1860, NPG. UNKNOWN, hs, woodcut, for *Illust London News*, 12 June 1875, NPG.

RUSSELL, Sir Charles, 3rd Bart (1826–1883) soldier and politician.

C CARLO PELLEGRINI ('Ape'), wl, profile, w/c study, for *Vanity Fair*, 2 Feb 1878, NPG 4740.

RUSSELL, Charles William (1812–1880) divine and writer.

P GAGLIARDI, 1883, St Patrick's College, Maynooth.

RUSSELL, Francis Charles Hastings, see 9th Duke of Bedford.

RUSSELL, Sir George, 4th Bart (1828–1898) judge.

C SIR LESLIE WARD ('Spy'), wl, profile, w/c study, for *Vanity Fair*, 2 March 1889, NPG 4741.

PH SIR BENJAMIN STONE, wl, print, NPG.

RUSSELL, Henry (1812–1900) singer and song writer.

PR UNKNOWN, two prints, hl seated at piano, and wl seated at piano, both stipple, BM.

RUSSELL, Herbrand Arthur, see 11th Duke of Bedford.

RUSSELL, John Scott (1808–1882) naval architect.

P H.W.PHILLIPS, SNPG 876.

G H.W.PHILLIPS, 'The Royal Commissioners for the Great Exhibition, 1851', oil, V & A.

PR W.H.MOTE, after a photograph by Mayall, hl seated with plans, semi-profile, stipple, NPG.

PH LOCK & WHITFIELD, hs, oval, woodburytype, for *Men of Mark*, 1878, NPG.

RUSSELL, Odo William Leopold, see 1st Baron Ampthill.

RUSSELL, Sir Thomas Wallace, 1st Bart (1841–1920) politician.

P SARAH PURSER, NGI 1101.

D SIR WILLIAM ORPEN, Municipal Gallery of Modern Art, Dublin.

C SIR FRANCIS CARRUTHERS GOULD, wl seated, chalk, sketch, NPG 2869. SIR LESLIE WARD ('Spy'), wl, w/c study, for *Vanity Fair*, 24 March 1888, NPG 3295.

PH SIR BENJAMIN STONE, two prints, both wl, NPG.

RUSSELL, William Clark (1844–1911) novelist.

G P.NAUMANN & R.TAYLOR & CO, 'Our Literary Contributors – Past and Present', one of a series of woodcuts, for *Illust London News*, 14 May 1892, BM, NPG.

PR UNKNOWN, after a photograph by Elliott & Fry, hs, wood engr, for *Harper's Mag*, June 1888, NPG.

RUSSELL, Sir William Howard (1820–1907) war correspondent.

P LOWES DICKINSON, c1860, wl seated at desk, Times Newspapers Ltd, London.

G HENRY NELSON O'NEIL, 'The Billiard Room of the Garrick Club', oil, 1869, Garrick Club, London.

SC BERTRAM MACKENNAL, 1909, memorial bust, St Paul's Cathedral, London.

PR Several prints and woodcuts, NPG.

C HARRY FURNISS, wl seated, pen and ink sketch, NPG 3602. CARLO PELLEGRINI ('Ape'), wl, w/c study, for *Vanity Fair*, 16 Jan 1875, NPG 3268.

PH T.CRANFIELD, wl, carte, NPG AX7537. C.D.FREDERICKS & CO, tql, carte, NPG. LOCK & WHITFIELD, hs, oval, woodburytype, for *Men of Mark*, 1876, NPG. LONDON STEREOSCOPIC CO, tql seated, carte, NPG (Album 40). MAYALL, wl, carte, NPG. SCHIER & SCHOEFFT, hs, carte, NPG X8722.

RUSSELL of Killowen, Charles Russell, 1st Baron (1832–1900) lord chief-justice of England.

P JAMES DOYLE PENROSE, 1896, wl in robes, DoE (Law Courts). J.S.SARGENT, 1900, replica, hl seated, NPG 1907. EDWIN WARD, hl seated, Reform Club, London.

D S.P.HALL, various sketches, some made at the sessions of the Parnell Commission, NPG 2230, 2239–41, 2250–1, 2295 and 2318. RUDOLPH LEHMANN, 1891, hs, BM. FREDERICK PEGRAM, various pencil sketches, V & A.

SC SIR THOMAS BROCK, marble statue, DoE (Law Courts).

C HARRY FURNISS, pen and ink sketch, NPG 3601. FRANCOIS VERHEYDEN, hl, w/c study, for *Vanity Fair*, 5 May 1883, NPG 2740. 'QUIZ', hl in court, chromo-lith, for *Vanity Fair*, 29 March 1890, NPG.

PH BARRAUD, tql seated, print, for *Men and Women of the Day*, vol II, 1889, NPG AX5466. W. & D.DOWNEY, hl, woodburytype, for Cassell's *Cabinet Portrait Gallery*, vol II, 1891, NPG.

RUTHERFORD, Mark (pseudonym), see William Hale WHITE.

RUTHERFORD, William (1839–1899) physiologist.

PR W.HOLE, wl, etch, for *Quasi Cursores*, 1884, NPG.

RUTHERFORD, William Gunion (1853–1907) classical scholar.

D SEYMOUR LUCAS, RA 1895, tql seated, chalk, Westminster School, London.

C SIR LESLIE WARD ('Spy'), wl, profile, chromo-lith, for *Vanity Fair*, 3 March 1898, NPG.

RUTLAND, Charles Cecil John Manners, 6th Duke of (1815-1888) politician.

P Several portraits by SIR FRANCIS GRANT: 1846, hs; 1876, on his pony, with his dog, Prince; tql; all at Belvoir Castle, Leics.

PR JOSEPH BROWN, after a photograph by Mayall, hs, stipple, for *Baily's Mag*, 1863, NPG. UNKNOWN, after a photograph by Broadhead, hs, wood engr, for *Illust London News*, 24 March 1888, NPG. G.R.WARD, hl, mezz, BM.

C UNKNOWN, wl, chromo-lith, for *Vanity Fair*, 16 Sept 1871, NPG.

PH CAMILLE SILVY, 1861, wl, carte, NPG (Album 2).

RUTLAND, Lord John James Robert Manners, 7th Duke of (1818-1906) politician.

P SIR FRANCIS GRANT, 1853, wl, Belvoir Castle, Leics; replica?, Hughenden Manor (NT), Bucks. SIR FRANCIS GRANT, c1860, hs, Belvoir. J.R.HERBERT, tql, Belvoir. SIR HUBERT VON HERKOMER, wl, Belvoir. W.W.OULESS, 1886, tql seated, NPG 2945.

D H.T.WELLS, 1872, hs, chalk, NPG 2679.

G HENRY GALES, 'The Derby Cabinet of 1867', w/c, NPG 4893.

PR W.WALKER, after R.Buckner, hl, oval, mezz, pub 1853, BM, NPG. E.LACRETELLE, hl seated, etch, pub 1874, NPG. UNKNOWN, hl, lith, for *Civil Service Review*, 1877, BM. G.COOK, after a photograph by S.A.Walker, tql seated, stipple and line, NPG.

C CARLO PELLEGRINI ('Ape'), wl, chromo-lith, for *Vanity Fair*, 20 Nov 1869, NPG. THÉOBALD CHARTRAN ('T'), wl seated in 'Birth, Behaviour and Business', chromo-lith, for *Vanity Fair*, 5 July 1881, NPG. 'BEDE', 'A Fox Hunting Constellation', mechanical repro, for *Vanity Fair*, 7 Dec 1905, NPG. SIR MAX BEERBOHM, 1926, drg, Sheffield City Art Gallery. Several popular prints, NPG.

PH BASSANO, hs, print, for *Our Conservative and Unionist Statesmen*, vol III, NPG (Album 20). ELLIOTT & FRY, tql seated, cabinet, NPG. LOCK & WHITFIELD, hs, oval, woodburytype, for *Men of Mark*, 1878, NPG. LONDON STEREOSCOPIC CO, tql seated, cabinet, NPG.

RUSSELL & SONS, 1891, hs, woodburytype, NPG. RUSSELL & SONS, hs, print, for *Our Conservative Statesmen*, vol I, NPG (Album 16).

RYAN, Vincent William (1816-1888) divine.

P UNKNOWN, 1854, hl, Hertford College, Oxford.

RYDER, Sir Alfred Phillipps (1820-1888) admiral.

PR 'R.T.', after a photograph by Symonds & Son, hs, profile, wood engr, for *Illust London News*, 12 May 1888, NPG.

RYDER, Dudley Francis Stuart, see 3rd Earl of Harrowby

RYDER, John (1814-1885) actor.

PR Several prints, Harvard Theatre Collection, Cambridge, Mass, USA.

RYLANDS, Peter (1820-1887) politician.

PR 'R.T.', after a photograph by Russell & Sons, hs, profile, wood engr, for *Illust London News*, 19 Feb 1887, NPG.

C SIR LESLIE WARD ('Spy'), wl, profile, w/c study, for *Vanity Fair*, 25 Jan 1879, NPG 4742.

RYLE, Herbert Edward (1856-1925) dean of Westminster.

P WILLIAM CARTER, RA 1913, hl, Farnham Castle, Hants. H.G.RIVIERE, Queen's College, Cambridge.

C 'WH', wl, chromo-lith, for *Vanity Fair*, 27 March 1912, NPG. SIR MAX BEERBOHM, 1924, 'Our Abbey', drg, Art Gallery of New South Wales, Sydney, Australia.

PH UNKNOWN, hs, print, NPG (Anglican Bishops).

RYLE, John Charles (1816-1900) bishop of Liverpool.

P UNKNOWN, hl, a leaving portrait, Eton College, Berks.

PR W.HOLL, after a photograph, hl seated, stipple, NPG. UNKNOWN, hs, stipple, NPG.

C CARLO PELLEGRINI ('Ape'), tql, w/c study, for *Vanity Fair*, 26 March 1881, NPG 4743.

PH BARRAUD, hs, print, for *Men and Women of the Day*, vol I, 1888, NPG AX5420. DELANY & CO, tql seated, carte, NPG AX7497. DELANY & CO, wl, carte, NPG. LOCK & WHITFIELD, hs, oval, woodburytype, for *Men of Mark*, 1883, NPG. UNKNOWN, tql print, NPG (Anglican Bishops).

SACKVILLE of Knole, Sir Lionel Sackville Sackville-West, 2nd Baron (1827-1908) diplomat.
D P.A.DE LÁSZLÓ, pastel, Knole (NT), Kent.

SACKVILLE-WEST, Sir Charles Richard, see 6th Earl and 12th Baron DE La Warr.

SADLER, Thomas (1822-1891) divine.
PR R.T., hs, wood engr, for *Illust London News*, 19 Sept 1891, NPG.

ST ALDWYN, Sir Michael Edward Hicks Beach, 1st Earl (1837-1916) statesman.
P SIR A.S.COPE, 1906, tql, NPG 2948.
D S.P.HALL, three pencil sketches, two hs, one hl, NPG 2320.
PR UNKNOWN, hl, lith, for *Civil Service Review*, 1877, BM.
C SIR FRANCIS CARRUTHERS GOULD, hl seated with Balfour and Chamberlain, NPG 2864. CARLO PELLEGRINI ('Ape'), wl, semi-profile, chromo-lith, for *Vanity Fair*, 22 Aug 1874, NPG.
PH BASSANO, tql seated, profile, cabinet, NPG X4981. LOCK & WHITFIELD, hs, oval, woodburytype, for *Men of Mark*, 1876, NPG. BARRAUD, tql seated, profile, print, for *Men and Women of the Day*, vol IV, 1891, NPG AX5521. W.& D.DOWNEY, tql woodbury-type, for Cassell's *Cabinet Portrait Gallery*, vol III, 1892, NPG. SIR BENJAMIN STONE, 1897 and 1898, two prints, both wl, NPG. RUSSELL & SONS, hs, profile, print, for *Our Conservative Statesmen*, vol I, NPG (Album 16).

ST HELIER, Francis Henry Jeune, Baron (1843-1905) judge.
P SIR HUBERT VON HERKOMER, 1895, tql seated in President's robes, Inner Temple, London.
SC EMIL FUCHS, marble bust, DoE (Law Courts, London).
C (Possibly H.C.SEPPING) WRIGHT ('Stuff'), hs at bench, chromo-lith, for *Vanity Fair*, 11 April 1891, NPG.

SAINTON, Prosper Philippe Catherine (1813-1890) violinist.
G C.BAUGNIET, 'The Musical Union, 1851', lith, BM.

SAINTON-DOLBY, Charlotte Helen (1821-1885) contralto singer.
PR C.BAUGNIET, tql, lith, pub 1844, BM. S.GAZENAVE, after a photograph by Mayall, tql, lith, NPG. Several theatrical prints, liths, Harvard theatre collection, Cambridge, Mass, USA.
PH Two cartes by unknown photographers, wl, profile, and wl seated, NPG.

SAINTSBURY, George Edward Bateman (1845-1933) literary critic and historian.
P SIR WILLIAM NICHOLSON, 1925, hs, Merton College, Oxford.
PH WALTER STONEMAN, 1919, hs, NPG (NPR).

SALA, George Augustus Henry (1828-1896) journalist.
D S.P.HALL, two drgs, hl, profile, and hl, semi-profile, seated, made at the sessions of the Parnell Commission, pencil, NPG 2260-1. POLLIE VERNAY, 1894, wl, back-view, ink, NPG 1689a.
G P.NAUMANN and R.TAYLOR & Co, 'Our Literary Contributors – Past and Present', hs, one of a series of woodcuts, for *Illust London News*, 14 May 1892, NPG.
PR D.J.POUND, after a photograph by J. & C.Watkins, tql, stipple

and line, NPG. Several popular prints, NPG.
C HARRY FURNISS, pen and ink sketch, NPG 3507. CARLO PELLEGRINI ('Ape'), wl, profile, chromo-lith, for *Vanity Fair*, 25 Sept 1875, NPG.
PH UNKNOWN, early 1850s, oval, print, NPG X5182. JOHN & CHARLES WATKINS, two cartes, both wl seated, NPG. UNKNOWN, tql seated, print, NPG.

SALAMAN, Charles Kensington (1814-1901) composer.
PR R.J.LANE, after S.A.Hart, hl, lith, for *The Musical Keepsake*, 1834, BM, NPG.

SALISBURY, Enoch Robert Gibbon (1819-1890) barrister.
PR UNKNOWN, after a photograph by John Watkins, hl, oval, woodcut, for *Illust London News*, May 1857, NPG.

SALISBURY, Robert Arthur Talbot Gascoyne-Cecil, 3rd Marquess of (1830-1903) prime minister.
P J.GRIFFITHS, 1865, hs, V & A. GEORGE RICHMOND, c1872, wl in robes of Chancellor of University of Oxford, Hatfield House, Herts. ANTON VON WERNER, 1878, hs, Hatfield. G.F.WATTS, 1882, hl, semi-profile, in robes, NPG 1349. SIR J.E.MILLAIS, RA 1883?, tql, NPG 3242. HORSBURGH, 1886, tql seated, Hatfield. SIR HUBERT VON HERKOMER, RA 1894?, hs in gown and mortar board, as Chancellor of University of Oxford, DoE (Foreign Office). UNKNOWN, hs, Hatfield.
D Several drgs at Hatfield: GEORGE RICHMOND, 1861, hs, profile, chalk; EMILY BARNARD, 1887, hs, pencil; VIOLET, DUCHESS OF RUTLAND, 1889, hs, profile, pencil; E.FUCHS, 1901, hl seated, profile, pencil. S.P.HALL, several pencil sketches, NPG 2339-42.
SC Three busts at Hatfield: WILLIAM THEED, 1875, marble; ALBERT BRUCE JOY, 1888, bronze; SIR GEORGE FRAMPTON, 1903, bronze. SIR GEORGE FRAMPTON, 1906, seated statue, Hatfield. HERBERT HAMPTON, 1909, marble statue, in Garter robes, DoE (Foreign Office). SIR WILLIAM GOSCOMBE JOHN, RA 1912, bronze effigy, Salisbury Chapel, Hatfield. UNKNOWN, marble bust, NPG 2012.
PR Various prints and popular prints, NPG.
C CARLO PELLEGRINI ('Ape'), wl, profile, chromo-lith, for *Vanity Fair*, 10 July 1869, NPG. PHIL MAY, 1893, wl seated, profile, pen and ink, NPG 1610. SIR LESLIE WARD, wl, w/c, related to cartoon pub *Vanity Fair*, 20 Dec 1900, NPG 5004. Drgs by SIR FRANCIS CARRUTHERS GOULD and HARRY FURNISS, various dates and sizes, NPG 2861-2, 2873, 3409-11 and 3603. HARRY FURNISS, wl seated with Gladstone, in railway carriage, pen and ink, NPG. SIR JOHN TENNIEL, two pencil drgs, political satires, for *Punch*, 8 March 1873, and 28 Nov 1885, V & A, and one pencil cartoon, for *Punch*, 23 April 1892, Fitzwilliam Museum, Cambridge.
PH LONDON STEREOSCOPIC Co, c1870, hs, profile, cabinet, NPG X6853. LOCK & WHITFIELD, hs, oval, woodburytype, for *Men of Mark*, 1877, NPG. ELLIOTT & FRY, hs, carte, NPG. JOHN RUSSELL & SONS, hs, print, for *Our Conservative and Unionist Statesmen*, vol IV, NPG (Album 21). JOHN WATKINS, hs, carte, NPG (Album 99).

SALMON, George (1819-1904) mathematician and divine.
P SARAH PURSER, exhib 1887, tql seated, Trinity College, Dublin. BENJAMIN CONSTANT, 1897, hl, Trinity College.
SC JOHN HUGHES, 1911, marble seated statue, Trinity College. ALBERT BRUCE JOY, posthumous bronze bas-relief (head), on

memorial, St Patrick's Cathedral, Dublin.

SALT, Sir Titus (1803–1876) manufacturer.
sc JOHN ADAMS ACTON, seated statue, Lister Park, Bradford. JOHN ADAMS ACTON, marble bust, City of Bradford Art Gallery. FRANCIS DERWENT WOOD, statue, Roberts Park, Saltaire, Yorks. UNKNOWN, medallion, Bradford Wool Exchange.
PR W.HOLL, after a photograph by Appleton & Co of Bradford, tql seated, stipple, NPG; woodcut after similar photograph for *Illust London News*, 2 Oct 1869, NPG. UNKNOWN, hs, chromolith, NPG.

SALTER, William (1804–1875) painter.
PR UNKNOWN, hs, woodcut, for *Illust London News*, 22 Jan 1876, BM.

SALTING, George (1835–1909) art collector and benefactor.
D JOSEPH OPPENHEIMER, 1905, hs, profile, pencil, NPG 1790.
PH DR ROSENHEIM, two prints, both tql seated, the first holding an oriental vase, the second holding a bronze, BM (Engr Ports Coll).

SAMBOURNE, Edwin Linley (1844–1910) cartoonist and designer.
P SIR GEORGE REID, 1882, hs, oval, MacDonald Collection, Aberdeen Art Gallery.
D Self-portrait, 1891, hl, pen and ink, NPG 3034. Self-portrait, wearing kilt, with gun, pen and ink, The Athenaeum, London.
C HARRY FURNISS, three pen and ink sketches, NPG 3508–9 and 3619. SIR LESLIE WARD ('Spy'), wl, profile, chromo-lith, for *Vanity Fair*, 16 Jan 1892, NPG.
PH ELLIOTT & FRY, two cabinets, tql seated and hl seated, the second in middle age, NPG.

SAMSON, George (1858–1918) see Alexander.

SAMUDA, Joseph d'Aguilar (1813–1885) engineer.
C UNKNOWN, wl, profile, chromo-lith, for *Vanity Fair*, 15 Feb 1873, NPG.

SAMUEL, Marcus, see 1st Viscount Bearsted.

SAMUELSON, Sir Bernhard, 1st Bart (1820–1905) ironmaster and promoter of technical education.
SC FANTACHIOTTI, replica, bust, Queen Victoria Memorial Hospital Annex, Mont Boron, Nice.

SANDAY, William (1843–1920) theological scholar.
P L.CAMPBELL TAYLOR, 1908, tql seated, semi-profile, Christ Church, Oxford.
PH WALTER STONEMAN, 1917, hs, NPG (NPR).

SANDEMAN, Sir Robert Groves (1835–1892) major.
PR UNKNOWN, hs, woodcut, NPG.

SANDERSON, Frederick William (1857–1922) schoolmaster.
P UNKNOWN, after a photograph, Oundle School, Peterborough.

SANDERSON, Sir John Scott Burdon-, see BURDON-Sanderson.

SANDERSON, Thomas James Cobden-, see COBDEN-Sanderson.

SANDERSON, Thomas Sanderson, 1st Baron (1841–1923) under-secretary of state.
C SIR LESLIE WARD ('Spy'), wl, w/c study, for *Vanity Fair*, 10 Nov 1898, NPG 2968.

SANDFORD, Sir Francis Richard John Sandford, 1st Baron (1824–1893) secretary to the Royal Commissioners for the international exhibition.
PR DALZIEL, hs, circle, woodcut, for *What do you think of the Exhibition*, 1862, BM. UNKNOWN, hs, woodcut, for *Illust London News*, 22 March 1862, NPG. R.T., hs, wood engr, for *Illust London*

News, 17 Jan 1891, NPG.

SANDFORD, Sir Herbert Bruce (1826–1892) colonel.
PR UNKNOWN, after a photograph by Gutekunst of Philadelphia, hs woodcut, for *Illust London News*, 29 July 1876, NPG.

SANDHURST, Sir William Rose Mansfield, 1st Baron (1819–1876) general.
D EGRON LUNDGREN, 1858, hs, w/c, National Museum, Stockholm THEODORE BLAKE WIRGMAN, with Lord Clyde, pencil, SNPG 1976.
PR UNKNOWN, after a photograph by Hering, hs, woodcut, for *Illust London News*, 13 May 1865, NPG. UNKNOWN, after a photograph by Thomas Cranfield, tql seated in uniform, woodcut, for *Illust London News*, 29 April 1871, NPG.
C CARLO PELLEGRINI ('Ape'), wl seated, chromo-lith, for *Vanity Fair*, 30 May 1874, NPG.
PH UNKNOWN, with Lord Clyde and Sir James Hope Grant, print NPG X1588. Several prints, National Army Museum, London.

SANDS, Sir Christopher Nicholson Johnston, Lord (1857–1934) Scottish judge.
P HENRY LINTOTT, exhib 1930, Church of Scotland Assembly Hall Edinburgh. HENRY LINTOTT, tql, Faculty of Advocates, Parliament Hall, Edinburgh.

SANDWITH, Humphry (1822–1881) army physician.
PR D.J.POUND, after a photograph by Watkins, hl, stipple, NPG.

SANDYS, (Anthony) Frederick (Augustus) (1829–1904) painter.
P ANTHONY SANDYS (his father), 1848, hl seated, NPG 1741. Self portrait, 1848, hs, Castle Museum, Norwich. Self-portrait, hs Uffizi Gallery, Florence.
M ANTHONY SANDYS, hs, as a child, drg, Fitzwilliam Museum Cambridge.
PR ANTHONY SANDYS, c1848–9, hl, etch, Fitzwilliam Museum.
PH UNKNOWN, hs, print, BM (Engr Ports coll).

SANDYS, Sir John Edwin (1844–1922) classical scholar.
PH WALTER STONEMAN, 1917, hs, NPG (NPR).

SANT, James (1820–1916) painter.
P Self-portraits: wl seated in studio, NPG 4093, and hs, oval MacDonald Collection, Aberdeen Art Gallery.
G G.GRENVILLE MANTON, 'Conversazione at the Royal Academy 1891', w/c, NPG 2820.
PR UNKNOWN, tql seated, woodcut, for *The Graphic*, 7 May 1870 NPG.
PH ELLIOTT & FRY, hs, profile, carte, NPG (Album 103). LOCK & WHITFIELD, hs, oval, woodburytype, for *Men of Mark*, 1877, NPG RALPH W.ROBINSON, wl seated, print, for *Members and Associate of the Royal Academy of Arts, 1891*, NPG X7390. JOHN RUSSELL & SONS, hl, print, for *National Photographic Record*, vol I, NPG. JOHN & CHARLES WATKINS, tql seated, carte, NPG (Album 104).

SANTLEY, Sir Charles (1834–1922) singer.
PR UNKNOWN, hs, chromo-lith, NPG.
C SIR LESLIE WARD ('Spy'), wl seated, chromo-lith, for *Vanity Fair* 27 Feb 1902, NPG.
PH Various cartes by ELLIOTT & FRY, H.N.KING, MAYER BROTHERS HERBERT WATKINS and H.J.WHITLOCK, various dates and sizes some in character, NPG. ELLIOTT & FRY, hs, cabinet, NPG BARRAUD, hs, print, for *Men and Women of the Day*, vol III, 1890 NPG AX5509. W. & D.DOWNEY, hl, woodburytype, for Cassell' *Cabinet Portrait Gallery*, vol V, 1894, NPG.

SAPHIR, Adolph (1831–1891) theologian.
PR UNKNOWN, after a photograph by T.Rodger, hs, oval, proce print, NPG.

PH EDWARD SEELEY, tql seated, profile, carte, NPG.

SARGANT, Sir Charles Henry (1856-1942) judge.
D SIR WILLIAM ROTHENSTEIN, chalk, New College, Oxford.
PH ELLIOTT & FRY, wl seated in robes, print, NPG.

SARGEAUNT, John (1857-1922) teacher and scholar.
SC F.W.POMEROY, c1924, relief panel, Westminster School, London.

SARGENT, John Singer (1856-1925) painter.
P Several self-portraits: 1886, hs, oval, MacDonald Collection, Aberdeen Art Gallery; 1892, hs, National Academy of Design, New York, USA; 1906, hs, Uffizi Gallery, Florence.
G SIR HUBERT VON HERKOMER, 'The Council of the Royal Academy', oil, 1908, TATE 2481.
SC AUGUSTUS SAINT-GAUDENS, 1880, bronze medal, American Academy of Arts and Letters, New York; copies, Metropolitan Museum of Art, New York, Museum of Fine Arts, Boston and Salle du Jeu de Paume, Paris.
PR W.ROTHENSTEIN, 1897-8, hl, lith, BM, NPG. GIOVANNI BOLDINI, 1902, hs, profile, drypoint, Museo Boldini, Ferrara.
C SIR MAX BEERBOHM, several cartoons: c1900, drg, TATE 3199; tql, 'A Great Realist', Hentschel-Colourtype, for Vanity Fair, 24 Feb 1909, NPG; 1911, 'Mr Sargent in Venice', drg, Johannesburg Art Gallery; c1912, 'The Strong man of the Royal Academy', drg, Ashmolean Museum, Oxford; wl, profile, drg, V & A. SIR BERNARD PARTRIDGE, wl at easel, pen and ink, for Punch, 1925, (unpublished), NPG.
PH J.E.PURDY of Boston, 1903, tql seated, print, NPG X11845. ALVIN LANGDON COBURN, 1907, hs, photogravure, for Men of Mark, 1913, NPG AX7779.

SARTORIS, Adelaide, née Kemble (1814?-1879) singer and writer.
PR Various prints and theatrical prints, BM, NPG, Harvard Theatre Collection, Cambridge, Mass, USA.
PH CAMILLE SILVY, 1860, wl, carte, NPG (Album 1). J.G. & E.SHORT, wl, profile, carte, NPG.

SASSOON, Sir Albert Abdullah David, 1st Bart (1818-1896) philanthropist.
PR UNKNOWN, after a photograph by Dickinson and Foster, hs, wood engr, for Illust London News, 31 Oct 1896, NPG.
C SIR LESLIE WARD ('Spy'), wl, profile, chromo-lith, for Vanity Fair, 16 Aug 1879, NPG. 'PET', wl, chromo-lith, for Supplement to The Monetary Gazette, 4 April 1877, NPG.

SATOW, Sir Ernest Mason (1843-1929) diplomat and historian.
C SIR LESLIE WARD ('Spy'), wl, profile, chromo-lith, for Vanity Fair, 23 April 1903, NPG.

SAUNDERS, William Wilson (1809-1879) entomologist.
PH MAULL & POLYBLANK, 1855, tql seated, print, NPG P120 (4).

SAUNDERSON, Edward James (1837-1906) Irish politician.
SC SIR WILLIAM GOSCOMBE JOHN, 1910, bronze statue, Portadown, N Ireland.
PR W.BURTON, after a photograph by Elliott & Fry, hs, profile, etch, NPG.
C CARLO PELLEGRINI ('Ape'), wl, profile, chromo-lith, for Vanity Fair, 26 Feb 1887, NPG.

SAVILE of Rufford, John Savile, 1st Baron (1818-1896) diplomat.
SC SAIBAS VAN DEN KERKHOVE, bronze bust, DoE (British Embassy, Brussels).

SAVILE of Rufford, John Savile Lumley-Savile, 2nd Baron (1853-1931) diplomat and sportsman.

C SIR LESLIE WARD ('Spy'), wl, w/c study, for Vanity Fair, 15 April 1908, NPG 4608.
PH J.RUSSELL & SONS, 1904, with Edward VII and others in large shooting-party group, neg, NPG x8461. J.RUSSELL & SONS, with Edward VII and others in large house party group, neg, NPG x8466.

SAVORY, Sir William Scovell, 1st Bart (1826-1895) surgeon.
P W.W.OULESS, 1893, tql seated, St Bartholomew's Hospital, London.
G HENRY JAMYN BROOKS, 'Council of the Royal College of Surgeons of England 1884-85', oil, Royal College of Surgeons, London.
SC H.R.HOPE PINKER, marble bust, St Bartholomew's Hospital; replica, 1896, Royal College of Surgeons.

SAXE-COBURG-GOTHA, Duke of, see ALFRED Ernest Albert.

SAXE-WEIMAR, Prince Edward of, see Edward.

SAYCE, Archibald Henry (1845-1933) orientalist and comparative philologist.
P MRS ATTWOOD MATHEWS, c1902, tql seated, Queen's College, Oxford. GEORGE FIDDES WATT, 1919, tql seated, Queen's College.

SAYERS, Tom (1826-1865) boxer.
SC A.BEZZI, plaster cast of statuette, NPG 2465; bronze cast, NPG 2465a.
PR R.CHILDS, wl, coloured lith, pub 1860, BM.
PH UNKNOWN, c1860, tql seated, print, V & A.

SCHAFER, Sir Edward Albert Sharpey-, see SHARPEY-Schafer.

SCHARF, Sir George (1820-1895) art historian; first director of the National Portrait Gallery.
P W.W.OULESS, 1885, hl seated, NPG 985.
D Self-portrait, 1869, wl seated, pen and ink, NPG 5344. Self-portrait, 1872, hl seated, w/c, NPG 3865. Self-portraits, two w/cs, both hs, NPG 3863-4. Self-portrait, wl, ink and w/c, BM. A.LANGDON, hl seated, chalk, NPG 4583.
G HENRY JAMYN BROOKS, 'Private view of the Old Masters Exhibition, Royal Academy, 1888', oil, NPG 1833.
PH Various cartes by ERNEST EDWARDS, MAULL & POLYBLANK, NADAR, SOUTHWELL BROS and unknown photographers, various dates and sizes, NPG (Albums 116 and 117). MAULL & POLYBLANK, 1861, tql seated, print, NPG. UNKNOWN, 1876, tql seated, profile, oval, cabinet, NPG X1368. BASSANO, 1885, two cabinets, tql and tql seated, NPG. J.FISHER, 1889, wl, profile, oval, cabinet, NPG. J.C.STODART, tql seated with an unknown man, cabinet, NPG.

SCHARLIEB, Dame Mary Ann Dacomb (1845-1930) gynaecological surgeon.
P H.G.RIVIERE, 1908, tql seated, Royal Free Hospital (School of Medicine), London.

SCHLESWIG-HOLSTEIN, Princess Christian of, see Princess HELENA Augusta Victoria.

SCHLICH, Sir William (1840-1925) forester.
PH WALTER STONEMAN, 1921, hs, NPG (NPR).

SCHMITZ, Leonhard (1807-1890) scholar.
PR R.T., hs, wood engr, for Illust London News, 7 June 1890, NPG.

SCHNADHORST, Francis (1840-1900) secretary of the National Liberal Association.
C (Possibly H.C.SEPPING) WRIGHT ('Stuff'), wl seated, w/c study, for Vanity Fair, 2 July 1892, NPG 1774a.

PH W. & D.DOWNEY, hl, woodburytype, for Cassell's *Cabinet Portrait Gallery*, vol III, 1892, NPG.

SCHOLEFIELD, William (1809-1867) politician.
SC PETER HOLLINS, 1860, bust, Birmingham City Art Gallery.
PR D.J.POUND, after a photograph by Whitlock of Birmingham, tql seated, stipple and line, for *The Drawing Room Portrait Gallery of Eminent Personages*, NPG.

SCHOMBURGK, Sir Robert Hermann (1804-1865) traveller.
D WILLIAM BROCKEDON, 1840, hl, chalk, NPG 2515 (91).
PR M.GAUCI, after a drg by E.U.Eddis, hl, lith, pub 1840, BM.

SCHORLEMMER, Carl (1834-1892) chemist.
PH WALKER & BOUTALL, after a photograph by Warwick Brookes, hs, photogravure, NPG.

SCHREIBER, Lady Charlotte Elizabeth, née Bertie (1812-1895) Welsh scholar and collector.
PR W.WALKER, after R.Buckner, tql in evening dress, mezz, pub 1852, BM.

SCHREINER, William Philip (1857-1919) South African lawyer and statesman.
P JOHN ST HELIER LANDER, Downing College, Cambridge.
PH JOHN RUSSELL & SONS, hs, print, for *National Photographic Record*, vol II, NPG.

SCHUSTER, Sir Arthur (1851-1934) mathematical physicist.
P JOHN COLLIER, 1907, Manchester University.

SCHUSTER, Sir Felix Otto, 1st Bart (1854-1936) banker.
C SIR LESLIE WARD ('Spy'), wl, mechanical repro, for *Vanity Fair*, 28 June 1906, NPG.

SCLATER-BOOTH, George, see 1st Baron Basing.

SCOTT, Archibald (1837-1909) Scottish divine and leader of the general assembly of the Church of Scotland.
P SIR GEORGE REID, 1902, Church of Scotland, Edinburgh.
SC JAMES PITTENDRIGH MACGILLIVRAY, 1907, bronze bust, St George's Church, Edinburgh.

SCOTT, Charles Prestwich (1846-1932) journalist, editor of the *Manchester Guardian*.
P T.C.DUGDALE, Manchester Press Club.
D EDMOND KAPP, 1931, Barber Institute of Fine Arts, Birmingham.
SC SIR JACOB EPSTEIN, c1926, bronze bust, Manchester City Art Gallery.
PR FRANCIS DODD, 1916, wl seated, etch, NPG 3997.
PH UNKNOWN, hl seated at his desk, print, The Guardian Newspaper.

SCOTT, Lord Charles Thomas Montagu-Douglas (1839-1911) admiral.
P SIR FRANCIS GRANT, 1842, wl with spaniel, Buccleuch Estates, Selkirk, Scotland.
D GEORGE RICHMOND, 1853, hs, semi-profile, oval, chalk, Buccleuch Estates.

SCOTT, Clement William (1841-1904) dramatic critic.
G P.NAUMANN and R.TAYLOR & CO, 'Our Literary Contributors – Past and Present', hs, one of a series of woodcuts, for *Illust London News*, 14 May 1892, BM, NPG.

SCOTT, David (1806-1849) artist.
P Self-portrait, 1832, SNPG 1450. ROBERT SCOTT LAUDER, 1839, tql, SNPG 1608. CHARLES LEES, hl seated, Royal Scottish Academy, Edinburgh.
SC SIR JOHN STEELL, plaster bust, SNPG 1312. SIR JOHN STEELL, marble bust, NGS.
PR UNKNOWN, head, woodcut, for *Art Journal*, 1849, BM.

W.B.SCOTT, after D.Scott, head, etch, for *Memoir* of him b[y] W.B.Scott, 1850, BM. W.B.SCOTT, on his deathbed, from [a] pencil sketch, etch, BM.

SCOTT, Dukinfield Henry (1854-1934) palaeobotanist.
P JAMES KERR-LAWSON, hs, semi-profile, Jodrell laboratory, Kew Gardens.

SCOTT, Sir George Gilbert (1811-1878) architect.
P GEORGE RICHMOND, RA 1878, hl seated, RIBA, London; 1877, hs, chalk study, NPG 1061 and small variant version (oil), c1870, Royal Academy, London.
D C.B.BIRCH, 1859, hs, pencil, NPG 2475.
SC G.G.ADAMS, RA 1884, medallion, NPG (for the Art Union).
PR J.D.MILLER, after W.B.Richmond, hs, mezz, pub 1880, BM. Three woodcuts after photographs by John Watkins, M[r] Dolamore, and London Stereoscopic Co, for *Illust London News*, 23 Feb 1861, 3 Aug 1872 and 13 April 1878, NPG.
PH ERNEST EDWARDS, wl, print, for *Men of Eminence*, ed L.Reeve, vol I, 1863, NPG. LONDON STEREOSCOPIC CO, wl, carte, NPG (Album 102). UNKNOWN, tql seated, print, NPG AX7340.

SCOTT, Henry Young Darracott (1822-1883) major general.
PR UNKNOWN, hs, wood engr, for *Illust London News*, 5 May 1883, NPG.

SCOTT, Sir John (1841-1904) judicial adviser to the Khedive.
D MISS E.G.HILL (his sister-in-law), 1883, hl seated in robes, chalk, Pembroke College, Oxford.

SCOTT, Sir Percy Moreton, 1st Bart (1853-1924) admiral.
P JOHN COLLIER, 1904, HMS *Excellent*, Portsmouth.
C SIR LESLIE WARD ('Spy'), wl, w/c study, for *Vanity Fair*, 17 Sep 1903, NPG 2998.

SCOTT, Robert (1811-1887) divine.
P UNKNOWN, tql seated in robes, Balliol College, Oxford.
PR UNKNOWN, after a photograph by Samuel A.Walker, hs, profile, wood engr, for *Illust London News*, 17 Dec 1887, NPG.

SCOTT, Walter Francis, see 5th Duke of Buccleuch.

SCOTT, William Bell (1811-1890) poet and artist.
P Self-portrait, 1867, SNPG 1849. DAVID SCOTT, c1832, hl, NGS 2118, on loan to SNPG (L314).
D THOMAS SIBSON, hs, pen and ink, V & A.
PR Self-portrait, hs, aged 20, oval, etch, BM. W.B.SCOTT, afte[r] A.Boyd, hl, etch, 1875, BM. Self-portraits, 1875, two etching[s,] both hl in skull-cap, one in profile, BM.
PH W. & D.DOWNEY, 1863, wl, with D.G.Rossetti and Joh[n] Ruskin, carte, NPG (Album 110).

SCRATCHLEY, Sir Peter Henry (1835-1885) major general.
PR UNKNOWN, hs, wood engr, for *Illust London News*, 12 Dec 188[5,] NPG.

SCRUTTON, Sir Thomas Edward (1856-1934) judge.
C 'APE JUNIOR', wl, profile, in robes, Hentschel-Colourtype, fo[r] *Vanity Fair*, 28 June 1911, NPG.
PH OLIVE EDIS, two prints, hs and hs, profile, NPG. WALTE[R] STONEMAN, 1917, hs, NPG (NPR).

SCULLY, Vincent (1810-1871) Irish political writer.
PH MAULL & POLYBLANK, wl seated, carte, NPG AX8681.

SEALE-HAYNE, Charles Hayne (1833-1903) libera[l] politician.
PH SIR BENJAMIN STONE, wl, print, Birmingham Reference Library.

SEDDING, John Dando (1838-1891) architect.
SC H.R.HOPE PINKER, bust, The Art Workers' Guild, London.

SEDDON, Richard John (1845-1906) premier of New Zealand.
P ELLEN VON MAYERN, hs, City of Auckland Art Gallery, New Zealand.
SC UNKNOWN, memorial bust, St Paul's Cathedral, London.
C UNKNOWN, wl, semi-profile, chromo-lith, for *Vanity Fair*, 17 April 1902, NPG.
PH GUNN & STUART, hl, photogravure, NPG.

SEDGWICK, Adam (1854-1913) zoologist.
D WILLIAM STRANG, 1909, hs, chalk, Department of Zoology, University of Cambridge.

SEDGWICK, Amy (afterwards Mrs Parkes, Mrs Pemberton and Mrs Goostry) (1830-1897) actress.
D WALTER GOODMAN, hs, pastel, Garrick Club, London.
SC UNKNOWN, marble bust, Brighton Art Gallery.
PR D.J.POUND, after a photograph by Juliane, tql seated as Hester in Taylor's *An Unequal Match*, stipple and line, supplement to *Illustrated News of the World*, BM, NPG. UNKNOWN, tql seated, woodcut, for Balou's *Pictorial Drawing-Room Companion*, 1858, Harvard Theatre Collection, Cambridge, Mass, USA.
PH Two cartes by unknown photographers, wl and tql seated, NPG.

SEELEY, Sir John Robert (1834-1895) historian.
P CLARA EWALD, 1896, hl seated, Divinity School, University of Cambridge; versions, Christ's College, Cambridge and Gonville and Caius College, Cambridge.
C G.MILNER GIBSON, ink, Christ's College.
PH CRELLIN, tql seated, carte, NPG (Album 99). W. & D.DOWNEY, hs, carte, NPG (Album 102). ELLIOTT & FRY, hs, profile, carte, NPG (Album 40). UNKNOWN, print, Christ's College.

SEEMANN, Berthold Carl (1825-1871) botanist.
PR VINCENT BROOKS, hs, lith, NPG.

SELBORNE, Sir Roundell Palmer, 1st Earl of (1812-1895) lord chancellor.
P W.W.OULESS, 1872, tql seated in chancellor's robes, Magdalen College, Oxford. H.T.WELLS, RA 1874, wl in chancellor's robes, Mercers' Hall, London. E.M.BUSK, RA 1889, hl seated in chancellor's robes, Trinity College, Oxford; copy by J.M.Stewart, NPG 1448. H.A.OLIVIER, RA 1892, with Bishop Gore-Browne, the Athenaeum, London. G.F.WATTS, 1893, hl seated, Lincoln's Inn, London.
D H.W.PETHERICK, 1884, head, pencil, NPG 2138.
G JOHN PHILLIP, 'The House of Commons, 1860', oil, Palace of Westminster, London.
PR W.HOLL, after G.Richmond, hs, stipple, one of 'Grillion's Club' series, BM. N.SANDERS, after Sir F.Grant, hs, mezz, pub 1864, NPG.
C UNKNOWN, wl, chromo-lith, for *Vanity Fair*, 16 March 1872, NPG. THÉOBALD CHARTRAN ('T'), 'Purse, Pussy, Piety and Prevarication', chromo-lith, for *Vanity Fair*, 5 July 1882, NPG.
PH ALEXANDER BASSANO, tql in robes, carte, NPG X 12651. L.CALDESI & CO, wl, carte, NPG (Album 120). ELLIOTT & FRY, hs, photogravure, NPG X 12652. LOCK & WHITFIELD, hs, oval, woodburytype, for *Men of Mark*, 1876. NPG. MAULL & POLYBLANK, wl, carte, NPG (Album 136). W. WALKER & SONS, tql, carte, NPG X 12650. JOHN & CHARLES WATKINS, hs, carte, NPG (Album 99).

SELBORNE, William Waldegrave Palmer, 2nd Earl of (1859-1942) statesman.
P P.A.DE LÁSZLÓ, 1911, wl in garter robes, Mercer's Hall, London. P.A.DE LÁSZLÓ, 1931, hs, Church House, Westminster.
C SIR LESLIE WARD ('Spy'), wl, chromo-lith, for *Vanity Fair*, 3 Oct 1901, NPG.
PH BASSANO, hs, print, for *Our Conservative and Unionist Statesmen*,

vol II, NPG (Album 25). LONDON STEREOSCOPIC CO, tql, print, NPG. LONDON STEREOSCOPIC CO, hs, cabinet, NPG. JOHN RUSSELL & SONS, hs, print, for *National Photographic Record*, vol I, NPG. WALTER STONEMAN, three portraits, 1917, 1928 and 1939, all hs, NPG (NPR).

SELBY, William Court Gully, 1st Viscount (1835-1909) speaker of the House of Commons.
P JOHN COLLIER, 1898, tql in speaker's robes, Inner Temple, London. SIR GEORGE REID, wl, Palace of Westminster, London.
C SIR LESLIE WARD ('Spy'), wl, semi-profile, chromo-lith, for *Vanity Fair*, 17 Sept 1896, NPG.
PH BASSANO, hs, cabinet, NPG. SIR BENJAMIN STONE, four prints, all wl, NPG.

SELFRIDGE, Harry Gordon (1858-1947) businessman.
P SIR WILLIAM ORPEN, 1927, tql, Selfridges, London.
D EDMOND KAPP, 1928, Barber Institute of Fine Arts, Birmingham.
C ROBERT S.SHERRIFFS, wl seated, ink and pencil, NPG 5224(1). ALICK P.F.RITCHIE, wl, chromo-lith, for *Vanity Fair*, 6 Dec 1911, NPG.

SELLAR, William Young (1825-1890) professor of Latin in Edinburgh University.
PR W.HOLE, tql, etch, for *Quasi Cursores*, 1884, NPG. R.T., hs, wood engr, for *Illust London News*, 25 Oct 1890, NPG.

SELOUS, Frederick Courtenay (1851-1917) hunter and explorer.
D OLIVIA M.BRYDEN, posthumous, hs, pastel, NPG 2795.
SL UNKNOWN, hs, NPG.
SC W.R.COLTON, RA 1919, memorial bronze bust, BM (Natural History).
C UNKNOWN, wl in hunting dress, chromo-lith, for *Vanity Fair*, 26 April 1894, NPG.

SELOUS, Henry Courtney (1811-1890) painter and lithographer.
P Self-portrait, 1871, hs, NPG 4848.

SELWIN-IBBETSON, Sir Henry John, 7th Bart, see Baron Rookwood.

SELWYN, Sir Charles Jasper (1813-1869) lawyer.
PR UNKNOWN, hs in robes, woodcut, for *Illust London News*, 24 Aug 1867, NPG.
PH MAYLAND, wl with Canon Selwyn, carte, NPG (Album 120).

SELWYN, George Augustus (1809-1878) bishop of Lichfield.
P GEORGE RICHMOND, 1855, hl, St John's College, Cambridge. UNKNOWN, over a photograph by Mason & Co, c1867, hs, oval, oil, NPG 2780.
PR S.COUSINS, after G.Richmond, tql, mezz, pub 1842, BM, NPG. several prints after photographs, BM, NPG. UNKNOWN, hs, woodcut, for *Illust London News*, 14 Dec 1867, NPG.
PH MASON & CO, tql seated, carte, NPG. UNKNOWN, hs, carte, NPG (Album 38).

SELWYN, William (1806-1875) divine.
SC ALBERT BRUCE JOY, 1878, marble bust, Divinity School, University of Cambridge.

SEMON, Sir Felix (1849-1921) laryngologist.
P SIR HUBERT VON HERKOMER, RA 1906, hl, The Royal Society of Medicine, London.
C SIR LESLIE WARD ('Spy'), wl, chromo-lith, for *Vanity Fair*, 1 May 1902, NPG.

SENDALL, Sir Walter Joseph (1832-1904) colonial governor.

SC EDOUARD LANTERI, 1902, marble bust, NPG 4859.

SETON, George (1822-1908) advocate.
D THOMAS CRAWFORD HAMILTON, 1890, pencil, SNPG 1815.

SEVERN, Ann Mary, see Newton.

SEWELL, James Edwards (1810-1903) warden of New College, Oxford.
P SIR HUBERT VON HERKOMER, 1886, hl seated in robes, New College, Oxford; related etch, BM.
C SIR LESLIE WARD ('Spy'), wl, profile, chromo-lith, for *Vanity Fair*, 5 April 1894, NPG.

SEYMOUR, Edward Adolphus Seymour, see 12th Duke of Somerset.

SEYMOUR, Sir Edward Hobart (1840-1929) admiral of the fleet.
P HERMAN G.HERKOMER, hl, The Admiralty, Devonport.
C SIR LESLIE WARD ('Spy'), wl in uniform, chromo-lith, for *Vanity Fair*, 31 Oct 1901, NPG.

SEYMOUR, Sir Francis (1813-1890) general.
PR UNKNOWN, hs in uniform, with medals, wood engr, for *Illust London News*, 26 July 1890, NPG.
C CARLO PELLEGRINI ('Ape'), wl, profile, chromo-lith, for *Vanity Fair*, 11 Aug 1877, NPG.

SEYMOUR, Frederick Beauchamp Paget, see Baron Alcester.

SEYMOUR, Sir Michael (1802-1887) admiral.
P MISS MAUD PORTER, after a crayon drg by de Solomé of 1864, The Admiralty, Portsmouth.

SEYMOUR, William Digby (1822-1895) lawyer.
PR UNKNOWN, after a daguerreotype by Beard, hs, woodcut, NPG.

SHADWELL, Charles Lancelot (1840-1919) college archivist and translator of Dante.
P GEORGE FIDDES WATT, tql seated, semi-profile, in robes, Oriel College, Oxford.

SHAFTESBURY, Antony Ashley Cooper, 7th Earl of (1801-1885) philanthropist and reformer.
P Attrib SIR FRANCIS GRANT, *c*1840-50, wl, Palace of Westminster, London. G.F.WATTS, 1862, hs, semi-profile, NPG 1012. JOHN COLLIER, 1877, tql, NPG 1728. SIR J.E.MILLAIS, 1877, tql, British and Foreign Bible Society, London. T.RODWELL, Broadlands, Hants.
D FREDERICK SARGENT, hl seated, pencil, NPG 1834cc.
G SIR GEORGE HAYTER, 'The House of Commons, 1833', oil, NPG 54.
SC MATTHEW NOBLE, 1859, marble bust, Wimborne St Giles Parish Church, Dorset. SIR J.E.BOEHM, 1875, plaster bust, NPG 862. WALTER MERRETT, plaster bust, Guildhall Art Gallery, London.
PR W.J.EDWARDS, after F.Sandys, hs, stipple, pub 1855, BM, NPG. F.C.LEWIS, after J.Slater, hs, stipple, for 'Grillion's Club' series, BM, NPG. H.ROBINSON, after G.Richmond, hs, stipple, BM, NPG. J.THOMSON, after Sir W.C.Ross, hl in cloak, octagon, stipple, for *Eminent Conservative Statesmen*, BM. Several popular prints and prints after photographs, BM, NPG.
C JOHN DOYLE, several political satires, drgs, BM. CARLO PELLEGRINI ('Ape'), wl, profile, chromo-lith, for *Vanity Fair*, 13 Nov 1869, NPG.
PH ANNAN & SWAN, after a photograph by Bassano, hs, profile, photogravure, NPG. ASHFORD BROTHERS & CO, wl, carte, NPG. H.HERING, wl, carte, NPG (Album 102). LOCK & WHITFIELD, hs, semi-profile, woodburytype, oval, for *Men of Mark*, 1876, NPG. MAULL & CO, hs, profile, carte, NPG. Attrib MAULL & POLY-

BLANK, tql, print, NPG AX7307. UNKNOWN, tql, carte, NPG (Album 38).

SHAIRP, John Campbell (1819-1885) professor of Latin at St Andrews and professor of poetry at Oxford.
P ROBERT HERDMAN, University of St Andrews.
PR UNKNOWN, tql, mezz, NPG.

SHAND, Alexander Burns Shand, 1st Baron (1828-1904) judge.
P SIR GEORGE REID, nearly tql in robes, Gray's Inn, London.
C SIR LESLIE WARD ('Spy'), wl seated, w/c study, for *Vanity Fair*, 23 July 1903, NPG 2969.

SHANDON, Ignatius John O'Brien, Baron (1857-1930) lord chancellor of Ireland.
PH WALTER STONEMAN, 1918, hs, NPG (NPR).

SHARP, Cecil James (1859-1924) musician, author, and collector and arranger of English folk-songs and dances.
D SIR WILLIAM ROTHENSTEIN, 1920, head, crayon, Cecil Sharp House, London. ESTHER B.MACKINNON, 1921, two drgs: hs, chalk, NPG 2517; hl seated, profile, playing piano, pencil, NPG 2518.
PH Several prints, Cecil Sharp House.

SHARP, William (1855-1905) author and poet writing under the pseudonym of Fiona Macleod.
P D.A.WEHRSCHMIDT, 1898, tql, SNPG 1214.
D WILLIAM STRANG, hs, metalpoint, BM, NPG.
PR W.STRANG, head, semi-profile, etch, BM.

SHARPE, Daniel (1806-1856) geologist.
PR UNKNOWN, after a photograph, hs, semi-profile, galvano-graphic process, BM.
PH MAULL & POLYBLANK, 1855, tql seated, print, NPG P120(19).

SHARPEY, William (1802-1880) physiologist.
SC SIR WILLIAM HAMO THORNYCROFT, RA 1872, marble bust, University College, London; reduced model, plaster, University Museum, Oxford.
PH MAULL & POLYBLANK, 1855, tql, print, NPG P120(21).

SHARPEY-SCHAFER, Sir Edward Albert (1850-1935) physiologist.
SC C.D'O.PILKINGTON JACKSON, bronze medal, NPG 4581, and two bronze medals, dated 1922, SNPG 1826 and 1827.

SHAUGHNESSY, Thomas George Shaughnessy, 1st Baron (1853-1923) Canadian railway administrator.
C SIR LESLIE WARD ('Spy'), wl, Hentschel-Colourtype, for *Vanity Fair*, 26 Aug 1908, NPG.
PH WALTER STONEMAN, 1919, hs, NPG (NPR).

SHAW, Sir Eyre Massey (1830-1908) head of the London Metropolitan Fire Brigade.
P HENRY WEIGALL, RA 1871, London Fire Brigade.
C CARLO PELLEGRINI ('Ape'), wl, profile, chromo-lith, for *Vanity Fair*, 3 June 1871, NPG.
PH BARRAUD, tql, print, for *Men and Women of the Day*, vol III, 1890, NPG.

SHAW, George Bernard (1856-1950) playwright.
P AUGUSTUS JOHN, 1915, three portraits, all hs, Shaw's Corner (NT), Herts, Fitzwilliam Museum, Cambridge and Royal Coll. LADY HAZEL LAVERY, 1925, hs, Manchester City Art Gallery. SIR JOHN LAVERY, wl seated in his study, Municipal Gallery of Modern Art, Dublin. JOHN COLLIER, 1927, NGI 899. DAME LAURA KNIGHT, RA 1933, hs, Hereford Art Gallery. FELIKS TOPOLSKI, 1939, hl with umbrella, Glasgow City Art Gallery. FELIKS TOPOLSKI, 1943, wl, University of Texas, Austin, USA. CLARE WINSTEN,

1945, University of Texas.

D ALBERT LUDOVICI, 1892, wl, pencil and w/c, BM. ALICE PIKE BARNEY, 1908, pastel, National Collection of Fine Arts, Washington DC, USA. DAME LAURA KNIGHT, Castle Museum, Nottingham. SIR WILLIAM ROTHENSTEIN, several drgs: 1916, pencil, Manchester City Art Gallery; 1928, crayon, University of Texas; chalks, Abbey Theatre, Dublin. EDMOND KAPP, 1930, Barber Institute of Fine Arts, Birmingham. FELIKS TOPOLSKI, ink, Royal Academy of Dramatic Art, London.

SC AUGUSTE RODIN, 1906, bronze bust, Rodin Museum, Philadelphia, USA; marble replica, Municipal Gallery of Modern Art, Dublin. JO DAVIDSON, 1929, bronze, University of Texas. JOSEPH COPLANS, 1932, bronze, NGI 8146. J.COPLANS, head, National Book League, London. SIR JACOB EPSTEIN, 1934, bronze busts, NPG 4047; University of Texas; City Museum and Art Gallery, Birmingham; Metropolitan Museum of Art, New York; National Gallery of Canada, Ottawa. PAUL TROUBETZKOY, 1926, bronze, TATE 4274. PAUL TROUBETZKOY, 1927, bronze statue, NGI 8105. PAUL TROUBETZKOY, plaster statuette, seated in an arm chair, Shaw's Corner. KATHLEEN, LADY KENNET, bronze bust, Russell-Cotes Art Gallery, Bournemouth. ROSIE BANKS DANE-COURT, relief figure on brass door knocker, Shaw's Corner. CLARE WINSTEN, 1946, bronze, University of Texas.

W CAROLINE TOWNSHEND, 1910, wl figure, Beatrice Webb House, Leith Hill, Surrey.

PR W.ROTHENSTEIN, 1920, hl, etch, NPG. W.STRANG, hs, etch, NPG.

C SIR MAX BEERBOHM, various cartoons, drgs, most are c1901–1924, New York Public Library, USA; Yale University, New Haven, USA; University of Texas; BM; University of California at Los Angeles; Fitzwilliam Museum; Cornell University Library, USA. HORACE BRODZKY, coloured print, V & A. HARRY FURNISS, several pen and ink sketches, various sizes, NPG 3510–12, 3604. EINAR NERMAN, wl seated, pen and ink?, V & A. SIR BERNARD PARTRIDGE, several w/cs: 1894, wl, NPG 4229; c1925, wl, NPG 4228; Municipal Gallery of Modern Art, Dublin. ROBERT S.SHERRIFFS, two sketches, wl, with the Sitwells, wash, and wl, ink and charcoal?, for The Sketch, 12 Aug 1936, NPG. SIR MAX BEERBOHM ('Ruth'), wl, mechanical repro, for Vanity Fair, 28 Dec 1905, NOG. ALICK P.F.RITCHIE, wl, Hentschel-Colourtype, for Vanity Fair, 16 Aug 1911, NPG.

PH There are numerous photographs in public collections, eg: FREDERICK HENRY EVANS, 1896, hs, print, NPG P113. FREDERICK HOLLYER, several prints, in middle age, V & A. EMERY WALKER, various negs, mostly hs, in middle age, NPG. E.J.STEICHEN, c1902, tql, Royal Photographic Society, Bath. ALVIN LANGDON COBURN, 1904, hs, photogravure, for Men of Mark, NPG AX7768. A.L.COBURN, 1908, hl, print, Royal Photographic Society. A.L.COBURN, wl, profile, seated naked in the pose of Rodin's The Thinker, International Museum of Photography, Rochester, New York. HOWARD COSTER, various prints and negs, c1932–4, various sizes, NPG. MADAME YEVONDE, several prints, NPG. Various prints and negs by G.C.BERESFORD, WALTER BIRD, ALLAN CHAPPELOW, W. & D.DOWNEY, OLIVE EDIS, RICHARD HALL, H.LAMBERT, RUSSELL & SONS, WALTER STONEMAN and others, British Library, NPG, V & A, National Theatre, Royal Academy of Dramatic Arts.

SHAW, James Johnston (1845-1910) county court judge.
P SYDNEY ROWLEY, c1911, Queen's University, Belfast.

SHAW, Mary (1814-1876) dramatic singer.
PR Several theatrical prints, Harvard Theatre Collection, Cambridge, Mass, USA.

SHAW, Richard Norman (1831-1912) architect.
P J.C.HORSLEY, RA 1886, MacDonald Collection, Aberdeen Art

Gallery.
SC SIR WILLIAM HAMO THORNYCROFT, portrait plaque, Old Scotland Yard, London.
PH LOCK & WHITFIELD, hs, oval, woodburytype, for Men of Mark, 1883, NPG. RALPH W.ROBINSON, wl seated, print, for Members and Associates of the Royal Academy of Arts, 1891, NPG X7391.

SHAW, Thomas (1850-1937), see 1st Baron Craigmyle.

SHAW, Sir (William) Napier (1854-1945) meteorologist.
P SIR WALTER RUSSELL, hl, profile, Emmanuel College, Cambridge.
PH WALTER STONEMAN, 1917, hs, NPG (NPR).

SHAW-LEFEVRE, George John, see Baron Eversley.

SHEARMAN, Sir Montague (1857-1930) judge.
C 'WAG', wl, profile, chromo-lith, for Vanity Fair, 4 July 1895, NPG.

SHEE, Sir William (1804-1868) judge.
PR D.J.POUND, after a photograph by Mayall, tql, stipple and line, for Drawing Room Portrait Gallery of Eminent Personages, 1859, NPG. UNKNOWN, after a photograph by John & Charles Watkins, hl, woodcut, for Illust London News, 2 Jan 1864, NPG.

SHEFFIELD, Edward Lyulph Stanley, 4th Baron (1839-1925) politician.
PH WALTER STONEMAN, 1917, hs, NPG (NPR).

SHEPSTONE, Sir Theophilus (1817-1893) South African statesman.
PR UNKNOWN, hs, woodcut, for Illust London News, 30 June 1877, NPG.

SHERBORN, Charles William (1831-1912) engraver.
D ARTHUR ELLIS, 1898, hl seated at work in his studio, wash, BM, engr William Fowler Hopson, 1903, wood engr, University College, London.
PR Self-portrait, 1900, hs, etch, NPG. Self-portrait, hs, etch, BM. S.L.SMITH, hl, etch, BM.
PH UNKNOWN, hl seated in his studio, print, BM (Engr Ports Coll).

SHERBROOKE, Robert Lowe, 1st Viscount (1811-1892) chancellor of the exchequer.
P G.F.WATTS, c1874, hs, profile, NPG 1013. ETHEL MORTLOCK, c1878, Castle Museum, Nottingham.
D RUDOLPH LEHMANN, 1874, hs, BM.
G LOWES CATO DICKINSON, 'Gladstone's Cabinet of 1868', oil, NPG 5116.
SC CARLO PELLEGRINI, 1873, terracotta statuette, NPG 5106.
PR C.BAUGNIET, tql seated, lith, BM. F.HOLL, after G.RICHMOND, hs, stipple, one of 'Grillion's Club' series, BM. Several popular prints, NPG.
C HARRY FURNISS, two pen and ink drgs, NPG 3605–06. CARLO PELLEGRINI ('Ape'), wl, profile, chromo-lith, for Vanity Fair, 27 Feb 1869, NPG.
PH LOCK & WHITFIELD, hs, oval, woodburytype, for Men of Mark, 1878, NPG. H.S.MENDELSSOHN, tql seated with ribbon and star, print, NPG X6825. UNKNOWN, hs, photogravure, NPG. Various cartes by ELLIOTT & FRY, A.J.MELHUISH and JOHN & CHARLES WATKINS, various sizes, NPG.

SHERIDAN, Helen Selina, see Countess of DUFFERIN and Claneboye.

SHERRING, Matthew Atmore (1826-1880) missionary at Benares and Mirzapore.
PR J.COCHRAN, after a photograph, hl seated, stipple, NPG.

SHERRINGTON, Sir Charles Scott (1857-1952) physiologist.

P AUGUSTUS JOHN, RA 1924, hl seated, University Club, Liverpool. R.G.EVES, *c*1927, hl seated, NPG 3828; related charcoal drg, NPG 3829. R.G.EVES, 1927, tql seated, The Royal Society, London. SIR WILLIAM RUSSELL FLINT, 1929, hl, Magdalen College, Oxford.

D R.J.BRACKEN, 1944, hs, semi-profile, pencil, Fitzwilliam Museum, Cambridge.

PH WALTER STONEMAN, three portraits, 1917, 1933 and 1943, NPG (NPR).

SHERRINGTON, Helen Lemmens-, see LEMMENS-Sherrington.

SHIELDS, Frederic James (1833-1911) painter and decorative artist.

P FORD MADOX BROWN, head, as the figure of Wicklyffe, in 'Wicklyffe on his Trial', fresco, Manchester Town Hall.

SHIRLEY, Walter Waddington (1828-1866) regius professor of ecclesiastical history at Oxford.

P UNKNOWN, *c*1881, based on photographs, hl seated, Keble College, Oxford.

SHIRREFF, Emily Anne Eliza (1814-1897) pioneer of women's education.

PH UNKNOWN, print, Girton College, Cambridge.

SHORT, Augustus (1802-1883) bishop of Adelaide.

PR J.THOMSON, after G.Richmond, hs, stipple, pub 1849, BM, NPG.

SHORT, Sir Francis (Frank) Job (1857-1945) etcher and engraver.

P ARTHUR HACKER, RA 1918, tql seated, Royal Academy, London.

D A.W.PETERS, *c*1914, head, chalk, NPG 3776. SIR WILLIAM ROTHENSTEIN, 1921, hs, lithographic chalk, NPG 4804.

PR MALCOLM OSBORNE, 1931, tql in his studio, drypoint, NPG. W.STRANG, hs, etch?, (or drg), The Art Worker's Guild, London.

PH UNKNOWN, 1914, hs, print, NPG.

SHORTER, Clement King (1857-1926) journalist and author.

C SIR LESLIE WARD ('Spy'), wl seated, chromo-lith, for *Vanity Fair*, 20 Dec 1894, NPG.

PH OLIVE EDIS GALSWORTHY, 1916, hl seated, with Augustine Birrell, print, NPG X12402.

SHUCKBURGH, Evelyn Shirley (1843-1906) classical scholar.

SC ERNEST GILLICK, bronze relief, Emmanuel College, Cambridge.
PH UNKNOWN, print, Emmanuel College, Cambridge.

SIDDAL, Elizabeth Eleanor (*d*1862) wife of Dante Gabriel Rossetti; model for numerous Pre-Raphaelite paintings.

P Elizabeth Siddal sat as a model for a number of paintings, eg: WILLIAM HOLMAN HUNT, 1850, 'A Converted British Family Sheltering a Christian Priest from the Persecution of the Druids', Ashmolean Museum, Oxford, and 1851, 'Valentine rescuing Sylvia from Proteus', City Museum and Art Gallery, Birmingham. SIR J.E.MILLAIS, 1851-2, wl as Ophelia, TATE 1506; pencil study, City Museum and Art Gallery, Birmingham. DANTE GABRIEL ROSSETTI, 1857, wl as St Catherine, TATE 4603. D.G.ROSSETTI, 1860, hs, 'Regina Cordium', Johannesburg Art Gallery. D.G.ROSSETTI, 1864, posthumous, hl, semi-profile, 'Beata Beatrix', TATE 1279; pencil study, William Morris Gallery, Walthamstow. D.G.ROSSETTI, 1874, 'The Boat of Love' (unfinished), (model for Beatrice), Birmingham City Art Gallery; studies, pencil and w/c, Birmingham City Art Gallery.

D D.G.ROSSETTI, numerous drgs and sketches, various dates, sizes and media: Birmingham City Museum and Art Gallery;

Courtauld Institute of Art, London; Fitzwilliam Museum, Cambridge; V & A; Cecil Higgins Art Gallery, Bedford; Ashmolean Museum; Wightwick Manor (NT), W Midlands; BM; TATE; Leicester Museum and Art Gallery; Manchester City Art Gallery; Norfolk Museum, Virginia, USA; National Gallery of Victoria, Melbourne; Aldrich Collection, Iowa Historical and General Library, Des Moines, USA. D.G.ROSSETTI, 1853, Rossetti sitting to Elizabeth Siddal, pen and ink, Birmingham City Art Gallery, and 1853-62, seated with Rossetti, pen and sepia, Fondazione Horne, Florence. As a model for drgs by ROSSETTI: 1850, wl, 'Rossovestita', w/c over pen and ink, Birmingham City Art Gallery; 1853, 'The First Anniversary pf the Death of Beatrice', w/c, Ashmolean Museum; pencil studies, as Delia, Birmingham City Art Gallery and Fitzwilliam Museum; 1855, as Rachel in 'Dante's vision of Rachel and Leah', w/c, TATE 5228 (pencil study, wl seated, Birmingham City Art Gallery); 1857, as Mary Nazarene, w/c, TATE 2860; 1857-8, in 'A Christmas Carol', w/c, Fogg Museum of Art, Harvard University, USA; 1862, in 'St George and the Princess Sabra', w/c, TATE 5231.

SIDGWICK, Eleanor Mildred (1845-1936) principal of Newnham College, Cambridge.

P J.J.SHANNON, Newnham College, Cambridge.

SIDGWICK, Henry (1838-1900) philosopher.

P LOWES DICKINSON, 1902, hl seated, Trinity College, Cambridge. J.J.SHANNON, Newnham College, Cambridge.

PH SAMUEL A.WALKER, tql seated, cabinet, NPG. UNKNOWN, hs, print, NPG. UNKNOWN, print, Girton College, Cambridge.

SIEMENS, Sir William (1823-1883) metallurgist and electrician.

P M.THOMAS, 1876, Institution of Electrical Engineers, London. RUDOLPH LEHMANN, Institution of Civil Engineers, London. RUDOLPH LEHMANN, 1882, hl seated, NPG 2632.

PR G.J.STODART, after a photograph by Van der Weyde, hs, stipple, NPG. Two woodcuts, both hs, NPG.

PH LOCK & WHITFIELD, hs, oval, woodburytype, for *Men of Mark*, 1883, NPG.

SIEVEKING, Sir Edward Henry (1816-1904) physician.

P W.S.HERRICK, *c*1860?, hl seated, Royal College of Physicians, London. R.TOUSSE, Royal Society of Medicine, London.

PR 'R.T.', hs, wood engr, for *Illust London News*, 27 March 1886, NPG.

SIKES, Sir Charles William (1818-1889) projector of post-office savings banks.

P UNKNOWN, Huddersfield Town Hall.

PR R.TAYLOR, hs, wood engr, for *Illust London News*, 2 Nov 1889, NPG.

SILLERY, Charles Doyne (1807-1837) poet.

SL AUGUSTIN EDOUART, 1830, SNPG 1174.

SIMMONS, Sir John Lintorn Arabin (1821-1903) field-marshal.

P FRANK HOLL, 1883, tql in uniform, Royal Engineers HQ Mess, Chatham, Kent.

PR R.T., hs in uniform, wood engr, for *Illust London News*, 31 May 1890, NPG.

C CARLO PELLEGRINI ('Ape'), wl, w/c study, for *Vanity Fair*, 1 Dec 1877, NPG 3269.

SIMMS, Frederic Walter (1803-1865) engineer.

PH MAULL & POLYBLANK, 1855, tql seated, print, NPG P120(8).

SIMON, Sir John (1816-1904) surgeon and sanitary reformer.

SC THOMAS WOOLNER, 1876, marble bust, Royal College of

Surgeons, London.
PR C.BAUGNIET, tql seated, aged 32, lith, BM.

SIMON, Sir John (1818-1897) serjeant-at-law.
C SIR LESLIE WARD ('Spy'), wl, profile, chromo-lith, for *Vanity Fair*, 25 Sept 1886, NPG.

SIMPSON, Sir James Young, 1st Bart (1811-1870) discoverer of chloroform.
P SIR JOHN WATSON GORDON, *c*1860, tql, Edinburgh University.
SC WILLIAM BRODIE, 1877, bronze seated statue, West Princes Street Gardens, Edinburgh. W.BRODIE, 1879, bust, Westminster Abbey, London. JOHN STEVENSON RHIND, after Patric Park, marble bust, SNPG 426.
PR DALZIEL, hs, circle, woodcut, BM. UNKNOWN, after a photograph by Bingham, hs, woodcut, for *Illust London News*, 24 Feb 1866, NPG. W.HOLE, hs, etch, for *Quasi Cursores*, 1884, NPG.
PH BINGHAM, wl seated, carte, NPG. J.MOFFAT, hs, cabinet, NPG.

SIMPSON, Sir John William (1858-1933) architect.
P SIR A.S.COPE, 1922, tql, RIBA, London.
PH UNKNOWN, hs, print, NPG. WALTER STONEMAN, 1930, hl, NPG (NPR).

SIMPSON, Thomas (1808-1840) arctic explorer.
PR J.COOK, after G.P.Green, hl, stipple and line, pub 1845, BM, NPG.

SIMPSON, William (1823-1899) artist.
G UNKNOWN, hs, one of a series of woodcuts, 'Our Artists – Past and Present', for *Illust London News*, 14 May 1892, NPG.

SIMPSON, Sir William John Ritchie (1855-1931) physician and pioneer in tropical medicine.
SC FRANK BOWCHER, bust, London School of Hygiene and Tropical Medicine.

SIMSON, William (1800-1847) artist.
SC DAVID SIMSON, plaster bust, SNPG 179.

SINCLAIR, James (1821-1881), see 14th Earl of Caithness.

SIRR, Henry Charles (1807-1872) barrister, writer on China.
PH UNKNOWN, wl seated with dog, print, NPG.

SKAE, David (1814-1873) physician.
PH UNKNOWN, 1861, hl seated, oval, print, NPG X7999.

SKEAT, Walter William (1835-1912) philologist.
P C.E.BROCK, 1899, tql seated, Christ's College, Cambridge.
PR C.W.WALTON, hs, lith, Department of English, King's College, London and British Academy, London.

SKELTON, Sir John (1831-1897) author.
SC CHARLES MATTHEW, 1890, wax medallion, SNPG 570.

SKENE, William Forbes (1809-1892) historian and Celtic scholar.
P SIR GEORGE REID, hs, SNPG 428.
SL AUGUSTIN EDOUART, SNPG 802.

SKETCHLEY, Arthur, see George Rose.

SKIPSEY, Joseph (1832-1903) Northumberland miner and poet.
P After J.KOSTER of 1896, hs, Laing Museum and Art Gallery, Newcastle-upon-Tyne.
PR R.T. & Co, hs, wood engr, for *Illust London News*, 16 April 1892, NPG.

SLADE, Sir Adolphus (1804-1877) vice-admiral.
PR UNKNOWN, after a photograph, hs in uniform, woodcut, for *Illust London News*, 1 Dec 1877, NPG.

SLADEN, Sir Charles (1816-1884) Australian statesman.
PR UNKNOWN, National Gallery of Victoria, Melbourne.

SLADEN, Sir Edward Bosc (1827-1890) Indian officer.
PR R.T., hs in uniform, wood engr, for *Illust London News*, 12 Dec 1885, NPG.

SLANEY, William Slaney Kenyon-, see KENYON-Slaney.

SLATIN, Rudolph Carl von Slatin, Baron (1857-1932) administrator in Sudan.
C SIR LESLIE WARD ('Spy'), wl, w/c study, for *Vanity Fair*, 15 June 1899, NPG 3001.

SLEIGH, William Campbell (1818-1887) serjeant-at-law.
PR 'R.T.', hs, woodcut, for *Illust London News*, 5 Feb 1887, NPG.

SMART, Henry Hawley (1833-1893) novelist.
PH BARRAUD, tql, print, for *Men and Women of the Day*, vol II, 1889, NPG AX5456.

SMART, Henry Thomas (1813-1879) organist and composer.
PR UNKNOWN, hs, woodcut, BM.

SMARTT, Sir Thomas William (1858-1929) South African politician.
PH WALTER STONEMAN, 1921, hs, NPG (NPR).

SMEDLEY, Francis Edward (1818-1864) novelist.
PH C.COMBES, hs, carte, NPG AX7522.

SMEE, Alfred (1818-1877) surgeon and metallurgist.
PR UNKNOWN, after a photograph by Grillet of Naples, hs, woodcut, for *Illust London News*, 27 Jan 1877, NPG.

SMETHAM, James (1821-1889) painter and essayist.
P Self-portrait, hs, Ashmolean Museum, Oxford.
D Self-portrait, *c*1845, hs, chalk and wash, NPG 4487.

SMILES, Samuel (1812-1904) social reformer, author of *Self Help*.
P SIR GEORGE REID, hs, profile, NPG 1377. Two portraits by SIR GEORGE REID, 1879 and 1891, SNPG 1243 and 631.
D LOUISE JOPLING-ROWE, hs, chalk, NPG 1856.
C SIR LESLIE WARD ('Spy'), wl, semi-profile, chromo-lith, for *Vanity Fair*, 14 Jan 1882, NPG.
PH W.WALKER & SONS, hs, carte, NPG.

SMILLIE, Robert (1857-1940) labour leader and politician.
C SIR BERNARD PARTRIDGE, pen and ink drg, for *Punch*, 29 Sept 1920, NPG.

SMITH, Albert Richard (1816-1860) novelist and lecturer.
G P.NAUMANN & R.TAYLOR & Co, 'Our Literary Contributors – Past and Present', one of a series of woodcuts, for *Illust London News*, 14 May 1892, NPG.
PR C.BAUGNIET, 1844, tql seated, lith, BM, NPG. C.BAUGNIET, 1855, tql in mountaineering dress, seated, lith, BM, NPG. R.J.LANE, after F.Talfourd, hs, lith, BM, NPG. D.J.POUND, after a photograph by Mayall, tql seated, stipple and line, supplement to *Illust News of the World*, BM, NPG. Several woodcuts and popular prints, NPG.

SMITH, Alexander (1830-1867) poet and writer.
SC WILLIAM BRODIE, plaster medallion, SNPG 883.
PR DALZIEL, tql seated, woodcut, BM.

SMITH, Aquilla (1806-1890) Irish physician and antiquary.
P STEPHEN CATTERSON SMITH jun, exhib 1891, Royal College of Physicians, Dublin.
PR J.KIRKWOOD, after F.W.Burton, hl, 1843, etch, for Sainthill's *Olla Podrida*, BM, NPG.

SMITH, Archibald (1813-1872) mathematician.
D T.C.WAGEMAN, 1835?, w/c, Trinity College, Cambridge.

SMITH, Sir Archibald Levin (1836-1901) judge.
C SIR LESLIE WARD ('Spy'), wl, profile, in robes, chromo-lith, for *Vanity Fair*, 3 Nov 1888, NPG.

SMITH, Arthur Lionel (1850-1924) historian, master of Balliol.
P FRANCIS DODD, 1914, tql, Balliol College, Oxford; related pastel sketch, hs, Balliol College.
PR FRANCIS DODD, 1915, tql, etch, NPG 3996.
PH UNKNOWN, hs, Balliol College.

SMITH, Benjamin Leigh (1828-1913) explorer.
P STEPHEN PEARCE, 1886, hs, profile, NPG 924; replica, Jesus College, Cambridge.

SMITH, Sir Charles Bean Euan-, see EUAN-Smith.

SMITH, Charles Roach (1807-1890) antiquary.
SC GIOVANNI GIUSEPPE FONTANA, marble relief medallion, Walker Art Gallery, Liverpool.
PR 'R.T.', hs, wood engr, for *Illust London News*, 30 Aug 1890, NPG.

SMITH, Donald Alexander, see 1st Baron STRATHCONA and Mount Royal.

SMITH, Sir Francis Pettit (1808-1874) inventor of screw-propeller for steamships.
P SIR WILLIAM BOXALL, Science Museum, London.
PR UNKNOWN, after a photograph by Maull & Co, hs, woodcut, for *Illust London News*, 9 Sept 1871, NPG.

SMITH, Sir Frederick (1857-1929) major-general.
P DOROFIELD HARDY, Royal College of Veterinary Surgeons, London.
PH WALTER STONEMAN, 1918, hs, NPG (NPR).

SMITH, George (1815-1871) bishop of Victoria.
P UNKNOWN, c1849, hl seated, Hertford College, Oxford.
PR F.HOLL, after G.Richmond, hs, stipple, BM, NPG.

SMITH, George (1824-1901) publisher and founder of the *Dictionary of National Biography*.
P JOHN COLLIER, posthumous, hs, NPG 1620.

SMITH, George (1831-1895) philanthropist.
PR UNKNOWN, hs, woodcut, for *The Graphic*, 24 May 1879, NPG.

SMITH, George (1840-1876) Assyriologist.
PR UNKNOWN, after a photograph by N.Briggs, hs, woodcut, for *Illust London News*, 10 April 1875, NPG.
PH UNKNOWN, print, BM.

SMITH, Sir George Adam (1856-1942) Old Testament scholar and theologian.
P SIR WILLIAM ORPEN, 1927, King's College, Aberdeen. J.B.SOUTER, Trinity Hall, Aberdeen.

SMITH, George Barnett (1841-1909) author.
PR M.MENPES, hl, drypoint, 1879, BM.

SMITH, Goldwin (1823-1910) historian and political writer.
P E.WYLY GRIER, 1894, tql seated, Bodleian Library, Oxford. JOHN RUSSELL, 1907, replica, Corporation of Reading. MARGARET CARPENTER, hs, Art Gallery of Ontario, Toronto, Canada. J.W.L.FORSTER, two portraits, Art Gallery of Ontario, and Cornell University, USA.
D CATHERINE LYONS, 1848 or 1868, probably after George Richmond of 1840s, hl seated, w/c, Art Gallery of Ontario.
M UNKNOWN, hl seated, University Museum, Oxford.
SC ALEXANDER MUNRO, plaster bust, Bodleian Library.
PR G.E.PERINE of New York, hl seated, mixed engr, for *The Eclectic*, NPG.
PH J.GUGGENHEIM, 1874, tql seated, cabinet, NPG X4985. LOCK & WHITFIELD, hs, oval, woodburytype, for *Men of Mark*, 1878, NPG. HATCH & SON, hl, carte, NPG AX7518. MAYALL, tql seated, carte, NPG (Album 102).

SMITH, Henry John Stephen (1826-1883) mathematician.
D ALEXANDER MACDONALD, 1884, tql seated, pencil, Corpus Christi College, Oxford.
SC SIR J.E.BOEHM, 1883, marble bust, University Museum, Oxford; related busts, terracotta, NPG 787; bronze, Corpus Christi College, Oxford; stone, Balliol College, Oxford.

SMITH, James Elimalet (1801-1857) 'Shepherd Smith' divine and essayist.
PH J.LÖWY, hs, photogravure, NPG.

SMITH, John Russell (1810-1894) bookseller.
PR W.J.ALAIS, after a photograph, hl, stipple, for his *Cat of Engraved Portraits*, 1883, BM, NPG.

SMITH, Robert Payne (1819-1895) dean of Canterbury.
P J.CORBETT, 1871, tql seated, The Deanery, Canterbury.

SMITH, Robert Vernon, see 1st Baron Lyveden.

SMITH, Samuel (1836-1906) politician and philanthropist.
P W.E.LOCKHART, tql seated, Walker Art Gallery, Liverpool.
PR UNKNOWN, hs, wood engr, for *Illust London News*, 9 Feb 1884, NPG.
C SIR LESLIE WARD ('Spy'), wl, profile, w/c study, for *Vanity Fair*, 4 Aug 1904, NPG 2984.

SMITH, Stephen Catterson (1806-1872) painter.
P Self-portrait, hs, semi-profile, NGI 122. Self-portrait, Royal Hibernian Academy, Dublin.

SMITH, Thomas (1817-1906) missionary and mathematician.
P J.H.LORIMER, 1903, New College, Edinburgh.

SMITH, Sir Thomas, 1st Bart (1833-1909) surgeon.
P JOHN COLLIER, 1901, tql, St Bartholomew's Hospital, London.
G HENRY JAMYN BROOKS, 'Council of the Royal College of Surgeons of England 1884-85', oil, Royal College of Surgeons, London.

SMITH, Walter Chalmers (1824-1908) Free Church minister and poet.
P SIR GEORGE REID, hs, SNPG 2207.

SMITH, William (1808-1876) printseller and antiquary.
P MARGARET CARPENTER, 1856, hl seated, NPG 1692.
PR W.CARPENTER, two etchings, both hl, one after NPG 1692, BM.
PH CALDESI, BLANFORD & CO, 1860, wl, carte, NPG (Album 117). G & R.LAVIS, tql seated, carte, NPG (Album 104).

SMITH, Sir William (1813-1893) lexicographer.
PR C.W.WALTON, hs, lith, Dr Williams's Library, London. UNKNOWN, after a photograph by Elliott & Fry, hs, woodcut, for *Harper's Mag*, 1888, NPG.
PH CRELLIN, tql seated, carte, NPG.

SMITH, William Henry (1825-1891) statesman.
D S.P.HALL, 1887, with John Bright and others, pencil sketch, NPG 2322.
SC ALBERT BRUCE JOY, marble bust, Palace of Westminster, London. FREDERICK WINTER, 1891, plaster bust, NPG 1742.
PR Two liths, hs and hl, the second for *Civil Service Review*, 1876, BM. J.D.MILLER, after G.Richmond, hl, mezz, pub 1882, BM, NPG. Various woodcuts and popular prints, BM, NPG.
C HARRY FURNISS, pen and ink sketch, NPG 3607. UNKNOWN, wl seated, chromo-lith, for *Vanity Fair*, 9 March 1872, NPG. SIR LESLIE WARD ('Spy'), wl seated, chromo-lith, for *Vanity Fair*, 12 Nov 1887, NPG.
PH LOCK & WHITFIELD, hs, oval, woodburytype, for *Men of Mark*, 1881, NPG. BARRAUD, tql seated, profile, print, for *Men and Women of the Day*, vol II, 1889, NPG AX5439. LOMBARDI, tql seated, carte, NPG AX8600.

SMITH, William Robertson (1846-1894) theologian and Semitic scholar.
P SIR GEORGE REID, two portraits, SNPG 680 and Christ's College, Cambridge.
PH UNKNOWN, tql seated, print, NPG.

SMITH, William Tyler (1815-1873) obstetrician.
PH M.WYNTER, wl with dog, carte, NPG (Album 110).

SMITH-DORRIEN, Sir Horace Lockwood (1858-1930) general.
P SIR OSWALD BIRLEY, 1935, tql in uniform, Harrow School, Middx.
D FRANCIS DODD, 1918, charcoal and w/c, IWM.
C SIR LESLIE WARD ('Spy'), wl, profile, chromo-lith, for *Vanity Fair*, 5 Dec 1901, NPG.
PH BASSANO, The Convent, Gibraltar. JOHN RUSSELL & SONS, hl, semi-profile, in uniform, for *National Photographic Record*, vol I, NPG. SWAINE, hs in uniform, print, NPG.

SMITHSON, Harriet Constance, (afterwards Madame Berlioz) (1800-1854) actress.
P UNKNOWN, wl, Garrick Club, London.
PR J.HOPWOOD, after R.Drummond, hl, stipple, for *Ladies' Monthly Museum*, 1819, BM, NPG. R.COOPER, after G.Clint, wl as Miss Dorrillon in *Wives as they were and Maids as they are*, coloured stipple for Terry's *Theatrical Gallery*, 1822, BM, NPG. G.MAILE, after C.M.Dubufe, tql seated, mezz, BM. UNKNOWN, wl seated, lith, BM.

SMYTH, Dame Ethel Mary (1858-1944) composer.
P NEVILLE LYTTON, EARL OF LYTTON, 1936, tql seated in robes, Royal College of Music, London.
D ANTONIO MANCINI, 1900, chalks, Royal College of Music. J.S.SARGENT, 1901, hl, profile, charcoal, NPG 3243.
SC GILBERT BAYES, 1939, bust, Sadler's Wells Theatre, London.
PH H.S.MENDELSSOHN, 1884, hs, profile, cabinet, NPG. UNKNOWN, 1891, hl seated with her dog 'Marco', print, NPG. HERBERT LAMBERT, hs, profile, photogravure, for *Modern British Composers*, 1923, NPG AX7742. HOWARD COSTER, 1930s, five negs, various sizes, NPG. HOWARD COSTER, two prints, both hs, semi-profile, NPG X2104-5.

SMYTH, Sir Henry Augustus (1825-1906) general and colonel commandant.
SL UNKNOWN, hs, NPG.

SMYTH, Sir Leicester (1829-1891) general.
PR 'R.T.', hs, profile, in uniform, wood engr, for *Illust London News*, 7 Feb 1891, NPG.

SMYTH, Richard (1826-1878) Irish politician.
PR UNKNOWN, after a photograph by A.Ayton, hs, circle, woodcut, for *Illust London News*, 18 July 1874, NPG.

SMYTH, Sir Warington Wilkinson (1817-1890) geologist.
PR R.T., after a photograph by Abel Lewis, hs, wood engr, for *Illust London News*, 28 June 1890, NPG.

SMYTHE, George Augustus Frederick Percy Sydney, see 7th Viscount Strangford.

SMYTHE, Percy Ellen Frederick William, see 8th Viscount Strangford.

SMYTHIES, Charles Alan (1844-1894) bishop of Central Africa.
P CLARA REYNOLDS, 1899, hs in robes, Trinity College, Cambridge.
PH UNKNOWN, tql, print, NPG (Anglican Bishops).

SOLOMON, Abraham (1823-1862) painter.

PH CUNDALL, DOWNES & CO, wl seated, carte, NPG (Album 104).

SOLOMON, Sir Richard (1850-1913) South African statesman.
SC FRANCIS DERWENT WOOD, RA 1922, posthumous marble bust, Cape Town Legislative Assembly, South Africa.

SOLOMON, Simeon (1840-1905) painter and draughtsman.
D Self-portrait, 1859, pencil, TATE 3410.

SOMERSET, Edward Adolphus Seymour Seymour, 12th Duke of (1804-1885) statesman.
C CARLO PELLEGRINI ('Ape'), wl, profile, chromo-lith, for *Vanity Fair*, 7 Aug 1869, NPG.

SOMERSET, Lady Isabella Caroline, Lady Henry Somerset, née Somers (1851-1921) devoted herself to temperance work.
P G.F.WATTS, 1861, hs, with her sister Adeline, as children, Eastnor Castle, Hereford and Worcester. G.F.WATTS, 1871, Eastnor Castle.
D CANAVARI, Eastnor Castle.
PH JULIA MARGARET CAMERON, 1864, hs, with her sister Adeline, print, NPG P18(34). JOHN RUSSELL & SONS, hs, profile, print, for *National Photographic Record*, vol I, NPG.

SOMERSET, Poulett George Henry (1822-1875) politician, aide-de-camp to Lord Raglan.
PH MAULL & POLYBLANK, wl, carte, NPG AX8624.

SOMERVILLE, Alexander (1811-1885) social reformer.
PR Two prints: one tql seated, after a photograph, lith, the second engr W.Wood, after P.Wilkinson, tql seated, stipple and line, NPG.

SORBY, Henry Clifton (1826-1908) geologist.
P M.L.WALKER, 1906, Sheffield University.
SC UNKNOWN, marble bust, Sheffield University.

SOTHERN, Edward Askew (1826-1881) actor.
P G.E.TUSON, 1862, hs as Lord Dundreary in *Our American Cousin*, Garrick Club, London. C.R., over a photograph, tql as Lord Dundreary, Garrick Club.
PR Various theatrical woodcuts and liths, Harvard Theatre Collection, Cambridge, Mass, USA.
C Various prints, Harvard Theatre Collection.
PH UNKNOWN, tql, woodburytype, carte, NPG AX7604. several cartes by ELLIOTT & FRY, H.HERING, LONDON STEREOSCOPIC CO, and SARONY, various sizes, NPG.

SOTHERON-ESTCOURT, Thomas Henry Sutton, see Estcourt.

SOUTAR, Ellen, (Mrs Robert) see Farren.

SOUTHESK, James Carnegie, 9th Earl of (1827-1905) poet and antiquary.
PR R.J.LANE, after J.R.Swinton, 1861, hl, lith, NPG.

SOUTHEY, Sir Richard (1808-1901) South African official.
P F.WOLF, hl, Civil Service Club, Cape Town, South Africa.

SOYER, Alexis Benoît (1809-1858) cook.
G JERRY BARRETT, sketch for 'Florence Nightingale at Scutari', oil, c1856, NPG 4305; pen and ink study, NPG 2939a.
PR H.B.HALL, after E.Soyer, hl, stipple, for his *Memoirs*, by Volant and Warren, 1858, BM, NPG.

SOYER, Elizabeth Emma, née Jones (1813-1842) painter.
PR H.B.HALL, after E.Soyer, hl with crayon, oval, stipple, BM, NPG.

SPEDDING, James (1808-1881) editor of Francis Bacon.
P SAMUEL LAURENCE, 1881-2, posthumous, hs, Trinity College, Cambridge.

D G.F.WATTS, c1853, head, profile, chalk, NPG 2059.

SC THOMAS WOOLNER, 1882, marble medallion, Trinity College, Cambridge.

PH JULIA MARGARET CAMERON, 1864, hs, profile, print, NPG P18(10).

SPEKE, John Hanning (1827-1864) African explorer and discoverer of the source of the Nile.

SC LOUIS GARDIE, 1864, plaster bust, NPG 1739. L.GARDIE, 1865, bust, Royal Geographical Society, London. E.G.PAPWORTH sen, RA 1865, bust, Shire Hall, Taunton. S.C.PIERONI, bust, Royal Albert Memorial Museum, Exeter.

PR Several woodcuts and popular prints, NPG. S.HOLLYER, after a photograph by Southwell Bros, wl, stipple and line, NPG.

PH Cartes by DISDERI and AUBREY PAUL, tql and hl seated, NPG.

SPENCE, James (1812-1882) surgeon.

P JAMES IRVINE, hs, replica of a tql portrait exhib 1881, Royal College of Surgeons, Edinburgh.

SPENCER, Herbert (1820-1903) philosopher.

P J.B.BURGESS, 1872, tql seated, NPG 1358. JOHN McLURE HAMILTON, c1895, hl seated, profile, NPG 4092. SIR HUBERT VON HERKOMER, 1898, tql seated, SNPG 618. ALICE GRANT, 1904, hl seated, The Athenaeum, London.

SC SIR J.E.BOEHM, c1884, marble bust, NPG 1359.

PR E.GULLAND, after H.Herkomer, hl, Herkomertype, pub 1899, BM.

C HARRY FURNISS, hs, pen and ink sketch, NPG 3609. SIR FRANCIS CARRUTHERS GOULD ('CG'), wl, w/c study, for *Vanity Fair*, 26 April 1879, NPG 2601.

PH BARRAUD, hl, print, for *Men and Women of the Day*, vol I, 1888, NPG AX5412. BARRAUD, hs, cabinet, NPG. ELLIOTT & FRY, hs, profile, cabinet, NPG. LONDON STEREOSCOPIC Co, tql seated, cabinet, NPG. MAYALL, tql seated, print, NPG. JOHN WATKINS, hs, carte, NPG.

SPENCER, John Poyntz Spencer, 5th Earl (1835-1910) statesman and viceroy of Ireland.

P FRANK HOLL, 1888, tql seated with Garter ribbon, Althorp, Northants. SIR T.A.JONES, tql with orders, Althorp. HENRY WEIGALL, wl, Althorp.

D S.P.HALL, pencil sketch, NPG 2346.

G F.R.LEE and JOHN HOLLINS, 'Salmon Fishing on the River Awe', oil, 1854, Althorp. H.T.WELLS, 'Wimbledon, 1864', oil, Althorp. JOHN CHARLTON, four portraits of hunting groups, three dated 1878, oil, Althorp. HENRY JAMYN BROOKS, 'Private view of the old Masters Exhibition, Royal Academy, 1888', oil, NPG 1833.

SC ARTHUR POLLEN, 1933, bust, Palace of Westminster, London.

PR J.BROWN, after a photograph by J.E.Mayall, hl, stipple, for *Baily's Mag*, 1862, BM, NPG. J.BROWN, after H.T.Wells, hs, stipple, one of 'Grillion's Club' series, BM. S.COUSINS, after H.T.Wells, hl, mezz, BM. G.ROBINSON, after F.Holl, tql seated, mezz, pub 1890, BM.

C HARRY FURNISS, two pen and ink sketches, NPG 3412 and 3608. SIR FRANCIS CARRUTHERS GOULD, wl, sketch, NPG 2874. CARLO PELLEGRINI ('Ape'), wl seated, chromo-lith, for *Vanity Fair*, 2 June 1870, NPG. SIR LESLIE WARD ('Spy'), 'Mixed Political Wares', chromo-lith, for *Vanity Fair*, 3 Dec 1892, NPG.

PH G.C.BERESFORD, 1903, several negs and prints, all hs, or hs, profile, NPG x6592-3 and x12919-22. R.BONING, wl seated, carte, NPG AX7451. LONDON STEREOSCOPIC Co, two prints, both hs, NPG. J.RUSSELL & SONS, tql seated, carte, NPG.

SPIELMANN, Marion Harry (1858-1948) art historian.

P J.H.F.BACON, 1904, hs, NPG 4352.

G W.H.BARTLETT, 'Saturday Night at the Savage Club', oil, Savage Club, London. G.GRENVILLE MANTON, 'Conversazione at the Royal Academy, 1891', w/c, NPG 2820. J.H.AMSCHEWITZ, 1907, wl with others, pen and ink, NPG 3047.

C HARRY FURNISS, pen and ink sketch, NPG 3516.

PH UNKNOWN, hs, print, NPG.

SPOFFORTH, Frederick Robert (1853-1926) Australian cricketer.

C SIR LESLIE WARD ('Spy'), wl, profile, chromo-lith, for *Vanity Fair*, 13 July 1878, NPG.

SPOONER, William Archibald (1844-1930) warden of New College, Oxford.

P H.G.RIVIERE, 1913, tql seated, New College, Oxford.

D S.P.HALL, pencil sketch, NPG 2377.

C SIR LESLIE WARD ('Spy'), wl, profile, chromo-lith, for *Vanity Fair*, 21 April 1898, NPG.

PH WALTER STONEMAN, 1924, hs, NPG (NPR).

SPOTTISWOODE, William (1825-1883) mathematician and physicist.

P JOHN COLLIER, 1884, hl, Royal Society, London.

SC R.C.BELT, RA 1880, marble bust, Royal Institution, London. THOMAS WOOLNER, marble bust, Royal Society.

PR UNKNOWN, hs, profile, lith, NPG. UNKNOWN, hs, woodcut, for *Illust London News*, 7 July 1883, NPG. G.J.STODART, after a photograph by Van der Weyde, hs, stipple, NPG.

SPRIGG, Sir John Gordon (1830-1913) South African statesman.

C SIR LESLIE WARD ('Spy'), wl, profile, chromo-lith, for *Vanity Fair*, 16 Sept 1897, NPG.

SPRY, Henry Harpur (1804-1842) writer on India.

PR UNKNOWN, wl, profile, lith, NPG.

SPURGEON, Charles Haddon (1834-1892) Baptist preacher.

P ALEXANDER MELVILLE, 1885, tql seated, NPG 2641.

PR Various popular prints, some after photographs, NPG.

C HARRY FURNISS, two pen and ink sketches, NPG 3517 and 3610. CARLO PELLEGRINI ('Ape'), wl, chromo-lith, for *Vanity Fair*, 10 Dec 1870, NPG.

PH LOCK & WHITFIELD, hs, oval, woodburytype, for *Men of Mark*, 1880, NPG. BARRAUD, tql seated, print, for *Men and Women of the Day*, vol II, 1889, NPG AX5441. ELLIOTT & FRY, tql seated, photogravure, NPG. LONDON STEREOSCOPIC Co, hl seated, woodburytype, NPG. Various cartes by W. & D.DOWNEY, ELLIOTT & FRY, INSKIP, LONDON STEREOSCOPIC Co and RICHARD SMITH, various dates and sizes, one with his wife and child, NPG.

'SPY', see Sir Leslie WARD.

SQUIRE, William Barclay (1855-1927) assistant in the British Museum, musical critic.

D WILLIAM STRANG, 1902, hl, chalk, Royal College of Music, London.

STAFFORD, Richard Anthony (1801-1854) surgeon.

PR J.COCHRAN, after W.Salter, hl, stipple and line, BM, NPG.

STAINER, Sir John (1840-1901) organist and composer.

P SIR HUBERT VON HERKOMER (replica), tql seated, Faculty of Music, Oxford. GERALD E.MOIRA, 1892, hs, Magdalen College, Oxford.

G WILLIAM HOLMAN HUNT, 'May Morning on Magdalen Tower', oil, 1890, Lady Lever Art Gallery, Port Sunlight.

C SIR LESLIE WARD ('Spy'), wl seated, chromo-lith, for *Vanity Fair*, 29 Aug 1891, NPG.

PH LOCK & WHITFIELD, hs, oval, woodburytype, for *Men of Mark*, 1878, NPG.

STALBRIDGE, Richard de Aquila Grosvenor, 1st Baron (1837-1912) railway administrator and politician.

PH CALDESI, BLANFORD & CO, wl seated, carte, NPG AX8583.

STAMER, Sir Lovelace Tomlinson, 3rd Bart (1829-1908) bishop-suffragan of Shrewsbury.

PR R.T., hs, semi-profile, wood engr, for *Illust London News*, 18 Feb 1888, NPG.

PH WHITLOCK & SONS, tql seated, postcard, NPG. UNKNOWN, tql, print, NPG (Anglican Bishops).

STAMFORDHAM, Arthur John Bigge, Baron (1849-1931) private secretary to King George V.

D FRANCIS DODD, 1931, charcoal, Royal Coll.

C SIR LESLIE WARD ('Spy'), wl, profile, chromo-lith, for *Vanity Fair*, 6 Sept 1900, NPG.

PH WALTER STONEMAN, 1917, hs, NPG (NPR).

STANFORD, Sir Charles Villiers (1852-1924) composer.

P SIR HUBERT VON HERKOMER, 1882, tql, Royal College of Music, London. SIR WILLIAM ORPEN, 1920, tql seated in robes, Trinity College, Cambridge.

D EDMOND KAPP, 1913, Barber Institute of Fine Arts, Birmingham. SIR WILLIAM ROTHENSTEIN, c1920, head, pencil and chalk, NPG 4067.

PR W.ROTHENSTEIN, 1897, hl, lith, BM, NPG.

C SIR LESLIE WARD ('Spy'), wl, chromo-lith, for *Vanity Fair*, 2 Feb 1905, NPG.

PH W. & D.DOWNEY, hl, woodburytype, for Cassell's *Cabinet Portrait Gallery*, vol V, 1894, NPG. E.O.HOPPÉ, print, Royal College of Music, London.

STANHOPE, Edward (1840-1893) cabinet minister.

PR J.BROWN, after H.T.Wells, hs, stipple, one of 'Grillion's Club' series, BM, NPG. UNKNOWN, after a photograph, hl, lith, BM, NPG.

C SIR LESLIE WARD ('Spy'), wl, profile, chromo-lith, for *Vanity Fair*, 12 April 1879, NPG.

PH LONDON STEREOSCOPIC CO, woodburytype, for Cornelius Brown's *Life of Earl of Beaconsfield*, 1881, NPG. RUSSELL & SONS, hs, print, for *Our Conservative Statesmen*, vol I, NPG (Album 16).

STANHOPE, Philip Henry Stanhope, 5th Earl of (1805-1875) historian and a founder of the National Portrait Gallery.

P SIR GEORGE HAYTER, 1834, hl seated, study for NPG 54, NPG 4336. JOHN PARTRIDGE, 1845, tql, study for NPG 342, Society of Antiquaries, London. E.M.WARD, 1854, wl seated in his study, Hughenden Manor (NT), Bucks.

D SIR GEORGE SCHARF, 1873 or 1876, tql seated, presiding at the Society of Antiquaries, pencil, pen and ink, BM.

G SIR GEORGE HAYTER, 'The House of Commons, 1833', oil, NPG 54. JOHN PARTRIDGE, 'The Fine Arts Commissioners, 1846', NPG 342, 3.

SC H.H.ARMSTEAD, after Lawrence Macdonald of 1854, marble bust, NPG 499. After a medallion by FREDERICK THOMAS, c1894, plaster cast, NPG 955.

PR W. & F.HOLL, after J.Lucas, hl in cloak, octagon, stipple, for *Eminent Conservative Statesmen*, 1839, BM, NPG. F.C.LEWIS, after J.Slater, hs, stipple, one of 'Grillion's Club' series, BM. UNKNOWN. after L.Dickinson, hl, oval, stipple, pub 1873, NPG.

C JOHN DOYLE, 1830, two pencil sketches, 'A Pair of very Riotous Fellows', and 'Guy Fawkes, or the Anniversary of the Popish Plot', BM. CARLO PELLEGRINI ('Ape'), wl, profile, chromo-lith, for *Vanity Fair*, 23 May 1874, NPG.

PH MAULL & POLYBLANK, wl, profile, carte, NPG AX7443. HERBERT WATKINS, 1857, hs, oval, print, NPG AX7906.

STANLEY, Arthur Penrhyn (1815-1881) dean of Westminster.

PH E.U.EDDIS, before 1853, tql, University College, Oxford. L.C.DICKINSON, RA 1860?, hs, NPG 1536. G.F.WATTS, RA 1867, tql seated, Bodleian Library, Oxford. HEINRICH VON ANGELI, hs, Royal Coll.

D EMILY J.HARDING, exhib 1877, hs, chalk, NPG 4701.

M UNKNOWN, hl, NPG 1072.

SC SIR J.E.BOEHM, recumbent effigy on monument, Westminster Abbey, London; plaster cast, NPG 867. MARY GRANT, c1882-4, marble bust, Royal Coll. UNKNOWN, plaster statuette, Balliol College, Oxford.

PR DALZIEL, hs, profile, woodcut, BM. Various prints, some after photographs, NPG.

C UNKNOWN, tql in pulpit, chromo-lith, for *Vanity Fair*, 21 Sept 1872, NPG.

PH UNKNOWN, tql seated, print, NPG P35. LOCK & WHITFIELD, hs, oval, woodburytype, for *Men of Mark*, 1880, NPG. Various prints by H.N.KING, LONDON STEREOSCOPIC CO, S.A.WALKER, JOHN & CHARLES WATKINS and unknown photographers, cartes and cabinets, various sizes, NPG X12925-33 and AX11949.

STANLEY, Edward Henry, see 15th Earl of Derby.

STANLEY, Edward Lyulph, see 4th Baron Sheffield.

STANLEY, Frederick Arthur, see 16th Earl of Derby.

STANLEY, Sir Henry Morton (1841-1904) explorer and journalist.

P ROBERT GIBB, 1885, tql, Livingstone Memorial, Blantyre, Scotland. SIR HUBERT VON HERKOMER, RA 1887, hl seated, Bristol City Art Gallery. HEINRICH VON ANGELI, 1890, hl in uniform, Royal Coll.

D RUDOLPH LEHMANN, 1890, hs, BM.

SC CHARLOTTE DUBRAY, RA 1878, bronze bust, Royal Geographical Society, London.

PR Various popular prints, some representing his meeting with Livingstone, BM, NPG, Livingstone Memorial, Blantyre.

C UNKNOWN, hl, chromo-lith, for *Vanity Fair*, 2 Nov 1872, NPG. SIR MAX BEERBOHM, 1897, wl, ink and wash, NPG 3857.

PH LOCK & WHITFIELD, hs, oval, woodburytype, for *Men of Mark*, 1880, NPG. BARRAUD, tql, print, for *Men and Women of the Day*, vol III, 1890, NPG AX5497. SIR BENJAMIN STONE, 1897, wl, print, Birmingham Reference Library, NPG. EVELEEN MYERS, tql seated, print, NPG P145. Various prints by LONDON STEREOSCOPIC CO, RUSSELL & SONS and others, NPG, Livingstone Memorial and Royal Geographical Society.

STANLEY of Alderley, Edward John Stanley, 2nd Baron (1802-1869) statesman.

G SIR GEORGE HAYTER, 'The House of Commons, 1833', oil, NPG 54.

PR R.J.LANE, after E.U.Eddis, hl, lith, 1856, NPG.

STANMORE, Arthur Charles Hamilton-Gordon, 1st Baron (1829-1912) colonial governor.

P JOHN LUCAS, hl as a boy, Haddo House, Grampian region, Scotland. FRANK SALISBURY, 1911, tql seated, DoE.

PR UNKNOWN, after a photograph by Bassano, hs, profile, woodcut, for *Illust London News*, 10 April 1875, NPG.

STANNARD, Henrietta Eliza Vaughan, née Palmer (1856-1911) novelist, wrote under the pseudonym of John Strange Winter.

PH BARRAUD, hs, print, for *Men and Women of the Day*, vol III, 1890, NPG AX5489. SIR BENJAMIN STONE, 1904, wl with her daughters, NPG.

STANSFELD, Sir James (1820-1898) politician.

C CARLO PELLEGRINI ('Ape'), wl, semi-profile, chromo-lith, for

Vanity Fair, 10 April 1869, NPG. 'FAUSTIN', wl, chromo-lith, a 'Figaro' cartoon, NPG.

PH W.E.DEBENHAM, wl, carte, NPG AX8615. JOHN WATKINS, hs, carte, NPG (Album 99).

STANTON, Arthur Henry (1839–1913) Anglo-Catholic divine.

SC ALFRED DRURY, *c*1917, bronze recumbent effigy, St Alban's Church, Holborn, London. FREDERICK LESSORE, plaster bust, NPG 3830.

PH SAMUEL A.WALKER, *c*1863, hs, carte, NPG x8352.

STAUNTON, Howard (1810–1874) chess player and editor of Shakespeare.

G P.NAUMANN & R.TAYLOR & CO, hs, one of a series of woodcuts, 'Our Literary Contributors – Past and Present', for *Illust London News*, 14 May 1892, NPG.

PR R. & E.TAYLOR, hs, oval, woodcut, for *Illust London News*, 4 July 1874, NPG.

STAVELEY, Sir Charles William Dunbar (1817–1896) general.

PR UNKNOWN, hs, profile, in uniform, lith, NPG.

STEAD, William Thomas (1849–1912) journalist.

D S.P.HALL, three sketches, the first two made at the sessions of the Parnell Commission, pencil, NPG 2250, 2257 and 2288. FREDERICK PEGRAM, pencil sketch, V & A.

SC SIR GEORGE FRAMPTON, RA 1917, memorial plaque, Victoria Embankment, London.

C SIR FRANCIS CARRUTHERS GOULD, with others, ink and w/c, V & A.

PH W. & D.DOWNEY, tql seated, woodburytype, for Cassell's *Cabinet Portrait Gallery*, vol IV, 1893, NPG. A.D.LEWIS, wl seated, cabinet, NPG x12924. LONDON STEREOSCOPIC CO, wl seated, cabinet, NPG. LONDON STEREOSCOPIC CO, hs, print, NPG. MEDRINGTON'S GRAND STUDIO, hs, cabinet, NPG x12923. NATIONAL ENGRAVERS LTD, hs, photogravure, NPG. UNKNOWN, tql, profile, print, NPG.

STEELE, Sir Thomas Montague (1820–1890) general.

C CARLO PELLEGRINI ('Ape'), wl, profile, chromo-lith, for *Vanity Fair*, 20 July 1878, NPG.

PH UNKNOWN, tql in uniform, photogravure, BM (Engr Ports Coll).

STEELL, Sir John (1804–1891) sculptor.

P ROBERT SCOTT LAUDER, 1832, head, oval, SNPG 2042. SIR GEORGE REID, MacDonald Collection, Aberdeen Art Gallery.

SC DAVID WATSON STEVENSON, plaster bust, SNPG 611.

PH D.O.HILL & ROBERT ADAMSON, hl seated, print, NPG P6(52). LOTHIAN, hs, carte, NPG (Album 106).

STEERE, Edward (1828–1882) missionary bishop.

PH UNKNOWN, hs, print, NPG (Anglican Bishops).

STEPHEN, Sir Alexander Condie (1850–1908) diplomat.

C SIR LESLIE WARD ('Spy'), wl, chromo-lith, for *Vanity Fair*, 18 Dec 1902, NPG.

PH ADÈLE of Vienna, tql seated, cabinet, NPG.

STEPHEN, Sir Alfred (1802–1894) chief-justice of New South Wales.

P JOHN PRESCOTT KNIGHT, RA 1861, tql, Supreme Court of New South Wales, Sydney, Australia.

STEPHEN, George, see 1st Baron Mount Stephen.

STEPHEN, Sir James Fitzjames, 1st Bart (1829–1894) judge.

P After G.F.WATTS, 1886, hs, DoE (Master of the Rolls).

D G.F.WATTS, *c*1855, hs, chalk, NPG 3076.

C SIR LESLIE WARD ('Spy'), hs at bench, chromo-lith, for *Vanity Fair*, 7 March 1885, NPG.

PH LOCK & WHITFIELD, hs, oval, woodburytype, for *Men of Mark*, 1882, NPG.

STEPHEN, James Kenneth (1859–1892) author.

PR R.T. & CO, hs, wood engr, for *Illust London News*, 13 Feb 1892, NPG.

STEPHEN, Sir Leslie (1832–1904) first editor of the *Dictionary of National Biography*, man of letters and philosopher.

D SIR WILLIAM ROTHENSTEIN, *c*1903, head, chalk, NPG 2098.

PR A.L.MERRITT, hs, etch, BM.

PH G.C.BERESFORD, 1902, two negs, both hs, NPG x6595–6, and two prints, both hs, NPG x12917–8. G.C.BERESFORD, 1902, hs, profile, with his daughter Virginia, print, NPG x4600. JULIA MARGARET CAMERON, hs, carte, NPG. SWAN ELECTRIC ENGRAVING CO, after J.Caswall-Smith, hs, photogravure, NPG.

STEPHENS, Edward Bowring (1815–1882) sculptor.

PR UNKNOWN, hs, woodcut, for *Illust London News*, 13 Aug 1864, NPG.

PH JOHN & CHARLES WATKINS, hs, carte, NPG (Album 104).

STEPHENS, Frederic George (1828–1907) Pre-Raphaelite painter and art critic.

P WILLIAM HOLMAN HUNT, 1847, hs, TATE 4624.

D FORD MADOX BROWN, 1852, hs, study for 'Jesus washing Peter's feet' (TATE 1394), TATE T571. SIR J.E.MILLAIS, 1853, head, pencil, NPG 2363.

G SIR J.E.MILLAIS, 'Lorenzo and Isabella', Stephens was the model for the servant, oil, 1849, Walker Art Gallery, Liverpool.

STEPHENS, George (1813–1895) runic archaeologist.

P TALBOT HUGHES, 1894, Det Nationalhistoriske Museum Paa Frederiksborg, Denmark.

STEPHENS, Joseph Rayner (1805–1879) agitator.

PR PROSSLEWHITE, tql, stipple, NPG. W.READ, after Garside, hl, stipple, NPG.

STEPHENSON, Sir Frederick Charles Arthur (1821–1911) general.

C SIR LESLIE WARD ('Spy'), wl, profile, in uniform, chromo-lith, for *Vanity Fair*, 18 June 1887, NPG.

PH UNKNOWN, tql in uniform, photogravure, BM (Engr Ports Coll).

STEPHENSON, George Robert (1819–1905) civil engineer.

PH BROWN & WHEELER, wl, carte, NPG.

STEPHENSON, Robert (1803–1859) civil engineer.

P Several portraits by JOHN LUCAS: 1845, Philosophical Institute, Newcastle-on-Tyne; 1850, wl with Menai Bridge in background, Institution of Civil Engineers, London; 1851, seated, with his father, George, Institution of Civil Engineers; hs, oval, Department of Civil Engineering, University of Newcastle. H.W.PHILLIPS, posthumous, 1866, tql seated, Institution of Civil Engineers.

G H.W.PHILLIPS, 'The Royal Commissioners for the Great Exhibition, 1851', oil, V & A. JOHN LUCAS, with his family at Killingworth, oil, *c*1857, Science Museum, London. JOHN LUCAS, 'Conference of Engineers· at Britannia Bridge', oil, Institution of Civil Engineers.

SC CHARLES M.MABEY, after E.W.Wyon of *c*1855–6, 1897, marble bust, NPG 5079. BARON CARLO MAROCHETTI, bronze statue, Euston Square, London.

PR H.HARRA, after photograph by Robert Howlett, 1858, wl with the great hydraulic ram used in launching the Leviathan, woodcut, NPG. F.HOLL, after G.Richmond, hs, stipple, 1860, BM. Various prints, after photographs by Claudet, Kilburn and Mayall, NPG.

PH MAULL & POLYBLANK, 1856, tql, print, NPG AX7276. MAYALL, hs, print, NPG X1394. UNKNOWN, hs, daguerreotype, NPG P4.

STERLING, Antoinette, see MacKinlay.

STERLING, John (1806-1844) author.
PR J.BROWN, 1870, after Delacour of 1830, tql seated, stipple, NPG.

STERNDALE, William Pickford, Baron (1848-1923) judge.
P FRED STRATTON, 1923, hl in robes, Inner Temple, London.
PH WALTER STONEMAN, 1917, hs in wig and robes, NPG (NPR).

STEVENS, Alfred (1818-1875) sculptor and designer.
P Self-portrait, 1832, hs, TATE 3805.
D Two self-portraits, hs, pencil, TATE. Self-portrait, c1835-40, wl seated, pencil, NPG 1526. A.LEGROS, 1907, partly based on a photograph, silverpoint, TATE 2433.
SC REUBEN TOWNROE, 1875, plaster cast of death mask, NPG 1413. WILLIAM ELLIS, c1876, marble bust, Mappin Art Gallery, Sheffield. EDOUARD LANTERI, bronze bust, TATE 2853; plaster cast, Manchester City Art Gallery.
PH ADAMS & STILLIARD, hs, carte, NPG. UNKNOWN, c1867, hs, print, NPG.

STEVENS, Marshall (1852-1936) one of the founders and first general manager of the Manchester Ship Canal Company.
C 'ELF', wl, profile, Hentschel-Colourtype, for Vanity Fair, 14 Sept 1910, NPG.

STEVENSON, Sir Daniel Macaulay, Bart (1851-1944) merchant, civil administrator and philanthropist.
P J.B.ANDERSON, Glasgow City Art Gallery. D.S.EWART, University of Glasgow.
SC ALEXANDER PROUDFOOT, bronze bust, Glasgow University.

STEVENSON, Joseph (1806-1895) historian and archivist.
SC CHARLES MATTHEW, 1889, wax and bronze medallions, SNPG 550 and 1008. CHARLES MATTHEW, plaster medallion, NPG 982.

STEVENSON, Robert Alan Mowbray (1847-1900) painter and art critic.
D P.S.KROGER, 1879, hs, Den Hirschsprungske Samling, Copenhagen.

STEVENSON, Robert Louis (1850-1894) essayist, poet and novelist.
P J.S.SARGENT, 1884, wl seated, The Taft Museum, Cincinnati, Ohio, USA. SIR W.B.RICHMOND, 1887, hl seated, NPG 1028. COUNT GIROLAMO NERLI, 1892, hs, SNPG 847.
D J.S.SARGENT, 1875 or 1884-5?, Yale University, New Haven, USA. COUNT GIROLAMO NERLI, 1892, hs, pastel, SNPG 1361. P.F.S.SPENCE, 1893, hs, pencil, NPG 1184. WILLIAM STRANG, Municipal Gallery of Modern Art, Dublin.
SC AUGUSTUS SAINT GAUDENS, portrait reliefs, three versions: first version, 1887-89, electrotype, wl seated, Saint-Gaudens National Historic Site, Cornish, New Hampshire, USA; second version, 1887-89, bronze medallion, tql seated, Saint-Gaudens National Historic Site; third version, 1899-1900, bronze plaque, wl seated, Dartmouth College Art Collection, Hanover, New Hampshire; numerous copies in public collection, eg NPG 2349, TATE 3431, Municipal Gallery of Modern Art, Dublin, Metropolitan Museum of Art, New York, National Collection of Fine Arts, Smithsonian Institution, Washington DC, Salle du Jeu de Paume, Paris, Edinburgh Cathedral. ALLEN HUTCHINSON, 1893, bronze bust, NPG 2454. DAVID WATSON STEVENSON, 1894-5, marble bust, SNPG 548. T.J.CLAPPERTON, 1909, bronze statue, University of Texas, Austin, USA.
PR M.L.MENPES, 1879, hs, etch, NPG. R.E.J.BUSH, 1892, hs, etch, NPG. W.STRANG, two etchings, hs and tql seated, BM.
C HARRY FURNISS, wl reclining, pen and ink sketch, NPG 3518.

PH J.DAVIS, with his wife, mother, Lloyd Osbourne and others, print, NPG X4630. J.MOFFAT, 1891-4, two prints, wl with a native, and wl seated with Lloyd Osbourne and two others, NPG X4627-8. DEW SMITH, hl, print, NPG X1345. UNKNOWN, c1885, hl seated, photogravure, NPG X4626.

STEVENSON, Thomas (1818-1887) lighthouse and harbour engineer.
P SIR GEORGE REID, tql, SNPG 568.

STEVENSON, Sir Thomas (1838-1908) scientific analyst and toxicologist.
C 'WAG', tql, profile, chromo-lith, for Vanity Fair, 30 Nov 1899, NPG.

STEWART, Alan Plantagenet, see 10th Earl of Galloway.

STEWART, Alexander (1830-1872) whaling officer.
P STEPHEN PEARCE, c1854, hl, NPG 1220.

STEWART, Sir Donald Martin, 1st Bart (1824-1900) commander-in-chief in India.
P FRANK BROOKS, 1903, hs in uniform, NPG 1622.
C CARLO PELLEGRINI ('Ape'), wl, profile, w/c study, probably for Vanity Fair, 15 Jan 1887, SNPG 1560; chromo-lith, NPG.
PH FRY & SONS, c1895, tql, print, National Army Museum, London.

STEWART, Sir Herbert (1843-1885) major-general.
P FRANK HOLL, 1886, posthumous, tql in uniform, 1888, Staff College, Camberley, Surrey. R.C.WOODVILLE, c1888, '"Too Late", Sir Herbert Stewart in sight of the Nile, Jan 1885', Royal Coll.
SC SIR J.E.BOEHM, medallion on mural monument, St Paul's Cathedral, London.
PR ZAPP & BENNETT, hs, chromo-lith, supplement to the Pictorial World, 26 Feb 1885, NPG.

STEWART, James (1831-1905) African missionary and explorer.
P JOHN BOWIE, United Free Church Assembly Hall, Edinburgh.

STEWART, John Alexander (1846-1933) professor of moral philosophy at Oxford.
PR J.WHEATLEY, hl seated, aged 76, etch, BM.

STEWART, Patrick (1832-1865) director of telegraphs in India.
PR C.H.JEENS, after a photograph, hl, stipple and line, for Goldsmid's Telegraph and Travel, 1874, BM, NPG. UNKNOWN, hl, woodcut, for Illust London News, 8 July 1865, NPG.

STEWART, Sir Thomas Grainger (1837-1900) physician.
PR W.HOLE, hl, etch, for Quasi Cursores, 1884, NPG.

STIRLING, Sir James (1836-1916) judge.
P SIR WILLIAM ORPEN, 1907, tql seated in robes, Lincoln's Inn, London.
C SIR LESLIE WARD ('Spy'), hs at bench, chromo-lith, for Vanity Fair, 28 Jan 1897, NPG.

STIRLING, James Hutchison (1820-1909) Scottish philosopher.
D UNKNOWN, replica, University of St Andrews.

STIRLING, Mary Ann (Fanny), née Kehl, afterwards Lady Gregory (1815-1895) actress.
P H.W.PHILLIPS, before 1857, hs as Peg Woffington in Masks and Faces, Garrick Club, London. M.J.RORSINGER, c1860-70, hs, Museum of London. ANNA LEA MERRITT, 1883, wl as the Nurse, with Ellen Terry as Juliet, Garrick Club. WALTER GOODMAN, hl, Garrick Club.
PR D.J.POUND, after a photograph by John & Charles Watkins, tql seated, stipple and line, NPG. Theatrical prints, BM, NPG, Harvard

Theatre Collection, Cambridge, Mass, USA.
PH W. & D.DOWNEY, c1885, hl as the Nurse, with Mary Anderson as Juliet, print, NPG x79. F.R.WINDOW, wl, carte, NPG (Album 108).

STIRLING-MAXWELL, Caroline Elizabeth Sarah, Lady, (Caroline Norton) (1808-1877) poet, society wit and beauty.
P H.W.PICKERSGILL, possibly RA 1829, tql seated, the Beaverbrook Art Gallery, Fredericton, Canada. SIR GEORGE HAYTER, 1832, hl seated, Chatsworth, Derbys. WILLIAM ETTY, c1845, hs, oval, Pollok House, Glasgow. W.ETTY, c1847, hl with her two sisters, oval, Manchester City Art Gallery. G.F.WATTS, hs, NGI 279.
D JOHN HAYTER, hl, chalk, NGI 2664, engr J.Thomson, stipple, for *New Monthly Mag*, 1831, BM, NPG. SIR EDWIN LANDSEER, tql seated?, Nottingham College of Art. Attrib MRS EMMA FERGUSON of Raith, 1860, w/c, SNPG 332.
G FRANK STONE, wl seated with Samuel Rogers and Mrs Phipps, c1845, oil, NPG 1916. DANIEL MACLISE, 'Justice', (Lady Stirling-Maxwell was the model for the figure of Justice), fresco, 1848–49, House of Lords, Palace of Westminster, London.
SC LORD GIFFORD, marble bust, as a young woman, Pollok House. F.J.WILLIAMSON, 1873, plaster bust, NPG 729.
PR I.W.SLATER, after a drg by J.Slater, hl, lith, pub 1829, BM. D.MACLISE, wl seated at breakfast table, making tea, lith, for *Fraser's Mag*, 1831, BM, NPG. H.ROBINSON, after T.Carrick, hl seated, oval, stipple, BM, NPG. J.C.BROMLEY, after E.T.Parris, wl seated with lyre, mezz, BM.
C SIR EDWIN LANDSEER, c1835, hl with General Edmund Phipps and 2nd Baron Alvanley at the theatre, pen and wash, NPG 4918.
PH LONDON STEREOSCOPIC CO, wl seated, carte, NPG.

STIRLING-MAXWELL, Sir William, 9th Bart (1818-1878) historian and collector.
P WILLIAM DOUGLAS, as a child, Pollok House, Glasgow.
SC F.J.WILLIAMSON, 1873, bronze bust, SNPG 558; related plaster bust, NPG 728.
PR W.HOLL, after a drg by G.Richmond, hs, profile, stipple, one of 'Grillion's Club' series, BM. UNKNOWN, hs, oval, woodcut, for *Illust London News*, 25 Nov 1871, NPG.
PH THOMAS RODGER, wl, carte, NPG (Album 101).

STOCKS, Lumb (1812-1892) engraver.
P A.STOCKS, 1884, MacDonald Collection, Aberdeen Art Gallery.
PH ELLIOTT & FRY, hs, carte, NPG (Album 103). LOCK & WHITFIELD, hs, oval, woodburytype, for *Men of Mark*, 1883, NPG. M'LEAN & HAES, wl seated, carte, NPG (Album 105). RALPH W.ROBINSON, tql seated, print, for *Members and Associates of the Royal Academy of Arts, 1891*, NPG x7392.

STODDART, Charles (1806-1842) soldier and diplomat.
D WILLIAM BROCKEDON, 1835, hs, chalk, NPG 2515(74).

STODDART, Thomas Tod (1810-1880) angler and author.
PR UNKNOWN, after a photograph by Macintosh and Co, hs, profile, woodcut, for *Illust London News*, 11 Dec 1880, NPG.

STOKES, Sir George Gabriel, 1st Bart (1819-1903) mathematician and physicist.
P SIR HUBERT VON HERKOMER, 1891, tql seated, Royal Society, London. LOWES DICKINSON, Pembroke College, Cambridge.
D T.C.WAGEMAN, w/c, Trinity College, Cambridge.
SC After HENRY WILES, 1887, plaster bust, Philosophical Library, University of Cambridge. SIR WILLIAM HAMO THORNYCROFT, c1898, marble busts, Fitzwilliam Museum, Cambridge and Pembroke College. SIR W.H.THORNYCROFT, memorial medallion bust, Westminster Abbey, London. G.W.DE SAULLES, 1899, gold medallion, Fitzwilliam Museum, Cambridge; bronze version, NPG 2758.

PR C.H.JEENS, after a photograph, hs, stipple, BM.
PH RUSSELL & SONS, hs, cabinet, NPG.

STOKES, John Lort (1812-1885) admiral.
P STEPHEN PEARCE, RA 1879, tql, NMM, Greenwich.

STOKES, Margaret M'Nair (1832-1900) Irish archaeologist.
D WALTER OSBORNE, chalks, NGI 2550.

STOKES, Whitley (1830-1909) Celtic scholar.
SC UNKNOWN, marble bust, Jesus College, Oxford.

STOKES, William (1804-1878) physician.
D SIR F.W.BURTON, hs, chalk, NGI 2347.
SC J.H.FOLEY, statue, Royal College of Physicians, Dublin.

STONE, Darwell (1859-1941) Anglo-Catholic theologian.
P SIR JAMES GUNN, 1935, Pusey House, Oxford.

STONE, Frank (1800-1859) painter.
P Self-portraits, both hs, Manchester City Art Gallery and Art Gallery of New South Wales, Australia.
PR UNKNOWN, after a photograph by Mayall, hl seated, woodcut, for *Illust London News*, 1859, NPG.

STONE, Sir John Benjamin (1838-1914) photographer and traveller.
C SIR LESLIE WARD ('Spy'), wl, w/c study, for *Vanity Fair*, 20 Feb 1902, NPG 2985.
PH Six self-portrait prints, 1897–1902, all wl, NPG. Various prints, some in groups, Birmingham Reference Library.

STONE, Marcus (1840-1921) painter.
P Self-portrait, 1883, hs, MacDonald Collection, Aberdeen Art Gallery.
G HENRY JAMYN BROOKS, 'Private view of the Old Masters Exhibition, Royal Academy, 1888', oil, NPG 1833. G.GRENVILLE MANTON, 'Conversazione at the Royal Academy, 1891', w/c, NPG 2820.
PH LUCAS, tql, carte, and MAULL & POLYBLANK, wl, carte, NPG (Album 104). LOCK & WHITFIELD, hs, oval, woodburytype, for *Men of Mark*, 1882, NPG. LONDON STEREOSCOPIC CO, hs, carte, NPG (Album 106). ERNEST H.MILLS, hl seated, cabinet, NPG. RALPH W.ROBINSON, wl, print, for *Members and Associates of the Royal Academy of Arts, 1891*, NPG x7393. UNKNOWN, with Dickens and others in a group, print, 1857, Dickens House, London.

STONE, William (1857-1958) 'The Squire of Piccadilly'.
C HARRY FURNISS, 1905, wl seated, pen and ink sketch, for *The Garrick Gallery*, NPG 4095(10).

STONEY, George Johnstone (1826-1911) mathematical physicist.
P SIR THOMAS JONES, 1883, Royal Dublin Society.

STOPFORD, Sir Frederick William (1854-1929) general.
PH WALTER STONEMAN, 1923, hs in uniform, NPG (NPR).

STOREY, George Adolphus (1834-1919) painter.
G H.T.WELLS, 'Friends at Yewden', oil, Hamburger Kunsthalle, Hamburg.
C HARRY FURNISS, two pen and ink sketches, NPG 3519–20.
PH MAULL & FOX, tql with palette, cabinet, NPG. RALPH W.ROBINSON, wl seated, print, for *Members and Associates of the Royal Academy of Arts, 1891*, NPG x7394. JOHN RUSSELL & SONS, hl, print, for *National Photographic Record*, vol I, NPG. UNKNOWN, wl seated, with his wife?, print, NPG x1376. UNKNOWN, in his studio, print, NPG x1377.

STORKS, Sir Henry Knight (1811-1874) lieutenant-general.
G JERRY BARRETT, sketch for 'Florence Nightingale at Scutari', oil, c1856, NPG 4305; pen and ink study, NPG 2939a.

c CARLO PELLEGRINI ('Ape'), wl, profile, w/c study, for *Vanity Fair*, 24 Dec 1870, NPG 2602.

STORY, Robert Herbert (1835-1907) principal of Glasgow University.

p SIR GEORGE REID, two portraits, one owned by the Church of Scotland, Edinburgh and the other, tql seated in robes, University of Glasgow.

STOUGHTON, John (1807-1897) ecclesiastical historian.

p UNKNOWN, hl, Dr Williams's Library, London.

STOUT, Sir Robert (1844-1930) prime minister and chief justice of New Zealand.

PH WALTER STONEMAN, 1921, hs, NPG (NPR).

STOWELL, William Hendry (1800-1858) congregational minister at Rotherham.

PR J.COCHRAN, after H.Room, hl, stipple, for *Evangelical Mag*, BM,. NPG.

STRACHAN-DAVIDSON, James Leigh (1843-1916) classical scholar.

p SIR GEORGE REID, 1909-10, tql, Balliol College, Oxford.

d SIR HUBERT VON HERKOMER, hs, w/c, Balliol College.

STRACHEY, Sir Edward, 4th Bart (1858-1936), see 1st Baron Strachie.

STRACHEY, Sir John (1823-1907) Anglo-Indian administrator.

PH ELLIOTT & FRY, wl with Sir Richard Strachey, print, NPG X13066. HILLS & SAUNDERS, wl seated in large family group, print, NPG.

STRACHEY, Sir Richard (1817-1908) lieutenant-general, scientist and engineer.

p LOWES DICKINSON, 1889, hl, Oriental Club, London.

d SIMON BUSSY, wl, seated, profile, pastel, NPG 4596.

PH Several prints by H.LENTHALL, ELLIOTT & FRY, MAULL & FOX, FREDERICK HOLLYER, and unknown photographers, cartes, cabinets, etc, various dates and sizes, one with Lady Strachey and one with Sir John Strachey, NPG X13035-41 and X13064-66.

STRACHIE, Sir Edward Strachey, 4th Bart, 1st Baron (1858-1936) politician and landowner.

PH SIR BENJAMIN STONE, 1898, wl, print, NPG.

STRAFFORD, George Henry Charles Byng, 3rd Earl of (1830-1898) politician.

PR UNKNOWN, hl, woodcut, for *Illust London News*, 1 April 1865, NPG.

c ADRIANO CECIONI, wl, profile, w/c study, for *Vanity Fair*, 14 Sept 1872, NPG 3272.

STRAFFORD, George Stevens Byng, 2nd Earl of (1806-1886) politician.

G SIR GEORGE HAYTER, 'The House of Commons, 1833', oil, NPG 54.

PR R.J.LANE after A.D'Orsay, hl, profile, lith, BM, NPG. J.BROWN, after J.E.Mayall, hs, stipple, for *Baily's Mag*, 1863, NPG.

STRANG, William (1859-1921) artist.

p Several self-portraits: 1912, hl, TATE 3606; 1917, hs, NPG 4533; 1919, hl seated with palette, TATE 3629; 1919, hl, Fitzwilliam Museum, Cambridge; hs, SNPG 966; hl with palette, SNPG 2198.

d Self-portrait, 1895, hl, black lead, BM. Self-portrait, 1902, hs, chalk, NPG 2927.

SC SIR GEORGE FRAMPTON, c1903, bronze bust, Royal Academy, London.

PR W.ROTHENSTEIN, hl, profile, lith, BM, NPG. Several self-portrait etchings, various sizes, BM, NPG.

PH UNKNOWN, hl, print, NPG X12826.

STRANGE, Alexander (1818-1876) lieutenant-colonel and man of science.

PR UNKNOWN, hs, woodcut, for *Illust London News*, 1 April 1876, NPG.

STRANGFORD, George Augustus Frederick Percy Sydney Smythe, 7th Viscount (1818-1857) statesman and writer.

p RICHARD BUCKNER, tql seated, Hughenden Manor (NT), Bucks.

STRANGFORD, Percy Ellen Frederick William Smythe, 8th Viscount (1826-1869) philologist.

p A.GLASGOW, 1869, posthumous, hs, Merton College, Oxford.

STRANGWAYS, Arthur Henry Fox (1859-1948) music critic.

D SIR WILLIAM ROTHENSTEIN, 1915, hs, pencil, University of Hull; related pencil drg, NPG L168(5).

STRATHCLYDE, Alexander Ure, Baron (1853-1928) lawyer and politician.

PH SIR BENJAMIN STONE, 1897, wl, print, NPG.

STRATHCONA and MOUNT ROYAL, Donald Alexander Smith, 1st Baron (1820-1914) Canadian financier.

c SIR LESLIE WARD ('Spy'), wl, chromo-lith, for *Vanity Fair*, 19 April 1900, NPG.

PH ELLIOTT & FRY, hs, profile, cabinet, NPG.

STRATHMORE and KINGHORNE, Claude George Bowes-Lyon, 14th and 1st Earl of (1855-1944) father of Queen Elizabeth, the Queen Mother.

PH WALTER STONEMAN, 1928, hs in uniform, NPG (NPR).

STRATHNAIRN, Sir Hugh Henry Rose, 1st Baron (1801-1885) field-marshal.

p UNKNOWN, after a photograph by Bassano, formerly United Service Club, London (c/o The Crown Commissioners).

D UNKNOWN, w/c and pencil, SNPG 1736.

SC EDWARD ONSLOW FORD, c1895, bronze equestrian statue, Albert Gate, Knightsbridge; related plaster bust (sketch for the head of the statue), NPG 1331.

PR EDWARD MORTON, hs, semi-profile, lith, NPG.

c CARLO PELLEGRINI ('Ape'), wl, profile, chromo-lith, for *Vanity Fair*, 20 Aug 1870, NPG.

STRAUSS, Gustave Louis Maurice (1807?-1887) miscellaneous writer.

PR 'R.T.', after a photograph by Fradelle and Young, hs, wood engr, for *Illust London News*, 17 Sept 1887, NPG.

STREET, George Edmund (1824-1881) architect.

SC H.H.ARMSTEAD, bust, RIBA, London. H.H.ARMSTEAD, 1886, marble statue, DoE (Law Courts, London).

PR UNKNOWN, after a photograph, hl, profile, woodcut, for *Illust London News*, 14 Jan 1882, BM, NPG. Several popular prints, NPG.

PH LOCK & WHITFIELD, hs, profile, oval, woodburytype, for *Men of Mark*, 1878, NPG.

STRICKLAND, Hugh Edwin (1811-1853) naturalist.

PR T.H.MAGUIRE, after F.W.Wilkins, tql seated, lith, 1837, NPG.

STRONG, Sir Samuel Henry (1825-1909) chief justice of Canada.

p UNKNOWN, Supreme Court, Ottawa, Canada.

STRUTHERS, Sir John (1823-1899) anatomist.

p SIR GEORGE REID, tql seated, profile, Royal College of Surgeons, Edinburgh.

STRUTHERS, Sir John (1857-1925) educationist.

p MAURICE GREIFFENHAGEN, 1922, SNPG 1019. M.GREIFFENHAGEN, 1922, tql seated, NPG 3141.

PH WALTER STONEMAN, 1921, hs, NPG (NPR).

STRUTT, John William, see 3rd Baron Rayleigh.

STUART, Lord Dudley Coutts (1803-1854) advocate of Polish independence.

D COUNT ALFRED D'ORSAY, 1839, hs, profile, pencil, DoE (Warsaw).

G SIR GEORGE HAYTER, 'The House of Commons, 1833', oil, NPG 54. PLOSZCZYNSKI, after C.Compton, 'Banquet Given by the Reformers of Marylebone, 1st Dec 1847', lith, BM.

PR A.OLESZCZYNSKI, after G.Hayter, hl, line, oval, 1855, BM.

STUART, Edmund Archibald, see 15th Earl of Moray.

STUART, Henry Windsor Villiers (1827-1895) politician, writer on Egypt.

PR R.J.LANE, hl, octagon, lith, BM.

STUART, John McDouall (1815-1866) explorer.

PR UNKNOWN, wl, woodcut, for *Illust London News*, 11 April 1863, NPG. UNKNOWN, hs, woodcut, for *Illust London News*, 14 Jan 1865, NPG.

STUART, John Patrick Crichton, see 3rd Marquess of Bute.

STUART-WORTLEY, Charles Stuart-Wortley, 1st Baron (1851-1926) parliamentary under-secretary of state for Home Department.

C SIR LESLIE WARD ('Spy'), wl, profile, w/c study, for *Vanity Fair*, 11 Sept 1886, NPG 4627.

STUART-WORTLEY, Lady Emmeline Charlotte Elizabeth (1806-1855) poet and writer.

P SIR FRANCIS GRANT, 1837, wl seated, Belvoir Castle, Leics.

STUART-WORTLEY, James Archibald (1805-1881) politician.

PR W.HOLL, two stipple engravings after George Richmond, both hl, one for 'Grillion's Club' series, BM. F.C.LEWIS, after G.Richmond, hl, stipple, for 'Grillion's Club' series, BM, NPG.

STUART-WORTLEY, John, see 2nd Baron Wharncliffe.

STUBBS, William (1825-1901) historian, bishop of Chester and Oxford.

P SIR HUBERT VON HERKOMER, c1885, tql seated, Bodleian Library, Oxford. C.W.FURSE, 1892, hl in robes, Trinity College, Oxford.

D H.AITCHISON, 1884, hs, chalk, NPG 2469.

PH UNKNOWN, hs, print, NPG (Anglican Bishops).

STUDD, Sir (John Edward) Kynaston, 1st Bart (1858-1944) philanthropist.

P ALICE BURTON, RA 1929, as lord mayor, Polytechnic of Central London.

STURDEE, Sir Frederick Charles Doveton, 1st Bart (1859-1925) admiral of the fleet.

P GLYN PHILPOT, 1918, IWM, London.

D FRANCIS DODD, 1917, charcoal and w/c, IWM.

G SIR A.S.COPE, 'Naval Officers of World War I, 1914-18', oil, NPG 1913; hl study, NMM, Greenwich.

PH WALTER STONEMAN, 1917, hs in uniform, NPG (NPR).

STURT, Henry Gerard, see 1st Baron Alington.

SULLIVAN, Alexander Martin (1830-1884) Irish politician.

SC THOMAS FARRELL, plaster death mask, NGI 8195.

PR 'R.T.', after a photograph by Russell & Sons, hs, semi-profile, wood engr, for *Illust London News*, 1 Nov 1884, NPG.

SULLIVAN, Sir Arthur Seymour (1842-1900) composer, collaborated with W.S.Gilbert.

P SIR J.E.MILLAIS, 1888, tql seated, NPG 1325.

SC SIR WILLIAM GOSCOMBE JOHN, several portraits: 1902, marble bust, Royal College of Music, London; c1902, bronze bas-relief, St Paul's Cathedral, London; 1903, bronze memorial bust, Victoria Embankment, London.

PR R. & E.TAYLOR, hs, oval, woodcut, for *The Illustrated Review*, 25 Oct 1873, NPG.

C CARLO PELLEGRINI ('Ape'), wl, chromo-lith, for *Vanity Fair*, 14 March 1874, NPG.

PH SARONY, wl, carte, and HERBERT WATKINS, hs, carte, NPG (Album 110). WALERY, tql, print, NPG x8018. LONDON STEREOSCOPIC CO, a print taken in The Green Room on the occasion of an amateur performance of *Sheep in Wolf's Clothing* and *Cox and Box*, in aid of the Bennett fund, Watts Society and NPG.

SULLIVAN, Barry (1821-1891) actor.

PR J.MOORE, after a daguerreotype, wl as Hamlet, stipple and line, for Tallis's *Drawing Room Table Book*, BM, NPG. Several theatrical prints, Harvard Theatre Collection, Cambridge, Mass, USA.

SUMMERS, Charles (1825-1878) sculptor.

P MARGARET THOMAS, State Library of Victoria, Melbourne, Australia.

SC MARGARET THOMAS, 1880, marble bust, Shire Hall, Taunton.

PR UNKNOWN, engr, for *The Australasian Sketcher*, 15 Feb 1879, State Library of Victoria.

SUMNER, John Andrew Hamilton, Viscount (1859-1934) judge.

P SIR WILLIAM ORPEN, 1919, hs, NPG 2760. SIR OSWALD BIRLEY, 1931, hl seated, Inner Temple, London.

SUTHERLAND, George Granville William Sutherland Leveson-Gower, 3rd Duke of (1828-1892).

PR S.COUSINS, after E.Landseer, as a child, seated, with his sister Lady Evelyn, who stands feeding a fawn, mezz, pub 1841, BM. W.O.BURGESS, after D.Chisholm, hl, as a child, in highland dress, mezz, pub 1853 (originally pub 1840), BM, NPG. MACLURE & MACDONALD, hs, semi-profile, oval, lith, NPG.

C CARLO PELLEGRINI ('Ape'), wl, chromo-lith, for *Vanity Fair*, July 1870, NPG.

PH W. & D.DOWNEY, tql seated, carte, NPG AX7410.

SUTHERLAND, Harriet Elizabeth Georgiana Leveson-Gower, née Howard, Duchess of (1806-1868) mistress of the robes and friend of Queen Victoria.

P SIR THOMAS LAWRENCE, RA 1828, wl seated with her daughter, Dunrobin Castle, Highland region, Scotland. C.R.LESLIE, c1839, wl in coronation robes with page, Wolverhampton Art Gallery. F.X.WINTERHALTER, wl, Dunrobin Castle.

D SIR GEORGE HAYTER, c1838, pencil study for coronation picture, BM. S.F.DIEZ, 1841, tql seated, Staatliche Museen zu Berlin.

M H.P.BONE, after Mrs Mee, hl, enamel, Arundel Castle, W Sussex. SIR W.C.ROSS, Wallace Collection, London.

G SIR GEORGE HAYTER, 'The Coronation of Queen Victoria', oil, 1838, Royal Coll. C.R.LESLIE, 'Queen Victoria receiving the Sacrament at her Coronation', oil, 1838, Royal Coll.

SC MATTHEW NOBLE, 1868, recumbent effigy, St Mary and All Saints Church, Trentham Park, Staffs. MATTHEW NOBLE, 1869, statue, Dunrobin Castle. MATTHEW NOBLE, c1869, marble bust, Alnwick Castle, Northumberland; related plaster bust, NPG 808.

PR H.ROBINSON after A.E.Chalon, tql seated, octagon, stipple, BM, NPG.

SUTHERLAND, John (1808-1891) promoter of sanitary science.

PR 'R.T.', hs, wood engr, for *Illust London News*, 1 Aug 1891, NPG.

SUTHERLAND, Sir Thomas (1834-1922) chairman of P and O Steamship Company.

P J.H.LORIMER, 1882, SNPG 2055.

c CARLO PELLEGRINI ('Ape'), wl, profile, w/c study, for *Vanity Fair*, 22 Oct 1887, NPG 2603.
PH SIR BENJAMIN STONE, 1897, wl, print, NPG.

SUTTON, Sir John Bland-, see BLAND-Sutton.

SWAIN, Charles (1801-1874) poet.
P There are several portraits by WILLIAM BRADLEY, all similar and of the same date. WILLIAM BRADLEY, *c*1833: hs, NPG 4014; hs, Salford Art Gallery; hs, Manchester City Art Gallery; oil sketch, Central Library, Manchester.
D WILLIAM BRADLEY, hs, Manchester City Art Gallery.
M WILLIAM BRADLEY, hs, Manchester City Art Gallery.
SC E.G.PAPWORTH, 1860, marble bust, Manchester City Art Gallery.
PR WILLIAM BRADLEY, Central Library, Manchester. F.J.SMYTH, hl, woodcut, BM.

SWAIN, Joseph (1820-1909) wood engraver.
PH UNKNOWN, hs, print, BM (Engr Ports Coll).

SWAINE, John Barak (1815?-1838) artist.
PR J.SARTAIN, after G.Scharf, wl as a boy, seated at an easel, drawing, etch, BM.

SWAINSON, Charles Anthony (1820-1887) theologian.
D UNKNOWN, hs, chalk, Divinity School, University of Cambridge. EDWIN WILSON, 1901, pencil and wash sketch, Christ's College, Cambridge.

SWAN, John Macallan (1847-1910) painter and sculptor.
G SIR HUBERT VON HERKOMER, 'The Council of the Royal Academy', oil, 1908, TATE 2481.
SC SIR WILLIAM GOSCOMBE JOHN, *c*1910, bronze bust, Royal Academy, London.
PR T.B.WIRGMAN, hl, holding up statuette, woodcut, BM.
PH LONDON STEREOSCOPIC CO, hl, cabinet, NPG X13213.

SWAN, Sir Joseph Wilson (1828-1914) chemist and electrical inventor.
P W.PAGET, 1929, posthumous, Institution of Electrical Engineers, London.
D MINNIE AGNES COHEN, 1894, hs, pencil, NPG 1781c.
PR UNKNOWN, hs, stipple and line, NPG.
PH ELLIOTT & FRY, hs, print, NPG X13215. Attrib LAFAYETTE, hl, print, NPG X13214. UNKNOWN, tql seated, photogravure, NPG X13216.

SWANBOROUGH, Mrs Arthur, see Eleanor Bufton.

SWANSEA, Sir Henry Hussey Vivian, 1st Baron (1821-1894) copper merchant and politician.
c SIR LESLIE WARD ('Spy'), wl, profile, chromo-lith, for *Vanity Fair*, 5 June 1886, NPG.

SWAYTHLING, Samuel Montagu, 1st Baron (1832-1911) foreign exchange banker and philanthropist.
c LIBERIO PROSPERI ('Lib'), wl, profile, chromo-lith, for *Vanity Fair*, 6 Nov 1886, NPG.

SWEET, Henry (1845-1912) phonetician, comparative philologist and English scholar.
PH UNKNOWN, hl, print, Department of Phonetic Linguistics, School of Oriental and African Studies, London.

SWETE, Henry Barclay (1835-1917) regius professor of divinity at Cambridge.
P H.G.RIVIERE, 1906, Caius College, Cambridge.

SWETTENHAM, Sir Frank Athelstan(e) (1850-1946) colonial administrator.
P J.S.SARGENT, 1904, tql, NPG 4837.

PH WALTER STONEMAN, 1917, hs, profile, NPG (NPR).

SWINBURNE, Algernon Charles (1837-1909) poet.
P WILLIAM BELL SCOTT, 1860, tql, sea in background, Balliol College, Oxford. G.F.WATTS, 1867, hs, NPG 1542. R.M.B.PAXTON, 1909, wl, profile, NPG 4002.
D D.G.ROSSETTI, 1861, hs, w/c, Fitzwilliam Museum, Cambridge. SIR WILLIAM ROTHENSTEIN, 1895, hs, chalk, Municipal Gallery of Modern Art, Dublin. R.P.STAPLES, 1900, hs, chalk, NPG 2217.
G GEORGE RICHMOND, 1843, wl with his sisters, Edith and Alice, w/c, NPG 1762. SIR EDWARD BURNE-JONES, 'The Adoration of the Magi', oil, 1861, (Swinburne was the model for the shepherd), TATE 4743.
c ALFRED BRYAN, wl, sepia, NPG 3016. HARRY FURNISS, pen and ink sketch, NPG 3611. CARLO PELLEGRINI ('Ape'), wl, w/c study, for *Vanity Fair*, 21 Nov 1874, NPG 2216. SIR MAX BEERBOHM, several posthumous drgs, for example those at the Tate Gallery, Merton College, Oxford and Ashmolean Museum, Oxford.
PH ELLIOTT & FRY, hs, cabinet, NPG X12830. LONDON STEREOSCOPIC Co, hs, carte, NPG (Album 99), and (smaller version) NPG X12831. HOWARD M.KING, copy, in a group at Lady Jane Swinburne's funeral, print, NPG X12832.

SWINFEN, Charles Swinfen Eady, 1st Baron (1851-1919) judge.
c SIR LESLIE WARD ('Spy'), hl at bench, chromo-lith, for *Vanity Fair*, 13 Feb 1902, NPG.
PH ELLIOTT & FRY, wl in robes, cabinet, NPG X12825. WALTER STONEMAN, 1917, hs in wig and robes, NPG (NPR).

SYDENHAM of Combe, George Sydenham Clarke (1848-1933) administrator.
P LEIGH PEMBERTON, 1949, posthumous, hl in robe, with insignia of the Star of India, Royal Engineers HQ Mess, Chatham, Kent.
SC SIR THOMAS BROCK, *c*1918, statue, Bombay.
PH WALTER STONEMAN, 1920, hs, NPG (NPR).

SYDNEY, Emily, Viscountess, née Paget (1810-1893) wife of 3rd Viscount and 1st Earl Sydney.
M WILLIAM EGLEY, 1836, hs, NPG L152(39).

SYDNEY, John Robert Townshend, 3rd Viscount and 1st Earl (1805-1890) politician.
P SIR GEORGE HAYTER, hl, Eton College, Berks.
D GEORGE RICHMOND, 1877, head, study, chalk, Fitzwilliam Museum, Cambridge.
M WILLIAM EGLEY, 1836, hs, NPG L152(38).
SC SIR J.E.BOEHM, 1882, marble bust, Royal Coll. SIR J.E.BOEHM (completed by Sir Alfred Gilbert), marble recumbent effigy, Church of St Nicholas, Chislehurst.
PR T.L.ATKINSON, after Heinrich von Angeli, hs, mezz, pub 1881, NPG.
c CARLO PELLEGRINI ('Ape'), wl, profile, chromo-lith, for *Vanity Fair*, 1 May 1869, NPG.

SYLVESTER, James Joseph (1814-1897) mathematician.
PR G.J.STODART, after a photograph by J.Stilliard & Co, hs, stipple, NPG.

SYMES-THOMPSON, Edmund (1837-1906) physician.
D UNKNOWN, crayon, Royal Society of Medicine, London.

SYMONDS, Sir Charters James (1852-1932) surgeon.
PH WALTER STONEMAN, 1918, hl in uniform, NPG (NPR).

SYMONDS, John Addington (1807-1871) physician.
PH UNKNOWN, hl seated, print, NPG X13217.

SYMONDS, John Addington (1840-1893) man of letters.
D CARLO ORSI, hl, chalk, NPG 1427.
PR J.BROWN, after a drg by E.Clifford, hs, profile, stipple, NPG.

TADEMA, Lady Laura Alma-, see ALMA-Tadema.

TADEMA, Sir Lawrence Alma-, see ALMA-Tadema.

TAGLIONI, Marie (1809-1884) dancer; the foremost ballerina of the century.
P GUILLAUME LEPAULLE, *c*1835, wl with her brother, Paul, in the costumes for *La Sylphide*, Louvre, Paris.
D A.E.CHALON, *c*1831, wl performing the Tyrolienne dance in Rossini's *Guillaume Tell*, w/c, NPG 1962(l). QUEEN VICTORIA, 1833-4, three sketches, Royal Coll.
PR Various theatrical and popular prints, Harvard Theatre Collection, Cambridge, Mass, USA, V & A, NPG.
PH L.HAASE & CO, wl seated, carte, NPG X7807.

TAIT, Archibald Campbell (1811-1882) archbishop of Canterbury.
P JAMES SANT, *c*1865, tql, NPG 4580. SYDNEY HODGES, *c*1869, wl, Fulham Palace, London. GEORGE RICHMOND, 1879, hl seated, Lambeth Palace, London; 1885, replica, Balliol College, Oxford.
D LOWES CATO DICKINSON, 1867, hs, chalk, NPG 1431.
SC WILLIAM BEHNES, RA 1861, marble bust, Lambeth Palace, London. SIR J.E.BOEHM, RA 1883, marble bust, Royal Coll; plaster cast, NPG 859. UNKNOWN, marble medallion on panel, Balliol College. UNKNOWN, plaster cast of death mask, NPG 2352.
PR DALZIEL, hs, woodcut, BM. G.PILOTELL, hs, profile, drypoint, BM. D.J.POUND, after a photograph by Mayall, tql seated, stipple and line, NPG. G.ZOBEL, after J.R.Swinton, hl, mezz, pub 1860, BM, NPG.
C UNKNOWN, wl, profile, chromo-lith, for *Vanity Fair*, 25 Dec 1869, NPG.
PH LOCK & WHITFIELD, hs, oval, woodburytype, for *Men of Mark*, 1876, NPG. Various cartes by BINGHAM, HILLS & SAUNDERS, MAYALL, WALKER & SONS and an unknown photographer, various sizes, NPG X12970-5 and AX7466. UNKNOWN, hl, woodburytype, NPG X12976.

TAIT, Peter Guthrie (1831-1901) physicist.
P SIR GEORGE REID, 1882, tql, Edinburgh University. SIR GEORGE REID, 1891, Royal Society of Edinburgh; replicas, SNPG 600 and Peterhouse, Cambridge.
D T.C.WAGEMAN, w/c, Trinity College, Cambridge.
PR W.HOLE, tql, etch, for *Quasi Cursores*, 1884, NPG.

TAIT, Robert Lawson (1845-1899) surgeon.
PH JOHN COLLIER, hl, cabinet, NPG X12977.

TALBOT, Christopher Rice Mansel (1803-1890) politician.
P SIR GEORGE HAYTER, 1834, hl, Penrice Castle, West Glamorgan.
D COUNT ALFRED D'ORSAY, 1834, hs, profile, pencil and chalk, NPG 4026 (55).
G SIR GEORGE HAYTER, 'The House of Commons, 1833', oil, NPG 54.

TALBOT, Edward Stuart (1844-1934) bishop of Winchester.
P GEORGE RICHMOND, 1876, hl seated, Keble College, Oxford. HENRY HARRIS BROWN, RA 1912, tql seated with mantle of the Prelate of the order of the Garter, Christ Church, Oxford.
G S.P.HALL, 'The Bench of Bishops, 1902', w/c, NPG 2369.
SC CECIL THOMAS, recumbent effigy, Southwark Cathedral.
C SIR LESLIE WARD ('Spy'), wl, w/c study, for *Vanity Fair*, 21 April

1904, NPG 3004. 'RAY', wl seated in Garter robes, chromo-lith for *Vanity Fair*, 11 Oct 1911, NPG.
PH SIR BENJAMIN STONE, 1909, wl, print, Birmingham Reference Library. OLIVE EDIS, *c*1912, tql seated, autochrome, NPG X7209. OLIVE EDIS, hs, profile, print, NPG X12980. WALTER STONEMAN, 1918, hl, profile, neg, for NPR, NPG X516. ELLIOTT & FRY, hl seated, print, NPG X12979. UNKNOWN, hs, print, NPG (Anglican Bishops).

TALBOT, William Henry Fox (1800-1877) pioneer of photography.
PH UNKNOWN, *c*1840s, hs, daguerreotype, Lacock Collection, Lacock Abbey (NT), Wilts. ANTOINE CLAUDET, *c*1845-6, tql seated, daguerreotype, Lacock Collection. JOHN MOFFAT, 186-, tql seated with camera, print, Science Museum, London. Various daguerreotypes and prints, Lacock Collection and Science Museum.

TALBOT de Malahide, James Talbot, 4th Baron (1805-1883) politician and president of the Archaeological Society.
D FREDERICK SARGENT, hl, seated, profile, pencil, NPG 1834 (ee).
G SIR GEORGE HAYTER, 'The House of Commons, 1833', oil, NPG 54.
PH LOCK & WHITFIELD, hs, oval, woodburytype, for *Men of Mark*, 1876, NPG.

TANGYE, Sir Richard (1833-1906) engineer.
P E.R.TAYLOR, Birmingham School of Art.
SC W.R.COLTON, RA 1916, bronze memorial plate with relief portrait, Birmingham City Art Gallery.

TANKERVILLE, Charles Augustus Bennet, 6th Earl of (1810-1899) man of affairs.
D COUNT ALFRED D'ORSAY, 1842, hl, profile, chalk, NPG 4026 (56).

TATA, Jamsetji Nasarwanji (1839-1904) pioneer of Indian industries.
SC W.R.COLTON, 1912, bronze statue, Bombay.

TATE, Sir Henry, 1st Bart (1819-1899) public benefactor.
P SIR HUBERT VON HERKOMER, 1897, tql seated, TATE 3517.
SC SIR THOMAS BROCK, RA 1898, bronze bust, TATE 1765. SIR T.BROCK, *c*1905, bronze bust, Library Garden, Brixton Road, London.

TAYLER, Frederick (1802-1889) landscape painter.
PR UNKNOWN, after a photograph by John Watkins, hs, wood eng, for *Illust London News*, 6 July 1889, NPG.

TAYLOR, Alfred Swaine (1806-1880) medical jurist.
M UNKNOWN, hs, profile, Royal College of Physicians, London.

TAYLOR, Charles (1840-1908) master of St John's College, Cambridge.
SC FLORENCE NEWMAN, 1908, bronze relief medallion, University Library, Cambridge.

TAYLOR, Harriette Deborah (1807-1874) actress.
D S.DRUMMOND, hs, pastel, Garrick Club, London.
PR Various theatrical prints, Harvard Theatre Collection, Cambridge, Mass, USA.

TAYLOR, Sir Henry (1800-1886) poet, essayist and civil servant.

P G.F.WATTS, hs, NPG 1014.
SC LAWRENCE MACDONALD, 1843, marble bust, NPG 2619.
PH JULIA MARGARET CAMERON, eight prints in the 'Herschel Album': 1864, two, both hs, P 18 (7, 21); 1864, two, hl as Fiar Laurence, with Mary Ann Hillier as Juliet, P 18 (61, 62); 1865, tql seated, P 18 (71); 1865, hs, 'Prospero', P 18 (75); 1865, tql seated as King Ahasuerus with Mary Ryan and Mary Kellaway, P 18 (77); 1866, tql seated as King David, P 18 (70). O.REJLANDER, hs, carte, NPG X12982.

TAYLOR, Henry Martyn (1842-1927) mathematician.
D GILBERT SPENCER, 1927, pencil, Trinity College, Cambridge.

TAYLOR, Isaac (1829-1901) archaeologist and philologist.
PH UNKNOWN, hs, print, NPG.

TAYLOR, James (1813-1892) minister and author.
P SIR DANIEL MACNEE, 1873, SNPG 690.

TAYLOR, Peter Alfred (1819-1891) politician.
G BELLIN, after J.R.Herbert, 'Meeting of the Council of the Anti Corn Law League', mixed engr, pub 1850, BM, NPG.
PR DALZIEL, hs, oval, woodcut, BM.

TAYLOR, (Philip) Meadows (1808-1876) Indian officer; author of *Confessions of a Thug*.
PR J.KIRKWOOD, after C.Grey, wl seated, etch, for *Dublin University Mag*, 1841, BM, NPG; 1840, original pen sketch, NGI 593.

TAYLOR, Thomas Edward (1811-1883) politician and soldier.
C CARLO PELLEGRINI ('Ape'), wl, chromo-lith, for *Vanity Fair*, 4 July 1874, NPG.
PH W. & D.DOWNEY, tql seated, carte, NPG AX8568

TAYLOR, Tom (1817-1880) dramatist and art critic, editor of *Punch*.
D RUDOLPH LEHMANN, 1872, hs, crayon, BM.
PR D.J.POUND, after a photograph by John & Charles Watkins, tql seated, stipple and line, for *Drawing Room Portrait Gallery of Eminent Personages*, BM, NPG. UNKNOWN, after a photograph by John Watkins, hs, woodcut, for *The Illust Review*, 8 May 1873, NPG.
C SIR LESLIE WARD ('Spy'), wl, profile, chromo-lith, for *Vanity Fair*, 11 March 1876, NPG.
PH LOCK & WHITFIELD, hs, oval, woodburytype, for *Men of Mark*, 1881, NPG. Various cartes by ELLIOTT & FRY, MAULL & POLYBLANK, SOUTHWELL BROS and JOHN & CHARLES WATKINS, various sizes, NPG.

TEALE, Thomas Pridgin (1831-1923) surgeon.
SC THOMAS EARLE, 1867, bust, Leeds General Infirmary.
PH UNKNOWN, print, Royal Society, London.

TEALL, Sir Jethro Justinian Harris (1849-1924) geologist.
PH WALTER STONEMAN, 1918, NPG (NPR).

TEESDALE, Sir Christopher Charles (1833-1893) soldier.
PR D.J.POUND, after a photograph by Watkins, tql in uniform, line, BM, NPG.
PH UNKNOWN, 1856, with Sir William Williams, print, NPG X8021. P.SEBAH, c1863, hs, carte, NPG X8357. W. & D.DOWNEY, 1868, two prints, in groups with Queen Victoria and others, NPG P22 (2, 24). W. & D.DOWNEY, tql, woodburytype, for Cassell's *Cabinet Portrait Gallery*, vol II, 1891, NPG.

TEMPLE, Frederick (1821-1902) archbishop of Canterbury.
P G.F.WATTS, RA 1880, Rugby School, Warwicks. SIR HUBERT VON HERKOMER, 1896, tql seated, Fulham Palace, London; replica, Lambeth Palace. E.A.FELLOWES PRYNNE, hl, Bishop's Palace, Exeter.
G S.P.HALL, 'The Bench of Bishops, 1902', w/c, NPG 2369.

SC THOMAS WOOLNER, c1871, bust, Rugby School. SIR GEORGE FRAMPTON, c1904, bronze bust, Sherborne School, Dorset; bronze replica, Rugby School. F.W.POMEROY, 1905, panel, wl kneeling, St Paul's Cathedral, London. SIR THOMAS BROCK, medallion, Rugby School Chapel.
PR Various popular prints and woodcuts, NPG.
C SIR FRANCIS CARRUTHERS GOULD, two sketches, NPG 2870–1. HARRY FURNISS, pen and ink sketch, NPG 3522. UNKNOWN, wl seated, chromo-lith, for *Vanity Fair*, 6 Nov 1869, NPG. SIR LESLIE WARD ('Spy'), hl in pulpit, chromo-lith, for *Vanity Fair*, 11 Sept 1902, NPG.
PH Various prints by LONDON STEREOSCOPIC CO, T.RODGER, H.J.WHITLOCK and unknown photogtaphers, various dates and sizes, cartes and prints, NPG X12986–92 and AX7486. UNKNOWN, hs, print, NPG (Anglican Bishops).

TEMPLE, Sir Richard, 1st Bart (1826-1902) Anglo-Indian administrator.
SC SIR THOMAS BROCK, c1884, marble statue, Bombay Town Hall.
C SIR LESLIE WARD ('Spy'), wl, profile, with ribbon and star, chromo-lith, for *Vanity Fair*, 15 Jan 1881, NPG.

TEMPLE, Sir Richard Carnac, 2nd Bart (1850-1931) soldier and oriental scholar.
PH WALTER STONEMAN, 1925, hs, NPG (NPR).

TEMPLETON, John (1802-1886) singer.
PR C.BAUGNIET, tql, lith, pub 1844, BM. MACLURE & MACDONALD, after A.Keith, hl, lith, NPG.

TENNANT, Sir Charles, Bart (1823-1906) manufacturer, politician and patron of art.
G HENRY JAMYN BROOKS, 'Private View of the Old Masters Exhibition, Royal Academy, 1888', oil, NPG 1833.
PR J.W.WATT, hl, lith, NPG.
C FRANÇOIS VERHEYDEN, wl, profile, w/c study, for *Vanity Fair*, 9 June 1883, NPG 4745.

TENNANT, James (1808-1881) mineralogist.
PR UNKNOWN, after a photograph by H.N.King, hs, woodcut, for *Illust London News*, 12 March 1881, NPG.

TENNENT, Sir James Emerson, 1st Bart (1804-1869) politician and author.
SC PATRICK MACDOWELL, marble bust, Belfast Corporation.
PR R.A.ARTLETT, after G.Richmond, hl seated, octagon, stipple, for Ryall's *Eminent Conservative Statesmen*, 1836, BM, NPG. UNKNOWN, wl, lith, pub 1852, NPG.

TENNIEL, Sir John (1820-1914) cartoonist and illustrator.
P Self-portrait, 1882, hs, MacDonald Collection, Aberdeen Art Gallery. FRANK HOLL, hs, profile, NPG 1596. EDWIN WARD, tql, Reform Club, London.
D 'G.J.R.', 1844, hs, profile, pencil, NPG 2002. Self-portrait, 1889, hs, pen and ink, NPG 2818.
C HARRY FURNISS, several pen and ink sketches, NPG 3525–7 and 3612. SIR LESLIE WARD ('Spy'), wl, profile, chromo-lith, for *Vanity Fair*, 26 Oct 1878, NPG.
PH ELLIOTT & FRY, two cartes, both hs, NPG (Albums 104 and 106). ELLIOTT & FRY, two cabinets, tql seated, and tql, NPG X6399 and X12993. UNKNOWN, The Green Room on the occasion of the amateur performances of *Sheep in Wolf's Clothing* and *Cox and Box*, in aid of the Bennett fund, print, Watts Society, and NPG.

TENNYSON, Alfred Tennyson, 1st Baron (1809-1892) poet laureate.
P SAMUEL LAURENCE, c1840, hs, semi-profile, NPG 2460. G.F.WATTS, several portraits: 1857, hl, profile, National Gallery of Victoria, Melbourne, Australia; 1858-9, hl, 'the great moonlight portrait', Eastnor Castle, Hereford and Worcester;

1863–4, hs, NPG 1015; 1890, hl in Oxford DCL gown, Trinity College, Cambridge (preliminary drg, Usher Art Gallery, Lincoln); 1890, hl in peer's robes, Art Gallery of South Australia, Adelaide. E.G.GIRARDOT, c1864, based on photograph by Mayall, Usher Art Gallery, Lincoln. SIR J.E.MILLAIS, 1881, tql, Lady Lever Art Gallery, Port Sunlight.

D Attrib JAMES SPEDDING, c1831, tql seated, pencil, NPG 3940. RICHARD DOYLE, c1850, three drgs, BM. D.G.ROSSETTI, 1855, wl seated, reading 'Maud' at Browning's house, 27 Sept 1855, Birmingham City Art Gallery. L.C.DICKINSON, 1892, based on Mayall photograph of 1864, Usher Art Gallery. L.C.DICKINSON, hs, chalk, Trinity College, Cambridge. M.ARNAULT, after Mayall photograph, hs, semi-profile, oval, chalk, NPG 970. SIR HUBERT VON HERKOMER, 1879, hs, w/c, Lady Lever Art Gallery, Port Sunlight; related chalk drg, Usher Art Gallery. RUDOLPH LEHMANN, based on photograph by Barraud, BM. W.H.MARGETSON, 1891, after a photograph by Barraud of 1882, tql, w/c, NPG 4343.

SL UNKNOWN, 1824, hs, called Tennyson, Usher Art Gallery.

SC THOMAS WOOLNER, several portraits: 1850–1, bronze cast of medallion, Usher Art Gallery, Lincoln (1856, related plaster medallion, NPG 3847); 1856–7, marble bust, Trinity College, Cambridge (marble replicas, Museum and Art Gallery, Ipswich, and Westminster Abbey, London, and marble copy by Mary Grant, 1893, NPG 947); 1864, alto-relievo medallion, marble and bronze versions, Usher Art Gallery; 1873, marble bust, Art Gallery of South Australia, Adelaide (plaster cast, NPG 1667 and Lincoln Central Library, marble version of 1876, Usher Art Gallery, and bronze cast, St Margaret's Church, Somersby). ALPHONSE LEGROS, c1882, bronze cast of medallion, Manchester City Art Gallery; plaster cast, Usher Art Gallery. J.W.MINTON, c1884, bronze medal, Usher Art Gallery. F.J.WILLIAMSON, 1893, marble bust, Guildhall Art Gallery; replica, Royal Coll and plaster casts, NPG 1178 and Usher Art Gallery. G.F.WATTS, c1898–1905, bronze statue, Lincoln. W.H.THORNYCROFT, c1910, marble statue, Trinity College, Cambridge.

PR H.LINTON, after drg by E.Morin (after Mayall), hl, woodcut, BM, engr in reverse by unknown artist, NPG. P.RAJON, c1880, etch, Museum of Fine Arts, Boston. S.HOLLYER, after C.Roberts, in his study at Aldworth, etch, 1885, Usher Art Gallery. After a w/c by H.Allingham, 1890, in his study, engr, Lincoln Central Library. UNKNOWN, on his deathbed, woodcut, from Illust London News, Usher Art Gallery. Various popular prints and prints after photographs, BM, NPG.

C CARLO PELLEGRINI ('Ape'), tql, profile, chromo-lith, for Vanity Fair, 22 July 1871, NPG.

PH JULIA MARGARET CAMERON, 1865–7, seven prints in the 'Herschel album', hs, and hs, profile, NPG P18 (3, 6, 72, 73, 74, 76, 84). JULIA MARGARET CAMERON, 1869, two prints, both hs, NPG P9 and P124. Various prints by BARRAUD, H.H.H.CAMERON, J.M.CAMERON, ELLIOTT & FRY, W.JEFFREY, LONDON STEREOSCOPIC CO, MAYALL, JAMES MUDD, O.REJLANDER, B.SCOTT & SON and others, various dates and sizes, NPG, Usher Art Gallery, Lincoln Central Library. THE CAMERON STUDIO, 1890, wl seated with Lady Tennyson and their son Hallam, print, NPG X7955.

TENNYSON, Frederick (1807–1898) poet.

PR R.TAYLOR & Co, after a photograph, hl, profile, woodcut, for Illust London News, 26 Sept 1891, BM.

TENTERDEN, Charles Stuart Aubrey Abbott, 3rd Baron (1834–1882) under-secretary for foreign affairs.

C CARLO PELLEGRINI ('Ape'), wl, semi-profile, chromo-lith, for Vanity Fair, 17 Aug 1878, NPG.

TERRISS, William (1847–1897) actor.

C AUBREY BEARDSLEY, in character in Tennyson's Becket, pen and pencil, for The Pall Mall Budget, 9 Feb 1893, V & A.

PH BARRAUD, c1885, hl as Romeo, woodburytype, for The Theatre, NPG X13221. BASSANO, tql, cabinet, NPG X4176. BONING & SMALL, hs, carte, NPG X13219. UNKNOWN, tql seated as Henry VIII, photogravure, NPG X13223.

TERRY, Dame (Alice) Ellen (1847–1928) actress.

P G.F.WATTS, 1863?, hl seated with her sister Kate, Eastnor Castle, Hereford and Worcester. G.F.WATTS, c1864, hs, profile, 'Choosing', NPG 5048. G.F.WATTS, c1864–5, hs, profile, NPG 2274. G.F.WATTS, hl as Ophelia, Watts Gallery, Compton, Surrey. SIR JOHNSTON FORBES-ROBERTSON, 1876, hs, NPG 3789. ANNA LEA MERRITT, 1883, wl as Juliet, with Mrs Stirling as the Nurse in Romeo and Juliet, Garrick Club, London. J.S.SARGENT, 1888–9, wl as Lady Macbeth, TATE 2053. J.S.SARGENT, 1889, wl, grisaille, NPG 2273. WALFORD GRAHAM ROBERTSON, 1922, tql, NPG 3132. E.M.HALE, hl, Russell-Cotes Art Gallery, Bournemouth. WALFORD GRAHAM ROBERTSON, replica of his pastel drg, Ellen Terry Memorial Museum, Smallhythe Place (NT), Kent. UNKNOWN, tql as Portia, Garrick Club.

D C.J.BECKER, 1913, head, pencil, Royal Shakespeare Memorial Theatre Museum, Stratford-upon-Avon. EDWARD GORDON CRAIG, as Mrs Page in The Merry Wives of Windsor, pen, ink and wash, V & A. CYRIL ROBERTS, 1923, hs, chalk, NPG 3662. UNKNOWN, hs, pencil, Garrick Club.

G G.Grenville MANTON, 'Conversazione at the Royal Academy, 1891', w/c, NPG 2820. JOHN COLLIER, a scene from The Merry Wives of Windsor, with Herbert Tree as Falstaff and Madge Kendal as Mrs Ford, oil, 1904, Garrick Club.

SC WILLIAM BRODIE, 1879, marble bust, Royal Shakespeare Memorial Theatre Museum. UNKNOWN, plaster cast of death mask, NPG 3657.

PR Various prints, theatrical, popular and after photographs, BM, NPG, Harvard Theatre Collection, Cambridge, Mass, USA.

C 'HM', wl with Irving, pen and ink, Theatre Museum (V & A), London.

PH UNKNOWN, 1856, wl as Mamillius, with Charles Kean print, NPG. BARRAUD, tql seated, print, for Men and Women of the Day, vol I, 1888, NPG AX5411. MRS A.BROOM, in a group with Lady Alexander and others, at a fête, neg, NPG X1140. JULIA MARGARET CAMERON, print, Gernsheim Collection, University of Texas, Austin, USA. Various cabinets by WINDOW & GROVE, various sizes, as different characters, NPG. Numerous miscellaneous prints, some in character, NPG, Theatre Museum.

THACKERAY, William Makepeace (1811–1863) novelist.

P FRANK STONE, c1839, hs, NPG 4210. SAMUEL LAURENCE, c1864, after a drg of 1862, hs, semi-profile, NPG 725. SIR JOHN GILBERT, 1864, hl seated, profile, Garrick Club, London. SAMUEL LAURENCE, 1881, almost wl, Reform Club, London. W.LOCKHART BOGLE, 1893, hs, Trinity College, Cambridge.

D DANIEL MACLISE, 1832, wl seated, pencil, Garrick Club, London. D.MACLISE, 1833, tql seated, pencil, Garrick Club. Self-portrait, 1834, pen and wash, The Athenaeum, London. D.MACLISE, c1840, hl, pencil, NPG 4209. RICHARD DOYLE, 1848, pencil and w/c, SNPG 143, and hl, pencil, BM. SAMUEL LAURENCE, 1852, replicas, Berg Collection, New York Public Library, USA, and BM. CHARLES MARTIN, 1853, pencil, BM. E.GOODWIN LEWIS, 1863, hs, chalks, Kensington Public Library. Self-portrait, tql, lecturing, w/c, Huntington Library and Art Gallery, San Marino, USA. Self-portrait, hs, pencil, Walsall Museum and Art Gallery.

M UNKNOWN, c1835, Pierpont Morgan Library, New York, USA.

G GEORGE CHINNERY, 1814, wl with his parents, pencil and wash, Harris Museum and Art Gallery, Preston. D.MACLISE, 'The

Fraserians', lith, for *Fraser's Mag*, Jan 1835, V & A.
SC Sir J.E.BOEHM, after a plaster bust by J.S.Deville of 1824–5, plaster cast, NPG 620. BRUCCIANI & Co, 1863, plaster death mask, NPG 1501. JOSEPH DURHAM, 1864, plaster bust, NPG 495. Sir J.E.BOEHM, 1864, plaster statuette, NPG 1282. BARON CARLO MAROCHETTI, *c*1866, later altered by Edward Onslow Ford, bust, Poet's Corner, Westminster Abbey, London. N.N.BURNARD, *c*1867, marble bust, NPG 738. LEONARD JENNINGS, 1911, marble bust, Thackeray Memorial, Calcutta.
PR F.HOLL, after S.Laurence, hs, stipple, pub 1853, BM, NPG.
C Sir EDWIN LANDSEER, 1857, head, pen, ink and wash, NPG 3925.
PH HERBERT WATKINS, hl seated, profile, print, NPG AX7334. Various cartes by BLANFORD & Co, CUNDALL, DOWNES & Co, ERNEST EDWARDS, HERBERT WATKINS and unknown photographers, various dates and sizes, NPG. J.H.WHITEHURST, 1855, hs, daguerreotype, Boston Public Library, USA.

THEED, William (1804-1891) sculptor.
SC CALDESI & Co, wl, carte, NPG (Album 104).

THERRY, Sir Roger (1800-1874) judge in New South Wales.
SC CHARLES SUMMERS, RA 1871, marble bust, Mitchell Library, Sydney, Australia.

THESIGER, Alfred Henry (1838-1880) lord justice of appeal.
D Sir J.E.MILLAIS, hs, chalk, Inner Temple, London.
PR UNKNOWN, after a photograph by the Surrey Photographic Company, hs, profile, woodcut, for *Illust London News*, 17 Nov 1877, NPG.
PH LOCK & WHITFIELD, hs, oval, woodburytype, for *Men of Mark*, 1880, NPG.

THESIGER, Frederic Augustus, see 2nd Baron Chelmsford.

THISELTON-DYER, Sir William Turner (1843-1928) botanist.
PH ELLIOTT & FRY, hl, print, Royal Botanic Gardens, Kew.

THOMAS, Arthur Goring (1850-1892) composer.
D F.I.THOMAS, 1889, hs, semi-profile, chalk, NPG 1316.

THOMAS, David Alfred, see Viscount Rhondda.

THOMAS, George Housman (1824-1868) painter.
G UNKNOWN, hs, one of a series of woodcuts, 'Our Artists – Past and Present', for *Illust London News*, 14 May 1892, BM, NPG.
PR M.JACKSON, hl seated, woodcut, BM.

THOMAS, Hugh Owen (1834-1891) surgeon.
P H.FLEURY, *c*1890, hs, NPG 3167.

THOMAS, James Havard (1854-1921) sculptor.
D JAMES KERR-LAWSON, two portraits: 1910, the sitter is asleep, pencil sketch, TATE 4187, and hs, pencil, NPG 2115. Sir WILLIAM ROTHENSTEIN, 1920, hs, chalk, TATE 4009.

THOMAS, John (1813-1862) sculptor.
PR C.BAUGNIET, tql with statue, lith, 1847, BM. UNKNOWN, tql seated, woodcut, BM. UNKNOWN, after W.B.Scott, hs, woodcut, for *The Art Journal*, NPG.

THOMAS, John (1826-1913) harpist.
D S.P.HALL, pencil sketch, NPG 2380.
SC UNKNOWN, marble bust, Royal College of Music, London.

THOMAS, Sidney Gilchrist (1850-1885) metallurgist.
D UNKNOWN, head, chalk, NPG 2615.

THOMAS, William Luson (1830-1900) wood engraver; founder of *The Graphic*.
PR H.HERKOMER, hs, Herkomergravure, BM.
C Sir LESLIE WARD ('Spy'), tql, semi-profile, chromo-lith, for *Vanity Fair*, 13 Dec 1894, NPG.

THOMAS, William Moy (1828-1910) novelist and journalist.
PH BARRAUD, hs, woodburytype, for *The Theatre*, July 1885, NPG.

THOMPSON, see also THOMSON.

THOMPSON, Sir Edward Maunde (1840-1929) director and principal librarian of the British Museum.
P Sir E.J.POYNTER, 1909, tql seated, BM.

THOMPSON, Francis (1859-1907) poet.
D NEVILLE LYTTON, 3RD EARL OF LYTTON, 1907, hs, profile, chalk, NPG 2940.
SC EVERARD MEYNELL, plaster cast of life-mask, NPG 5271.

THOMPSON, George (1804-1878) Slavery abolitionist.
G B.R.HAYDON, 'The Anti-Slavery Society Convention, 1840', oil, NPG 599.
PR C.TURNER, after G.Evans, tql, mezz, pub 1842, BM. UNKNOWN, after a photograph by C.Braithwaite of Leeds, hs, semi-profile, woodcut, for *Illust London News*, 19 Oct 1878, NPG.
C HARRY FURNISS, tql, pen and ink sketch, NPG 3523.

THOMPSON, Sir Henry, 1st Bart (1820-1904) surgeon.
P Sir LAWRENCE ALMA-TADEMA, 1878, hs, oval, Fitzwilliam Museum, Cambridge. Sir J.E.MILLAIS, 1881, tql, TATE 1941.
D RUDOLPH LEHMANN, 1902, hs, crayon, BM.
SC F.W.POMEROY, bust, Golder's Green, London.
C CARLO PELLEGRINI ('Ape'), wl, semi-profile, chromo-lith, for *Vanity Fair*, 1 Aug 1874, NPG.
PH LOCK & WHITFIELD, hs, oval, woodburytype, for *Men of Mark*, 1882, NPG. WALERY, tql, print, NPG. UNKNOWN, tql seated, woodburytype, carte, NPG AX7734.

THOMPSON, Sir (Henry Francis) Herbert, 2nd Bart (1859-1944) Egyptologist.
P Sir LAWRENCE ALMA-TADEMA, 1877, hs, profile, Fitzwilliam Museum, Cambridge.

THOMPSON, Henry Langhorne (1829-1856) soldier.
PR UNKNOWN, hs, lith, NPG.

THOMPSON, Henry Yates (1838-1928) book-collector.
PH Sir BENJAMIN STONE, 1906, wl, print, NPG.

THOMPSON, Jacob (1806-1879) landscape painter.
PH UNKNOWN, hs, print, Carlisle City Art Gallery.

THOMPSON, James (1817-1877) journalist and local historian.
P W.P.MILLER, hl, Leicester Museum.

THOMPSON, Sir James (1835-1906) manager of Caledonian Railway.
C Sir LESLIE WARD ('Spy'), wl, w/c study, for *Vanity Fair*, 15 Aug 1895, NPG 2991.

THOMPSON, Lydia, (Mrs Alexander Henderson) (1836-1908) actress.
PR Various theatrical prints and prints after photographs, BM, NPG, Harvard Theatre Collection, Cambridge, Mass, USA.
PH SOUTHWELL BROS, wl in costume, carte, NPG X13225. UNKNOWN, hs, profile, woodburytype, carte, NPG AX7652.

THOMPSON, Silvanus Phillips (1851-1916) physicist.
P Sir HUBERT VON HERKOMER, after 1892, tql seated, on loan to Imperial College, London.
PH UNKNOWN, 1912, in a group, print, Royal Society, London.

THOMPSON, Theophilus (1807-1860) physician.
PH MAULL & POLYBLANK, 1855, tql seated, print, NPG P120 (32).

THOMPSON, William (1805-1852) Irish naturalist.
PR T.H.MAGUIRE, tql seated, lith, 1849, one of set of *Ipswich Museum Portraits*, BM, NPG.

THOMPSON, William (1811-1889) pugilist, known as Bendigo.
p THOMAS EARL, 1850, hs, NPG 4191.

THOMPSON, William Hepworth (1810-1886) classical scholar.
p SAMUEL LAURENCE, 1869, tql seated, Trinity College, Cambridge. SIR HUBERT VON HERKOMER, 1881, tql seated, Trinity College, Cambridge.
d SAMUEL LAURENCE, 1841, hs, profile, chalk, NPG 1743. JAMES SPEDDING, pencil, Trinity College.

THOMPSON, William Marcus (1857-1907) journalist.
p J.B.YEATS, National Liberal Club, London.

THOMS, William John (1803-1885) antiquary.
PH POULTON, 1861, wl seated, carte, NPG (Album 117).

THOMSON, see also THOMPSON.

THOMSON, Alexander (1817-1875) architect.
SC JOHN MOSSMAN, 1877, marble bust, Kelvingrove Art Gallery, Glasgow.

THOMSON, Sir Charles Wyville (1830-1882) naturalist.
PR UNKNOWN, hs, woodcut, for *Illust London News*, 8 July 1876, NPG. C.H.JEENS, after a photograph, hs, stipple, for his *Voyage of the 'Challenger'*, 1877, BM, NPG. W.HOLE, hs, etch, for *Quasi Cursores*, 1884, NPG.

THOMSON, John (1805-1841) music writer.
p UNKNOWN, tql, seated, Edinburgh University.

THOMSON, John (1856-1926) paediatrician.
SC C.D'O.PILKINGTON JACKSON, 1929, bronze medal, SNPG 2352.

THOMSON, Joseph (1858-1894) explorer.
SC C.McBRIDE, 1896, marble bust, Royal Geographical Society, London.
PR R.T., hs, woodcut, for *Illust London News*, 20 Dec 1884, NPG.

THOMSON, Sir Joseph John (1856-1940) physicist.
p ARTHUR HACKER, 1903, hl seated, Cavendish Laboratory, Cambridge University. GEORGE FIDDES WATT, 1922, tql seated, Royal Society, London. RENÉ DE L'HÔPITAL, 1923-4, Royal Institution, London. SIR WILLIAM NICHOLSON, 1924, tql seated, Trinity College, Cambridge.
d WILLIAM STRANG, 1909, hs, chalk, Royal Coll. SIR WILLIAM ROTHENSTEIN, 1915, head, pencil, NPG 4796. FRANCIS DODD, 1920, tql, charcoal, Fitzwilliam Museum, Cambridge. SIR W.T.MONNINGTON, 1932, head, pencil, NPG 3256.
SC FRANCIS DERWENT WOOD, 1925, marble bust, Trinity College, Cambridge.
PR F.DODD, hl, etch, NPG.
PH WALTER STONEMAN, 1933, hs, profile, NPG (NPR).

THOMSON, Robert William (1822-1873) engineer.
PR R. & E.TAYLOR, after a photograph by Peterson of Copenhagen, hs, profile, woodcut, for *Illust London News*, 29 March 1873, NPG.

THOMSON, Thomas (1817-1878) naturalist.
PH MAULL & POLYBLANK, 1855, tql seated, print, NPG P120 (31).

THOMSON, William (1819-1890) archbishop of York.
p W.W.OULESS, RA 1886, tql seated, Bishopthorpe Palace, York.
PR DALZIEL, hs, woodcut, BM. W.HOLL, after a photograph, hl seated, profile, stipple and line, NPG. D.J.POUND, after a photograph by Mayall, wl, stipple and line, presented with *Illust News of the World*, BM, NPG.
c CARLO PELLEGRINI ('Ape'), wl, profile, chromo-lith, for *Vanity Fair*, 24 June 1871, NPG.
PH LOCK & WHITFIELD, hs, oval, woodburytype, for *Men of Mark*, 1878, NPG. MASON & CO, hs, semi-profile, carte, NPG X13226.

MOIRA & HAIGH, wl seated, carte, NPG AX7455. JOHN WATKINS, hs, profile, carte, NPG (Album 117).

THOMSON, William (1824-1907), see 1st Baron Kelvin.

THORBURN, Robert (1818-1885) miniature painter.
PH ELLIOTT & FRY, hs, profile, carte, NPG (Album 104).

THORNBURY, George Walter (1828-1876) author.
PR UNKNOWN, after a photograph by Charles Watkins, hs, woodcut, for *Illust London News*, 24 June 1876, NPG.

THORNE, William (Will) James (1857-1946) labour leader.
p MARGARETTA HICKS, National Union of General and Municipal Workers. F.SLATER, 1934, hs, Woodstock College, Surrey. UNKNOWN, hs, Woodstock College.
d UNKNOWN, head, pencil, Woodstock College.
PH Various prints by CLAUDE HARRIS, JARCHE and unknown photographers, NPG (Daily Herald Archive). WALTER STONEMAN, 1921 and 1938, two portraits, both hs, NPG (NPR).

THORNTON, Sir Edward (1817-1906) diplomat.
c CARLO PELLEGRINI ('Ape'), wl, profile, w/c study, for *Vanity Fair*, 27 March 1886, NPG 2742.

THORNTON, William Thomas (1813-1880) author.
PR UNKNOWN, tql seated, lith, NPG.

THORNYCROFT, Sir John Isaac (1843-1928) naval architect.
p A.J.NOWELL, RA 1905, tql seated, Institution of Mechanical Engineers, London.
c SIR LESLIE WARD ('Spy'), wl, profile, chromo-lith, for *Vanity Fair*, 19 Jan 1905, NPG.

THORNYCROFT, Mary (1814-1895) sculptor.
SC MARY ALYCE THORNYCROFT (her daughter), *c*1892, bronze bust, NPG 4065.

THORNYCROFT, Thomas (1815-1885) sculptor.
PH ERNEST EDWARDS, wl seated, print, for *Men of Eminence*, ed L.Reeve, vol II, 1864, NPG.

THORNYCROFT, Sir (William) Hamo (1850-1925) sculptor; son of Mary Thornycroft.
p T.B.WIRGMAN, 1884, hs, profile, MacDonald Collection, Aberdeen Art Gallery.
d T.B.WIRGMAN, 1880, wl seated, profile, pen and ink, NPG 2218.
c REGINALD CLEAVER, 'Hanging Committee, Royal Academy 1892', pen and ink, NPG 4245.
c SIR LESLIE WARD ('Spy'), wl, profile, w/c study, for *Vanity Fair*, 20 Feb 1892, NPG 3933.
PH Four cabinets by DONE & BALL, F.W.EDWARDS (two) and MAULL & FOX, three hs, one working on a sculpture of General Gordon, NPG X12593-6. RALPH W.ROBINSON, wl seated in his studio, print, for *Members and Associates of the Royal Academy of Arts*, 1891, NPG X7395. UNKNOWN, *c*1914, hs, profile, print, NPG X1104. WALTER STONEMAN, 1917, hs, NPG (NPR).

THOROLD, Anthony Wilson (1825-1895) bishop of Rochester.
p Attrib E.U.EDDIS, hl seated, St Giles-in-the-Fields, London.
c SIR LESLIE WARD ('Spy'), wl, profile, w/c study, for *Vanity Fair*, 10 Jan 1885, NPG 4746.
PH LOCK & WHITFIELD, hs, oval, woodburytype, for *Men of Mark*, 1881, NPG.

THRING, Edward (1821-1887) headmaster of Uppingham School.
p CYRUS JOHNSON, RA 1880, Uppingham School, Leics.
SC SIR THOMAS BROCK, RA 1892, marble statue, seated, Uppingham School Chapel.

PH EMERY WALKER, tql seated, neg, NPG.

THRING, Sir Henry Thring, 1st Baron (1818-1907) parliamentary draftsman.
C SIR LESLIE WARD ('Spy'), wl, profile, chromo-lith, for *Vanity Fair*, 29 June 1893, NPG.
PH C.W.CAREY, hs, print, NPG.

THRUPP, Frederick (1812-1895) sculptor.
PH UNKNOWN, tql, profile, when old, print, BM (Engrs Ports Coll). UNKNOWN, copied by J.C.DINHAM, hl, profile, cabinet, NPG X13227.

THURSTON, Sir John Bates (1836-1897) colonial governor.
PR BALL, hs, semi-profile, wood engr, NPG.

THYNNE, Lord Henry Frederick (1832-1904) politician and courtier.
C SIR LESLIE WARD ('Spy'), wl, back view, face in profile, w/c study, for *Vanity Fair*, 26 May 1877, NPG 4747.

TIMBS, John (1801-1875) writer.
M T.J.GULLICK, c1855, tql seated, NPG 5011.

TINSLEY, William (1831-1902) publisher.
C HARRY FURNISS, pen and ink sketch, NPG 3524.

TINWORTH, George (1843-1913) modeller.
PH DONE & BALL, hs, profile, cabinet, NPG.

TITCOMB, Jonathan Holt (1819-1887) bishop of Rangoon.
PR R.T., hs, wood engr, for *Illust London News*, 16 April 1887, NPG.

TITIENS (TIETJENS), Teresa Caroline Johanna (1831-1877) singer.
PR Various theatrical prints and prints after photographs, BM, NPG, Harvard Theatre Collection, Cambridge, Mass, USA.
PH ELLIOTT & FRY, wl, cabinet, NPG (Album 117). LONDON STEREOSCOPIC CO, wl, cabinet, NPG X5573. Several cartes by LONDON STEREOSCOPIC CO and one by WINDOW & BRIDGE, NPG.

TODD, Elliott d'Arcy (1808-1845) soldier and political agent.
PR C.G., 1842, tql, line, NPG.

TODD, Robert Bentley (1809-1860) physician.
SC MATTHEW NOBLE, 1860, marble bust, Royal College of Physicians, London. M.NOBLE, 1862, marble statue, King's College Hospital, Denmark Hill, London.
PR J.H.LYNCH, after E.Armitage, tql, lith, BM. T.H.MAGUIRE, tql, lith, 1848, BM.

TODHUNTER, Isaac (1820-1884) mathematician.
D T.C.WAGEMAN, w/c, Trinity College, Cambridge.
SC UNKNOWN, medallion portrait, St John's College, Cambridge.

TOMBS, Sir Henry (1824-1874) major-general.
PR Two woodcuts, by unknown artists, both hs, NPG.

TOMES, Sir John (1815-1895) dental surgeon.
P G.MEISTNER, tql seated, Royal College of Surgeons, London.

TOOLE, John Lawrence (1830-1906) actor and theatrical manager.
P JOHN COLLIER, 1887, tql seated, Garrick Club, London. SIGISMUND GOETZE, exhib 1893, tql seated, Guildhall Art Gallery, London.
D S.P.HALL, pencil sketch, made at the sessions of the Parnell Commission, NPG 2264. FREDERICK PEGRAM, pencil sketch, V & A.
PR Various theatrical prints and prints after photographs, NPG, Harvard Theatre Collection, Cambridge, Mass, USA.
C ALFRED BRYAN, wl, chalk, NPG 3074. HARRY FURNISS, pen and ink sketch, NPG 3528. SIR LESLIE WARD ('Spy'), wl, chromo-lith, for *Vanity Fair*, 29 July 1876, NPG.
PH BARRAUD, hs, print, for *Men and Women of the Day*, vol II, 1889, NPG.

NPG AX5448. W. & D.DOWNEY, hl, woodburytype, for Cassell's *Cabinet Portrait Gallery*, vol III, 1892, NPG. Various prints by LONDON STEREOSCOPIC CO, W.WALKER, MARCUS WARD and others, various sizes, cartes, photogravures, woodburytypes, various sizes, some in character, NPG.

TOPHAM, Francis William (1808-1877) painter.
G UNKNOWN, hs, one of a series of woodcuts, 'Our Artists – Past and Present', for *Illust London News*, 14 May 1892, BM, NPG.
PR UNKNOWN, wl as T.Homespun in an artists' amateur performance of *The Heir at Law*, woodcut, for *Illust London News*, 6 May 1848, NPG. UNKNOWN, after a photograph by Elliott & Fry, hs, woodcut, for *Illust London News*, 14 April 1877, BM, NPG.
PH ELLIOTT & FRY, hs, cartè, NPG (Album 104).

TORRENS, Sir Arthur Wellesley (1809-1855) major-general.
PR G.SANDERS, after Lowes Dickinson, wl seated, mezz, pub 1864, NPG.

TORRENS, William Torrens McCullagh (1813-1894) politician.
C SIR LESLIE WARD ('Spy'), wl, profile, chromo-lith, for *Vanity Fair*, 8 Dec 1883, NPG.

TOSTI, Sir Francesco Paolo (1847-1916) song writer.
P SIR JOHN LAVERY, 1903, hl, Royal College of Music, London.
D GEORGE WASHINGTON LAMBERT, hs, pencil, NPG 3137.
C SIR MAX BEERBOHM, in a group 'An audition', ink, w/c over chalk, 1908, BM.
PH WALERY, wl, print, NPG.

TOTTENHAM, Arthur Loftus (1838-1887) politician.
C SIR LESLIE WARD ('Spy'), wl, w/c study, for *Vanity Fair*, 15 April 1882, NPG 4748.

TOUT, Thomas Frederick (1855-1929) historian and teacher.
P? UNKNOWN, St David's University College, Lampeter.
PH LAFAYETTE, print, Pembroke College, Oxford. WALTER STONEMAN, 1917, hs, NPG (NPR).

TOWNSEND, Richard (1821-1884) mathematician.
P SARAH PURSER, after a photograph, tql seated, Trinity College, Dublin.

TOWNSHEND, John Robert, see 3rd Viscount and 1st Earl Sydney.

TOWNSHEND, John Townshend, 5th Marquess (1831-1899) politician and landowner.
C ALFRED THOMPSON, wl, w/c study, for *Vanity Fair*, 26 Feb 1870, NPG 2604.
PH W.WALKER & SONS, tql seated, carte, NPG AX7426.

TOYNBEE, Arnold (1852-1883) economist and social reformer.
SC SIR J.E.BOEHM, posthumous marble medallion, Balliol College, Oxford; plaster cast, NPG 2486.

TOYNBEE, Joseph (1815-1866) aural surgeon.
D R.H.RUSHTON, Royal Society of Medicine, London.

TOYNBEE, Paget Jackson (1855-1932) Dante scholar.
PH WALTER STONEMAN, 1921, hs, NPG (NPR).

TRAILL, Henry Duff (1842-1900) journalist and writer.
C HARRY FURNISS, pen and ink sketch, NPG 3529.
PH UNKNOWN, tql, cabinet, NPG X13233.

TREE, Ann Maria, see Bradshaw.

TREE, Ellen (Mrs Charles Kean) (1805-1880) actress.
P Attrib GEORGE CLINT, wl in costume for *Love's Sacrifice*, Harvard University, Cambridge, Mass, USA.

PR Various theatrical prints, Harvard Theatre Collection, Cambridge, Mass.

TREE, Sir Herbert Beerbohm (1852-1917) actor-manager.
P CHARLES BUCHEL, three portraits, as 'The Beloved Vagabond', as Hamlet, and ? as Richard III, Royal Academy of Dramatic Art, London. J.S.SARGENT, hs as Svengali in *Trilby*, Garrick Club, London.
D CHARLES BUCHEL, *c*1903, as Zakkuri in *The Darling of the Gods*, charcoal, V & A. S.P.HALL, hs, profile, pencil sketch, made at the sessions of the Parnell Commission, NPG 2263. ALFRED MORROW, hs as Svengali, w/c, Garrick Club.
M ETHEL WEBLING, 1892, Russell-Cotes Art Gallery, Bournemouth.
G JOHN COLLIER, a scene from *The Merry Wives of Windsor*, with Ellen Terry and Madge Kendal, oil, 1904, Garrick Club.
SC SIR GEORGE FRAMPTON, 1918, plaster cast of death mask, NPG 2392.
C SIR LESLIE WARD ('Spy'), wl, profile, chromo-lith, for *Vanity Fair*, 12 July 1890, NPG. HARRY FURNISS, 1905, wl, pen and ink, for *The Garrick Gallery*, NPG 4095(11). SIR MAX BEERBOHM, *c*1908, tql, drg, Ashmolean Museum, Oxford, and wl, back view, drg, V & A. 'NIBS', wl, Hentschel-Colourtype, for *Vanity Fair*, 5 April 1911, NPG.
PH W. & D.DOWNEY, tql as Hamlet, woodburytype, for Cassell's *Cabinet Portrait Gallery*, vol III, 1892, NPG. W. & D.DOWNEY, tql, cabinet, NPG X12557. ELLIS & WALERY, hs, photogravure, NPG X5601. Various woodburytypes, photogravures and postcards, some in character, NPG.

TRELOAR, Sir William Purdie, Bart (1843-1923) manufacturer and philanthropist.
P PHILIP TENNYSON COLE, 1907, hl, cut down from wl, Guildhall Art Gallery, London.
C HARRY FURNISS, pen and ink sketch, NPG 3613. SIR LESLIE WARD ('Spy'), wl, semi-profile, in mayor's robes, chromo-lith, for *Vanity Fair*, 8 March 1894, NPG.

TRENCH, Richard Chenevix (1807-1886) archbishop of Dublin, poet and philologist.
P SIR T.A.JONES, Archbishop of Dublin. UNKNOWN, The Deanery, Westminster.
D SAMUEL LAURENCE, *c*1841, head, chalk, NPG 1685. GEORGE RICHMOND, 1859, two drgs, See House, Dublin, and Synod Hall, Dublin. THOMAS BRIDGFORD, Alexandra College, Dublin.
PR J.R.JACKSON, after G.Richmond, hl, mezz, pub 1863, BM, NPG. Various prints and woodcuts, some after photographs, NPG.
PH H.HERING, tql seated, carte, NPG X13234. MASON & CO, hs, carte, NPG X13235. W.WALKER & SONS, tql seated, carte, NPG AX7457. HERBERT WATKINS, 1857, hs, oval, print, NPG AX7923. UNKNOWN, tql seated, print, NPG AX7319. UNKNOWN, *c*1874, tql seated, woodburytype, NPG X6016.

TRENT, Jesse Boot, 1st Baron (1850-1931) businessman and philanthropist.
SC C.L.J.DOMAN, bust, Nottingham University.

TREVELYAN, Sir Charles Edward, 1st Bart (1807-1886) governor of Madras.
PR D.J.POUND, after a photograph by John Watkins, tql seated, stipple and line, NPG.
PH W. & D.DOWNEY, tql seated, cabinet, NPG X4988. SOUTHWELL BROS, wl, carte, NPG X13236. JOHN WATKINS, hs, carte, NPG X13237.

TREVELYAN, Sir George Otto, 2nd Bart (1838-1928) statesman and historian; nephew of Lord Macaulay.
P JAMES ARCHER, RA 1872, wl seated, Wallington Hall (NT),

Northumberland. FRANK HOLL, 1886, tql, Trinity College, Cambridge.
D FANNY, LADY HOLROYD, 1911, hs, w/c, NPG 2224.
C SIR LESLIE WARD ('Spy'), wl, semi-profile, chromo-lith, for *Vanity Fair*, 2 Aug 1873, NPG 2743.
PH W. & D.DOWNEY, hl, woodburytype, for Cassell's *Cabinet Portrait Gallery*, vol IV, 1893, NPG.

TREVES, Sir Frederick, Bart (1853-1923) surgeon.
P SIR LUKE FILDES, 1896, tql, London Hospital; reduced replica, NPG 2917.
C SIR LESLIE WARD ('Spy'), tql, chromo-lith, for *Vanity Fair*, 19 July 1900, NPG.
PH WALTER STONEMAN, 1918, hs, NPG (NPR).

TREVETHIN, Sir Alfred Tristram Lawrence, 1st Baron (1843-1936) lord chief justice of England.
P R.G.EVES, RA 1922, tql seated in robes, Middle Temple, London.
C SIR LESLIE WARD ('Spy'), hl at bench, mechanical repro, for *Vanity Fair*, 16 Oct 1907, NPG.
PH WALTER STONEMAN, 1925, hs, NPG (NPR).

TRISTRAM, Henry Baker (1822-1906) canon of Durham.
PH LOCK & WHITFIELD, hs, oval, woodburytype, for *Men of Mark*, 1883, NPG.

TROLLOPE, Anthony (1815-1882) novelist.
P SAMUEL LAURENCE, *c*1864, hs, NPG 1680. HENRY NELSON O'NEIL, 1873, tql seated, Garrick Club, London.
G HENRY NELSON O'NEIL, 'The Billiard Room of the Garrick Club', oil, 1869, Garrick Club.
C SIR LESLIE WARD ('Spy'), wl, w/c study, for *Vanity Fair*, 5 April 1873, NPG 3915.
PH JULIA MARGARET CAMERON, 1864, hs, print, NPG P18 (32). ASHFORD BROS, wl, carte, NPG X12817. ELLIOTT & FRY, hs, carte, NPG X12818. LOCK & WHITFIELD, hs, oval, woodburytype, for *Men of Mark*, 1878, NPG. LONDON STEREOSCOPIC CO, hs, carte, NPG X12820. NAUDIN, wl, carte, NPG AX7541. MARCUS WARD, hs, carte, NPG X12819. HERBERT WATKINS, three cartes, all wl, NPG X12821-2 and X12824.

TROLLOPE, Edward (1817-1893) bishop of Nottingham and antiquary.
PH SAMUEL A.WALKER, *c*1889, tql, print, NPG X13254.

TROTTER, Coutts (1837-1887) vice-master of Trinity College, Cambridge.
SC THOMAS WOOLNER, 1888, marble bust, Trinity College, Cambridge.

TROUBRIDGE, Sir Thomas St Vincent Hope Cochrane (1815-1867) colonel.
PR UNKNOWN, hs, woodcut, for *Illust London News*, 19 Oct 1867, NPG.

TRURO, Charles Robert Claude Wilde, 2nd Baron (1816-1891) lawyer.
C CARLO PELLEGRINI ('Ape'), wl, profile, w/c study, for *Vanity Fair*, 1 Jan 1887, NPG 4749.

TRYON, Sir George (1832-1893) vice-admiral.
SL UNKNOWN, hs, profile, NPG.
PR UNKNOWN, from a drg by C.W.Walton (from a photograph of 1891), hs in uniform, engr, NPG.

TUCKER, Alfred Robert (1849-1914) bishop of Eastern Equatorial Africa.
PR R.T., after a photograph by Samuel A.Walker, hs, wood engr, for *Illust London News*, 17 May 1890, NPG.
PH UNKNOWN, hl, print, NPG (Anglican Bishops).

TUCKER, Sir Charles (1838-1935) general.

P H.A.OLIVIER, two portraits in the mantle of a Knight Grand Cross of the Bath, Staffordshire Regimental Museum, Lichfield.

TUFNELL, Henry (1805-1854) secretary to the treasury.
PR W.HOLL, after G.Richmond, hs, profile, stipple, one of 'Grillion's Club' series, BM, NPG.

TUFNELL, Thomas Jolliffe (1819-1885) surgeon.
P SIR T.A.JONES, exhib 1875, Royal College of Surgeons, Dublin.

TUKE, Henry Scott (1858-1929) painter.
PH ELLIOTT & FRY, hl, cabinet, NPG X13238.

TULLOCH, Sir Alexander Murray (1803-1864) major-general.
PR UNKNOWN, hl seated in uniform, woodcut, for *Illust London News*, 2 July 1864, NPG.

TULLOCH, John (1823-1886) theologian, principal of St Andrews University.
P ROBERT HERDMAN, 1879, wl, University of St Andrews; 1880, tql replica, SNPG 219. SIR GEORGE REID, RA 1881, hs, Royal Coll.
G A.E.EMSLIE, 'Dinner at Haddo House, 1884', oil, NPG 3845.
PH J.MOFFAT, hs, cabinet, NPG X6862. T.RODGER, hl, carte, NPG X13239.

TUPPER, Sir Charles, 1st Bart (1821-1915) Canadian statesman.
PR 'R.T.', hs, wood engr, for *Illust London News*, 31 July 1886, NPG.
C 'OWL', wl seated, mechanical repro, for *Vanity Fair*, 30 July 1913, NPG.
PH BARRAUD, hl, print, for *Men and Women of the Day*, vol IV, 1891, NPG AX5514. W. & D.DOWNEY, hs, woodburytype, for Cassell's *Cabinet Portrait Gallery*, vol II, 1891, NPG.

TUPPER, Martin Farquhar (1810-1889) poet, writer and barrister.
D FRANÇOIS THEODORE ROCHARD, 1846, tql, w/c, NPG 4381.
PR W.WALKER, after H.W.Pickersgill, hl, stipple, NPG. J.BAKER, after a photograph?, hs, profile, stipple, NPG. D.J.POUND, after a photograph by Mayall, tql seated, stipple and line, NPG.
PH DUTHIE, hs, carte, NPG (Album 102). ERNEST EDWARDS, tql seated, print, for *Men of Eminence*, vol III, 1865, NPG. SOUTHWELL BROS, wl, carte, NPG AX7509.

TURNBULL, William Barclay David Donald (1811-1863) antiquary and genealogist.
PR J.ARCHER, hs, lith, NPG.

TURNER, James Smith (1832-1904) dentist.
P SIDNEY HODGES, 1890, British Dental Association, London.

TURNER, Sir William (1832-1916) principal of Edinburgh University.
P SIR JAMES GUTHRIE, 1912, tql seated in academic robes, Edinburgh University.
D W.GRAHAM BOSS, pencil, SNPG 1709.
PR W.HOLE, tql, etch, for *Quasi Cursores*, 1884, NPG.

TWEEDDALE, Arthur Hay, 9th Marquess of (1824-1878)

soldier and naturalist.
PR UNKNOWN, after Barraud and Jerrard, hs, woodcut, for *Illust London News*, 18 Jan 1879, NPG.
PH T.R.WILLIAMS, c1860, hs, print, NPG X1505.

TWEEDDALE, William Montagu Hay, 10th Marquess of (1826-1911) landowner.
PR UNKNOWN, after a photograph by W.Kurtz of New York, hs, woodcut, for *Illust London News*, 9 Feb 1884, NPG.
C CARLO PELLEGRINI ('Ape'), wl, profile, w/c study, for *Vanity Fair*, 12 Dec 1874, NPG 4750.

TWEEDMOUTH, Edward Marjoribanks, 2nd Baron (1849-1909) politician.
C SIR LESLIE WARD ('Spy'), wl, chromo-lith, for *Vanity Fair*, 12 July 1894, NPG. SIR MAX BEERBOHM, 1907, drg, New Club, Edinburgh.

TYABJI, Badruddin (1844-1906) Indian judge and reformer.
P HAITE, Bombay High Court, India.

TYLOR, Sir Edward Burnett (1832-1917) anthropologist.
P W.E.MILLER, hl seated, semi-profile, Balliol College, Oxford.
D GEORGE BONAVIA, 1860, hs, chalk and pastel, NPG 1912.

TYNDALL, John (1820-1893) scientist.
P JOHN MCLURE HAMILTON, 1893, hl seated, NPG 1287; related lith, Walker Art Gallery, Liverpool.
D GEORGE RICHMOND, 1864, Royal Institution, London.
SC THOMAS WOOLNER, 1876, medallion, Royal Institution.
PR C.H.JEENS, after a photograph, hs, stipple, for *Nature*, 1874, BM.
C HARRY FURNISS, two pen and ink sketches, NPG 3530, 3614. ADRIANO CECIONI, tql, chromo-lith, for *Vanity Fair*, 6 April 1872, NPG.
PH ERNEST EDWARDS, wl, print, for *Men of Eminence*, ed L.Reeve, vol II, 1864, NPG. F.GUTEKUNST, 1873, tql seated, print, NPG X13250. LOCK & WHITFIELD, hs, oval, woodburytype, for *Men of Mark*, 1877, NPG. BARRAUD, hl, print, for *Men and Women of the Day*, vol II, 1889, NPG AX5469. W. & D.DOWNEY, tql seated, woodburytype, for Cassell's *Cabinet Portrait Gallery*, vol V, 1894, NPG. ALEXANDER BASSANO, hs, cabinet, NPG X13243. ELLIOTT & FRY, two cartes, hs and hl, NPG X13245-6. G.JERRARD, hs, cabinet, NPG X13244. MAULL & POLYBLANK, wl, carte, NPG X13247.

TYNTE, Charles John Kemeys (1800-1882) MP for Somerset West.
G SIR GEORGE HAYTER, 'The House of Commons, 1833', oil, NPG 54.

TYRRELL, Robert Yelverton (1844-1914) classical scholar.
P A.A.WOLMARK, 1907, Trinity College, Dublin.

TYRWHITT, Richard St John (1827-1895) writer on art.
PH C.L.DODGSON ('Lewis Carroll'), c1856, tql seated, print, NPG P7(17).

TYSSEN-AMHERST, William Amhurst, see 1st Baron AMHERST of Hackney.

U

ULLSWATER, James William Lowther, 1st Viscount (1855-1949) speaker of the House of Commons.

P P.A.DE LÁSZLÓ, 1907, hs, Inner Temple, London. P.A.DE LÁSZLÓ, Law Courts, Carlisle. GEORGE FIDDES WATT, 1922, wl seated in speaker's gown, Palace of Westminster, London. GEORGE FIDDES WATT, RA 1922, tql in robes, on loan to County Hall, Ipswich.

PR R.T. & CO, hs, wood engr, for *Illust London News*, 10 Oct 1891, NPG.

C HARRY FURNISS, pen and ink sketch, NPG 3615. SIR LESLIE WARD ('Spy'), wl, w/c study, for *Vanity Fair*, 19 Dec 1891, NPG 4610. SIR LESLIE WARD ('Spy'), wl in speaker's robes, profile, mechanical repro, for *Vanity Fair*, 24 Oct 1906, NPG.

PH HENRY MAYSON, hs, print, NPG. JOHN RUSSELL & SONS, hs, print, for *National Photographic Record*, vol I, NPG. RUSSELL & SONS, hs, print, for *Our Conservative Statesmen*, vol I, NPG (Album 16). SIR BENJAMIN STONE, two prints, both wl, NPG.

PR ALPHONSE LEGROS, etch, Imperial College, London.

UNDERHILL, Edward Bean (1813-1901) missionary advocate.

PR UNKNOWN, hl seated, stipple, NPG.

UNWIN, William Cawthorne (1838-1933) engineer.

P WILFRID WALTER, 1914, tql seated, Institution of Civil Engineers, London. HAROLD SPEED, 1920, tql seated, Institute of Mechanical Engineers, London.

URE, Alexander, see Baron Strathclyde.

URWICK, William (1826-1905) non-conformist divine and chronicler.

PR J.COCHRAN, after a photograph by Maull & Polyblank, hl seated, stipple, NPG.

V

VALLANCE, William Fleming (1827-1904) artist.
D J.R.ABERCROMBY, wash, SNPG 1748.

VANDENHOFF, Charlotte Elizabeth (Mrs T.Swinbourne) (1818-1860) actress.
PR Several theatrical prints, and prints after photographs, BM, NPG, Harvard Theatre Collection, Cambridge, Mass, USA.

VANE-TEMPEST, George Henry Robert Charles William, see 5th Marquess of Londonderry.

VANE-TEMPEST-STEWART, Charles Stewart, see 6th Marquess of Londonderry.

VAUGHAN, Bernard John (1847-1922) Jesuit priest.
C SIR LESLIE WARD ('Spy'), wl, mechanical repro, for *Vanity Fair*, 30 Jan 1907, NPG.
PH G.C.BERESFORD, 1905, two negs, hs, and hs, profile, NPG x6604-5. RUSSELL & SONS, tql seated, cabinet, NPG x12581. SARONY & CO, hs, profile, photogravure, NPG x13256.

VAUGHAN, Charles John (1816-1897) dean of Llandaff.
P GEORGE RICHMOND, c1866-7, tql, Harrow School, Middx. W.W.OULESS, 1895, tql seated, Trinity College, Cambridge.
D GEORGE RICHMOND, 1853, hs, chalk, Inner Temple, London.
SC SIR WILLIAM GOSCOMBE JOHN, c1900, recumbent marble effigy, Llandaff Cathedral.
PR Several popular prints, NPG.
C UNKNOWN, hl, profile, in pulpit, chromo-lith, for *Vanity Fair*, 24 Aug 1872, NPG.
PH ELLIOTT & FRY, hs, profile, carte, NPG x13257. LOCK & WHITFIELD, hs, oval, woodburytype, for *Men of Mark*, 1882, NPG. LONDON STEREOSCOPIC CO, hs, cabinet, NPG x13258. SAMUEL A.WALKER, hs, profile, cabinet, NPG x4989. UNKNOWN, wl, carte, NPG x13259.

VAUGHAN, David James (1825-1905) canon of Peterborough.
PR C.H.JEENS, tql, seated, stipple, BM.

VAUGHAN, Henry Halford (1811-1885) historian.
PH JULIA MARGARET CAMERON, 1864, hs, oval, print, P18(20).

VAUGHAN, Herbert Alfred (1832-1903) cardinal.
SC UNKNOWN, recumbent figure, Westminster Cathedral, London.
C SIR LESLIE WARD ('Spy'), wl, profile, chromo-lith, for *Vanity Fair*, 7 Jan 1893, NPG.
PH LONDON STEREOSCOPIC CO, hl, print, NPG x13260.

VAUGHAN, Kate (1852?-1903) actress.
PR Several theatrical prints, Harvard Theatre Collection, Cambridge, Mass, USA.
PH W. & D.DOWNEY, tql, one of thirteen woodburytypes grouped to form a panel, 'Some leading Actresses', for Cassell's *Cabinet Portrait Gallery*, vol I, 1890, NPG. KINGSBURY & NOTCUTT, tql, cabinet, NPG x4180.

VAUX of Harrowden, George Charles Mostyn, 6th Baron (1804-1883) representative peer.
D FREDERICK SARGENT, hl, pencil, NPG 1834 (ff).

VEITCH, Sir Harry James (1840-1924) horticulturist.
P H.G.RIVIERE, 1909, Royal Horticultural Society, London.

VENABLES, George Stovin (1810-1888) journalist.
D UNKNOWN, chalk, Jesus College, Cambridge.

VENN, John (1834-1923) man of letters.
P C.E.BROCK, Gonville and Caius College, Cambridge.
D E.CLIFFORD, 1889, crayon, Queen's College, Cambridge.

VERNEY, Sir Harry, 2nd Bart (1801-1894) soldier, traveller and politician.
G SIR GEORGE HAYTER, 'The House of Commons, 1833', oil, NPG 54.
C SIR LESLIE WARD ('Spy'), wl, profile, chromo-lith, for *Vanity Fair*, 15 July 1882, NPG.

VERNEY, Margaret Maria Verney, Lady (1844-1930) historical writer.
P SIR W.B.RICHMOND, c1868, wl in her wedding dress, Claydon House (NT), Bucks.

VERNON, Augustus Henry Vernon, 6th Baron (1829-1883) president of the Royal Agricultural Society.
P ANGELO ROMAGNOLI, 1884, Sudbury Hall (NT), Derbys.
D GEORGE RICHMOND, 1866, chalk, Sudbury Hall.

VERNON, George John Warren Vernon, 5th Baron (1803-1866) politician and Dante scholar.
P JOHN COLLIER, Sudbury Hall (NT), Derbys.
D SIR GEORGE HAYTER, head, pencil and ink, BM.
G SIR GEORGE HAYTER, 'The House of Commons, 1833', oil, NPG 54.
PR UNKNOWN, hl, profile, mezz, pub 1839, BM.

VERNON, Robert, see Baron Lyveden.

VERRALL, Arthur Woollgar (1851-1912) classical scholar.
P TADELL, tql seated, Trinity College, Cambridge.
D SIR WILLIAM ROTHENSTEIN, 1908, hs, chalk, Fitzwilliam Museum, Cambridge. EDMOND KAPP, 1911, Barber Institute of Fine Arts, Birmingham.
PH UNKNOWN, hs, print, BM (Engr Ports Coll).

VESTEY, William Vestey, 1st Baron (1859-1940) director of the Union Cold Storage Company.
PH WALTER STONEMAN, 1924, hs, NPG (NPR).

VEZIN, Hermann (1829-1910) actor.
PR E.MATTHEWS & SONS, hs, oval, lith, NPG.
C A.B., wl, lith, NPG.
PH UNKNOWN, hs, profile, print, for *The Theatre*, 1878, BM (Engr Ports Coll). BARRAUD, hs, print, for *Men and Women of the Day*, vol IV, 1891, NPG AX5529. DAILY MIRROR STUDIOS, 1909, two postcards, with others, in character, NPG x8736 and x8738.

VEZIN, Jane Elizabeth (1827-1902) actress, formerly Mrs Charles Young.
PH UNKNOWN, hs, woodburytype, carte, NPG AX7618.

VICTOR Ferdinand Franz Eugen Gustaf Adolf Constantin Friedrich of Hohenlohe-Langenburg, Prince, see Count GLEICHEN.

VICTORIA, Queen (1819-1901) reigned 1837-1901.
P SIR WILLIAM BEECHEY, 1821, wl with her mother, Royal Coll. WILLIAM FOWLER, 1827, tql, Royal Coll. RICHARD WESTALL, 1830, wl, Royal Coll. A.J.DUBOIS DRAHONET, 1832, Royal Coll.

SIR GEORGE HAYTER, 1837, seated in robes of state, Guildhall Art Gallery, London. SIR GEORGE HAYTER, 1838, wl seated in coronation robes, Royal Coll; replica, NPG 1250. SIR GEORGE HAYTER, 1838, taking the coronation oath, Queen's University, Belfast. THOMAS SULLY, 1838, tql, Wallace Collection, London. AGOSTINO AGLIO, c1838, wl, Palace of Westminster, London. SIR FRANCIS GRANT, 1839–40, on horseback, with Lord Melbourne and others, Royal Coll. SIR EDWIN LANDSEER, 1839, tql, profile, Royal Coll. SIR EDWIN LANDSEER, c1839, several related equestrian paintings, for example, one with dogs and a cavalry escort, in front of Windsor Castle, Royal Coll, and another with dogs, attendants and a dead stag, in Windsor Home Park, Wolverhampton Art Gallery. SIR DAVID WILKIE, 1840, wl, Lady Lever Art Gallery, Port Sunlight. JOHN PARTRIDGE, 1840, tql, Royal Coll. F.X.WINTERHALTER, 1840, hl in bridal veil, Royal Coll. WILLIAM FOWLER, c1840, hl with Garter ribbon, Royal Coll. SIR M.A.SHEE, 1842, Royal Academy, London. F.X.WINTERHALTER, 1842, tql, profile, Royal Coll. SIR EDWIN LANDSEER, 1842, with Prince Albert, dressed as Queen Philippa and Edward III for a bal costumé, Royal Coll. SIR FRANCIS GRANT, 1843, formerly United Service Club, London (c/o Crown Commissioners). F.X.WINTERHALTER, 1843, wl in garter robes, Royal Coll. F.X.WINTERHALTER, 1843, hl with loose, flowing hair, Royal Coll. F.X.WINTERHALTER, 1845, wl, Royal Coll. SIR FRANCIS GRANT, 1845, on horseback, Christ's Hospital, Horsham, Sussex. SIR EDWIN LANDSEER, 1845, dressed as Catherine the Great for a bal costumé, Royal Coll. COUNT ALFRED D'ORSAY, 1846, wl on horseback, DoE. F.X.WINTERHALTER, 1846, with The Prince of Wales, Royal Coll. H.J.STEWART, 1847, landing at Dumbarton, Dumbarton County Council. F.X.WINTERHALTER, 1850, wl seated with Prince Arthur, Royal Coll. SIR FRANCIS GRANT, 1850, on horseback, Army and Navy Club, London. F.X.WINTERHALTER, 1852, with the Duchess of Nemours, Royal Coll. E.BOUTIBONNE and J.F.HERRING, 1856, on horseback, Royal Coll. F.X.WINTERHALTER, 1856, hl in red, Royal Coll. F.X.WINTERHALTER, 1859, seated in robes of state, Royal Coll. ALBERT GRAEFLE, 1864, tql, Royal Coll. HEINRICH VON ANGELI, 1875, tql, Royal Coll; w/c copy, NPG 708. HEINRICH VON ANGELI, 1885, Royal Coll. STEPHEN CATTERSON SMITH jun, 1887, Royal College of Surgeons, Dublin. HENRY GRANT, 1888, Corporation of Devizes. HEINRICH VON ANGELI, 1893, Royal Coll. LAURITS TUXEN, 1894, Kunsthistorisk Pladearkiv, Copenhagen. J.H.BENTLEY, c1897, Guildhall, Lincoln. BENJAMIN CONSTANT, 1899, Royal Coll. H.VON ANGELI, 1899, Royal Coll. F.X.WINTERHALTER, with a wreath of corn in her hair, Royal Coll. L.CASABIANCA, Corporation of London. HENRY WEIGALL, Burghley House, Northants. SIR J.J.SHANNON, SNPG 1124.

D S.P.DENNING, 1823, wl, w/c, Dulwich College Picture Gallery, London. S.CATTERSON SMITH, 1828, Royal Coll. R.J.LANE, 1829, Royal Coll. JOHN HAYTER, 1830, Royal Coll. SIR GEORGE HAYTER, 1834, with her mother, Royal Coll. CARL VOGEL, 1834, Küpferstichkabinett, Staatliche Kunstsammlungen, Dresden. LOUISA COSTELLO, 1837, Royal Coll. A.E.CHALON, 1838, in robes of state, w/c, Royal Coll of Belgium. A.E.CHALON, 1838, wl seated on a terrace at Windsor Castle, SNPG 1000. A.E.PENLEY, c1840, tql, w/c, NPG 4108. F.X.WINTERHALTER, 1851, with Prince Albert, dressed as Catherine of Braganza and Charles II for a bal costumé, Royal Coll, EUGÈNE LAMI, 1853, w/c V & A. F.X.WINTERHALTER, 1855, w/c Royal Coll. SIR J.NOEL PATON, 1863, study for the unfinished picture of 'Royal Family mourning Prince Albert', at Kew Palace, Royal Coll. ADOLPHE DE BATHE, 1880s–90s, hl, profile, pencil, NPG 4042. SIR HUBERT VON HERKOMER, 1901, on her death-bed, w/c, Royal Coll.

M Various, by J.P.FISCHER (1819), ATHONY STEWART (c1822 and c1826), HENRY COLLEN (c1837), SIR W.C.ROSS (1837, c1840 and 1841), ROBERT THORBURN (1844, and 1847, copy of a miniature with Prince Alfred and Princess Helena), Royal Coll. SIR W.C.ROSS, 1847, Trinity College, Cambridge. MRS CORBOULD-ELLIS, c1896, Corporation of London. MISS M.H.CARLISLE, hs, profile, NPG 2088.

G Numerous family groups and groups depicting royal occasions, eg: SIR DAVID WILKIE, 'The Queen Presiding over her First Council, 1837', oil, 1837, Royal Coll. J.H.NIXON, 'Queen Victoria's Progress to the Guildhall', oil, 1837, Corporation of London. SIR GEORGE HAYTER, 'The Coronation of Queen Victoria', oil, 1838, Royal Coll. C.R.LESLIE, 'Queen Victoria receiving the Sacrament at her Coronation', oil, 1838, Royal Coll. R.B.DAVIS, 'Queen Victoria and her Suite' (on horseback), oil, 1839, Plas Newydd (NT), Gwynedd. SIR GEORGE HAYTER, 'Marriage of Queen Victoria and Prince Albert', oil, 1840, Royal Coll. C.R.LESLIE, 'Christening of the Princess Royal', oil, 1841, Royal Coll. SIR GEORGE HAYTER, 'The Christening of the Prince of Wales', oil, 1842, Royal Coll. SIR EDWIN LANDSEER, 'Windsor Castle in Modern Times', oil, 1842, Royal Coll. SIR FRANCIS GRANT, 1842, wl seated with the Prince of Wales and the Princess Royal, Royal Coll. SIR EDWIN LANDSEER, 1842, with the Prince of Wales and the Princess Royal, oil, Royal Coll. F.X.WINTERHALTER, 'Reception of Queen Victoria and Prince Albert by Louis Philippe, at the Château d'Eu', oil, 1843, Musée de Versailles. F.X.WINTERHALTER, 'Reception of Louis Philippe at Windsor', oil, 1844, Musée de Versailles. ALEXANDER BLAIKLEY, 'Queen Victoria opening Parliament, 1845', oil, Palace of Westminster. F.X.WINTERHALTER, 1846, with her family, Royal Coll. H.C.SELOUS, 'The Opening of the Crystal Palace', oil, 1851, V & A. F.X.WINTERHALTER, 'May the First, 1851', oil, Royal Coll. E.M.WARD, 'Queen Victoria visiting the Tomb of Napoleon I', and 'Queen Victoria Investing Napoleon III with the order of the Garter at Windsor Castle', both oil, 1855, Royal Coll. G.H.THOMAS, 'Queen Victoria Decorating Crimean War Heroes', oil, 1855, Royal Coll. JOHN PHILLIP, 'The Marriage of the Princess Royal', oil, 1858, Royal Coll. G.H.THOMAS, 'Queen Victoria and Prince Albert at a Military Review at Aldershot', oil, 1859, Royal Coll. THOMAS JONES BARKER, 'Queen Victoria Presenting a Bible in the Audience Chamber at Windsor', oil, c1861, NPG 4969. UNKNOWN, 'The Last Moments of the Prince Consort', c1861, Wellcome Institute of the History of Medicine, London. G.H.THOMAS, 'The Marriage of Princess Alice to Prince Louis of Hesse', oil, 1862, Royal Coll. W.P.FRITH, 'The Marriage of the Prince of Wales', oil, 1863, Royal Coll. J.C.HORSLEY, 1865, with her children (made to look as in c1850), oil, Royal Society of Arts, London. CHRISTIAN MAGNUSSEN, 'The Marriage of Princess Helena', 1866, Royal Coll. SIR EDWIN LANDSEER, on horseback with John Brown and two of her daughters, oil, 1866, Royal Coll. JAMES SANT, c1872, with three of her grandchildren, Royal Coll. NICHOLAS CHEVALIER, 'The Marriage of the Duke of Edinburgh', 1874. Royal Coll. S.P.HALL, 'The Marriage of the Duke of Connaught', 1879, Royal Coll. SIR J.D.LINTON, 'The Marriage of the Duke of Albany', 1882, Royal Coll. R.C.WOODVILLE, 'The Marriage of Princess Beatrice and Prince Maurice of Battenberg', 1885, Royal Coll. LAURITS TUXEN, 'The Royal Family at the Time of the Jubilee', oil, 1887, Royal Coll. SIR JOHN LAVERY, 'Queen Victoria's visit to the Glasgow Exhibition of 1888', oil, Corporation of Glasgow. SIR GEORGE REID, 'Baptism of Prince Maurice of Battenburg', oil, 1891, Royal Coll. LAURITS TUXEN, 'Marriage of George V and Queen Mary', 1893, and 'Marriage of Princess Maud and Prince Charles of Denmark', both Royal Coll. SIR W.Q.ORCHARDSON, 'The Four Generations', oil, 1897, Royal Agricultural Society, London; study, NPG 4536.

SC Numerous busts and statues, eg: WILLIAM BEHNES, 1829, marble bust, Royal Coll. SIR JOHN STEELL, 1838, plaster bust, SNPG 168. SIR FRANCIS CHANTREY, 1839, marble bust, Royal Coll; replica, NPG 1716 and preliminary drgs, NPG 316a (125–6). JOHN FRANCIS, 1840, marble bust, Reform Club, London, and c1842, marble bust, Guildhall Art Gallery, London. JOHANN FLATTERS, 1843, marble bust, V & A. SIR JOHN STEELL, 1844, statue, Royal Institution, Edinburgh. JOHN GIBSON, c1844, marble statue, Royal Coll. JOHN THOMAS, 1845, statue, Lincoln's Inn Library, London. J.G.LOUGH, 1845, marble statue, Royal Exchange, London. JOHN GIBSON, c1848, marble bust, Corporation of Liverpool. JOHN GIBSON, 1850–5, marble statue, Palace of Westminster, JOHN FRANCIS, 1850, marble bust, with Prince Albert, Geological Museum, London. THOMAS THORNYCROFT, 1853, bronze statuette, Royal Coll; related statue, 1860, on horseback, Liverpool. MATTHEW NOBLE, 1854, statue, Manchester, and 1856, marble bust, Palace of Westminster. WILLIAM THEED, 1860, marble bust, Grocers Hall, London. THOMAS EARLE, 1861, bust, Royal Coll. ALEXANDER BRODIE, 1865, marble statue, Aberdeen. JOSEPH DURHAM, 1866, statue, Public Record Office, London. WILLIAM THEED, 1868, marble statue, with Prince Albert, both dressed as Anglo-Saxons, Royal Coll. SIR J.E.BOEHM, 1871, marble statue, seated, Royal Coll; related plaster cast of bust, NPG 858. COUNT GLEICHEN, 1875, marble bust, Walker Art Gallery, Liverpool. C.B.BIRCH, 1876, bronze statue, Victoria Embankment, London. PRINCESS LOUISE, 1876, marble bust, Royal Academy, London. THOMAS WOOLNER, 1883, marble statue, Council House, Birmingham. F.J.WILLIAMSON, 1887, marble statue, Royal Coll. SIR J.E.BOEHM, 1887, bronze statue, in front of Windsor Castle. SIR ALFRED GILBERT, 1887, statue, Winchester. PRINCESS LOUISE, 1893, marble statue in coronation robes and made to look as in c1838, Kensington Gardens, London. SIR W.H.THORNYCROFT, 1896, statue, Royal Exchange, London. EDWARD ONSLOW FORD, 1897, marble bust, Royal Coll. SIR THOMAS BROCK, c1897, marble statue, Carlton House Terrace, London. EDWARD ONSLOW FORD, 1899, marble bust, Mansion House, London. E.R.MULLINS, 1900, statue, Port Elizabeth, South Africa. SIR GEORGE FRAMPTON, 1901, bronze statue, Victoria Memorial Hall, Calcutta. H.L.FLORENCE, 1904, bust, Victoria Monument, Kensington High Street, London. SIR T.BROCK and SIR A.WEBB, c1911, 'The Victoria Memorial', The Mall, London.

PR Numerous prints and popular prints, BM, NPG, Royal Coll.

PH Numerous prints by W.BAMBRIDGE, A.BASSANO, L.CALDESI, W. & D.DOWNEY, HILLS & SAUNDERS, J.RUSSELL & SONS, MAYALL, JABEZ HUGHES, HUGHES & MULLINS, ROBERT MILNE, WALERY and others, various dates and sizes, singly and in family groups, NPG, Royal Coll. Various prints by ROGER FENTON and others, V & A.

VICTORIA Adelaide Mary Louise, Princess Royal, later Empress of Germany (1840–1901) eldest daughter of Queen Victoria and Prince Albert.

P Various portraits in the Royal Coll: SIR EDWIN LANDSEER, 1841, wl lying in a chair, with 'Eos' the greyhound; SIR FRANCIS GRANT, 1842, wl with the Prince of Wales; T.M.JOY, 1842, wl with the Prince of Wales; F.X.WINTERHALTER, 1842, wl seated holding flowers; SIR EDWIN LANDSEER, 1842, with Java pony and St Bernard dog; JOHN LUCAS, 1844, tql; F.X.WINTERHALTER, c1844, with the Prince of Wales, playing in a forest near Balmoral; F.X.WINTERHALTER, 1851, hs, oval, part of a set of

portraits of the royal children; C.L.MÜLLER, 1856, hl; F.X.WINTERHALTER, 1857, tql holding fan; ALBERT GRAEFLE, c1860, tql; F.X.WINTERHALTER, 1867, hs; HEINRICH VON ANGELI, 1876, hl. F.X.WINTRHALTER, 1856, wl holding bouquet, oil sketch, Schloss Friedrichshof, Germany. HEINRICH VON ANGELI, several portraits: 1880, tql in fancy dress, Staatliche Schlosser und Gärten, Potsdam-Sanssouci; 1882, hl, Wallace Collection, London, and 1893, hl seated in widow's weeds, Schloss Friedrichshof, Germany. JOSEPH MORDECAI, after a photograph of c1900, hs, NPG 4430.

D Various drgs by QUEEN VICTORIA, 1841–2, Royal Coll. SIR EDWIN LANDSEER, 1842, on her father's lap, Royal Coll. SIR GEORGE HAYTER, 1842, holding a doll, Royal Coll. F.X.WINTERHALTER, 1850, with Princess Alice, in 18th century costumes, w/c, Royal Coll.

M SIR W.C.ROSS, 1841, hl as a cherub, Royal Coll. SIR W.C.ROSS, 1845, hl, part of set of miniatures of the royal children, Royal Coll. SIR W.C.ROSS, 1850, wl in Turkish dress, Royal Coll. H.C.HEATH, c1860, after A.Hahnisch, Royal Coll. ZEHNGRAFF, post 1888, probably after a photograph, in mourning costume, Royal Coll.

G C.R.LESLIE, 'Christening of the Princess Royal', oil, 1841, Royal Coll. SIR FRANCIS GRANT, 1842, with Queen Victoria and the Prince of Wales, oil, Royal Coll. SIR EDWIN LANDSEER, 'Windsor Castle in Modern Times', oil, 1842, Royal Coll. SIR EDWIN LANDSEER, 1842, with Queen Victoria and the Prince of Wales, oil, Royal Coll. F.X.WINTERHALTER, 'Reception of Queen Victoria and Prince Albert by Louis Philippe at the Château d'Eu', oil, 1843, Musée de Versailles. F.X.WINTERHALTER, 'Reception of Louis Philippe at Windsor Castle', oil, 1844, Musée de Versailles. F.X.WINTERHALTER, a family group, oil, 1846, Royal Coll. SIR EDWIN LANDSEER, 'The Queen sketching at Loch Laggan with the Prince of Wales and the Princess Royal', oil, 1847, Royal Coll. F.X.WINTERHALTER, with Princesses Alice, Helena and Louise, oil, 1849, Royal Coll. H.C.SELOUS, 'The Opening of the Crystal Palace', oil, 1851, V & A. E.M.WARD, 'Queen Victoria Visiting the Tomb of Napoleon I', oil, 1855, Royal Coll. E.M.WARD, 'Queen Victoria Investing Napoleon III with the Order of the Garter at Windsor Castle', oil, 1855, Royal Coll. JOHN PHILLIP, 'The Marriage of the Princess Royal', oil, 1858, Royal Coll. A.MENZEL, 'Coronation of Wilhem I at Königsberg', oil, 1861, Staatliche Schlosser und Gärten, Potsdam. F.X.WINTERHALTER, 1862, wl with her husband and two sons, Royal Coll. W.P.FRITH, 'The Marriage of the Prince of Wales', oil, 1863, Royal Coll. J.C.HORSLEY, 1865, with Queen Victoria and other royal children (made to look as in c1850), oil, Royal Society of Arts, London. S.P.HALL, 'The Marriage of the Duke of Connaught', oil, 1879, Royal Coll. A.VON WERNER, 'The Baptism of Crown Prince Wilhelm', w/c, 1882, Staatliche Schlosser und Gärten, Potsdam. LAURITS TUXEN, 'The Royal Family at the time of the Jubilee', oil, 1887, Royal Coll. A.VON WERNER, 'Opening of the Reichstag under Wilhelm II', oil, 1888, Staatliche Schlosser und Gärten, Potsdam.

SC EMIL WOLFF, 1841, marble bust, Royal Coll. MARY THORNYCROFT, 1846, marble bust, Royal Coll. MARY THORNYCROFT, 1847, marble statue, as 'Summer', Royal Coll. HUGO HAGEN, c1858, marble bust (said to be c1874 but showing the sitter around the time of her marriage), Royal Coll. SUSAN D.DURANT, 1866, marble medallion, Royal Coll; small related ormolu medallion, NPG 2023a(5,6).

PR R.J.LANE, after W.C.ROSS (1841), hl, lith, BM, NPG. R.J.LANE, after W.C.ROSS, after a sketch by Queen Victoria (1841), wl seated, playing with a hound, lith, BM, NPG. H.ROBINSON, after W.C.ROSS, hl with Prince of Wales, stipple, pub 1842, BM.

J.B.HUNT, after A.Hunt, tql, stipple, for *Ladies' Companion*, 1853, BM, NPG. R.J.LANE, after F.X.Winterhalter, tql, lith, pub 1855, NPG. Various popular prints and prints after photographs, BM, NPG.
c C.DE GRIMM ('Nemo'), wl, chromo-lith, for *Vanity Fair*, 7 June 1884, NPG.
PH Numerous prints, singly and in family groups by W.BAMBRIDGE, L.CALDESI, ELLIOTT & FRY, HEINRICH GRAF, HERMAN GÜNTHER, L.HAASE & CO, HILLS & SAUNDERS, MAYALL, ROBERT MILNE, MONDEL & JACOB, CAMILLE SILVY and others, various dates and sizes, cartes, cabinets, etc, NPG, Royal Coll, V & A.

VÍGFÚSSON, Gúdbrandr (1828-1889) Icelandic scholar.
P H.M.PAGET, RA 1890, hl, Bodleian Library, Oxford.

VILLIERS, Augustus (1810-1847) soldier.
D COUNT ALFRED D'ORSAY, 1841, hs, profile, chalk, NPG 4026 (58).

VILLIERS, Charles Pelham (1802-1898) politician.
P SIR A.S.COPE, RA 1885, hs, Reform Club, London.
G S.BELLIN, after J.R.Herbert, 'Meeting of the Council of the Anti Corn Law League', mixed engr, pub 1850, BM, NPG.
SC WILLIAM THEED, 1879, statue, Wolverhampton.
PR S.W.REYNOLDS jun, after C.du Val, tql seated, octagon, mezz, pub 1844, BM, NPG. J.H.LYNCH, after a daguerreotype, hs, lith, NPG.
c UNKNOWN, wl, chromo-lith, for *Vanity Fair*, 31 Aug 1872, NPG.
PH W. & D.DOWNEY, tql seated, carte, NPG X13263. W.WALKER & SONS, tql seated, carte, NPG AX8667.

VILLIERS, George William Frederick, see 4th Earl of Clarendon.

VILLIERS, Henry Montagu (1813-1861) bishop of Durham.
PR C.BAUGNIET, tql, lith, BM, NPG. W.J.EDWARDS, after G.Richmond, hs, stipple, pub 1856, NPG. D.J.POUND, after a photograph by Mayall, tql, seated, stipple and line, for *Drawing Room Portrait Gallery of Eminent Personages*, NPG.
PH CUNDALL & DOWNES, hs, carte, NPG X13264.

VILLIERS, Margaret Elizabeth Child-, see Countess of Jersey.

VILLIERS, Victor Albert George Child-, see 7th Earl of Jersey.

VILLIERS STUART, Henry Windsor, see Stuart.

VINCENT, Sir (Charles Edward) Howard (1849-1908) director of criminal investigations.
c SIR LESLIE WARD ('Spy'), wl, profile, w/c study, for *Vanity Fair*, 22 Dec 1883, NPG 2744.
PH SIR BENJAMIN STONE, 1897–1901, three prints, all wl, NPG.

VINCENT, Sir Edgar, see Viscount D'Abernon.

VINES, Sydney Howard (1849-1934) botanist.
P JOHN COLLIER, 1905, Linnean Society, London.
PH ELLIOTT & FRY, print, Christ's College, Cambridge.

VINING, George James (1824-1875) actor.
PR Three theatrical prints, Harvard Theatre Collection, Cambridge, Mass, USA.
PH SOUTHWELL BROS, wl as Mercutio in *Romeo and Juliet*, carte, NPG X13265.

VINOGRADOFF, Sir Paul Gavrilovitch (1854-1925) jurist and historian.
P HENRY LAMB, *c*1925, hs, Examination Schools, Oxford.

PH EMERY WALKER, after Lafayette, 1913, hl, photogravure, NPG X13275. WALTER STONEMAN, 1918, hs, NPG (NPR).

VIVIAN, Sir Charles Crespigny Vivian, 2nd Baron (1808-1886) lord-lieutenant of Cornwall.
PR J.BROWN, after a photograph by Mayall, hl, stipple, for *Baily's Mag*, 1867, BM, NPG.
c SIR LESLIE WARD ('Spy'), wl, profile, chromo-lith, for *Vanity Fair*, 19 Aug 1876, NPG.

VIVIAN, Sir Henry Hussey, see 1st Baron Swansea.

VIVIAN, Sir Hussey Crespigny Vivian, 3rd Baron (1834-1893) diplomat.
PH LOCK & WHITFIELD, hl seated, carte, NPG X13266.

VIVIAN, Sir Robert John Hussey (1802-1887) general.
PR D.J.POUND, after a photograph by John Watkins, tql seated in uniform, stipple, presented with *Illust News of the World*, BM, NPG.

VIZETELLY, Henry (1820-1894) wood-engraver and publisher.
PR UNKNOWN, hs, woodcut, for *Illust London News*, 1892, BM.

VOELCKER, John Christopher Augustus (1822-1884) agricultural chemist.
PR J.B.HUNT, after a photograph, hl, stipple, pub 1869, NPG.

VOGEL, Sir Julius (1835-1899) prime minister of New Zealand.
PR UNKNOWN, hs, woodcut, for *Illust London News*, 3 July 1875, NPG.

VOKES, Frederick Mortimer (1846-1888) actor and dancer.
PR UNKNOWN, in a scene from a pantomime at Drury Lane, woodcut, for *Illust London News*, 13 Jan 1877, NPG
PH UNKNOWN, hl, woodburytype, carte, NPG AX7631.

VOKES, Jessie Catherine Biddulph (1851-1884) actress and dancer.
PR Two prints, one in a group, Harvard Theatre Collection, Cambridge, Mass, USA.
PH LOCK & WHITFIELD, *c*1876, two cartes, hl, semi-profile, and hl with her sisters Victoria and Rosina, woodburytypes, NPG AX7628 and AX7681.

VOKES, Rosina (1858-1894) actress.
PR Two lithographs, Harvard Theatre Collection, Cambridge, Mass, USA.
PH LOCK & WHITFIELD, *c*1876, two cartes, hl, and hl with her sisters Jessie and Victoria, woodburytypes, NPG AX7630 and AX7681.

VOKES, Victoria (1853-1894) actress and singer.
PR Two theatrical prints, Harvard Theatre Collection, Cambridge, Mass, USA.
PH LOCK & WHITFIELD, *c*1876, two cartes, hl, and hl with her sisters Jessie and Rosina, woodburytypes, NPG AX7629 and AX7681.

VOYSEY, Charles (1828-1912) theistic preacher.
c UNKNOWN, tql, chromo-lith, for *Vanity Fair*, 21 Oct 1871, NPG.
PH H.J.WHITLOCK, hl seated, semi-profile, carte, NPG (Album 40).

VOYSEY, Charles Francis Annesley (1857-1941) architect.
P HAROLD SPEED, 1905, hl seated, profile, NPG 5140. G.MEREDITH FRAMPTON, RA 1925, hs, The Art Workers' Guild, London.
D HAROLD SPEED, 1896, hs, profile, chalk, NPG 4116.
G S.P.HALL, 'The St John's Wood Arts Club, 1895', chalk and wash, NPG 4404.

W

WACE, Henry (1836-1924) dean of Canterbury.
P WILLIAM LOGSDAIL, 1903, tql seated, The Deanery, Canterbury.

WADDINGTON, John (1810-1880) divine.
PR J.COCHRAN, after a photograph, hs, stipple, NPG.

WADE, Sir Thomas Francis (1818-1895) diplomat.
PR UNKNOWN, after a photograph by Mrs Myers, hs, wood engr, for *Illust London News*, 10 Aug 1895, NPG.

WAGHORN, Thomas (1800-1850) pioneer of the overland route to India.
P SIR GEORGE HAYTER, hl, NPG 974.
SC H.H.ARMSTEAD, *c*1889, statue, Chatham, Kent.
PR DAY & HAGHE, after C.Baxter, hl, lith, pub 1837, NPG. G.B.BLACK, after Sabatier, hl seated in uniform, lith, NPG.

WAKEFIELD, Charles Cheers Wakefield, Viscount (1859-1941) businessman and philanthropist.
P FRANK BERESFORD, Worshipful Company of Haberdashers, London. SIR JOHN LAVERY, RA 1916, tql, Corporation of Hythe. SIR OSWALD BIRLEY, two portraits, 1932, tql seated, formerly Royal Aero Club, London (c/o Crown Commissioners), and 1934. Bethlem Royal Hospital, Beckenham, Kent.
G FRED ROE, 'Swearing in the City Guard at the Guildhall', oil, 1919-20, Corporation of London (on exhibition at Royal Military College, Shrivenham); hs study, drg, NPG.

WALDEGRAVE, Frances Elizabeth Anne Waldegrave, née Braham, Countess (1821-1879) leader of London Society.
PR A.MACLURE, tql with pug dog, lith, for *Whitehall Review*, 1876, BM. J.A.VINTER, after M.Tekusch, hs, lith, BM. UNKNOWN, hl, standing before mirror, lith, BM.

WALDEGRAVE, Samuel (1817-1869) bishop of Carlisle.
PR J.COCHRAN, after a photograph by Maull, tql seated, stipple, NPG.
PH T.RODGER, wl, carte, NPG AX7474.

WALKER, Sir Andrew Barclay, 1st Bart (1824-1893) benefactor of Liverpool.
P After SIR W.Q.ORCHARDSON of *c*1891, wl seated, Walker Art Gallery, Liverpool. UNKNOWN, wl seated with gun, Walker Art Gallery.
C LIBERIO PROSPERI ('Lib'), wl, profile, chromo-lith, for *Vanity Fair*, 7 June 1890, NPG.

WALKER, Sir Baldwin Wake, 1st Bart (1802-1876) admiral in the Turkish navy.
PR J.NASH, after D.Wilkie, hl in Turkish uniform, lith, for Sir D.Wilkie's *Oriental Sketches*, 1843, BM.

WALKER, Sir Byron Edmund (1848-1924) Canadian banker.
P SIR JOHN LAVERY, National Gallery of Canada, Ottawa.

WALKER, Charles Vincent (1812-1882) electrical engineer.
P M.THOMAS, 1876, Institution of Electrical Engineers, London.

WALKER, David (1837-1917) surgeon and naturalist.
P STEPHEN PEARCE, RA 1860, hl with Arctic medal, NPG 922.

WALKER, Elizabeth, née Reynolds (1800-1876) miniature painter.
PR E.REYNOLDS, after J.Opie, hl, as a child, mezz, BM. T.WOOLNOTH, after a miniature by E.Reynolds, tql seated, painting, stipple, for *Ladies' Monthly Museum*, 1825, BM, NPG.

WALKER, Sir Emery (1851-1933) process engraver and printer.
P SIR GEORGE CLAUSEN, RA 1926, hs, The Art Worker's Guild, London.
PR W.STRANG, hl, line, BM.
PH HOWARD COSTER, two negs, NPG. ELLIOTT & FRY, hs, print, NPG. Two negs, by himself or an unknown assistant, hl with cat and wl in a large group, NPG.

WALKER, Frederick (1840-1875) painter and illustrator.
D Self-portrait, head, w/c, NPG 1498. UNKNOWN, Barber Institute of Fine Arts, Birmingham.
SC H.H.ARMSTEAD, marble medallion, Cookham Church.
PR Several woodcuts, one by F.BARNARD, for *Fun*, 1873, another by H.SCHEU, after J.E.Hodgson, wl with fishing rod, R.Ansdell seated by him, the others by unknown artists, BM. Self-portrait, hs, etch, BM.
PH LONDON STEREOSCOPIC CO, two cartes, wl and tql in Directoire dress, NPG X13281-2. JOHN WATKINS, tql seated, carte, NPG (Album 104). DAVID WILKIE WYNFIELD, *c*1860s, hs, profile, print, NPG P84. Various prints, various dates and sizes, several in fancy dress, BM (Engr Ports Coll).

WALKER, Frederick William (1830-1910) schoolmaster.
P SIR WILLIAM ROTHENSTEIN, *c*1906, tql seated, St Paul's School, London.
SC H.R.HOPE PINKER, 1889, marble bust, St Paul's School.
C SIR LESLIE WARD ('Spy'), wl, seated, chromo-lith, for *Vanity Fair*, 27 June 1901, NPG.
PH Several prints, Manchester Grammar School and St Paul's School.

WALKER, Sir Frederick William Edward Forestier Forestier-, see FORESTIER-Walker.

WALKER, Sir Mark (1827-1902) general.
P UNKNOWN, after a photograph?, tql in uniform, formerly United Services and Royal Aero Club, London (c/o Crown Commissioners).

WALKLEY, Arthur Bingham (1855-1926) dramatic and literary critic.
C SIR MAX BEERBOHM, several drgs, including, 1907, 'Dramatic Critics arboricultural and otherwise', The William Andrews Clark Memorial Library, University of California at Los Angeles, USA, and an untitled sketch at the University of Texas, Austin, USA.

WALLACE, Alfred Russel (1823-1913) naturalist.
P UNKNOWN, oil over a photograph by Thomas Sims, *c*1863-6, tql seated, NPG 1765.
D WILLIAM STRANG, 1908, hs, chalk, Royal Coll.
SC ALBERT BRUCE JOY, 1906, bronze medallion, Linnean Society, London; plaster cast, NPG 1764.
PR W.ROTHENSTEIN, hl, lith, NPG.
PH Various prints by MISS CHANT, REGINALD HAINES, E.O.HOPPÉ, THOMAS SIMS, TABER and unidentified photographers, various dates and sizes, NPG X5108-22 and X5124.

WALLACE, Sir Donald Mackenzie (1841-1919) newspaper correspondent, editor and author.
PH JOHN RUSSELL & SONS, hl seated, print, for *National Photographic Record*, vol I, NPG. WALTER STONEMAN, before 1917, hs, NPG (NPR).

WALLACE, Sir Richard, 1st Bart (1818-1890) connoisseur and collector.
p W.R.Symonds, 1885, hs, Wallace Collection, London.
d Candide Blaize, 1826, w/c, v & a.
g A.C.F.Decaen, 'A Shooting Party at the Great Wood, Sudbourn Hall, 1876', oil, Orford Town Hall, Suffolk. Henry Jamyn Brooks, 'Private view of the Old Masters Exhibition, Royal Academy, 1888', oil, NPG 1833.
sc Emmanuel Hannaux, 1899, marble bust, with Bath Star, Wallace Collection.
pr J.Jacquemart, after P.Baudry, tql, etch, for *Gazette des Beaux Arts*, vol vii, BM, NPG.
c Sir Leslie Ward ('Spy'), wl, chromo-lith, for *Vanity Fair*, 29 Nov 1873, NPG.
ph Adolphe, 1871, with members of the British Charitable Fund after the siege of Paris, print, NPG x8892. J.Thomson, 1888, tql seated, print, NPG.

WALLACE, Robert (1831-1899) divine and radical politician.
ph Sir Benjamin Stone, 1898, wl, print, NPG.

WALLACE, William Vincent (1813-1865) musical composer.
pr Unknown, after a photograph, tql seated, oval, lith, for supplement to *The Orchestra*, 1865, BM. Unknown, hl, woodcut, for *Illust London News*, 18 Nov 1865, NPG.

WALLAS, Graham (1858-1932) political psychologist.
d Sir William Rothenstein, 1923, hs, sanguine, London School of Economics. Robert Austin, London School of Economics.

WALLIS, George (1811-1891) Keeper of South Kensington museum.
p Alphonse Legros, hs, oil sketch, v & a.

WALLOP, Isaac Newton, see 5th Earl of Portsmouth.

WALMISLEY, Thomas Attwood (1814-1856) musician.
d Unknown, hs, Royal College of Music, London.

WALPOLE, Sir Spencer (1839-1907) historian and civil servant.
d H.G.Riviere, c1903, hs, chalk, NPG 3632.
ph Unknown, 'Members of the Imperial Penny Postage Conference, 1898', print, NPG.

WALPOLE, Spencer Horatio (1806-1898) home secretary.
g John Phillip, 'The House of Commons, 1860', oil, Palace of Westminster, London. Henry Gales, 'The Derby Cabinet of 1867', w/c, NPG 4893.
sc Conrad Dressler, 1882, plaster relief, NPG 5215.
pr W.Holl, after G.Richmond, hs, stipple, one of 'Grillion's Club' series, BM. G.Cook, after a photograph by S.A.Walker, tql seated, stipple, NPG.
c Adriano Cecioni, wl, w/c study, for *Vanity Fair*, 10 Feb 1872, NPG 2745.
ph W. & D.Downey, hs, carte, NPG AX8627. Lock & Whitfield, hs, oval, woodburytype, for *Men of Mark*, 1876, NPG. Walker & Sons, tql seated, carte, NPG (Album 120). John Watkins, hs, carte, NPG (Album 99).

WALSH, John Henry (1810-1888) pseudonym 'Stonehenge', writer on sport.
pr Unknown, hs, wood engr, for *Illust London News*, 25 Feb 1888, NPG.

WALSH, William Pakenham (1820-1902) bishop of Ossory.
ph Unknown, tql, print, NPG (Anglican Bishops).

WALSINGHAM, Thomas de Grey, 6th Baron (1843-1919) naturalist and sportsman.
c Théobald Chartran, wl, profile, w/c study, for *Vanity Fair*, 9 Sept 1882, NPG 4636.

WALTER, John (1818-1894) proprietor of *The Times*.
p Sir Hubert von Herkomer, 1889?, tql seated, The Times Newspapers Ltd, London.
pr S.Bellin, after J.Lucas, wl, mezz, pub 1853, BM. D.J.Pound, after a photograph by Mayall, tql seated, stipple and line, for *The Drawing Room Portrait Gallery of Eminent Personages*, NPG.
c Sir Leslie Ward ('Spy'), wl, profile, chromo-lith, for *Vanity Fair*, 10 Sept 1881, NPG.
ph Barraud, tql, print, for *Men and Women of the Day*, vol IV, 1891, NPG AX5515.

WALTON, Sir John Lawson (1852-1908) lawyer.
c Sir Leslie Ward ('Spy'), tql seated, profile, chromo-lith, for *Vanity Fair*, 6 March 1902, NPG.

WALTON, Sir Joseph (1845-1910) judge.
d Unknown, charcoal, Trinity College, Cambridge.
c Sir Leslie Ward ('Spy'), hs at bench, chromo-lith, for *Vanity Fair*, 24 July 1902, NPG.

WANOSTROCHT, Nicholas (1804-1876) 'N.Felix', cricketer and artist.
g G.H.Phillips, after W.Drummond and C.J.Basebe, 'A Cricket Match between Sussex and Kent', coloured lith, Marylebone Cricket Club, London. N.Ploszczynski, after a w/c drg by N.Felix, 'The Eleven of England Selected to contend in the great Cricket Matches of the North for the year 1847', coloured lith, Marylebone Cricket Club.
pr Self-portrait, wl, coloured lith, Marylebone Cricket Club.

WANTAGE, Robert James Lindsay, afterwards Loyd-Lindsay, Baron (1832-1901) soldier and politician.
p Unknown, 1895?, tql in uniform, University of Reading.
g Henry Jamyn Brooks, 'Private view of the Old Masters Exhibition, Royal Academy, 1888', oil, NPG 1833.
pr Violet, Duchess of Rutland, 1891, hs, lith, NPG.
c Sir Leslie Ward ('Spy'), wl, profile, in uniform, chromo-lith, for *Vanity Fair*, 4 Nov 1876, NPG.
ph Unknown, hs, print, NPG (Album 38).

WARD, Sir Adolphus William (1837-1924) historian.
p Sir Hubert von Herkomer, Manchester University H.G.Riviere, Peterhouse, Cambridge.
ph Walter Stoneman, 1918, hs, NPG (NPR).

WARD, Edward Matthew (1816-1879) history painter.
d George Richmond, 1859, hs, chalk, NPG 2072. C.W.Cope, c1862, head, profile, NPG 3182(10).
pr J.Smyth, after T.Brigstocke, tql seated, line, for *Art Union Journal*, 1847, BM, NPG. D.J.Pound, after a photograph by Mayall, tql, semi-profile, stipple and line, for *Illust News of the World*, BM, NPG. Several woodcuts, BM.
c Sir Leslie Ward ('Spy'), his son, wl, w/c study, for *Vanity Fair*, 20 Dec 1873, NPG 2746.
ph Elliott & Fry, hs, carte, NPG (Album 106). Lock & Whitfield, hs, oval, woodburytype, for *Men of Mark*, 1878, NPG. Maull & Polyblank, wl seated, carte, NPG AX11918. John & Charles Watkins, hl seated, carte, NPG (Album 104). Window & Bridge, tql seated, carte, NPG AX 7566.

WARD, Sir Edward Willis Duncan, 1st Bart (1853-1928) soldier and military administrator.
c Sir Leslie Ward ('Spy'), wl in uniform, chromo-lith, for *Vanity Fair*, 30 May 1901, NPG.
ph Walter Stoneman, 1918, hs, NPG (NPR).

WARD, Harry Marshall (1854-1906) botanist.
d Unknown, chalks, Christ's College, Cambridge.

WARD, James (1800-1885) pugilist and artist.
PR H.Adlard, after T.Wageman, hl, stipple, BM.

WARD, James (1843-1925) philosopher and psychologist.
P Ambrose McEvoy, 1913, hl seated, semi-profile, Fitzwilliam Museum, Cambridge.

WARD, Sir Joseph George, 1st Bart (1856-1930) prime minister of New Zealand.
P Sir William Orpen, 1919, hs, NPG 2640.
PH Sir Benjamin Stone, 1909, wl, print, Birmingham Reference Library.

WARD, Sir Leslie (1851-1922) 'Spy'; caricaturist.
C Jean de Paleologu ('Pal'), wl seated, w/c study, for *Vanity Fair*, 23 Nov 1889, NPG 3007.
PH Sir Benjamin Stone, 1901, wl, print, NPG.

WARD, Mary Augusta, née Arnold, (Mrs Humphry Ward) (1851-1920) novelist.
P J.R.Story, 1889, tql seated, NPG 2650.
D Lucy Graham Smith, 1889, hs, semi-profile, pastel, Somerville College, Oxford. Rudolph Lehmann, 1890, head, semi-profile, chalk, BM. Albert Steiner, crayon, Mary Ward Centre, London.
PH C.L.Dodgson ('Lewis Carroll'), 1872, hl seated, print, NPG P69. Barraud, tql, print, for *Men and Women of the Day*, vol II, 1889, NPG AX5470. W. & D.Downey, tql, woodburytype, for Cassell's *Cabinet Portrait Gallery*, vol I, 1890, NPG. Edwin Arnold, 1898?, tql seated, print, Somerville College, Oxford. Elliott & Fry, hl seated, print, NPG X13284. Crowdy & Loud, after Elliott & Fry, hl seated, photogravure, NPG X13286.

WARD, William George (1812-1882) Roman Catholic theologian and philosopher.
PR Unknown, hs, wood engr, for *Illust London News*, 29 July 1882, NPG.

WARING, John Burley (1823-1875) architect.
PR Unknown, hl, oval, lith, BM.

WARNER, Charles (1846-1909) actor.
PH Barraud, hs, print, for *The Theatre*, NPG. Lock & Whitfield, hs, woodburytype, carte, NPG AX7664. Lock & Whitfield, hs, woodburytype, for *The Theatre*, NPG. Walery, hl, print, for *The Theatre*, Feb 1891, NPG.

WARNER, Sir George Frederic (1845-1936) palaeographer and scholar.
PH Walter Stoneman, 1917, hs, NPG (NPR). Unknown, hl, photogravure, BM (Engr Ports Coll).

WARNER, Mary Amelia, née Huddart (1804-1854) actress.
PR R.J.Lane, wl as Joan of Arc in Serle's *Joan of Arc*, lith, pub 1837, BM, NPG. Unknown, after a daguerreotype, wl as Hermione in *The Winter's Tale*, line and stipple, for Tallis's *Drawing Room Table Book*, BM, NPG.

WARRE, Edmond (1837-1920) headmaster and provost of Eton.
P J.S.Sargent, 1906, wl, Eton College, Berks.
C Sir Leslie Ward ('Spy'), wl, profile, chromo-lith, for *Vanity Fair*, 20 June 1885, NPG.
PH Barraud, hl, print, for *Men and Women of the Day*, vol I, 1888, NPG AX5433. W. & D.Downey, hl, woodburytype, for Cassell's *Cabinet Portrait Gallery*, vol I, 1890, NPG.

WARRE-CORNISH, Francis Warre (1839-1916) teacher, author and bibliophile.
C Sir Leslie Ward ('Spy'), wl, chromo-lith, for *Vanity Fair*, 26 Sept 1901, NPG.

WARREN, Sir Charles (1840-1927) lieutenant-general and archaeologist.
C Carlo Pellegrini ('Ape'), wl, chromo-lith, for *Vanity Fair*, 6 Feb 1886, NPG.
PH Barraud, hl in uniform, print, for *Men and Women of the Day*, vol I, 1888, NPG AX5432. Walter Stoneman, hs, NPG (NPR).

WARREN, George John Vernon, see 5th Baron Vernon.

WARREN, Samuel (1807-1877) lawyer and author.
P Attrib John Linnell, c1835-40, hl, NPG 1441. Sir John Watson Gordon, RA 1856, hl seated, SNPG L286.
PR Various prints, some after photographs, NPG.
PH Ernest Edwards, wl seated, print, for *Men of Eminence*, ed L.Reeve, vol II, 1864, NPG.

WARREN, Sir Thomas Herbert (1853-1930) president of Magdalen College, Oxford.
P Sir W.B.Richmond, 1899, hl seated, Magdalen College, Oxford.
C Sir Leslie Ward ('Spy'), wl, chromo-lith, for *Vanity Fair*, 8 April 1893, NPG.
PH Unknown, hl seated, print, NPG X1687.

WARRINGTON of Clyffe, Thomas Rolls Warrington, Baron (1851-1937) judge.
D Sir William Rothenstein, 1932, chalk, The Athenaeum, London.
C Sir Leslie Ward ('Spy'), tql, mechanical repro, for *Vanity Fair*, 27 Nov 1907, NPG.
PH Walter Stoneman, 1917, hs, NPG (NPR).

WATERFORD, Louisa Stuart, Marchioness of (1818-1891) artist and illustrator.
P Attrib Sir Francis Grant, c1845, wl, NPG 3176. C.Spindler, wl with her sister, Charlotte, Countess Canning, Musée Historique de la Ville Strasbourg.
D J.R.Swinton, 1851, hs, semi-profile, oval, chalk, Harewood House, W Yorks.
M Robert Thorburn, wl with Countess Canning, SNPG 1530. Robert Thorburn, wl with Countess Canning, Harewood House, W Yorks.
PR W.H.Egleton, after J.Hayter, tql, profile, stipple, pub 1839, BM, NPG. W.Roffe, two prints, both wl, one after a sketch by Sir J.Leslie, the other after a photograph, both stipple and line, NPG.

WATERHOUSE, Alfred (1830-1905) architect.
P Sir A.S.Cope, 1886, hs, profile, MacDonald Collection, Aberdeen Art Gallery. Sir W.Q.Orchardson, tql, RIBA, London.
PH Ralph W.Robinson, hl seated, semi-profile, print, for *Members and Associates of the Royal Academy of Arts*, 1891, NPG X7396.

WATERHOUSE, George Robert (1810-1888) naturalist.
PR T.H.Maguire, tql seated, octagon, lith, one of set of *Ipswich Museum Portraits*, 1851, BM.

WATERLOW, Sir Ernest Albert (1850-1919) painter.
P Sir Lawrence Alma-Tadema, 1889, Royal Academy, London. Self-portrait, 1890, hs, profile, MacDonald Collection, Aberdeen Art Gallery.
PH Ralph W.Robinson, hl seated, semi-profile, print, for *Members Associates of The Royal Academy of Arts*, 1891, NPG X7398. Unknown, hs, profile, print, NPG.

WATERLOW, Sir Sydney Hedley, 1st Bart (1822-1906) alderman and philanthropist.
P Sir Hubert von Herkomer, 1892, St Bartholomew's Hospital, London. Unknown, hl, Stationer's Hall, London.
SC Joseph Durham, 1873, marble bust, St Bartholomew's Hospital. F.M.Taubman, c1900, bronze statue, Waterlow Park, Highgate,

London; replica, Westminster City School, London.

c UNKNOWN, wl, profile, chromo-lith, for *Vanity Fair*, 9 Nov 1872, NPG.

PH W. & D.DOWNEY, hl, woodburytype, for Cassell's *Cabinet Portrait Gallery*, vol III, 1892, NPG. LONDON STEREOSCOPIC CO, hs, woodburytype, NPG. WALERY, tql, print, NPG.

WATKIN, Sir Edward William, 1st Bart (1819-1901) railway promoter.

P A.H.FOX, 1891, hs, Museum of British Transport, York.

PR UNKNOWN, after a photograph by J. & C.Watkins, tql seated, woodcut, for *Illust London News*, 23 July 1864, NPG.

c CARLO PELLEGRINI ('Ape'), wl, chromo-lith, for *Vanity Fair*, 6 Nov 1875, NPG. 'PET', wl, chromo-lith, for *The Monetary Gazette*, 17 Jan 1877, NPG.

PH BARRAUD, hl, profile, print, for *Men and Women of the Day*, vol II, 1889, NPG AX5450.

WATSON, Albert (1828-1904) principal of Brasenose College, Oxford.

P AMBROSE MCEVOY, 1905, posthumous, based on photographs, tql seated, Brasenose College, Oxford.

WATSON, Henry William (1827-1903) mathematician.

D T.C.WAGEMAN, w/c, Trinity College, Cambridge.

WATSON, John (1850-1907) 'Ian Maclaren', presbyterian divine and author.

P ROBERT MORRISON, Sefton Park Church, Liverpool. SIR GEORGE REID, hs, Walker Art Gallery, Liverpool.

WATSON, John Dawson (1832-1892) artist.

D FREDERICK WALKER, pencil and wash, Manchester City Art Gallery.

PH ELLIOTT & FRY, tql seated, carte, NPG (Album 104). DAVID WILKIE WYNFIELD, c1862-4, hs, semi-profile, print, NPG P85.

WATSON, Sir (John) William (1858-1935) poet and critic.

P R.G.EVES, 192(9?), hl, NPG 3839.

c SIR MAX BEERBOHM, wl, profile, drg, Princeton University Library, USA.

PH Two cabinets by ELLIOTT & FRY and LONDON STEREOSCOPIC CO, both hs, NPG. JOHN RUSSELL & SONS, hl, print, for *National Photographic Record*, vol I, NPG.

WATSON, Musgrave Lewthwaite (1804-1847) sculptor, etcher and painter in water-colours.

SC GEORGE NELSON, portrait relief medallion, Carlisle Cathedral.

WATSON, Robert Spence (1837-1911) political, social and educational reformer.

P PERCY BIGLAND, University of Newcastle-upon-Tyne. LILIAN ETHERINGTON, University of Newcastle-upon-Tyne. SIR GEORGE REID, two portraits, National Liberal Club, London, and Laing Art Gallery, Newcastle-upon-Tyne.

WATSON, William Watson, Lord (1827-1899) judge.

P J.S.SARGENT, RA 1898, wl, Faculty of Advocates, Parliament Hall, Edinburgh.

WATTS, George Frederic (1817-1904) painter.

P Various self-portraits: c1834, hl, unfinished, Watts Gallery, Compton, Surrey; c1840, hs, Watts Gallery; c1844-5, hs, a fresco fragment, V & A; 1853, nearly wl in robe, Watts Gallery; c1860, hs, NPG 5087; 1863?, tql in armour, 'Eve of Peace', Dunedin Public Art Gallery, New Zealand; 1862-4, hl, TATE 1561 (related oil sketch, hs, semi-profile, Municipal Gallery of Modern Art, Dublin); 1879-80, hl, profile, with palette, standing in front of his painting, 'Time, Death and Judgement', Uffizi Gallery, Florence (related portraits, 1879, hl, profile, Watts Gallery, and hs, profile, NPG 1406); 1882, hs, oval, MacDonald Collection,

Aberdeen Art Gallery; c1882, hl seated, unfinished, Parish of Compton; 1904, hl, based on a late photograph, Watts Gallery. H.W.PHILLIPS, c1850, hl, profile, NPG 1378. SIR PHILIP BURNE-JONES, c1888-9, wl in his studio at work on his statue of 'Physical Energy', Johannesburg Art Gallery. SIR CHARLES HOLROYD, 1897, hs, profile, TATE 3397. LOUIS DEUCHARS, after a photograph of 1897, wl seated in garden, NPG 5223. J.V.GIBSON, after a photograph, hs, Watts Gallery.

D Self-portrait, c1840, head, study for a picture of 'Fear', Watts Gallery. Two early self-portrait drgs, one hl, the other on horseback, shielding his eyes, Watts Gallery. CHARLES COUZENS, c1849, wl, w/c, Watts Gallery. RUDOLPH LEHMANN, 1868, hs in skull cap, crayon, BM. MRS WATTS, 1894, propped up in bed, w/c, Watts Gallery.

M ETHEL WEBLING, 1899, after a photograph, hs, oval, Watts Gallery.

G HENRY JAMYN BROOKS, 'Private view of the old Masters Exhibition, Royal Academy, 1888', oil, NPG 1833.

SC SIR ALFRED GILBERT, 1888-9, bronze cast of bust, TATE 1949; reduced bronze cast, Watts Gallery. UNKNOWN, 1897, bronze medallion, Watts Gallery, SIR CHARLES HOLROYD, c1897, bronze medallion, NPG 1980. SIR GEORGE FRAMPTON, 1905, posthumous, marble bust, South London Art Gallery. THEODORE SPICER-SIMSON, c1905, cast of bronze medallion, Watts Gallery. T.H.WREN, c1905, two small plaster recumbent effigies, Watts Gallery, and cloisters of Watts Memorial Chapel, Compton. REGINALD GOULDEN, 1909, statue, Cromwell Road Facade, V & A. HENRY POOLE, bronze statuette, NPG 2480. UNKNOWN, statuette, Postmen's Park, Aldersgate Street, London. UNKNOWN, bronze statuette (holding hat behind his back), Watts Gallery.

PR ALPHONSE LEGROS, c1880, etch, NGS, Municipal Gallery of Modern Art, Dublin, Watts Gallery, NPG. MORTIMER MENPES, hs, profile, etch, NPG.

c SIR LESLIE WARD ('Spy'), wl, profile, chromo-lith, for *Vanity Fair*, 26 Dec 1891, NPG.

PH JAMES SOAME, 1858, wl, print, NPG P68. JULIA MARGARET CAMERON, several prints: c1863-8, tql seated, NPG P125; 1864, hs, NPG P18(38); 1864, hl and tql seated, NPG P18(8,9). DAVID WILKIE WYNFIELD, 1860s, hs, print, NPG P96. LOCK & WHITFIELD, hs, profile, oval, woodburytype, for *Men of Mark*, 1882, NPG. RALPH W.ROBINSON, wl seated with model of his statue of 'Physical Energy', print, for *Members and Associates of the Royal Academy of Arts, 1891*, NPG X7399. Various prints by H.CAMERON, ELLIOTT & FRY, FREDERICK HOLLYER and JOHN WATKINS, cartes, cabinets etc, various dates and sizes, NPG. Various prints, copy prints and copy negs, Watts Gallery.

WATTS, Sir Philip (1846-1926) naval architect.

c SIR LESLIE WARD ('Spy'), wl, profile, Hentschel-Colourtype, for *Vanity Fair*, 7 April 1910, NPG.

WATTS-DUNTON, Theodore (1832-1914) critic, novelist and poet.

D D.G.ROSSETTI, 1874, hs, pastel, NPG 4888. HENRY TREFFRY DUNN, 1882, wl seated with D.G.Rossetti, w/c, NPG 3022.

WAUGH, Benjamin (1839-1908) philanthropist.

P EDNA CLARKE, LADY HALL (his daughter), hs, NPG 3909.

PH A.MONTIVILLE, hs, profile, print, NPG. UNKNOWN, tql, seated, print, NPG.

WAUGH, Edwin (1817-1890) Lancashire poet and miscellaneous writer.

P WILLIAM PERCY, 1882, hl, Manchester City Art Gallery.

SC E.E.GEFLOWSKI, 1878, marble bust, Gawsworth Hall, Cheshire.

WAY, Albert (1805–1874) antiquary.
PR R. & E.TAYLOR, after a photograph by G.Evans, hs, semi-profile, woodcut, for *Illust London News*, 25 April 1874, NPG.

WEBB, Allan Becher (1839–1907) dean of Salisbury and bishop in South Africa.
PH UNKNOWN, hs, print, NPG (Anglican Bishops).

WEBB, Sir Aston (1849–1930) architect and president of the Royal Academy.
P SOLOMON J.SOLOMON, two portraits, RA 1906, tql seated, RIBA, London, and version, *c*1906, hl seated, NPG 2489. SIR WILLIAM LLEWELLYN, RA 1921, hl, Royal Academy, London.

WEBB, Benjamin (1819–1885) ecclesiologist.
SC H.H.ARMSTEAD, RA 1889, marble relief, St Paul's Cathedral, London.

WEBB, Francis William (1836–1906) civil engineer.
P GEORGE HALL NEALE, 1903, tql, Museum of British Transport, York.

WEBB, (Martha) Beatrice, see Lady Passfield.

WEBB, Matthew (1848–1883) swimmer.
C CARLO PELLEGRINI ('Ape'), wl, profile, w/c study, for *Vanity Fair*, 9 Oct 1875, NPG 4751.
PH UNKNOWN, hl, profile, print, NPG X5584. UNKNOWN, hl, woodburytype, carte, NPG AX7659.

WEBB, Philip (Speakman) (1831–1915) architect.
D CHARLES FAIRFAX MURRAY, 1873, hs, wash, NPG 4310.
PH Several snapshot negs by EMERY WALKER, NPG.

WEBB, Sidney James, see Baron Passfield.

WEBSTER, Augusta, née Davies (1837–1894) poet.
PR UNKNOWN, after a photograph by Ferrando, hs, wood engr, NPG.

WEBSTER, Richard Everard, see Viscount Alverstone.

WEBSTER, Thomas (1800–1886) painter.
P J.C.HORSLEY, 1886, hs, oval, MacDonald Collection, Aberdeen Art Gallery.
D E.M.WARD, 1862, head, profile, pencil, NPG 2879.
PR Several woodcuts after photographs, BM, NPG.
PH LOCK & WHITFIELD, hs, oval, woodburytype, for *Men of Mark*, 1878, NPG. Several cartes by LONDON STEREOSCOPIC CO, MAULL & POLYBLANK and JOHN & CHARLES WATKINS, various dates and sizes, NPG AX11925, AX11920, AX11929 and in Album 104.

WEEKES, Henry (1807–1877) sculptor.
G UNKNOWN, hs, one of a series of woodcuts, 'Members of the Royal Academy in 1857', for *Illust London News*, 2 May 1857, BM, NPG. UNKNOWN, hs, 'Members of the Royal Academy in 1863', for *Illust London News*, 25 July 1863, BM, NPG.
PH ELLIOTT & FRY, hs, profile, carte, NPG (Album 103).

WEIR, Harrison William (1824–1906) animal painter and author.
G UNKNOWN, hs, one of a series of woodcuts, 'Our Artists – Past and Present', for *Illust London News*, 14 May 1892, BM, NPG.
PH ELLIOTT & FRY, hs, carte, NPG (Album 104).

WEISS, Willoughby Hunter (1820–1867) singer and composer.
PR UNKNOWN, hs, oval, woodcut, for *Illust London News*, 9 Nov 1867, NPG.

WELBY, Reginald Earle Welby, 1st Baron (1832–1915) public servant.
P JOHN COLLIER, 1913, hl, Society of Dilettanti, Brooks's Club, London.

WELLDON, James Edward Cowell (1854–1937) divine,

headmaster of Dulwich College and Harrow.
P JOHN COLLIER, 1898, tql, Harrow School, Middx. SIR GERALD KELLY, 1921, tql, Manchester City Art Gallery.
D S.P.HALL, pencil sketch, NPG 2347.
C ARNOLD, 8TH EARL OF ALBEMARLE, in pulpit, pencil and w/c, Fitzwilliam Museum, Cambridge. SIR LESLIE WARD ('Spy'), wl, profile, chromo-lith, for *Vanity Fair*, 17 Nov 1898, NPG.
PH BARRAUD, tql, print, for *Men and Women of the Day*, vol II, 1889, NPG AX5444. ELLIOTT & FRY, hl, print, NPG (Anglican Bishops). JOHN RUSSELL & SONS, hs, print, for *National Photographic Record*, vol I, NPG. SIR BENJAMIN STONE, 1902, wl, print, Birmingham Reference Library.

WELLESLEY, Frederick Arthur (1844–1931) soldier and diplomat.
C CARLO PELLEGRINI ('Ape'), wl, profile, w/c study, for *Vanity Fair*, 25 May 1878, NPG 4752.

WELLESLEY, Gerald Valerian (1809–1882) dean of Windsor.
P HEINRICH VON ANGELI, hs, Royal Coll.
G E.M.WARD, 'Queen Victoria Investing Napoleon III with the Order of the Garter at Windsor Castle', oil, 1855, Royal Coll.
SC G.G.ADAMS, 1882, monument, Stratfield Saye, Hants.
PR UNKNOWN, after a photograph by Samuel A.Walker, hs, woodcut, for *The Pictorial World*, 30 Sept 1882, NPG.
C SIR LESLIE WARD ('Spy'), wl, profile, chromo-lith, for *Vanity Fair*, 8 April 1876, NPG.

WELLESLEY, Henry (1846–1900), see 3rd Duke of Wellington.

WELLESLEY, Henry Richard Charles, see 1st Earl Cowley.

WELLINGTON, Henry Wellesley, 3rd Duke of (1846–1900) soldier and member of parliament.
P ETHEL MORTLOCK, tql seated, Stratfield Saye, Hants.
C CARLO PELLEGRINI ('Ape'), wl, w/c study, for *Vanity Fair*, 3 Jan 1885, NPG 4630.

WELLS, Henry Tanworth (1828–1903) portrait painter.
P Self-portrait, 1882, MacDonald Collection, Aberdeen Art Gallery.
G G.GRENVILLE MANTON, 'Conversazione at the Royal Academy, 1891', w/c, NPG 2820.
PR UNKNOWN, hs, profile, woodcut, for *Illust London News*, 30 June 1866, NPG.
PH LOCK & WHITFIELD, hs, oval, woodburytype, for *Men of Mark*, 1878, NPG. RALPH W.ROBINSON, hl seated, print, for *Members and Associates of the Royal Academy of Arts, 1891*, NPG X7400.

WELLS, Sir Thomas Spencer, 1st Bart (1818–1897) surgeon.
P RUDOLPH LEHMANN, RA 1884, tql seated, Royal College of Surgeons, London.
G HENRY JAMYN BROOKS, 'Council of the Royal College of Surgeons of England, 1884–85', oil, Royal College of Surgeons.
SC R.LIEBREICH, RA 1879, marble bust, Royal Naval Hospital, Haslar. UNKNOWN, plaster statuette, Royal College of Surgeons.

WELSBY, William Newland (1802?–1864) legal writer.
PR G.BLACK, 1847, hs, lith, NPG.

WEMYSS and MARCH, Francis Wemyss-Charteris-Douglas, 10th earl of (1818–1914) politician.
P P.A.de LÁSZLÓ, 1908, SNPG 1403.
D SIR JOHN LESLIE, pen and pencil sketch, Shugborough (NT), Staffs. UNKNOWN, pastel, SNPG 963.
SL AUGUSTIN EDOUART, SNPG 778.
G JOHN PHILLIP, 'The House of Commons, 1860', oil, Palace of Westminster, London.

PR Several prints by J.BROWN, D.J.POUND and an unknown artist, after photographs, all tql in uniform, BM.

C CARLO PELLEGRINI ('Ape'), wl, chromo-lith, for *Vanity Fair*, 23 July 1870, NPG.

PH L.CALDESI, wl in uniform, carte, NPG. D.O.HILL & ROBERT ADAMSON, 1843–8, hl seated, print, NPG P6 (17). JOHN & CHARLES WATKINS, wl seated, carte, NPG AX8596.

WENLOCK, Beilby Lawley, 3rd Baron (1849–1912) governor of Madras.

C 'BINT', wl, w/c study, for *Vanity Fair*, 28 Jan 1893, NPG 2971.

WERNHER, Sir Julius Charles, 1st Bart (1850–1912) financier and philanthropist.

P SIR HUBERT VON HERKOMER, 1910, tql, Luton Hoo, Beds; replica, Johannesburg Art Gallery.

SC PAUL MONTFORD, bust, with Alfred Beit, Imperial College, London.

PH LONDON STEREOSCOPIC CO, hs, print, NPG.

WESLEY, Samuel Sebastian (1810–1876) organist and composer.

P UNKNOWN, c1835, Royal College of Music, London. W.K.BRIGGS, 1849, Royal College of Music.

WEST, Sir Algernon Edward (1832–1921) chairman of the Board of Inland Revenue.

C SIR LESLIE WARD ('Spy'), wl, w/c study, for *Vanity Fair*, 13 Aug 1892, NPG 2986.

PH JOHN RUSSELL & SONS, hs, print, for *National Photographic Record*, vol I, NPG.

WEST, Sir Charles Richard Sackville-, see 6th Earl and 12th Baron DE La Warr.

WEST, Lionel Sackville-, see 2nd Baron SACKVILLE of Knole.

WESTBURY, Richard Bethell, 1st Baron (1800–1873) lord chancellor.

P SIR FRANCIS GRANT, RA 1865, tql seated in robes, Middle Temple, London. MICHELE GORDIGIANI, hs, NPG 1941. M.GORDIGIANI, hs, semi-profile, DoE (Privy Council).

SC JOHN BAILEY, 1852, bust, Wadham College, Oxford.

PR D.J.POUND, after a photograph by Mayall, tql seated, stipple and line, supplement to *Illust News of the World*, BM, NPG.

C CARLO PELLEGRINI ('Ape'), tql, chromo-lith, for *Vanity Fair*, 15 May 1869, NPG.

PH W.WALKER & SONS, tql, carte, NPG. JOHN WATKINS, hs, profile, carte, NPG (Album 40). UNKNOWN, c1860, tql seated, carte, NPG AX5063. UNKNOWN, wl in robes, carte, NPG. UNKNOWN, tql, print, NPG AX7314.

WESTCOTT, Brooke Foss (1825–1901) bishop of Durham.

P W.E.MILLER, hs, Trinity College, Cambridge. SIR W.B.RICHMOND, RA 1890, tql seated, Fitzwilliam Museum, Cambridge. H.A.OLIVIER, RA 1906, tql seated, Sherborne School, Dorset.

PH ELLIOTT & FRY, two cabinets, hs and tql seated, NPG. UNKNOWN, hs, print, NPG (Anglican Bishops).

WESTLAKE, John (1828–1913) jurist.

P ALICE WESTLAKE (his wife), c1896–7, hs, NPG 4847. MARIANNE STOKES, 1902, hs, profile, NPG 1890. C.H.SHANNON, 1910, tql, seated in academic gown, Trinity College, Cambridge.

SC SIR GEORGE FRAMPTON, 1912, marble bust, Squire Law Library, Cambridge.

PH G.JERRARD, hs, profile, cabinet, NPG.

WESTMINSTER, Hugh Lupus Grosvenor, 1st Duke of (1825–1899) politician.

P SIR J.E.MILLAIS, 1872, wl in hunting dress, Ragley Hall, Warwicks. UNKNOWN, in dress of Cheshire Hunt, Chester Town Hall. WILLIAM CARTER, RA 1901, hl seated, Westminster City Library, Buckingham Palace Road, London.

G H.T.WELLS, 'Wimbledon, 1864', oil, Althorp, Northants.

SC UNKNOWN, bas-relief portrait on bronze tablet, Chesham Buildings, Brown Street, Duke Street, Grosvenor Square, London.

PR J.BROWN, after a photograph by Southwell, hl, stipple, for *Baily's Mag*, 1864, BM. W.HOLL, after G.Richmond, hs, stipple, one of 'Grillion's Club' series, BM. G.PILOTELL, hs, semi-profile, drypoint, BM. Several popular prints, NPG.

C CARLO PELLEGRINI ('Ape'), wl, profile, chromo-lith, for *Vanity Fair*, 16 July 1870, NPG.

PH W. & D.DOWNEY, hs, woodburytype, for Cassells' *Cabinet Portrait Gallery*, vol I, 1890, NPG. CALDESI, BLANFORD & CO, wl, carte, NPG AX8606.

WESTMORLAND, Francis William Henry Fane, 12th Earl of (1825–1891) colonel.

PR J.BROWN, after a photograph by Mayall, hl, stipple, for *Baily's Mag*, 1864, BM. HANHART, tql, lith, NPG.

WESTON, Dame Agnes Elizabeth (1840–1918) nautical philanthropist.

P UNKNOWN, hs, oval, NPG 4437.

WESTWOOD, John Obadiah (1805–1893) entomologist and antiquary.

P UNKNOWN, before 1876, hl seated, University Museum, Oxford. SIR HUBERT VON HERKOMER, 1890, tql seated, Ashmolean Museum, Oxford.

PR T.H.MAGUIRE, tql seated, octagon, lith, one of set of *Ipswich Museum Portraits*, 1851, BM.

PH ERNEST EDWARDS, wl seated, print, for *Men of Eminence*, ed L.Reeve, vol II, 1864, NPG.

WET, Christiaan Rudolph de, see DE Wet.

WEYMAN, Stanley John (1855–1928) novelist.

PH LONDON STEREOSCOPIC CO, tql seated, cabinet, NPG.

WHALLEY, George Hammond (1813–1878) politician.

C CARLO PELLEGRINI ('Ape'), hl, chromo-lith, for *Vanity Fair*, 18 Feb 1871, NPG.

PH JOHN & CHARLES WATKINS, hs, carte, NPG AX8582. UNKNOWN, tql seated, carte, NPG.

WHARNCLIFFE, Edward Montagu-Wortley-Mackenzie, 1st Earl of (1827–1899) railway chairman, politician and collector.

G HENRY JAMYN BROOKS, 'Private view of the Old Masters Exhibition, Royal Academy, 1888', oil, NPG 1833.

C CARLO PELLEGRINI ('Ape'), wl, profile, w/c study, for *Vanity Fair*, 14 Aug 1875, NPG 4699.

WHARNCLIFFE, John Stuart-Wortley, 2nd Baron (1801–1855) politician.

PR F.C.LEWIS, after J.Slater, hs, stipple, one of 'Grillion's Club' series, BM.

WHARTON, Edward Ross (1844–1896) philologer and genealogist.

PH UNKNOWN, hs, semi-profile, coloured print?, Jesus College, Oxford.

WHARTON, Sir William James Lloyd (1843–1905) hydrographer.

P HARRY ALLEN, two posthumous portraits, after photographs, both hl in uniform, NPG 1497, and NMM, Greenwich.

WHEATSTONE, Sir Charles (1802–1875) scientist and inventor.

P CHARLES MARTIN, RA 1870, tql seated, Royal Society, London. UNKNOWN, Institution of Electrical Engineers, London.

D WILLIAM BROCKEDON, 1837, hs, chalk, NPG 2515(84). SAMUEL LAURENCE, 1868, hs, chalk, NPG 726.

PR Several woodcuts and prints after photographs, BM, NPG.

PH LONDON STEREOSCOPIC CO, tql seated, carte, NPG. MAYALL, hs, semi-profile, carte, NPG (Album 40).

WHIBLEY, Charles (1859-1930) scholar, critic and journalist.

P SIR GERALD KELLY, RA 1926, tql seated, profile, Jesus College, Cambridge.

D POWYS EVANS, 1929, hs, semi-profile, pen and ink, NPG 4395.

WHICHCORD, John (1823-1885) architect.

P SIR LAWRENCE ALMA-TADEMA, RA 1882, tql seated, RIBA, London.

WHISTLER, James Abbott McNeill (1834-1903) painter and etcher.

P SIR WILLIAM BOXALL, hl, University of Glasgow. Various self-portraits: 1857-8, hs with hat, Freer Gallery of Art, Washington DC, USA; 1867-8, wl, 'The Artist in his Studio', Art Institute of Chicago, USA; 1872, hl with brushes, 'Arrangement in Grey', Detroit Institute of Arts, USA; 1870-5, hl, Freer Gallery of Art; 1893-4, tql, Fogg Art Museum, Harvard University, Cambridge, Mass, USA; 1895-1900, wl, 'Brown and Gold', Hunterian Museum and Art Gallery, University of Glasgow; c1896-8, hl, 'Gold and Brown', National Gallery of Art, Washington DC, USA (c1896, two related portraits, both hl, Hunterian Museum and Art Gallery, University of Glasgow). WALTER GREAVES, 1877, hl, Museum of Art, Toledo, Ohio, USA. WALTER GREAVES, hl, NPG 4497. WILLIAM MERRITT CHASE, 1885, wl, Metropolitan Museum of Art, New York, USA. GIOVANNI BOLDINI, 1897, wl, Brooklyn Museum.

D Self-portrait, hl, pen, Pennell Collection, Library of Congress, Washington DC. ALICE PIKE BARNEY, 1898, hs, pastel, National Collection of Fine Arts, Smithsonian Institution, Washington DC. WALTER GREAVES, hl seated, wash, V & A. H.D.MARTIN, head, pencil, Princeton University Art Museum. SIR ROBERT PONSONBY STAPLES, 1901, two heads, hs, and hs profile, chalk, NPG 2188. UNKNOWN, hs, 'Penny Whistler', pencil, V & A.

SC SIR J.E.BOEHM, 1872, terracotta bust, NPG (Smithsonian Institution), Washington DC.

PR Self-portrait, 1859, hs, etch, Art Institute of Chicago, USA. C.A.CORWIN, 1880, hs, profile, monotype, Metropolitan Museum of Art, New York. GIOVANNI BOLDINI, 1897, hl asleep, drypoint, Museo Boldini, Ferrara. SIR WILLIAM NICHOLSON, 1899, wl, coloured woodcut, NPG. PAUL HELLEU, hl, drypoint, Cabinet des Estampes, Louvre. MORTIMER MENPES, hs, drypoint, Cleveland Museum of Art, Ohio. JACQUES REICH, wl, etch, University of Missouri (Museum of Art and Archaeology), Columbia, USA.

C J.C.CLARKE ('Kyd'), in front of a picture by Velasquez, w/c, V & A. HARRY FURNISS, two pen and ink sketches, NPG 3617-18. ERNEST HASKELL, hs, profile, drg, Cleveland Museum of Art, Ohio, and hs, etch, V & A. FINCH MASON, wl, pencil and w/c, V & A. SIR BERNARD PARTRIDGE, wl, w/c, NPG 3541. SIR LESLIE WARD ('Spy'), tql, w/c study, for *Vanity Fair*, 12 Jan 1878, NPG 1700. SIR MAX BEERBOHM, several cartoons, some posthumous, eg University of Glasgow, Birmingham City Art Gallery, Harvard College Library, Cambridge, Mass, USA.

PH LONDON STEREOSCOPIC CO, tql, cabinet, NPG X12544. UNKNOWN, tql, print, Glasgow University Library.

WHITE, Adam (1817-1879) naturalist, assistant in the British Museum.

PR J.RICHARDSON JACKSON, after J.P.Knight, seated in armchair, mezz, 1849, NPG.

PH Two prints by unknown photographers, tql, aged 42, and hl, as an old man, BM (Engr Ports Coll).

WHITE, Sir George Stuart (1835-1912) field-marshal.

P P.A.DE LÁSZLÓ, hl in uniform, Royal Coll.

SC JOHN TWEED, c1915, bronze equestrian statue, Portland Place, London.

C SIR LESLIE WARD ('Spy'), two chromo-liths, wl, profile, in uniform, for *Vanity Fair*, 14 June 1900, and 'A General Group', for *Vanity Fair*, 29 Nov 1900, NPG.

PH COWELL, 1894, hs, print, National Army Museum, London.

WHITE, Henry (1836-1890) clergyman.

C CARLO PELLEGRINI ('Ape'), wl, chromo-lith, for *Vanity Fair*, 26 Dec 1874, NPG 4634.

WHITE, Henry Julian (1859-1934) Latin biblical scholar and dean of Christ Church, Oxford.

P ERNEST MOORE, 1928, two portraits, Christ Church, Oxford.

PH ELLIOTT & FRY, tql seated, print, NPG.

WHITE, John Campbell, see 1st Baron Overtoun.

WHITE, Sir William Arthur (1824-1891) diplomat.

PH J.JOHNSTONE, c1863, tql seated, carte, NPG x8355.

WHITE, William Hale (1831-1913) novelist (under the pseudonym of Mark Rutherford).

D ARTHUR HUGHES, 1887, hs, crayon, Cecil Higgins Art Gallery, Bedford.

WHITE, Sir William Hale- (1857-1949), see HALE-White.

WHITE, Sir William Henry (1845-1913) naval architect.

P UNKNOWN, c1902-3, tql, NMM, Greenwich.

WHITEING, Richard (1840-1928) journalist and novelist.

PH JOHN RUSSELL & SONS, hs, print, for *National Photographic Record*, vol II, NPG.

WHITESIDE, James (1804-1876) lord chief-justice of Ireland.

P? A.SCOTT, Kings Inns, Dublin.

D CHARLES GREY, wl seated, pencil, original drg for etch pub in *Dublin University Mag*, 1849, NGI 2595. J.B.YEATS, 1866, hl, pen, NGI 2575.

SC Attrib PATRICK MACDOWELL, RA 1861?, marble bust, Trinity College, Dublin. ALBERT BRUCE JOY, RA 1880, marble statue, St Patrick's Cathedral, Dublin. THOMAS WOOLNER, 1880, statue, Four Courts, Dublin.

PR D.J.POUND, after a photograph by Mayall, tql seated, stipple and line, presented with *Illust News of the World*, BM, NPG. Several woodcuts, NPG.

WHITLA, Sir William (1851-1933) physician.

PH WALTER STONEMAN, 1921, hs, NPG (NPR).

WHITWORTH, Sir Joseph, 1st Bart (1803-1887) engineer.

P LOUIS DESANGES, wl, Whitworth Institute, Darley Dale, Derbys. Attrib SIR E.J.POYNTER, 18?6, hl, Science Museum, London. J.E.WHINFIELD, Institution of Mechanical Engineers, London.

SC PATRIC PARK, 1855, marble bust, Gawsworth Hall, Cheshire.

PR DALZIEL, hs, circle, woodcut, BM. Several popular prints and prints after photographs, NPG.

PH C.A.DUVAL & CO, hs, carte, NPG (Album 117). UNKNOWN, 1850, in a group, with his gun, print, Manchester Public Libraries. Several prints, Institution of Civil Engineers, London and Institution of Mechanical Engineers, London.

WHYMPER, Edward (1840-1911) artist and mountaineer.

PR O.HAUCK, after C.Whymper, hl with ice-axe, woodcut, BM. UNKNOWN, hs, wood engr, for *Illust London News*, 28 May 1881, NPG.

WHYMPER, Josiah Wood (1813-1903) wood engraver.
PH JOHN & CHARLES WATKINS, hs, carte, NPG (Album 105).

WHYTE, Alexander (1836-1921) principal of New College, Edinburgh.
P SIR JAMES GUTHRIE, hl seated, profile, SNPG 2194.
SC PAUL WISSAERT, 1915, bronze medallion, SNPG 855.

WHYTE-MELVILLE, George John (1821-1878) novelist.
P UNKNOWN, wl in uniform, Royal and Ancient Golf Club of St Andrews, Fife, Scotland.
SC SIR J.E.BOEHM, 1879, marble bust, NPG 3836; related medallion on fountain, St Andrews, Scotland.
PR J.BROWN, after a photograph by Mayall, hl, stipple, for *Baily's Mag*, 1867, BM. UNKNOWN, hs, woodcut, for *Illust London News*, 28 Dec 1878, NPG. JUDD & CO, hs, semi-profile, lith, for *The Whitehall Review*, 11 Jan 1879, NPG.
C UNKNOWN, hl seated, chromo-lith, for *Vanity Fair*, 23 Sept 1871, NPG.
PH T.RODGER, hs, carte, NPG AX7524.

WICKENS, Sir John (1815-1873) judge.
P MARGARET CARPENTER, hl, Eton College, Berks.
PR UNKNOWN, after a photograph by John Watkins, hs, woodcut, for *Illust London News*, 6 May 1871, NPG.

WICKHAM, Edward Charles (1834-1910) dean of Lincoln.
P RENÉ DE L'HÔPITAL, tql, Wellington College, Berks. SIR W.B.RICHMOND, tql, seated, New College, Oxford.

WIGAN, Alfred Sydney (1814-1878) actor.
PR Several theatrical prints, Harvard Theatre Collection, Cambridge, Mass, USA.
PH CAMILLE SILVY, wl, carte, NPG.

WIGAN, Horace (1818?-1885) actor and adapter of plays.
PH CAMILLE SILVY, wl, carte, NPG.

WIGAN, Leonora, née Pincott (1805-1884) actress.
PR T.HOLLIS, after a daguerreotype by Mayall, with her husband A.S.Wigan, as Virginia and Tourbillon in *To Parents and Guardians*, stipple and line, for Tallis's *Drawing Room Table Book*, BM, NPG.

WIGHTWICK, George (1802-1872) architect.
PR E.SCRIVEN, after R.R.Scanlan, hs, stipple, for Arnold's *Library of the Fine Arts*, 1832, BM, NPG.

WILBERFORCE, Ernest Roland (1840-1907) bishop of Chichester.
P CHARLES GOLDSBOROUGH ANDERSON, replica, hl seated, Bishop's Palace, Chichester.
PR UNKNOWN, hs, woodcut, for *Illust London News*, 29 July 1882, NPG.

WILBERFORCE, Samuel (1805-1873) successively bishop of Oxford and Winchester.
P F.R.SAY, RA 1846, tql, Lambeth Palace, London. GEORGE RICHMOND, 1864–5, tql, Bishop of Oxford, Cuddesdon College, Oxon; study, NPG 1054. GEORGE RICHMOND, 1868, hl seated, Royal Academy, London; version, The Deanery, Westminster. 'E.W.R.', 1873, tql, Society for the Propagation of the Gospel, London. UNKNOWN, tql seated, Oriel College, Oxford.
D CLARA PUSEY, c1856, two sketches, one wl with Edward Pusey and others, pen and ink, the other, hl, in pulpit, pencil and w/c, NPG 4541 (9,11). GEORGE RICHMOND, 1868, hs, charcoal and chalk, NPG 4974.
G E.M.WARD, 'Queen Victoria Investing Napoleon III with the Order of the Garter at Windsor Castle', oil, 1855, Royal Coll.
SC UNKNOWN, 1876, wooden bust, Christ Church, Oxford. H.H.ARMSTEAD, 1890, recumbent effigy, Winchester.

PR R.WOODMAN, after G.Richmond of 1843, hs, stipple, NPG. H.ROBINSON, after a drg by G.Richmond, hs, stipple, pub 1845, BM, NPG. W.HOLL, after a drg by G.Richmond of c1851, hs, semi-profile, stipple, for 'Grillion's Club' series, BM, NPG. Several woodcuts and engravings after photographs, NPG.
C CARLO PELLEGRINI ('Ape'), wl, w/c study, for *Vanity Fair*, 24 July 1869, NPG 1993.
PH MAULL & POLYBLANK, tql seated, profile, print, NPG AX7271. HERBERT WATKINS, 1857, hs, print, NPG X6390. Various cartes by ADAMS & STILLIARD, CALDESI, BLANFORD & CO, GUGGENHEIM, KILBURN, H.N.KING, LONDON STEREOSCOPIC CO, JOHN WATKINS and others, various dates and sizes, NPG. Various prints in 'Wilberforce Albums', NPG (Albums 46 and 47).

WILDE, Charles Robert Claude, see 2nd Baron Truro.

WILDE, James, see 1st Baron Penzance.

WILDE, Oscar (1856-1900) wit and dramatist.
D A.S.BOYD ('TWYM'), 1883, pencil, NGI 3774. S.P.HALL, 1888–9, pencil sketch, hs, profile, made at the sessions of the Parnell Commission, NPG 2265. FREDERICK PEGRAM, pencil sketch, made at the sessions of the Parnell Commission, V & A. Self-portrait, wl, Cabinet des Estampes, Bibliotèque Nationale, Paris. J.A.McNEILL WHISTLER, wl in top hat, pen, brush and ink, University of Glasgow.
C CARLO PELLEGRINI ('Ape'), wl, w/c study, for *Vanity Fair*, 24 May 1884, NPG 3653. AUBREY BEARDSLEY, design for Frontispiece to John Davidson's Plays, 1894, TATE 4172. SIR MAX BEERBOHM, several drgs: 1894, hl, Ashmolean Museum, Oxford; 1898, with John Toole, Princeton University Library, USA; 1916 and 1926, posthumous drgs, TATE 5391 (xxiii) and University of Texas, Austin, USA. J.A.McNEILL WHISTLER, two pen and ink sketches, as a pig and as a jockey, University of Glasgow.
PH NAPOLEON SARONY, 1882, two prints, wl and wl seated, panels, NPG P24 and P25. NAPOLEON SARONY, 1882, wl, print, Gernsheim Collection, University of Texas, Austin, USA. W. & D.DOWNEY, tql seated, woodburytype, for Cassell's *Cabinet Portrait Gallery*, vol II, 1891, NPG.

WILDE, Sir William Robert Wills (1815-1876) surgeon and Irish antiquary.
D ERSKINE NICOL, 1854, w/c, NGI 2208.
SC UNKNOWN, plaster bust, Royal Victoria Eye and Ear Hospital, Dublin.

WILKINS, Augustus Samuel (1843-1905) classical scholar.
P JOHN COLLIER, c1904, Manchester University.

WILKINSON, George Howard (1833-1907) bishop of St Andrews.
SC SIR GEORGE FRAMPTON, memorial, St Ninian's Cathedral, Perth.
PR UNKNOWN, after a photograph by Lock & Whitfield, hs, wood engr, for *Illust London News*, 10 Feb 1883, NPG.
C SIR LESLIE WARD ('Spy'), wl, profile, w/c study, for *Vanity Fair*, 26 Dec 1885, NPG 4753.
PH UNKNOWN, tql, print, NPG (Anglican Bishops).

WILKS, Sir Samuel, 1st Bart (1824-1911) physician.
P PERCY BIGLAND, 1897, tql seated in robes, Royal College of Physicians, London. GEORGE SEPHTON, 1910, tql, Royal College of Physicians.
C SIR LESLIE WARD ('Spy'), tql, chromo-lith, for *Vanity Fair*, 1 Oct 1892, NPG.

WILLES, Sir George Ommanney (1823-1901) admiral.
P UNKNOWN, The Admiralty, Portsmouth.

WILLES, Sir James Shaw (1814-1872) judge.
PR R. & E.TAYLOR, hs, oval, woodcut, for *Illust London News*, 12

Oct 1872, NPG.

WILLETT, William (1856-1915) builder, and the originator of 'daylight' saving.
P CHARLES SHANNON, c1923, Chelsea Town Hall.
PH SIR BENJAMIN STONE, 1909, wl, print, Birmingham Reference Library, NPG.

WILLIAMS, Charles James Blasius (1805-1889) physician.
PR R.T., after a photograph by Window & Grove, hs, wood engr, for *Illust London News*, 20 April 1889, NPG.

WILLIAMS, Sir Edward Leader (1828-1910) engineer.
PR UNKNOWN, hs, wood engr, for *Illust London News*, 10 Oct 1885, NPG.

WILLIAMS, Sir George (1821-1905) founder of YMCA.
P JOHN COLLIER, replica of portrait of 1887, hs, NPG 2140. JOHN COLLIER, 1912, YMCA, London; replicas, 1923, YMCA, Chicago, USA, and The Guildhall, London. UKNOWN, tql seated, YMCA Dunford Management College, Midhurst.
SC SIR GEORGE FRAMPTON, c1909, bust on monument, St Paul's Cathedral, London.
PH UNKNOWN, tql, print, National Council of YMCA, London.

WILLIAMS, Isaac (1802-1865) poet and theologian.
P W.H.CUBLEY, c1859, hl seated, Trinity College, Oxford.

WILLIAMS, John Carvell (1821-1907) nonconformist politician.
PH SIR BENJAMIN STONE, 1897, wl, print, Birmingham Reference Library, NPG.

WILLIAMS, Sir Monier Monier-, see MONIER-Williams.

WILLIAMS, Montagu Stephen (1835-1892) police magistrate
PR P.NAUMANN, hs, woodcut, for *Illust London News*, 31 Dec 1892, BM, NPG.
C SIR LESLIE WARD ('Spy'), wl, profile, chromo-lith, for *Vanity Fair*, 1 Nov 1879, NPG.

WILLIAMS, Owen Lewis Cope (1836-1904) lieutenant-general.
D S.P.HALL, pencil sketch, NPG 2291.
C CARLO PELLEGRINI ('Ape'), wl, profile, chromo-lith, for *Vanity Fair*, 19 Jan 1878, NPG.

WILLIAMS, Sir Roland Bowdler Vaughan (1838-1916) judge.
P W.T.MAUD, tql seated in robe, DoE (Law Courts, London).
C 'QUIZ', hl seated, profile, chromo-lith, for *Vanity Fair*, 13 Dec 1890, NPG. 'C.G.D.', wl, profile, chromo-lith, for *Vanity Fair*, 2 March 1899, NPG.

WILLIAMS, Rowland (1817-1870) Anglican divine.
P J.ROBERTSON, 1862, tql seated, King's College, Cambridge.

WILLIAMS, Rowland, 'Hwfa Môn' (1823-1905) archdruid of Wales.
PR UNKNOWN, after a photograph by Lettsome & Sons, hs, wood engr, NPG.

WILLIAMS, William (1800-1879?) bishop of Waiapu, New Zealand.
P UNKNOWN, 1868, hl, Hertford College, Oxford.

WILLIAMS, William (1801-1869) Welsh poet, 'Caledfryn'.
P WILLIAM WILLIAMS, 1861, hl, National Museum of Wales 674, Cardiff.
SC J.MILO GRIFFITH, 1870, plaster relief, oval, National Museum of Wales 1184.

WILLIAMS, Sir William Fenwick, Bart (1800-1883)
general.
P WILLIAM GUSH, RA 1860, wl, Nova Scotia Legislative Library, Halifax, Canada.
PR C.BAUGNIET, hs in uniform, oval, lith, BM, NPG. W.J.EDWARDS, tql in uniform, line, BM, NPG. T.H.MAGUIRE, after P.C.French, tql seated, semi-profile, lith, BM. T.MAGUIRE, after W.Maddox, hl, lith, pub 1855, NPG. Various prints after photographs by Mayall and John Watkins, various sizes and media, in uniform, BM, NPG.
PH MAULL & POLYBLANK, tql seated, print, NPG AX7306. UNKNOWN, 1856, with Sir Christopher Teesdale, print, NPG X8021. UNKNOWN, hl seated in uniform, print, NPG.

WILLIAMS-BULKELEY, Sir Richard Bulkeley, Bart (1801-1875) MP for Anglesey, sportsman.
G SIR GEORGE HAYTER, 'The House of Commons, 1833', oil, NPG 54.
PR S.W.REYNOLDS jun, after F.Grant, tql, mezz, BM. J.BROWN, after a photograph by Mayall, hl, stipple, for *Baily's Mag*, 1862, BM, NPG.

WILLIAMS-WYNN, Charles (1822-1896) politician.
C SIR LESLIE WARD ('Spy'), wl, profile, w/c study, for *Vanity Fair*, 28 June 1879, NPG 2605.

WILLIAMS-WYNN, Charlotte (1807-1869) diarist.
P Attrib H.W.PICKERSGILL, tql, National Museum of Wales 394, Cardiff.

WILLIAMS-WYNN, Sir Watkin, Bart (1820-1885) land-owner and politician.
PR W.SHARP, after T.Lawrence, head, as a child, lith, pub 1830, BM, NPG. M.GAUCI, after C.Brocky, hl, lith, pub 1841, BM. J.BROWN, after a photograph by Mayall, hl, stipple, for *Baily's Mag*, 1863, BM, NPG. R.J.LANE, after J.Cranc, tql seated, lith, BM.
C SIR LESLIE WARD ('Spy'), wl, w/c study, for *Vanity Fair*, 14 June 1873, NPG 2606.
PH UNKNOWN, three cartes, all wl, NPG X1490-2.

WILLIAMSON, Alexander William (1824-1904) chemist.
P JOHN COLLIER, 1888, University College, London. W.BISCOMBE GARDNER, 1894-5, Department of Chemistry, University College, London.
PR UNKNOWN, hs, profile, woodcut, for *Illust London News*, 20 Sept 1873, NPG.

WILLIS, Sir George Harry Smith (1823-1900) general.
PR UNKNOWN, hs in uniform, wood engr, for *Illust London News*, 12 Aug 1882, NPG.

WILLMORE, James Tibbitts (1800-1863) line-engraver.
P UNKNOWN, Birmingham City Art Gallery.

WILLMOTT, Robert Aris (1809-1863) author.
PR H.B.HALL, hl seated, stipple, NPG.

WILLOUGHBY, Sir John Christopher, 5th Bart (1859-1918) soldier.
C SIR LESLIE WARD ('Spy'), wl, profile, w/c study, for *Vanity Fair*, 6 Sept 1884, NPG 4754.

WILLS, Sir George Alfred, 1st Bart, of Blagdon (1854-1928) president of the Imperial Tobacco Company; philanthropist.
P H.G.RIVIERE, 1925, Bristol University. GLYN PHILPOT, Imperial Tobacco Company, London.

WILLS, William Gorman (1828-1891) dramatist.
PR R.T., after a photograph by Van der Weyde, hs, wood engr, for *Illust London News*, 19 Dec 1891, NPG.

WILLS, William Henry (1810-1880) miscellaneous writer.
PH UNKNOWN, print, V & A.

WILLS, William Henry (1830-1911), see Baron Winterstoke.

WILLS, William John (1834-1861) Australian explorer.
SC CHARLES SUMMERS, statue on monument, with statue of Robert O'Hara Burke, Collins Street, Melbourne, Australia.

WILMOT, Sir John Eardley Eardley-, 2nd Bart (1810-1892) barrister and politician.
C SIR LESLIE WARD ('Spy'), wl, profile, w/c study, for *Vanity Fair,* 9 May 1885, NPG 3296.

WILMOT, Sir Sainthill Eardley- (1852-1929) forester.
PH WALTER STONEMAN, 1918, hs, NPG (NPR).

WILSON, Sir Archdale, 1st Bart (1803-1874) general in India.
PR D.J.POUND, after a photograph by Mayall, tql in uniform, stipple and line, supplement to *Illust News of the World,* BM, NPG. G.J.STODART, after a photograph, hl in uniform, stipple, for Nolan's *History of the war against Russia,* BM, NPG.

WILSON, Arthur (1836-1909) shipowner and benefactor.
PR J.BROWN, after a photograph by Barry, hs, stipple, for *Baily's Mag,* 1887, NPG.

WILSON, Sir Arthur Knyvet, 3rd Bart (1842-1921) admiral of the fleet.
D WILLIAM STRANG, hs in uniform, chalk, Royal Coll.
PH WALTER STONEMAN, 1921, hs, NPG (NPR).

WILSON, Charles Henry, see 1st Baron Nunburnholme.

WILSON, Sir Charles Rivers (1831-1916) civil servant and financier.
C CARLO PELLEGRINI ('Ape'), wl, profile, chromo-lith, for *Vanity Fair,* 9 Nov 1878, NPG.
PH LOCK & WHITFIELD, hs, semi-profile, oval, woodburytype, for *Men of Mark,* 1881, NPG.

WILSON, Sir Charles William (1836-1905) major-general.
PR R.T., hs in uniform, wood engr, for *Illust London News,* 13 Sept 1884, NPG.

WILSON, Sir Daniel (1816-1892) antiquary.
P SIR GEORGE REID, 1891, three hs portraits on one canvas, SNPG 429.

WILSON, George (1808-1870) chairman of the Anti Corn Law League.
G S.BELLIN, after J.R.Herbert, 'Meeting of the Council of the Anti Corn Law League', mixed engr, pub 1850, BM, NPG.
SC H.S.LEIFCHILD, 1871, bust, Manchester Town Hall.
PR S.W.REYNOLDS jun, after C.A.du Val, hl seated, octagon, stipple, pub 1843, BM, NPG. R.TAYLOR, after a photograph, hs, woodcut, for *Illust London News,* 21 Jan 1871, NPG.

WILSON, George (1818-1859) chemist and religious writer.
PR L.STOCKS, tql seated, line, BM.

WILSON, Sir Jacob (1836-1905) agriculturist.
PR UNKNOWN, after a photograph by W. & D.Downey, hs, wood engr, for *Illust London News,* 20 July 1889, NPG.

WILSON, James (1805-1860) politician and founder of *The Economist.*
P SIR JOHN WATSON GORDON, 1858, tql seated, NPG 2189.
G S.BELLIN, after J.R.Herbert, 'Meeting of the Council of the Anti Corn Law League', mixed engr, pub 1850, BM, NPG.
SC SIR JOHN STEELL, 1859, marble bust, SNPG 968; related plaster cast, Hawick Museum. SIR J.STEELL, 1865, marble statue, Dalhousie Institute, Calcutta.
PR DALZIEL, tql seated, woodcut, BM. D.J.POUND, after a photograph by Davy of Plymouth, tql seated, stipple and line, for

Drawing Room Portrait Gallery of Eminent Personages, BM, NPG.
C RICHARD DOYLE, BM

WILSON, James Maurice (1836-1931) schoolmaster, divine and antiquary.
P UNKNOWN, copy after a photograph, Clifton College, Bristol.
PH M.GUTTENBERG, hs, carte, NPG (Album 40).

WILSON, John (1800-1849) singer and composer of songs.
P SIR DANIEL MACNEE, SNPG 755.
PR Various theatrical prints, Harvard Theatre Collection, Cambridge, Mass, USA.

WILSON, John (1812-1888) agriculturist.
PR W.HOLE, tql, etch, for *Quasi Cursores,* 1884, NPG.

WILSON, John Dove (1833-1908) Scottish legal writer.
PH UNKNOWN, print, Advocates' Library, Aberdeen.

WILSON, John Mackay (1804-1835) author of *Tales of The Borders.*
P JAMES SINCLAIR, 1831, SNPG 1300.
PR UNKNOWN, hl, stipple, pub 1837, NPG.

WILSON, Mary Anne (1802-1867) singer.
PR C.PICART, after J.Jackson, hl, stipple, pub 1821, BM, NPG. Several popular prints and theatrical prints, BM, NPG.

WILSON, Sir William James Erasmus (1809-1884) surgeon.
P JOHN LEWIS REILLY, after Stephen Pearce (RA 1872), tql in gown, Royal College of Surgeons, London. Attrib S.PEARCE, hl (cut down), Royal College of Physicians, London.
SC SIR THOMAS BROCK, 1888, marble bust, Royal College of Surgeons.

WILSON-PATTEN, John, see 1st Baron Winmarleigh.

WINCHILSEA, George Finch-Hatton, 11th Earl of (1815-1887) politician.
D COUNT ALFRED D'ORSAY, 1840, hl, profile, pencil and chalk, NPG 4026(60).
PR G.HOLLIS, after T.Phillips, hl, octagon, stipple and line, BM, NPG.
C SIR LESLIE WARD ('Spy'), wl, profile, chromo-lith, for *Vanity Fair,* 2 Oct 1880, NPG.

WINDHAM, Sir Charles Ash (1810-1870) general.
P GEORGE CLINT, 1833, hl in uniform, Felbrigg Hall (NT), Norfolk.
PR J.H.LYNCH, tql seated, lith, pub 1856, BM, NPG. D.J.POUND, after a photograph by Mayall, tql in uniform, line, supplement to *Illust News of the World,* BM, NPG.

WINDUS, William Lindsay (1822-1907) artist.
P Self-portrait, hs, as a young man, Walker Art Gallery, Liverpool.

WINGATE, Sir James Lawton (1846-1924) artist.
P Self-portrait, exhib 1913, hs, Royal Scottish Academy, Edinburgh.
D HENRY WRIGHT KERR, 1917, hs, w/c, SNPG 2140.
PH OLIVE EDIS, two prints, tql and tql seated, in his studio, NPG.

WINMARLEIGH, John Wilson-Patten, 1st Baron (1802-1892) politician.
P FRANK HOLL, RA 1883, Royal Albert Hospital, Lancaster.
G SIR GEORGE HAYTER, 'The House of Commons, 1833', oil, NPG 54. JOHN PHILLIP, 'The House of Commons, 1860', oil, Palace of Westminster, London.
SC G.G.ADAMS, marble bust, Gawsworth Hall, Cheshire. JOHN WARRINGTON WOOD, 1872, marble bust, Gawsworth Hall. H.H.ARMSTEAD, 1893, marble monumental effigy, St Elphin's Church, Warrington, Cheshire.
PR S.COUSINS, after G.Richmond, tql in militia uniform, mezz, BM. T.LUPTON, after Bostock, tql, Mezz, 1838, NPG. F.C.LEWIS, after J.Slater, hs, stipple, one of 'Grillion's Club' series, BM.

PH C.A.DUVAL, tql, carte, NPG AX8610. LOCK & WHITFIELD, hs, oval, woodburytype, for *Men of Mark*, 1877, NPG.

WINNINGTON-INGRAM, Arthur Foley (1858-1946) bishop of London.
P SIR HUBERT VON HERKOMER, 1908, tql seated, Fulham Palace, London; replica, Keble College, Oxford. GEORGE HALL NEALE, *c*1916, tql in robes, London Diocesan House.
G S.P.HALL, 'The Bench of Bishops, 1902', w/c, NPG 2369.
C SIR LESLIE WARD ('Spy'), wl, profile, chromo-lith, for *Vanity Fair*, 23 May 1901, NPG. SIR BERNARD PARTRIDGE, pen and ink cartoon, for *Punch*, 16 June 1909, NPG. 'W.H.', wl playing tennis, chromo-lith, for *Vanity Fair*, 22 May 1912, NPG.
PH OLIVE EDIS, three autochromes, two tql seated and one wl in robes and mitre, NPG x7190-2. OLIVE EDIS, four prints, two hs and two tql seated, JOHN RUSSELL & SONS, hs, print, for *National Photographic Record*, vol I, NPG. WALTER STONEMAN, 1917, hs, NPG (NPR). PAUL TANQUERAY, hs, print, NPG. UNKNOWN, hs, print, NPG (Anglican Bishops).

WINSLOW, Forbes Benignus (1810-1874) physician.
G G.B.BLACK, from daguerreotypes by Mayall, 'English Physicians', lith, pub 1851, BM.
PR H.LINTON, after a photograph by John Watkins, hs, line, NPG.
PH ERNEST EDWARDS, wl seated, print, for *Men of Eminence*, ed L.Reeve, vol II, 1864, NPG.

WINTERBOTHAM, Henry Selfe Page (1837-1873) politician.
PR UNKNOWN, after a photograph by London Stereoscopic Co, hs, woodcut, for *Illust London News*, 17 Jan 1874, NPG.

WINTERHALTER, Franz Xavier (1806-1873) portrait painter.
P Self-portrait, hs, semi-profile, Uffizi Gallery, Florence; copy by Enrico Belli, 1874, Royal Coll.
D COUNT ALFRED D'ORSAY, 1843, hs, profile, pencil, DoE.
PR UNKNOWN, after a photograph by Caldesi, hs, woodcut, for *Illust London News*, 23 Aug 1873, BM, NPG.
PH L.CALDESI & Co, tql, carte, NPG (Album 105).

WINTERSTOKE, Sir William Henry Wills, Baron (1830-1911) benefactor to Bristol.
P Two portraits, one by E.J.GREGORY (exhib 1880), the other by H.G.RIVIERE (1907), Bristol City Art Gallery.
C SIR LESLIE WARD ('Spy'), wl, chromo-lith, for *Vanity Fair*, 23 Nov 1893, NPG.

WINTON, Archibald William Montgomerie, 1st Earl of, see 13th Earl of Eglinton.

WISEMAN, Nicholas Patrick Stephen (1802-1865) cardinal-archbishop of Westminster.
P Two portraits, one by THOMAS FURSE of *c*1840, the other by an unknown artist, English College at Rome. J.R.HERBERT, RA 1842, tql seated, St Mary's College, Oscott.
D H.E.DOYLE, 1858, hs, w/c, NGI 2080. H.E.DOYLE, hs, chalk, NPG 4237. Attrib H.E.DOYLE, tql seated, chalk, NPG 2074.
SC E.W.PUGIN, monument, Westminster Cathedral, London.
PR G.E.MADELEY, after M.R.Giberne (1846), hs, lith, NPG. G.S.SHURY, tql seated, mixed engr, pub 1850, NPG. UNKNOWN, after Sir F.Grant?, wl, engr, NPG. Various engravings after photographs, NPG.
C Attrib RICHARD DOYLE, tql, profile, pen and ink, NPG 4619. TOUCHSTONE, 1850-1, several cartoons of religious groups, NPG.
PH MOIRA & HAIGH, wl seated, print, NPG AX7341. MOIRA & HAIGH, wl, carte, NPG. FRANCK, tql seated, carte, NPG (Album 118). HERBERT WATKINS, two cartes, tql seated and hs, the second in Album 40, NPG.

WODEHOUSE, John Gurdon, see 1st Earl of Kimberley.

WODEHOUSE, Sir Philip Edmond (1811-1887) governor of Bombay.
P MALCOLM STEWART, hs, Government House, Cape Town.
PR MAGUIRE, after W.Carpenter, tql seated, lith, BM.

WOLF, Josef (1820-1899) illustrator of animal books.
P LANCE CALKIN, hl, Royal Zoological Society, London.

WOLFE-BARRY, Sir John Wolfe (1836-1918) civil engineer.
P SIR HUBERT VON HERKOMER, 1912, replica of RA 1900?, Institute of Civil Engineers, London.
C SIR LESLIE WARD ('Spy'), wl, profile, w/c study, for *Vanity Fair*, 26 Jan 1905, The Athenaeum, London.
PH JOHN RUSSELL & SONS, hl, print, for *National Photographic Record*, vol I, NPG.

WOLFF, Sir Henry Drummond Charles (1830-1908) diplomat.
PR Two wood engrs, both hs, for *Illust London News*, 22 Aug 1885 and 30 Jan 1892, NPG.
C CARLO PELLEGRINI ('Ape'), wl, profile, chromo-lith, for *Vanity Fair*, 5 Sept 1874, NPG.
PH UNKNOWN, hl, print, NPG.

WOLSELEY, Garnet Joseph Wolseley, 1st Viscount (1833-1913) field-marshal.
P P.A.BESNARD, 1880, wl in uniform with horse, NPG 1789. CARL SOHN jun, 1882, hs in uniform, Royal Coll. FRANK HOLL, 1886, tql in uniform, NGI 777, related hs portrait, Hove Library, Sussex. H.SCHADOW, 1896, tql in uniform, DoE (War Office, London). HELEN DONALD SMITH, *c*1905, hs, Hove Library. UNKNOWN, hs in uniform, Staff College, Camberley, Surrey.
D WILLIAM STRANG, 1908, hl, chalk, NPG 4059.
SC SIR J.E.BOEHM, 1883, bronze cast of bust, NPG 1840. Attrib SIR J.E.BOEHM, marble bust, DoE (War Office). UNKNOWN, after 1894, wax figure, tql in robe, Hove Library. SIR WILLIAM GOSCOMBE JOHN, 1918, bronze equestrian statue, Horse Guards Parade, London.
PR Various woodcuts and popular prints, NPG.
C CARLO PELLEGRINI ('Ape'), wl in uniform, chromo-lith, for *Vanity Fair*, 18 April 1874, NPG.
PH LOCK & WHITFIELD, hs, oval, woodburytype, for *Men of Mark*, 1876, NPG. BARRAUD, hl in uniform, print, for *Men and Women of the Day*, vol I, 1888, NPG AX5415. W. & D.DOWNEY, hl, woodburytype, for Cassell's *Cabinet Portrait Gallery*, vol III, 1892, NPG. MRS A.BROOM, 1911, with 1st Earl Roberts in George V's coronation procession, neg, NPG x751. Various prints by A.BASSANO, FRADELLE, LONDON STEREOSCOPIC CO, MAULL & CO and WINDOW & GROVE, various dates and sizes, cartes and cabinets, NPG. Several prints, Scottish United Services Museum, Edinburgh.

WOLVERHAMPTON, Henry Hartley Fowler, 1st Viscount (1830-1911) statesman.
P SIR A.S.COPE, RA 1893, Wolverhampton Town Hall. SIR A.S.COPE, RA 1896, Law Society, London.
C HARRY FURNISS, pen and ink sketch, NPG 3533. SIR LESLIE WARD ('Spy'), wl in group, 'Mixed Political Wares', chromo-lith, for *Vanity Fair*, 3 Dec 1892, NPG.
PH LONDON STEREOSCOPIC CO, *c*1902, two cabinets, both hs, NPG x11847-48. SIR BENJAMIN STONE, wl, print, NPG. UNKNOWN, tql seated, profile, photogravure, NPG x11849.

WOLVERTON, George Grenfell Glyn, 2nd Baron (1824-1887) postmaster-general.
PR J.BROWN, after a photograph by Mayall, hl, stipple, for *Baily's*

Mag, 1875, BM.

C UNKNOWN, wl, chromo-lith, for *Vanity Fair*, 24 Feb 1872, NPG.

WOOD, Sir Charles (1800-1885), see 1st Viscount Halifax.

WOOD, Sir Charles Lindley, see 2nd Viscount Halifax.

WOOD, Ellen, née Price, (Mrs Henry Wood) (1814-1887) author of *East Lynne*.
P SYDNEY HODGES, 1875, tql seated, The Guildhall, Worcester.
PR L.STOCKS, after R.Easton, hl seated, oval, stipple and line, BM.

WOOD, Sir (Henry) Evelyn (1838-1919) field-marshal.
P W.W.OULESS, 1906, tql in uniform, Fishmonger's Hall, London.
PR FLORA LION, 1915, hs, lith, NPG 3949. Several popular prints, NPG.
C SIR LESLIE WARD ('Spy'), wl, profile, w/c study, for *Vanity Fair*, 15 Nov 1879, NPG 4756.
PH LOCK & WHITFIELD, hs, oval, woodburytype, for *Men of Mark*, 1883, NPG. BARRAUD, tql, print, for *Men and Women of the Day*, vol III, 1890, NPG AX5485. OLIVE EDIS, 1914, two autochromes, tql seated and tql, both in uniform, NPG X7211 and X8003. MAULL & FOX, hl in uniform, cabinet, NPG. UNKNOWN, hl in uniform, print, NPG. UNKNOWN, hs in uniform, carte, NPG.

WOOD, John (1825-1891) surgeon.
D C.B.BIRCH, *c*1858, head, with G.D.Leslie and Sir Charles Eastlake, pencil, NPG 2477.
G HENRY JAMYN BROOKS, two groups, 'Council of Royal College of Surgeons of England, 1884–85', and 'Court of Examiners', 1894, both oil, both Royal College of Surgeons, London.

WOOD, John George (1827-1889) writer on natural history.
PR R.T., after a photograph by Negretti & Zambra, hs, profile, woodcut, for *Illust London News*, 16 March 1889, BM, NPG.

WOOD, Mary Ann, née Paton (1802-1864) opera singer.
P THOMAS SULLY, 1836, wl seated, as Amina in *La Sonnambula*, Royal College of Music, London; study, hs, NPG 1351. JOHN NEAGLE, 1848, replica of portrait of 1836, hs, Pennsylvania Academy of the Fine Arts, Philadelphia, USA. SAMUEL CHINN, Guildhall Art Gallery, London.
D JAMES STEWART, wl as Susanna in *The Marriage of Figaro*, w/c, Garrick Club, London.
M J.W.CHILDE, Guildhall Art Gallery.
PR R.NEWTON, after W.J.Newton, tql holding music, line, pub 1823, BM. Various theatrical prints, BM, NPG, Harvard Theatre Collection, Cambridge, Mass, USA.

WOOD, Thomas McKinnon (1855-1927) politician.
P LEONARD WATTS, 1899, London County Council.

WOOD, Western (1804-1863) chemist.
PR UNKNOWN, hl, semi-profile, woodcut, for *Illust London News*, 15 Feb 1862, NPG.

WOOD, William Page, see Baron Hatherley.

WOODALL, William (1832-1901) philanthropist.
P W.M.PALIN, Wedgwood Institute, Burslem, Staffs.
G W.H.BARTLETT, 'A Saturday Night at the Savage Club', oil, *c*1891, Savage Club, London.
C SIR LESLIE WARD ('Spy'), tql, w/c study, for *Vanity Fair*, 15 Oct 1896, NPG 2987.
PH SIR BENJAMIN STONE, 1897, wl, print, NPG.

WOODARD, Nathaniel (1811-1891) founder of the Woodard schools.
P UNKNOWN, hl, Lancing College, Sussex.

WOODFORD, James Russell (1820-1885) bishop of Ely.
PR W.B.GARDNER, after a photograph by Russell & Sons, hs, woodcut, for *Illust London News*, 30 Aug 1873, NPG.
PH LOCK & WHITFIELD, hs, semi-profile, oval, woodburytype, for

Men of Mark, 1880, NPG.

WOODINGTON, William Frederick (1806-1893) painter
PR R. & E.TAYLOR, hs, semi-profile, woodcut, for *Illust London News*, 13 May 1876, NPG.

WOODS, Sir Albert William (1816-1904) Garter King o Arms.
PR C.F.KELL, tql with insignia of grand director of ceremonies o freemasons, lith, for Sadler's *Notes on the Ceremony of Installatio* BM. UNKNOWN, hs, with chain of office, woodcut, for *Illus London News*, 8 May 1875, NPG.

WOODS, Edward (1814-1903) civil engineer.
P MISS PORTER, 1898, tql seated, Institution of Civil Engineers London.

WOODS, Margaret Louisa, née Bradley (1856-1945) write and poet.
PH JULIA MARGARET CAMERON, 1864, hs, print, NPG P18(27).

WOODWARD, Benjamin (1815-1861) architect.
SC ALEXANDER MUNRO, marble medallion, University Museum Oxford.

WOOLAVINGTON, James Buchanan, 1st Baron (1849 1935) philanthropist and race-horse owner.
C SIR LESLIE WARD ('Spy'), wl, Hentschel-Colourtype, for *Vanit Fair*, 20 Nov 1907, NPG.
PH WALTER STONEMAN, 1925, hs, NPG (NPR).

WOOLGAR, Sarah Jane, see Mellon.

WOOLNER, Thomas (1825-1892) sculptor and poet.
P A.C.GOW, 1883, hs, Macdonald Collection, Aberdeen Ar Gallery.
D D.G.ROSSETTI, 1852, hs, pencil, NPG 3848.
PR UNKNOWN, after T.B.Wirgman, wl in his studio, working on bust, woodcut, for *Century Mag*, 1883, BM. J.M.JOHNSTONE after a photograph, hs, semi-profile, woodcut, for *Mag of Ar* 1891, BM.
PH ERNEST EDWARDS, wl seated, print, for *Men of Eminence*, e L.Reeve, vol II, 1864, NPG. LOCK & WHITFIELD, hs, ova woodburytype, for *Men of Mark*, 1877, NPG. J.P.MAYALL, hl i his studio, working on a bust, cabinet, NPG X13286. RALPI W.ROBINSON, hl, profile, at easel, print, for *Members an Associates of the Royal Academy of Arts, 1891*, NPG X7402. Variou prints by THE AUTOTYPE CO, ELLIOTT & FRY, FRADELLE & MARSHALL, W.JEFFREY, LOCK & WHITFIELD, J.P.MAYALI NEGRETTI & ZAMBRA, J.G.SHORT and unidentified photograp hers, cartes, cabinets, etc, various dates and sizes, one in a grou with his workmen, NPG X5126–44.

WORBOISE, Emma Jane, afterwards Mrs Guyton (1825 1887) author.
PR T.W.HUNT, tql seated, stipple, NPG.

WORDSWORTH, Charles (1806-1892) bishop of : Andrews.
PR W.WALKER, after G.Richmond, hs, stipple, pub 1848, B UNKNOWN, after a photograph, hs, woodcut, for *Illust Lond News*, 10 Dec 1892, BM.
PH T.RODGER, wl, carte, NPG AX7480. UNKNOWN, tql, print, N (Anglican Bishops).

WORDSWORTH, Christopher (1807-1885) bishop Lincoln.
P EDWIN LONG, 1878, Diocese of Lincoln.
D GEORGE RICHMOND, 1853, hs, chalk, Harrow School, Midd
PR UNKNOWN, hl, woodcut, for *Illust London News*, 28 March 188 NPG.

WORDSWORTH, Dame Elizabeth (1840-1932) principal of Lady Margaret Hall, Oxford.
P J.J.SHANNON, 1891, tql seated, Lady Margaret Hall, Oxford.
D A.G.WALKER, c1909, hl seated, chalk, and T.BINNEY GIBBS, 1922, head, pencil, Lady Margaret Hall.
PH Two prints by unknown photographers, both wl in academic robes, NPG.

WORDSWORTH, John (1805-1839) classical scholar.
SC HENRY WEEKES, 1840, marble bust, Trinity College Chapel, Cambridge.

WORDSWORTH, John (1843-1911) bishop of Salisbury.
P SIR GEORGE REID, 1905, tql seated, Bishop's Palace, Salisbury; reduced copy by E.S.Carlos, 1906, Brasenose College, Oxford.
G S.P.HALL, 'The Bench of Bishops, 1902', w/c, NPG 2369.
PH ROTARY PHOTO, tql seated, postcard, NPG. UNKNOWN, hl, print, NPG (Anglican Bishops).

WORMS, Henry de, see Baron Pirbright.

WORNUM, Ralph Nicholson (1812-1877) art critic and keeper of the National Gallery.
PR UNKNOWN, after a photograph, hs, woodcut, for *Illust London News*, 5 Jan 1878, NPG.

WRENBURY, Henry Burton Buckley, 1st Baron (1845-1935) judge.
C SIR LESLIE WARD ('Spy'), hl at bench, chromo-lith, for *Vanity Fair*, 5 April 1900, NPG.
PH WALTER STONEMAN, 1917 and 1928, both hs, NPG (NPR).

WRIGHT, Edward Richard (1813-1859) actor.
PR R.KEMP, wl as Splash, in Rodwell's *The Young Widow*, chromo-lith, NPG. Various theatrical prints, Harvard Theatre Collection, Cambridge, Mass, USA.

WRIGHT, Joseph (1855-1930) philologist.
P ERNEST MOORE, Taylor Institution, Oxford.
PH UNKNOWN, wl in library, print, NPG.

WRIGHT, Sir Robert Samuel (1839-1904) judge.
C (Possibly H.C.SEPPING) WRIGHT ('Stuff'), hs at bench, chromo-lith, for *Vanity Fair*, 27 June 1891, NPG.

WRIGHT, Thomas (1810-1877) antiquary.
SC G.G.FONTANA, marble bust, Walker Art Gallery, Liverpool.
PR D.J.POUND, after a photograph by Maull & Polyblank, tql seated, stipple and line, for *Drawing Room Portrait Gallery of Eminent Personages*, NPG. UNKNOWN, after a photograph by Charles Watkins, hs, woodcut, for *Illust London News*, 12 Jan 1878, NPG.

WRIGHT, Whitaker (1845-1904) company promoter.
C HARRY FURNISS, pen and ink sketch, NPG 3534.

WRIGHT, William (1830-1889) orientalist.
SC J.HUTCHINSON, 1890, marble bust, Fitzwilliam Museum, Cambridge.

WRIGHT, William Aldis (1831-1914) Shakespearian and Biblical scholar.
P W.W.OULESS, 1887, tql seated, Trinity College, Cambridge.
D WILLIAM STRANG, 1910, hs, chalk, Fitzwilliam Museum, Cambridge.
PH A.G.DEW SMITH, hl seated, print, NPG X4631.

WROTTESLEY, Arthur Wrottesley, 3rd Baron (1824-1910) philanthropist in Staffordshire.
D FREDERICK SARGENT, hl seated, pencil, NPG 1834 (hh).
C (Possibly H.C.SEPPING) WRIGHT ('Stuff'), wl, profile, w/c study, for *Vanity Fair*, 20 June 1895, NPG 2972.

WYATT, Sir Matthew Digby (1820-1877) architect.
P ALESSANDRO OSSANI, hl, RIBA, London.
PR UNKNOWN, after a photograph, hs, profile, woodcut, for *Illust London News*, 2 June 1877, BM. Several woodcuts, NPG.
PH UNKNOWN, hs, profile, print, RIBA, London.

WYATT, Thomas Henry (1807-1880) architect.
P GEORGE RICHMOND, RA 1878, hs, RIBA, London.
D Attrib GEORGE RICHMOND, hs, chalk, RIBA.

WYKE, Sir Charles Lennox (1815-1897) diplomat.
C SIR LESLIE WARD ('Spy'), hl, profile, w/c study, for *Vanity Fair*, 9 Feb 1884, NPG 4757.

WYLD, James (1812-1887) geographer and politician.
PR UNKNOWN, after a photograph by Mayall, hs, oval, woodcut, for *Illust London News*, May 1857, NPG.

WYLDE, Henry (1822-1890) Gresham Professor of Music, London.
PR PN, hs, wood engr, for *Illust London News*, 22 March 1890, NPG.

WYLIE, James Aitken (1808-1890) protestant writer.
PR UNKNOWN, hl, stipple, NPG.

WYLLIE, John William Shaw (1835-1870) Indian civilian.
SC UNKNOWN, marble medallion on monument, Cheltenham College Chapel.

WYLLIE, Sir William (1802-1891) general.
PR UNKNOWN, hs, profile, in uniform, wood engr, for *Illust London News*, 6 June 1891, NPG.

WYLLIE, William Lionel (1851-1931) painter.
PH RALPH W.ROBINSON, wl seated in studio, print, for *Members and Associates of the Royal Academy of Arts*, 1891, NPG X7403. UNKNOWN, 1914, tql, profile, painting, print, NPG.

WYNDHAM, Sir Charles (1837-1919) actor-manager.
P JOHN PETTIE, RA 1888, tql as David Garrick, Garrick Club, London.
D S.P.HALL, pencil sketch, NPG 2373.
C 'ASH', wl, mechanical repro, supplement to *Vanity Fair*, NPG. SIR MAX BEERBOHM, two drgs, V & A, and one, University of Texas, Austin, USA. HARRY FURNISS, c1905, wl seated, pen and ink, NPG 3535.
PH BARRAUD, 1888, two cabinets, tql and wl, both as David Garrick, NPG X12587 and X12580. BARRAUD, 1888, tql with Mary Moore in *David Garrick*, carte, NPG X12589. BARRAUD, tql, print, for *Men and Women of the Day*, vol II, 1889, NPG AX5459. L.BERTIN, hs, profile, woodburytype, carte NPG X12598. LANGFIER, tql, cabinet, NPG X12586. Two photogravures, both hl seated, NPG.

WYNDHAM, Percy Scawen (1835-1911) landowner and connoisseur.
P SIR WILLIAM ORPEN, c1907, hl seated in drawing room, Petworth, W Sussex.
PR J.BROWN, after a photograph by A.J.Melhuish, hs, stipple, for *Baily's Mag*, 1884, NPG.
C SIR LESLIE WARD ('Spy'), tql, profile, w/c study, for *Vanity Fair*, 30 Oct 1880, NPG 4758.

WYNDHAM, Robert Henry (1814-1894) actor and theatrical manager.
P HUGH COLLINS, 1872, SNPG 849.

WYNDHAM-QUIN, Windham Thomas, see 4th Earl of DUNRAVEN and Mount-Earl.

WYNFIELD, David Wilkie (1837-1887) painter and photographer.
PH Self-portrait, 1860s, hs, print, NPG P97.

WYNN-CARRINGTON, Charles Robert, see 1st Marquess

of Lincolnshire.

WYNN, Williams-, see WILLIAMS-Wynn.

WYON, Joseph Shepherd (1836–1873) medallist.
PR UNKNOWN, head, woodcut, BM.

Y

YARROW, Sir Alfred Fernandez, 1st Bart (1842–1932)
marine engineer and shipbuilder.
P H.G.RIVIERE, replica of portrait of *c*1908, hl, Institution of Civil
Engineers, London.
PH WALTER STONEMAN, 1924, hs, NPG (NPR).

YATES, Edmund (1831–1894) novelist and journalist.
PR J.BROWN, after a photograph by Adolphe Beau, hl seated, stipple
and line, NPG.
C SIR LESLIE WARD ('Spy'), tql, chromo-lith, for *Vanity Fair*, 16
Nov 1878, NPG. 'H.H.E.'?, wl, w/c, pub 1884, NPG 4546.
PH WALERY, wl seated, print, NPG. JOHN & CHARLES WATKINS, wl,
carte, NPG AX7544. JOHN WATKINS, hl, carte, NPG X13298.

YEAMES, William Frederick (1835–1918) painter.
P Self-portrait, hs, MacDonald Collection, Aberdeen Art Gallery.
G G.GRENVILLE MANTON, 'Conversazione at the Royal Academy,
1891', w/c, NPG 2820. H.T.WELLS, 'Friends at Yewden', oil,
Hamburger Kunsthalle, Hamburg.
PR UNKNOWN, hs, woodcut, for *Illust London News*, 30 June 1866,
NPG.
PH DAVID WILKIE WYNFIELD, 1860s, hs, print, NPG P98. LOCK &
WHITFIELD, hs, profile, oval, woodburytype, for *Men of Mark*,
1883, NPG. RALPH W.ROBINSON, wl seated in studio, print, for
Members and Associates of the Royal Academy of Arts, 1891, NPG
X7404. JOHN & CHARLES WATKINS, hs, carte, NPG (Album 104).

YEATS, John Butler (1839–1922) painter.
P Self-portrait, *c*1904, hs, North Western University, Evanston,
Illinois, USA, ROBERT HENRI, 1909, hl seated, Hirshhorn
Museum and Sculpture Garden, Smithsonian Institution, Wash-
ington DC, USA. Self-portrait, 1911, hl, Dartmouth College
Collection, Hanover, New Hampshire, USA. ANNE
GOLDTHWAITE, hs, Baltimore Museum of Art, USA. WALT
KUHN, hl seated, Municipal Gallery of Modern Art, Dublin.
D Various self-portrait studies for an oil painting: 1919, tql,
Princeton University Library, USA; 1920, hl, chalk, NPG 4104;
1920 and 1922, two hs sketches, John Sloan Collection, Delaware
Art Museum; hl, pencil, NPG 6313. WALT KUHN, Municipal
Gallery of Modern Art, Dublin. JOHN SLOAN, 1923, wl seated,
Delaware Art Museum.
G JOHN SLOAN, 'Yeats at Petitpas', oil, 1910, The Corcoran Gallery
of Art, Washington DC, USA.
C Self-portrait, John Sloan Collection, Delaware Art Museum.

YONGE, Charlotte Mary (1823–1901) novelist and writer
of books for children.
D GEORGE RICHMOND, 1844, tql, w/c and chalk, NPG 2193.
PH C.L.DODGSON ('Lewis Carroll'), 1866, two prints, tql, and tql

seated with her mother, Gernsheim Collection, University of
Texas, USA. WALKER & COCKERELL, after Miss Anna Bramston,
tql seated, photogravure, NPG X13299. UNKNOWN, hs, profile,
print, NPG X5575.

YORKE, Charles Philip, see 5th Earl of Hardwicke.

YOUNG, Sir Allen William (1827–1915) sailor and explorer.
P STEPHEN PEARCE, 1876, hs, profile, NPG 920.

YOUNG, Mrs Charles, see Jane Elizabeth Vezin.

YOUNG, George Young, Lord (1819–1907) Scottish judge.
SC MRS WALLACE, bust, Faculty of Advocates, Parliament House,
Edinburgh.

YOUNG, Sir John (1807–1876), see Baron Lisgar.

YOUNG, Sydney (1857–1937) chemist.
PH WALTER STONEMAN, 1918, hs, NPG (NPR).

**YOUNGER of Leckie, Sir George Younger, 1st Viscount
(1851–1929)** politician.
P SIR WILLIAM ORPEN, replica, Carlton Club, London.
C 'H.C.O.', wl, Hentschel-Colourtype, for *Vanity Fair*, 6 Jan 1910,
NPG.

YOXALL, Sir James Henry (1857–1925) educationist.
PH SIR BENJAMIN STONE, 1898–1901, three prints, all wl, NPG.

**YPRES, John Denton Pinkstone French, 1st Earl of
(1852–1925)** field-marshal.
P UNKNOWN, 1908, hl in uniform, National Army Museum,
London. By or after JOHN ST HELIER LANDER, *c*1910–1915, tql in
uniform and great coat. Cavalry and Guards Club, London.
J.S.SARGENT, hs, NPG 2654.
D FRANCIS DODD, 1917, charcoal and w/c, IWM. JOSEPH SIMPSON,
wash and pencil, IWM.
G J.S.SARGENT, 'General Officers of World War I, 1914–18', oil,
1922, NPG 1954; hs, charcoal study, Corcoran Gallery of Art,
Washington DC, USA.
SC UNKNOWN, bronze bust, Cavalry and Guards Club.
C G.D.G., wl on horseback, chromo-lith, for *Vanity Fair*, 12 July
1900, NPG. SIR LESLIE WARD ('Spy'), 'A General Group',
chromo-lith, for *Vanity Fair*, 29 Nov 1900, NPG.
PH JOHN RUSSELL & SONS, hs in uniform, print, for *National
Photographic Record*, vol I, NPG. WALTER STONEMAN, 1918, hs,
semi-profile, in uniform, NPG (NPR).

YULE, Sir Henry (1820–1889) geographer.
P T.B.WIRGMAN, hl seated, Royal Engineers, Chatham, Kent.
D T.B.WIRGMAN, ink, SNPG 1988.

Z

ZOUCHE, Robert Curzon, 14th Baron (1810-1873)
diplomat.
PR W.HOLL, after G.Richmond, hs, stipple, one of 'Grillion's Club' series, BM, NPG.
PH Studio of RICHARD BEARD, c1845, hs, daguerreotype, NPG P116.

ZUKERTORT, Johannes Hermann (1842-1888) chess player.
G A.ROSENBAUM, 'Chess players', oil, 1880, NPG 3060.
PR UNKNOWN, after a photograph by A.E.Fradelle, hs, woodcut, for *Illust London News*, 7 Sept 1878, NPG.